The O'Leary Series

Microsoft Word 2002

Introductory Edition

Timothy J. O'Leary

Arizona State University

Linda I. O'Leary

InformationTechnology

**McGraw-Hill
Irwin**

Boston   Burr Ridge, IL   Dubuque, IA   Madison, WI   New York
San Francisco   St. Louis   Bangkok   Bogotá   Caracas   Kuala Lumpur
Lisbon   London   Madrid   Mexico City   Milan   Montreal   New Delhi
Santiago   Seoul   Singapore   Sydney   Taipei   Toronto

McGraw-Hill Higher Education

A Division of The McGraw-Hill Companies

MICROSOFT® WORD 2002, INTRODUCTORY EDITION
Published by McGraw-Hill/Irwin, an imprint of the McGraw-Hill Companies, Inc. 1221 Avenue of the Americas, New York, NY, 10020.

Some ancillaries, including electronic and print components, may not be available to customers outside the United States.

Disclaimer: This book is designed to help you improve your computer use. However, the author and publisher assume no responsibility whatsoever for the uses made of this material or for decisions based on their use, and make no warranties, either expressed or implied, regarding the contents of this book, its merchantability, or its fitness for any particular purpose.

Neither the publisher nor anyone else who has been involved in the creation, production, or delivery of this product shall be liable for any direct, incidental, or consequential damages, such as, but not limited to, loss of anticipated profits or benefits resulting from its use or from any breach of warranty. Some states do not allow the exclusion or limitation of direct, incidental, or consequential damages, so the above disclaimer may not apply to you. No dealer, company, or person is authorized to alter this disclaimer. Any representation to the contrary will not bind the publisher or author.

This book is printed on acid-free paper.

domestic   1 2 3 4 5 6 7 8 9 0 QPD/QPD 0 9 8 7 6 5 4 3 2 1
international   1 2 3 4 5 6 7 8 9 0 QPD/QPD 0 9 8 7 6 5 4 3 2 1

ISBN 0-07-247234-0

Publisher: *George Werthman*
Sponsoring editor: *Daniel Silverburg*
Marketing manager: *Paul Murphy*
Project manager: *Jim Labeots*
Manager, new book production: *Melonie Salvati*
Freelance design coordinator: *Gino Cieslik*
Cover & interior design: *Maureen McCutcheon*
Cover image: *Digitalvision*
Photo research coordinator: *David A. Tietz*
Supplement coordinator: *Marc Mattson*
New media: *David Barrick*
Compositor: *Rogondino & Associates*
Typeface: *10.5/13 New Aster*
Printer: *Quebecor World Dubuque Inc.*

Library of Congress Control Number 2001095799

INTERNATIONAL EDITION ISBN 0-07-112099-8

www.mhhe.com

InformationTechnology

Information Technology at McGraw-Hill/Irwin

At McGraw-Hill Higher Education, we publish instructional materials targeted at the higher education market. In an effort to expand the tools of higher learning, we publish texts, lab manuals, study guides, testing materials, software, and multimedia products.

At McGraw-Hill/Irwin (a division of McGraw-Hill Higher Education), we realize that technology has created and will continue to create new mediums for professors and students to use in managing resources and communicating information to one another. We strive to provide the most flexible and complete teaching and learning tools available as well as offer solutions to the changing world of teaching and learning.

McGraw-Hill/Irwin is dedicated to providing the tools for today's instructors and students to successfully navigate the world of Information Technology.

- **Seminar Series** McGraw-Hill/Irwin's Technology Connection seminar series offered across the country every year demonstrates the latest technology products and encourages collaboration among teaching professionals.

- **McGraw-Hill/Osborne** This division of The McGraw-Hill Companies is known for its best-selling Internet titles, *Internet & Web Yellow Pages* and the *Internet Complete Reference*. For more information, visit Osborne at **www.osborne.com**.

- **Digital Solutions** McGraw-Hill/Irwin is committed to publishing digital solutions. Taking your course online doesn't have to be a solitary adventure, nor does it have to be a difficult one. We offer several solutions that will allow you to enjoy all the benefits of having your course material online.

- **Packaging Options** For more information about our discount options, contact your McGraw-Hill/Irwin Sales representative at 1-800-338-3987 or visit our web site at **www.mhhe.com/it**.

APPROVED COURSEWARE

What does this logo mean?

It means this courseware has been approved by the Microsoft® Office User Specialist Program to be among the finest available for learning *Microsoft Word 2002, Microsoft Excel 2002, Microsoft Access 2002,* and *Microsoft PowerPoint 2002.* It also means that upon completion of this courseware, you may be prepared to become a Microsoft Office User Specialist.

What is a Microsoft Office User Specialist?

A Microsoft Office User Specialist is an individual who has certified his or her skills in one or more of the Microsoft Office desktop applications of Microsoft Word, Microsoft Excel, Microsoft PowerPoint®, Microsoft Outlook® or Microsoft Access, or in Microsoft Project. The Microsoft Office User Specialist Program typically offers certification exams at the "Core" and "Expert" skill levels.* The Microsoft Office User Specialist Program is the only Microsoft approved program in the world for certifying proficiency in Microsoft Office desktop applications and Microsoft Project. This certification can be a valuable asset in any job search or career advancement.

More Information:

To learn more about becoming a Microsoft Office User Specialist, visit www.mous.net

To purchase a Microsoft Office User Specialist certification exam, visit www.DesktopIQ.com

To learn about other Microsoft Office User Specialist approved courseware from McGraw-Hill/Irwin, visit http://www.mhhe.com/catalogs/irwin/cit/mous/index.mhtml

---

* The availability of Microsoft Office User Specialist certification exams varies by application, application version and language. Visit www.mous.net for exam availability.

Microsoft, the Microsoft Office User Specialist Logo, PowerPoint and Outlook are either registered trademarks or trademarks of Microsoft Corporation in the United States and/or other countries.

Who benefits from Microsoft, Office User Specialist certification?

Employers

Microsoft Office User Specialist ("MOUS") certification helps satisfy employers' needs for qualitative assessments of employees' skills. Training, coupled with MOUS certification, offers organizations of every size, the ability to enhance productivity and efficiency by enabling their employees to unlock many advanced and laborsaving features in Microsoft Office applications. MOUS certification can ultimately improve the bottom line.

Employees

MOUS certification demonstrates employees' productivity and competence in Microsoft Office applications, the most popular business applications in the world. Achieving MOUS certification verifies that employees have the confidence and ability to use Microsoft Office applications in meeting and exceeding their work challenges.

Instructors

MOUS certification validates instructors' knowledge and skill in using Microsoft Office applications. It serves as a valuable credential, demonstrating their potential to teach students these essential applications. The MOUS Authorized Instructor program is also available to those who wish to further demonstrate their instructional capabilities.

Students

MOUS certification distinguishes students from their peers. It demonstrates their efficiency in completing assignments and projects, leaving more time for other studies. Improved confidence toward meeting new challenges and obstacles is yet another benefit. Achieving MOUS certification gives students the marketable skills necessary to set them apart in the competitive job market.

To learn more about MOUS certification, visit www.mous.net

To purchase a MOUS certification exam, visit www.DesktopIQ.com

Brief Contents

Detailed Contents

Lab
2 Revising And Refining A Document   WD2.1

Lab 6 Creating a Web Site WD6.1

Working Together 2: Linking and Document Collaboration WDWT2.1

Acknowledgments

The new edition of The O'Leary Series has been made possible only through the enthusiasm and dedication of a great team of people. Because the team spans the country, literally from coast to coast, we have utilized every means of working together including conference calls, FAX, e-mail, and document collaboration. We have truly tested the team approach and it works!

Leading the team from McGraw-Hill/Irwin are George Werthman, Publisher and Alexandra Arnold, Developmental Editor. Their renewed commitment, direction, and support have infused the team with the excitement of a new project.

The production staff is headed by James Labeots, Project Manager, whose planning and attention to detail has made it possible for us to successfully meet a very challenging schedule. Members of the production team include: Gino Cieslik, Designer; Pat Rogondino, Compositor; Susan Defosset, Copy Editor; Melonie Salvati, Production Supervisor; Marc Mattson, Supplement Coordinator; and David Barrick, Media Producer. We would particularly like to thank Pat and Susan—team members for many past editions whom we can always depend on to do a great job.

Finally, we are particularly grateful to a small but very dedicated group of people who helped us develop the manuscript. Colleen Hayes, Susan Demar, and Kathy Duggan have helped on the last several editions and continue to provide excellent developmental and technical support. To Steve Willis and Carol Cooper who provide technical expertise, youthful perspective, and enthusiasm, my thanks for helping get the manuscripts out the door and meeting the deadlines.

Preface

Introduction

The 20th century not only brought the dawn of the Information Age, but also rapid changes in information technology. There is no indication that this rapid rate of change will be slowing— it may even be increasing. As we begin the 21st century, computer literacy will undoubtedly become prerequisite for whatever career a student chooses. The goal of the O'Leary Series is to assist students in attaining the necessary skills to efficiently use these applications. Equally important is the goal to provide a foundation for students to readily and easily learn to use future versions of this software. This series does this by providing detailed step-by step instructions combined with careful selection and presentation of essential concepts.

About the Authors

Tim and Linda O'Leary live in the American Southwest and spend much of their time engaging instructors and students in conversation about learning. In fact, they have been talking about learning for more than 25 years. Something in those early conversations convinced them to write a book, to bring their interest in the learning process to the printed page. Today, they are as concerned as ever about learning, about technology, and about the challenges of presenting material in new ways, both in terms of content and the method of delivery.

   A powerful and creative team, Tim combines his years of classroom teaching experience with Linda's background as a consultant and corporate trainer. Tim has taught courses at Stark Technical College in Canton, Ohio, Rochester Institute of Technology in upper New York state, and is currently a professor at Arizona State University in Tempe, Arizona. Tim and Linda have talked to and taught students from ages 8 to 80, all of them with a desire to learn something about computers and the applications that make their lives easier, more interesting, and more productive.

About the Book

Times are changing, technology is changing, and this text is changing, too. Do you think the students of today are different from yesterday? There is no doubt about it—they are. On the positive side, it is amazing how much effort students will put toward things they are convinced are relevant to them. Their effort directed at learning application programs and exploring the Web seems at times limitless. On the other hand, students can often be shortsighted, thinking that learning the skills to use the application is the only objective. The mission of the series is to build upon and extend this interest by not only teaching the specific application skills but by introducing the concepts that are common to all applications, providing students with the confidence, knowledge, and ability to easily learn the next generation of applications.

What's New in This Edition?

- **Introduction to Computer Essentials**—A brief introduction to the basics of computer hardware and software (Appears in Office XP, Volume I Only).

- **Introduction to Windows 2000**—Two hands-on labs devoted to Windows 2000 basics (Appears in Office XP, Volume I Only).

- **Introduction to the WWW: Internet Explorer and E-mail**—Hands-on introductions for using Internet Explorer to browse the WWW and using e-mail (Appears in Office XP, Volume I. Only).

- **Topic Reorganization**—The text has been reorganized to include main and subtopic heads by grouping related tasks. For example, tasks such as changing fonts and applying character effects appear under the "Formatting" topic head. This results in a slightly more reference-like approach, making it easier for students to refer back to the text to review. This has been done without losing the logical and realistic development of the case.

- **Clarified Marginal Notes**—Marginal notes have been enhanced by more clearly identifying the note content with box heads and the use of different colors.

    Additional Information—Brief asides with expanded discussion of features.

    Having Trouble?—Procedural tips advising students of possible problems and how to overcome.

    Another Method—Alternative methods of performing a procedure.

- Larger **Screen Figures**—Make it easier to identify elements and read screen content.

- All **Numbered Steps** and bullets appear in left margin space making it easy not to miss a step.

- A **MOUS (*Microsoft Office User Specialist*) Skills** table, appearing at the end of each chapter, contains page references to MOUS skills learned in the lab.

- **Two New References**

    File Finder—Helps organize all data and solution files.

    MOUS (*Microsoft Office User Specialist*) Certification Guide—Links all MOUS objectives to text content and end-of-chapter exercises.

Same Great Features as the Office 2000 Series

- **Relevant Cases**—Four separate running cases demonstrate the features in each application. Topics are of interest to students—At Arizona State University, over 600 students were surveyed to find out what topics are of interest to them.

- **Focus on Concepts**—Each chapter focuses on the concepts behind the application. Students learn the essentials, so they can succeed regardless of the software package they might be using.

- **Steps**—Numbered procedural steps clearly identify each hands-on task needed to complete the step.

- **Screens**—Plentiful screen illustrations illustrate the completion of each numbered step to help students stay on track.

- **Callouts**—Meaningful screen callouts identify the results of the steps as well as reinforce the associated concept.

- **End-of-Chapter Material**

  Terminology—Questions and exercises test recall of the basic information and terminology in the lab.

  - Screen Identification
  - Matching
  - Multiple Choice

  Concepts—Questions and exercises review students' understanding of concepts and ability to integrate ideas presented in different parts of the lab.

  - Fill-In
  - Discussion Questions

  Hands-On Practice Exercises—Students apply the skills and concepts they learned to solve case-based exercises. Many cases in the practice exercises tie to a running case used in another application lab. This helps to demonstrate the use of the four applications across a common case setting. For example, the Adventure Travel Tours case used in the Word labs is continued in practice exercises in Excel, Access, and PowerPoint.

  - Step-by-Step
  - On Your Own
  - On The Web

- **Rating System**—The 3-star rating system identifies the difficulty level of each practice exercise in the end-of-chapter materials.

- **Working Together Labs**—At the completion of the brief and introductory texts, a final lab demonstrates the integration of the MS Office applications and the WWW.

Instructor's Guide

We understand that, in today's teaching environment, offering a textbook alone is not sufficient to meet the needs of the many instructors who use our books. To teach effectively, instructors must have a full complement of supplemental resources to assist them in every facet of teaching from preparing for class, to conducting a lecture, to assessing students' comprehension. *The O'Leary Series* offers a fully-integrated supplements package and Web site, as described below.

Instructor's Resource Kit

The **Instructor's Resource Kit** contains a computerized Test Bank, an Instructor's Manual, and PowerPoint Presentation Slides. Features of the Instructor's Resource Kit are described below.

- **Instructor's Manual** The Instructor's Manual contains lab objectives, concepts, outlines, lecture notes, and command summaries. Also included are answers to all end-of chapter material, tips for covering difficult materials, additional exercises, and a schedule showing how much time is required to cover text material.

- **Computerized Test Bank** The test bank contains over 1,300 multiple choice, true/false, and discussion questions. Each question will be accompanied by the correct answer, the level of learning difficulty, and corresponding page references. Our flexible Diploma software allows you to easily generate custom exams.

- **PowerPoint Presentation Slides** The presentation slides will include lab objectives, concepts, outlines, text figures, and speaker's notes. Also included are bullets to illustrate key terms and FAQs.

Online Learning Center/Web Site

Found at **www.mhhe.com/oleary**, this site provides additional learning and instructional tools to enhance the comprehension of the text. The OLC/Web Site is divided into these three areas:

- **Information Center** Contains core information about the text, supplements, and the authors.

- **Instructor Center** Offers instructional materials, downloads, additional exercises, and other relevant links for professors.

- **Student Center** Contains chapter competencies, chapter concepts, self-quizzes, flashcards, projects, animations, additional Web links, and more.

Skills Assessment

SimNet (Simulated Network Assessment Product) provides a way for you to test students' software skills in a simulated environment. SimNet is available for Microsoft Office 97, Microsoft Office 2000, and Microsoft Office XP. SimNet provides flexibility for you in your course by offering:

- Pre-testing options
- Post-testing options
- Course placement testing
- Diagnostic capabilities to reinforce skills
- Proficiency testing to measure skills
- Web or LAN delivery of tests.
- Computer-based training tutorials (new for Office XP)
- MOUS preparation exams

For more information on skills assessment software, please contact your local sales representative, or visit us at **www.mhhe.com/it**.

Digital Solutions to Help You Manage Your Course

PageOut is our Course Web Site Development Center that offers a syllabus page, URL, McGraw-Hill Online Learning Center content, online exercises and quizzes, gradebook, discussion board, and an area for student Web pages.

Available free with any McGraw-Hill/Irwin product, PageOut requires no prior knowledge of HTML, no long hours of coding, and a way for course coordinators and professors to provide a full-course web site. PageOut offers a series of templates—simply fill them with your course information and click on one of 16 designs. The process takes under an hour and leaves you with a professionally designed Web site. We'll even get you started with sample web sites, or enter your syllabus for you! PageOut is so straightforward and intuitive, it's little wonder why over 12,000 college professors are using it. For more information, visit the PageOut Web site at **www.pageout.net**.

Online courses are also available. Online Learning Centers (OLCs) are your perfect solutions for Internet-based content. Simply put, these Centers are "digital cartridges" that contain a book's pedagogy and supplements. As students read the book, they can go online and take self-grading quizzes or work through interactive exercises. These also provide students appropriate access to lecture materials and other key supplements.

Online Learning Centers can be delivered through any of these platforms:

McGraw-Hill Learning Architecture (TopClass)

Blackboard.com

Ecollege.com (formerly Real Education)

WebCT (a product of Universal Learning Technology)

McGraw-Hill has partnerships with WebCT and Blackboard to make it even easier to take your course online. Now you can have McGraw-Hill content delivered through the leading Internet-based learning tool for higher education. At McGraw-Hill, we have the following service agreements with WebCT and Blackboard:

Instructor Advantage   Instructor Advantage is a special level of service McGraw-Hill offers in conjuction with WebCT designed to help you get up and running with your new course. A team of specialists will be immediately available to ensure everything runs smoothly through the life of your adoption.

Instructor Advantage Plus   Qualified McGraw-Hill adopters will be eligible for an even higher level of service. A certified WebCT or Blackboard specialist will provide a full day of on-site training for you and your staff. You will then have unlimited e-mail and phone support through the life of your adoption. Please contact your local McGraw-Hill representative for more details.

Technology Connection Seminar Series

McGraw-Hill/Irwin's Technology Connection seminar series offered across the country every year demonstrates the latest technology products and encourages collaboration among teaching professionals.

Computing Essentials

Available alone, or packaged with the O'Leary Series, *Computing Essentials* offers a unique, visual orientation that gives students a basic understanding of computing concepts. *Computing Essentials* is one of the few books on the market that is written by a professor who still teaches the course every semester and loves it! While combining current topics and technology into a highly illustrated design geared to catch students' interest and motivate them in their learning, this text provides an accurate snapshot of computing today. When bundled with software application lab manuals, students are given a complete representation of the fundamental issues surrounding the personal computing environment.

The text includes the following features:

- **A "Learn By Doing" approach** encourages students to engage in activity that is more interactive than the traditional learning pattern students typically follow in a concepts course. The exercises, explorations, visual orientation, inclusion of screen shots and numbered steps, and integrated internet references combine several methods to achieve an interactive learning environment for optimum reinforcement.

- **Making IT Work For You** sections visually demonstrate how technology is used in everyday life. Topics covered include how find a job online and how to protect a computer against viruses. These"gallery" style boxes combine text and art to take students step-by-step through technological processes that are both interesting and useful. As an added bonus, the *CE 2001-2002 Making IT Work Video Series* has been created to compliment the topics presented throughout the text.

- **On the Web Explorations** appear throughout the margins of the text and encourage students to go to the Web to visit several informative and established sites in order to learn more about the chapter's featured topic.

- **On the Web Exercises** present thought-provoking questions that allow students to construct articles and summaries for additional practice on topics relevant to that chapter while utilizing Web resources for further research. These exercises serve as additional reinforcement of the chapter's pertinent material while also allowing students to gain more familiarity with the Web.

- **A Look to the Future** sections provide insightful information about the future impact of technology and forecasts of how upcoming enhancements in the world of computing will play an important and powerful role in society.

- **Colorful Visual Summaries**, appearing at the end of every chapter, provide dynamic, graphical reviews of the important lessons featured in each chapter for additional reinforcement.

- **End-of-Chapter Review** material follows a three-level format and includes exercises that encourage students to review terms, concepts, and applications of concepts. Through matching, true/false, multiple choice, short answer completion, concept matching, and critical thinking questions, students have multiple review opportunities.

PowerWeb

PowerWeb is an exciting new online product available from McGraw-Hill. A nominally priced token grants students access through our web site to a wealth of resources—all corresponding to computer literacy. Features include an interactive glossary; current events with quizzing, assessment, and measurement options; Web survey; links to related text content; and WWW searching capability via Northern Lights, an academic search engine. Visit the PowerWeb site at **www.dushkin.com/powerweb**.

Interactive Companion CD-ROM

This free student CD-ROM, designed for use in class, in the lab, or at home by students and professors alike, includes a collection of interactive tutorial labs on some of the most popular and difficult topics in information technology. By combining video, interactive exercises, animation, additional content, and actual "lab" tutorials, we expand the reach and scope of the textbook. The lab titles are listed below.

- Binary Numbers
- Basic Programming
- Computer Anatomy
- Disk Fragmentation
- E-mail Essentials
- Multimedia Tools
- Workplace Issues (ergonomics/privacy/security)
- Introduction to Databases
- Programming II
- Network Communications
- Purchasing Decisions
- User Interfaces
- File Organization
- Word Processing and Spreadsheets
- Internet Overview
- Photo Editing
- Presentation Techniques
- Computer Troubleshooting
- Programming Overview
- SQL Queries

Student's Guide

As you begin each lab, take a few moments to read the **Case Study** and the **Concept Overview**. The case study introduces a real-life setting that is interwoven throughout the entire lab, providing the basis for understanding the use of the application. Also, notice the **Additional Information**, **Having Trouble?**, and **Another Method** boxes scattered throughout the book. These tips provide more information about related topics, help to get you out of trouble if you are having problems and offer suggestions on other ways to perform the same task. Finally, read the text between the steps. You will find the few minutes more it takes you is well worth the time when you are completing the practice exercises.

Many learning aids are built into the text to ensure your success with the material and to make the process of learning rewarding. The pages that follow call your attention to the key features in the text.

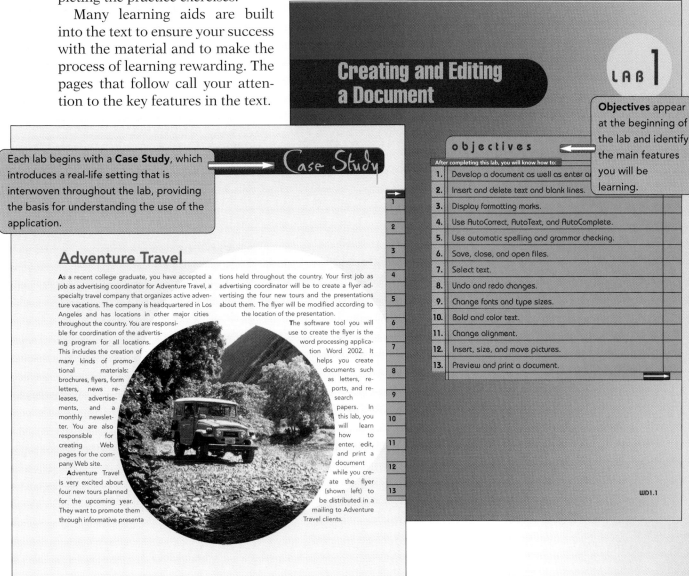

Creating and Editing a Document

LAB 1

Each lab begins with a **Case Study**, which introduces a real-life setting that is interwoven throughout the lab, providing the basis for understanding the use of the application.

Objectives appear at the beginning of the lab and identify the main features you will be learning.

Case Study

objectives

After completing this lab, you will know how to:

1.	Develop a document as well as enter and edit text.
2.	Insert and delete text and blank lines.
3.	Display formatting marks.
4.	Use AutoCorrect, AutoText, and AutoComplete.
5.	Use automatic spelling and grammar checking.
6.	Save, close, and open files.
7.	Select text.
8.	Undo and redo changes.
9.	Change fonts and type sizes.
10.	Bold and color text.
11.	Change alignment.
12.	Insert, size, and move pictures.
13.	Preview and print a document.

Adventure Travel

As a recent college graduate, you have accepted a job as advertising coordinator for Adventure Travel, a specialty travel company that organizes active adventure vacations. The company is headquartered in Los Angeles and has locations in other major cities throughout the country. You are responsible for coordination of the advertising program for all locations. This includes the creation of many kinds of promotional materials: brochures, flyers, form letters, news releases, advertisements, and a monthly newsletter. You are also responsible for creating Web pages for the company Web site.

Adventure Travel is very excited about four new tours planned for the upcoming year. They want to promote them through informative presenta

tions held throughout the country. Your first job as advertising coordinator will be to create a flyer advertising the four new tours and the presentations about them. The flyer will be modified according to the location of the presentation.

The software tool you will use to create the flyer is the word processing application Word 2002. It helps you create documents such as letters, reports, and research papers. In this lab, you will learn how to enter, edit, and print a document while you create the flyer (shown left) to be distributed in a mailing to Adventure Travel clients.

WD1.1

xxv

Using Word Wrap

Now you will continue entering more of the paragraph. As you type, when the text gets close to the right margin, do not press ⬅Enter to move to the next line. Word will automatically wrap words to the next line as needed.

concept 6

Word Wrap

6 The **word wrap** feature automatically decides where to end a line and wrap text to the next line based on the margin settings. This saves time when entering text, as you do not need to press ⬅Enter at the end of a full line to begin a new line. The only time you need to press ⬅Enter is to end a paragraph, to insert blank lines, or to create a short line such as a salutation. In addition, if you change the margins or insert or delete text on a line, the program automatically readjusts the text on the line to fit within the new margin settings. Word wrap is common to all word processors.

> The **Concepts** that are common to all applications are emphasized— providing you with the confidence, knowledge, and ability to easily learn the next generation of applications.

❶ ● Press →.

● Type: about some of the earth's greatest unspoiled habitats and to find out how you can experience the adventure of a lifetime.

Your screen should be similar to Figure 1.22

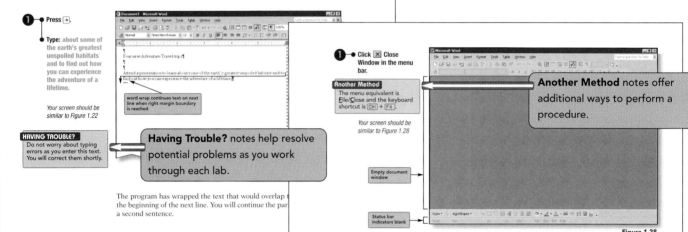

word wrap continues text on next line when right margin boundary is reached

HAVING TROUBLE?
Do not worry about typing errors as you enter this text. You will correct them shortly.

> **Having Trouble?** notes help resolve potential problems as you work through each lab.

The program has wrapped the text that would overlap the beginning of the next line. You will continue the par a second sentence.

❶ ● Click ☒ Close Window in the menu bar.

Another Method
The menu equivalent is File/Close and the keyboard shortcut is Ctrl + F4.

Your screen should be similar to Figure 1.28

> **Another Method** notes offer additional ways to perform a procedure.

Empty document window

Status bar indicators blank

Figure 1.28

Because you did not make any changes to the document since saving it, the document window is closed immediately. If you had made additional changes, Word would ask if you wanted to save the file before closing it. This prevents the accidental closing of a file that has not been saved first. Now the Word window displays an empty document window, and the status bar indicators are blank because there are no open documents.

Opening a File

You asked your assistant to enter the remaining information in the flyer for you while you attended the meeting. Upon your return, you find a note from your assistant on your desk. The note explains that he had a little trouble entering the information and tells you that he saved the revised file as Flyer2. You want to open the file and continue working on the flyer.

❶ ● Move to Z (second line of paragraph below tour list).

● Drag to the right until all the text including the space before the word "locations" is highlighted.

HAVING TROUBLE?
Hold down the left mouse button while moving the mouse to drag.

Additional Information
When you start dragging over a word, the entire word including the space after it is automatically selected.

Your screen should be similar to Figure 1.41

> Clear **Step-by-Step Instructions** detail how to complete a task, or series of tasks.

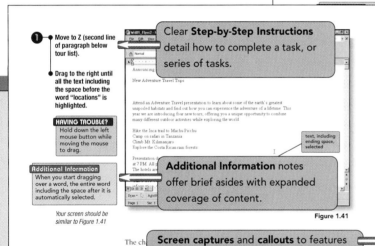

text, including ending space, selected

> **Additional Information** notes offer brief asides with expanded coverage of content.

Figure 1.41

The ch be mo remov

❷ ● Press Delete.

> **Screen captures** and **callouts** to features show how your screen should look at the completion of a step.

Location to open files

Changes dialog box view

Figure 1.29

You also decide to delete the entire last sentence of the paragraph. You can quickly select a standard block of text. Standard blocks include a sentence, paragraph, page, tabular column, rectangular portion of text, or the entire document. The following table summarizes the techniques used to select standard blocks.

To Select	Procedure
Word	Double-click in the word.
Sentence	Press Ctrl and click within the sentence.
Line	Click to the left of a line when the mouse pointer is ⬧.
Multiple lines	Drag up or down to the left of a line when the mouse pointer is ⬧.
Paragraph	Triple-click on the paragraph or double-click to the left of the paragraph when the mouse pointer is ⬧.
Multiple paragraphs	Drag to the left of the paragraphs when the mouse pointer is ⬧.
Document	Triple-click or press Ctrl and click to the left of the text when the mouse pointer is ⬧.
	Use Edit/Select All or the keyboard shortcut Ctrl + Alt.

> **Tables** provide quick summaries of toolbar buttons, key terms, and procedures for specific tasks.

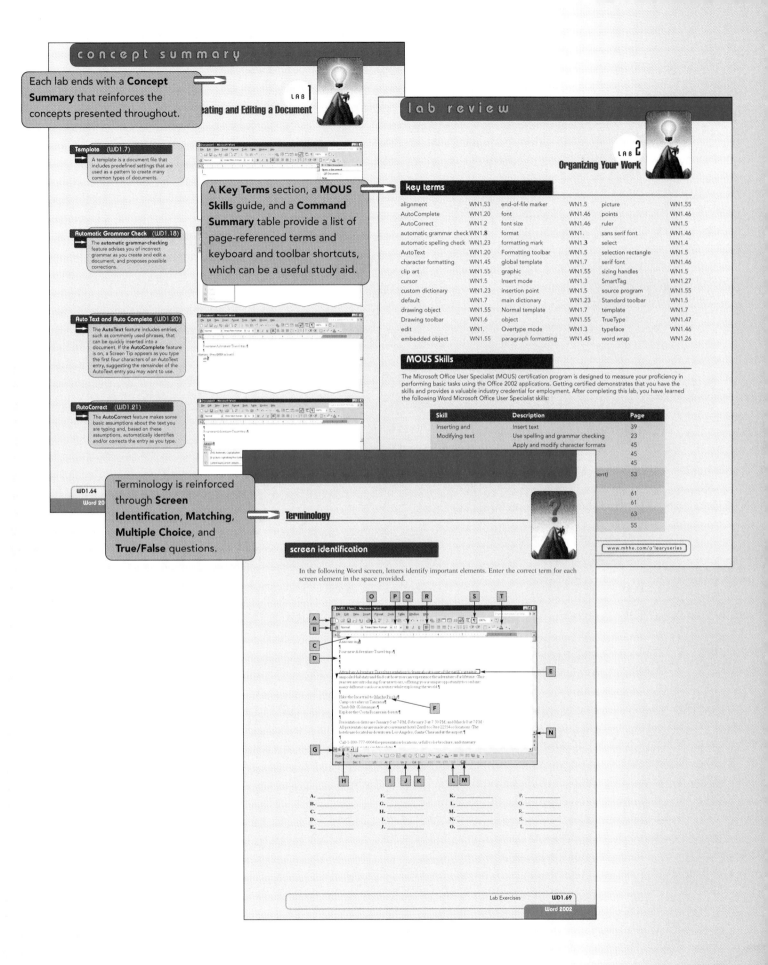

Each lab ends with a **Concept Summary** that reinforces the concepts presented throughout.

concept summary

LAB 1
...eating and Editing a Document

Template (WD1.7)
A template is a document file that includes predefined settings that are used as a pattern to create many common types of documents.

Automatic Grammar Check (WD1.18)
The automatic grammar-checking feature advises you of incorrect grammar as you create and edit a document, and proposes possible corrections.

A **Key Terms** section, a **MOUS Skills** guide, and a **Command Summary** table provide a list of page-referenced terms and keyboard and toolbar shortcuts, which can be a useful study aid.

Auto Text and Auto Complete (WD1.20)
The AutoText feature includes entries, such as commonly used phrases, that can be quickly inserted into a document. If the AutoComplete feature is on, a Screen Tip appears as you type the first four characters of an AutoText entry, suggesting the remainder of the AutoText entry you may want to use.

AutoCorrect (WD1.21)
The AutoCorrect feature makes some basic assumptions about the text you are typing and, based on these assumptions, automatically identifies and/or corrects the entry as you type.

WD1.64
Word 20...

Terminology is reinforced through **Screen Identification**, **Matching**, **Multiple Choice**, and **True/False** questions.

lab review

LAB 2
Organizing Your Work

key terms

alignment	WN1.53	end-of-file marker	WN1.5	picture	WN1.55
AutoComplete	WN1.20	font	WN1.46	points	WN1.46
AutoCorrect	WN1.2	font size	WN1.46	ruler	WN1.5
automatic grammar check	WN1.8	format	WN1.	sans serif font	WN1.46
automatic spelling check	WN1.23	formatting mark	WN1.3	select	WN1.4
AutoText	WN1.20	Formatting toolbar	WN1.5	selection rectangle	WN1.5
character formatting	WN1.45	global template	WN1.7	serif font	WN1.46
clip art	WN1.55	graphic	WN1.55	sizing handles	WN1.5
cursor	WN1.5	Insert mode	WN1.3	SmartTag	WN1.27
custom dictionary	WN1.23	insertion point	WN1.5	source program	WN1.55
default	WN1.7	main dictionary	WN1.23	Standard toolbar	WN1.5
drawing object	WN1.55	Normal template	WN1.7	template	WN1.7
Drawing toolbar	WN1.6	object	WN1.55	TrueType	WN1.47
edit	WN1.	Overtype mode	WN1.3	typeface	WN1.46
embedded object	WN1.55	paragraph formatting	WN1.45	word wrap	WN1.26

MOUS Skills

The Microsoft Office User Specialist (MOUS) certification program is designed to measure your proficiency in performing basic tasks using the Office 2002 applications. Getting certified demonstrates that you have the skills and provides a valuable industry credential for employment. After completing this lab, you have learned the following Word Microsoft Office User Specialist skills:

Skill	Description	Page
Inserting and	Insert text	39
Modifying text	Use spelling and grammar checking	23
	Apply and modify character formats	45
		45
		45
...ent)	53
		61
		61
		63
		55

www.mhhe.com/o'learyseries

Terminology

screen identification

In the following Word screen, letters identify important elements. Enter the correct term for each screen element in the space provided.

A. _____ F. _____ K. _____ P. _____
B. _____ G. _____ L. _____ Q. _____
C. _____ H. _____ M. _____ R. _____
D. _____ I. _____ N. _____ S. _____
E. _____ J. _____ O. _____ T. _____

lab exercises

Concepts

Fill-in questions

1. A small blue box appearing under a word or character indicates that the _____ feature was applied.

2. If a word is underlined with purple dots, this indicates a(n) _____.

3. The _____ feature displays each page of your document in a reduced size so you can see the page layout.

4. To size a graphic evenly, click and drag the _____ in one corner of the graphic.

5. It is good practice to use only _____ types of fonts in a document.

6. When you use _____, new text replaces existing text as you type.

7. The _____ sits on the right side of the window and contains buttons and icons to help you perform common tasks, such as opening a blank document.

8. Use _____ when you want to keep your existing document with the original name and make a copy with a new name.

9. The _____ window displays a reduced view of how the current page will appear when printed.

10. The _____ feature includes entries, such as commonly used phrases, that can be quickly inserted into a document.

discussion questions

1. Discuss several uses you may have for a word processor. Then e2002lain the steps you would follow to create a document.

2. Discuss how the AutoCorrect and Spelling and Grammar Checker features help you as you type. es of corrections does the AutoCorrect feature make?

ow word wrap works. What happens when text is added? What happens when text is

ree ways you can select text. Discuss when it would be appropriate to use the different

ow the Undo and Redo features work. What are some advantages of these features?

ow graphics can be used in a document. What should you consider when adding graphics ? Can the use of a graphic change the reader's response to a document?

> Concepts are reinforced in **Fill-In** and **Discussion** questions.

Lab 1: Creating and Editing a Document

www.mhhe.com/o'learyseries

2

Hands-On Exercises

rating system
★ Easy
★★ Moderate
★★★ Difficult

step-by-step

★ **Writing a Memo**

1. Universal Industries is starting a casual Friday policy. Ms. Jones, the Vice President of Human Resources, has sent a memo informing employees of this new policy. Your completed memo is shown here.

   a. Open a blank Word document and create the memo with the following text. Press Tab twice after you type colons (:) in the To, From, Date, and RE lines. This will make the information following the colons line up evenly. Enter a blank line below the RE line and between paragraphs.

   To: [Your Name]
   From: Ms. Jones
   Date: [Current date]
   RE: Business Casual Dress Code

   Effective next Friday, business casual will be allowed in the corporate facility on Fridays and the day before a holiday break. Business casual is sometimes difficult to interpret. For men, it is a collared shirt and tailored trousers. For women, it is a pantsuit or tailored trousers or skirt. Business casual is not jeans, t-shirts, or exercise clothes. A detailed dress code will be available on the company intranet.

   Thank you for your cooperation in this matter.

   CSJ/xxx

   b. Correct any spelling and grammar errors that are identified.
   c. Change the font for the entire memo to 14 pt.
   d. Change the alignment of the memo body to justified.
   e. Insert a blank line under the Date line and insert the AutoText reference line "RE:".
   f. Press Tab and type "Business Casual Dress Code".
   g. Save the document as Dress Code on your data disk.
   h. Preview and print the document.

> **Hands-on Exercises** develop critical thinking skills and offer step-by-step practice. These exercises have a rating system from easy to difficult, and test your ability to apply the knowledge you have gained in each lab.

Lab Exercises   **WD1.73**

Word 2002

Introduction to Microsoft Office XP

What is Office XP?

Microsoft Office XP is a suite of applications that can be used individually and that are designed to work together seamlessly. The applications include tools used to create, discuss, communicate, and manage projects. If you share a lot of documents with other people, these features facilitate access to common documents. This version has expanded and refined the communication and collaboration features and integration with the World Wide Web. In addition, several new interface features are designed to make it easier to perform tasks and help users take advantage of all the features in the applications.

The Office XP suite is packaged in different combinations of components. The major components and a brief description are provided in the following table.

Component	Description
Word 2002	Word processor
Excel 2002	Spreadsheet
Access 2002	Database manager
PowerPoint 2002	Presentation graphics
Outlook 2002	Desktop information manager
FrontPage 2002	Web page authoring
Publisher	Desktop publishing
SharePoint	Team Web sites

The four main components of Office XP—Word, Excel, Access, and PowerPoint—are described in more detail in the following sections.

Word 2002

Word 2002 is a word processing software application whose purpose is to help you create text-based documents. Word processors are one of the most flexible and widely used application software programs. A word processor can be used to manipulate text data to produce a letter, a report,

I.

a memo, an e-mail, message or any other type of correspondence. Two documents you will produce in the first two Word labs, a letter and flyer, are shown here.

February 18, 2001

Dear Adventure Traveler,

Imagine hiking and paddling your way through the rain forests of Costa Rica, under the stars in Africa, or following in the footsteps of the ancient Inca as you backp the Inca trail to Machu Picchu. Turn these dreams of adventure into memories you w forever by joining Adventure Travel Tours on one of our four new adventure tours.

To tell you more about these exciting new adventures, we are offerin presentations in your area. These presentations will focus on the features and cultu region. We will also show you pictures of the places you will visit and activities participate in, as well as a detailed agenda and package costs. Plan on attending o following presentations:

Date	Time	Location	Room
January 5	7:00 PM	Town Center Hotel	Room 284B
February 3	7:30 PM	Airport Manor	Conference Room A
March 8	7:00 PM	Country Inn	Mountainside Room

In appreciation of your past patronage, we are pleased to offer you a 10% disco price of any of the new tour packages. You must book the trip at least 60 days pr departure date. Please turn in this letter to qualify for the discount.

Our vacation tours are professionally developed solely for your enjoyment. W almost everything in the price of your tour while giving you the best possible valu dollar. All tours include:

- Professional tour manager and local guides
- All accommodations and meals
- All entrance fees, excursions, transfers and tips

We hope you will join us this year on another special Adventure Travel Tour Your memories of fascinating places and challenging physical adventures should li long, long time. For reservations, please see your travel agent, or contact Adventure Tr at 1-800-777-0004. You can also visit our new Web site at www.AdventureTravelTour

Best regards,

Student Name

A letter containing a tabbed table, indented paragraphs, and text enhancements is quickly created using basic Word features.

Announcing
New Adventure Travel Tours

This year we are introducing four new tours, offering you a unique opportunity to combine many different outdoor activities while exploring the world.

Hike the Inca trail to Machu Picchu
Camp on safari in Tanzania
Climb Mt. Kilimanjaro
Explore the Costa Rican rain forests

Attend an Adventure Travel presentation to learn about some of the earth's greatest unspoiled habitats and find out how you can experience the adventure of a lifetime.

Presentation dates and times are January 5 at 7 PM, February 3 at 7:30 PM, and March 8 at 7 PM. All presentations are held at convenient hotel locations located in downtown Los Angeles, Santa Clara and at the airport.

Call us at 1-800-777-0004 for presentation locations, a full color brochure, and itinerary information, costs, and tour dates.

Visit Our
Web site at
AdventureTravelTours.com

A flyer incorporating many visual enhancements such as colored text, varied text styles, and graphic elements is both eye-catching and informative.

The beauty of a word processor is that you can make changes or corrections as you are typing. Want to change a report from single spacing to double spacing? Alter the width of the margins? Delete some paragraphs and add others from yet another document? A word processor allows you to do all these things with ease.

Word 2002 includes many group collaboration features to help streamline how documents are developed and changed by group members. You can also create and send e-mail messages directly from within Word using all its features to create and edit the message. You can also send an entire document as your e-mail message, allowing the recipient to edit the document directly without having to open or save an attachment.

Word 2002 is also closely integrated with the World Wide Web, detecting when you type a Web address and automatically converting it to a hyperlink. You can also create your own hyperlinks to locations within documents, or to other documents, including those at external locations such as a Web site or file server. Its many Web-editing features, including a Web Page Wizard that guides you step by step, help you quickly create a Web page. You will see how easy it is when you create the Web page shown below in the Working Together tutorial.

A Web page created in Word and displayed in the Internet Explorer browser.

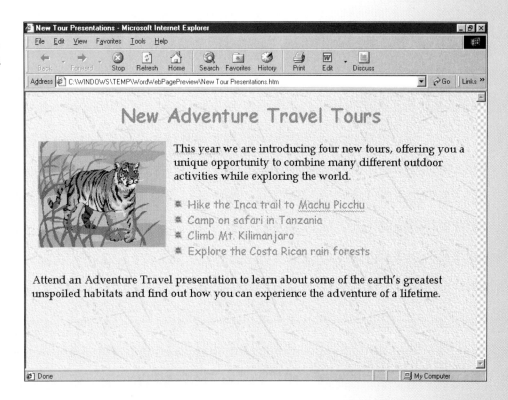

Excel 2002

Excel 2002 is an electronic worksheet that is used to organize, manipulate, and graph numeric data. Once used almost exclusively by accountants, worksheets are now widely used by nearly every profession. Marketing professionals record and evaluate sales trends. Teachers record grades and calculate final grades. Personal trainers record the progress of their clients. Excel includes many features that not only help you create a well-designed worksheet, but one that produces accurate results. Formatting features include visual enhancements such as varied text styles, colors, and graphics. Other features help you enter complex formulas and identify and correct formula errors. You can also produce a visual display of data in the form of graphs or charts. As the values in the worksheet change, charts referencing those values automatically adjust to reflect the changes.

Excel also includes many advanced features and tools that help you perform what-if analysis and create different scenarios. And like all Office XP applications, it is easy to incorporate data created in one application into another. Two worksheets you will produce in Labs 2 and 3 of Excel are shown here.

A worksheet showing the quarterly sales forecast containing a graphic, text enhancements, and a chart of the data is quickly created using basic Excel features.

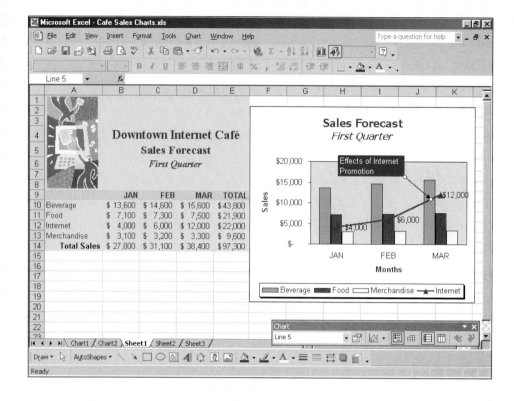

A large worksheet incorporating more complex formulas, visual enhancements such as colored text, varied text styles, and graphic elements is both informative and attractive.

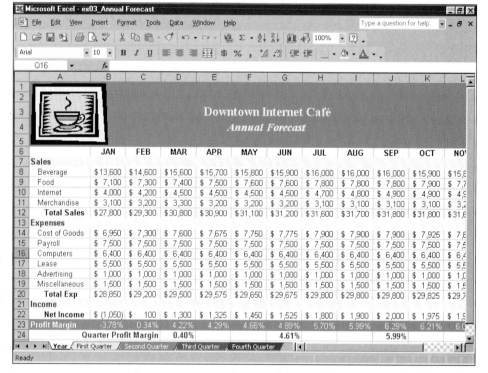

You will see how easy it is to analyze data and make projections using what-if analysis and what-if graphing in Lab 3 and to incorporate Excel data in a Word document as shown in the figures below.

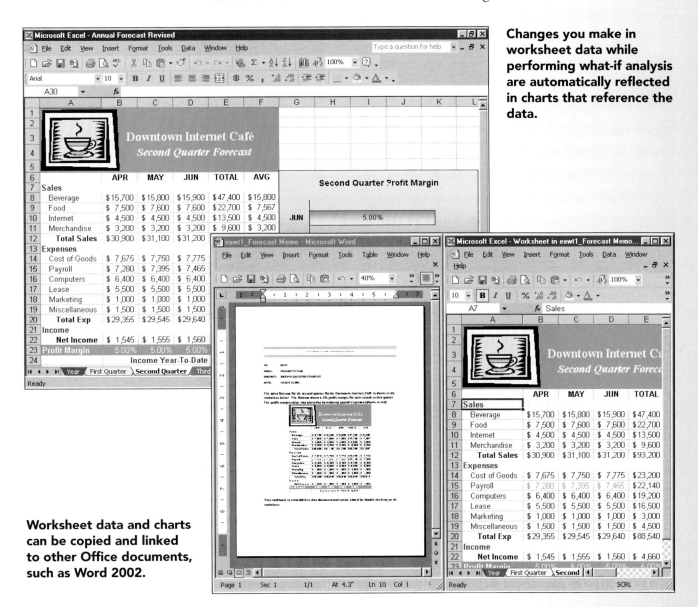

Changes you make in worksheet data while performing what-if analysis are automatically reflected in charts that reference the data.

Worksheet data and charts can be copied and linked to other Office documents, such as Word 2002.

Access 2002

Access 2002 is a relational database management application that is used to create and analyze a database. A database is a collection of related data. In a relational database, the most widely used database structure, data is organized in linked tables. Tables consist of columns (called fields) and rows (called records). The tables are related or linked to one another by a common field. Relational databases allow you to create smaller and more manageable database tables, since you can combine and extract data between tables.

The program provides tools to enter, edit, and retrieve data from the database as well as to analyze the database and produce reports of the output. One of the main advantages of a computerized database is the ability to quickly add, delete, and locate specific records. Records can also be easily rearranged or sorted according to different fields of data, resulting in multiple table arrangements that provide more meaningful information for different purposes. Creation of forms makes it easier to enter and edit data as well. In the Access labs you will create and organize the database table shown below.

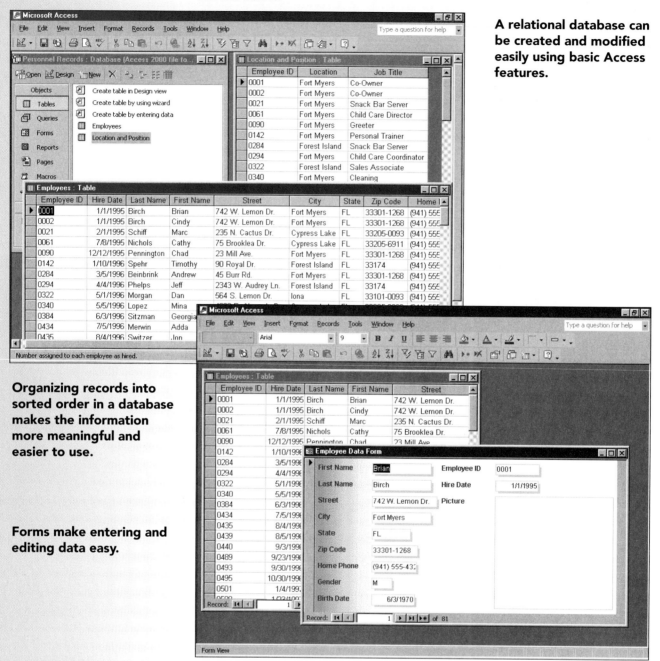

A relational database can be created and modified easily using basic Access features.

Organizing records into sorted order in a database makes the information more meaningful and easier to use.

Forms make entering and editing data easy.

Another feature is the ability to analyze the data in a table and perform calculations on different fields of data. Additionally, you can ask questions or query the table to find only certain records that meet specific conditions to be used in the analysis. Information that was once costly and time-consuming to get is now quickly and readily available. This information can then be quickly printed out in the form of reports ranging from simple listings to complex, professional-looking reports in different layout styles, or with titles, headings, subtotals, or totals.

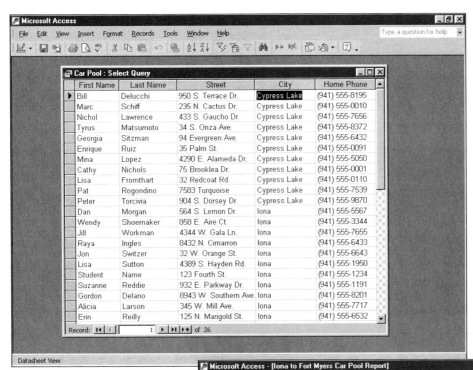

A database can be queried to locate and display only specified information.

A professional-looking report can be quickly generated from information contained in a database.

PowerPoint 2002

PowerPoint 2002 is a graphics presentation program designed to help you produce a high-quality presentation that is both interesting to the audience and effective in its ability to convey your message. A presentation can be as simple as overhead transparencies or as sophisticated as an on-screen electronic display. In the first two PowerPoint labs you will create and organize the presentation shown on the next page.

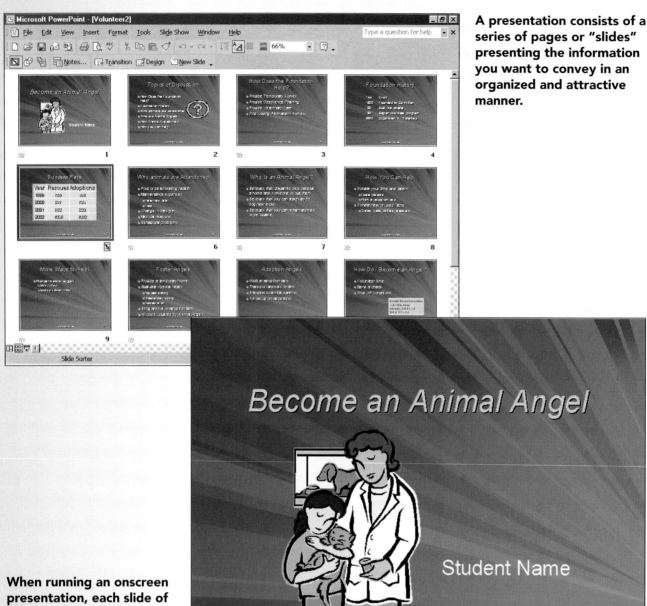

A presentation consists of a series of pages or "slides" presenting the information you want to convey in an organized and attractive manner.

When running an onscreen presentation, each slide of the presentation is displayed full-screen on your computer monitor or projected onto a screen.

Common Office XP Features

Additional Information

Please read the Before You Begin and Instructional Conventions sections in the Overview to Word 2002 (WDO.4) before starting this section.

Now that you know a little about each of the applications in Microsoft Office XP, we will take a look at some of the features that are common to all Office applications. This is a hands-on section that will introduce you to the features and allow you to get a feel for how Office XP works. Although Word 2002 will be used to demonstrate how the features work, only common features will be addressed. These features include using menus, the Office Assistant and Office Help, task panes, toolbars, and starting and exiting an application. The features that are specific to each application will be introduced individually in each lab.

Starting an Office Application

There are several ways to start an Office application. One is to use the New Office Document command on the Start menu and select the type of document you want to create. Another is to use the Documents command on the Start menu and select the document name from the list of recently used documents. This starts the associated application and opens the selected document at the same time. The two most common ways to start an Office XP application are by choosing the application name from the Start menu or by clicking a desktop shortcut for the program if it is available.

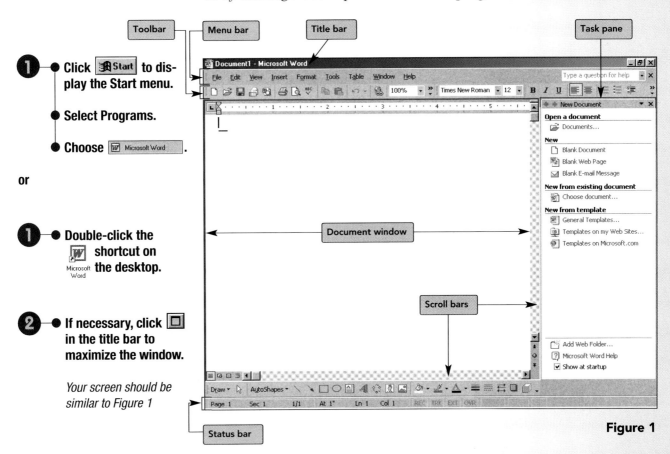

1 ● Click **Start** to display the Start menu.

● Select Programs.

● Choose **Microsoft Word**.

or

1 ● Double-click the **W** Microsoft Word shortcut on the desktop.

2 ● If necessary, click ☐ in the title bar to maximize the window.

Your screen should be similar to Figure 1

Figure 1

Additional Information

Application windows can be sized, moved, and otherwise manipulated like any other windows on the desktop. Refer to your text or, if available, to the *Introduction to Windows 2000* labs for information about working with windows.

The Word program is started and displayed in a window on the desktop. The left end of the application window title bar displays the file name followed by the program name, Microsoft Word. The right end of the title bar displays the ▬ Minimize, ◱ Restore, and ☒ Close buttons. They perform the same functions and operate in the same way as in Windows 98 and 2000.

The **menu bar** below the title bar displays the application's program menu. The right end displays the document window's ☒ Close button. As you use the Office applications, you will see that the menu bar contains many of the same menus, such as File, Edit, and Help. You will also see several menus that are specific to each application.

The **toolbars** located below the menu bar contain buttons that are mouse shortcuts for many of the menu items. Commonly, the Office applications will display two toolbars when the application is first opened: Standard and Formatting. They may appear together on one row (as in Figure 1), or on separate rows.

The large center area of the program window is the **document window** where open application files are displayed. Currently, there is a blank Word document open. The **task pane** is displayed on the right side of the document window. Task panes provide quick access to features as you are using the application. As you perform certain actions, different task panes automatically open. In this case, since you just started an application, the New Document task pane is automatically displayed, providing different ways to create a new document or open an existing document.

The **status bar** at the bottom of the window displays location information and the status of different settings as they are used. Different information is displayed in the status bar for different applications.

On the right and bottom of the document window, are vertical and horizontal scroll bars. A **scroll bar** is used with a mouse to bring additional lines of information into view in a window. The vertical scroll bar is used to move up or down, and the horizontal scroll bar moves side to side in the window.

As you can see, many of the features in the Word window are the same as in other Windows applications. The common user interface makes learning and using new applications much easier.

Using Menus

A **menu** is one of many methods you can use to accomplish a task in a program. When opened, a menu displays a list of commands.

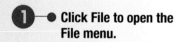
Click File to open the File menu.

Your screen should be similar to Figure 2

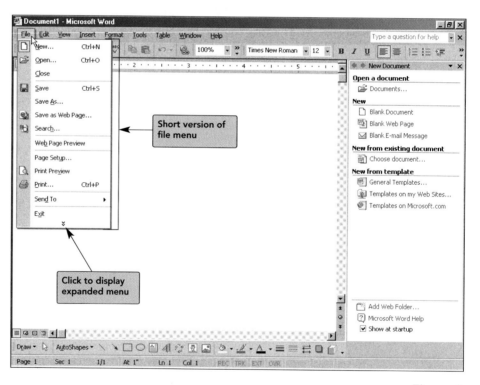

Figure 2

When an Office program menu is first opened, it may display a short version of commands. The short menu is a personalized version of the menu that displays basic and frequently used commands and hides those used less often. An expanded version will display automatically after the menu is open for a few seconds (see Figure 3).

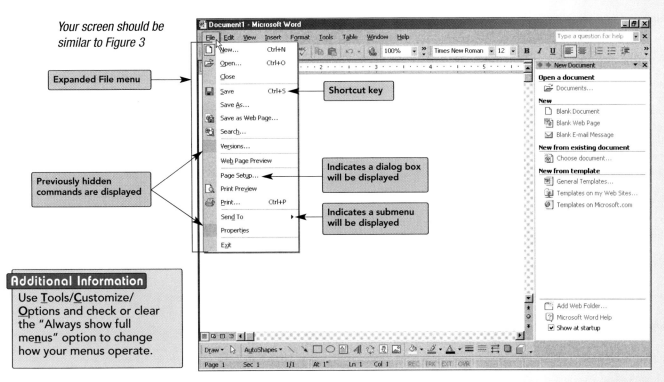

*Your screen should be
similar to Figure 3*

Expanded File menu

**Previously hidden
commands are displayed**

Shortcut key

**Indicates a dialog box
will be displayed**

**Indicates a submenu
will be displayed**

Additional Information
Use **T**ools/**C**ustomize/
Options and check or clear
the "Always show full
me**n**us" option to change
how your menus operate.

Figure 3

When the menu is expanded the hidden commands are displayed. Once one menu is expanded, others are expanded automatically until you choose a command or perform another action.

2 ● **Point to each menu in the menu bar to see the full menu for each.**

● **Point to the File menu again.**

Many commands have images next to them so you can quickly associate the command with the image. The same image appears on the toolbar button for that feature. Menus may include the following features (not all menus include all features):

Feature	Meaning
Ellipsis (...)	Indicates a dialog box will be displayed
▶	Indicates a submenu will be displayed
Dimmed	Indicates the command is not available for selection until certain other conditions are met
Shortcut key	A key or key combination that can be used to execute a command without using the menu
Checkmark	Indicates a toggle type of command. Selecting it turns the feature on or off. A checkmark indicates the feature is on.

Common Office XP Features

I.11

Word 2002

Once a menu is open, you can select a command from the menu by pointing to it. A colored highlight bar, called the **selection cursor**, appears over the selected command.

3 ● **Point to the Send To command to select it and display the submenu.**

Your screen should be similar to Figure 4

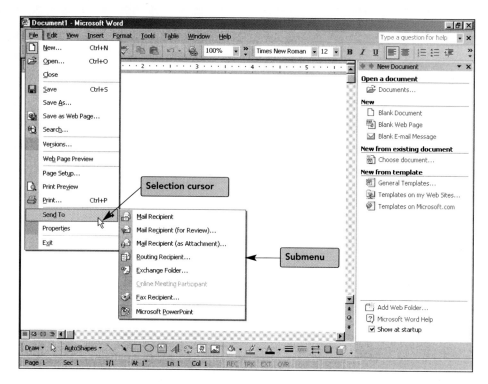

Figure 4

Then to choose a command, you click on it. When the command is chosen, the associated action is performed. You will use a command in the Help menu to access the Microsoft Office Assistant and Help features.

Note: If your screen displays the Office Assistant character as shown in Figure 5, skip step 4.

4 ● **Point to Help.**

● **Click Show the Office Assistant to choose the command.**

Your screen should be similar to Figure 5

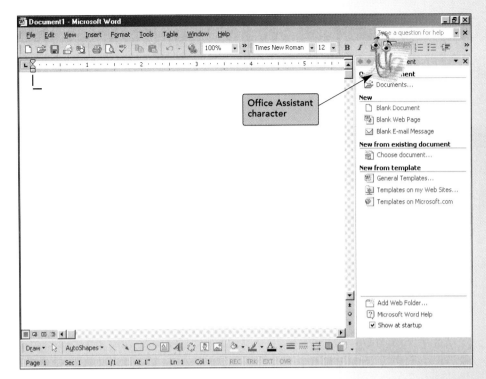

Office Assistant character

Figure 5

HAVING TROUBLE?
If the Assistant does not appear, this feature has been disabled. If this is the case, choose <u>H</u>elp/Microsoft Word <u>H</u>elp or press F1 and skip to the section "Using Help."

The command to display the Office Assistant has been executed, and the Office Assistant character is displayed. The default Assistant character is Clippit shown in Figure 5. Because there are eight different characters from which you can select, your screen may display a different Assistant character.

Using the Office Assistant

When the Office Assistant is on, it automatically suggests help topics as you work. It anticipates what you are going to do and then makes suggestions on how to perform a task. In addition, you can activate the Assistant at any time to get help on features in the Office application you are using. Clicking on the Assistant character activates it and displays a balloon in which you can type the topic you want help on. You will ask the Office Assistant to provide information on the different ways you can get help while using the program.

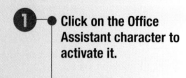

① ● Click on the Office Assistant character to activate it.

● Type *How do I get help?* in the text box.

● Click ⌷Search⌷.

Your screen should be similar to Figure 6

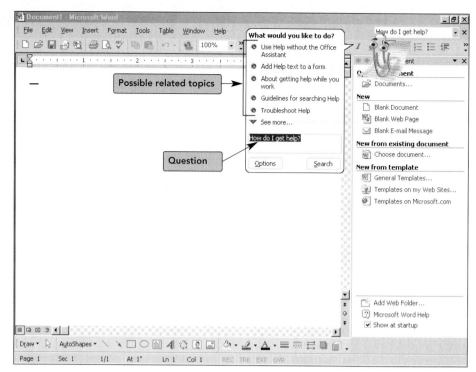

Figure 6

The balloon displays a list of related topics from which you can select.

② ● Select About getting help while you work.

Your screen should be similar to Figure 7

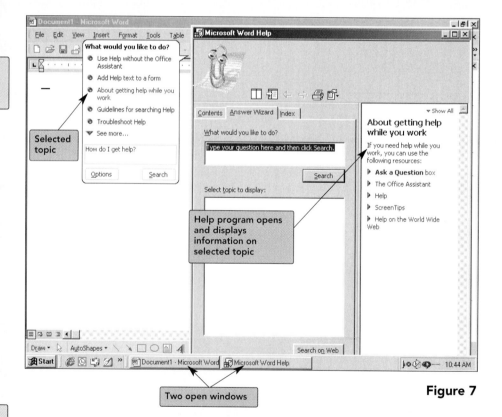

Figure 7

The Help program opens and displays the selected topic. Because Word Help is a separate program within Office, it appears in its own window. The Help window overlaps the Word window so that it is easy to read the information in Help while referring to the application window. The taskbar displays a button for both open windows.

Now that Help is open, you no longer need to see the Assistant. To access commands to control the Office Assistant, you will display the object's shortcut menu by right-clicking on the Assistant character. **Shortcut menus** display the most common menu options related to the selected item only.

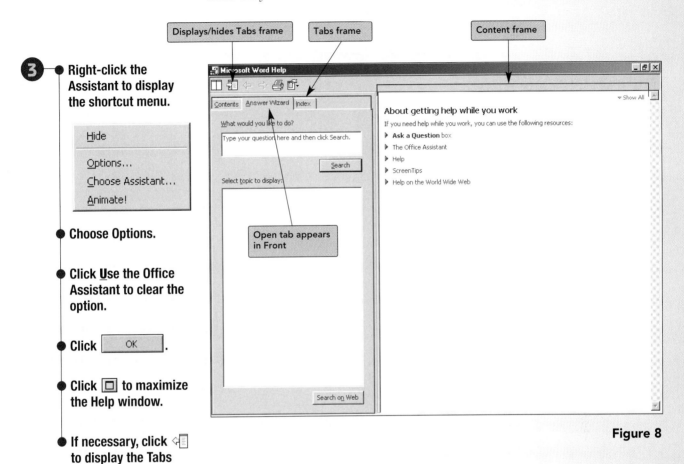

3 ● Right-click the Assistant to display the shortcut menu.

● Choose Options.

● Click **U**se the Office Assistant to clear the option.

● Click   OK   .

● Click ▢ to maximize the Help window.

● If necessary, click ◁▤ to display the Tabs frame.

Your screen should be similar to Figure 8

Figure 8

Using Help

In the Help window, the toolbar buttons help you use different Help features and navigate in Help.

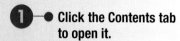
The Help window is divided into two vertical frames. **Frames** divide a window into separate, scrollable areas that can display different information. The left frame in the Help window is the Tabs frame. It contains three folder-like tabs, Contents, Index, and Search, that provide three different means of getting Help information. The open tab appears in front of the other tabs and displays the available options for the feature. The right frame is the content frame where the content for the selected topic is displayed.

1 ● **Click the Contents tab to open it.**

HAVING TROUBLE?

If you cannot see the Contents tab, click the ◄ tab scroll button to bring it into view.

Your screen should be similar to Figure 9

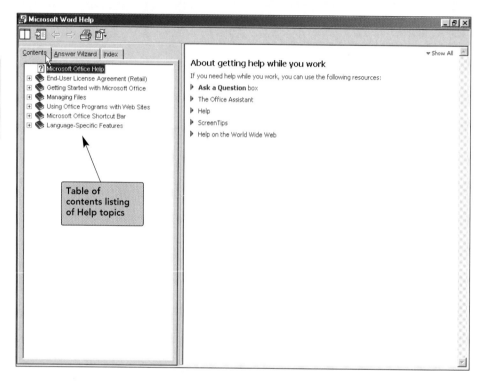

Table of contents listing of Help topics

Figure 9

Using the Contents Tab

The Contents tab displays a table of contents listing of topics in Help. Clicking on an item preceded with a ⊞ opens a "chapter," which expands to display additional chapters or specific Help topics.

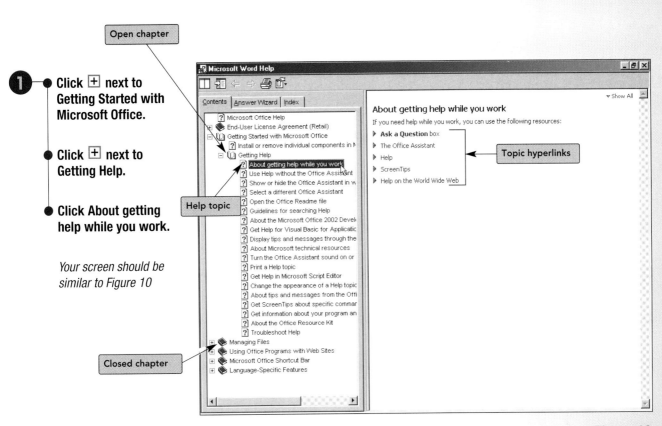

Open chapter

1 ● Click ⊞ next to
  **Getting Started with
  Microsoft Office.**

● Click ⊞ next to
  Getting Help.

● Click **About getting
  help while you work.**

*Your screen should be
similar to Figure 10*

Help topic

Closed chapter

Topic hyperlinks

Figure 10

You have opened two chapters and selected a Help topic. Open chapters are preceded with a 📖 icon and topics with a ⁇ icon.

Using a Hyperlink

The Help topic tells you about five resources you can use to get help. Each resource is a **hyperlink** or connection to additional information in the current document, in online Help, or on the Microsoft Office Web site. It commonly appears as colored or underlined text. Clicking the hyperlink accesses and displays the information associated with the hyperlink. A hyperlink preceded with a ▶ indicates clicking the link will display additional information about the topic.

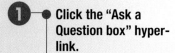

1 ● Click the "Ask a Question box" hyperlink.

● Click the "The Office Assistant" hyperlink.

Your screen should be similar to Figure 11

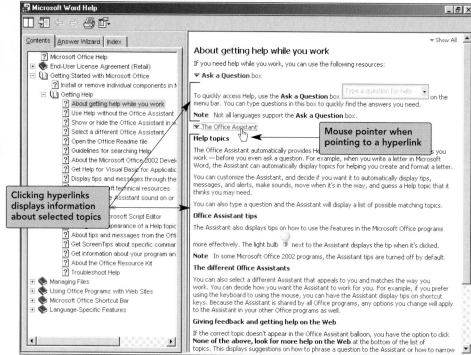

Figure 11

Additional Information

Clicking the scroll arrows scrolls the text in the frame line by line, and dragging the scroll box up or down the scroll bar moves to a general location within the frame area.

The content frame displays additional information about the two selected topics. Now, because there is more information in the content frame than can be displayed at one time, you will need to use the vertical scroll bar to scroll the additional information into the frame as you read the Help information. Also, as you are reading help, you may see text that appears as a hyperlink. Clicking on the text will display a definition of a term.

2 ● Using the scroll bar, scroll the content frame to read the information on this topic.

● Click the "shortcut keys" hyperlink.

Your screen should be similar to Figure 12

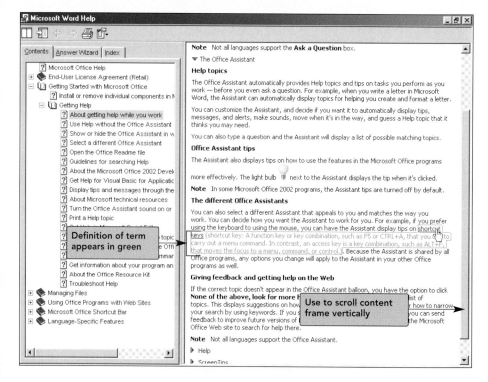

Figure 12

Scrolling the frame displays the information at the bottom of the frame while the information at the top of the frame is no longer visible. The end of the Help information is displayed in the frame. A definition of the term "shortcut keys" is displayed in green text.

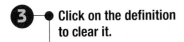

3 ● **Click on the definition to clear it.**

● **Click on the Use Help without the Office Assistant topic in the Contents tab.**

Additional Information

Pointing to a topic in the content frame that is not fully visible displays the full topic in a ScreenTip box.

Your screen should be similar to Figure 13

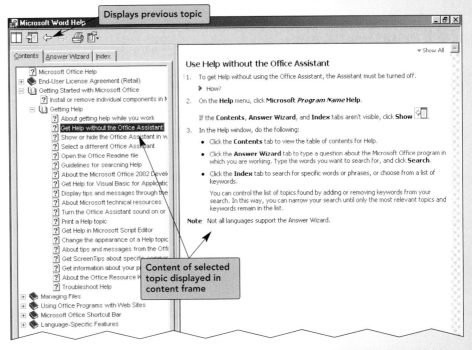

Figure 13

The content frame now displays the Help information about the selected topic. To quickly return to the previous topic,

4 ● **Click** ⇐ **Back.**

Your screen should be similar to Figure 14

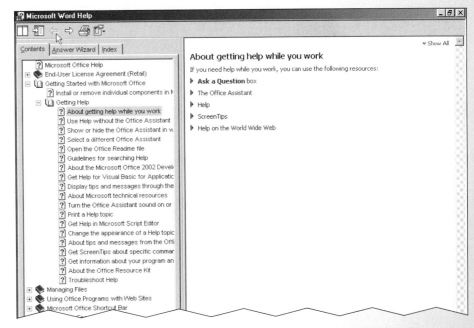

Figure 14

The topic is redisplayed as it originally appeared, without the topic selections expanded.

Using the Index Tab

To search for Help information by entering a word or phrase for a topic, you can use the Index tab.

1 Open the Index tab.

HAVING TROUBLE?
If the Index tab is not visible in the frame, click the ▶ scroll button to display it.

Your screen should be similar to Figure 15

Open tab

Enter word or phrase to locate

Alphabetical list of keywords

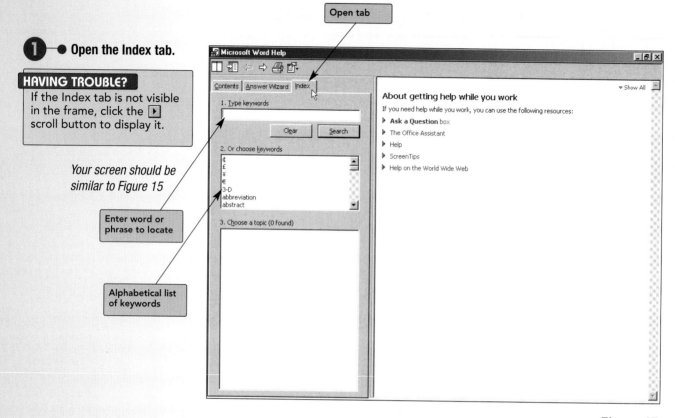

Figure 15

The Index tab consists of a text box where you can type a word or phrase that best describes the topic you want to locate. Below it is a list box displaying a complete list of Help keywords in alphabetical order. You want to find information about using the Index tab.

2 ● **Type index in the text box.**

● **Click [Search].**

Your screen should be similar to Figure 16

19 Help topics containing keyword "index"

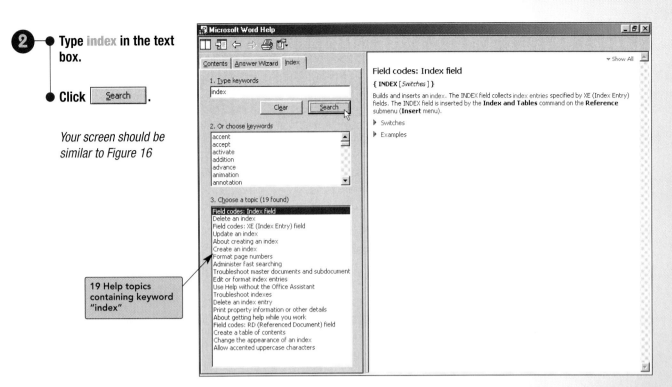

Figure 16

The topic list displays 19 Help topics containing this word, and the content frame, displays the information on the first topic. However, many of the located topics are not about the Help Index feature. To narrow the search more, you can add another word to the keyword text box.

3 ● **Click in the text box.**

● **Type help following the word "index."**

● **Click [Search].**

Your screen should be similar to Figure 17

Two topics contain both keywords

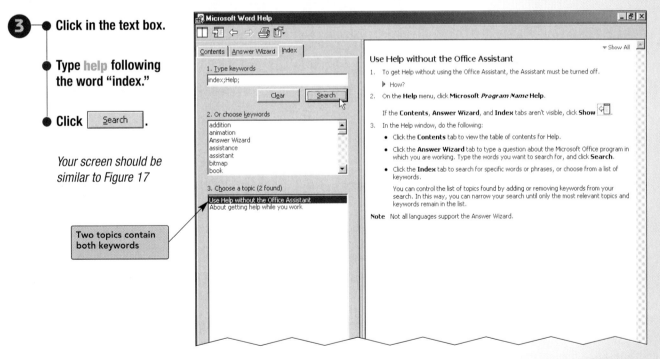

Figure 17

Now only two topics were located that contain both keywords. The first topic in the list is selected and displayed in the content frame.

Using the Answer Wizard

Another way to locate Help topics is to use the Answer Wizard tab. This feature works just like the Office Assistant and the Answer box to locate topics. You will use this method to locate information on toolbars.

1 ● **Open the Answer Wizard tab.**

● **Type** How do I use toolbars? **in the text box.**

● **Click** Search .

Your screen should be similar to Figure 18

Topics related to your search

Additional Information

The search term does not need to be worded as a question. It can also be a word or phrase.

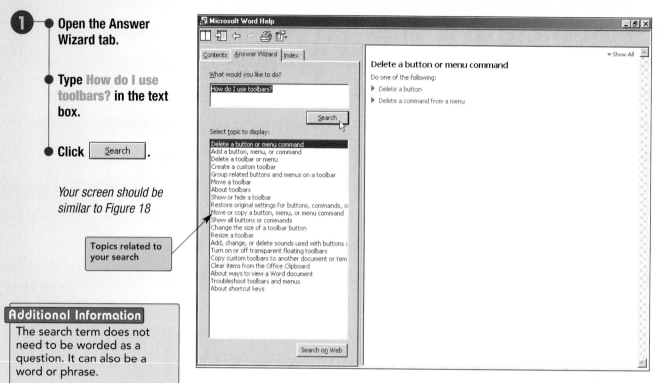

Figure 18

The topic list box displays all topics that the Answer Wizard considers may be related to the question you entered.

2 ● **Select "About toolbars" from the topic list.**

● **Click Show All.**

Your screen should be similar to Figure 19

Selected topic

Selected topic is displayed in Content frame

Displays/hides all topic information

Topic information fully displayed

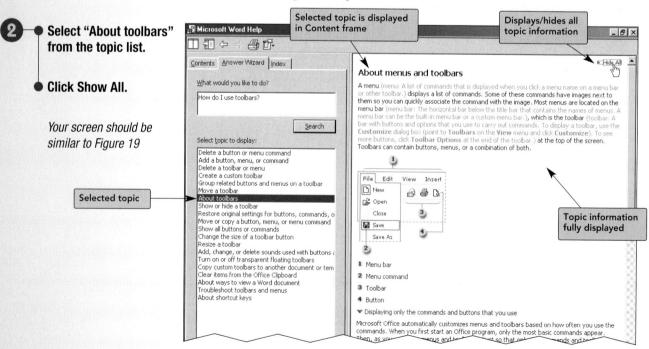

Figure 19

All topics are expanded and definitions displayed.

3 ● **Read the information about this topic.**

● **Click ☒ to close Help.**

Your screen should be similar to Figure 20

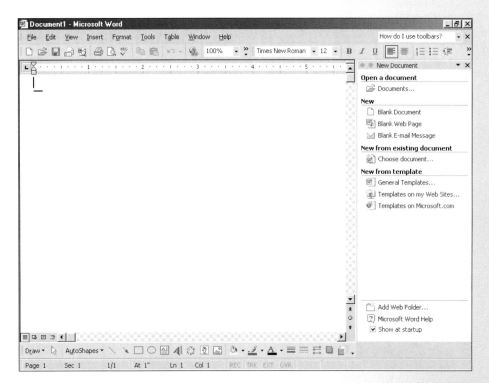

Figure 20

The Help window is closed, and the Word window is displayed again.

HAVING TROUBLE?

Your system must have an Internet connection to access the Microsoft Office Web site. If you do not have that, skip this section.

Getting Help on the Web

A final source of Help information is the Microsoft Office Web site. If a Help topic begins with "Web," clicking it takes you to the Web site and displays the topic in your Help window. You can also connect directly to this site from any Office application using the Help menu.

1 ● Choose **H**elp/Office on the **W**eb.

● If necessary, enter your user information and make the appropriate selections to connect to the Internet.

● If necessary, click United States.

Your screen should be similar to Figure 21

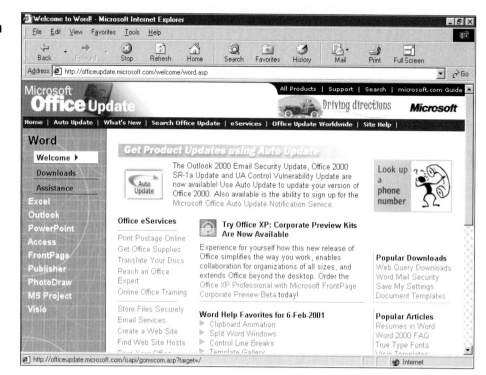

Figure 21

The browser application on your system is started and displays the Microsoft Office Web site. Now you could select any of the hyperlinks to further explore the site.

1 ● Read the information on this page.

● Click ☒ to close the browser.

● If necessary, disconnect from the Internet.

The Word application window is displayed again.

Using Toolbars

While using Office XP, you will see that many toolbars open automatically as different tasks are performed. Toolbars initially display the basic buttons. Like menus, they are personalized automatically, displaying those buttons you use frequently and hiding others. The More Buttons ⁑ button located at the end of a toolbar displays a drop-down button list of those buttons that are not displayed. When you use a button from this list, it then is moved to the toolbar, and a button that has not been used recently is moved to the More Buttons list.

Initially, Word displays two toolbars, Standard and Formatting, on one row below the menu bar (see Figure 22). The Standard toolbar contains buttons that are used to complete the most frequently used menu commands. The Formatting toolbar contains buttons that are used to change the appearance or format of the document.

HAVING TROUBLE?
Your screen may display different toolbars in different locations. This is because the program displays the settings that were in effect when it was last exited.

1 ● **Right-click on any toolbar to display the shortcut menu.**

Your screen should be similar to Figure 22

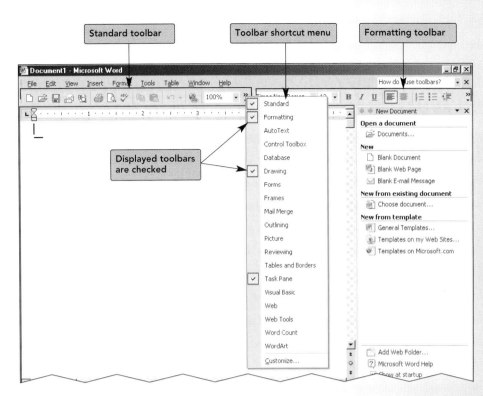

Figure 22

Additional Information

The customize option can be used to change features of toolbars and menus.

The toolbar shortcut menu displays a list of toolbar names. The Formatting, Standard, and Task Pane options should be checked, indicating they are displayed. Clicking on a toolbar from the list will display it on-screen. Clicking on a checked toolbar will hide the toolbar.

2 ● **Click Task Pane to clear the checkmark.**

Your screen should be similar to Figure 23

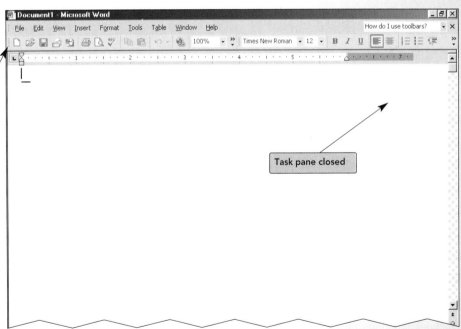

Figure 23

The task pane is closed. When a toolbar is open, it may appear docked or floating. A docked toolbar is fixed to an edge of the window and displays a vertical bar called the move handle ▐, on the left edge of the toolbar. Dragging this bar up or down allows you to move the toolbar. If multiple toolbars share the same row, dragging the bar left or right adjusts the size of the toolbar. If docked, a toolbar can occupy a row by itself, or several can be on a row together. A floating toolbar appears in a separate window.

3 ● **Drag the move handle of the Standard toolbar into the document window.**

Another Method

You can also double-click the top or bottom edge of a docked toolbar to change it to a floating toolbar.

Your screen should be similar to Figure 24

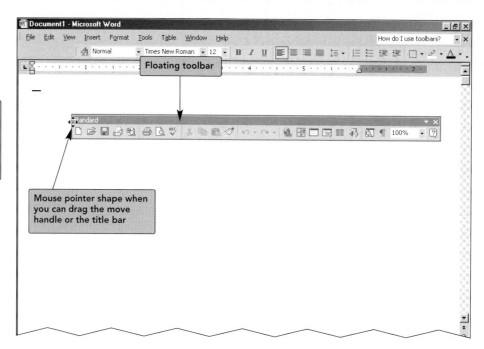

Figure 24

The Standard toolbar is now floating and can be moved to any location in the window by dragging the title bar. If you move it to the edge of the window, it will attach to that location and become a docked toolbar. A floating toolbar can also be sized by dragging the edge of toolbar.

4 ● **Drag the title bar of the floating toolbar to move it to the row below the Formatting toolbar.**

● **Move the Formatting toolbar below the Standard toolbar.**

Your screen should be similar to Figure 25

Additional Information

You can permanently display the toolbars on two rows using Tools/Customize/ Options or by choosing Customize from the toolbar shortcut menu and selecting "Show Standard and Formatting toolbars on two rows."

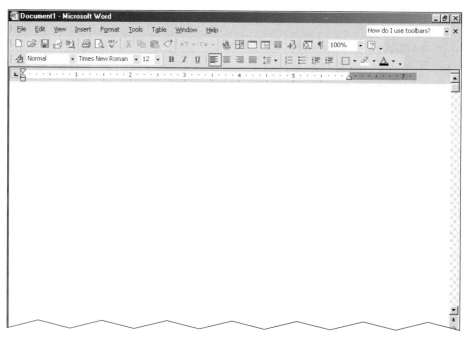

Figure 25

The two toolbars now occupy two rows. To quickly identify the toolbar buttons, you can display the button name by pointing to the button.

5 Point to any button on the Standard toolbar.

Your screen should be similar to Figure 26

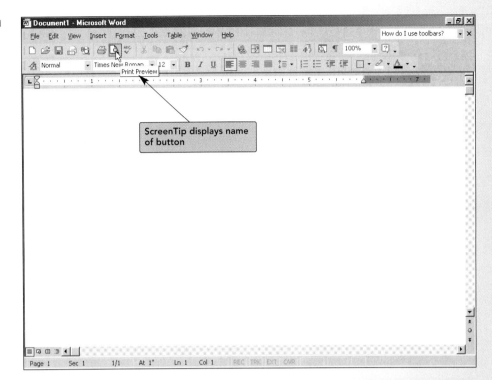

ScreenTip displays name of button

Figure 26

A ScreenTip containing the button name appears next to the mouse pointer.

Exiting an Office Application

The Exit command on the File menu can be used to quit most Windows programs. Alternatively, you can click the ☒ Close button in the program window title bar.

1 Click ☒ Close.

The program window is closed and the desktop is visible again.

Starting an Office Application

command summary

Command	Shortcut	Button	Action
Start/Programs			Opens program menu
File/Exit	Alt + F4		Exits Office program
View/Toolbars			Hides or displays toolbars
View/Task Pane			Hides or displays task pane
Tools/Customize/Options	F4		Changes settings associated with toolbars and menus
Help/Microsoft Word Help	F1	?	Opens Help window
Help/Show the Office Assistant			Displays Office Assistant

Overview of Word 2002

What Is Word Processing?

Word 2002 is a word processing software application whose purpose is to help you create any type of written communication. A word processor can be used to manipulate text data to produce a letter, a report, a memo, an e-mail message or any other type of correspondence. Text data is any letter, number, or symbol that you can type on a keyboard. The grouping of the text data to form words, sentences, paragraphs, and pages of text results in the creation of a document. Through a word processor you can create, modify, store, retrieve, and print part or all of a document.

February 18, 2001

Dear Adventure Traveler,

Imagine hiking and paddling your way through the rain forests of Costa Rica under the stars in Africa, or following in the footsteps of the ancient Inca as you backp the Inca trail to Machu Picchu. Turn these dreams of adventure into memories you w forever by joining Adventure Travel Tours on one of our four new adventure tours.

To tell you more about these exciting new adventures, we are offerin presentations in your area. These presentations will focus on the features and cultu region. We will also show you pictures of the places you will visit and activities participate in, as well as a detailed agenda and package costs. Plan on attending o following presentations:

Date	Time	Location	Room
January 5	7:00 PM	Town Center Hotel	Room 284B
February 3	7:30 PM	Airport Manor	Conference Room A
March 8	7:00 PM	Country Inn	Mountainside Room

In appreciation of your past patronage, we are pleased to offer you a 10% disco price of any of the new tour packages. You must book the trip at least 60 days pr departure date. Please turn in this letter to qualify for the discount.

Our vacation tours are professionally developed solely for your enjoyment. W almost everything in the price of your tour while giving you the best possible value dollar. All tours include:

- **Professional tour manager and local guides**
- **All accommodations and meals**
- **All entrance fees, excursions, transfers and tips**

We hope you will join us this year on another special Adventure Travel Tour Your memories of fascinating places and challenging physical adventures should li long, long time. For reservations, please see your travel agent, or contact Adventure Tr at 1-800-777-0004. You can also visit our new Web site at www.AdventureTravelTour

Best regards,

Student Name

Announcing
New Adventure Travel Tours

This year we are introducing four new tours, offering you a unique opportunity to combine many different outdoor activities while exploring the world.

Hike the Inca trail to Machu Picchu
Camp on safari in Tanzania
Climb Mt. Kilimanjaro
Explore the Costa Rican rain forests

Attend an Adventure Travel presentation to learn about some of the earth's greatest unspoiled habitats and find out how you can experience the adventure of a lifetime.

Presentation dates and times are January 5 at 7 PM, February 3 at 7:30 PM, and March 8 at 7 PM. All presentations are held at convenient hotel locations located in downtown Los Angeles, Santa Clara and at the airport.

Call us at 1-800-777-0004 for presentation locations, a full color brochure, and itinerary information, costs, and tour dates.

Visit Our
Web site at
AdventureTravelTours.com

A letter and flyer created using Word 2002.

Word processors are one of the most widely used applications software programs. Putting your thoughts in writing, from the simplest note to the most complex book, is a time-consuming process. Even more time-consuming is the task of editing and retyping the document to make it better. Word processors make errors nearly nonexistent—not because they are not made, but because they are easy to correct. Word processors let you throw away the correction fluid, scissors, paste, and erasers. Now, with a few keystrokes, you can easily correct errors, move paragraphs, and reprint your document.

Word 2002 Features

Word 2002 excels in its ability to change or edit a document. Editing involves correcting spelling, grammar, and sentence-structure errors. In addition, you can easily revise or update existing text by inserting or deleting text. For example, a document that lists prices can easily be updated to reflect new prices. A document that details procedures can be revised by deleting old procedures and inserting new ones. This is especially helpful when a document is used repeatedly. Rather than recreating the whole document, you change only the parts that need to be revised.

Revision also includes the rearrangement of selected areas of text. For example, while writing a report, you may decide to change the location of a single word or several paragraphs or pages of text. You can do it easily by cutting or removing selected text from one location, then pasting or placing the selected text in another location. The selection can also be copied from one document to another.

Another time saver is word wrap. As you enter text you do not need to decide where to end each line, as you do on a typewriter. When a line is full, the program automatically wraps the text down to the next line.

To help you produce a perfect document, Word 2002 includes many additional support features. The AutoCorrect feature checks the spelling and grammar in a document as text is entered. Many common errors are corrected automatically for you. Others are identified and a correction suggested. While you enter text, the AutoComplete feature may suggest entire phrases that can be quickly inserted based on the first few characters you type. The words and phrases are included in a list of AutoText entries provided with Word 2002, or they may be ones you have included yourself. A thesaurus can be used to display alternative words that have a meaning similar or opposite to a word you entered. A Find and Replace feature can be used to quickly locate specified text and replace it with other text throughout a document.

A variety of Wizards are included in Word 2002 that provide step-by-step assistance while you produce many common types of documents, such as business letters, faxes, resumes, or reports. Templates also can be used to produce many of these documents without the step-by-step guidance provided by the Wizard.

You can also easily control the appearance or format of the document. Formatting includes such operations as changing the line spacing and margin widths, adding page numbers, and displaying page headers and footers. You can also quickly change how your text is aligned with the left or right margin. For example, text can be centered between the margins, or justified—evenly aligned on both the left and right margins. Perhaps the most noticeable formatting feature is the ability to apply different fonts (type styles and sizes) and text appearance changes such as bold, italics, and color to all or selected portions of the document. Additionally, you can add color shading behind individual pieces of text or entire paragraphs and pages to add emphasis. Automatic formatting can be turned on to automatically format text as you type by detecting when to apply selected formats to text as it is entered. In addition, Word 2002 includes a variety of tools that automate the process of many common tasks, such as creating tables, form letters, and columns.

Group collaboration on projects is common in industry today. Word 2002 includes many features to help streamline how documents are developed and changed by group members. A discussion feature allows multiple people to insert remarks in the same document without having to route the document to each person or reconcile multiple reviewers' comments. A feature called versioning allows you to save multiple versions of the same document so that you can see exactly who did what on a document and when. You can easily consolidate all changes and comments from different reviewers in one simple step and accept or reject changes as needed.

To further enhance your documents, you can insert many different types of graphic elements. You can select from over 150 borderline styles that can be applied to areas of text such as headings, or around graphics or entire pages. The drawing tools supplied with Word 2002 can be used to create your own drawings, or you can select from over 100 adjustable AutoShapes and modify them to your needs. All drawings can be further enhanced with 3-D effects, shadows, colors, and textures. Additionally, you can produce fancy text effects using the WordArt tool. More complex pictures can be inserted in documents by scanning your own, using supplied or purchased clip art, or downloading images from World Wide Web.

Word 2002 is closely integrated with the World Wide Web. It detects when you are typing a Web address and converts it to a hyperlink automatically for you. You can also create your own hyperlinks to locations within documents, or to other documents, including those at external locations such as a Web site or file server. Word's many Web-editing features help you quickly create a Web page. Among these is a Web Page Wizard that guides you step by step through the process of creating a Web page. Themes can be used to quickly apply unified design elements and color schemes to your Web pages. Frames can be created to make your Web site easier for users to navigate. Pictures, graphic elements, animated graphics, sound, and movies can all be used to increase the impact of your Web pages.

You can also create and send e-mail messages directly from within Word 2002, using all its features to create and edit the message. You can also send an entire document directly by e-mail. The document becomes the message. This makes collaboration easy because you can edit the document directly without having to open or save an attachment.

Case Study for Word 2002 Labs

As a recent college graduate, you have accepted a job as advertising coordinator for Adventure Travel Tours, a specialty travel company that organizes active adventure vacations. The company is headquartered in Los Angeles and has locations in other major cities throughout the country. Your duties include the creation of brochures, flyers, form letters, news releases, advertisements, and a monthly newsletter, all of which promote Adventure Travel's programs. You are also responsible for working on the company Web site.

Brief Version

Lab 1: Adventure Travel has developed four new tours for the upcoming year and needs to promote them, partly through informative presentations held throughout the country. Your first job as advertising coordinator is to create a flyer advertising the four new tours and the presentations about them.

Lab 2: Your next project is to create a letter to be sent to past clients along with your flyer. The letter briefly describes Adventure Travel's four new tours and invites clients to attend an informational presentation.

Lab 3: Part of your responsibility as advertising coordinator is to gather background information about the various tour locations. You will write a report providing information about Tanzania and Peru for two of the new tours.

Working Together: Adventure Travel has a company Web site. You will convert the flyer you developed to promote the new tours and presentations to be used on the Web site.

Before You Begin

To the Student

The following assumptions have been made:

- Microsoft Word 2002 has been properly installed on your computer system.

- You have the data files needed to complete the series of Word 2002 labs and practice exercises. These are supplied by your instructor.

- You are already familiar with how to use Microsoft Windows and a mouse.

To the Instructor

A complete installation of Office XP is required in which all components are available to students while completing the labs.

Please be aware that the following settings are assumed to be in effect for the Word 2002 program. These assumptions are necessary so that the screens and directions in the labs are accurate.

- The New Document Task Pane is displayed when Word is started. (Use Tools/Options/View/Startup Task Pane.)

- The ScreenTips feature is active. (Use Tools/Customize/Options/Show ScreenTips on Toolbar.)

- The status bar is displayed. (Use Tools/Options/View/Status bar.)

- The horizontal and vertical scroll bars are displayed. (Use Tools/Options/View.)
- The Wrap to Window setting is off. (Use Tools/Options/View.)
- The SmartTags feature is installed and active. (Use Tools/Options/View/SmartTags.)
- The Mark Formatting inconsistencies option is off. (Use Tools/Options/Edit.)
- The Paste Options buttons are displayed. (Use Tools/Options/Edit/Show Paste Options buttons.)
- Background repagination is on. (Use Tools/Options/General.)
- The Standard and Formatting toolbars are displayed on two rows. (Tools/Customize/Options.)
- Full menus are always displayed. (Use Tools/Customize/Options.)
- The Normal view is on. Zoom is 100 percent. (Use View/Normal; View/Zoom/100%.)
- The Drawing toolbar is on and displayed at the bottom of the window. (Use View/Toolbars/Drawing.)
- Language is set to English (US). (Use Tools/Language/Set Language.)
- The Office Assistant feature is off. (Right-click on the Assistant character, choose Options, and clear the Use the Office Assistant option.)
- All default settings for the Normal document template are in effect.

In addition, all figures in the manual reflect the use of a standard VGA display monitor set at 800 by 600. If another monitor setting is used, there may be more or fewer lines of text displayed in the windows than in the figures. This setting can be changed using Windows setup.

Microsoft Office Shortcut Bar

The Microsoft Office Shortcut Bar (shown below) may be displayed automatically on the Windows desktop. Commonly, it appears in the right side of the desktop; however, it may appear in other locations, depending upon your setup. The Shortcut Bar on your screen may also display different buttons. This is because the Shortcut Bar can be customized to display other toolbar buttons.

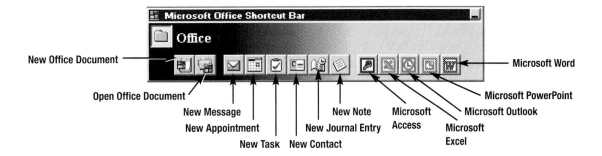

The Office Shortcut Bar makes it easy to open existing documents or to create new documents using one of the Microsoft Office applications. It can also be used to send e-mail, add a task to a to-do list, schedule appointments using Schedule+, or access Office Help.

Instructional Conventions

Hands-on instructions you are to perform appear as a sequence of numbered steps. Within each step, a series of bullets identifies the specific actions that must be performed. Step numbering begins over within each topic heading throughout the lab.

Command sequences you are to issue appear following the word "Choose." Each menu command selection is separated by a /. If the menu command can be selected by typing a letter of the command, the letter will appear underlined and bold. Items that need to be selected will follow the word "Select" and will appear in black text. You can select items with the mouse or directional keys. (See Example A.)

Example A

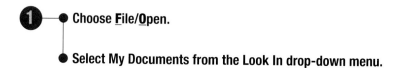

1 ● Choose **File/Open**.

● Select My Documents from the Look In drop-down menu.

Commands that can be initiated using a button and the mouse appear following the word "Click." The icon (and the icon name if the icon does not include text) is displayed following "Click." The menu equivalent and keyboard shortcut appear in an Another Method margin note when the action is first introduced. (See Example B.)

Example B

1 ● Click 🗁 Open.

Another Method
The menu equivalent is
File/**O**pen and the keyboard
shortcut is ⌈Ctrl⌉+O.

Plain blue text identifies file names you need to select or enter. Information you are asked to type appears in blue and bold. (See Example C.)

Example C

1 ● **Open the document** wd01_Flyer.

● **Type** Adventure Travel presents four new trips.

The O'Leary Series

Microsoft® Word 2002

Brief Edition

Creating and Editing a Document

LAB **1**

objectives

1.	Develop a document as well as enter and edit text.
2.	Insert and delete text and blank lines.
3.	Display formatting marks.
4.	Use AutoCorrect, AutoText, and AutoComplete.
5.	Use automatic spelling and grammar checking.
6.	Save, close, and open files.
7.	Select text.
8.	Undo and redo changes.
9.	Change fonts and type sizes.
10.	Bold and color text.
11.	Change alignment.
12.	Insert, size, and move pictures.
13.	Preview and print a document.

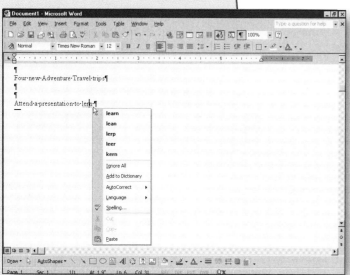

Entering and editing text is simplified with many of Word's AutoCorrect features.

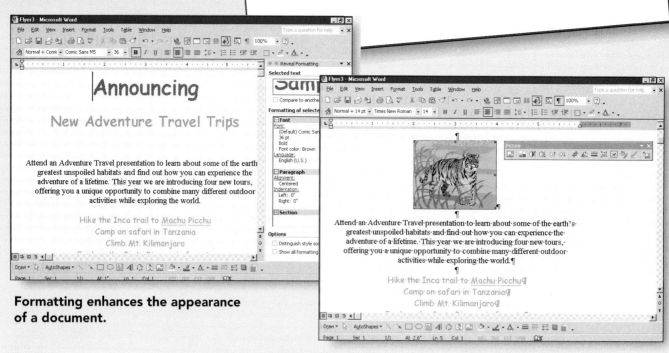

Formatting enhances the appearance of a document.

Pictures add visual interest to a document.

Adventure Travel Tours

As a recent college graduate, you have accepted a job as advertising coordinator for Adventure Travel Tours, a specialty travel company that organizes active adventure vacations. The company is headquartered in Los Angeles and has locations in other major cities throughout the country. You are responsible for coordination of the advertising program for all locations. This includes the creation of many kinds of promotional materials: brochures, flyers, form letters, news releases, advertisements, and a monthly newsletter. You are also responsible for creating Web pages for the company Web site.

Adventure Travel is very excited about four new tours planned for the upcoming year. They want to promote them through informative presentations held throughout

the country. Your first job as advertising coordinator will be to create a flyer advertising the four new tours and the presentations about them. The flyer will be modified according to the location of the presentation.

The software tool you will use to create the flyer is the word processing application Microsoft® Word 2002. It helps you create documents such as letters, reports, and research papers. In this lab, you will learn how to enter, edit, and print a document while you create the flyer (shown left) to be distributed in a mailing to Adventure Travel Tours clients.

© Corbis

Introducing Word 2002

Adventure Travel Tours has recently upgraded their computer systems at all locations across the country. As part of the upgrade, they have installed the latest version of the Microsoft Office suite of applications, Office XP. You are very excited to see how this new and powerful application can help you create professional letters and reports as well as eye-catching flyers and newsletters.

Starting Word 2002

You will use the word processing application included in the Office suite, Word 2002, to create a flyer promoting the new tours and presentations.

① ● **Start the Word application.**

HAVING TROUBLE?
See "Common Office XP Features" on page I.9 for information on how to start the application and for a discussion of features common to all Office XP applications.

● **If necessary, maximize the Word application window.**

● **To display the standard window view, choose View/Normal.**

Your screen should be similar to Figure 1.1

Additional Information
You will learn about the different Word views shortly.

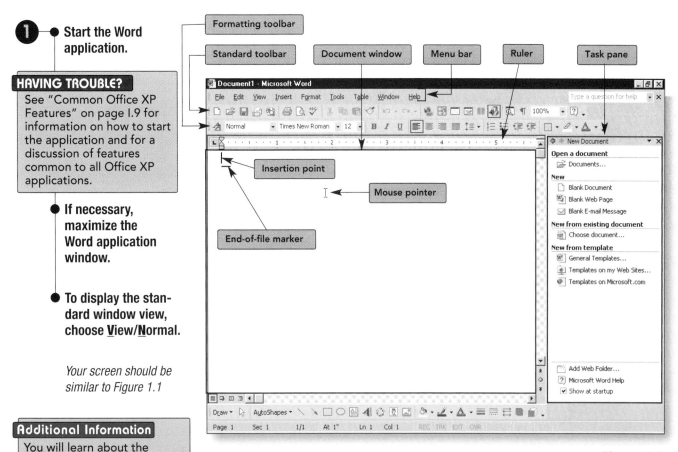

Figure 1.1

HAVING TROUBLE?
If your toolbars are on a single row, choose Tools/Customize/Options/Show Standard and Formatting toolbars on two rows.

HAVING TROUBLE?
If your task pane is not displayed, choose View/Task Pane. If the ruler is not displayed, choose View/Ruler.

Exploring the Word Window

The menu bar below the title bar displays the Word program menu. It consists of nine menus that provide access to the commands and features you will use to create and modify a document.

The toolbars, normally located below the menu bar, contain buttons that are mouse shortcuts for many of the menu items. The **Standard toolbar** contains buttons for the most frequently used menu commands. The **Formatting toolbar** contains buttons that are used to change the appearance or format of the document. Word includes 19 toolbars, many of which appear automatically as you use different features. Your screen may display other toolbars if they were on when the program was last exited.

The task pane is displayed on the right side of the window. Word includes eight task panes, which are displayed depending on the task being performed. Since you just started Word, the New Document task pane is automatically displayed. This task pane provides different ways to create a new document or open an existing document.

The large area to the left of the task pane is the document window. It currently displays a blank Word document. The **ruler**, displayed at the top of the document window, shows the line length in inches and is used to set margins, tab stops, and indents. The **insertion point**, also called the **cursor**, is the blinking vertical bar that marks your location in the document. The solid horizontal line is the **end-of-file marker**. Because there is nothing in this document, the insertion point appears at the first character space on the first line.

The mouse pointer may appear as an I-beam I (see Figure 1.1) or a left- or right-facing arrow, depending on its location in the window. When it appears as an I-beam, it is used to move the insertion point, and when it appears as an arrow, it is used to select items.

1 • Move the mouse pointer into the left edge of the document window to see it appear as $\nwarrow$.

• Move the mouse pointer to the menu bar to see it appear as $\k$.

Your screen should be similar to Figure 1.2

Drawing toolbar →

Status bar →

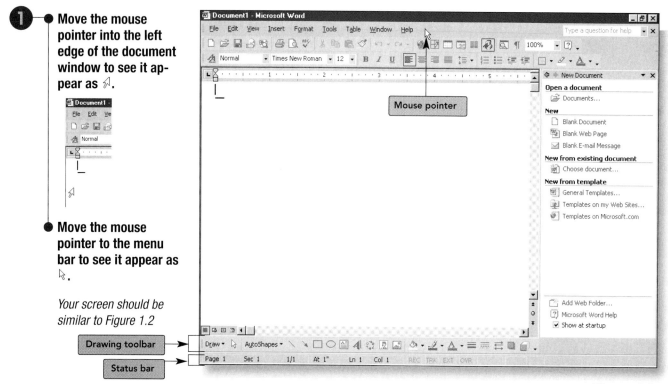

Figure 1.2

HAVING TROUBLE?

If the Drawing toolbar is not displayed, choose View/Toolbars/Drawing.

Below the document window, the **Drawing toolbar** is displayed. It contains buttons that are used to create and enhance drawing objects.

The indicators on the **status bar** show both the location of the text that is displayed in the document window as well as the location of the insertion point in a document. The numbers following the indicators specify the exact location in the document. The indicators are described in the following table.

Indicator	Meaning
Page	Indicates the page of text displayed onscreen.
Sec	Indicates the section of text displayed onscreen. A large document can be broken into sections.
1/1	Indicates the number of the pages displayed on screen, and the total number of pages in the document.
At	Indicates the vertical position in inches of the insertion point from the top of the page.
Ln	Indicates the line of text where the insertion point is located.
Col	Indicates the horizontal position of the insertion point in number of characters from the left margin.

Creating New Documents

When you first start Word 2002, a new blank Word document is opened. It is like a blank piece of paper that already has many predefined settings. These settings, called **default** settings, are generally the most commonly used settings and are stored as a document template.

concept 1

Template

1 A **template** is a document file that includes predefined settings that can be used as a pattern to create many common types of documents. Every Word document is based on a document template (see the examples below).

Default document settings are stored in the **Normal template**. Whenever you create a new document using this template, the same default settings are used. The Normal document template is referred to as a **global template** because it contains settings that are available to all documents.

Many other templates are available within Word and at the Microsoft Office Template Gallery on the Microsoft Web site that are designed to help you create professional-looking documents. They include templates for different styles of memos, letters, reports, faxes, and Web pages. Unlike global templates, the settings included in these specialized templates are available only to documents based on that template. You can also design and save your own document templates.

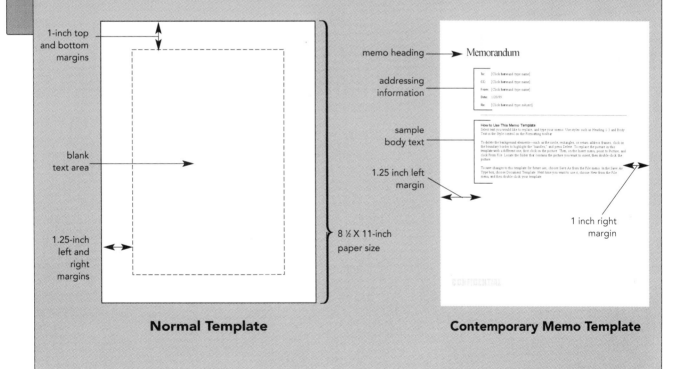

Normal Template

Contemporary Memo Template

Using the Normal Template

When you first start Word, it displays a new blank document based on the Normal template. The Normal document template settings include 1-inch top and bottom margins, and 1.25-inch left and right margins. Other default settings include a standard paper-size setting of 8.5 by 11 inches, tab stops at every half inch, and single line spacing.

To verify several of the default settings, you can look at the information displayed in the status bar (see Figure 1.3). As you can see from the first three indicators in the status bar, page 1 of section 1 of a document consisting of only 1 page (1/1) is displayed on your screen. The next three indicators show the position of the insertion point. Currently, the insertion point is positioned at the 1-inch location from the top of the page, on line 1 from the top margin and column 1 from the left margin. The ruler displays dimmed tab marks below each half-inch position, showing the default tab stops of every half inch.

Viewing and Zooming a Document

To more easily verify several of the Normal template settings, you can switch to another document view. Word includes several views that are used for different purposes. You can change views using the View menu commands or the view buttons located to the left of the horizontal scroll bar. The main document views are described in the table below.

Document View	Command	Button	Effect on Text
Normal	View/Normal		Shows text formatting and simple layout of the page. This is the best view to use when typing, editing, and formatting text.
Web Layout	View/Web Layout		Shows the document as it will appear when viewed in a Web browser. Use when creating Web pages or documents that will be displayed on the screen only.
Print Layout	View/Print Layout		Shows how the text and objects will appear on the printed page. This is the view to use when adjusting margins, working in columns, drawing objects, and placing graphics.
Outline	View/Outline		Shows the structure of the document. This is the view to use to move, copy, and reorganize text in a document.

The view you see when first starting Word is the view that was in use when the program was last exited. Currently, your view is normal view, as shown in Figure 1.3. You can tell which view is in use by looking at the view buttons. The button for the view that is in use appears recessed as if it were depressed.

In addition, you can change the amount of information displayed in the document window by "zooming in" to get a close-up view or "zooming out" to see more of the document at a reduced view. The default display, 100 percent, shows the characters the same size they will be when printed. You can increase the onscreen character size up to five times normal display (500 percent) or reduce the character size to 10 percent. You will "zoom out" on the document to see the entire width of the page.

1 ● **Open the** `100%` **Zoom drop-down menu (on the Standard toolbar).**

HAVING TROUBLE?

Click the ▼ in the `100%` button to open the drop-down menu.

● **Choose Page Width.**

Another Method

The menu equivalent is View/Zoom/Page Width.

Your screen should be similar to Figure 1.3

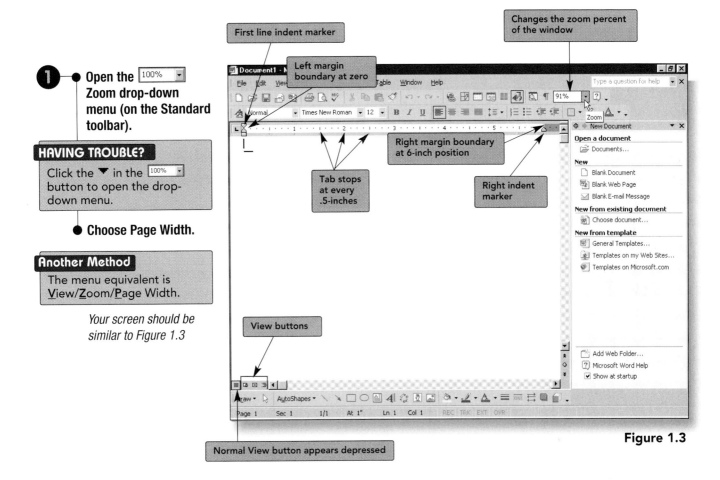

Figure 1.3

HAVING TROUBLE?

If your zoom percentage is different, this is a function of the monitor you are using.

To view the document at page width, the zoom percentage as shown in the Zoom box is 91percent. You can verify several more Normal template settings by looking at the information displayed in the ruler. The margin boundaries on both ends of the ruler show the location of the left and right margins. The symbol ▽ at the zero position on the ruler is the first line indent marker and marks the location of the left paragraph indent. The symbol △ on the right end of the ruler line at the 6-inch position marks the right paragraph indent. The default paragraph indent locations are the same as the margin settings. The ruler shows that the distance between the left and right margins is 6 inches. Knowing that the default page size is 8.5 inches wide, this leaves 2.5 inches for margins: 1.25 inches for equal-sized left and right margins.

Although in normal view at page width you can see the default document settings, they are even easier to see when you are in print layout view. The zoom for each view is set independently.

2 ● Click ▣ **Print Layout View** (located to the left of the horizontal scroll bar).

Additional Information
The view buttons display the button name in a ScreenTip when you point to them.

● **If your screen does not display the top and sides of the page as in Figure 1.4, change the zoom to Page Width.**

● **Move the mouse pointer to the center of the document.**

Your screen should be similar to Figure 1.4

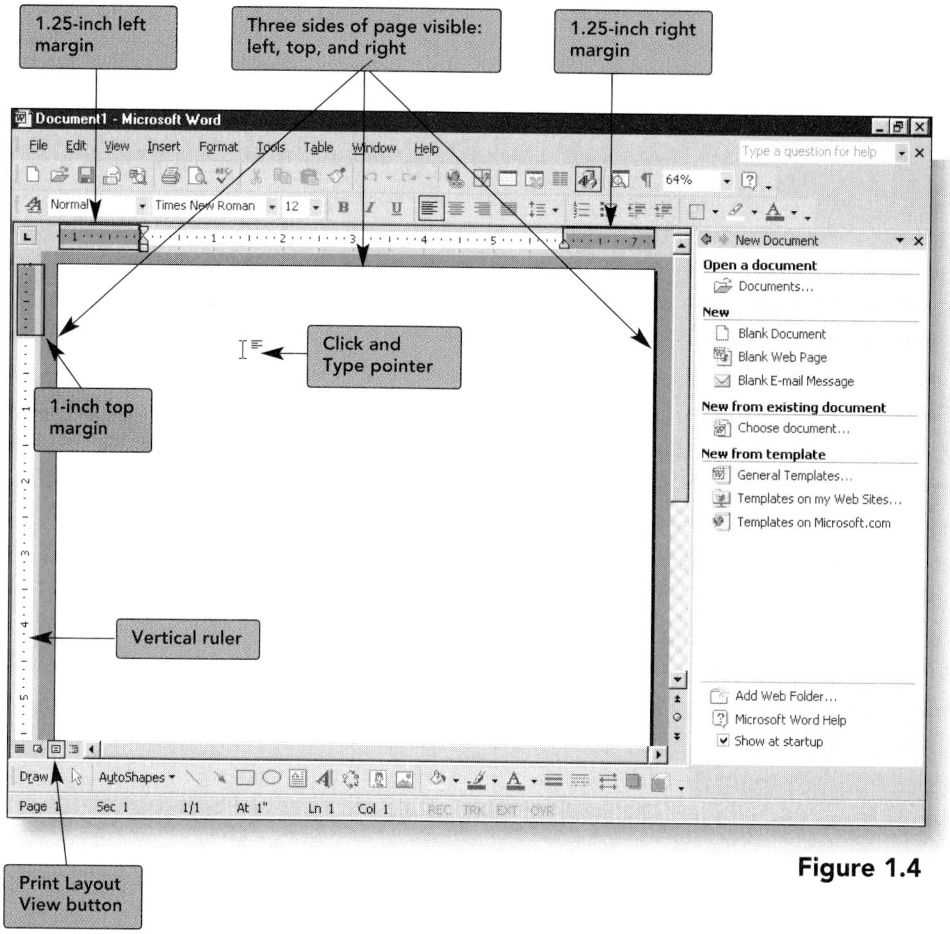

1.25-inch left margin

Three sides of page visible: left, top, and right

1.25-inch right margin

Click and Type pointer

1-inch top margin

Vertical ruler

Print Layout View button

Figure 1.4

Print layout view displays the current page of your document as it will appear when printed. The top edge of the paper is visible below the horizontal ruler, and the left and right edges are visible along the sides of the window. The top margin is 1 inch from the top of the page, and the left margin setting is 1.25 inches from the left edge of the page.

This view also displays a vertical ruler that shows the vertical position of text. Also notice in this view that the mouse pointer appears as I￪ when positioned over the document. This is the Click and Type pointer, which indicates the Click and Type feature is on. This feature allows you to quickly insert text into a blank area of a document while applying certain design features automatically. You will learn more about this feature in later labs.

You will use the Normal template in Normal view at the standard zoom percentage of 100 percent to create the flyer about this year's new tours. You will also close the New Document task pane to allow more space in the document window for viewing the document.

3 • Click ▤ to switch back to Normal view.

• Open the `100%` ▾ Zoom drop-down menu and change the zoom percent to 100%.

• Click ☒ in the task pane title bar to close the task pane.

Another Method
The <u>V</u>iew/Ta<u>s</u>k Pane command can also be used to display and hide the task pane.

Your screen should be similar to Figure 1.5

Normal view button depressed

Task pane closed

Zoom percent at 100%

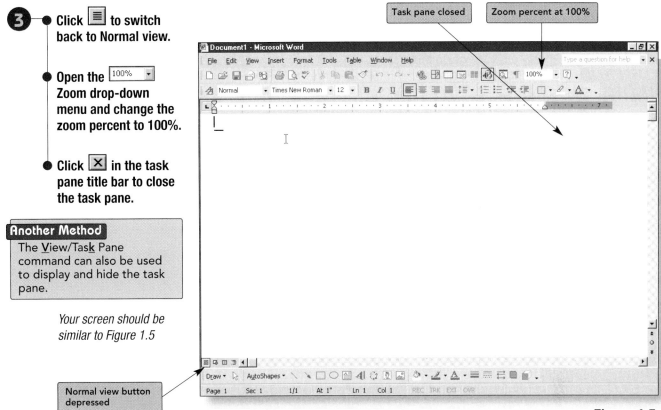

Figure 1.5

Developing a Document

Your first project with Adventure Travel Tours is to create a flyer about four new tours. The development of a document follows several steps: plan, enter, edit, format, and preview and print.

Step	Description
Plan	The first step in the development of a document is to understand the purpose of the document and to plan what your document should say.
Enter	After planning the document, you enter the content of the document by typing the text using the keyboard. Text can also be entered using the handwriting and speech recognition features.
Edit	Making changes to your document is called **editing**. While typing, you are bound to make typing and spelling errors that need to be corrected. This is one type of editing. Another is to revise the content of what you have entered to make it clearer, or to add or delete information.
Format	Enhancing the appearance of the document to make it more readable or attractive is called **formatting**. This step is usually performed when the document is near completion. It includes many features such as boldfaced text, italics, and bulleted lists.
Preview and Print	The last step is to preview and print the document. Previewing displays the document onscreen as it will appear when printed, allowing you to check the document's overall appearance and make any final changes before printing.

You will find that you will generally follow these steps in the order listed above for your first draft of a document. However, you will probably retrace steps such as editing and formatting as the final document is developed.

During the planning phase, you spoke with your manager regarding the purpose of the flyer and the content in general. The primary purpose of the flyer is to promote the new tours. A secondary purpose is to advertise the company in general.

You plan to include specific information about the new tours in the flyer as well as general information about Adventure Travel Tours. The content also needs to include information about the upcoming new tour presentations. Finally, you want to include information about the Adventure Travel Web site.

Entering Text

Now that you understand the purpose of the flyer and have a general idea of the content, you are ready to enter the text.

Text is entered using the keyboard. As you type, many of Word's features make entering text much easier. These features include checking for spelling and grammar errors, auto correction, and word wrap. You will see how these features work next.

Typing Text

To enter text in a new document, simply begin typing the text. On the first line of the flyer you will enter "Announcing four new Adventure Travel trips." As you enter the text, do not be concerned if you make errors. You will learn how to correct them shortly.

1 ● **Type** Announcing four new Adventure Travel trips.

Your screen should be similar to Figure 1.6

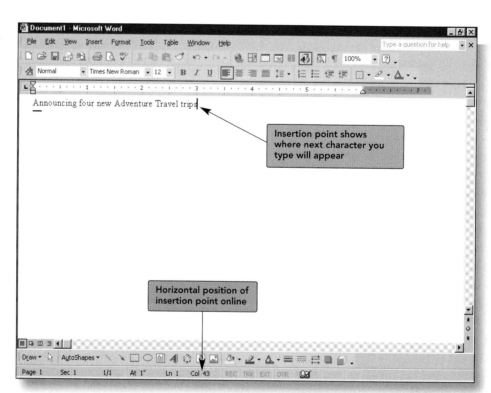

Insertion point shows where next character you type will appear

Horizontal position of insertion point online

Figure 1.6

Notice that as you type, the insertion point moves to the right and the character appears to the left of the insertion point. The location of the insertion point shows where the next character will appear as you type. Also, the status bar reflects the new horizontal position of the insertion point on the line. It shows the insertion point is currently positioned on column 43 of line 1.

Ending a Line and Inserting Blank Lines

Now you are ready to complete the first line of the announcement. To end a line and begin another line, you simply press ←Enter. The insertion point moves to the beginning of the next line. If you press ←Enter at the beginning of a line, a blank line is inserted into the document. If the insertion point is in the middle of a line of text and you press ←Enter, all the text to the right of the insertion point moves to the beginning of the next line.

1 ● **Press** ←Enter **3 times.**

Three blank lines

Your screen should be similar to Figure 1.7

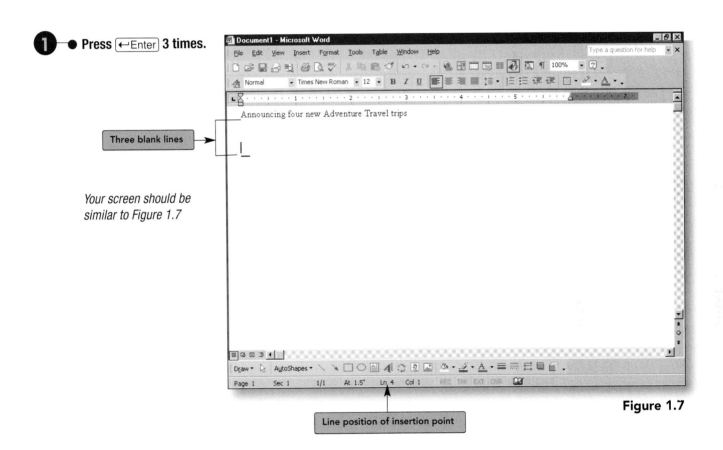

Line position of insertion point

Figure 1.7

Pressing the first ←Enter ended the first line of text and inserted a blank line. The next two inserted blank lines. The status bar now shows that the insertion point is positioned on line 4, column 1 of the page.

Displaying Formatting Marks

While you are creating your document, Word automatically inserts **formatting marks** that control the appearance of your document. Word's default screen display does not show this level of detail. Sometimes, however, it is helpful to view the underlying formatting marks. Displaying these marks makes it easy to see, for example, if you have added an extra space between words or at the end of a sentence.

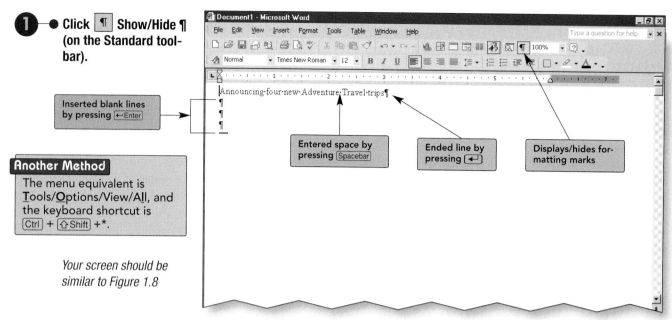

Inserted blank lines by pressing ←Enter

Entered space by pressing Spacebar

Ended line by pressing ←

Displays/hides formatting marks

Another Method

The menu equivalent is **T**ools/**O**ptions/View/A**l**l, and the keyboard shortcut is Ctrl + ⇧Shift +*.

Your screen should be similar to Figure 1.8

Figure 1.8

Additional Information

You can display selected formatting marks using **T**ools/**O**ptions/View and selecting the formatting marks you want to see.

The document now displays the formatting marks. The ¶ character on the line above the insertion point represents the pressing of ←Enter that created the blank line. The ¶ character at the end of the text represents the pressing of ←Enter that ended the line and moved the insertion point to the beginning of the next line. Between each word, a dot shows where the Spacebar was pressed. Formatting marks do not appear when the document is printed. You can continue to work on the document while the formatting marks are displayed, just as you did when they were hidden.

Moving through Text

Once text is entered into a document, it is important to know how to move around within the text to correct errors or make changes. Either the mouse or the keyboard can be used to move through the text in the document window. Depending on what you are doing, the mouse is not always the quickest means of moving. For example, if your hands are already on the keyboard as you are entering text, it may be quicker to use the keyboard rather than take your hands off to use the mouse. Therefore, you will learn how to move through the document using both methods.

Moving Using the Keyboard

You use the arrow keys located on the numeric keypad or the directional keypad to move the insertion point in a document. The directional keys and key combinations are described in the table on the next page.

Key	Movement
→	One character to right
←	One character to left
↑	One line up
↓	One line down
Ctrl + →	One word to right
Ctrl + ←	One word to left
Home	Left end of line
End	Right end of line

Additional Information

You can use the directional keys on the numeric keypad or the dedicated directional keypad area. If using the numeric keypad, make sure the Num Lock feature is off, otherwise numbers will be entered in the document. The Num Lock indicator light above the keypad is lit when on. Press Num Lock to turn it off.

Holding down a directional key or key combination moves quickly in the direction indicated, saving multiple presses of the key. Many of the Word insertion point movement keys can be held down to execute multiple moves. You will use many of these keys to quickly move through the text.

① Press ↑ 3 times.

● Press → 5 times.

● Press Ctrl + → 4 times.

● Press End.

● Hold down ← until the insertion point is positioned to the left of the A in Adventure. If you move too far to the left along the line, use → to move back to the correct position.

● Press Home.

Your screen should be similar to Figure 1.9

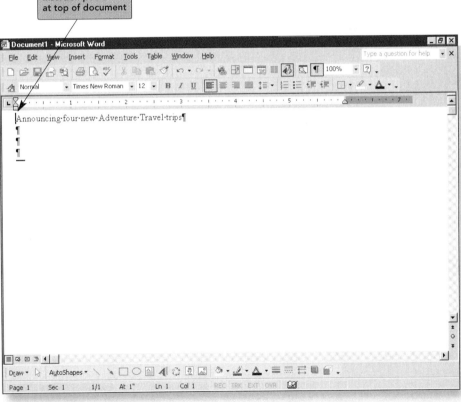

Figure 1.9

Additional Information

The insertion point will attempt to maintain its horizontal position in a line of text as you move up or down through the document.

The insertion point first moved up three lines, then five character spaces to the right, four words to the right, then quickly to the end of the line. You then held down the direction key to quickly move character by character to the left, and finally to the beginning of the line and down two lines to the blank line where you started.

Moving Using the Mouse

You use the mouse to move the insertion point to a specific location in a document. When you can use the mouse to move the insertion point, it is shaped as an I-beam. However, when the mouse pointer is positioned in the unmarked area to the left of a line (the left margin), it changes to an arrow ⟨. When the mouse is in this area, it can be used to highlight (select) text.

You have decided you want the flyer heading to be on two lines, with the word "Announcing" on the first line. To do this, you will insert a blank line after this word. To quickly move the insertion point to the location in the text where you want to insert the blank line,

Additional Information

You will learn about selecting text using this feature shortly.

1 • **Click on the "f" in "four."**

• **Move the mouse pointer out of the way so you can see the insertion point better.**

Your screen should be similar to Figure 1.10

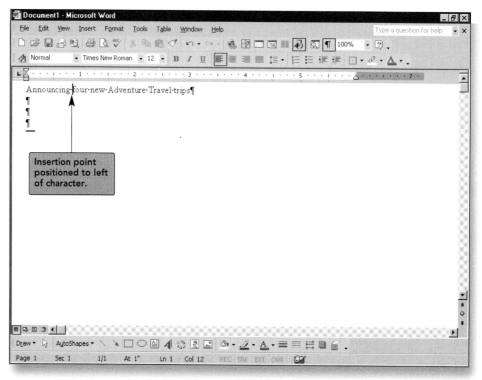

Insertion point positioned to left of character.

Figure 1.10

The insertion point should now be positioned on one side or the other of the f, with the status bar showing the new location of the insertion point. If it is positioned to the left of the f, this means that the I-beam was positioned more to the left side of the character when you clicked the mouse button. If it is positioned to the right of the f, this means the I-beam was positioned more to the right side of the character when you clicked the mouse button.

Additional Information

Throughout these labs, when instructed to move to a specific letter in the text, this means to move the insertion point to the *left* side of the character.

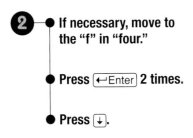

2 ● **If necessary, move to the "f" in "four."**

● **Press** Enter **2 times.**

● **Press** ↓.

Your screen should be similar to Figure 1.11

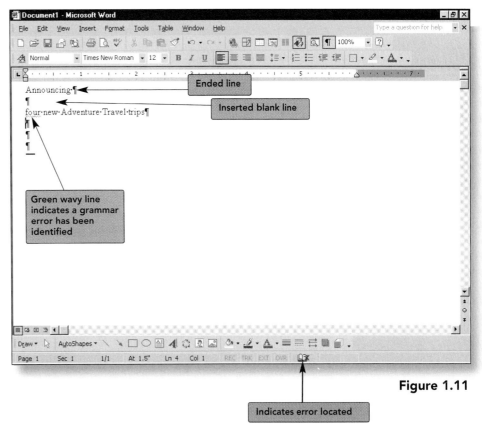

Ended line

Inserted blank line

Green wavy line indicates a grammar error has been identified

Figure 1.11

Indicates error located

HAVING TROUBLE?
If the green underline is not displayed, choose Tools/Options, open the Spelling and Grammar tab and select the "Check spelling as you type" and "Check grammar as you type" options.

The insertion point is positioned at the beginning of the blank line. As you continue to create a document, the formatting marks are automatically inserted and deleted. Notice that a green wavy underline appears under the word "four." This indicates Word has detected an error.

Using Word's Automatic Correcting Features

As you enter text, Word is constantly checking the document for spelling and grammar errors. The Spelling and Grammar Status icon 📖 in the status bar displays an animated pencil icon while you are typing, indicating Word is checking for errors as you type. When you stop typing, it displays either a red checkmark 📖, indicating the program does not detect any errors, or a red X 📖, indicating the document contains an error. In many cases, Word will automatically correct errors for you. In other cases, it identifies the error by underlining it. The different colors and designs of underlines indicate the type of error that has been identified. In addition to identifying the error, Word provides suggestions as to the possible correction needed.

Checking Grammar

In addition to the green wavy line under "four," the Spelling and Grammar Status icon appears as 📖. This indicates a spelling or grammar error has been located. The green wavy underline indicates it is a grammar error.

concept 2

Grammar Checker

2 The **grammar checker** advises you of incorrect grammar as you create and edit a document, and proposes possible corrections. Grammar checking occurs after you enter punctuation or end a line. If grammatical errors in subject-verb agreements, verb forms, capitalization, or commonly confused words, to name a few, are detected they are identified with a wavy green line. You can correct the grammatical error by editing it or you can display a suggested correction. Because not all identified grammatical errors are actual errors, you need to use discretion when correcting the errors.

1 ● **Right-click on the green underline.**

Your screen should be similar to Figure 1.12

Grammar shortcut menu

HAVING TROUBLE?

If the wrong shortcut menu appears, you probably did not have the I-beam exactly positioned on the green wavy line. Press Esc or click outside the menu to cancel it and try again.

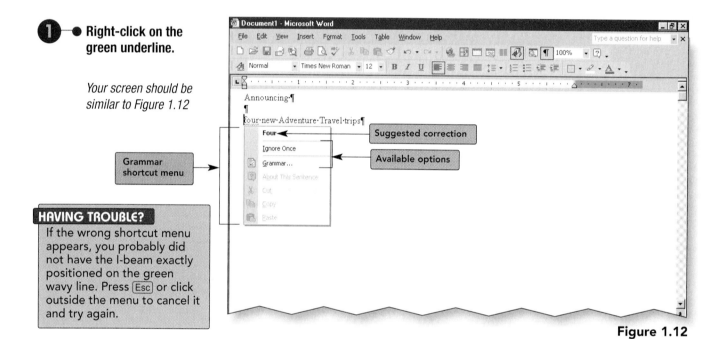

Figure 1.12

The first item on the Grammar shortcut menu is the suggested correction, "Four." It wants you to capitalize the first letter of the word because it is the beginning of a sentence. It also includes three available commands that are relevant to the item, described below.

Command	Effect
Ignore Once	Instructs Word to ignore the grammatical error in this sentence.
Grammar	Opens the grammar checker and displays an explanation of the error.
About This Sentence	Provides help about the grammatical error.

Additional Information

A dimmed menu option means it is currently unavailable.

To make this correction, you could simply choose the correction from the shortcut menu and the correction would be inserted into the document. Although in this case you can readily identify the reason for the error, sometimes the reason is not so obvious. In those cases, you can open the grammar checker to find out more information.

2 ● **Choose Grammar.**

Your screen should be similar to Figure 1.13

Line containing error is selected

Type of error

Location of error

Suggested correction

Click to make suggested correction

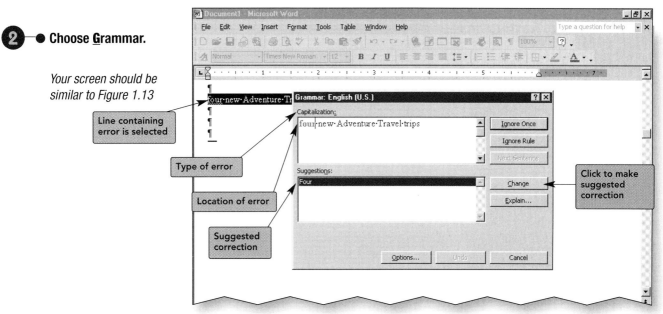

Figure 1.13

The Grammar dialog box identifies the possible grammatical error in the upper text box and the suggested correction in the Suggestions box. The line in the document containing the error is also highlighted (selected) to make it easy for you to see the location of the error. You will make the suggested change.

3 ● **Click** [Change] .

● **Move to the blank line at the end of the document.**

Your screen should be similar to Figure 1.14

Additional Information

Moving the insertion point using the keyboard or mouse deselects or removes the highlight from text that is selected.

Error corrected by capitalizing 'F'

No more errors located

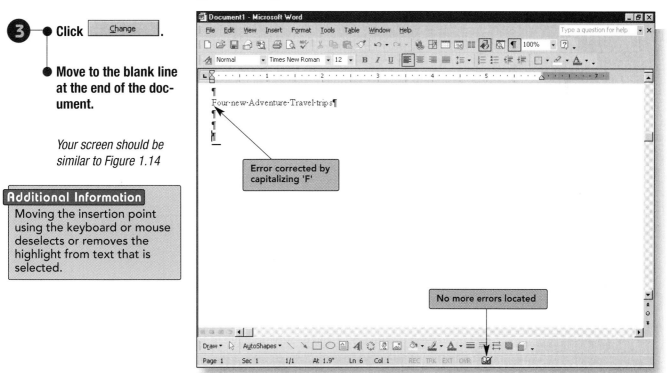

Figure 1.14

The error is corrected, the wavy green line is removed, and the Spelling and Grammar Status icon returns to 📖 .

Using AutoText and AutoComplete

Now you are ready to type the text for the first paragraph of the flyer.

Type atte.

Your screen should be similar to Figure 1.15

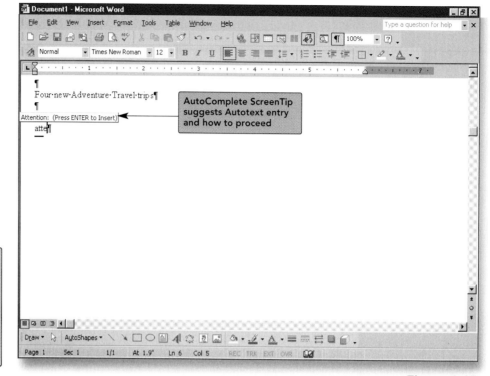

Figure 1.15

HAVING TROUBLE?
If a ScreenTip is not displayed, choose Insert/AutoText/AutoText, select Show AutoComplete Suggestions, and click ⬚OK⬚ to turn on this feature.

A ScreenTip appears displaying "Attention (Press ENTER to Insert):". This is Word's AutoText and AutoComplete feature.

concept 3

AutoText and AutoComplete

3 The **AutoText** feature includes entries, such as commonly used phrases, that can be quickly inserted into a document. The AutoText entries can be selected and inserted into the document using the Insert/AutoText command. Word's standard AutoText entries include salutations and closing phrases. You can also add your own entries to the AutoText list, which can consist of text or graphics you may want to use again.

Common uses are for a company name, mailing address, and a distribution list for memos.

Additionally, if the **AutoComplete** feature is on, a ScreenTip appears as you type the first few characters of an AutoText entry, suggesting the remainder of the AutoText entry you may want to use. You can choose to accept the suggestion to insert it into the document, or to ignore it.

The AutoComplete ScreenTip suggests that you may be typing the word "Attention." In this case, you do not want to enter the suggested word and will continue typing the word "attend."

**Type** nd.

Your screen should be similar to Figure 1.16

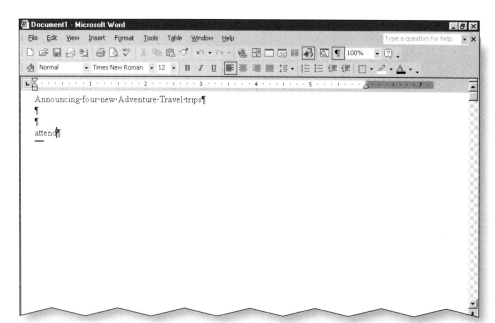

Figure 1.16

The AutoComplete ScreenTip has cleared, and the text as you typed it is displayed.

Using AutoCorrect

To end this word, you need to enter a space. As soon as you complete a word by entering a space or punctuation, the program checks the word for accuracy. This is part of the AutoCorrect feature of Word.

concept 4

AutoCorrect

4   The **AutoCorrect** feature makes some basic assumptions about the text you are typing and, based on these assumptions, automatically corrects the entry. The AutoCorrect feature automatically inserts proper capitalization at the beginning of sentences and in the names of days of the week. It will also change to lowercase letters any words that were incorrectly capitalized due to the accidental use of the Caps Lock key. In addition, it also corrects many common typing and spelling errors automatically.

One way the program automatically makes corrections is by looking for certain types of errors. For example, if two capital letters appear at the beginning of a word, Word changes the second capital letter to a lowercase letter. If a lowercase letter appears at the beginning of a sentence, Word capitalizes the first letter of the first word. If the name of a day begins with a lowercase letter, Word capitalizes the first letter.

Another way the program makes corrections is by checking all entries against a built-in list of AutoCorrect entries. If it finds the entry on the list, the program automatically replaces the error with the correction. For example, the typing error "aboutthe" is automatically changed to "about the" because the error is on the AutoCorrect list. You can also add words to the AutoCorrect list that you want to be automatically corrected.

A third method the program uses to automatically correct errors is to use suggestions from the spelling checker to automatically correct misspelled words. You will learn more about the spelling checker shortly.

1 ● Press [Spacebar].

● Point to the word "Attend."

Your screen should be similar to Figure 1.17

First letter of word capitalized automatically

Blue box indicates AutoCorrect feature was used

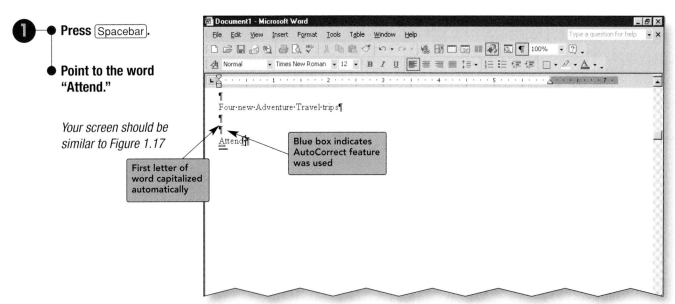

Figure 1.17

HAVING TROUBLE?

If your screen does not display the blue box, choose **T**ools/**A**utoCorrect Options and select the Show AutoCorrect Options button check box.

Word automatically capitalized the first letter of the word because it determined it is the first word in a sentence. When you rest the mouse pointer near text that has been corrected automatically or move the insertion point onto the word, a small blue box appears under the first character of the word. The blue box changes to the  AutoCorrect Options button when you point directly to it.

2 ● Point to the blue box.

● Click  AutoCorrect Options.

Your screen should be similar to Figure 1.18

AutoCorrect options button and menu

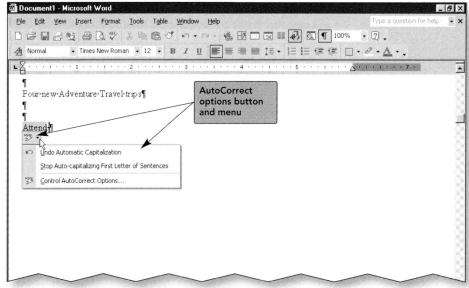

Additional Information

In some cases, you may want to exclude a word from automatic correction. You can do this by manually adding the word to an exception list using **T**ools/**A**utoCorrect Options/Exceptions.
Alternatively, if you use [Backspace] to delete an automatic correction and then type it again the way you want it to appear, the word will be automatically added to the exceptions list.

Figure 1.18

Each time Word uses the AutoCorrect feature, the AutoCorrect Options button is available. The AutoCorrect Options menu allows you to undo the AutoCorrection or permanently disable the AutoCorrection for the remainder of your document. The Control AutoCorrect Options command can also be used to change the settings for this feature. You want to keep this AutoCorrection.

3 ● Click outside the menu to close it.

Checking Spelling

Next you will continue entering the text for the paragraph. As you enter text, it is also checked for spelling accuracy.

concept 5

Spelling Checker

5 The **spelling checker** advises you of misspelled words as you create and edit a document, and proposes possible corrections. The spelling checker compares each word you type to a **main dictionary** of words supplied with the program. Although this dictionary includes most common words, it may not include proper names, technical terms, and so on. If the word does not appear in the main dictionary, it checks the **custom dictionary**, a dictionary that you can create to hold words you commonly use but that are not included in the main dictionary. If the word does not appear in either dictionary, the program identifies it as misspelled by displaying a red wavy line below the word. You can then correct the misspelled word by editing it. Alternatively, you can display a list of suggested spelling corrections for that word and select the correct spelling from the list to replace the misspelled word in the document.

You will continue to enter the text for the flyer. As you do, it will include several intentional errors. Type the text exactly as it appears.

1 ● If necessary, move to the end of the last line.

● Type a presentaation to lern.

● Press Spacebar.

Your screen should be similar to Figure 1.19

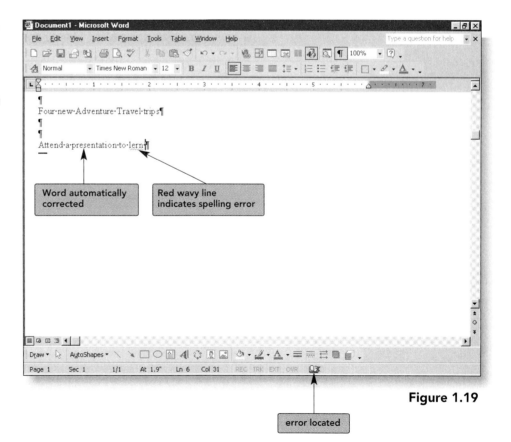

Figure 1.19

This time Word automatically corrected the spelling of "presentation" and identified the word "lern" as misspelled by underlining it with a wavy red line. The AutoCorrect feature corrected the spelling of presentation because it was the only suggested correction for the word supplied by the Spelling Checker. The word "lern" was not corrected because there are several suggested corrections on the Spelling shortcut menu.

The quickest way to correct a misspelled word is to select the correct spelling from a list of suggested spelling corrections displayed on the shortcut menu.

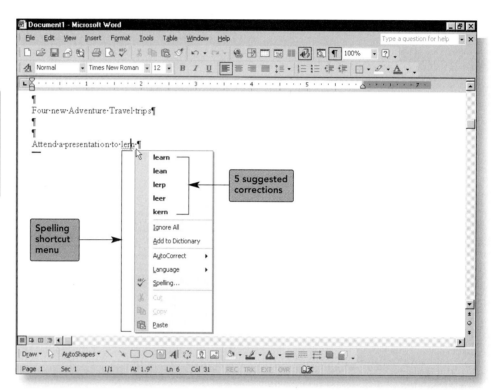

②— • **Right-click on lern to display the shortcut menu.**

Another Method

You can also position the insertion point on the item you want to display a shortcut menu for and press ⟨⇧ Shift⟩ + ⟨F10⟩ to open the shortcut menu.

Your screen should be similar to Figure 1.20

Figure 1.20

A shortcut menu of suggested correct spellings is displayed. In this case, five possible corrections are suggested. If the AutoCorrect feature is on and there is a single suggested spelling correction for a word, the program will automatically replace the incorrect spelling with the suggested replacement, as it did for the word "presentation."

The shortcut menu also includes several related menu options, described in the following table.

Option	Effect
Ignore All	Instructs Word to ignore the misspelling of this word throughout the rest of this session.
Add to Dictionary	Adds the word to the custom dictionary list. When a word is added to the custom dictionary, Word will always accept that spelling as correct.
AutoCorrect	Adds the word to the AutoCorrect list so Word can correct misspellings of it automatically as you type.
Language	Sets the language format, such as French, English or German, to apply to the word.
Spelling	Starts the spell-checking program to check the entire document. You will learn about this feature in Lab 2.

Sometimes there are no suggested replacements, because Word cannot locate any words in its dictionary that are similar in spelling; or the suggestions are not correct. If this happens, you need to edit the word manually. In this case, however the first suggestion is correct.

3 ➤● **Click learn.**

Your screen should be similar to Figure 1.21

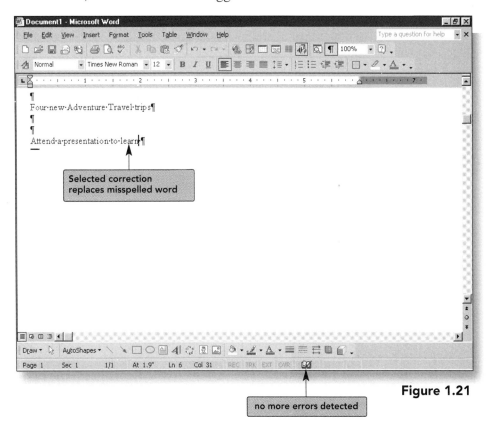

Figure 1.21

The spelling correction you selected replaces the misspelled word in the document. The Spelling and Grammar status icon returns to ☒ , indicating as far as Word is able to detect, the document is free from errors.

Using Word Wrap

Now you will continue entering more of the paragraph. As you type, when the text gets close to the right margin, do not press ←Enter to move to the next line. Word will automatically wrap words to the next line as needed.

concept 6

Word Wrap

6   The **word wrap** feature automatically decides where to end a line and wrap text to the next line based on the margin settings. This saves time when entering text, as you do not need to press ←Enter at the end of a full line to begin a new line. The only time you need to press ←Enter is to end a paragraph, to insert blank lines, or to create a short line such as a salutation. In addition, if you change the margins or insert or delete text on a line, the program automatically readjusts the text on the line to fit within the new margin settings. Word wrap is common to all word processors.

● Press →.

● **Type** about some of the earth's greatest unspoiled habitats and to find out how you can experience the adventure of a lifetime.

HAVING TROUBLE?
Do not worry about typing errors as you enter this text. You will correct them shortly.

Your screen should be similar to Figure 1.22

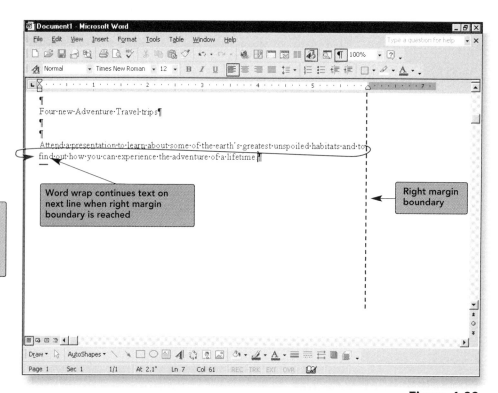

Figure 1.22

The program has wrapped the text that would overlap the right margin to the beginning of the next line. You will continue the paragraph by entering a second sentence.

② ● Press `Spacebar`.

● **Type** This year we are introducing four new tours and offering you a unique opportunity to combine many different outdoor activities while exploring the world.

● Press `←Enter`.

● Use the features you learned to correct any identified errors.

Your screen should be similar to Figure 1.23

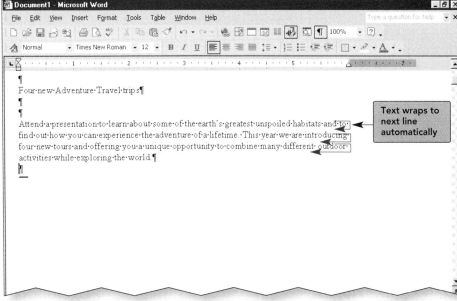

Figure 1.23

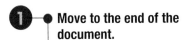 **Additional Information**

Generally, when using a word processor, separate sentences with one space after a period rather than two spaces, which was common when typewriters were used.

Using Smart Tags

You will be attending a meeting in a few minutes, and want to continue working on the document when you get back. You decide to add your name and the current date to the document.

HAVING TROUBLE?

If the SmartTag is not identified, choose **T**ools/**A**utoCorrect Options/SmartTags, select "Label text with smart tags" click Recheck Document , and click Yes . If it is still not available, the SmartTag feature has not been installed on your system.

① ● Move to the end of the document.

● Press `←Enter` to insert another blank line. Type your name.

● Press `←Enter`.

● Type the month and when the AutoText entry for the complete date appears, press `←Enter` to accept it.

● Press `←Enter`.

Your screen should be similar to Figure 1.24

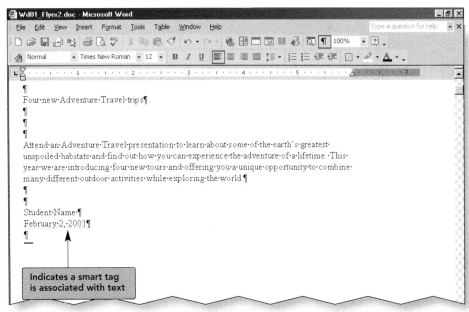

Figure 1.24

Notice that the date is underlined with a dotted purple line, which indicates a smart tag is attached to the text. The **smart tag** feature recognizes and labels data such as names, addresses, telephone numbers, dates, times,

Using Word's Automatic Correcting Features

and places as a particular type. The type of data it is recognized as determines what action can be performed with the data. For example, a name and address can be added directly from your document to the Microsoft Outlook Contacts folder. The date is recognized as a date item that can be added to the Outlook Calendar.

Since you do not need to perform any actions with the date, you will remove the Smart Tag. The purple dotted underline is removed indicating a smart tag is no longer associated with the text.

2 ● Point to the date to display the Smart Tag Actions button.

● Click 🛈 ▾ to open the Smart Tag Actions menu.

● Choose **R**emove this Smart Tag.

You will continue to see Smart Tags as you work through the labs.

Saving, Closing, and Opening Files

Before leaving to attend your meeting you want to save your work to a file and close the file. As you enter and edit text to create a new document, the changes you make are immediately displayed onscreen and are stored in your computer's memory. However, they are not permanently stored until you save your work to a file on a disk. Once a document is saved as a file, it can be closed and opened again at a later time to be further edited.

As a backup against the accidental loss of work due to power failure or other mishap, Word includes an AutoRecover feature. When this feature is on, as you work you may see a pulsing disk icon briefly appear in the status bar. This indicates the program is saving your work to a temporary recovery file. The time interval between automatic saving can be set to any period you specify; the default is every 10 minutes. After a problem has occurred, when you restart the program, the recovery file is automatically opened containing all changes you made up to the last time it was saved by AutoRecover. You then need to save the recovery file. If you do not save it, it is deleted when closed. While AutoRecover is a great feature for recovering lost work, it should not be used in place of regularly saving your work.

Saving a File

You will save the work you have done so far on the flyer. The Save or Save As command on the File menu is used to save files. The Save command or the 💾 Save button will save the active file using the same file name by replacing the contents of the existing file with the document as it appears on your screen. The Save As command allows you to save a file using a new file name or to a new location. This leaves the original file unchanged.

① ● Choose File/Save As.

Your screen should be similar to Figure 1.25

Additional Information

You could also use the Save command to save a new document for the first time, as it will display the Save As dialog box automatically.

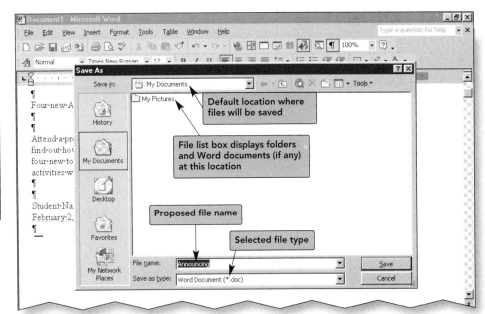

Figure 1.25

The Save As dialog box is used to specify the location to save the file and the file name. The Save In drop-down list box displays the default folder as the location where the file will be saved, and the File Name text box displays the proposed file name. The file list box displays the names of any Word documents in the default location. Only Word-type documents are listed, because Word Document is the specified file type in the Save As Type list box. First you need to change the location where the file will be saved to the drive containing your data disk.

② ● Open the Save In drop-down list box.

● Select the appropriate location where you want to save your file.

Your screen should be similar to Figure 1.26

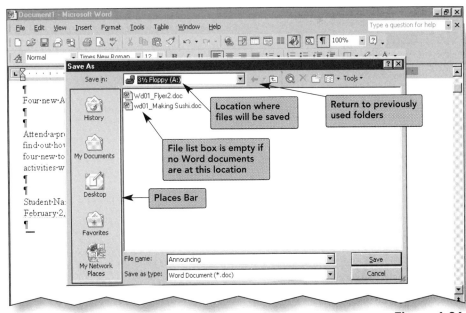

Figure 1.26

Now the large list box displays the names of all Word files, if any, at that location. You can also select the location to save your file from the Places bar along the left side of the dialog box. The icons bring up a list of recently accessed files and folders, the contents of the My Documents and Favorites folder, items on the Windows desktop, and the locations on a network. You can also click the ⬅ button in the toolbar to return to folders that were previously opened.

Next you need to enter a file name and specify the file type. The File Name box displays the default file name, consisting of the first few words from the document. The Save as Type box displays "Word Document" as the default format in which the file will be saved. Word documents are identified by the file extension .doc. The file type you select determines the file extension that will be automatically added to the file name when the file is saved. You will change the file name to Flyer and use the default document type.

3 • **Triple-click in the File Name text box.**

• **Type** Flyer.

• **Click** [Save].

Your screen should be similar to Figure 1.27

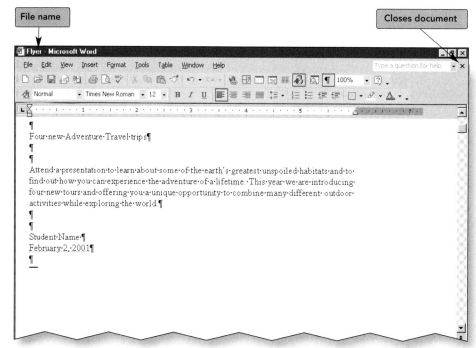

Figure 1.27

The document is saved as Flyer.doc at the location you selected, and the new file name is displayed in the Word title bar.

Closing a File

Finally, you want to close the document while you attend your meeting.

① ► Click ⊠ Close Window in the menu bar.

Another Method

The menu equivalent is File/Close and the keyboard shortcut is Ctrl + F4.

Your screen should be similar to Figure 1.28

Empty document window

Status bar indicators blank

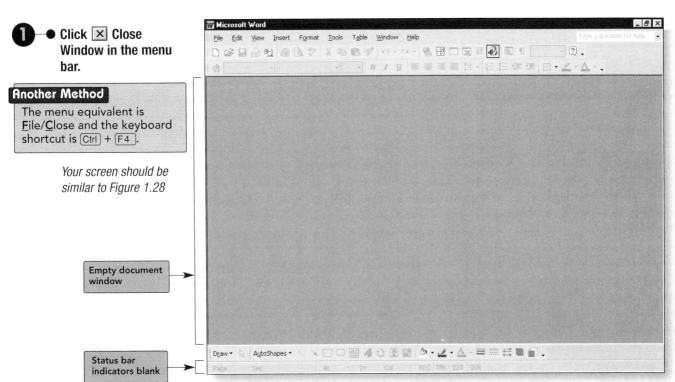

Figure 1.28

Another Method

The menu equivalent is File/Open and the keyboard shortcut is Ctrl + O. You can also click 📂 Open in the Standard Toolbar.

Additional Information

You can also quickly open a recently used file by selecting it from the list of file names displayed at the bottom of the File menu and at the top of the New Document task pane.

Because you did not make any changes to the document since saving it, the document window is closed immediately. If you had made additional changes, Word would ask if you wanted to save the file before closing it. This prevents the accidental closing of a file that has not been saved first. Now the Word window displays an empty document window, and the status bar indicators are blank because there are no open documents.

Opening a File

You asked your assistant to enter the remaining information in the flyer for you while you attended the meeting. Upon your return, you find a note from your assistant on your desk. The note explains that he had a little trouble entering the information and tells you that he saved the revised file as Flyer2. You want to open the file and continue working on the flyer.

① ► Choose View/Task Pane.

► Click 📂 More Documents (in the Task Pane).

Your screen should be similar to Figure 1.29

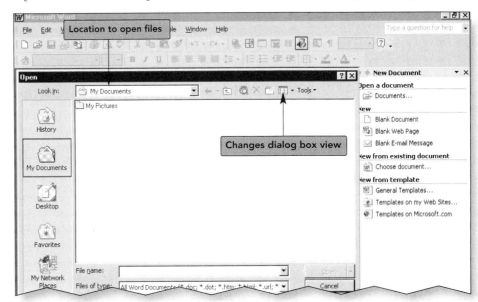

Figure 1.29

In the Open dialog box you specify the location and name of the file you want to open. The Look In drop-down list box displays the last specified location, in the case the location where you saved the Flyer document. The large list box displays the names of all Word documents with the file extensions displayed in the Files of type box. As in the Save As dialog box, the Places bar can be used to quickly access recently used files. When selecting a file to open, it may be helpful to see a preview of the file first. To do this you can change the dialog box view.

2 ● **If the Look In location is not correct, select the location containing your data files from the Look In drop-down list box.**

● **Open the** ⊞ **Views drop-down list.**

● **Choose** ⊞ **Preview.**

● **Select** wd01_Flyer2.doc.

Your screen should be similar to Figure 1.30

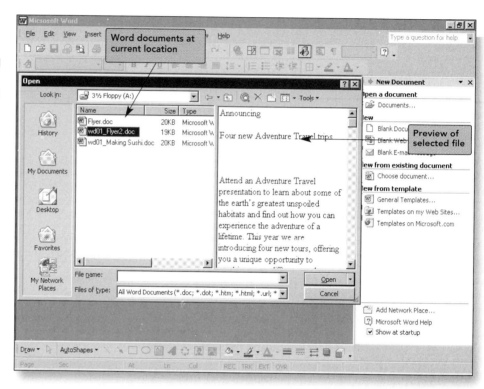

Figure 1.30

A preview of the selected file is displayed in the right pane of the dialog box. You will return the view to the list of file names and open this file.

3 ● **Open the** ⊞ **Views drop-down list.**

● **Choose List.**

● **Click** [Open].

Another Method

You could also double-click the file name to both select and open it.

Your screen should be similar to Figure 1.31

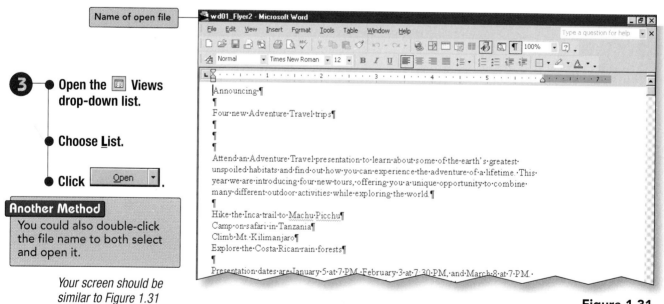

Figure 1.31

The file is opened and displayed in the document window. This file contains the text of the rest of the first draft of the flyer. The formatting marks are displayed because this feature is still on.

Navigating a Document

As documents increase in size, they cannot be easily viewed in their entirety in the document window and much time can be spent moving to different locations in the document. Word includes many features that make it easy to move around in a large document. The most basic is to scroll through a document using the scroll bar or keyboard. Another method is to move directly to a page or other identifiable item in the document, such as a table. You can also quickly return to a previous location, or browse through a document to a previous page or item.

Other features that help move through a large document include searching the document to locate specific items, and using the Document Map or a table of contents. Many of these features you will learn about in later labs.

Scrolling a Document

Additional Information
You can also scroll the document window horizontally using the horizontal scroll bar or the → and ← keys.

Now that more information has been added to the document, the document window is no longer large enough to display the entire document. To bring additional text into view in the window, you can scroll the document using either the scroll bars or the keyboard. Again, both methods are useful, depending on what you are doing. The table below explains the mouse and keyboard techniques that can be used to scroll a document.

Mouse	Action
Click ▼	Moves down line by line.
Click ▲	Moves up line by line.
Click above/below scroll box	Moves up/down window by window.
Drag scroll box	Moves up/down multiple windows.
Click ⬆	Moves to top of previous page.
Click ⬇	Moves to top of next page.
Click ⊙ Select Browse Object	Changes how you want the ⬆ and ⬇ buttons to browse through a document, such as by table or graphic. The default setting is by page.

Key	Action
↓	Down line by line
↑	Up line by line
Page Up	Top of window
Page Down	Bottom of window
Ctrl + Home	Beginning of document
Ctrl + End	End of document

You will use the scroll bar to view the text at the bottom of the flyer.

1 ● **Click ▾ in the verti-cal scroll bar 11 times.**

Your screen should be similar to Figure 1.32

Text scrolls up to allow more text to appear in window

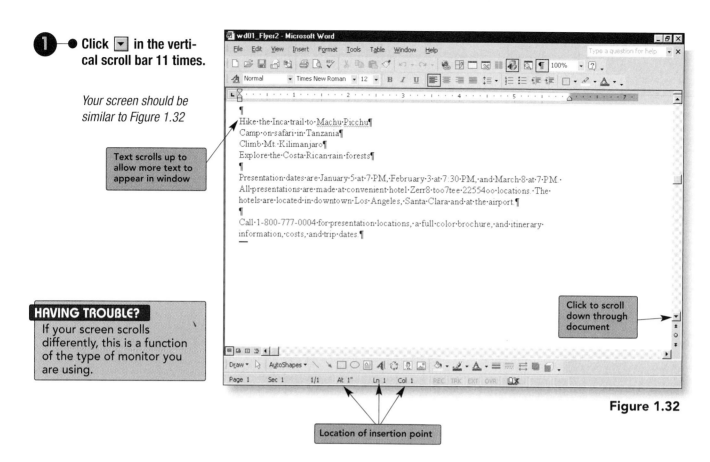

Click to scroll down through document

HAVING TROUBLE?
If your screen scrolls differently, this is a function of the type of monitor you are using.

Location of insertion point

Figure 1.32

The text at the beginning of the flyer has scrolled off the top of the document window, and the text at the bottom of the flyer is now displayed. Notice that the insertion point is no longer visible in the document window. The insertion point location information in the status bar shows that the insertion point is still positioned at the top of the document. To actually move the insertion point, you must click in a location in the window.

2 ● **Click anywhere in the last line.**

You can also scroll the document using the keyboard. While scrolling using the keyboard, the insertion point also moves. The insertion point attempts to maintain its position in a line as you scroll up and down through the document.

3 ● **Hold down ⬆ for several seconds until the insertion point is on the first line of the flyer.**

The document scrolled up in the document window, and the insertion point moved at the same time. In a large document, scrolling line by line can take a while. Observe how the document scrolls as you try out several of the scrolling features that move by larger jumps.

4 • **Click below the scroll box in the scroll bar.**

• **Drag the scroll box to the top of the scroll bar.**

• **Press** `Ctrl` + `End`.

Your screen should be similar to Figure 1.33

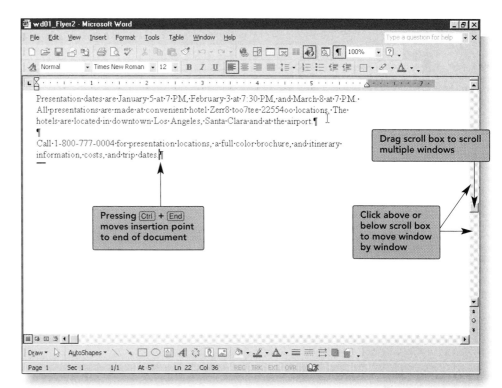

Pressing `Ctrl` + `End` moves insertion point to end of document

Drag scroll box to scroll multiple windows

Click above or below scroll box to move window by window

Figure 1.33

The insertion point is now at the end of the document. Using these features makes scrolling a large document much more efficient.

Editing Documents

While entering text and creating a document, you will find that you will want to edit or make changes and corrections to the document. Although many of the corrections are identified and made automatically for you, others must be made manually.

You have decided to make several changes to the text you just entered. The changes you want to make are shown below.

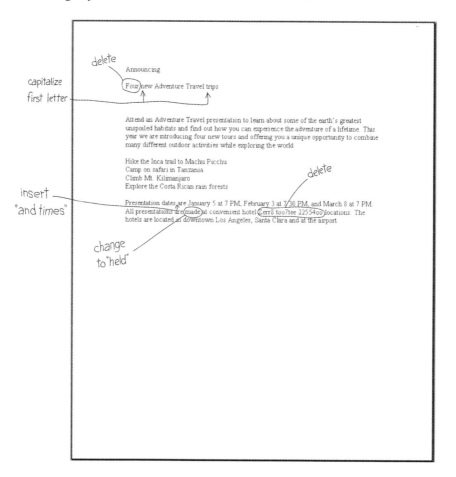

Using Backspace and Delete

Removing typing entries to change or correct them is one of the most basic editing tasks. Like many other features in Word, there are many ways to make corrections. Two of the most important editing keys are the [Backspace] key and the [Delete] key. The [Backspace] key removes a character or space to the left of the insertion point. It is particularly useful when you are moving from right to left (backward) along a line of text. The [Delete] key removes the character or space to the right of the insertion point and is most useful when moving from left to right along a line.

Because the formatting marks are displayed, you noticed there is an extra space after the word "Announcing" that can be deleted.

1 ● Press `Ctrl` + `Home` to move to the beginning of the document.

● Press `End`.

● Press `Backspace` once.

Your screen should be similar to Figure 1.34

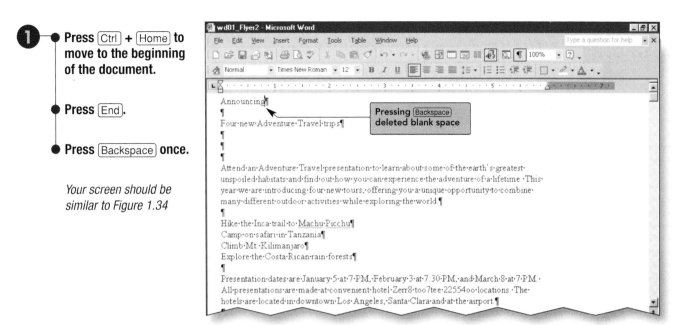

Figure 1.34

The blank space and the space formatting mark are deleted.
You also want to capitalize the first letter of each word in the flyer title.

2 ● Move to "t" in "trips."

HAVING TROUBLE?
Move to the left of the letter.

● Press `Delete` once.

● Type **T**.

● Move to the "e" in "new."

● Press `Backspace` once.

● Type **N**.

Your screen should be similar to Figure 1.35

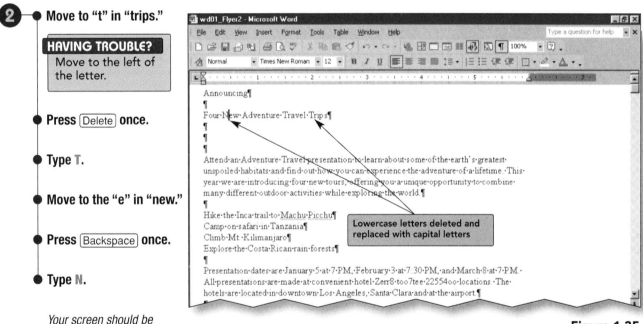

Figure 1.35

In many editing situations, it is helpful to display the formatting marks. However, for normal entry of text, you will probably not need the marks displayed.

3 ● **Click** ¶ **Show/Hide ¶.**

Your screen should be similar to Figure 1.36

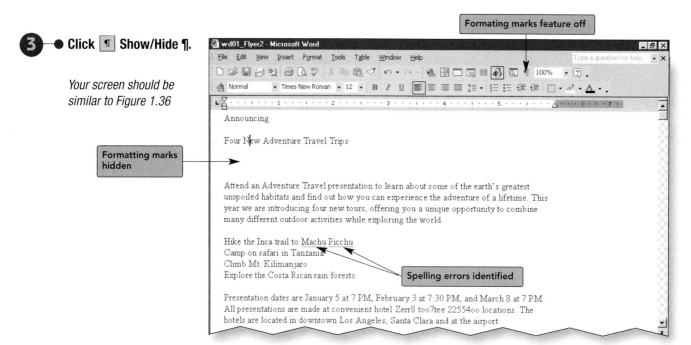

> Formating marks feature off

> Formatting marks hidden

> Spelling errors identified

Figure 1.36

The document returns to normal display. Now that you know how to turn this feature on and off, you can use it whenever you want when entering and editing text.

Ignoring Spelling Errors

After entering the text of a document, you should proofread it for accuracy and completeness and modify or edit the document as needed. You first notice that the spelling checker has identified the names of several locations as misspelled, though they are in fact spelled correctly. This is because they are not in the dictionary. You will instruct Word to accept the spelling of these words and all other words it encounters having the same spelling throughout the remainder of the current Word session.

1 ● **Right-click on Machu.**

● **Choose Ignore All.**

● **In the same manner, tell Word to ignore the spelling of Picchu.**

Your screen should be similar to Figure 1.37

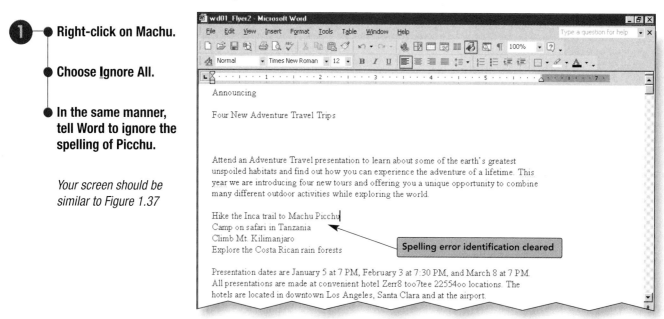

> Spelling error identification cleared

Figure 1.37

The red underlines are removed from each word. If you type any of these words again during this Word session, they will not be identified as misspelled.

Inserting Text

As you continue to check the document, you see that the first sentence of the paragraph below the list of trips is incorrect. It should read: "Presentation dates *and times* are . . ." The sentence is missing the words "and times." In addition, you want to change the word "made" to "held" in the following sentence. These words can easily be entered into the sentence without retyping using either Insert or Overtype mode.

In **Insert mode** new characters are inserted into the existing text by moving the existing text to the right to make space for the new characters. You will insert the words "and times" after the word "dates" in the first sentence.

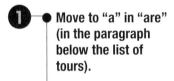

- Move to "a" in "are" (in the paragraph below the list of tours).

- Type **and times.**

- Press [Spacebar].

Your screen should be similar to Figure 1.38

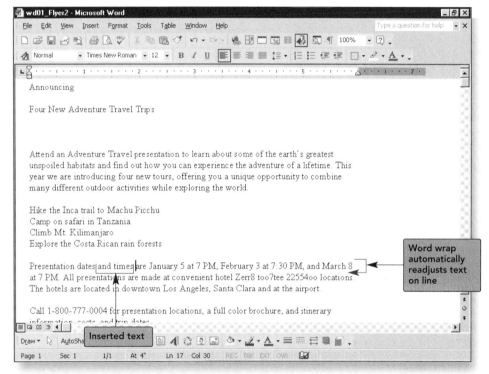

Figure 1.38

The inserted text pushes the existing text on the line to the right, and the word wrap feature automatically readjusts the text on the line to fit within the margin settings.

In the second sentence, you want to change the word "made" to "held." You could delete this word and type in the new word, or you can use the **Overtype mode** to enter text in a document. When you use Overtype mode, new text replaces existing text as you type. You will switch to this mode to change the word.

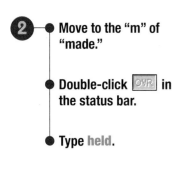

2 Move to the "m" of "made."

Double-click OVR in the status bar.

Type **held**.

Your screen should be similar to Figure 1.39

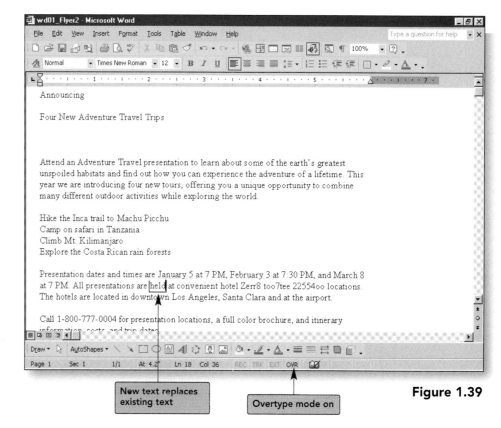

New text replaces existing text

Overtype mode on

Figure 1.39

As each character was typed, the selected character (or space) was replaced with the character being typed. Also notice that the OVR status indicator button letters are now bold, indicating the Overtype mode is on. To turn it off again,

3 Double-click OVR.

You can also turn Overtype mode on and off by pressing Insert or by choosing Tools/Options/Edit/Overtype mode.

Overtype mode is off and Insert mode is restored.

Deleting a Word

Looking back at the title, you decide to delete the word "Four" from the second line. The Ctrl + Delete key combination deletes text to the right of the insertion point to the beginning of the next group of characters. In order to delete an entire word, you must position the insertion point at the beginning of the word.

Additional Information

The Ctrl + Backspace key combination deletes text to the left of the insertion point to the beginning of the next group of characters.

1 ● Move to "F" in "Four" (second title line).

● Press `Ctrl` + `Delete`.

Entire word deleted using `Ctrl` + `Delete`

Your screen should be similar to Figure 1.40

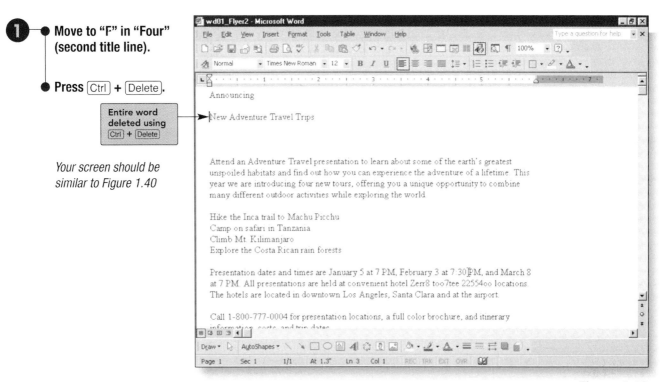

Figure 1.40

Selecting and Deleting Text

Additional Information

You can also select text with the keyboard by holding down `⇧Shift` while using the direction keys to expand the highlight in the direction indicated. Holding down `Ctrl` + `⇧Shift` while using the `→` or `←` keys selects word by word.

As you continue proofreading the flyer, you see that the second line of the paragraph below the list of trips contains several sections of junk characters. To remove these characters, you could use `Delete` and `Backspace` to delete each character individually, or `Ctrl` + `Delete` or `Ctrl` + `Backspace` to delete each word. This is very slow, however. Several characters, words, or lines of text can be deleted at once by first **selecting** the text and then pressing `Delete`. Text that is selected is highlighted. To select text, first move the insertion point to the beginning or end of the text to be selected, and then drag the mouse to highlight the text you want selected. You can select as little as a single letter or as much as the entire document.

The first area of characters you want to remove follow the word "hotel" in the second line of the paragraph below the list of trips.

1
- Move to "Z" (second line of paragraph below tour list).
- Drag to the right until all the text including the space before the word "locations" is highlighted.

HAVING TROUBLE?
Hold down the left mouse button while moving the mouse to drag.

Additional Information
When you start dragging over a word, the entire word including the space after it is automatically selected.

Your screen should be similar to Figure 1.41

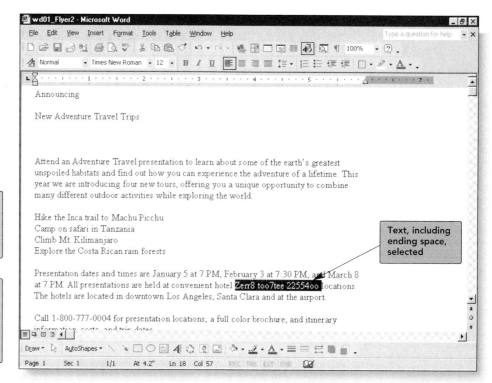

Figure 1.41

The characters you do not want are selected. Text that is selected can then be modified using many different Word features. In this case, you want to remove the selected text.

2
- Press Delete.

Another Method
The menu equivalent is Edit/Clear.

You also decide to delete the entire last sentence of the paragraph. You can quickly select a standard block of text. Standard blocks include a sentence, paragraph, page, tabular column, rectangular portion of text, or the entire document. The following table summarizes the techniques used to select standard blocks.

To Select	Procedure
Word	Double-click in the word.
Sentence	Press Ctrl and click within the sentence.
Line	Click to the left of a line when the mouse pointer is ⤢.
Multiple lines	Drag up or down to the left of a line when the mouse pointer is ⤢.
Paragraph	Triple-click on the paragraph or double-click to the left of the paragraph when the mouse pointer is a ⤢.
Multiple paragraphs	Drag to the left of the paragraphs when the mouse pointer is ⤢.
Document	Triple-click or press Ctrl and click to the left of the text when the mouse pointer is ⤢. Use Edit/Select All or the keyboard shortcut Ctrl + A.

You will select and delete the sentence.

3 ● Hold down Ctrl and click anywhere in the third sentence of the paragraph below the list of trips.

● Press Delete.

Your screen should be similar to Figure 1.42

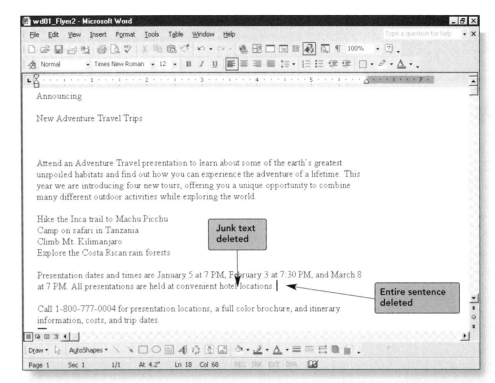

Figure 1.42

Undoing Editing Changes

After removing the sentence, you decide it may be necessary after all. To quickly restore this sentence, you can use  Undo to reverse your last action or command.

1 ● Click  Undo.

Your screen should be similar to Figure 1.43

Another Method

The menu equivalent is Edit/Undo (The action to be undone follows the command.) The keyboard shortcut is Ctrl + Z.

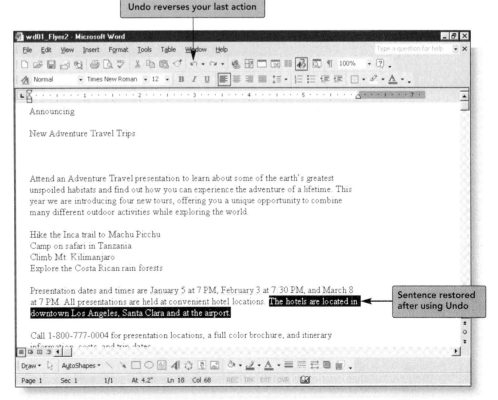

Figure 1.43

Undo returns your last deletion and restores it to its original location in the text, regardless of the current insertion point location. Notice that the Undo button includes a drop-down list button. Clicking this button displays a list of the most recent actions that can be reversed, with the most recent action at the top of the list. When you select an action from the drop-down list, you also undo all actions above it in the list.

2 • Open the [↶ ▾] Undo drop-down list.

most recent actions that can be reversed →

• Select Delete Word.

Your screen should be similar to Figure 1.44

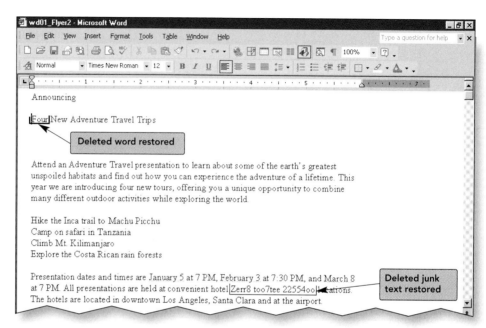

Figure 1.44

The junk characters and the word "Four" are restored. Immediately after you undo an action, the [↷ ▾] Redo button is available so you can restore the action you just undid. You will restore your corrections and then save the changes you have made to the document to a new file.

3 • Click [↷ ▾] Redo 2 times.

Another Method
The menu equivalent is Edit/Redo and the keyboard shortcut is Ctrl + Y.

• Choose File/Save As and save the document as Flyer3.

Your screen should be similar to Figure 1.45

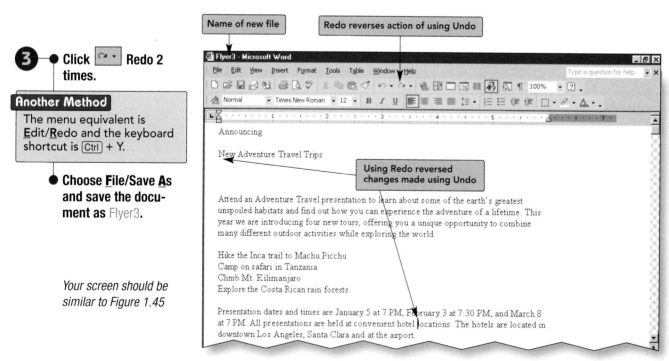

Figure 1.45

forms the actions in the list one by one. The new file name, Flyer3, is displayed in the window title bar. The original document file, wd01_Flyer2 is unchanged.

Formatting a Document

Because this document is a flyer, you want it to be easy to read and interesting to look at. Applying different formatting to characters and paragraphs can greatly enhance the appearance of the document. **Character formatting** consists of formatting features that affect the selected characters only. This includes changing the character style and size, applying effects such as bold and italics to characters, changing the character spacing and adding animated text effects. **Paragraph formatting** features affect an entire paragraph. A paragraph is all text up to and including the paragraph mark. Paragraph formatting features include how the paragraph is positioned or aligned between the margins, paragraph indentation, spacing above and below a paragraph, and line spacing within a paragraph.

Reviewing Document Formatting

Word allows you to quickly review the formatting in a document using the Reveal Formatting task pane.

1 • Choose Format/Reveal Formatting.

Your screen should be similar to Figure 1.46

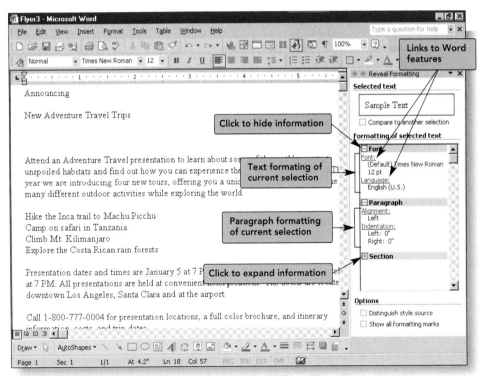

Figure 1.46

The Reveal Formatting task pane displays information about the formatting for the currently selected text and paragraph. It can also be used to modify these settings. The blue underlined text in the task pane indicates items that are direct links to Word features, providing faster access to the feature than using the menu. The mouse pointer appears as a 🖑 when pointing to a link. Clicking the link accesses the feature.

Changing Fonts and Font Sizes

The first formatting change you want to make is to use different fonts and font sizes in the flyer.

concept 7

Font and Font Size

7 A **font**, also commonly referred to as a **typeface**, is a set of characters with a specific design. The designs have names such as Times New Roman and Courier. Using fonts as a design element can add interest to your document and give readers visual cues to help them find information quickly.

There are two basic types of fonts, serif and sans serif. **Serif fonts** have a flair at the base of each letter that visually leads the reader to the next letter. Two common serif fonts are Roman and Times New Roman. Serif fonts generally are used for text in paragraphs. **Sans serif fonts** do not have a flair at the base of each letter. Arial and Helvetica are two common sans serif fonts.

Because sans serif fonts have a clean look, they are often used for headings in documents. It is good practice to use only two types of fonts in a document, one for text and one for headings. Too many styles can make your document look cluttered and unprofessional.

Each font has one or more sizes. **Font size** is the height and width of the character and is commonly measured in **points**, abbreviated "pt." One point equals about 1/72 inch, and text in most documents is 10 pt or 12 pt.

Several common fonts in different sizes are shown in the table below.

Font Name	Font Type	Font Size
Arial	Sans serif	This is 10 pt. This is 16 pt.
Courier New	Serif	This is 10 pt. This is 16 pt.
Times New Roman	Serif	This is 10 pt. This is 16 pt.

To change the font before typing the text, use the command and then type. All text will appear in the specified setting until another font setting is selected. To change a font setting for existing text, select the text you want to change and then use the command. If you want to apply font formatting to a word, simply move the insertion point to the word and the formatting is automatically applied to the entire word.

First you want to increase the font size of all the text in the flyer to make it easier to read.

1

Triple-click to the left of the text when the mouse pointer is 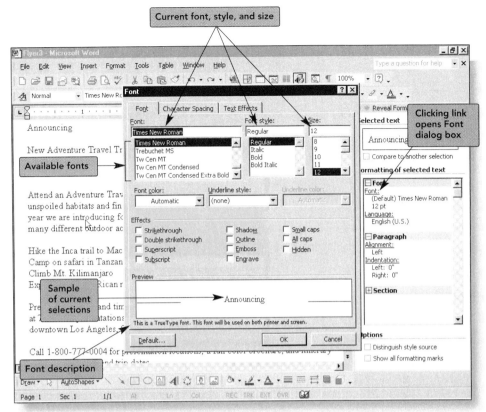 **to select the entire document.**

Another Method

The menu equivalent is Edit/Select All and the keyboard shortcut is Ctrl + A.

Click Font: in the task pane.

If necessary, click the Font tab to open it.

Another Method

The menu equivalent is Format/Font.

Your screen should be similar to Figure 1.47

Figure 1.47

The current font settings are displayed, reflecting the Normal template default of Times New Roman with a font size of 12 points. The Preview box displays an example of the currently selected font setting.

Notice the description of the font below the Preview box. It states that the selected font is a TrueType font. **TrueType** fonts are fonts that are automatically installed when you install Windows. They appear onscreen exactly as they will appear when printed. Some fonts are printer fonts, which are available only on your printer and may look different onscreen than when printed. Courier is an example of a printer font.

You will increase the font size to 14 points. As you select the option, the Preview box displays how it will appear.

2 ● Scroll the Size list box
and select 14.

● Click [OK].

Another Method

The menu equivalent
is F<u>o</u>rmat/<u>F</u>ont/Fon<u>t</u>/
<u>S</u>ize.

*Your screen should be
similar to Figure 1.48*

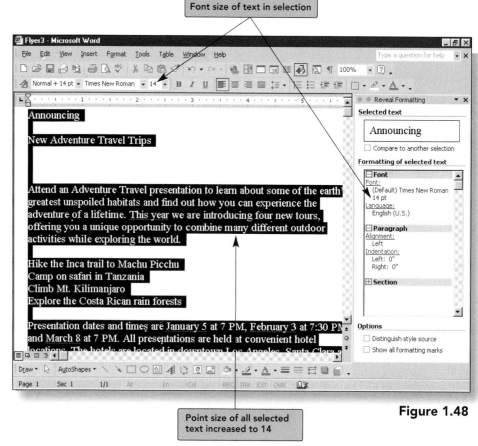

Font size of text in selection

Point size of all selected
text increased to 14

Figure 1.48

Additional Information

If a selection includes text of
various sizes, the Font Size
button will be blank.

The point size of all text in the document has increased to 14 points, making the text much easier to read. The Font Size button in the Formatting toolbar and in the task pane displays the new point size setting for the text at the location of the insertion point.

Next you will change the font and size of the two title lines. Another way to change the font and size is to use the toolbar buttons.

3 ● Click anywhere on the word "Announcing."

● Open the [Times New Roman ▼] Font drop-down list.

Additional Information

Font names appear in their actual font. Fonts used during the current session appear at the top of the list.

● Scroll the list and choose Comic Sans MS.

HAVING TROUBLE?

If this font is not available on your computer, choose a similar font.

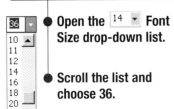

● Open the [14 ▼] Font Size drop-down list.

● Scroll the list and choose 36.

Your screen should be similar to Figure 1.49

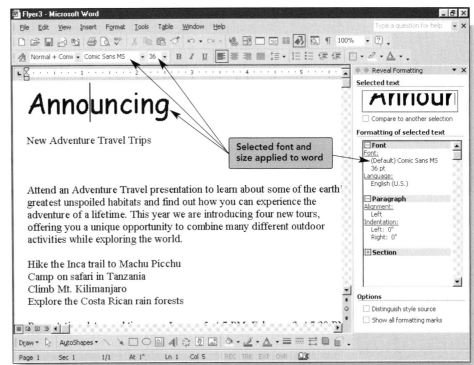

Figure 1.49

The selected font and size have been applied to the word, making the title line much more interesting and eye-catching. The font and font size buttons as well as the task pane reflect the settings in use at the location of the insertion point.

4 ● Select the second title line.

● Change the font to Comic Sans MS with a point size of 24.

● Select the list of four tours.

● Change the font to Comic Sans MS.

● Click anywhere on the highlighted text to deselect it.

Your screen should be similar to Figure 1.50

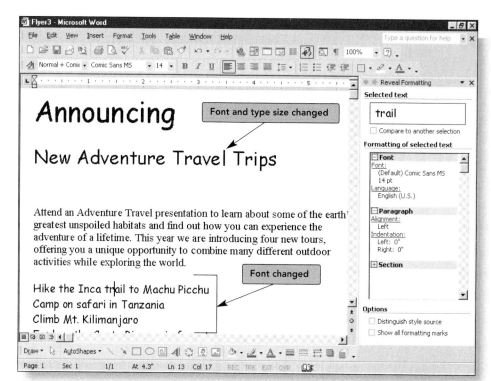

Figure 1.50

Applying Character Effects

Next you want to liven up the flyer by adding character effects such as color and bold to selected areas. The table below describes some of the effects and their uses.

Format	Example	Use
Bold, italic	**Bold** *Italic*	Adds emphasis
Underline	Underline	Adds emphasis
Strikethrough	~~Strikethrough~~	Indicates words to be deleted
Double strikethrough	~~Double Strikethrough~~	Indicates words to be deleted
Superscript	"To be or not to be."[1]	Used in footnotes and formulas
Subscript	H_2O	Used in formulas
Shadow	Shadow	Adds distinction to titles and headings
Outline	Outline	Adds distinction to titles and headings
Small caps	SMALL CAPS	Adds emphasis when case is not important
All caps	ALL CAPS	Adds emphasis when case is not important
Hidden		Prevents selected text from displaying or printing
Color	Color Color Color	Adds interest

First you will add color and bold to the top title line.

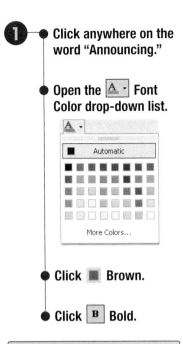

1 ● Click anywhere on the word "Announcing."

● Open the [A ▾] Font Color drop-down list.

● Click ■ Brown.

● Click [B] Bold.

Another Method

The menu equivalents are Format/Font/Font/Font Color and /Font Style/Bold. The Bold keyboard shortcut is Ctrl + B.

Your screen should be similar to Figure 1.51

Additional Information

Many of the formatting buttons are toggle buttons. This means that you can click the button to turn on the feature for the selection, and then click it again to remove it from the selection.

Figure 1.51

The selected color and bold effect have been applied to the entire word. The buttons and task pane information reflect the settings associated with the text at the insertion point. The Font Color button appears in the last selected color. This color can be quickly applied to other selections now simply by clicking the button.

Next you will add color and bold to several other areas of the flyer.

2 Select the entire second title line.

- Change the color to orange and add bold.

- Select the list of four trips.

- Click **A** to change the color to orange.

- Bold the last sentence of the flyer.

- Click in the document to deselect the text.

Your screen should be similar to Figure 1.52

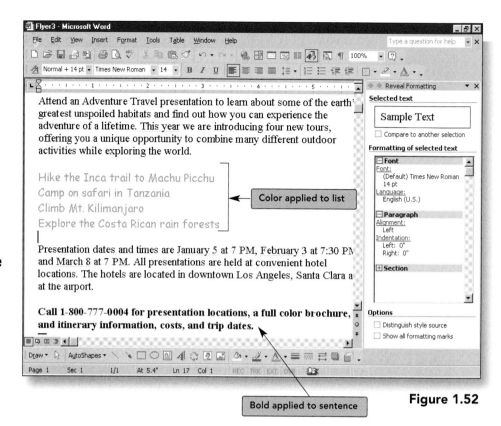

Figure 1.52

Setting Paragraph Alignment

The final formatting change you want to make is to change the paragraph alignment.

concept 8

Alignment

8 **Alignment** is how text is positioned on a line between the margins or indents. There are four types of paragraph alignment: left, center, right, and justified.

Alignment		Effect on Text Alignment
	Left	Aligns text against the left margin of the page, leaving the right margin ragged. This is the most commonly used paragraph alignment type and therefore the default setting in all word processing software packages.
	Center	Centers each line of text between the left and right margins. Center alignment is used mostly for headings or centering graphics on a page.
	Right	Aligns text against the right margin, leaving the left margin ragged. Use right alignment when you want text to line up on the outside of a page, such as a chapter title or a header.
	Justified	Aligns text against the right and left margins and evenly spaces out the words. Newspapers commonly use justified alignment so the columns of text are even.

The alignment settings affect entire paragraphs.

The commands to change paragraph alignment are under the Format/Paragraph menu. However, it is much faster to use the keyboard shortcuts or the buttons on the Formatting toolbar shown below.

Alignment	Command	Keyboard Shortcut	Button
Left	Format/Paragraph/Indents and Spacing/Alignment/Left	Ctrl + L	
Center	Format/Paragraph/Indents and Spacing/Alignment/Center	Ctrl + E	
Right	Format/Paragraph/Indents and Spacing/Alignment/Right	Ctrl + R	
Justified	Format/Paragraph/Indents and Spacing/Alignment/Justified	Ctrl + J	

You want to change the alignment of all paragraphs in the flyer from the default of left-aligned to centered.

1
- Press ⎡Ctrl⎤ + A to select the entire document.

- Click ☰ Center (on the Formatting toolbar).

- Press ⎡Ctrl⎤ + ⎡Home⎤.

Your screen should be similar to Figure 1.53

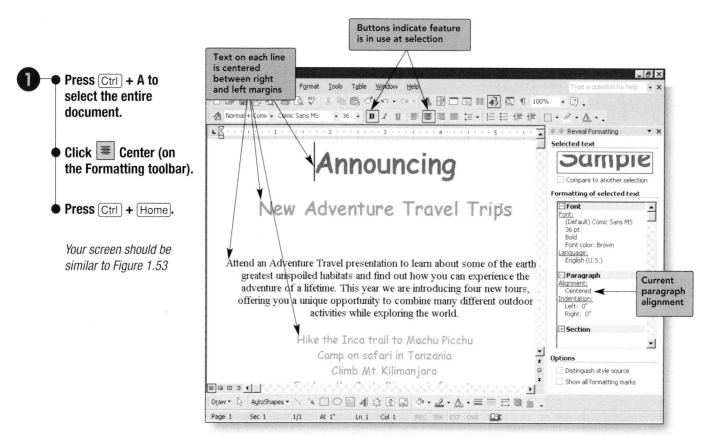

Figure 1.53

Each line of text is centered evenly between the left and right page margins. The task pane paragraph alignment setting shows the new alignment is centered. Now that you are finished with formatting the document, you will close the task pane and save the flyer again using the same file name.

2
- Click ⊠ Close in the task pane title bar.

- Click ⊞ Save to save the file using the same file name.

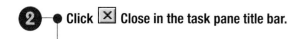
Additional Information

Saving a file frequently while you are making changes protects you from losing work due to a power outage or other mishap.

Working with Graphics

Finally, you want to add a graphic to the flyer to add interest.

concept 9

Graphics

9 A **graphic** is a non-text element or object, such as a drawing or picture, that can be added to a document. An **object** is an item that can be sized, moved, and manipulated.

A graphic can be a simple **drawing object** consisting of shapes such as lines and boxes that can be created using features on the Drawing toolbar. A drawing object is part of your Word document. A **picture** is an illustration such as a graphic illustration or a scanned photograph. Pictures are graphics that were created from another program and are inserted in your Word document as embedded objects. An **embedded object** becomes part of the Word document and can be opened and edited using the **source program**, the program in which it was created. Several examples of drawing objects and pictures are shown below.

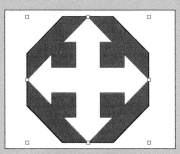
drawing object

graphic illustration

photograph

Add graphics to your documents to help the reader understand concepts, to add interest, and to make your document stand out from others.

Inserting a Picture

You want to add a picture to the flyer below the two title lines. Picture files can be obtained from a variety of sources. Many simple drawings called **clip art** are available in the Clip Organizer that comes with Office XP. You can also create picture files using a scanner to convert any printed document, including photographs, to an electronic format. Most images that are scanned and inserted into documents are stored as Windows bitmap files (.bmp). All types of pictures, including clip art, photographs, and other types of images, can be found on the Internet. These files are commonly stored as .jpg or .pcx files. Keep in mind that any images you locate on the Internet may be copyrighted and should only be used with permission. You can also purchase CDs containing graphics for your use.

You decide to check the Clip Organizer to find a suitable graphic.

Additional Information
You can also scan a picture and insert it directly into a Word document without saving it as a file first.

1 ● Click ¶ Show/Hide to display paragraph marks.

● Move to the middle blank line below the second title line.

● Click 🖼 Insert Clip Art (on the drawing toolbar).

Another Method

The menu equivalent is Insert/Picture/Clip Art.

Your screen should be similar to Figure 1.54

Figure 1.54

The Insert Clip Art task pane appears in which you can enter a word or phrase that is representative of the type of picture you want to locate. The pictures in the Clip Organizer are organized by topic and are identified with several keywords that describe the picture. You can also specify the locations to search and the type of media files, such as clip art, movies, photographs, or sound, to display in the results. You want to find clip art and photographs of animals.

2 ● In the Search text box, type animals.

● If All Collections is not displayed in the Search In text box, select Everywhere from the drop-down list.

HAVING TROUBLE?

Click the box next to an option to select or deselect (clear the checkmark) an option.

● Open the Results Should Be drop-down list, select Photographs and Clip Art and deselect all other options.

● Click Search .

Your screen should be similar to Figure 1.55

Figure 1.55

The Results area displays thumbnails, miniature representations of pictures, all located clip art and photographs of animals. You decide to try the picture of the tiger. Pointing to a thumbnail displays the keywords associated with the picture and information about the picture properties. It also displays a drop-down list bar that accesses the item's shortcut menu.

3 ● **Point to the thumbnail of the tiger.**

Keywords → animals, cats, natures, tigers...
Properties → 145 (w) x 117 (h) pixels, 18 KB, WMF

● **Click** ▾ **to open the shortcut menu.**

Additional Information
The shortcut menu commands are used to work with and manage the items in the Clip Organizer.

● **Choose Insert.**

Another Method
You could also simply click on the graphic to insert it in the document.

● **Click ⊠ in the task pane title bar to close it.**

Your screen should be similar to Figure 1.56

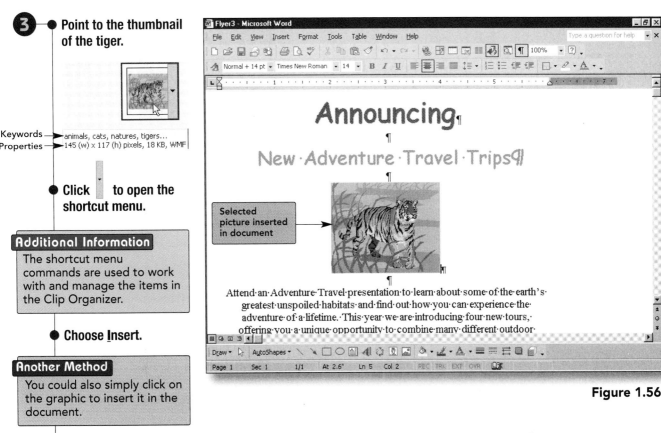

Figure 1.56

The picture is inserted in the document at the insertion point. It is centered because the paragraph formatting in which it was placed is centered. Although you think this graphic looks good, you want to see how a photograph of an elephant you recently received from a client would look instead. The photograph has been saved as a picture image.

4 ● Click 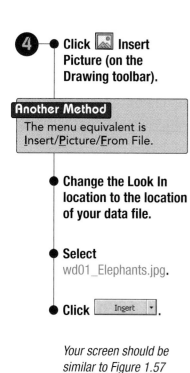 **Insert Picture (on the Drawing toolbar).**

Another Method
The menu equivalent is Insert/Picture/From File.

● **Change the Look In location to the location of your data file.**

● **Select** wd01_Elephants.jpg.

● **Click** Insert.

Your screen should be similar to Figure 1.57

Second picture of photograph inserted in document

Inserts picture from file

Figure 1.57

The elephant picture is inserted below the clip art. Although the photograph looks good, you think the clip art will look better when the flyer is printed.

5 ● Click Undo.

Your screen should be similar to Figure 1.58

Clicking Undo quickly reverses last action

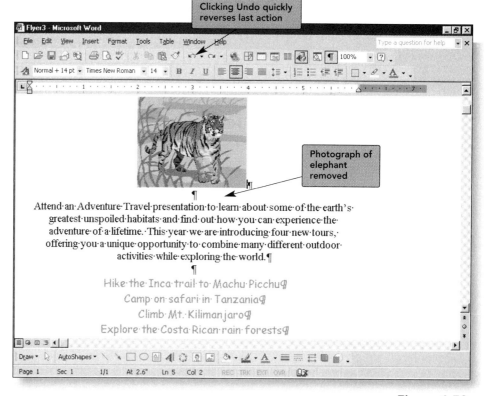

Photograph of elephant removed

Attend·an·Adventure·Travel·presentation·to·learn·about·some·of·the·earth's· greatest·unspoiled·habitats·and·find·out·how·you·can·experience·the· adventure·of·a·lifetime.·This·year·we·are·introducing·four·new·tours,· offering·you·a·unique·opportunity·to·combine·many·different·outdoor· activities·while·exploring·the·world.¶

Hike·the·Inca·trail·to·Machu·Picchu¶
Camp·on·safari·in·Tanzania¶
Climb·Mt.·Kilimanjaro¶
Explore·the·Costa·Rican·rain·forests¶

Figure 1.58

The last action you performed is reversed, and the photograph is removed from the document.

Sizing a Picture

Usually, when a graphic is inserted, its size will need to be adjusted. A graphic object can be manipulated in many ways. You can change its size, add captions, borders, or shading, or move it to another location. A graphic object can be moved anywhere on the page, including in the margins or on top of or below other objects, including text. The only places you cannot place a graphic object are into a footnote, endnote, or caption.

In this case, you want to increase the picture's size. To do this, you must first select the object.

Click on the picture.

Your screen should be similar to Figure 1.59

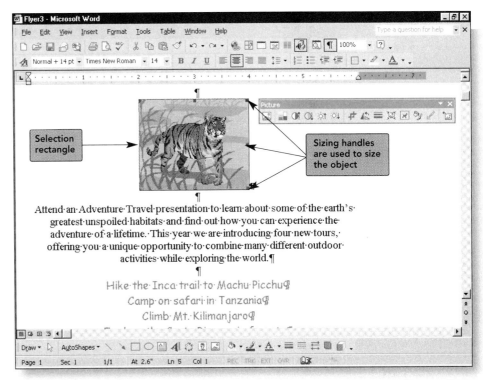

Figure 1.59

Additional Information

A selected graphic object can be moved by dragging it to the new location and deleted by pressing ⌊Delete⌋.

HAVING TROUBLE?

If the Picture toolbar is not displayed, right-click on any toolbar to open the shortcut menu and select Picture, or use **V**iew/**T**oolbars/Picture.

The picture is surrounded by a **selection rectangle** and eight boxes, called **sizing handles**, indicating it is a selected object and can now be deleted, sized, moved, or modified. The handles are used to size the object.

The Picture toolbar is also automatically displayed. Its buttons (identified below) are used to modify the selected picture object. Your Picture toolbar may be floating or may be docked along an edge of the window, depending on where it was when last used.

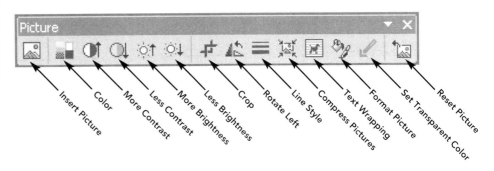

You want to increase the image to approximately 3 inches wide by 3.25 inches high.

2 ● **Point to the lower right corner handle.**

● **With the pointer as a ↖, drag outward from the picture to increase the size to approximately 3 by 3.25 inches (use the ruler as a guide and refer to Figure 1.60).**

● **Click anywhere in the document to deselect the graphic.**

● **Click ¶ Show/Hide.**

● **Click 🖫 Save.**

Your screen should be similar to Figure 1.60

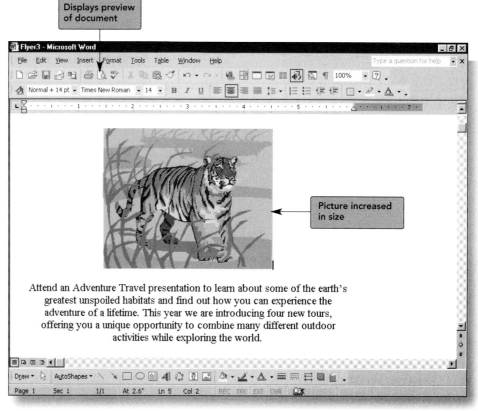

Displays preview of document

Picture increased in size

Attend an Adventure Travel presentation to learn about some of the earth's greatest unspoiled habitats and find out how you can experience the adventure of a lifetime. This year we are introducing four new tours, offering you a unique opportunity to combine many different outdoor activities while exploring the world.

Figure 1.60

Previewing and Printing a Document

Although you still plan to make several formatting changes to the document, you want to give a copy of the flyer to the manager to get feedback regarding the content and layout. To save time and unnecessary printing and paper waste, it is always a good idea to first preview onscreen how your document will appear when printed.

Previewing the Document

Previewing your document before printing it allows you to look over each page and make necessary adjustments before printing it.

1 ● Click ⬚ Print Preview (on the Standard toolbar).

Another Method
The menu equivalent is File/Print Preview.

● If necessary, change the zoom to Whole Page.

Your screen should be similar to Figure 1.61

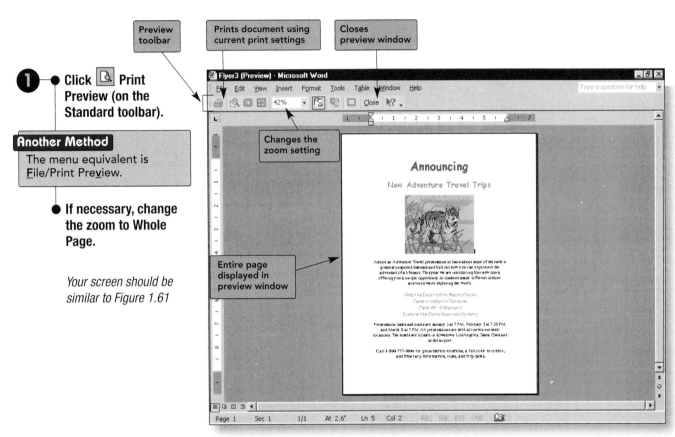

Figure 1.61

The print preview window displays a reduced view of how the current page will appear when printed. This view allows you to check your page layout before printing. The flyer looks good and does not appear to need any further modifications immediately.

The preview window also includes its own toolbar. You can print the letter directly from the preview window using the 🖨 Print button; however, you do not want to send the document directly to the printer just yet. First you need to add your name to the flyer and check the print settings.

2 Click `Close`.

● Add **your name at** before the phone number in the last sentence of the flyer.

● If necessary, make sure your printer is on and ready to print.

● Choose **File/Print**.

Another Method

The keyboard shortcut for the Print command is [Ctrl] + P. Clicking 🖨 Print on the Standard toolbar will print the active document immediately using the current print settings.

Your screen should be similar to Figure 1.62

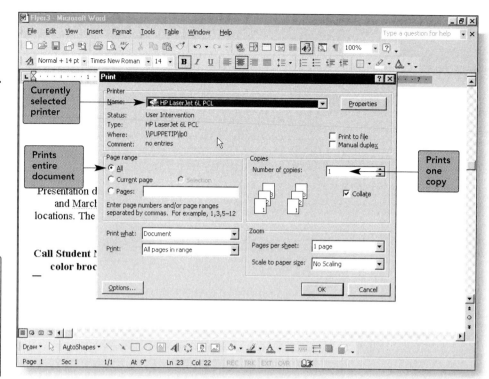

Figure 1.62

Note: Please consult your instructor for printing procedures that may differ from the following directions.

From the Print dialog box, you need to specify the printer you will be using and the document settings. The printer that is currently selected is displayed in the Name drop-down list box in the Printer section of the dialog box.

The Page Range area of the Print dialog box lets you specify how much of the document you want printed. The range options are described in the following table:

Option	Action
All	Prints entire document.
Current page	Prints selected page or page the insertion point is on.
Pages	Prints pages you specify by typing page numbers in the text box.
Selection	Prints selected text only.

The default range setting, All, is the correct setting. In the Copies section, the default setting of one copy of the document is acceptable. You will print using the default Print settings.

3 ● If you need to change the selected printer to another printer, open the Name drop-down list box and select the appropriate printer (your instructor will tell you which printer to select).

● Click [OK].

Your printer should be printing out the document. The printed copy of the flyer should be similar to the document shown here.

Exiting Word

The Exit command in the File menu is used to quit the Word program. Alternatively, you can click the [X] Close button in the application window title bar. If you attempt to close the application without first saving your document, Word displays a warning asking if you want to save your work. If you do not save your work and you exit the application, all your changes are lost.

1 ● Click [X] Close.

● Click [Yes] to save the changes you made to the file.

The Windows desktop is visible again.

Another Method

The keyboard shortcut for the Exit command is [Alt] + [F4].

LAB 1

Creating and Editing a Document

Template (WD1.7)

A template is a document file that includes predefined settings that are used as a pattern to create many common types of documents.

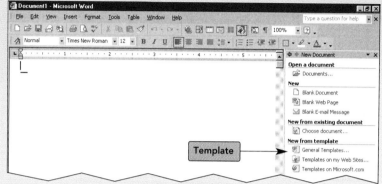

Grammar Checker (WD1.18)

The **grammar checker** advises you of incorrect grammar as you create and edit a document, and proposes possible corrections.

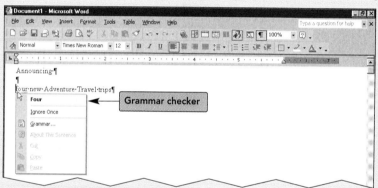

AutoText and AutoComplete (WD1.20)

The **AutoText** feature includes entries, such as commonly used phrases, that can be quickly inserted into a document. As you type the first few characters of an AutoText entry, the **AutoComplete** feature suggests the remainder of the AutoText entry you may want to use.

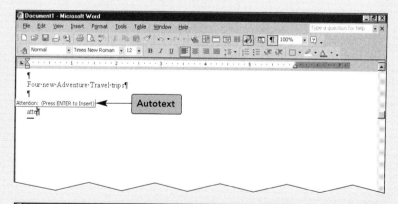

AutoCorrect (WD1.21)

The **AutoCorrect** feature makes some basic assumptions about the text you are typing and, based on these assumptions, automatically identifies and/or corrects the entry as you type.

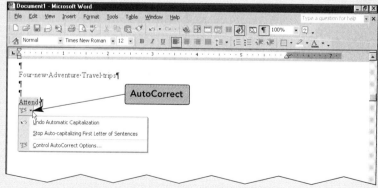

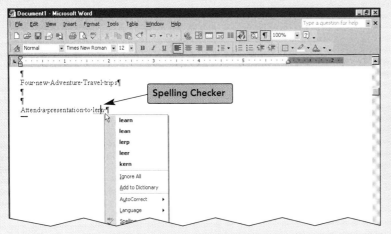

Spelling Checker (WD1.23)

The **spelling checker** advises you of misspelled words as you create and edit a document, and proposes possible corrections.

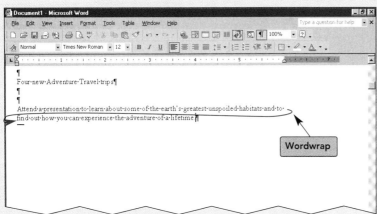

Word Wrap (WD1.26)

The **word wrap** feature automatically decides where to end a line and wrap text to the next line based on the margin settings.

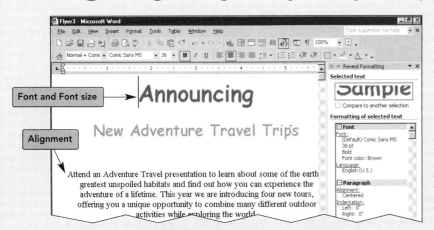

Font and Font Size (WD1.46)

A **font**, also commonly referred to as a typeface, is a set of characters with a specific design that has one or more font sizes.

Alignment (WD1.53)

Alignment is how text is positioned on a line between the margins or indents. There are four types of paragraph alignment: left, center, right, and justified.

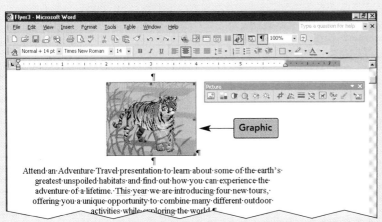

Graphics (WD1.55)

A **graphic** is a non-text element or object, such as a drawing or picture, that can be added to a document.

lab review

LAB 1

Creating and Editing a Document

key terms

alignment   WD1.53
AutoComplete   WD1.20
AutoCorrect   WD1.2
AutoText   WD1.20
character formatting   WD1.45
clip art   WD1.55
cursor   WD1.5
custom dictionary   WD1.23
default   WD1.7
drawing object   WD1.55
Drawing toolbar   WD1.6
edit   WD1.11
embedded object   WD1.55
end-of-file marker   WD1.5
font   WD1.46
font size   WD1.46

format   WD1.11
formatting mark   WD1.13
Formatting toolbar   WD1.5
global template   WD1.7
grammar checker   WD1.18
graphic   WD1.55
Insert mode   WD1.39
insertion point   WD1.5
main dictionary   WD1.23
Normal template   WD1.7
object   WD1.55
Overtype mode   WD1.39
paragraph formatting   WD1.45
picture   WD1.55
points   WD1.46
ruler   WD1.5

sans serif font   WD1.46
select   WD1.41
selection rectangle   WD1.59
serif font   WD1.46
sizing handles   WD1.59
SmartTag   WD1.27
source program   WD1.55
spelling checker   WD1.23
Standard toolbar   WD1.5
template   WD1.7
thumbnail   WD1.57
TrueType   WD1.47
typeface   WD1.46
word wrap   WD1.26

MOUS skills

The Microsoft Office User Specialist (MOUS) certification program is designed to measure your proficiency in performing basic tasks using the Office 2002 applications. Getting certified demonstrates that you have the skills and provides a valuable industry credential for employment. After completing this lab, you have learned the following Word Microsoft Office User Specialist skills:

Skill	Description	Page
Inserting and Modifying text	Insert, modify, and move text and symbols	WD1.39
	Correct spelling and grammar usage	WD1.23, WD1.18
	Apply and modify text formats	WD1.45
	Apply font and text effects	WD1.45
Creating and Modifying Paragraphs	Modify paragraph formats	WD1.53
Formatting Documents	Preview and print documents	WD1.61
Managing Documents	Save documents using different names and file formats	WD1.28
Working with Graphics	Insert images and graphics	WD1.55

command summary

Command	Shortcut	Key Button	Action
File/New	Ctrl + N	🗋	Opens new document
File/Open	Ctrl + O	📂	Opens existing document file
File/Close	Ctrl + F4	✖	Closes document
File/Save	Ctrl + S	💾	Saves document using same file name
File/Save As			Saves document using a new file name, type, and/or location
File/Print Preview		🔍	Displays document as it will appear when printed
File/Print	Ctrl + P	🖨	Prints document using selected print settings
File/Exit	Alt + F4	✖	Exits Word program
Edit/Undo	Ctrl + Z	↺ ▾	Restores last editing change
Edit/Redo	Ctrl + Y	↻ ▾	Restores last Undo or repeats last command or action
Edit/Select All	Ctrl + A		Selects all text in document
View/Normal		☰	Shows text formatting and simple layout of page
View/Web Layout		🖥	Shows document as it will appear when viewed in a Web browser
View/Print Layout		🖽	Shows how text and objects will appear on printed page
View/Outline		🖹	Shows structure of document
View/Task Pane			Displays or hides task pane
View/Toolbars			Displays or hides selected toolbar
View/Ruler			Displays horizontal ruler bar
View/Zoom/Page width			Fits display of document within right and left margins
Insert/AutoText/AutoText/Show AutoComplete suggestions			Turns on AutoComplete feature
Insert/Picture/Clip Art		🖾	Inserts selected clip art at insertion point
Insert/Picture/From File		🖼	Inserts selected picture at insertion point
Format/Font/Font/Font		Times New Roman ▾	Changes typeface
Format/Font/Font/Font Style/Bold	Ctrl + B	**B**	Makes selected text bold

lab review

command summary (continued)

Command	Shortcut	Key Button	Action
Format/Font/Font/Size		10	Changes font size
Format/Font/Font/Color		A	Changes text to selected color
Format/Paragraph/Indents and Spacing/Alignment/Center	Ctrl + E		Centers text between left and right margins
Format/Paragraph/Indents and Spacing/Alignment/Justified	Ctrl + J		Aligns text equally between left and right margins
Format/Paragraph/Indents and Spacing/Alignment/Left	Ctrl + L		Aligns text to left margin
Format/Paragraph/Indents and Spacing/Alignment/Right	Ctrl + R		Aligns text to right margin
Format/Reveal Formatting			Opens Reveal Formatting task pane
Format/Picture			Change format settings associated with selected picture
Tools/AutoCorrect Options/Show AutoCorrect Options buttons			Displays or hides AutoCorrect option buttons
Tools/Customize/Options/Show Standard and Formatting toolbars			Displays Standard and Formatting toolbars on two rows
Tools/Options/Edit/Overtype Mode	Insert	OVR	Switches between Insert and Overtype modes
Tools/Options/View/All	Ctrl + ⇧Shift + *	¶	Displays or hides formatting marks

Terminology

1. In the following Word screen, letters identify important elements. Enter the correct term for each screen element in the space provided.

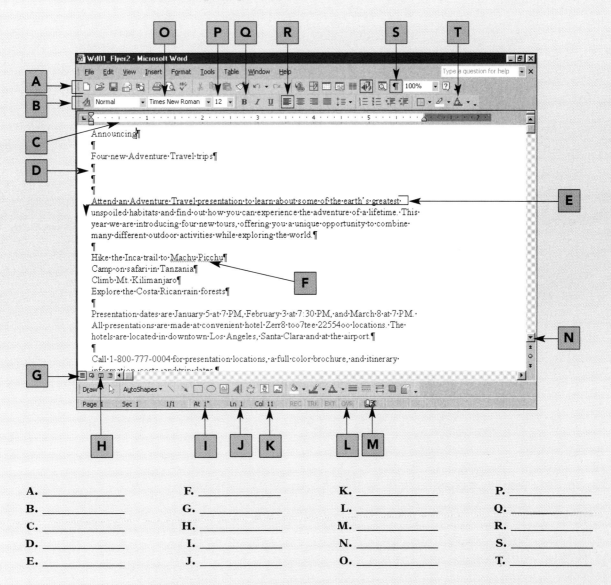

A. _____	F. _____	K. _____	P. _____
B. _____	G. _____	L. _____	Q. _____
C. _____	H. _____	M. _____	R. _____
D. _____	I. _____	N. _____	S. _____
E. _____	J. _____	O. _____	T. _____

matching

Match the item on the left with the correct description on the right.

1. 🔍   _____   **a.** new text writes over existing text

2. template   _____   **b.** type style that can be applied to text

3. font   _____   **c.** moves to the top of the document

4. OVR   _____   **d.** feature that automatically begins a new line when text reaches the right margin

5. alignment   _____   **e.** images that enhance a document

6. Ctrl + Home   _____   **f.** displays the print preview window

7. graphics   _____   **g.** predesigned document that is used as a pattern to create many common types of documents

8. 💾   _____   **h.** font size measurement

9. word wrap   _____   **i.** controls paragraph positioning between the margins

10. point   _____   **j.** saves a document using the same file name

multiple choice

Circle the correct response to the questions below.

1. Document development follows these steps.
   a. plan, edit, enter, format, preview, and print
   b. enter, edit, format, preview, and print
   c. plan, enter, edit, format, preview, and print
   d. design, enter, edit, format, preview, and print

2. The Word feature that makes some basic assumptions about the text entered and automatically makes changes based on those assumptions is _____.
   a. AutoChange
   b. AutoCorrect
   c. AutoText
   d. AutoFormat

3. Words that are not contained in the main dictionary can be added to the _____ dictionary.
   a. custom
   b. additional
   c. add to
   d. user defined

4. The feature that allows you to preview a document before it is printed is _____.
   a. print review
   b. page review
   c. page preview
   d. print preview

5. When text is evenly aligned on both margins it is _____.
   a. center aligned
   b. justified
   c. left aligned
   d. right aligned

6. Words that may be spelled incorrectly in a document are indicated by a _____.
   a. green wavy line
   b. red wavy line
   c. blue wavy line
   d. purple dotted underline

7. Font sizes are measured in _____.
   a. inches
   b. points
   c. bits
   d. pieces

8. A _____ is a document file that includes predefined settings that can be used as a pattern to create many common types of documents.
   a. template
   b. predesign
   c. design document
   d. format document

9. The _____ feature automatically decides where to end a line and where the next line of text begins based on the margin settings.
   a. line wrap
   b. word wrap
   c. wrap around
   d. end wrap

10. A set of characters with a specific design is called a(n) _____.
   a. style
   b. font
   c. AutoFormat
   d. design

true/false

Check the correct answer to the following questions.

		True	False
1.	A wavy red line indicates a potential grammar error.	True	False
2.	A template is a predesigned document.	True	False
3.	The first three steps in developing a document are: plan, enter, and edit.	True	False
4.	Text can be entered in a document in either the Insert or Overtype mode.	True	False
5.	The Delete key erases the character to the right of the insertion point.	True	False
6.	The automatic word wrap feature checks for typing errors.	True	False
7.	The Word document file name extension is .wrd.	True	False
8.	Font sizes are measured in inches.	True	False
9.	Word inserts hidden marks into a document to control the display of text.	True	False
10.	The AutoCorrect feature automatically identifies and corrects certain types of errors.	True	False

lab exercises

Concepts

fill-in

1. A small blue box appearing under a word or character indicates that the _____ feature was applied.

2. If a word is underlined with purple dots, this indicates a(n) _____.

3. The _____ feature displays each page of your document in a reduced size so you can see the page layout.

4. To size a graphic evenly, click and drag the _____ in one corner of the graphic.

5. It is good practice to use only _____ types of fonts in a document.

6. When you use _____, new text replaces existing text as you type.

7. The _____ sits on the right side of the window and contains buttons and icons to help you perform common tasks, such as opening a blank document.

8. Use _____ when you want to keep your existing document with the original name and make a copy with a new name.

9. The _____ window displays a reduced view of how the current page will appear when printed.

10. The _____ feature includes entries, such as commonly used phrases, that can be quickly inserted into a document.

discussion questions

1. Discuss several uses you may have for a word processor. Then explain the steps you would follow to create a document.

2. Discuss how the AutoCorrect and Spelling and Grammar Checker features help you as you type. What types of corrections does the AutoCorrect feature make?

3. Discuss how word wrap works. What happens when text is added? What happens when text is removed?

4. Discuss three ways you can select text. Discuss when it would be appropriate to use the different methods.

5. Describe how the Undo and Redo features work. What are some advantages of these features?

6. Discuss how graphics can be used in a document. What should you consider when adding graphics to a document? Can the use of a graphic change the reader's response to a document?

Hands-On Exercises

step-by-step

Writing a Memo

★ **1.** Universal Industries is starting a casual Friday policy. Ms. Jones, the Vice President of Human Resources, has sent a memo informing employees of this new policy. Your completed memo is shown here.

    a. Open a blank Word document and create the memo with the following text. Press `Tab` twice after you type colons (:) in the To, From, and Date lines. This will make the information following the colons line up evenly. Enter a blank line between paragraphs.

To:	**[Your Name]**
From:	**Ms. Jones**
Date:	**[Current date]**
RE:	**Business Casual Dress Code**

To: Student Name
From: Ms. Jones
Date: February 17, 2002
RE: Business Casual Dress Code

Effective next Friday, business casual will be allowed in the corporate facility on Fridays and the day before a holiday break. Business casual is sometimes difficult to interpret. For men, it is a collared shirt and tailored trousers. For women, it is a pantsuit or tailored trousers or skirt. Business casual is not jeans, t-shirts, or exercise clothes. A detailed dress code will be available on the company Intranet.

Thank you for your cooperation in this matter.

CSJ/xxx

Effective next Friday, business casual will be allowed in the corporate facility on Fridays and the day before a holiday break. Business casual is sometimes difficult to interpret. For men, it is a collared shirt and tailored trousers. For women, it is a pantsuit or tailored trousers or skirt. Business casual is not jeans, t-shirts, or exercise clothes. A detailed dress code will be available on the company Intranet.

Thank you for your cooperation in this matter.

CSJ/xxx

    b. Correct any spelling and grammar errors that are identified.
    c. Change the font size for the entire memo to 14 pt.
    d. Change the alignment of the memo body to justified.
    e. Insert a blank line under the Date line and insert the AutoText reference line "RE:".
    f. Press `Tab` twice and type **Business Casual Dress Code**.
    g. Save the document as Dress Code on your data disk.
    h. Preview and print the document.

Writing a Short Article

★★ **2.** You work for a health organization that produces a newsletter for patients. The upcoming issue will focus on the effects of stress and how to handle stress. You have located information about the top stresses and want to include this information in a short article. Your completed article is shown here.

a. Enter the following information in a new Word document, pressing [↵Enter] where indicated.

Top Stresses [↵Enter] (3 times)

The National Study of Daily Experiences has found over 50 different types of stress. However, 60 percent of all stresses people experience are from the top stresses listed below. [↵Enter] (2 times)

Arguments or tense moments [↵Enter]

Disagreement on how something gets done at work [↵Enter]

Concern over physical health of others [↵Enter]

Work overload and demands [↵Enter]

Worry about others' problems [↵Enter]

Financial issues [↵Enter]

Disciplining children [↵Enter]

Family disagreements [↵Enter]

Late for or miss an appointment [↵Enter]

Value differences [↵Enter]

Home overload and demands [↵Enter]

Household, car repairs [↵Enter]

Tension over chores [↵Enter]

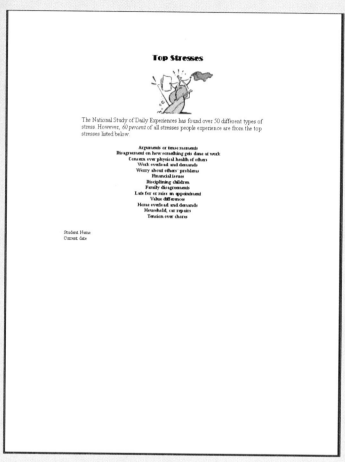

b. Correct any spelling or grammar errors. Save the document as Top Stresses.
c. Turn on the display of formatting marks. Remove any blank spaces at the end of short lines. *Hint:* Use Show/Hide Formatting marks.
d. Change the title font to Broadway (or a font of your choice), 16 pt.
e. Center the title.
f. Center and bold the list of stresses.
g. Add italics and bold to the text "60 percent."
h. Insert the clip art named wd01_Stress from your data file below the title. Size it appropriately and center it below the title.
i. Add your name and the current date on separate lines several lines below the list. Left-align both lines.
j. Preview, then print the document.
k. Save the document again.

Creating a Sales Promotion Flyer

★★★ **3.** You are owner of Executive Style, a new clothing boutique that specializes in career wear for men and women. In preparation for an upcoming sale, you want to create a flyer that you can give customers and also post in the window of other local businesses. Your completed flyer is shown here.

a. Open a new Word document and enter the following text, pressing ⏎Enter where indicated.

Celebrate their birthdays with style ⏎Enter
(2 times)
PRESIDENT'S DAY STOREWIDE SALE ⏎Enter
(4 times)
Starting Wednesday, February 14, we will be taking an additional 20% off all regularly priced spring fashion merchandise. Plus take an extra 25% off our entire stock of all fall and winter clearance fashions for a total savings of 40-60%. This sale ends Monday, February 19, so hurry in for the best selection. ⏎Enter (3 times)
Executive Style ⏎Enter (3 times)
2314 Telegraph Avenue ⏎Enter
Phone: 555-1010 ⏎Enter
Store Hours: Monday - Saturday 10 a.m. - 9 p.m. and Sunday 12 p.m. to 5:30 p.m. ⏎Enter

b. Correct any spelling and grammar errors that are identified.

c. Save the document as Executive Style.

d. Turn on the display of formatting marks. Center the entire document.

e. Change the first line to a font color of red, font type of Copperplate Gothic Light or a font of your choice, and size of 24 pt.

f. Change the second line to a font color of blue, font type of Copperplate Gothic Light or a font of your choice, and size of 36 pt.

g. Increase the font size of the paragraph to 16 points.

h. Bold the store name "Executive Style" and change the font color to red and the font size to 24 points.

i. Insert the pictures named wd01_Executive1 and wd01_Executive2 (from your data files) side by side on the middle blank line below the second title line.

j. Resize the graphics to be approximately 2 by 3 inches (they should be the same size) using the ruler as a guide.

k. Add your name and the current date, left-aligned, on separate lines two lines below the last line. Turn off the display of formatting marks.

l. Preview the document. If necessary, reduce the size of the pictures so the entire flyer fits on one page. Save and print the flyer.

Creating an Advertisement

★★
★ **4.** You own a bed and breakfast inn in the Pocono Mountains. You are going to advertise the B&B in a local travel guide. Your completed advertisement is shown here.

   a. Open a blank Word document and type the following information to create the first draft of the ad.

   Pocono Mountain Retreat

   124 Mountain Laurel Trail

   Pocono Manor, PA 18349

   Phone: 1-717-839-5555
   Host: [Your Name]

   Number of rooms: 4
   Number of private baths: 1
   Maximum number sharing baths: 4
   Double rate for shared bath: $85.00
   Double rate for private bath: $95.00
   Single rate for shared bath: $65.00
   Single rate for private bath: $75.00
   Open: All year
   Breakfast: Continental
   Children: Welcome, over 12

   Located in the heart of the Poconos is this rustic country inn where you can choose to indulge yourself in the quiet beauty of the immediate surroundings or take advantage of the numerous activities at nearby resorts, lakes, and parks.

   In the winter shuttle buses will transport you to the Jack Frost and Big Boulder ski resorts. We have trails for cross-country skiing right on the property. In the summer you can be whisked away to beautiful Lake Wallenpaupack for swimming and boating. The fall foliage is beyond compare. You can hike our nature trails and take in the breathtaking scenery at any time of year.

   In the evenings you can relax in front of a cozy fire or take advantage of the Pocono nightlife. The choice is yours!

   Be sure to call well in advance for reservations during the winter and summer months.

Pocono Mountain Retreat
124 Mountain Laurel Trail
Pocono Manor, PA 18349

Phone: 1-717-839-5555
Host: [Your Name]

Number of Rooms: 4
Number of private baths: 1
Maximum number sharing baths: 4
Double rate for shared bath: $85.00
Double rate for private bath: $95.00
Single rate for shared bath: $65.00
Single rate for private bath: $75.00
Open: All year
Breakfast: Continental
Pets: No
Children: Welcome, over 12

Located in the heart of the Poconos is this rustic country inn where you can choose to indulge yourself in the quiet beauty of the immediate surroundings or take advantage of the numerous activities at nearby resorts, lakes, and parks.

In the winter, shuttle buses will transport you to the Jack Frost and Big Boulder ski resorts. We have trails for cross-country skiing right on the property. In the summer you can be whisked away to beautiful Lake Wallenpaupack for swimming and boating. The fall foliage is beyond compare, and you can hike our nature trails and take in the breathtaking scenery at any time of year.

In the evenings, you can relax in front of a cozy fire take advantage of Pocono nightlife. The choice is yours!

Be sure to call well in advance for reservations during the winter and summer months.

   b. Correct any spelling and grammar errors that are identified. Ignore the spellings of proper names.

   c. Save the document as B&b Ad.

   d. Bold and center the first three lines. Change the font to Comic Sans MS (or a font of your choice), 16 pt. Add color of your choice to the three lines.

   e. Bold and center the phone number and host lines.

   f. Insert the text **Pets: No** above Children: Welcome, over 12.

   g. Center the list of features.

   h. Change the font size of the four paragraphs to 11 pt and change the alignment to justified.

   i. Insert the clip art named wd01_Sunshine (from your data files) above the phone number. Size it appropriately and center it.

   j. Save the document again. Preview and print the document.

Writing an Article for the Campus Newspaper

★★ **5.** Each month the campus newspaper runs a column on cooking. This month's article is about
★ making sushi. You started the column a few days ago and just need to continue the article by
adding instructions about making California rolls. Your completed article is shown here.

a. Open the file file named wd01_Making
Sushi and enter the following text at the
end of the document. Include one blank
line above and below the title and above
the Ingredients and Directions headings.

Making California Rolls

**California rolls are a great way to introduce
sushi to the novice, as there is no raw fish in
the roll. This recipe calls for imitation crabmeat, but if your budget can handle the cost,
use real crabmeat.**

Ingredients:
Nori seaweed
Prepared sushi rice
Avocado, peeled and cut into sixteenths
Imitation crabmeat
Cucumber, peeled, seeded, and julienned

Directions:
**Cut one sheet of Nori seaweed in half and
place on a bamboo mat. With a wooden
spoon, spread a thin layer of sushi rice on
the seaweed leaving a strip uncovered at
each end to seal the roll. At one end, add two
strips of cucumber, one slice of avocado, and
one piece of imitation crabmeat. Beginning
at the end with the cucumber, avocado, and crabmeat, roll the seaweed over once. Pull up the bamboo
mat and use it to help you roll the rest of the way until you reach the other end of the seaweed wrap.
Place the roll seam side down and with a sharp knife, cut the roll into 1/4 or 1/2-inch wide slices.**

Making Sushi

Your next dinner party can be a big success when you get everyone
involved in making sushi. You need just a few basic items for the
preparation. If you live in a large city, you may find these at your local
grocery store. Your best bet is to find an Asian grocery in your city.

Sushi Basics:
A bamboo-rolling mat (Makisu)
Cutting board
Sharp knife
Wasabi
Pickled ginger
Soy sauce

Making California Rolls

California rolls are a great way to introduce sushi to the novice, as there
is no raw fish in the roll. This recipe calls for imitation crabmeat, but if
your budget can handle the cost, use real crabmeat.

Ingredients:
Nori seaweed
Prepared sushi rice
Avocado, peeled and cut into sixteenths
Imitation crabmeat
Cucumber, peeled, seeded, and julienned

Directions:
Cut one sheet of Nori seaweed in half and place on a bamboo mat. With a wooden spoon,
spread a thin layer of sushi rice on the seaweed leaving a strip uncovered at each end to
seal the roll. At one end, add two strips of cucumber, one slice of avocado, and one piece
of imitation crabmeat. Beginning at the end with the cucumber, avocado, and crabmeat,
roll the seaweed over once. Pull up the bamboo mat and use it to help you roll the rest of
the way until you reach the other end of the seaweed wrap. Place the roll seam side down
and with a sharp knife, cut the roll into ¼ or ½-inch wide rolls.

Student Name - Current Date

b. Correct any spelling and grammar errors. Save the document as Making Sushi2.
c. Center the main title, "Making Sushi." Change the font to Impact with a point size of 24.
d. Center the subtitle "Making California Rolls." Change the font to Impact with a point size of
18.
e. Add a color of your choice to the title and subtitle.
f. Bold and increase to 14 pt the type size of the introductory sentences in each section.
g. Bold the words "Sushi Basics" and the colon that follows them.
h. Bold the word "Ingredients" and the colon that follows it.
i. Bold the word "Directions" and the colon that follows it.
j. Insert the pictue wd01_Sushi (from your data files) below the main title of the article.
k. Size the picture to be 2 inches wide (use the ruler as a guide). Center it below the title.
l. Add your name and the current date two lines below the last line.
m. Save the document again. Preview and print the document.

on your own

Writing a Career Report

★ **1.** Locate an article in the newspaper or magazine about careers and/or employment. Summarize the article in a few paragraphs. Add a title to the document and your name and the current date below the title. Center the title lines. Justify the paragraphs. Below the summary, include a reference to the source you used. Save the document as Career Report.

Creating a Family Reunion Invitation

★★ **2.** You are in charge of designing an invitation for an upcoming family reunion. The reunion will be held on July 26, 2002, at the Grand Hotel in Las Vegas. Design an invitation that includes all the information your relatives need to know to attend the event, including location, time, and family contacts. Be sure to use at least two colors of text, two sizes of text, two blank lines, and two kinds of paragraph alignment within your invitation. Include a graphic of your choice from the Clip Organizer. Save the document as Reunion.

Writing a Computer Lab Rules Memo

★★ **3.** Using Hands-On Exercise 1 as a model, create a memo from yourself to the rest of your class that explains the five most important rules to follow while working in the computer lab. Use a piece of clip art to liven up your memo. Format the document in the Arial typeface, 16 pt. Use different font colors for each rule. Save the document as Lab Rules.

Creating a Lost Animal Flyer

★★ **4.** You agreed to baby-sit your best friend's pet monkey, Pom-Pom. Everything was going well until
★ Pom-Pom ran away. Write and design a poster to place around your neighborhood and attract attention as much attention as possible. You want to make sure people will contact you with any information they may have about Pom-Pom. Insert a suitable graphic from the Clip Organizer to accent your poster. Size the graphic appropriately. Save the document as Pom-Pom.

Creating a Cruise Flyer

★★ **5.** Adventure Travel Tours is offering a great deal on a cruise to Spain, Italy, and Greece. Using the
★ formatting features of Word 2002 you have learned so far, create a flyer that will get your company off to a winning start. Search the Web to locate information about places in the tour countries and to obtain graphics you may want to include in the flyer. Right-click on the images you located and use the Save Image As command to download and save them. Insert them into the flyer using the Insert/Picture/From File command. Size and position them appropriately. Save the document as Cruise Flyer.

on the web

Improving Your Writing Skills

Word processors, when used skillfully, can help you improve the quality of your writing. Because word processors make it easy to make corrections and change what you type, they allow you to concentrate on expressing your ideas. However, you still need to decide how you want your ideas organized. The Web offers lots of information on how to improve your writing skills. Locate information about this topic, and create a list of ten tips that you think will be helpful when creating and editing documents. Save the document as Writing Tips.

Revising and Refining a Document

LAB 2

objectives

After completing this lab, you will know how to:

1.	Use the Spelling and Grammar tool and the Thesaurus.
2.	Move, cut, and copy text and formats.
3.	Work with multiple documents.
4.	Control document paging.
5.	Find and replace text.
6.	Insert the current date.
7.	Change margins, line spacing, and indents.
8.	Create a tabbed table and an itemized list.
9.	Add color highlighting and underlines to text.
10.	Create and remove a hyperlink.
11.	Add AutoText and Autoshapes.
12.	Edit in Print Preview.

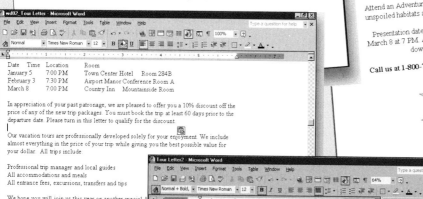

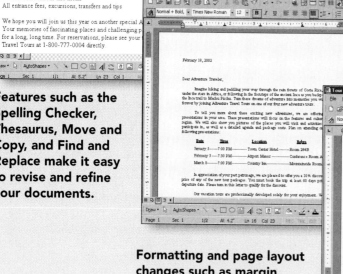

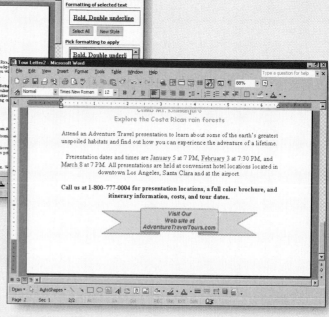

Features such as the Spelling Checker, Thesaurus, Move and Copy, and Find and Replace make it easy to revise and refine your documents.

Formatting and page layout changes such as margin adjustments, indented paragraphs, and tabbed tables help improve the readability and style of the document.

Graphic enhancements such as AutoShapes and additional color add interest to a document.

1
2
3
4
5
6
7
8

Adventure Travel Tours

After creating the rough draft of the trip announcement flyer, you showed the printed copy to your manager at Adventure Travel Tours. Your manager then made several suggestions for improving the flyer's style and appearance. In addition, you decided to write a letter to be sent to past clients along with your flyer. The letter briefly describes Adventure Travel's four new tours and invites clients to attend an informational presentation. Your manager likes the idea, but also wants the letter to include information about the new Adventure Travel Web site and a 10 percent discount for early booking.

In this lab, you will learn more about editing documents so you can reorganize and refine both your flyer and a rough draft of the letter to clients. You will also learn to use many more of the formatting features included in Word 2002 so you can add style and interest to your documents. Formatting features can greatly improve the appearance and design of any document you produce, so that it communicates its message more clearly. The completed letter and revised flyer are shown here.

© Corbis

1	**Thesaurus**	Word's Thesaurus is a reference tool that provides synonyms, antonyms, and related words for a selected word or phrase.
2	**Move and Copy**	Text and graphic selections can be moved or copied to new locations in a document or between documents, saving you time by not having to retype the same information.
3	**Page Break**	A page break marks the point at which one page ends and another begins. There are two types of page breaks that can be used in a document: soft page breaks and hard page breaks.
4	**Find and Replace**	To make editing easier, you can use the Find and Replace feature to find text in a document and replace it with other text as directed.
5	**Field**	A field is a placeholder that instructs Word to insert information into a document.
6	**Page Margin**	The page margin is the blank space around the edge of the page. Standard single-sided documents have four margins: top, bottom, left, and right.
7	**Indents**	To help your reader find information quickly, you can indent paragraphs from the margins. Indenting paragraphs sets them off from the rest of the document.
8	**Bulleted and Numbered Lists**	Whenever possible, use bulleted or numbered lists to organize information and make your writing clear and easy to read.

Revising a Document

After speaking with the manager about the letter's content, you planned the basic topics that need to be included in the letter: to advertise the new tours, invite clients to the presentations, describe the early-booking discount, and promote the new Web site. You quickly entered the text for the letter, saved it as Tour Letter, and printed out a hard copy. As you are reading the document again, you mark up the printout with the changes and corrections you want to make. The marked up copy is shown here.

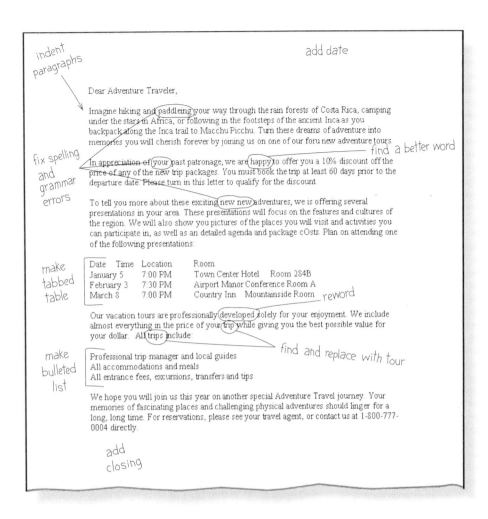

Spell-Checking the Entire Document

The first correction you want to make is to clean up the spelling and grammar errors that Word has identified.

1 • **Start Word and open the file** wd02_Tour Letter.

• **If necessary, switch to Normal view with a zoom of 100%.**

Your screen should be similar to Figure 2.1

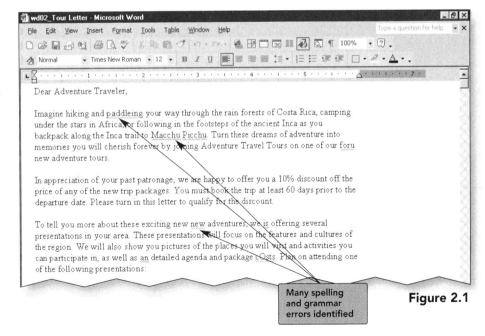

Figure 2.1

To correct the misspelled words and grammatical errors, you can use the shortcut menu to correct each individual word or error, as you learned in Lab 1. However, in many cases you may find it more efficient to wait until you are finished writing before you correct errors. Rather than continually breaking your train of thought to correct errors as you type, you can manually turn on the spelling and grammar checker to locate and correct all the errors in the document at once.

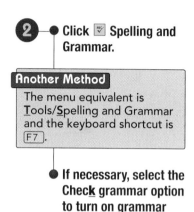

2 ● Click ✓ **Spelling and Grammar.**

Another Method

The menu equivalent is **Tools/Spelling and Grammar** and the keyboard shortcut is F7 .

● **If necessary, select the Check grammar option to turn on grammar checking.**

Your screen should be similar to Figure 2.2

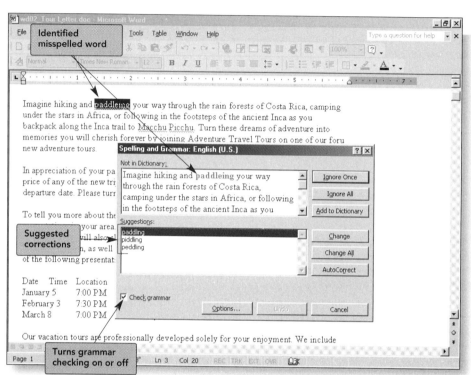

Figure 2.2

Additional Information

You can also double-click the Spelling and Grammar status icon ▣ to move to the next spelling or grammar error and open the spelling shortcut menu.

The Spelling and Grammar dialog box is displayed, and the spelling and grammar checker has immediately located the first word that may be misspelled, "paddleing." The sentence with the misspelled word in red is displayed in the Not in Dictionary text box, and the word is highlighted in the document.

The Suggestions list box displays the words the spelling checker has located in the dictionary that most closely match the misspelled word. The first word is highlighted. Sometimes the spelling checker does not display any suggested replacements. This occurs when it cannot locate any words in the dictionaries that are similar in spelling. If there are no suggestions, the Not in Dictionary text box simply displays the word that is highlighted in the text.

Additional Information

The Change All option replaces the same word throughout the document with the word you select in the Suggestions box.

To change the spelling of the word to one of the suggested spellings, highlight the correct word in the list and then choose Change . If there were no suggested replacements, and you did not want to use any of the option buttons, you could edit the word yourself by typing the correction in the Not in Dictionary box. In this case, the correct replacement, "paddling" is already highlighted.

3 • Click [Change].

Your screen should be similar to Figure 2.3

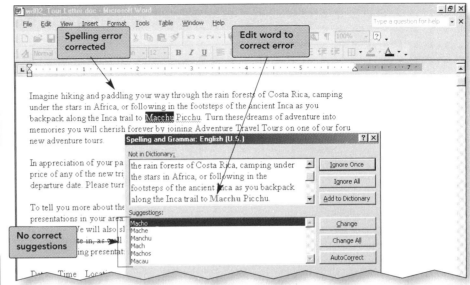

Figure 2.3

The spelling checker replaces the misspelled word with the selected suggested replacement and moves on to locate the next error. This time the error is the name of the Inca ruins at Machu Picchu. The word "Macchu" is spelled incorrectly; there is no correct suggestion, however, because the word is not found in the dictionary. You will correct the spelling of the word by editing it in the Not in Dictionary text box.

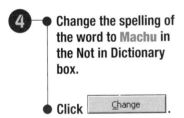

4 • Change the spelling of the word to **Machu** in the Not in Dictionary box.

• Click [Change].

Your screen should be similar to Figure 2.4

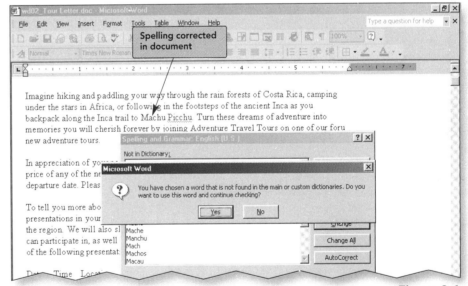

Figure 2.4

Word displays a question dialog box advising you that the correction to the word is not found in its dictionaries, and asking you to confirm that you want to continue.

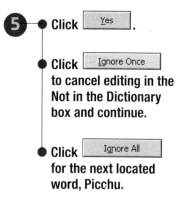

5 ● Click [Yes].

● Click [Ignore Once] to cancel editing in the Not in the Dictionary box and continue.

● Click [Ignore All] for the next located word, Picchu.

Your screen should be similar to Figure 2.5

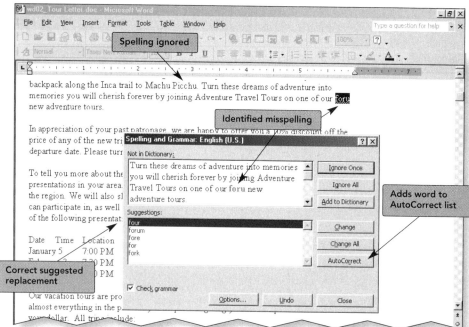

Figure 2.5

Additional Information

The [Ignore Once] option accepts the word as correct for this occurrence only.

The spelling of the word "Picchu" is ignored, and the word is no longer identified as misspelled.

The next located error, "foru," is a typing error that you make frequently when typing the word four. The correct spelling is selected in the Suggestions list box. You want to change it to the suggested word and add it to the list of words that are automatically corrected.

6 ● Click [AutoCorrect].

HAVING TROUBLE?

If a dialog box appears telling you an AutoCorrect entry already exists for this word, simply click [Yes] to continue.

Your screen should be similar to Figure 2.6

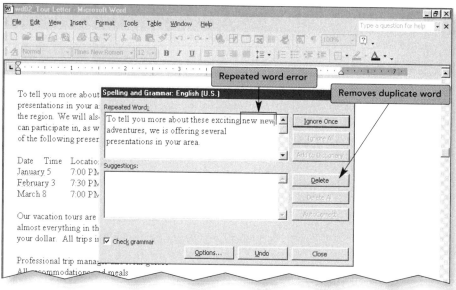

Figure 2.6

The word is corrected in the document. Because you also added it to the AutoCorrect list, in the future whenever you type this word incorrectly as "foru," it will automatically be changed to "four." The next located error identifies the duplicate words "new."

The next four errors that will be identified and their cause are shown in the following table

Identified Error	Cause	Action	Result
new	Repeated word	Delete	Duplicate word "new" is deleted
we is	Subject-verb disagreement	Change	we are
cOsts	Inconsistent capitalization	Change	costs
an detailed	Grammatical error	Change	a

7 ● Click [Delete] to delete the repeated word "new."

● Continue to respond to the Spelling and Grammar checker by clicking [Change] for the next three identified errors.

● Click [OK] in response to the message telling you that the spelling and grammar check is complete.

● Move to the top of the document and save the revised document as Tour Letter2 to the appropriate data file location.

Your screen should be similar to Figure 2.7

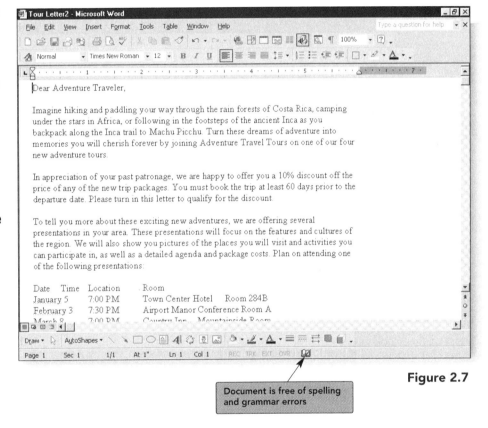

Document is free of spelling and grammar errors

Figure 2.7

Using the Thesaurus

The next text change you want to make is to find a better word for "happy" in the sentence about the 10 percent discount. To help find a similar word, you will use the thesaurus tool.

---

concept 1

Thesaurus

1 The **thesaurus** is a reference tool that provides synonyms, antonyms, and related words for a selected word or phrase. **Synonyms** are words with a similar meaning, such as "cheerful" and "happy." **Antonyms** are words with an opposite meaning, such as "cheerful" and "sad." Related words are words that are variations of the same word, such as "cheerful" and "cheer." The Thesaurus can help to liven up your documents by adding interest and variety to your text.

To identify the word you want looked up and to use the thesaurus,

1 ● Move to anywhere in the word "happy" (first sentence, second paragraph).

● Choose **Tools/Language/Thesaurus.**

Another Method

The keyboard shortcut is ⇧Shift + F7 . You can also choose Synonyms from the shortcut menu and select a word from the list.

Your screen should be similar to Figure 2.8

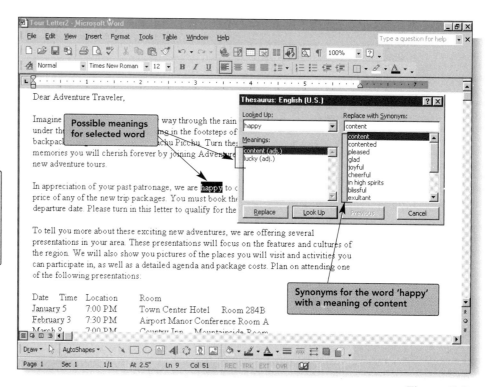

Figure 2.8

The Thesaurus dialog box displays a list of possible meanings for the selected word. From this list you can select the most appropriate meaning for the word. The currently selected meaning, "content," is appropriate for this sentence. The words in the Replace with Synonym box are synonyms for the word "happy" with a meaning of "content." The best choice from this list is "pleased."

② Select "pleased."

● Click Replace .

Your screen should be similar to Figure 2.9

Additional Information

If a synonym, antonym, or related word is not found, the thesaurus displays an alphabetical list of entries that are similar in spelling to the selected word.

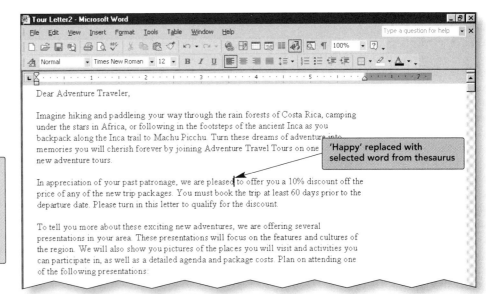

Figure 2.9

Word replaces the word "happy" with the word you selected from the thesaurus.

Moving and Copying Selections

After looking over the letter, you decide to add the company name in several other locations and to change the order of paragraphs. To quickly make these changes, you can move and copy selections.

---

concept 2

Move and Copy

2 Text and graphic selections can be moved or copied to new locations in a document or between documents, saving you time by not having to recreate the same information. A selection that is moved is cut from its original location, called the **source**, and inserted at a new location, called the **destination**. A selection that is copied leaves the original in the source and inserts a duplicate at the destination.

When a selection is cut or copied, the selection is stored in the system Clipboard, a temporary Windows storage area in memory. It is also stored in the Office Clipboard. The system Clipboard holds only the last art or copied items, whereas the Office Clipboard can store up to 24 items that have been cut or copied. This allows you to insert multiple items from various Office documents and paste all or part of the collection of items into another document.

Using Copy

You want to include the company name in the last paragraph of the letter in two places. Since the name is already entered in the first paragraph, instead of typing the name again, you will copy it.

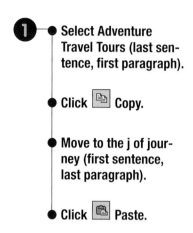

- Select Adventure Travel Tours (last sentence, first paragraph).

- Click  Copy.

- Move to the j of journey (first sentence, last paragraph).

- Click Paste.

Another Method

The menu equivalent to copy is Edit/Copy and the keyboard shortcut is Ctrl + C. The menu equivalent to paste is Edit/Paste and the keyboard shortcut is Ctrl + V.

Your screen should be similar to Figure 2.10

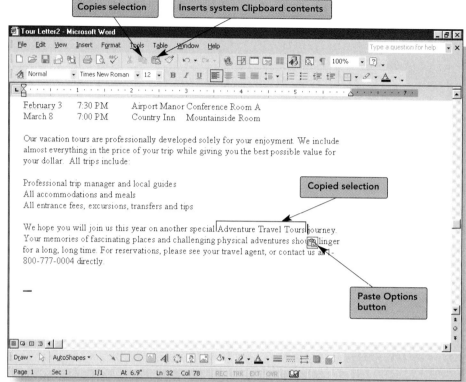

Figure 2.10

The copied selection is inserted at the location you specified. The Paste Options button appears automatically whenever a selection is pasted. It is used to control the format of the pasted item.

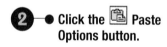

- Click the Paste Options button.

Your screen should be similar to Figure 2.11

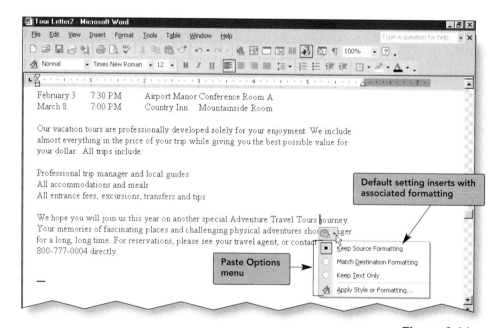

Figure 2.11

The options are used to specify whether to insert the item with the same formatting as it had in the source, to change it to the formatting of the surrounding destination text, or to insert text only (from a selection that is a combination of text and graphics). You can also apply new formatting to the selection. The default, to use the formatting from the source, is appropriate. Next, you want to insert the company name in place of the word "us" in the last sentence of the letter.

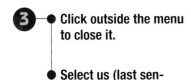

- Click outside the menu to close it.

- Select us (last sentence).

- Click 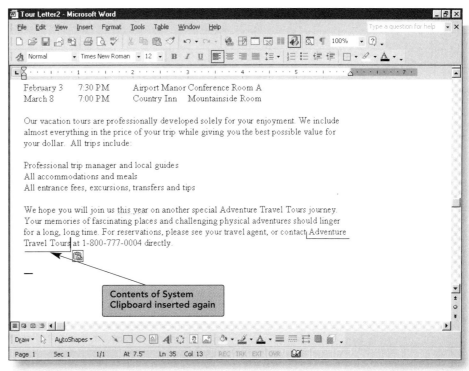 Paste.

Your screen should be similar to Figure 2.12

Figure 2.12

Additional Information

Using the 📋 Paste button or command equivalents inserts the system Clipboard contents, not the Office Clipboard contents. You will use the Office Clipboard in Lab 4.

The selected text was deleted and replaced with the contents of the system Clipboard. The system Clipboard contents remain in the Clipboard until another item is copied or cut, allowing you to paste the same item multiple times.

Using Cut and Paste

You want the paragraph about the 10 percent discount (second paragraph) to follow the list of presentation dates. To do this, you will move the paragraph from its current location to the new location. The Cut and Paste commands on the Edit menu are used to move selections. You will use the shortcut menu to select the Cut command.

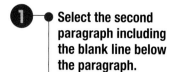

1 ● Select the second paragraph including the blank line below the paragraph.

HAVING TROUBLE?
Drag in the space to the left of the paragraph to select it.

● Right-click on the selection or press ⇧Shift + F10 to display the shortcut menu.

Another Method
The Cut shortcuts are ✂ or Ctrl + X.

● Choose Cu**t**.

Your screen should be similar to Figure 2.13

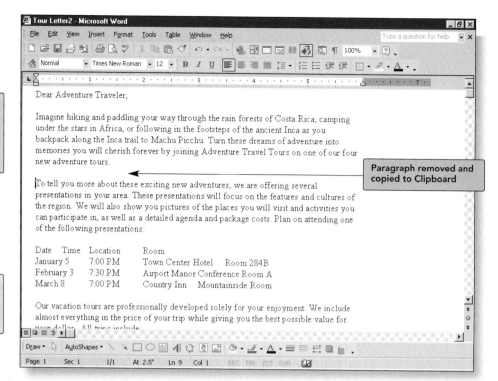

Figure 2.13

The selected paragraph is removed from the source and copied to the Clipboard. Next you need to move the insertion point to the location where the text will be inserted and paste the text into the document from the Clipboard.

2 ● Move to the "O" in "Our" (at the beginning of the paragraph below list of presentation dates).

● Click 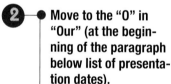 Paste.

Another Method
You can also choose Paste from the shortcut menu.

● If necessary, scroll down to view the pasted paragraph.

Your screen should be similar to Figure 2.14

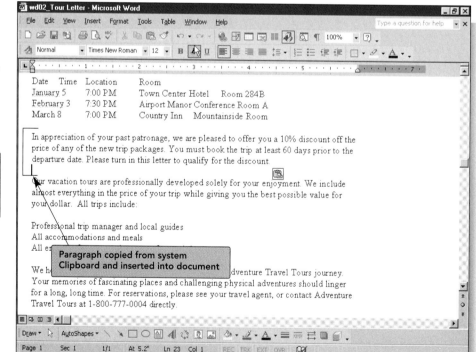

Figure 2.14

The deleted paragraph is reentered into the document at the insertion point location. That was a lot quicker than retyping the whole paragraph!

Using Drag and Drop

Additional Information

You can also use drag and drop to copy a selection by holding down Ctrl while dragging. The mouse pointer shape is ▨.

Finally, you also decide to move the word "directly" in the last paragraph so that the sentence reads ". . . contact Adventure Travel Tours directly at 1-888-777-0004." Rather than use Cut and Paste to move this text, you will use the **drag and drop** editing feature. This feature is most useful for copying or moving short distances in a document. To use drag and drop to move a selection, point to the selection and drag it to the location where you want the selection inserted. The mouse pointer appears as ▨ as you drag, and a temporary insertion point ▯ shows you where the text will be placed when you release the mouse button.

1 ● Select directly (last word in last paragraph).

● Drag the selection to before "at" in the same sentence.

Additional Information

You can also move or copy a selection by holding down the right mouse button while dragging. When you release the mouse button, a shortcut menu appears with the available move and copy options.

Your screen should be similar to Figure 2.15

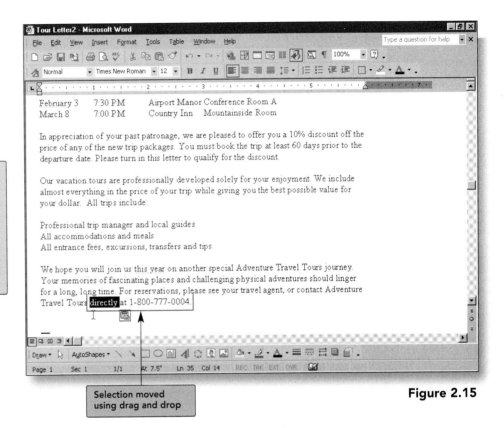

Selection moved using drag and drop

Figure 2.15

The selection is moved to the new location.

Working with Multiple Documents

Next you want to open the flyer document so that you can copy the flyer into the letter document. All Office XP applications allow you to open and use multiple files at the same time. Each file is displayed in a separate application window.

Opening a Second Document

Additional Information

It is always a good idea to save your work before opening another file.

You made several of the changes to the flyer suggested by the manager. You will save the document you are working with then open the revised flyer.

1
● Click 💾 Save.

● **Open the** wd02_Flyer4 **document.**

Additional Information
Sometimes you may want to open several files at once. To do this you can select multiple files by holding down Ctrl while clicking on each file name. If the files are adjacent, you can click the first file name, hold down ⇧Shift, and click on the name of the last file.

Your screen should be similar to Figure 2.16

Figure 2.16

The flyer document is opened and displayed in a separate window. It contains the insertion point, which indicates that it is the **active document**, or the document you can work in. The taskbar displays a button for each open document window; it can be used to quickly switch from one window to the other.

Copying between Documents

You plan to include the flyer with the letter to be mailed to clients. You also want to keep the flyer document in a separate file, because it will be printed separately to be given to clients when they come to the office. To include the flyer with the letter document, you will copy the flyer contents into the letter document.

1 ● **Select the entire flyer.**

HAVING TROUBLE?
Triple-click in the left margin to quickly select the entire document.

● **Click** 🔲 **Copy.**

● **Click** 📄 Tour Letter.... **in the taskbar.**

Another Method
You can also use Alt + Tab ⇆ or the Window menu to switch from one open document window to another.

● **Move to the blank line below the last paragraph of the letter.**

● **Click** 🔲 **Paste.**

Your screen should be similar to Figure 2.17

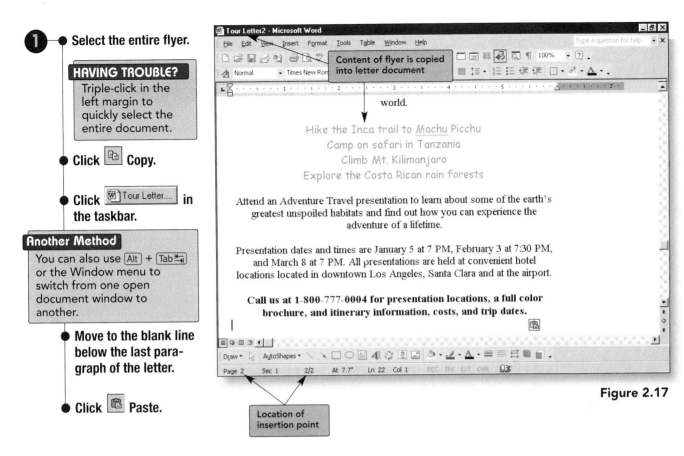

Figure 2.17

The letter now consists of two pages. Notice the status bar shows the insertion point location is on page 2/2.

Controlling Document Paging

As text and graphics are added to a document, Word automatically starts a new page when text extends beyond the bottom margin setting. The beginning of a new page is identified by a page break.

concept 3

Page Break

3 A **page break** marks the point at which one page ends and another begins. There are two types of page breaks that can be used in a document: soft page breaks and hard page breaks. As you fill a page with text or graphics, Word inserts a **soft page break** automatically when the bottom margin is reached and starts a new page. As you add or remove text from a page, Word automatically readjusts the placement of the soft page break.

Many times, however, you may want to force a page break to occur at a specific location. To do this you can manually insert a **hard page break**. This instructs Word to begin a new page regardless of the amount of text on the previous page. When a hard page break is used, its location is never moved regardless of the changes that are made to the amount of text on the preceding page. All soft page breaks that precede or follow a hard page break continue to automatically adjust. Sometimes you may find that you have to remove the hard page break and reenter it at another location as you edit the document.

Automatic (soft) page break →

Manual (hard) page break →

Page Break

To see where the second page begins,

1 ● Drag the scroll box upward until the flyer title is displayed.

Additional Information

As you drag the scroll box, a scroll tip displays the number of the page that is displayed in the window.

Your screen should be similar to Figure 2.18

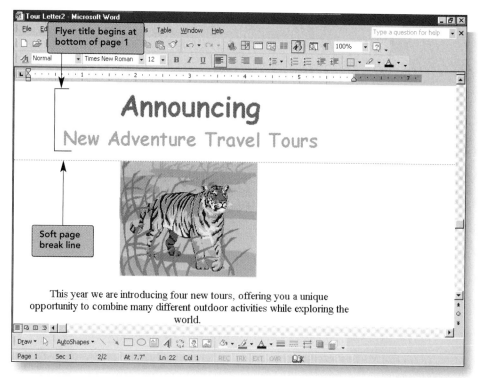

Figure 2.18

To show where one page ends and another begins, Word displays a dotted line across the page to mark the soft page break.

Inserting a Hard Page Break

Many times the location of the soft page break is not appropriate. In this case, the location of the soft page break displays the flyer title on the bottom of page 1 and the remaining portion of the flyer on page 2. Because you want the entire flyer to print on a page by itself, you will manually insert a hard page break above the flyer title.

1 ● **Move to the end of the last line of the letter.**

● **Press** Ctrl **+** ←Enter .

Another Method
The menu equivalent is Insert/**B**reak/**P**age break.

● **Save the document again.**

Your screen should be similar to Figure 2.19

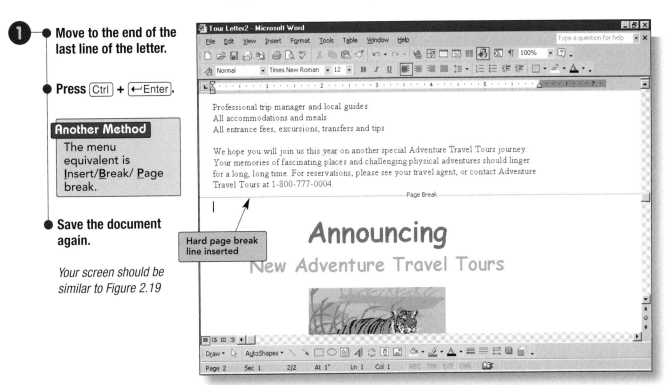

Figure 2.19

Additional Information
To remove a hard page break, simply select the hard page break line and press Delete .

A dotted line and the words "Page Break" appear across the page above the flyer title, indicating that a hard page break was entered at that position.

Finding and Replacing Text

As you continue proofing the letter, you notice that you frequently used the word "trip." You think that the letter would read better if the word "tour" was used in place of "trip" in some instances.

concept 4

Find and Replace

4 To make editing easier, you can use the Find and Replace feature to find text in a document and replace it with other text as directed. For example, suppose you created a lengthy document describing the type of clothing and equipment needed to set up a world-class home gym, and then you decided to change "sneakers" to "athletic shoes." Instead of deleting every occurrence of "sneakers" and typing "ath- letic shoes," you can use the Find and Replace feature to perform the task automatically.

You can also find and replace occurrences of special formatting, such as replacing bold text with italicized text, as well as find and replace formatting marks. This feature is fast and accurate; however, use care when replacing so that you do not replace unintended matches.

Finding Text

First you will use the Find command to locate all occurrences of the word "trip" in the document.

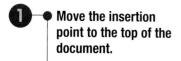

- Move the insertion point to the top of the document.

Another Method
Reminder: Use Ctrl + Home to quickly move to the top of the document.

- Choose Edit/Find.

Another Method
The keyboard shortcut is Ctrl + F. You can also open the Find and Replace dialog box by clicking the ☑ Select Browse Object button in the vertical scroll bar and selecting 🔍 Find from the menu.

Your screen should be similar to Figure 2.20

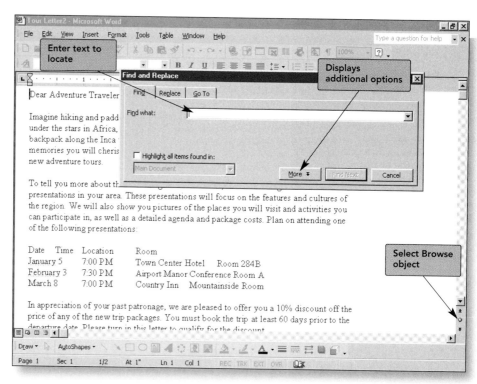

Figure 2.20

The Find and Replace dialog box is used to define the information you want to locate and replace. In the Find What text box, you enter the text you want to locate. In addition, you can use the search options to refine the search. To see these options,

② Click More ▼ .

Your screen should be similar to Figure 2.21

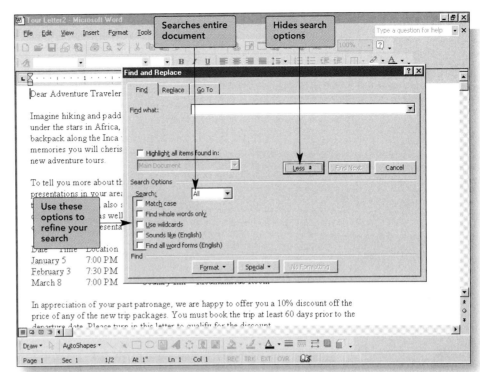

Figure 2.21

The additional options in the Find and Replace dialog box can be combined in many ways to help you find and replace text in documents. They are described in the table below.

Option	Effect on Text
Match case	Finds only those words in which the capitalization matches the text you typed.
Find whole words only	Finds matches that are whole words and not part of a larger word. For example, finds "cat" only and not "catastrophe" too.
Use wildcards	Fine-tunes a search; for example, c?t finds "cat" and "cot" (one-character matches), while c*t finds "cat" and "court" (searches for one or more characters).
Sounds like (English)	Finds words that sound like the word you type; very helpful if you do not know the correct spelling of the word you want to find.
Find all word forms (English)	Finds and replaces all forms of a word; for example, "buy" will replace "purchase," and "bought" will replace "purchased."

When you enter the text to find, you can type everything lowercase, because the Match Case option is not selected. If Match Case is not selected, the search will not be **case sensitive**. This means that lowercase letters will match both upper- and lowercase letters in the text.

Also notice that the Search option default setting is All, which means Word will search the entire document, including headers and footers. You can also choose to search Up or Down the document. These options search in the direction specified but exclude the headers, footers, footnotes, and comments from the area to search. Because you want to search the entire document, All is the appropriate setting. You will hide the search options again and begin the search.

Note: You will learn about headers, footers, footnotes, and comments in later labs.

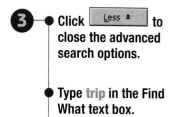
3 ● Click [Less ±] to close the advanced search options.

● Type **trip** in the Find What text box.

● Click [Find Next].

Your screen should be similar to Figure 2.22

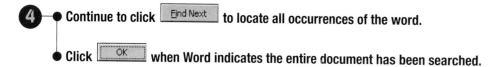

Figure 2.22

Additional Information
If the search does not begin at the top of the document, when Word reaches the end of the document it asks if you want to continue searching from the beginning of the document. You can also highlight text to restrict the search to a selection.

Word searches for all occurrences of the text to find beginning at the insertion point, locates the first occurrence of the word "trip" and highlights it in the document.

4 ● Continue to click [Find Next] to locate all occurrences of the word.

● Click [OK] when Word indicates the entire document has been searched.

The word "trip" is used six times in the document.

Replacing Text

You decide to replace three occurrences of the word "trip" in the letter with "tour" where appropriate. You will use the Replace function to specify the text to enter as the replacement text.

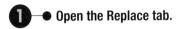
Open the Replace tab.

Your screen should be similar to Figure 2.23

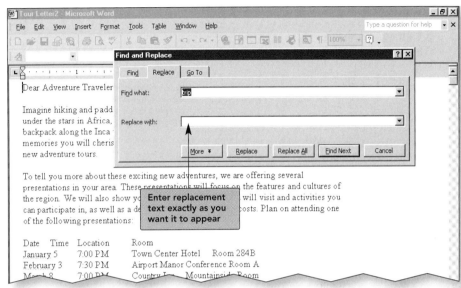

Figure 2.23

The Replace tab includes a Replace With text box in which you enter the replacement text. This text must be entered exactly as you want it to appear in your document. To find and replace the first occurrence of the word "trip" with "tour,"

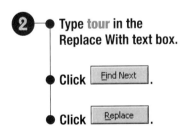
Type tour **in the Replace With text box.**

Click Find Next .

Click Replace .

Your screen should be similar to Figure 2.24

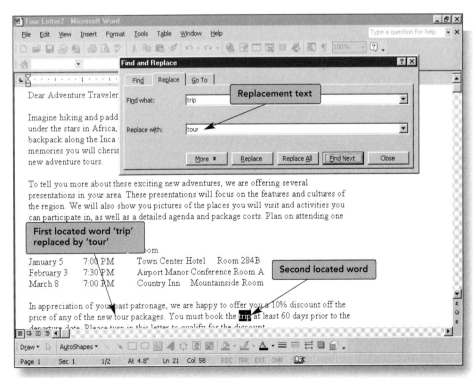

Figure 2.24

Word replaced the first located word with "tour" and has highlighted the second occurrence of the word "trip." You do not want to replace this occurrence of the word. To continue the search without replacing the highlighted text,

3 ● **Click** Find Next .

● **Replace the next located occurrence.**

● **Continue to review the document, replacing all other occurrences of the word "trip" with "tour,"** *except* **on the final line of the flyer.**

● **Click** Find Next .

● **Click** OK **to close the information dialog box.**

● **Click** Cancel **to close the Find and Replace dialog box.**

Your screen should be similar to Figure 2.25

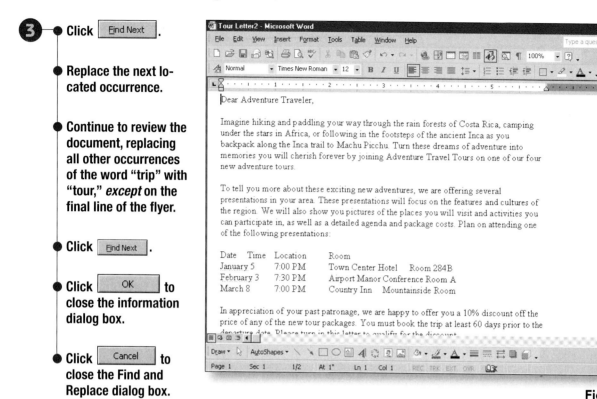

Figure 2.25

When using the Find and Replace feature, if you wanted to change all the occurrences of the located text, it is much faster to use Replace All . Exercise care when using Replace All, however, because the search text you specify might be part of another word and you may accidentally replace text you want to keep.

Inserting the Current Date

The last text change you need to make is to add the date to the letter. The Date and Time command on the Insert menu inserts the current date as maintained by your computer system into your document at the location of the insertion point. You want to enter the date on the first line of the letter, four lines above the salutation.

1 ● Move to the "D" in "Dear" at the top of the letter.

● Press ⬅Enter 4 times to insert four blank lines.

● Move to the first blank line.

● Choose **I**nsert/Date and **T**ime.

Your screen should be similar to Figure 2.26

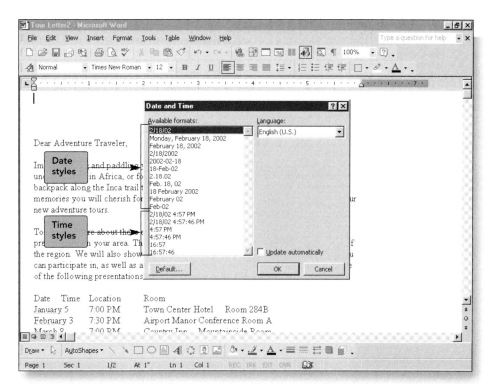

Figure 2.26

Additional Information

The current time can also be inserted into a document using the same procedure.

From the Date and Time dialog box, you select the style in which you want the date displayed in your document. The Available Formats list box displays the format styles for the current date and time. You want to display the date in the format Month XX, 2XXX, the third format setting in the list.

2 ● Select the third format setting.

Your screen should be similar to Figure 2.27

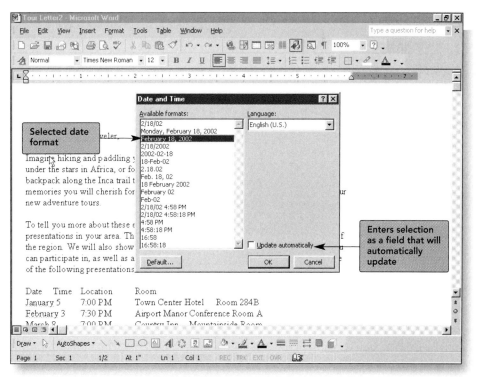

Figure 2.27

Automatically Updating the Date

You also want the date to be updated automatically whenever the letter is sent to new Adventure travelers. You use the Update Automatically option to do this by entering the date as a field.

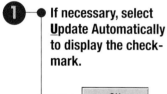

- If necessary, select **Update Automatically** to display the checkmark.

- Click  **OK**.

- Press ⏎.

Additional Information

You can use Alt + ⇧Shift + D to insert the current date as a field in the format MM/DD/YY.

Your screen should be similar to Figure 2.28

HAVING TROUBLE?

The date in Figure 2.28 will be different from the date that appears on your screen.

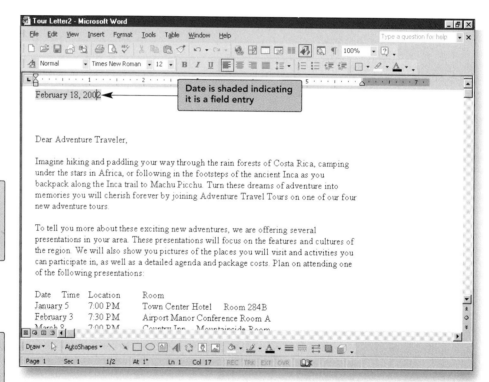

Figure 2.28

The date is entered in the document in the format you selected. When the insertion point is positioned on a field entry, it appears shaded. To see the underlying field code,

② ● **Right-click on the field.**

● **Choose Toggle Field Codes.**

Your screen should be similar to Figure 2.29

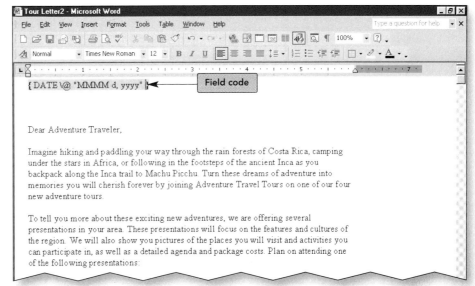

Figure 2.29

The field code includes the field characters, field type, and instructions. Whenever this document is printed, Word will print the current system date using this format.

③ ● **Press** ⇧Shift + F9.

● **Save the document again.**

Your screen should be similar to Figure 2.30

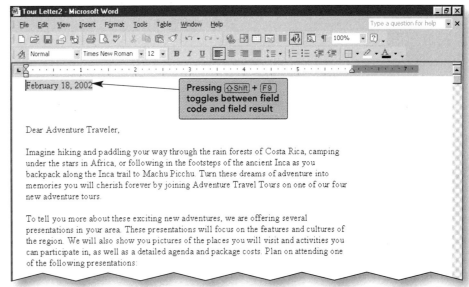

Figure 2.30

The field result is displayed again.

You can press Alt + F9 to show or hide field codes for all fields in a document.

Modifying Page Layout

Next the manager has suggested that you make several formatting changes to improve the appearance of the letter and flyer. Many formatting features that can be used in a document affect the layout of an entire page. These formatting features include page margin settings, vertical alignment of text on a page, headers and footers, and orientation of text on a page.

Changing Margin Settings

One of the first changes you will make is to change the page margin settings.

concept 6

Page Margin

6 The **page margin** is the blank space around the edge of a page. Generally, the text you enter appears in the printable area inside the margins. However, some items can be positioned in the margin space. You can set different page margin widths to alter the appearance of the document.

Standard single-sided documents have four margins: top, bottom, left, and right. Double-sided documents with facing pages, such as books and magazines, also have four margins: top, bottom, inside, and outside. These documents typically use mirror margins in which the left page is a mirror image of the right page. This means that the inside margins are the same width and the outside margins are the same width. (See the illustrations below.)

You can also set a "gutter" margin that reserves space on the left side of single-sided documents, or on the inside margin of double-sided documents, to accommodate binding. There are also special margin settings for headers and footers. (You will learn about these features in Lab 3.)

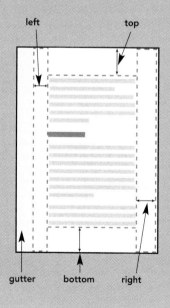

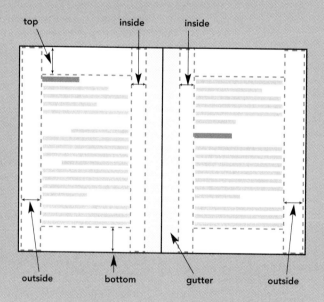

To make it easier to see how your planned margin setting changes will look on the page, you will first change the document view to Print Layout view and Page Width zoom.

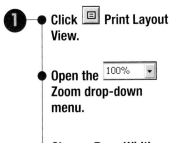

- Click Print Layout View.

- Open the [100%] Zoom drop-down menu.

- Choose **P**age Width.

Your screen should be similar to Figure 2.31

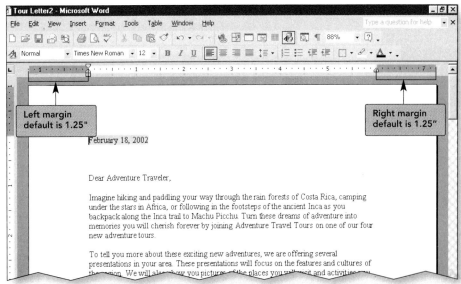

Figure 2.31

The default left and right margin settings of 1.25 inches are now easy to see. As you make changes to the margin settings next, you will be able to easily see the change in the layout of the document on the page.

You would like to see how the letter would look if you changed the right and left margin widths to 1 inch. The Page Setup command on the File menu is used to change settings associated with the layout of the entire document.

- Choose **F**ile/Page Set**u**p.

- If necessary, open the Margins tab.

Your screen should be similar to Figure 2.32

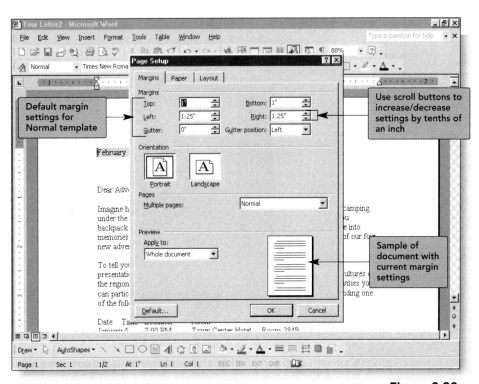

Figure 2.32

The Margins tab of the Page Setup dialog box displays the default margin settings for a single-sided document. The Preview box shows how the current margin settings will appear on a page. New margin settings can be entered by typing the value in the text box, or by clicking the ▲ and ▼ scroll buttons or pressing the ↑ or ↓ keys to increase or decrease the setting by tenths of an inch.

3 • Using any of these methods, set the left and right margins to 1 inch.

• Click [OK].

Your screen should be similar to Figure 2.33

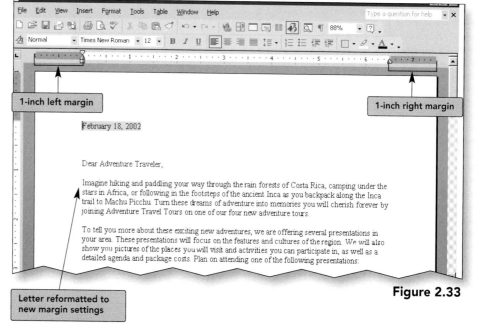

Figure 2.33

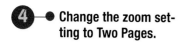

You can see that the letter has been reformatted to fit within the new margin settings. You would like to see what both pages look like at the same time.

4 • Change the zoom setting to Two Pages.

Your screen should be similar to Figure 2.34

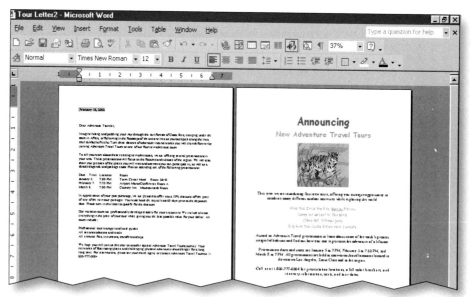

Figure 2.34

Both pages are displayed in the document window. Although the text is difficult to read, you can easily see the layout of the pages and that the margin settings have been changed for both pages.

More Paragraph Formatting

To give the document more interest, you can indent paragraphs, use tabs to create tabular columns of data, and change the line spacing. These formatting features are all paragraph formats that affect the entire selected paragraph.

Indenting Paragraphs

Business letters typically are either created using a block layout style or a modified block style with indented paragraphs. In a block style, all parts of the letter, including the date, inside address, all paragraphs in the body, and closing lines, are evenly aligned with the left margin. The block layout style of your letter has a very formal appearance. The modified block style, on the other hand, has a more casual appearance. In this style, certain elements such as the date, all paragraphs in the body, and the closing lines are indented from the left margin. You want to change the letter style from the block paragraph style to the modified block style.

concept 7

Indents

7   To help your reader find information quickly, you can indent paragraphs from the margins. Indenting paragraphs sets them off from the rest of the document. There are four types of indents you can use to stylize your documents.

Indent	Effect on Text	Indent	Effect on Text
Left	Indents the entire paragraph from the left margin. To outdent or extend the paragraph into the left margin, use a negative value for the left indent.	First Line	Indents the first line of the paragraph. All following lines are aligned with the left margin.
Right	Indents the entire paragraph from the right margin. To outdent or extend the paragraph into the right margin, use a negative value for the right indent.	Hanging	Indents all lines after the first line of the paragraph. The first line is aligned with the left margin. A hanging indent is typically used for bulleted and numbered lists.

You will begin by indenting the first line of the first paragraph.

1 ● **Return the zoom to Page Width.**

● **Move to anywhere in the first paragraph.**

● **Choose Format/Paragraph.**

● **If necessary, open the Indents and Spacing tab.**

Your screen should be similar to Figure 2.35

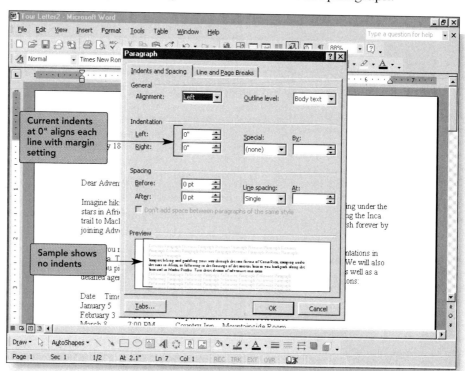

Current indents at 0" aligns each line with margin setting

Sample shows no indents

Figure 2.35

The Indents and Spacing tab shows that the left and right indentation settings for the current paragraph are 0. This setting aligns each line of the paragraph with the margin setting. Specifying an indent value would indent each line of the selected paragraph the specified amount from the margin. However, you only want to indent the first line of the paragraph.

2 ● **From the Special drop-down list box, select First line.**

Your screen should be similar to Figure 2.36

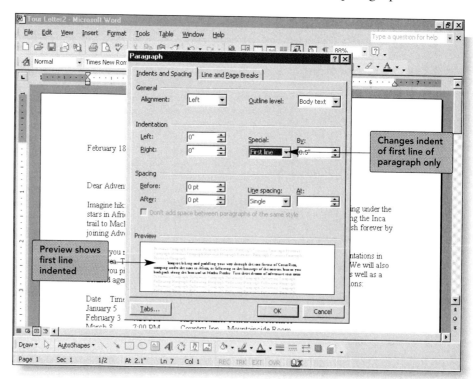

Changes indent of first line of paragraph only

Preview shows first line indented

Figure 2.36

The default first line indent setting of 0.5 inch displayed in the By text box is acceptable. The Preview area shows how this setting will affect a paragraph.

Click OK .

Your screen should be similar to Figure 2.37

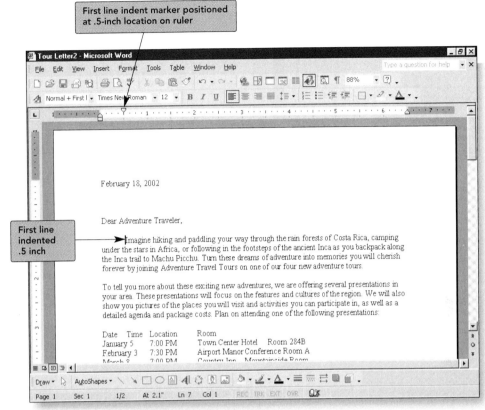

Figure 2.37

The first line of the paragraph indents a half inch from the left margin. The text in the paragraph wraps as needed, and the text on the following line begins at the left margin. Notice that the first line indent marker on the ruler moved to the 0.5-inch position. This marker controls the location of the first line of text in the paragraph.

A much quicker way to indent the first line of a paragraph is to press [Tab⇥] at the beginning of the paragraph. Pressing [Tab⇥] indents the first line of the paragraph to the first tab stop from the left margin. A **tab stop** is a marked location on the horizontal ruler that indicates how far to indent text when the [Tab] key is pressed. The default tab stops are every .5 inch.

4 ● Move to the beginning of the second paragraph.

● Press Tab.

Your screen should be similar to Figure 2.38

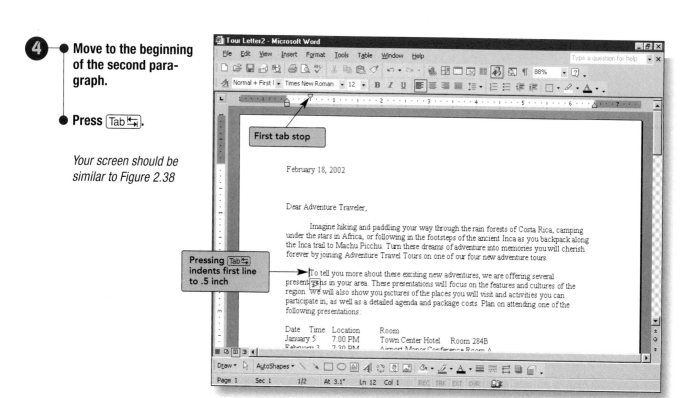

Figure 2.38

You can indent the remaining paragraphs individually, or you can select the paragraphs and indent them simultaneously by either using the Format menu or dragging the upper indent marker ▽ on the ruler.

5 ● Select the remaining text on page 1.

● Drag the First Line Indent marker on the ruler to the 0.5-inch position.

Additional Information
A ScreenTip identifies the First Line Indent marker when you point to it.

● If necessary, scroll the window to display the entire selection.

Your screen should be similar to Figure 2.39

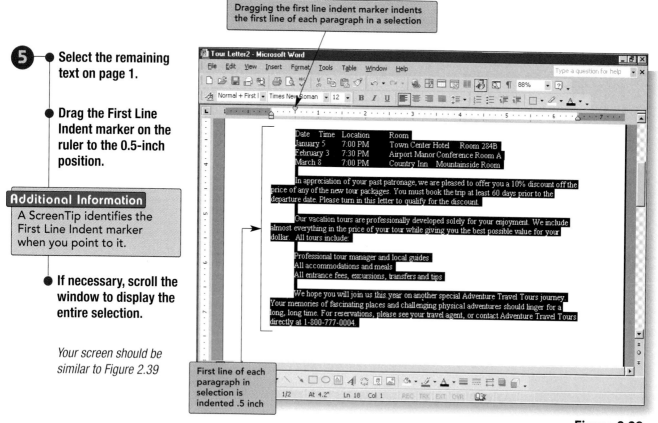

Figure 2.39

The first line of each paragraph in the selection is indented. Notice that each line of the date and time information is also indented. This is because each line ends with a paragraph mark. Word considers each line a separate paragraph.

Setting Tab Stops

Next you want to improve the appearance of the list of presentation times and dates. The date and time information was entered using tabs to separate the different columns of information. However, because the default tab stops are set at every 0.5 inch, the columns are not evenly spaced. You want to reformat this information to appear as a tabbed table of information so that it is easier to read as shown in the figure below.

Date	Time	Location	Room
January 5 ----- 7:00 PM ---------- Town Center Hotel ------- Room 284B			
February 3 ---- 7:30 PM ---------- Airport Manor ----------- Conference Room A			
March 8 ------- 7:00 PM ---------- Country Inn -------------- Mountainside Room			

To improve the appearance of the data, you will create custom tab stops that will align the data in evenly spaced columns. The default tab stops of every 0.5 inch are visible on the ruler as light vertical lines below the numbers. As with other default settings, you can change the location of tab stops in the document.

You can also select from five different types of tab stops that control how characters are positioned or aligned with the tab stop. The following table explains the five tab types, the tab marks that appear in the tab alignment selector box (on the left end of the horizontal ruler) and the effects on the text.

Tab Type	Tab Mark	Effects on Text	Example
Left	⌞	Extends text to right from tab stop	left
Center	⊥	Aligns text centered on tab stop	center
Right	⌟	Extends text to left from tab stop	right
Decimal	⊥.	Aligns text with decimal point	35.78
Bar	|	Draws a vertical line through text at tab stop	|

To align the data, you will place three left tab stops at the 1.5-inch, 2.75-inch, and 4.5-inch positions. You can quickly specify custom tab stop locations and types using the ruler. To select a type of tab stop, click the tab alignment selector box to cycle through the types. Then, to specify where to place the selected tab stop type, click on the location in the ruler. As you specify the new tab stop settings, the table data will align to the new settings.

1
- Select the line of table headings and the three lines of data.
- If necessary, click the tab alignment selector box until the left tab icon ∟ appears.
- Click the 1.5-inch position on the ruler.
- Click the 2.75-inch and the 4.5-inch positions on the ruler.
- Click anywhere in the table to deselect it.

Your screen should be similar to Figure 2.40

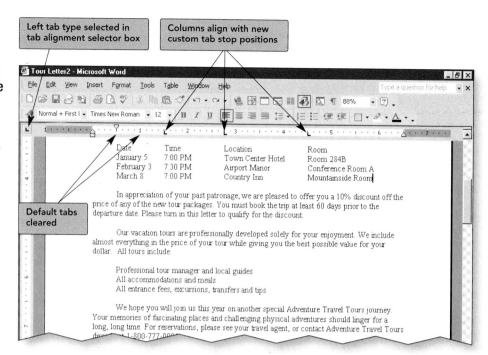

Figure 2.40

The three tabbed columns appropriately align with the new tab stops. All default tabs to the left of the custom tab stops are cleared. After looking at the columns, you decide the column headings would look better centered over the columns of data. To make this change, you will remove the three custom tabs for the heading line by dragging them off the ruler and then add three center tab stops.

2
- Move to anywhere in the heading line.
- Drag the three left tab stop marks off the ruler.
- Click the tab alignment selector box until the center tab icon ⊥ appears.
- Set a center tab stop at the .75-inch, 1.75-inch, 3.25-inch, and 5-inch positions.

Your screen should be similar to Figure 2.41

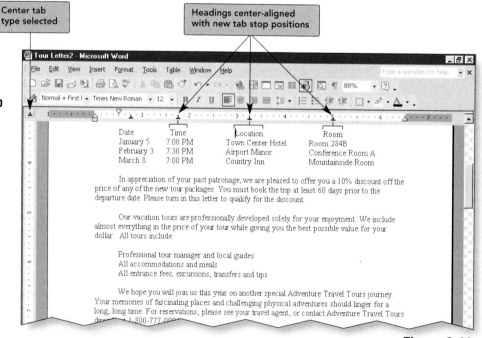

Figure 2.41

The Time, Location, and Room headings are appropriately centered on the tab stops. However, the Date heading still needs to be indented to the .75 tab stop position by pressing [Tab↹].

3 ● **If necessary, move to the "D" in "Date."**

● **Press [Tab↹].**

Your screen should be similar to Figure 2.42

Heading center-aligned at .75-inch position

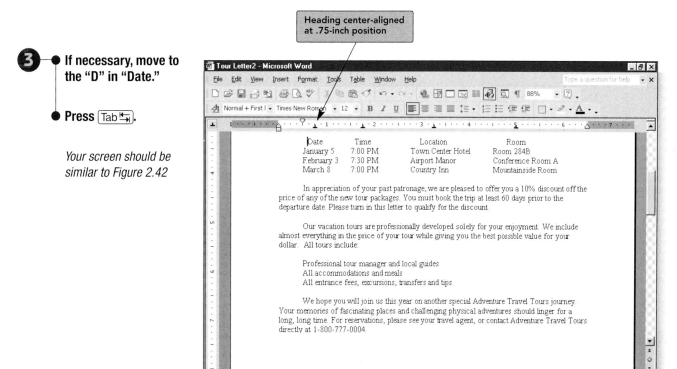

Figure 2.42

The Date heading is now centered at the .75-inch tab stop. As you can see, setting different types of tab stops is helpful for aligning text or numeric data vertically in columns. Using tab stops ensures that the text will indent to the same set location. Setting custom tab stops instead of pressing [Tab] or [Spacebar] repeatedly is a more professional way to format a document, as well as faster and more accurate. It also makes editing easier because you can change the tab stop settings for several paragraphs at once.

Adding Tab Leaders

To make the presentation times and location data even easier to read, you will add tab leaders to the table. **Leader characters** are solid, dotted, or dashed lines that fill the blank space between tab stops. They help the reader's eye move across the blank space between the information aligned at the tab stops.

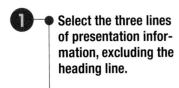

1 ● Select the three lines of presentation information, excluding the heading line.

● Choose F**o**rmat/**T**abs.

Your screen should be similar to Figure 2.43

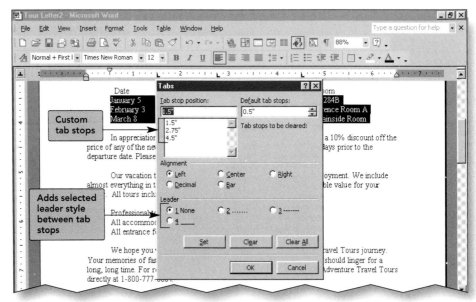

Figure 2.43

Notice that the Tabs dialog box displays the custom tabs you set on the ruler. You can set tab positions in the dialog box by entering the tab positions in the text box. The current tab leader setting is set to None for the 1.5-inch tab stop. You can select from three styles of tab leaders. You will use the third tab leader style, a series of dashed lines. The tab leader fills the empty space to the left of the tab stop. Each tab stop must have the leader individually set.

2 ● Select 3 -------.

● Click [Set].

● Select the 2.75-inch tab stop setting from the Tab Stop Position list box.

● Select 3 -------.

● Click [Set].

● In a similar manner, set the tab leader for the 4.5-inch tab.

● Click [OK].

● Click in the table to deselect the text.

Your screen should be similar to Figure 2.44

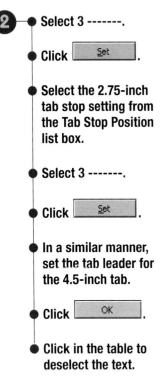

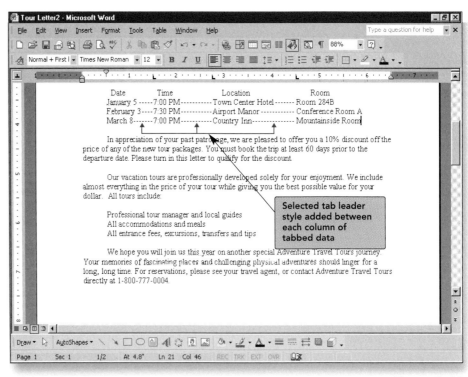

Figure 2.44

The selected leader style has been added to the blank space between each column of tabbed text.

Changing Line Spacing

You also want to increase the line spacing in the table to make the presentation data even easier to read. **Line spacing** is the vertical space between lines of text. The default setting of single line spacing accommodates the largest font in that line, plus a small amount of extra space.

1
- Select the table including the heading line.

- Choose **F**ormat/**P**aragraph.

- If necessary, open the **I**ndents and Spacing tab.

- Open the Li**n**e Spacing drop-down list.

Your screen should be similar to Figure 2.45

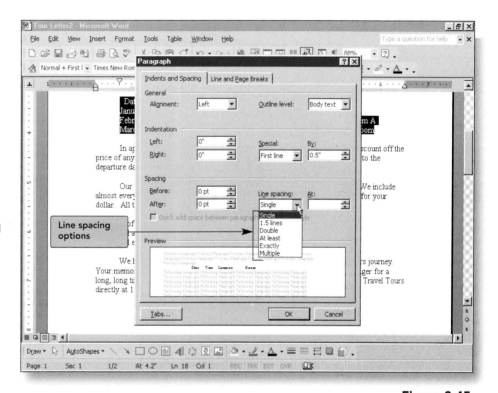

Figure 2.45

The line spacing options are described in the table below.

1.5 lines	Spacing is one and a half times that of single line spacing.
Double	Spacing is twice that of single line spacing.
At least	Uses a value specified in points in the At text box as the minimum line spacing amount that can accommodate larger font sizes or graphics that would not otherwise fit within the specified spacing.
Exactly	Uses a value specified in points in the At text box as a fixed line spacing amount that is not changed, making all lines evenly spaced.
Multiple	Uses a percentage value in the At text box as the amount to increase or decrease line spacing. For example, entering 1.3 will increase the spacing by 33 percent.

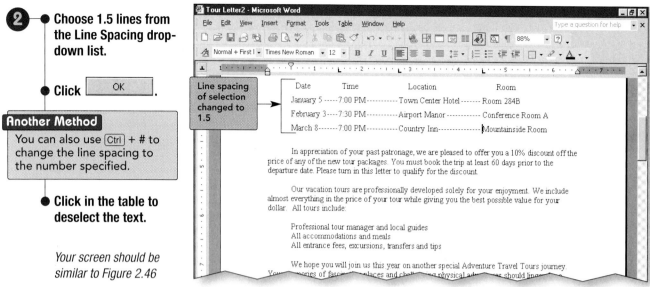

Figure 2.46

The line spacing within the selection has increased to 1.5 spaces.

Justifying Paragraphs

The final paragraph formatting change you want to make to the letter is to change the alignment of all paragraphs in the letter from the default of left-aligned to justified.

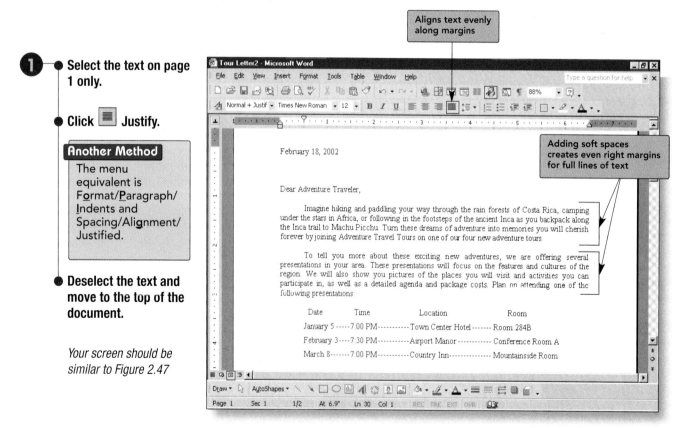

Figure 2.47

Additional Information

The alignment settings can also be specified before typing in new text. As you type, the text is aligned according to your selection until the alignment setting is changed to another setting.

All full lines now end even with the right margin. To do this, Word inserts extra spaces, called **soft spaces**, between words to push the text to the right margin. The soft spaces are adjusted automatically whenever additions and deletions are made to the text.

More Character Formatting

As you look at the letter, you still feel that the table of presentation dates and times does not stand out enough. You can add emphasis to information in your documents by formatting specific characters or words. Applying color shading behind text is commonly used to identify areas of text that you want to stand out. It is frequently used to mark text that you want to locate easily as you are revising a document. Italics, underlines, and bold are other character formats that add emphasis and draw the reader's attention to important items. Word applies character formatting to the entire selection or to the entire word at the insertion point. You can apply formatting to a portion of a word by selecting the area to be formatted first.

Adding Color Highlighting

First, you want to see how a color highlight behind the tabbed table of presentation times and locations would look.

1 ● Open the [✎▾] Highlight drop-down list.

● Select the turquoise color from the color palette.

Additional Information

The mouse pointer appears as [✎] when positioned on text, indicating the highlighting feature is on.

● Select the entire table.

Another Method

You can also select the area you want to highlight first and then click [✎▾] to apply the current color selection.

● Click [✎▾] to turn off the highlighting feature.

Another Method

You can also press [Esc] to turn off highlighting.

Your screen should be similar to Figure 2.48

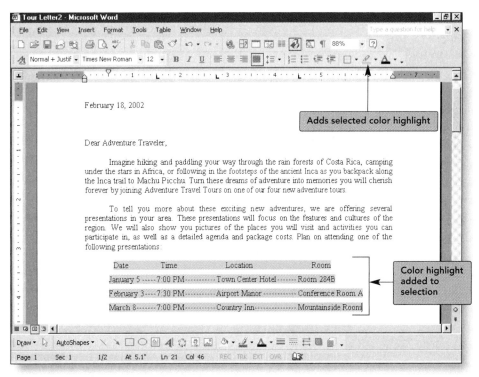

Figure 2.48

Although the highlight makes the table stand out, it does not look good.

Underlining Text

Instead, you decide to bold and underline the headings. In addition to the default single underline style, there are 15 other types of underlines.

1
- Click [↶ ▾] Undo.

- Click on the Date heading.

- Click **B** Bold.

- Choose F**o**rmat/**F**ont.

- If necessary, open the Fo**n**t tab.

- Open the **U**nderline style drop-down list box.

Your screen should be similar to Figure 2.49

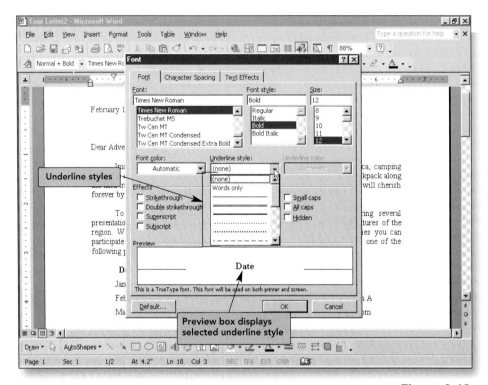

Figure 2.49

The None option removes underlining from a selection, and the Words Only option displays underlines under words in the selection only, not under the spaces between words. The Words Only option uses the default single underline style.

- Select several underline styles and see how they appear in the Preview box.

- Select the double underline style.

Another Method

You can also use ⓤ Underline or the keyboard shortcut Ctrl + U to add the default single underline style.

- Click [OK].

Your screen should be similar to Figure 2.50

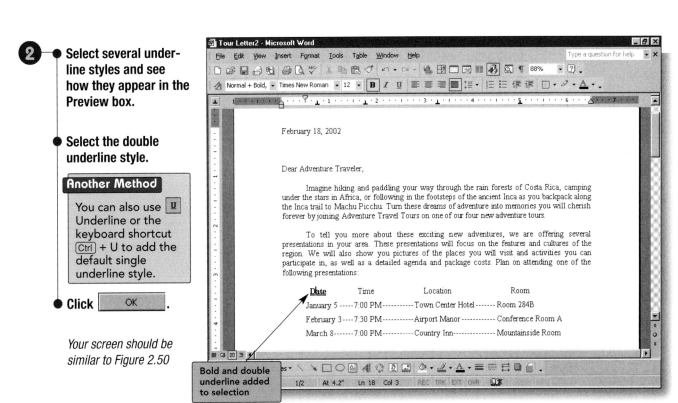

Bold and double underline added to selection

Figure 2.50

Copying Formats with Format Painter

You want to quickly apply the same formats to the other headings. To do this you can use the **Format Painter**. This feature applies the formats associated with the current selection to new selections. If the selection is a paragraph (including the paragraph mark), the formatting is applied to the entire paragraph. If the selection is a character, the format is applied to a character, word, or selection you specify. To turn on the feature, move the insertion point to the text whose formats you want to copy and click the 🖌 Format Painter button. Then select the text you want the formats applied to. The format is automatically applied to an entire word simply by clicking on the word. To apply the format to more or less text, you must select the area. If you double-click the 🖌 Format Painter button, you can apply the format multiple times.

Additional Information

When Format Painter is on, the mouse pointer appears as 🖌I.

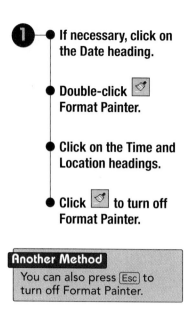

1 ● If necessary, click on the Date heading.

● Double-click ✦ Format Painter.

● Click on the Time and Location headings.

● Click ✦ to turn off Format Painter.

Another Method

You can also press [Esc] to turn off Format Painter.

Your screen should be similar to Figure 2.51

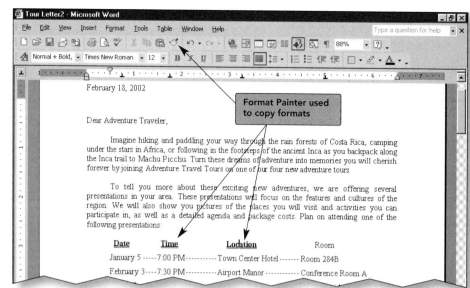

Format Painter used to copy formats

February 18, 2002

Dear Adventure Traveler,

Imagine hiking and paddling your way through the rain forests of Costa Rica, camping under the stars in Africa, or following in the footsteps of the ancient Inca as you backpack along the Inca trail to Machu Picchu. Turn these dreams of adventure into memories you will cherish forever by joining Adventure Travel Tours on one of our four new adventure tours.

To tell you more about these exciting new adventures, we are offering several presentations in your area. These presentations will focus on the features and cultures of the region. We will also show you pictures of the places you will visit and activities you can participate in, as well as a detailed agenda and package costs. Plan on attending one of the following presentations:

Date	Time	Location	Room
January 5	7:00 PM	Town Center Hotel	Room 284B
February 3	7:30 PM	Airport Manor	Conference Room A

Figure 2.51

Applying Formats Using the Styles and Formatting Task Pane

The last heading to format is Room. Another way to apply existing formatting is to use the Styles and Formatting task pane.

1 ● Click ▣ Styles and Formatting on the Formatting toolbar.

Your screen should be similar to Figure 2.52

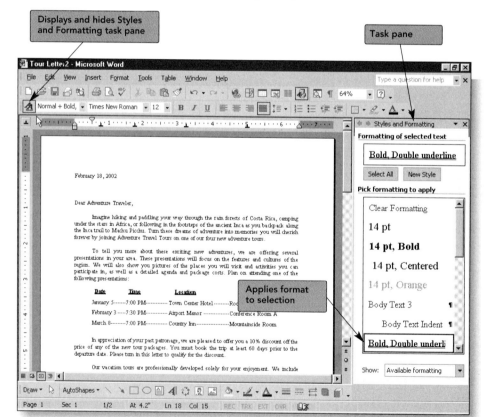

Displays and hides Styles and Formatting task pane

Task pane

Applies format to selection

Figure 2.52

This Styles and Formatting task pane displays the formatting associated with the selected text at the top of the pane. All other formatting in use in the document is listed in the scroll box. To apply an existing format to a selection, you can pick the format from this list.

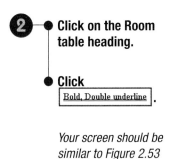

2 ● **Click on the Room table heading.**

● **Click** Bold, Double underline .

Your screen should be similar to Figure 2.53

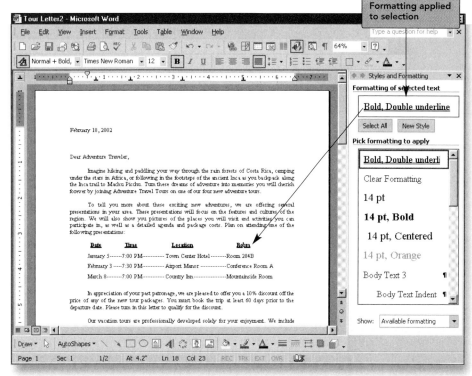

Figure 2.53

The selected formatting is applied to the word. The list box also now displays the last selected formatting at the top of the list to make it easier to select it again.

3 ● **Click** 🄰 **Styles and Formatting to turn off the task pane.**

● **Save the document again.**

Creating Lists

The next change you want to make is to display the three lines of information about tour features as an itemized list so that they stand out better from the surrounding text.

concept 8

Bulleted and Numbered Lists

8 | Whenever possible, use bulleted or numbered lists to organize information and to make your writing clear and easy to read. A list can be used whenever you present three or more related pieces of information.

Use a **bulleted list** when you have several items that logically fall out from a paragraph into a list. A bulleted list displays one of several styles of bullets before each item in the list. You can select from several types of symbols to use as bullets and you can change the color, size, and position of the bullet.

Use a **numbered list** when you want to convey a sequence of events, such as a procedure that has steps to follow in a certain order. A numbered list displays numbers or letters before the text. Word automatically increments the number or letter as you start a new paragraph. You can select from several different numbering schemes to create your numbered lists.

Use an **outline numbered list** style to display multiple outline levels that show a hierarchical structure of the items in the list. There can be up to nine levels.

Numbering a List

Because both bullet and number styles automatically will indent the items when applied, you first need to remove the indent from the three tour features. Then you will try a numbered list style to see how it looks.

1
- Select the three tour features.

- Drag the First Line Indent marker on the ruler back to the margin boundary.

- Choose F**o**rmat/Bullets and **N**umbering.

- Open the **N**umbered tab.

  Your screen should be similar to Figure 2.54

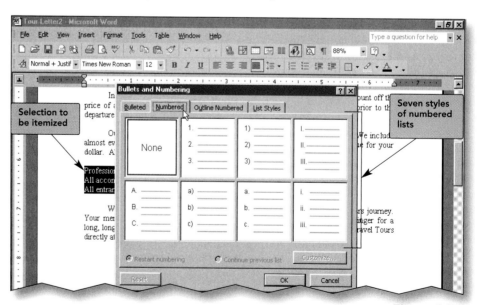

Figure 2.54

The Bullets and Numbering dialog box displays examples of seven numbered list styles. The document default is None. You can also change the appearance of the styles using the Customize option. The first style to the right of None is the style you will use.

2
● **Select the first numbered list style.**

● **Click** OK .

Another Method

You can also click [icon] Numbering to insert the last used numbering style.

Your screen should be similar to Figure 2.55

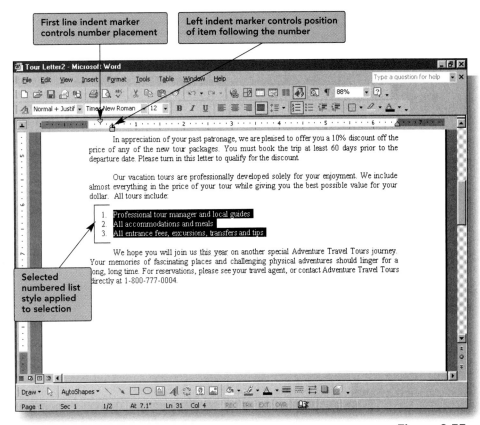

First line indent marker controls number placement

Left indent marker controls position of item following the number

Selected numbered list style applied to selection

Figure 2.55

Additional Information

You can also create bulleted and numbered lists as you type. To create a bulleted list, type an asterisk (*) followed by a space, and then type the text. To create a numbered list, type a number, type a period followed by a space, and then type the text. When you press ←Enter, Word automatically creates a list and adds numbers or bullets to the next line. To turn off the list, press ←Enter twice.

A number is inserted at the 0.25-inch position before each line, and the text following the number is indented to the 0.5-inch position. In an itemized list, the first line indent marker on the ruler controls the position of the number or bullet, and the left indent marker controls the position of the item following the number or bullet. The left indent marker creates a hanging indent. If the text following each bullet were longer than a line, the text on the following lines would also be indented to the 0.5-inch position.

Bulleting a List

After looking at the list, you decide it really would be more appropriate if it were a bulleted list instead of a numbered list.

① • Click 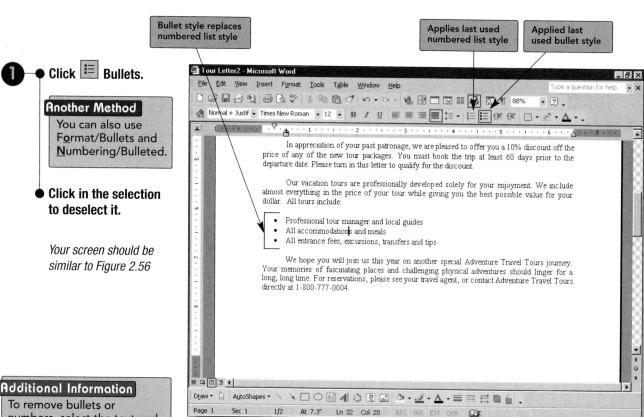 Bullets.

Another Method

You can also use Format/Bullets and Numbering/Bulleted.

• **Click in the selection to deselect it.**

Your screen should be similar to Figure 2.56

Additional Information

To remove bullets or numbers, select the text and choose Format/Bullets and Numbering, and then select the None option, or click 📋 or 📋 again.

Bullet style replaces numbered list style

Applies last used numbered list style

Applied last used bullet style

Figure 2.56

The last used bullet style replaces the number.

Using Hyperlinks

The manager has also asked you to add information about the company's Web site to the letter and flyer. You will include the Web site's address, called a **URL** (Uniform Resource Locator), in the document. Word automatically recognizes URLs you enter and creates a hyperlink of the entry. A **hyperlink** is a connection to a location in the current document, another document, or to a Web site. It allows the reader to jump to the referenced location by clicking on the hyperlink text when reading the document on the screen.

Creating a Hyperlink

First you will add the Web site address to the last line of the letter.

1 ● Add the following sentence after the phone number in the last paragraph: **You can also visit our new Web site at www.AdventureTravel Tours.com.**

● Press ⌐Enter twice.

Your screen should be similar to Figure 2.57

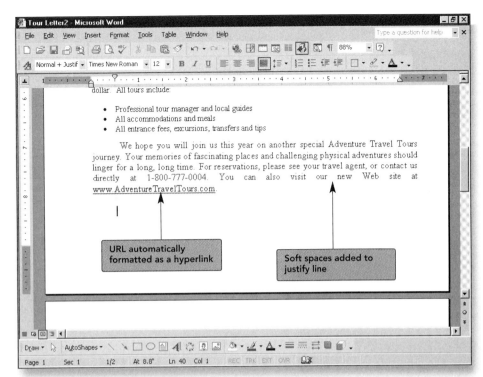

Figure 2.57

The Web address is automatically formatted in blue and underlined, indicating the entry is a hyperlink. The **AutoFormat** feature makes certain formatting changes automatically to your document. These formats include formatting a Web address, replacing ordinals (1st) with superscript (1st), fractions (1/2) with fraction characters (½) and applying a bulleted list format to a list if you type an asterisk (*) followed by a space at the beginning of a paragraph. These AutoFormat features can be turned off if the corrections are not needed in your document.

Removing a Hyperlink

Because this is a document you plan to print, you do not want the text displayed as a link. Since the hyperlink was created using the AutoFormat feature, you can undo the correction or turn it off using the AutoCorrect Options button. You also do not like how the line appears with the addition of soft spaces needed to justify it. To fix this, you decide to remove the word "directly" from the preceding sentence.

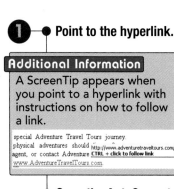

① ● **Point to the hyperlink.**

Additional Information

A ScreenTip appears when you point to a hyperlink with instructions on how to follow a link.

● **Open the AutoCorrect Options menu.**

Additional Information

You can turn off the AutoCorrect feature so the hyperlinks are not created automatically using **S**top Automatically Creating Hyperlinks.

● **Choose U**ndo **Hyperlink.**

Another Method

You could also click ↶ ▼ Undo to remove the hyperlink autoformatting, or right-click on the hyperlink and select **R**emove Hyperlink from the shortcut menu.

● **Delete the word "directly" from the previous sentence.**

Your screen should be similar to Figure 2.58

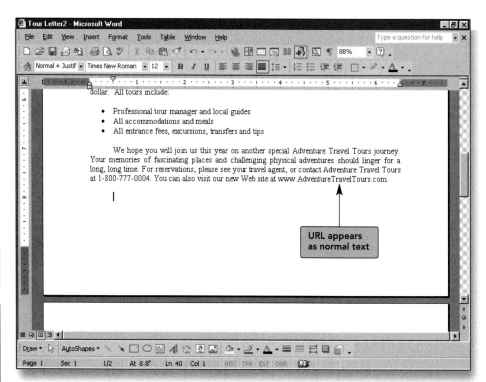

Figure 2.58

The Web address now appears as normal text. The appearance of the paragraph is also greatly improved with the deletion of the word.

Adding an AutoText Entry

While looking at the letter, you realize that the closing lines have not been added to the document. You can quickly insert text and graphics that you use frequently using the AutoText feature. As you learned in Lab 1, Word includes a list of standard AutoText entries that consists of standard phrases such as salutations and closings. You will use the AutoText feature to add a standard closing to the letter.

1 ● Move to the second blank line at the end of the letter.

● Choose **I**nsert/**A**utoText/ Closing.

● Choose Best regards.

● Press `←Enter` 3 times.

● Type *your name*.

● Finally, indent both closing lines to the 3.5-inch position.

● Save the document again.

Your screen should be similar to Figure 2.59

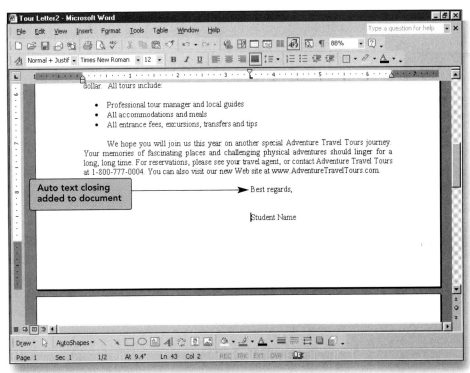

Figure 2.59

Using AutoShapes

You also want to add a special graphic to the flyer containing information about the Web site to catch the reader's attention. To quickly add a shape, you will use one of the ready-made shapes called **AutoShapes** that are supplied with Word. These include such basic shapes as rectangles and circles, a variety of lines, block arrows, flowchart symbols, stars and banners, and callouts. Additional shapes are available in the Clip Organizer. You can also combine AutoShapes to create more complex designs.

Inserting an AutoShape

You want to add a graphic of a banner to the bottom of the flyer.

1
- Press [Ctrl] + [End] to move to the bottom of the flyer.
- If necessary, click 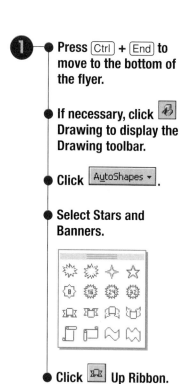 Drawing to display the Drawing toolbar.
- Click AutoShapes ▾ .
- Select Stars and Banners.
- Click 🎀 Up Ribbon.

Another Method
The menu equivalent is Insert/Picture/AutoShapes.

Your screen should be similar to Figure 2.60

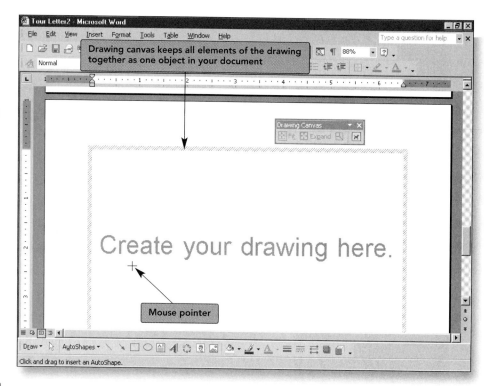

Figure 2.60

A drawing canvas is inserted in the document in which you can draw a picture. All items drawn in the drawing canvas stay as a complete picture within your document and can be moved and resized as a unit. The Drawing Canvas toolbar is used to control features associated with the drawing canvas.

2
- Click in the drawing canvas to insert the autoshape.
- Drag the side middle handles to increase the AutoShape size to that shown in Figure 2.61.

Additional Information
To maintain the height and width proportions of the AutoShape, hold down [Shift] while you drag.

Your screen should be similar to Figure 2.61

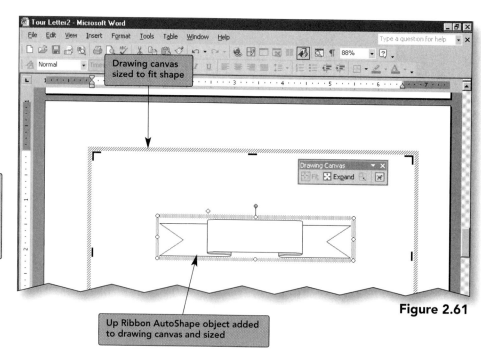

Figure 2.61

Filling the AutoShape with Color

The AutoShape can also be enhanced using many of the features on the Drawing toolbar, such as adding a fill color and line color.

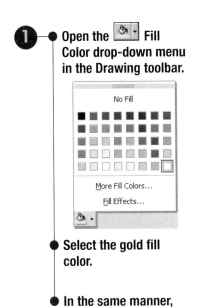

1 ● Open the [icon] Fill Color drop-down menu in the Drawing toolbar.

● Select the gold fill color.

● In the same manner, open the [icon] Line Color menu in the Drawing toolbar and select a color of your choice.

Your screen should be similar to Figure 2.62

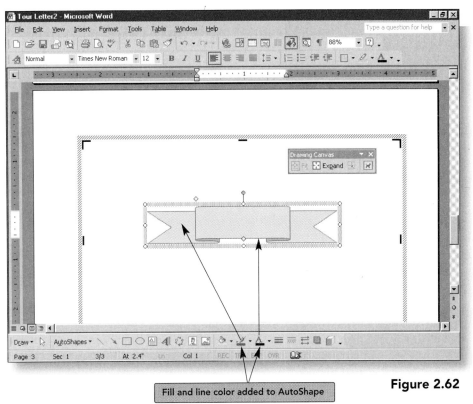

Fill and line color added to AutoShape

Figure 2.62

Adding Text to an AutoShape

Next you will add text to the AutoShape.

1
- Right-click on the shape to open the shortcut menu.
- Choose Add Te**x**t.
- Change the font settings to Arial, size 12, bold, italic, centered, and a font color of brown.
- Type Visit our.
- Press ⏎Enter.
- Type Web site at.
- Press ⏎Enter.
- Type AdventureTravel Tours.com.
- If necessary, adjust the AutoShape size to fully display the text.
- Zoom to Whole Page and scroll the window as in Figure 2.63.

  Your screen should be similar to Figure 2.63

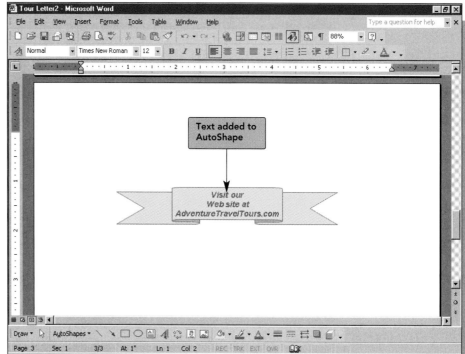

Figure 2.63

Next, you need to move the AutoShape to the bottom of the flyer. In order for the object to fit in this space, you can either make the drawing canvas smaller by sizing it to fit the AutoShape or delete the drawing canvas object. Since the Autoshape is a single object it is not necessary to use the drawing canvas (which is designed to keep multiple objects together). To remove the drawing canvas, you first need to drag the AutoShape off the drawing canvas, then select the drawing canvas and delete it.

2
- Drag the AutoShape object to move and center it between the margins in the space at the bottom of the flyer.
- Click on page 3 to select the drawing canvas and press Delete.
- Return the zoom to Page Width.

  Your screen should be similar to Figure 2.64

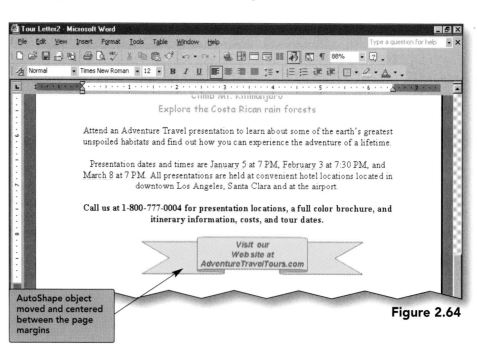

Figure 2.64

Editing While Previewing

Next you will preview and make any final changes to the letter before printing it. When previewing a large document, it is often useful to see multiple pages at the same time to check formatting and other items. Additionally, you can quickly edit while previewing, to make final changes to your document.

Previewing Multiple Pages

First, you want to display both pages of your document in the preview window. You can view up to six pages at the same time in the preview window.

● **Press** Ctrl **+** Home **to move to the top of the document.**

● **Click** Print Preview.

● **Click** Multiple pages.

● **Click to select 1x2 pages.**

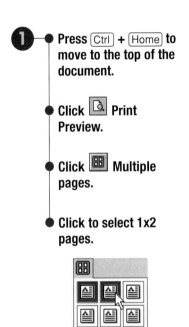

HAVING TROUBLE?

Point to the icons on the Multiple Pages drop-down menu to highlight the number of pages and click while selected.

Your screen should be similar to Figure 2.65

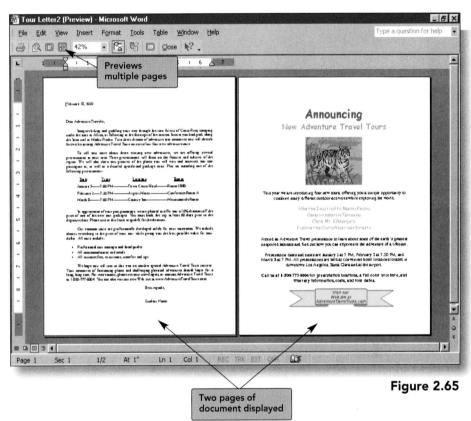

Figure 2.65

Editing in Print Preview

Now that you can see the entire letter, you see that the date needs to be indented to the 3.5-inch tab position. While in Print Preview, you can edit and format text. The mouse pointer can be a magnifying glass 🔍 or an I-beam when it is positioned on text in the document. The 🔍 indicates that when you click on a document, the screen will toggle between the Whole Page view you currently see and 100 percent magnification. The I-beam means you can edit the document.

- If your mouse pointer is not 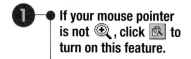, click to turn on this feature.

- Click near the date in the document.

Your screen should be similar to Figure 2.66

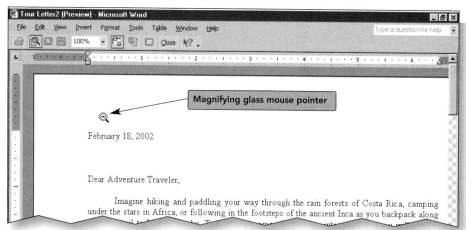

Magnifying glass mouse pointer

February 18, 2002

Dear Adventure Traveler,

Imagine hiking and paddling your way through the rain forests of Costa Rica, camping under the stars in Africa, or following in the footsteps of the ancient Inca as you backpack along

Figure 2.66

The text is displayed in the size it will appear when printed (100 percent zoom). Now that the document is large enough to work in, you will switch from zooming the document to editing it.

2

- Click  Magnifier.

- Move the mouse pointer to point to an area containing text.

Your screen should be similar to Figure 2.67

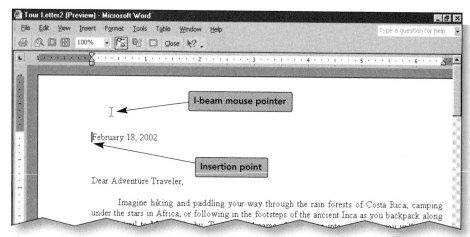

I-beam mouse pointer

February 18, 2002

Insertion point

Dear Adventure Traveler,

Imagine hiking and paddling your way through the rain forests of Costa Rica, camping under the stars in Africa, or following in the footsteps of the ancient Inca as you backpack along

Figure 2.67

When positioned near text, the mouse pointer changes to an I-beam and the insertion point is displayed. Now you can edit the document as in Normal view.

3

- If necessary, click View Ruler to display the ruler.

Additional Information

Pointing to the top or left edge of the window will temporarily display the ruler if the ruler display is off.

- Move to the beginning of the date.

- Indent the date to the 3.5-inch position.

Your screen should be similar to Figure 2.68

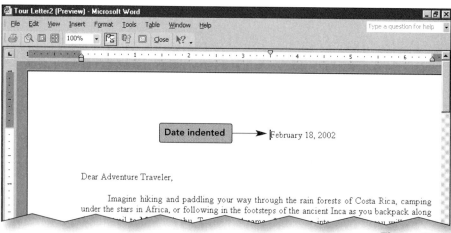

Date indented → February 18, 2002

Dear Adventure Traveler,

Imagine hiking and paddling your way through the rain forests of Costa Rica, camping under the stars in Africa, or following in the footsteps of the ancient Inca as you backpack along

Figure 2.68

While looking at the document, you decide to emphasize some of the text by adding bold. Because you are using Print Preview, the Formatting toolbar buttons are not displayed. You could display the Formatting toolbar or you could use the Format menu to change the text. Another quick way, however, is to use the keyboard shortcut.

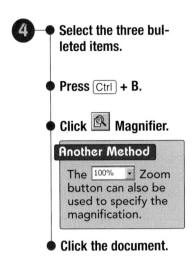

4 ● **Select the three bulleted items.**

● **Press** Ctrl **+ B.**

● **Click** 🔍 **Magnifier.**

Another Method

The 100% ▼ Zoom button can also be used to specify the magnification.

● **Click the document.**

Your screen should be similar to Figure 2.69

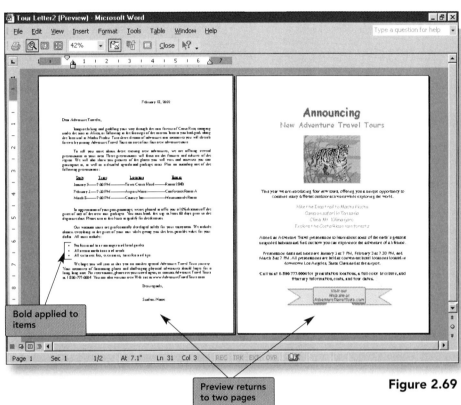

Figure 2.69

Now that the document has been edited and formatted the way you want, you will print a copy of the letter from the Print Preview window using the default print settings.

Note: If you need to specify a different printer, you will need to close the Preview window and use the Print command on the File menu.

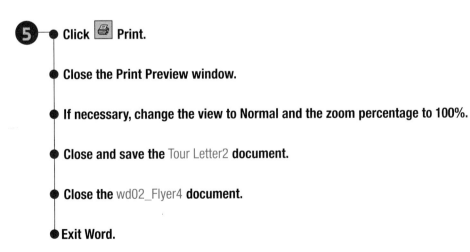

5 ● **Click** 🖶 **Print.**

● **Close the Print Preview window.**

● **If necessary, change the view to Normal and the zoom percentage to 100%.**

● **Close and save the** Tour Letter2 **document.**

● **Close the** wd02_Flyer4 **document.**

● **Exit Word.**

The printed output should be similar to the document shown in Figure 2.69.

Thesaurus (WD2.10)

Word's **Thesaurus** is a reference tool that provides synonyms, antonyms, and related words for a selected word or phrase.

Move and Copy (WD2.11)

Text and graphic selections can be **moved** or **copied** to new locations in a document or between documents, saving you time by not having to retype the same information.

Page Break (WD2.18)

A **page break** marks the point at which one page ends and another begins. There are two types of page breaks that can be used in a document: soft page breaks and hard page breaks.

Find and Replace (WD2.20)

To make editing easier, you can use the **Find and Replace** feature to find text in a document and replace it with other text as directed.

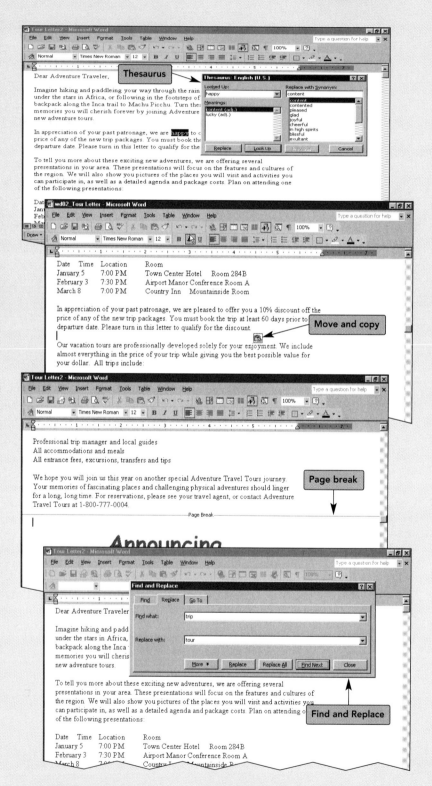

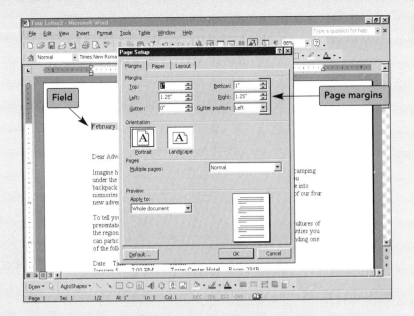
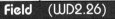

Field (WD2.26)

A **field** is a placeholder that instructs Word to insert information into a document.

Page Margins (WD2.28)

The **page margin** is the blank space around the edge of the page. Standard single-sided documents have four margins: top, bottom, left, and right.

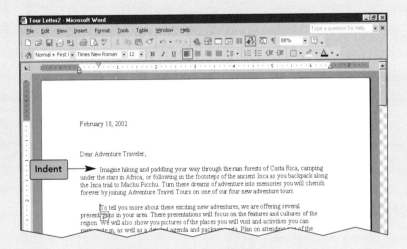

Indents (WD2.31)

To help your reader find information quickly, you can **indent** paragraphs from the margins. Indenting paragraphs sets them off from the rest of the document.

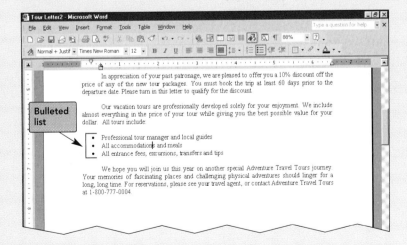

Bulleted and Numbered Lists (WD2.46)

Whenever possible, use **bulleted** or **numbered lists** to organize information and make your writing clear and easy to read.

lab review

key terms

active document   WD2.16
antonym   WD2.10
AutoFormat   WD2.49
AutoShape   WD2.51
bulleted list   WD2.46
case sensitive   WD2.21
destination   WD2.11
drag and drop   WD2.15
field   WD2.26

field code   WD2.26
field result   WD2.26
Format Painter   WD2.43
hard page break   WD2.18
hyperlink   WD2.48
leader character   WD2.37
line spacing   WD2.39
numbered list   WD2.46
outline numbered list   WD2.46

page break   WD2.18
page margin   WD2.28
soft page break   WD2.18
soft space   WD2.41
source   WD2.11
synonym   WD2.10
tab stop   WD2.33
Thesaurus   WD2.10
URL   WD2.48

mous skills

The Microsoft Office User Specialist (MOUS) certification program is designed to measure your proficiency in performing basic tasks using the Office XP applications. Getting certified demonstrates that you have the skills and provides a valuable industry credential for employment. After completing this lab, you have learned the following Microsoft Office User Specialist skills:

Skill	Description	Page
Inserting and Modifying text	Apply and modify text formats	WD2.48
	Correct spelling and grammar usage	WD2.5
	Apply font and text effects	WD2.41
	Enter and format Date and Time	WD2.24
Creating and Modifying paragraphs	Modify paragraph formats	WD2.28
	Set and modify tabs	WD2.31
	Apply bullet, outline, and numbering formats to paragraphs	WD2.46
Formatting Documents	Modify document layout and page setup options	WD2.28
	Preview and print documents, envelopes, and labels	

command summary

Command	Shortcut Keys	Button	Action
File/Page Set**u**p			Changes layout of page including margins, paper size, and paper source
Edit/Cu**t**	Ctrl + X	✂	Cuts selection to Clipboard
Edit/**C**opy	Ctrl + C	📋	Copies selection to Clipboard
Edit/**P**aste	Ctrl + V	📋	Pastes item from Clipboard
Edit/**F**ind	Ctrl + F		Locates specified text
Edit/Re**p**lace	Ctrl + H		Locates and replaces specified text
Insert/**B**reak/**P**age break	Ctrl + Enter		Inserts hard page break
Insert/Date and **T**ime			Inserts current date or time, maintained by computer system, in selected format
Insert/**A**utoText			Enters predefined text at insertion point
Insert/**P**icture/**A**utoShapes		AutoShapes ▾	Inserts selected AutoShape
F**o**rmat/**F**ont/Font/**U**nderline style/Single	Ctrl + U	U	Underlines selected text with a single line
F**o**rmat/**P**aragraph/**I**ndents and Spacing/**S**pecial/First Line			Indents first line of paragraph from left margin
F**o**rmat/**P**aragraph/**I**ndents and Spacing/Line Spacing	Ctrl + #		Changes amount of white space between lines
F**o**rmat/Bullets and **N**umbering		≣ ≣	Creates a bulleted or numbered list
F**o**rmat /**T**abs			Specifies types and position of tab stops
Tools/**S**pelling and Grammar	F7	✓	Starts Spelling and Grammar tool
Tools/**L**anguage/**T**hesaurus	Shift + F7		Starts Thesaurus tool

Terminology

screen identification

1. In the following Word screen, letters identify elements. Enter the correct term for each screen element in the space provided.

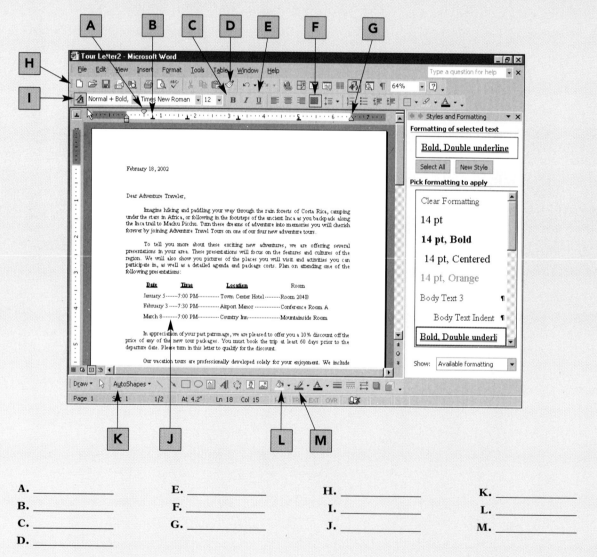

A. _____   E. _____   H. _____   K. _____

B. _____   F. _____   I. _____   L. _____

C. _____   G. _____   J. _____   M. _____

D. _____

matching

Match the item on the left with the correct description on the right.

1. [icon] _____   **a.** toggles between field text and field code

2. Shift + F9 _____   **b.** used to spell- and grammar-check the document

3. [icon] _____   **c.** adds bold to a selection

4. Ctrl + Enter _____   **d.** indents text to next tab stop

5. Ctrl + B _____   **e.** creates even left and right margins

6. [icon] _____   **f.** adds color shading behind selection

7. [icon] _____   **g.** removes text from the document and stores it in the system Clipboard

8. Tab _____   **h.** sets a centered tab stop

9. [icon] _____   **i.** creates a bulleted list

10. [icon] _____   **j.** inserts a hard page break

multiple choice

Circle the correct response to the questions below.

1. A _____ page break is inserted manually by the user.
   a. hard
   b. soft
   c. fixed
   d. floating

2. The _____ feature locates and automatically changes text in a document.
   a. search and replace
   b. find and change
   c. locate and change
   d. find and replace

3. The thesaurus in Word provides _____ .
   a. synonyms
   b. antonyms
   c. related words
   d. all the above

4. The field _____ contains the directions that tell Word what type of information to insert.
   a. results
   b. code
   c. placeholder
   d. format

lab exercises

5. The blank space around the edge of the page is called the _____ .
   a. gutter
   b. indent
   c. margin
   d. white space

6. The _____ indent positions the first line of a paragraph at the left margin with all following lines indented.
   a. left
   b. right
   c. first line
   d. hanging

7. To convey a sequence of events in a document, you should consider using a _____ .
   a. bulleted list
   b. numbered list
   c. organization list
   d. paragraph list

8. A tab stop is the_____ point along a line to which text will indent when you press Tab.
   a. starting
   b. stopping
   c. beginning
   d. ending

9. The feature most useful for copying or moving short distances in a document is _____ .
   a. drag and drop
   b. drop and drag
   c. move and place
   d. drag and place

10. _____ are solid, dotted, or dashed lines that fill the blank space between tab stops.
   a. tab leaders
   b. leader characters
   c. leader tabs
   d. tab characters

true/false

Circle the correct answer to the following questions.

1. The white space between the text and the edge of the paper is the margin.	True	False
2. A bulleted list conveys a sequence of events.	True	False
3. Indents are used to set paragraphs off from the rest of the text.	True	False
4. Tab leaders are used to separate columns of text.	True	False
5. The spelling checker identifies synonyms for common words.	True	False
6. The Find and Replace feature is used to locate misspelled words in a document.	True	False
7. Soft page breaks are automatically inserted whenever the text reaches the bottom margin.	True	False
8. Field placeholders define the information to be inserted in a document.	True	False
9. Hyperlinks are usually colored and underlined in Word documents.	True	False
10. Formatting and text editing can be done in the print preview window.	True	False

Concepts

fill-in

1. Use a _____ list to convey a sequence of events and a _____ when you have several items that logically fall out from a paragraph into a list.

2. A selection that is moved is cut from its original location, called the _____, and inserted at a new location, called the _____.

3. As you add or remove text from a page, Word automatically _____ the placement of the soft page break.

4. The thesaurus is a reference tool that provides _____, _____ and _____ for a selected word or phrase.

5. The page margin is the _____ space around the edge of a page.

6. A(n)_____ code instructs Word to insert the current date in the document using the selected format whenever the document is printed.

7. Line spacing is the _____ space between lines of text.

8. Use a(n) _____ list style to show a hierarchal structure of the items in the list.

9. Double-sided documents with facing pages typically use _____ margins in which the left page is a mirror image of the right page.

10. When a selection is moved or copied, the selection is stored in the _____ Clipboard, a temporary Windows storage area in memory.

discussion questions

1. Use Help for more information about the AutoFormat feature. Discuss how the AutoFormat feature works and the two ways it can be used.

2. Discuss how the AutoText feature works. When might you want to consider adding words to the AutoText feature? Will added words be recognized in other documents?

3. Discuss the different ways information can be moved within a document. Explain which method is most appropriate in certain circumstances.

4. Discuss how field codes are used in Word documents. What other field codes are available (list several)? Why are field codes important in documents that are reused?

5. Discuss the problems that can be associated with finding and replacing text. What can you do to avoid some of these problems?

Hands-On Exercises

step-by-step

Creating a Checklist

★ **1.** You work as a lab assistant in the computer lab. Each week, the lab assistants are responsible for cleaning the computers. You've decided to create a checklist of items that need to be performed to keep the computers clean. Your completed checklist is shown here:

a. Open the file wd02_Cleaning Checklist.

b. Use the spelling and grammar checker to correct the identified errors.

c. Set line spacing for the entire document to 1.5. Set the right and left margins to 1.5 inches.

d. Bold, color, center, and increase the font size of the main title to 24.

e. Center the introductory paragraph below the main title.

f. Move the second sentence in the introductory paragraph below the paragraph. Leave a blank line above and below the sentence. Highlight the sentence in yellow.

g. Bold, highlight, and center the subtitles, "Monitor," "Keyboard," and "CPU."

h. Find and delete each occurrence of "Once a week, " (Hint: leave the Replace With text box empty to delete). Capitalize the first word of the sentence where each deletion occurred.

i. Select the lines of text below each subtitle and create an itemized list using the solid square bullet style.

j. Use drag and drop to move the "CPU" section above the "Monitor" section.

k. Add the AutoShape "no" symbol from the Basic Shapes menu to the document.

l. Add the text Drinks in the Lab to the shape. Bold and center the text.

m. Add a red fill color to the shape. Move the AutoShape to the space below the introductory paragraph. Center the AutoShape between the margins.

n. Add your name and the current date several lines below the last line on the page.

o. Save the document as Cleaning Checklist2. Print the document.

Computer Cleaning Checklist

The following items need to be completed on a weekly basis. The cleaning supplies are located in the storeroom on the third shelf.

Before cleaning, always turn off the computer and unplug the keyboard.

CPU
- Clean the exterior of the box.
- Once a month, vacuum the exterior of the box.

Monitor
- Wipe the screen with a lint-free cloth that is lightly sprayed with an ammonia-free cleaner. Dry the screen thoroughly.
- Wipe the outside of the monitor case, paying special attention to the area around the air vents.

Keyboard
- Turn the keyboard 45 degrees on its edge with the keys facing down and tap the bottom to loosen dust, crumbs, and particles.
- Wipe down the keyboard with a cloth moistened with cleaner. Wrap your finger in the cloth and clean each key individually.

Student Name
Current Date

Creating a Table

★ 2. You recently attended a Career Fair and met with many different companies. At the end of the day, you decided to pursue job opportunities with four of the companies. To keep track of the companies, you want to put the key items into a table so you can easily compare them. Your completed document is shown here.

a. Open a new document and set the left and right page margins to 1 inch.

b. Set the line spacing to double.

c. Enter the title Final 4 Companies centered on the first line.

d. Apply formats of your choice to the title line.

e. Several lines below the title, place left tab stops at .25, 1.75, and 5.0 inches and a center tab at 4.25 inches on the ruler.

f. Enter the word Company at the first tab stop, Product/Service at the second tab stop, Size at the third tab stop, and Location at the fourth tab stop.

g. Enter the rest of the information shown here into the table.

Final 4 Companies

Company	Product/Service	Size	Location
Brown	Telecommunications	12,000	Memphis
GROTAN	Trucking	5,000	Minneapolis
Kriken	Software Development	2,500	San Jose
Matrox	Software Development	3,500	San Diego

Student Name

February 18, 2001

Brown	Telecommunications	1,200	Memphis
GROTAN	Trucking	5,000	Minneapolis
Kriken	Software development	2,500	San Jose
Matrox	Software development	3,500	San Diego

h. Change the font size of the table headings to 18 points and the remainder of the table to 14 points. Add bold, color, and an underline style of your choice to the table headings.

i. Add your name and the current date as a field using the Date and Time command several lines below the table.

j. Save the document as Career Fair and print it.

Preparing an Article

★ ★ 3. To complete this exercise, you must have completed Hands-On Exercise 5 in Lab 1. You are still working on the column for the campus newspaper. You need to add information to the article and make several formatting changes to the document. Your completed article is shown here:

a. Open the document Making Sushi2 you created in Practice Exercise 5 in Lab 1.

b. Copy the contents of the file wd02_Rice into the article above the "Making California Rolls" section.

c. Save the document using the file name Making Sushi3.

d. Format the newly inserted section using the same formats as in the "Making California Rolls" section.

e. Change the top margin to 1.5 inches. Change the right and left margins to 1 inch.

f. Indent all the lists to the 1-inch position.

g. Change the directions in both sections to an itemized numbered list.

h. Use the thesaurus to find a better word for "big" in the first sentence.

i. Replace the date in the last line with a date field.

j. Preview, and then print the document.

k. Save the document using the same file name.

Making Sushi

Your next dinner party can be a huge success when you get everyone involved in making sushi. You need just a few basic items for the preparation. If you live in a large city, you may find these at your local grocery store. Your best bet is to find an Asian grocery in your city.

Sushi Basics:
A bamboo-rolling mat (Makisu)
Cutting board
Sharp knife
Wasabi
Pickled ginger
Soy sauce

Making Sushi Rice

Great sushi starts with the rice. If you master this process all you need to add is really good fish. The trick involves fanning the rice as it cools to help evaporate the moisture. The end result should be sticky rice with a glossy texture.

Ingredients:
Medium grain rice
Water
1 tablespoon rice vinegar
1 tablespoon sugar
Dash salt

Directions:
1. Make the rice according to the package directions.
2. After the rice is cooked, put it into the wooden bowl and lightly flatten it.
3. Pour vinegar, sugar, and salt into a small bowl and mix until dissolved.
4. Drizzle the vinegar mixture onto the rice and mix it using the wooden spoon fanning the rice as you mix.
5. When the rice is sticky with a glossy texture, cover the bowl with a damp towel.
6. Let the rice reach room temperature before you use it.

Making California Rolls

California rolls are a great way to introduce sushi to the novice, as there is no raw fish in the roll. This recipe calls for imitation crabmeat but if your budget can handle the cost use real crabmeat.

Ingredients:
Nori seaweed
Prepared sushi rice
Avocado, peeled and cut into sixteenths
Imitation crabmeat
Cucumber, peeled, seeded, and julienned

Directions:
1. Cut one sheet of Nori seaweed in half and place on a bamboo mat.
2. With a wooden spoon, spread a thin layer of sushi rice on the seaweed leaving a strip uncovered at each end to seal the roll.
3. At one end, add two strips of cucumber, one slice of avocado, and one piece of imitation crabmeat.
4. Beginning at the end with the cucumber, avocado, and crabmeat, roll the seaweed over once. Pull up the bamboo mat and use it to help you roll the rest of the way until you reach the other end of the seaweed wrap.
5. Place the roll seam side down and with a sharp knife, cut the roll into ¼ or ½-inch wide rolls.

Student Name - April 18, 2001

Writing a Thank You Letter

★ ★ **4.** Your experience at the career fair was very positive. There is one company that you are very interested in and want to pursue further. You have quickly written a draft of a thank-you letter, but now need to revise it to fix mistakes and add more details of what you would like to discuss with the Human Resources representative. Your completed letter is shown below.

a. Open the file wd02_Thank-You Letter.

b. Replace "[Current Date]" with a date field using the form of the date shown in the final document. Indent the date to the 3-inch position.

c. Bullet the list using a bullet style of your choice.

d. Change the word "focus" in the first bulleted item to a similar word using the thesaurus to find a suitable synonym.

e. Change the left and right and top margins to 1.5 inch.

f. Using the AutoText feature, insert a closing on the second line under the last paragraph.

g. Replace "[Student Name]" with your name in the closing. Indent both closing lines to the 3-inch position.

h. Perform a spelling and grammar check to eliminate errors.

i. Save your letter as Thank-You Letter2 and print it. Sign it just above your name.

April 18, 2001

Brown Telecom
35 Pioneer Avenue
Memphis, TN 47143

Dear Ms. Jones:

Thank you for spending time with me at the West Valley Career Fair last Wednesday. I have attached another copy of my resume and want to point out some highlights that are of particular interest to your company:

- MBA with a concentration on the Global Economy
- Internship for major telecommunications firm in Munich
- Fluent in German and French

I am very interested in the position we discussed and would like to set up a time when we could explore the opportunity further. I will call you later this week to set up a time that is convenient for you.

Sincerely,

Student Name

Creating a Flyer

★ ★
★
5. You work for the Downtown Internet Cafe, which sells fresh roast coffee and coffee beverages. You want to create a document describing the roast coffee varieties and prices. Using tab settings, create a table of coffee varieties and prices according to the following specifications. Your completed flyer is shown here:

a. Open a new document.

b. Enter the title DownTown Internet Cafe on the first line.

c. Enter Roast Coffee below the title.

d. Center the first line, make it brown, and change the font size to 48 pt.

e. Center the second line, make it brown, and change the font size to 22 pt. Skip a line after the second line.

f. Place left tab stops at .75 and 2.5 inches and a center tab at 5.25 inches on the ruler.

g. Enter the word Coffee at the first tab stop, Description at the second tab stop, and Cost/Pound at the third tab stop.

h. Enter the rest of the information for the table shown in the final document.

i. Add tab leaders between the data in the table.

j. Increase the font of the table headings to 14 pt. Add bold, color, and an underline style of your choice to the table headings.

k. Open the file wd02_Coffee Flyer. Copy the first three paragraphs and insert them above "Roast Coffee" in the new document.

l. Center the words "Coffee Sale." Make them bold, font size 24 pt, and a color of your choice.

m. Make the paragraphs bold, centered, and 14 pt, and set their line spacing to double.

n. Increase the font size of the line above "Roast Coffee" to 18 pt. Reset its line spacing to single. Insert a blank line below it.

o. Copy the remaining paragraph from the wd02_Coffee Flyer document, and insert it at the bottom of the new document.

p. Bold and center the final paragraph.

q. Increase the left and right margins to 1.5 inch.

r. Insert the Explosion 1 AutoShape above the title line. Enter and center the word Sale in red within it, and choose the gold fill color.

s. Add your name and a field with the current date several lines below the final paragraph.

t. Save the document as Coffee Flyer2 and print it.

Applying for an Internship

★ 1. Your first year as a law student is going well and you are looking for a summer internship with a local law firm. You just had an interview with Christine Kent of the Kent, Johnson, and Smyth law firm and want to write a follow-up letter thanking her for her time and reiterating how you think you would be best qualified for this position. Write a business letter directed to Ms. Kent. Include your qualifications in the form of a bulleted list. Be sure to also include the date, a salutation, two justified paragraphs, a closing, and your name as a signature. Use the business letter in Hands-On Exercise 4 as a model. Save the document as Internship Letter and print the letter.

Insurance Survey

★ 2. The Arizona Department of Insurance conducted a survey in October, 2000 comparing the cost of a six-month car insurance premium in different areas of the state. The comparison was based on a 48-year-old married couple with a clean driving record. The same criteria for type and year of automobile and miles driven to work were used as well as the amount of insurance coverage.

Create a tabbed table using the information shown below. Bold and underline the column heads. Add style 2 tab leaders to the table entries. Above the table, write a paragraph explaining the table contents.

Insurance Company	Phoenix	Tucson	Flagstaff
AAA Preferred	$1,279	$1,116	$ 775
Farmers	1,461	1,432	1,023
Allstate	1,605	1,617	1,268
American Family	1,341	1,206	817

Include your name and the date below the table. Save the document as Insurance Comparison and print the document.

To-Do List

★★ 3. Many people create lists of things they need to do each day or each week. In this problem, you will create a list of things you need to do for the week. Create a numbered "to do" list of all the things you have to do this week (or all the things you would like to do this week) either in order of importance or in chronological order. Add a title that includes your name and the current date. Use the formatting techniques you have learned to improve the appearance of the list. Save the document as To Do List. Print the document.

New Employee Memo

★★ 4. Adventure Travel has recently hired a new sales representative, Amity Zeh. You need to write a memo introducing Amity to the sales staff. Address the memo to the sales staff and add appropriate From, Date, and RE: lines. Using a bulleted list, describe Amity Zeh's past experience as an assistant manager at a movie theater and the skills you think she learned there. Describe as well her new function of selling Adventure Travel tours. Justify your paragraphs and indent the first lines. Add two AutoShapes to accent your memo. Save the document as New Staff Memo and print the memo.

Advertising Flyer

★★ ★ **5.** Create a flyer to advertise something you have for sale (used car, used stereo, and so on). Integrate the following features into the flyer:

    Different fonts in different sizes, colors, and styles
    Bulleted or numbered list
    Indents
    An AutoShape
    A graphic
    A tabbed table with tab leaders

Include your name as the contact information. Save the document as For Sale Flyer and print the flyer.

on the web

Your political science class is studying the 2000 presidential election. Your instructor has divided the class into three groups and assigned each group a research project. Your group is to find out how Americans voted for the presidential candidates by age and sex. Use the Web to research this topic and write a one-page report on your findings. Include a table of the data you found. Use other features demonstrated in this lab, including AutoShapes, indents, bulleted lists, font colors, and so forth to make your report attractive and easy to read. Be sure to reference your sources on the Web for the data you located. Include your name and the current date below the report. Save the report as Election Results and print your report.

Creating Reports and Tables

LAB 3

objectives

After completing this lab, you will know how to:

1.	Create and modify an outline.
2.	Hide spelling and grammar errors.
3.	Use Click and Type.
4.	Apply styles.
5.	Create and update a table of contents.
6.	Create a section break.
7.	Center a page vertically.
8.	Create footnotes.
9.	Use Document Map.
10.	Wrap text around graphics.
11.	Add captions and cross-references.
12.	Create and format a simple table.
13.	Sort a reference list.
14.	Add headers, footers, and page numbers.
15.	Print selected pages and save to a new folder.

A table of contents listing can be created quickly from heading styles in a document.

Page 1 (Title page / Table of Contents)

Tanzania and Peru

Table of Contents

Student Name

Current Date

Page (Student Name 1)

Tanzania

Geography and Climate

"In the midst of a great wilderness, full of wild beasts…I fancied I saw a summit…covered with a dazzlingly white cloud (qtd. in Cole 56). This is how Johann Krapf, the first outsider to witness the splendor of Africa's highest mountain, described Kilimanjaro. The peak was real, though the white clouds he "fancied" he saw were the dense layer of snow that coats the mountain. [1]

Tanzania is primarily a plateau that slopes gently downward into the country's five hundred miles of Indian Ocean coastline. Nearly three-quarters of Tanzania is dry savannah, so much so that the Swahili word for the central plateau is *nyika*, meaning "wasteland." Winding through these flatlands is the Great Rift Valley, which forms narrow and shallow lakes in its long path. Several of these great lakes form a belt-like oasis of green vegetation. Contrasting with the severity of the plains are the coastal areas, which are lush with ample rainfall. In the north the plateau slopes dramatically into Mt. Kilimanjaro.

Figure 1. Lions in the Serengeti

Ngorongoro Conservation Area

Some of Tanzania's most distinguishing geographical features are found in the Ngorongoro Conservation Area. [2] The park is composed of many craters and gorges, as well as lakes, forest, and plains. Among these features is the area's namesake, the Ngorongoro Crater. The Crater is a huge expanse, covering more than one hundred square miles. On the Crater's floor, grasslands blend into swamps, lakes, rivers, and woodland. Also within the Conservation Area's perimeter is the Olduvai Gorge, commonly referred to as the "Cradle of Mankind," where in 1931 the stone tools of prehistoric man were found. This find subsequently led to the discovery of the remains of humans who lived 1.75 million years ago.

Serengeti Plain

Adjacent to the western edge of the Ngorongoro Conservation Area is the Serengeti Plain. Its area is approximately 5,700 square miles, and its central savanna supports many grazing animals with plentiful water and lush grasses. Its southern portion is dry, receiving an average of only twenty inches of rainfall annually. The north is wooded grassland with watercourses and tributaries to larger rivers. Only two seasons occur on the Serengeti: dry and wet. The dry season occurs between June and October and the wet season between November to May.

---

[1] Mt. Kilimanjaro is 19,340 feet high, making it the fourth tallest mountain in the world.
[2] The Conservation Area is a national preserve spanning 3,196 square miles.

Wrapping text around graphics, adding figure captions, footnotes, headers, and footers are among many features that can be used to enhance a report.

Page (Student Name 3)

coming from the east. Some areas in the south are considered drier than the Sahara. Conversely, there are a few areas in this region where mountain rivers meet the ocean that are green with life and do not give the impression of being in a desert at all.

La Sierra

Inland and to the east is the mountainous region called La Sierra, encompassing Peru's share of the Andes mountain range. The southern portion of this region is prone to volcanic activity, and some volcanoes are active today. La Sierra is subject to a dry season from May to September, which is winter in that part of the world. Temperatures are moderate by day, and can be freezing in some areas during the night. The weather is typically sunny, with moderate annual precipitation. The former Incan capital Cuzco is in this region, as well as the Sacred Valley of the Incas. This region also contains Lake Titicaca, the world's highest navigable lake[3]

La Selva

La Selva, a region of tropical rainforest, is the easternmost region in Peru. This region, with the eastern foot of the Andes Mountains, forms the Amazon Basin, into which numerous rivers flow. The Amazon River begins at the meeting point of the two dominant rivers, the Ucayali and Marañon. La Selva is extremely wet, with some areas exceeding an annual precipitation of 137 inches. Its wettest season occurs from November to April. The weather here is humid and extremely hot.

Region	Annual Rainfall (Inches)	Average Temperature (Fahrenheit)
La Costa	2	68
La Sierra	35	54
La Selva	137	80

Culture

Historical Culture

Peru is where the Incas built their homes and cities. They lived in the southern portion of La Sierra until around 1300 CE[4], when they moved north to the fertile Cuzco Valley. From here they built their empire, overrunning and assimilating neighboring lands and cultures. They organized into a socialist-type theocracy under an emperor – the Inca – whom they worshipped as a deity. The Inca Empire reached its maximum size by the late fifteenth and early sixteenth centuries.

In 1532 the Spanish explorer Francisco Pizarro landed in Peru. He saw great opportunity in seizing the empire because of the rich gold deposits in the Cuzco Valley, and did so with superior armament. This opened the door for masses of gold- and adventure-seeking conquistadors to join in the pursuit, who brought with them both modern weaponry and

---

[3] Lake Titicaca is 12,507 feet above sea level.
[4] Common Era (CE) is the period dating from the birth of Christ.

Including tables and using table formats makes the report attractive and easy to read.

Page (Student Name 5)

Works Cited

Camerapix Publishers International. Spectrum Guide to Tanzania. Edison: Hunter, 1992.

Cole, Tom. Geographic Expeditions. San Francisco: Geographic Expeditions, 1999.

Hudson, Rex A., ed "Peru: A Country Study." The Library of Congress – Country Studies. 1992. <http://lcweb2.loc.gov/frd/cs/petoc.html#pe0049> (11 Jan. 2001).

"The Living Edens: Manu – Peru's Hidden Rainforest." PBS Online <http://www.pbs.org/edens/manu> (11 Jan. 2001).

Valdizan, Mónica V. "Virtual Peru." 9 Jan. 1999. http://www.xs4all.nl/~govertme/visitperu/ (11 Jan. 2001).

Lists can be quickly sorted to appear in alphabetical order.

1
2
3
4
5
6
7
8

Adventure Travel Tours

Adventure Travel Tours gives out information on their tours in a variety of forms. Travel brochures, for instance, contain basic tour information in a promotional format and are designed to entice potential clients to sign up for a tour. More detailed regional information packets are given to people who have already signed up for a tour, so they can prepare for their vacation. These packets include facts about each region's climate, geography, and culture. Additional informational formats include pages on Adventure Travel's Web site and scheduled group presentations.

Part of your responsibility as advertising coordinator is to gather the information that Adventure Travel will publicize about each regional tour. Specifically, you have been asked to provide information for two of the new tours: the Tanzania Safari and the Machu Picchu trail. Because this information is used in a variety of formats, your research needs to be easily adapted. You will therefore present your facts in the form of a general report on Tanzania and Peru.

In this lab, you will learn to use many of the features of Word 2002 that make it easy to create an attractive and well-organized report. A portion of the completed report is shown on the left.

© Corbis

concept overview

The following concepts will be introduced in this lab:

1	**Style**	A style is a set of formats that is assigned a name and can be quickly applied to a selection.
2	**Section**	To format different parts of a document differently, you can divide a document into sections.
3	**Footnote and Endnote**	A footnote is a source reference or text offering additional explanation that is placed at the bottom of a page. An endnote is also a source reference or long comment that typically appears at the end of a document.
4	**Text Wrapping**	You can control how text appears around a graphic object by specifying the text wrapping style.
5	**Captions and Cross References**	A caption is a title or explanation for a table, picture, or graph. A cross-reference is a reference from one part of a document to related information in another part.
6	**Table**	A table is used to organize information into an easy-to-read format of horizontal rows and vertical columns.
7	**Sort**	Word can quickly arrange or sort paragraphs in alphabetical, numeric, or date order based on the first character in each paragraph.
8	**Header and Footer**	A header is a line or several lines of text at the top of each page just above the top margin line. A footer is text at the bottom of every page just below the bottom margin line.

Creating and Modifying an Outline

After several days of research, you have gathered many notes from various sources including books, magazines, and the Web. However, the notes are very disorganized and you are having some difficulty getting started on writing the report. Often the best way to start is by creating an outline of the main topics.

Word makes it easy to create and view document content as an outline using Outline view. Outline view shows the hierarchy of topics in a document by displaying the different heading levels indented to represent their level in the document's structure, as shown in the example at left. The arrangement of headings in a hierarchy of importance quickly shows the relationship between topics. You can use Outline view to help you create a new document or to view and reorganize the topics in an existing document.

- Tanzania
  - *Culture*
  - *Geography*
    - Climate
  - *Animal Life*
- Peru
  - *Culture*
    - Historical Culture
      - **Machu Picchu**
    - Current Culture
  - *Geography and Climate*
    - La Costa
    - La Sierra
    - La Selva
  - *Animal Life*

Using Outline View

You will use Outline view to help you organize the main topics of the report.

1 ● **Start Word.**

● **Close the task pane.**

● **Click** 🔲 **Outline View.**

Your screen should be similar to Figure 3.1

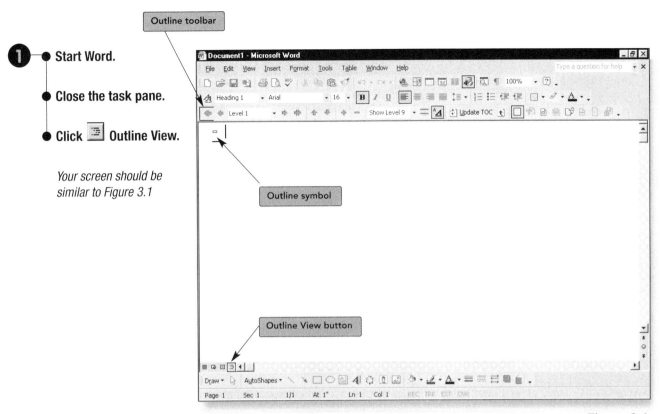

Figure 3.1

The Outline toolbar is displayed. It contains buttons that make it easy to modify the outline. The first line of the blank document displays an outline symbol. There are three outline symbols (□, ✛, and □) that are used to identify the levels of topics in the outline and to quickly reorganize topics. You will begin by entering the main topic headings for the report.

2 • Type the following headings, pressing ⏎Enter after each except the last:

Tanzania
Climate
Geography
Animal Life
Peru
Culture
Historical Culture
Machu Picchu
Current Culture
Geography and Climate
La Costa
La Sierra
La Selva
Animal Life (do not press ⏎Enter)

• Correct any misspelled words and use Ignore All for any identified proper names.

Your screen should be similar to Figure 3.2

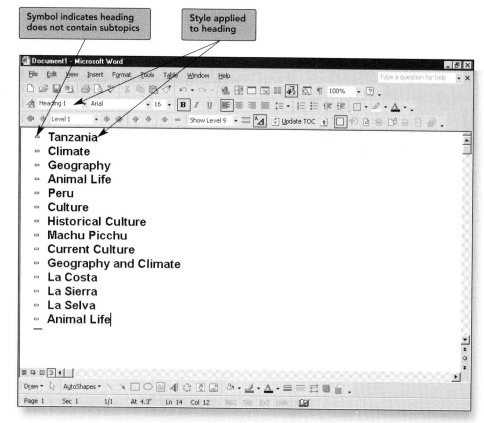

Symbol indicates heading does not contain subtopics

Style applied to heading

Figure 3.2

Each heading is preceded with the ▭ outline symbol, which indicates the heading does not contain subtopics. As you create a new document in Outline view, Word automatically applies built-in heading styles to the text as it is entered in the outline.

concept 1

Style

1 A **style** is a set of formats that is assigned a name and can be quickly applied to a selection. Word includes 75 predefined styles, and you can create your own custom styles. Many styles are automatically applied when certain features, such as footnotes, are used. Others must be applied manually to selected text.

Styles can be applied to characters or paragraphs. **Character styles** consist of a combination of any character formats in the Fonts dialog box that affect selected text. **Paragraph styles** are a combination of any character formats and paragraph formats that affect all text in a paragraph. A paragraph style can include all the font settings that apply to characters, as well as tab settings, indents, and line settings that apply to paragraphs. The default paragraph style is Normal, and it includes character settings of Times New Roman, 12 pt, and paragraph settings of left indent at 0, single line spacing, and left alignment. In addition, many paragraph styles are designed to affect specific text elements such as headings, captions, and footnotes.

Each topic you entered is initially formatted with a Heading 1 style. **Heading styles** are one of the most commonly used styles. They are designed to identify different levels of headings in a document. Heading styles include combinations of fonts, type sizes, bold, and italics. The first four heading styles and the formats associated with each are shown in the table below:

Heading Level	Appearance
Heading 1	Arial 16 pt bold
Heading 2	*Arial 14 pt bold, italic*
Heading 3	Arial 13 pt bold
Heading 4	Times New Roman 14 pt bold

The most important heading in a document should be assigned a Heading 1 style. This style is the largest and most prominent. The next most important heading should be assigned the Heading 2 style, and so on. Headings give the reader another visual cue about how the information is grouped in your document.

Changing Outline Levels

Next you need to arrange the headings by outline levels. As you rearrange the topic headings and subheadings, different heading styles are applied based upon the position or level of the topic within the outline hierarchy. Headings that are level 1 appear as the top level of the outline and appear in a Heading 1 style, level 2 headings appear indented below level 1 headings and appear in a Heading 2 style, and so on.

The outline symbols are used to select and move the heading to a new location or level within the document. Dragging the outline symbol to the right or left changes the level. To demote a heading to a lower level, drag the symbol to the right; to promote a heading to a higher level, drag the symbol to the left. As you drag the symbol, a vertical solid gray line appears at each outline level to show where the heading will be placed.

1 ● Drag the ▭ symbol of the **Climate** heading to the right one level.

Additional Information

The mouse pointer changes to ✛, indicating dragging it will move the heading.

Your screen should be similar to Figure 3.3

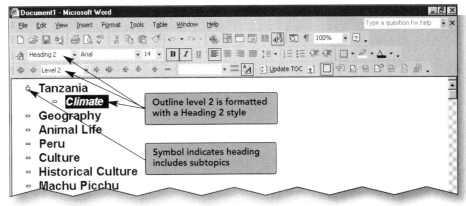

Figure 3.3

First you will make the Climate topic heading a subtopic below the main heading of Tanzania.

The Climate heading has changed to a Heading 2 style, and the heading is indented one level to show it is subordinate to the heading above it. The Tanzania heading now displays a ✥ outline symbol, which indicates the topic heading includes subtopics. You can also click ⇦ Promote and ⇨ Demote on the outlining toolabar to change outline levels.

2
- **Click on the Geography topic.**
- **Click ⇨ Demote 2 times.**

Your screen should be similar to Figure 3.4

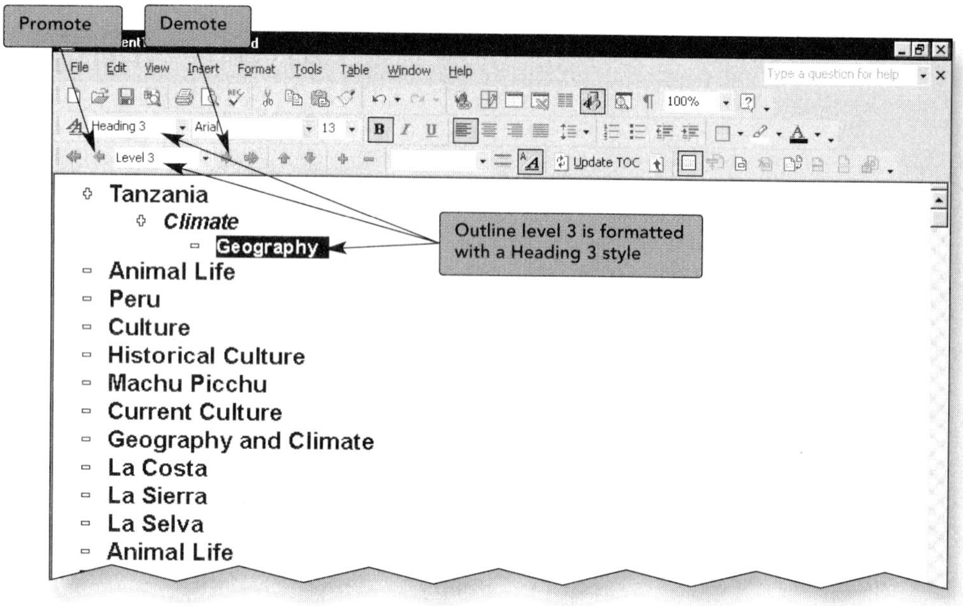

Figure 3.4

The Geography heading is now a Heading 3 style and is indented two levels in the outline.

3
- **Demote the remaining topics to the heading levels shown below.**

Animal Life	Level 2
Culture	Level 2
Historical Culture	Level 3
Machu Picchu	Level 4
Current Culture	Level 3
Geography and Climate	Level 2
La Costa	Level 3
La Sierra	Level 3
La Selva	Level 3
Animal Life	Level 2

Your screen should be similar to Figure 3.5

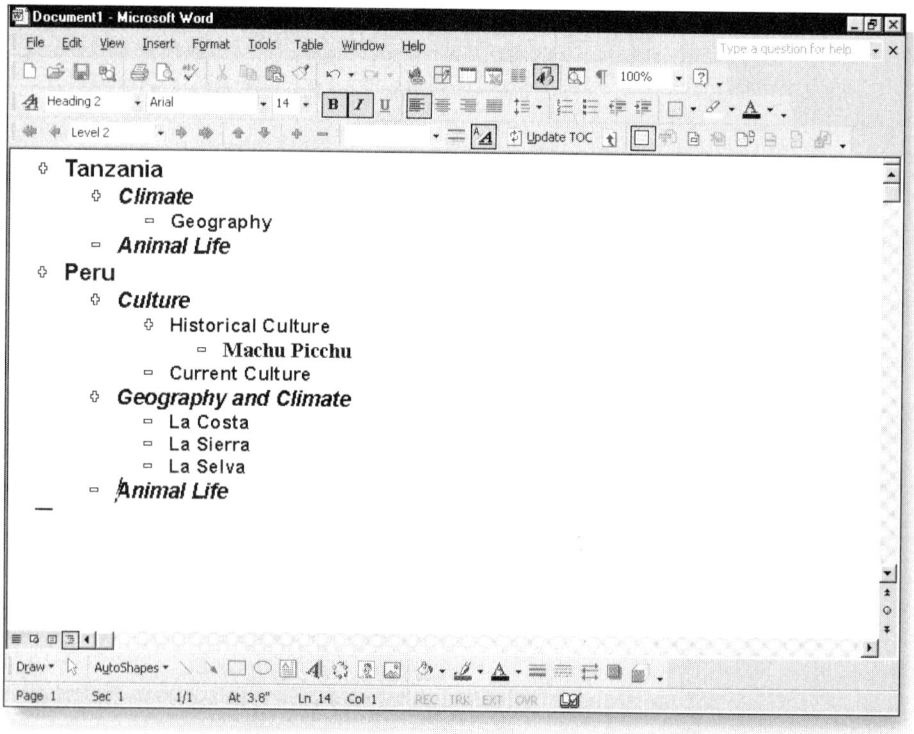

Figure 3.5

Moving and Inserting Outline Topics

Next you want to change the order of topics. To move a heading to a different location, drag the outline symbol up or down. As you drag, a horizontal line shows where the heading will be placed when you release the mouse button.

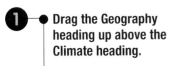

Another Method

You can also click ⬆ Move Up and ⬇ Move Down to move a topic.

- Drag the Geography heading up above the Climate heading.

- Promote the Geography heading to a level 2.

- Demote the Climate heading to a level 3.

  Your screen should be similar to Figure 3.6

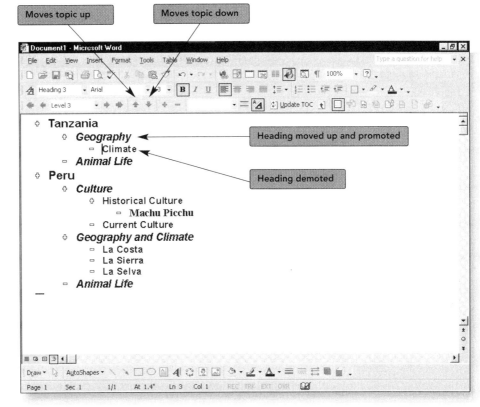

Figure 3.6

As you check the outline, you realize you forgot a heading for Culture under Tanzania.

- Move to the beginning of the Geography heading for Tanzania.

- Press ⏎Enter to insert a blank topic heading.

- Type **Culture** on the blank heading line.

  Your screen should be similar to Figure 3.7

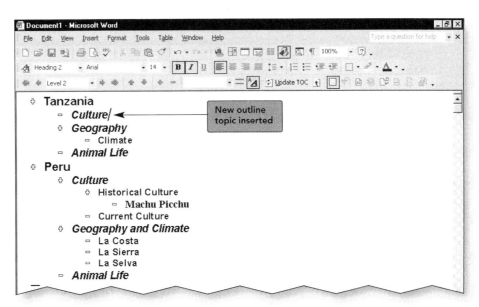

Figure 3.7

When you're satisfied with the organization, you can switch to Normal view or Print Layout view to add detailed body text and graphics.

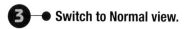 **Switch to Normal view.**

Your screen should be similar to Figure 3.8

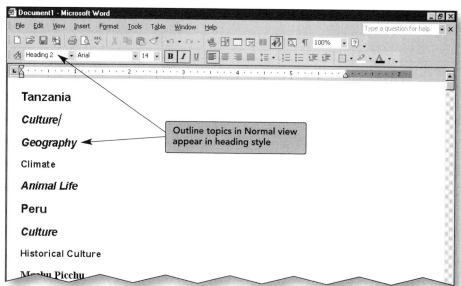

Figure 3.8

The topic headings appear left-aligned on the page in the style that was applied to the text as you created the outline.

Collapsing and Expanding the Outline

You have continued to work on the report during the day and have entered most of the information for the different topics. To see the information that has been added to the report,

1 ● **Open the file** wd03_Tour Research.

● **Switch to Outline view.**

● **Scroll the window to view the entire document.**

● **Return to the top of the document.**

Your screen should be similar to Figure 3.9

HAVING TROUBLE?
Your outline may display less text than in Figure 3.9. This is because Outline view reflects the settings that were in effect on your computer when this feature was last used.

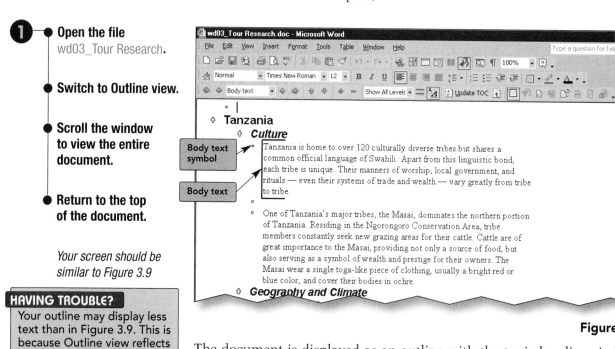

Figure 3.9

The document is displayed as an outline with the topic headings indented appropriately. The body text appears below the appropriate heading. Any text not identified with a heading style is considered body text. The small square to the left of a paragraph identifies it as body text.

In Outline view, you can display as much or as little of the document text as you want. To make it easier to view and reorganize the document's structure, you can "collapse" the document to show just the headings you want. Alternatively, you can display part of the body text below each heading or the entire body text. You can then easily move the headings around until the order is logical, and the body text will follow the heading. The table below shows how you can collapse and expand the amount of text displayed in Outline view.

To Collapse	Do This
Text below a specific heading level	Select the lowest heading you want to display from the [All] Show Level drop-down menu.
All subheadings and body text under a heading	Double-click ✛ next to the heading.
Text under a heading, one level at a time	Click the heading text, and then click [−] Collapse.
All body text	Select Show All Levels from the [Show Level 4 ▾] Show Level drop-down menu.
All body text except first line	Click [≡] Show First Line Only.

To Expand	Do This
All headings and body text	Select Show All Levels from the [Show Level 4 ▾] Show Level drop-down menu.
All collapsed subheadings and body text under a heading	Double-click ✛ next to the heading.
Collapsed text under a heading, one level at a time	Click the heading text, then click [✦] Expand.

To see more of the outline, you will collapse the display of the text under the Geography and Climate heading.

2 ➔● **Double-click ✛ of the Geography and Climate heading.**

Your screen should be similar to Figure 3.10

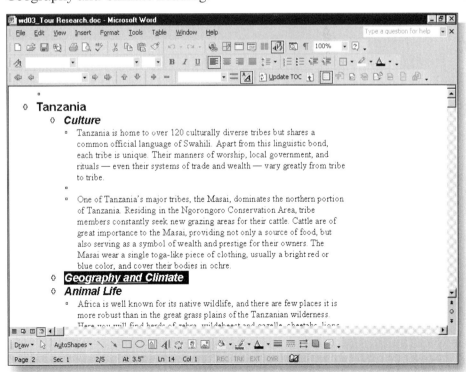

Figure 3.10

All the body text below this heading is hidden. You would like to see only the three heading levels of the document, not the body text, so you can quickly check its organization.

3 ● **Open the Show Level drop-down list.**

● **Choose Show Level 3.**

Your screen should be similar to Figure 3.11

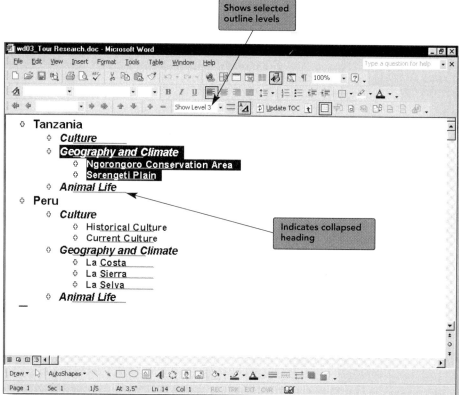

Figure 3.11

Now only the three heading levels are displayed. The gray line below a heading means the heading includes hidden or collapsed headings or body text.

As you look at the organization of the report, you decide to move the discussion of culture to follow the Geography and Climate section. Moving headings in Outline view quickly selects and moves the entire topic, including subtopics and all body text.

4 • Drag the Culture heading in the Tanzania section down to above the Animal Life heading in the same section.

• Drag the Culture heading in the Peru section down to above the Animal Life heading in the same section.

Your screen should be similar to Figure 3.12

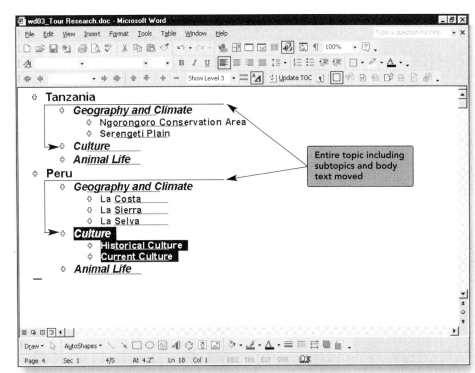

Figure 3.12

When you move or change the level of a heading that includes collapsed subordinate text, the collapsed text is also selected. Any changes you make to the heading, such as moving, copying, or deleting it, also affect the collapsed text. To verify this, you will display all body text again.

5 • Choose Show All Levels from the Show Level drop-down list.

• Scroll the report to see the top of the Peru Culture section.

• Click in the document to deselect the text.

Your screen should be similar to Figure 3.13

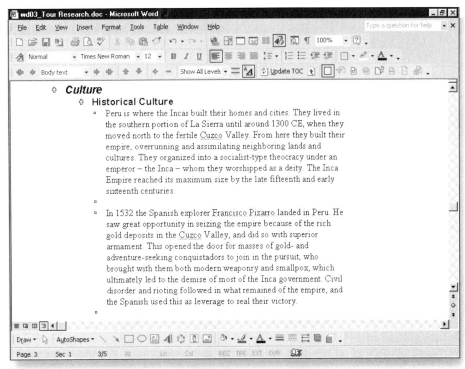

Figure 3.13

The subtopics and body text appear below the heading you moved.

Saving to a New Folder

Next you will save the unnamed document 1 and the changes you made to the research document in a folder that you will use to hold files related to the report. You can create a new folder at the same time you save a file.

1 ● Choose **File/Save As**.

● Change the Save In location to the appropriate location for your data files.

● Click  Create New Folder.

Your screen should be similar to Figure 3.14

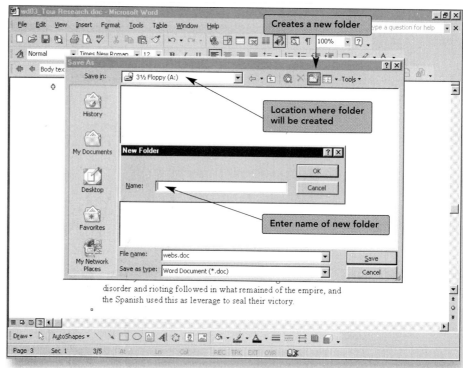

Figure 3.14

Additional Information
See "Saving, Closing, and Opening Files" in Lab 1 for file-naming rules.

In the New Folder dialog box, you enter the folder name. The rules for naming folders are the same as for naming files, except they typically do not include an extension.

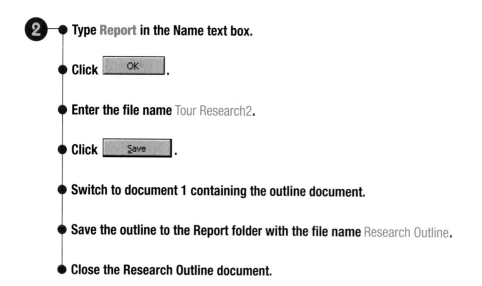

2 ● Type **Report** in the Name text box.

● Click [OK].

● Enter the file name Tour Research2.

● Click [Save].

● Switch to document 1 containing the outline document.

● Save the outline to the Report folder with the file name Research Outline.

● Close the Research Outline document.

The documents are saved in the newly created folder, Report.

Hiding Spelling and Grammar Errors

As you have been working on the report, you have noticed that many spelling and grammar errors are identified. However, they are mostly for proper names and words that are not in the dictionary. While working on a document, you can turn off the display of these errors so that they are not distracting as you work.

1 ● Choose **T**ools/**O**ptions.

● Open the Spelling & Grammar tab.

Your screen should be similar to Figure 3.15

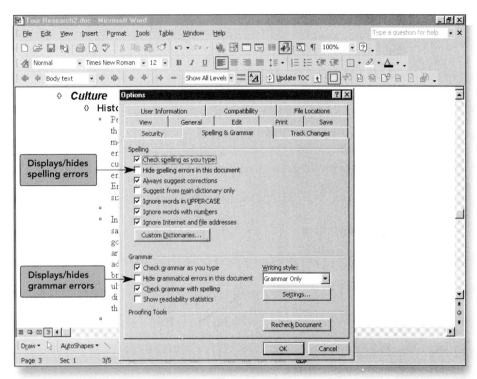

Figure 3.15

The Options dialog box is used to change the way many features in Word operate. The Spelling and Grammar tab displays options that control how these features operate. Checkmarks next to options indicate the setting is on. You want to turn off the display of spelling and grammar errors.

2 ● Select Hide **s**pelling errors in this document.

● Select Hide grammatical errors in this document.

● Click  OK .

Your screen should be similar to Figure 3.16

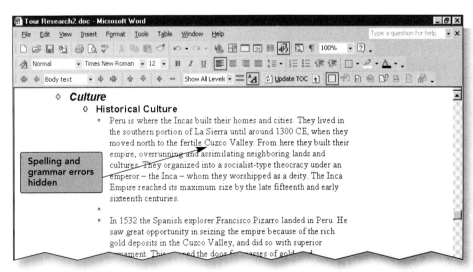

Figure 3.16

The red and green wavy lines are no longer displayed. You can still run spelling and grammar checking manually to check errors at any time.

Formatting Documents Automatically

Now that you are finished reorganizing the report, you want to add a title page. Generally, this page includes information such as the report title, the name of the author, and the date. You also want this page to include a table of contents list.

When preparing research reports, two styles of report formatting are commonly used: MLA (Modern Language Association) and APA (American Psychological Association). Although they require the same basic information, they differ in how this information is presented. For example, MLA style does not include a separate title page, but APA style does. The report you will create in this lab will use many of style requirements of the MLA. However, because this report is not a formal report to be presented at a conference or other academic proceeding, some liberties have been taken with the style to demonstrate features in Word.

Using Click and Type

You will create a new page above the first report topic and enter the title information in Print Layout view using the Click and Type feature. This feature, available in Print Layout and Web Layout views, is used to quickly insert text, graphics, and other items in a blank area of a document, avoiding the need to enter blank lines. This feature also applies the paragraph formatting needed to position an item at the location you clicked.

1 ● Switch to Print Layout view.

● Press Ctrl + Home to move to the top of the document.

● Press Ctrl + ←Enter to insert a hard page break and create a blank page above it.

● Move to the top of the blank new page.

● Move the mouse pointer from left to right across the page and observe the change in the mouse pointer.

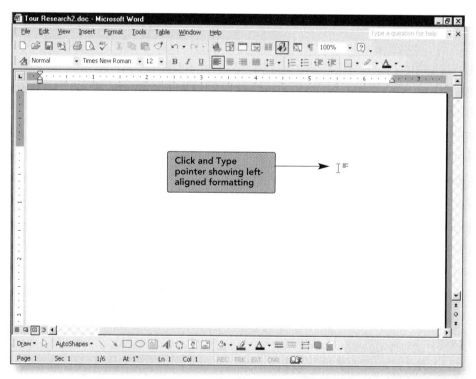

Figure 3.17

Your screen should be similar to Figure 3.17

Print Layout view includes formatting "zones" that control the formatting that will be applied. As you move the mouse pointer through the zones, the I-beam pointer displays an icon that indicates which formatting will be applied when you double-click at that location (See the following table). This is the Click and Type pointer.

Pointer shape	Formatting applied
	Align left
	Align center
	Align right
	Left indent
	Left text wrap
	Right text wrap

To enable the Click and Type pointer, first click on a blank area, then, as you move the mouse pointer the pointer shape indicates how the item will be formatted. Double-clicking on the location in the page moves the insertion point to that location and applies the formatting to the entry. You will enter the report title centered on the page.

2 ● **Click on the center of the page at the .5-inch vertical ruler position.**

● **Double-click at this location while the mouse pointer is a ☰.**

● **Type the report title, Tanzania and Peru.**

Your screen should be similar to Figure 3.18

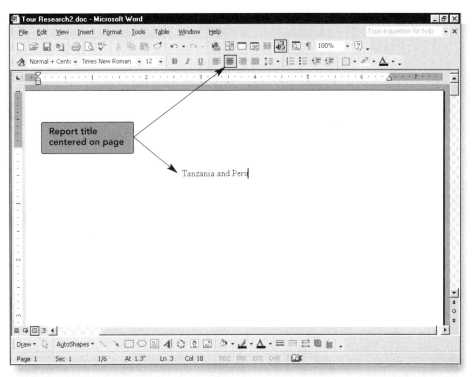

Report title centered on page

Tanzania and Peru

Figure 3.18

Next you will add a heading for the table of contents listing you will create, and you will enter your name and date at the bottom of the title page.

3 • Double-click on the center of the page at the 1.5-inch vertical ruler position while the mouse pointer is a ⊥ .

• Enter the title Table of Contents.

• In the same manner, enter your name centered at the 3-inch vertical ruler position.

• Press (←Enter).

• Enter the current date centered below your name.

Your screen should be similar to Figure 3.19

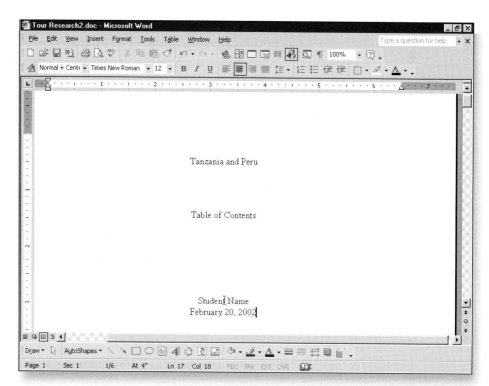

Figure 3.19

Applying Styles

Next you want to improve the appearance of the main title. You can do this quickly by applying a style to the title.

1 • Move to anywhere in the Tanzania and Peru title.

• Click [▲] Styles and Formatting.

Another Method
The menu equivalent is Format/Styles and Formatting.

Your screen should be similar to Figure 3.20

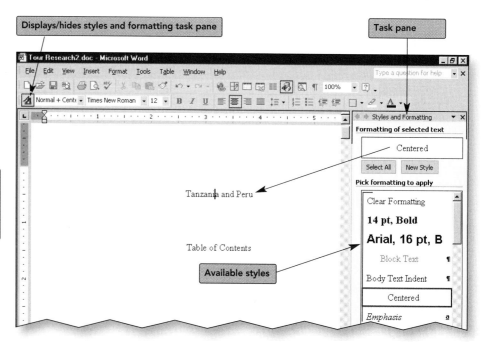

Figure 3.20

The Styles and Formatting task pane appears. Within this task pane, you can apply styles, create new styles, and modify existing styles. The "Formatting of selected text" box shows that the text of the current selection is centered. The "Pick formatting to apply" list box displays the names of all available formatting, including those that you have applied directly, in alphabetical order. The names are formatted using the associated formatting. You want to display the complete list of styles and apply the Title style to the text.

2 ● **Select All styles from the Show drop-down list box.**

● **Scroll the "Pick formatting to apply" list and choose Title.**

Additional Information

Pointing to the style name displays a ScreenTip of information about the format settings used in the style. Click on the style to choose it.

HAVING TROUBLE?

If you accidentally apply the wrong style, reselect the text and select the correct style. To return the style to the default, select Normal.

Your screen should be similar to Figure 3.21

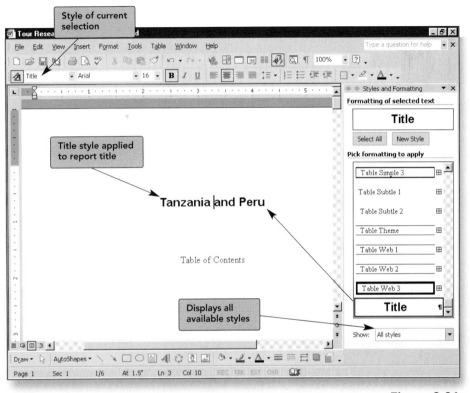

Figure 3.21

Notice that the entire title appears in the selected style. This is because a Title style is a paragraph style, affecting the entire paragraph at the insertion point. Also notice that the Style drop-down list button in the Formatting toolbar now displays "Title" as the style applied to the selection. This style includes formatting settings of Arial, 16 pt, and bold.

Next you want to apply a Subtitle style to the Table of Contents heading. Another way to select a style is from the [Normal ▼] Style drop-down menu.

3 ● **Close the Styles and Formatting task pane.**

● **Move the insertion point to anywhere in the Table of Contents heading.**

● **Open the** [Normal + Cente ▼] **Style drop-down menu.**

Your screen should be similar to Figure 3.22

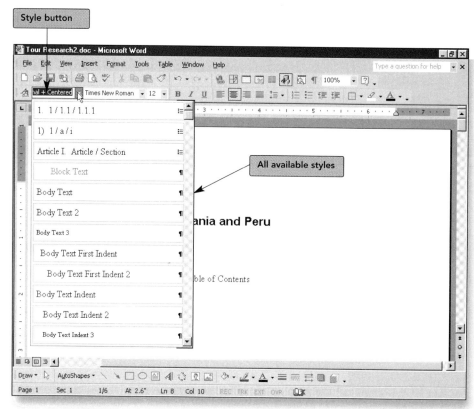

Figure 3.22

Additional Information
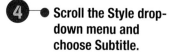

The symbols to the right of the style name indicate the type of style such as a paragraph style ¶ or a character style **a**.

The Style drop-down menu displays all available styles. The style names are listed in alphabetical order and appear formatted in that style.

4 ● **Scroll the Style drop-down menu and choose Subtitle.**

Your screen should be similar to Figure 3.23

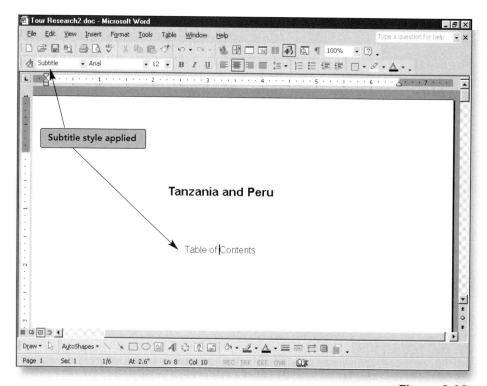

Figure 3.23

Creating a Table of Contents

Now you are ready to create the table of contents. A table of contents is a listing of the topic headings that appear in a document and their associated page references (see the sample below). It shows the reader at a glance what topics are included in the document and makes it easier for the reader to locate information. Word can generate a table of contents automatically once you have applied heading styles to the document headings.

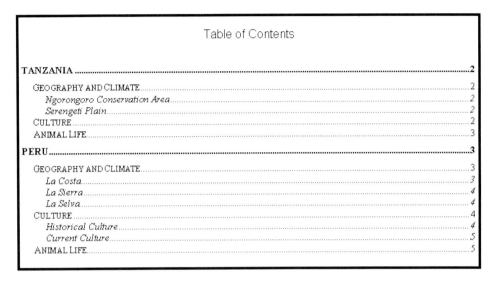

Generating a Table of Contents

You want the table of contents listing to be displayed several lines below the table of contents heading on the title page.

1 ● **Move to the second blank line below the Table of Contents heading.**

HAVING TROUBLE?

If needed, use ¶ Show/Hide to help locate the position in the document.

● **Choose Insert/ Reference/Index and Tables.**

● **Open the Table of Contents tab.**

Your screen should be similar to Figure 3.24

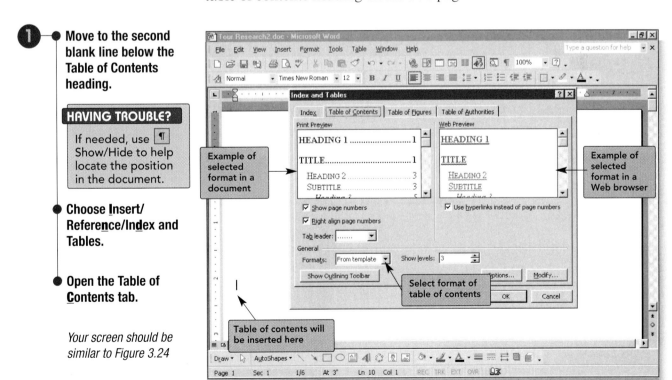

Figure 3.24

From the Table of Contents tab, you first need to select the format or design of the table of contents. The Formats drop-down list box displays the name of the default table of contents style, From Template, which is supplied with the Normal template. The Preview boxes display an example of how the selected format will look in a normal printed document or in a document when viewed in a Web browser. The From Template format option is used to design your own table of contents and save it as a template by modifying the existing format. You want to use one of the predesigned formats.

2 ● **Open the Formats drop-down list box.**

● **Choose Formal.**

Your screen should be similar to Figure 3.25

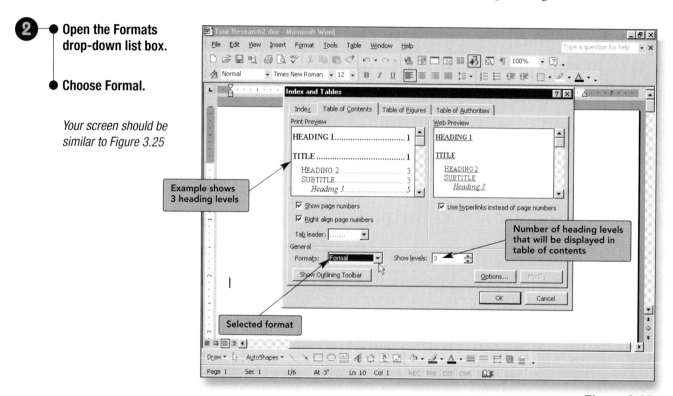

Figure 3.25

The Print Preview area shows this style will display the page numbers flush with the right margin, and with a series of tab leaders between the heading and the page number. This format will display in the table of contents all entries in the document that are formatted with Headings 1, 2, and 3, as well as Title and Subtitle styles. You want the table of contents to also include topics formatted with the Heading 4 style, but to exclude those formatted with the Title and Subtitle styles. You will modify the settings for the Formal format and turn off the use of these styles.

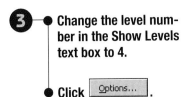

3 ● Change the level number in the Show Levels text box to 4.

● Click Options... .

Your screen should be similar to Figure 3.26

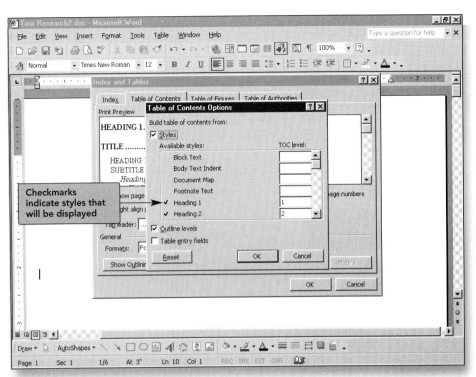

Figure 3.26

The Table of Contents Options dialog box shows the styles that are used to build the table of contents. The checkmark indicates which styles Word will look for in the document to use as items to include in the table of contents, and the number indicates the level at which they will be displayed. To clear a style selection, simply delete the number from the TOC level text box.

4 ● Scroll the Available Styles list to see the Subtitle and Title selections.

● Delete the numbers from the Subtitle and Title text boxes to clear the checkmarks.

● Click OK .

Your screen should be similar to Figure 3.27

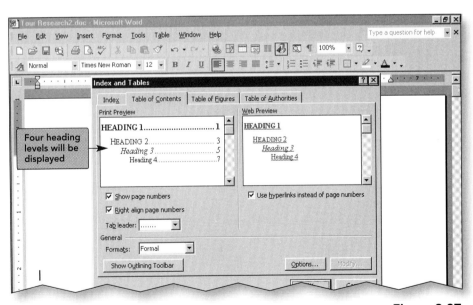

Figure 3.27

The Print Preview area now shows that four levels of headings will be reflected in the table of contents listing, and the title and subtitle will not be included. Now you are ready to generate the listing.

5 ● Click [OK].

Your screen should be similar to Figure 3.28

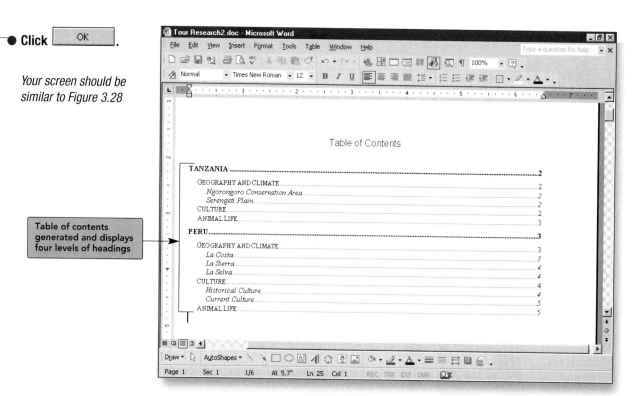

Table of contents generated and displays four levels of headings

Figure 3.28

Word searches for headings with the specified styles, sorts them by heading level, references their page numbers, and displays the table of contents using the Formal style in the document. The headings that were assigned a Heading 1 style are aligned with the left margin, and subordinate heading levels are indented as appropriate.

Using a Table of Contents Hyperlink

When a table of contents is generated, each entry is a field that is a hyperlink to the heading in the document.

1 ● Click anywhere in the table of contents list.

Your screen should be similar to Figure 3.29

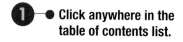

Additional Information

Pointing to an entry in a table of contents displays a ScreenTip with directions on how to follow the hyperlink.

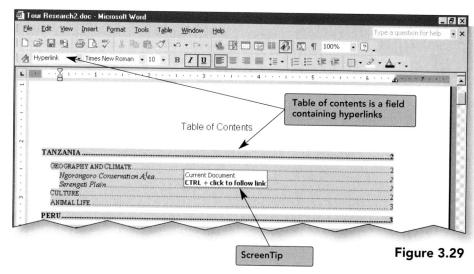

Table of contents is a field containing hyperlinks

ScreenTip

Figure 3.29

Notice that the text in the table of contents is shaded, indicating it is a field. This means it can be updated to reflect changes you may make at a later time in your document. Also notice that the Style list box displays "Hyperlink." Each line in the table of contents has been changed to a hyperlink. Now simply holding down Ctrl while clicking on a line will move you directly to that location in the document.

2 ● Hold down Ctrl and click the Peru table of contents line.

Additional Information
The mouse pointer shape changes to a 🖑 when holding down Ctrl and pointing to a hyperlink.

Your screen should be similar to Figure 3.30

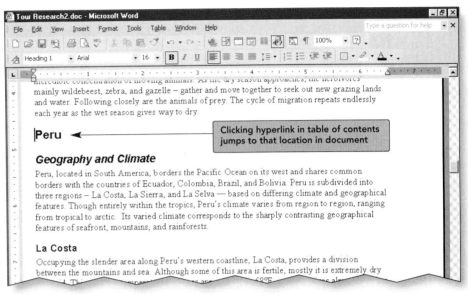

Figure 3.30

The insertion point jumps to that location in the document.

Formatting Document Sections

You want to change the layout of the title page so that the text on the page is centered vertically between the top and bottom page margins. Because page layout settings affect entire documents, to make this change to the title page only you need to divide the document into sections.

concept 2

Section

2 To format different parts of a document differently, you can divide a document into **sections**. Initially a document is one section. To separate it into different parts, you insert section breaks. The **section break** identifies the end of a section and stores the document format settings, such as margins and page layout, associated with that section of the document.

Creating a Section Break

Because the page layout you want to use on the title page is different than the rest of the document, you need to divide the document into two sections. You will delete the hard page break line you inserted and replace it with a section break.

● **Switch to Normal view.**

● **Move to the bottom of page 1.**

● **Delete the hard page break line.**

HAVING TROUBLE?
To remove a hard page break, click on the page break line and press [Delete].

● **Choose Insert/Break.**

Your screen should be similar to Figure 3.31

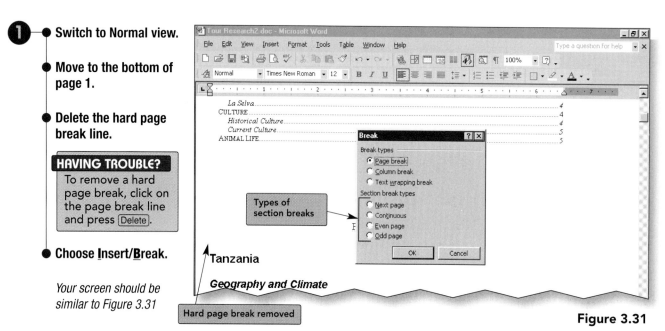

Figure 3.31

In the Break dialog box, you specify the type of section break you want to insert. The three types of section breaks, described in the following table, control the location where the text following a section break begins.

Option	Action
Next Page	Starts the new section on the next page.
Continuous	Starts the new section on the same page.
Odd or Even	Starts new section on the next odd or even numbered page.

You want the new section to start on the next page.

● **Select Next page.**

● **Click** OK **.**

● **Delete any blank lines above the Tanzania heading.**

Your screen should be similar to Figure 3.32

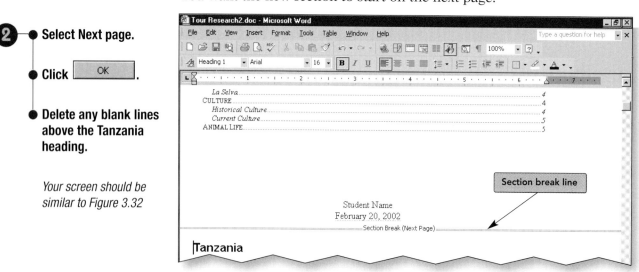

Figure 3.32

A double dotted line and the words "Section Break" identify the type of document break that was inserted.

Centering a Page Vertically

Finally, you are ready to change the layout of the title page to centered vertically.

- Switch back to Print Layout view.

- Move to anywhere in the title page.

- Zoom to Whole Page.

- Choose File/Page Setup.

- If necessary, open the Layout tab.

Your screen should be similar to Figure 3.33

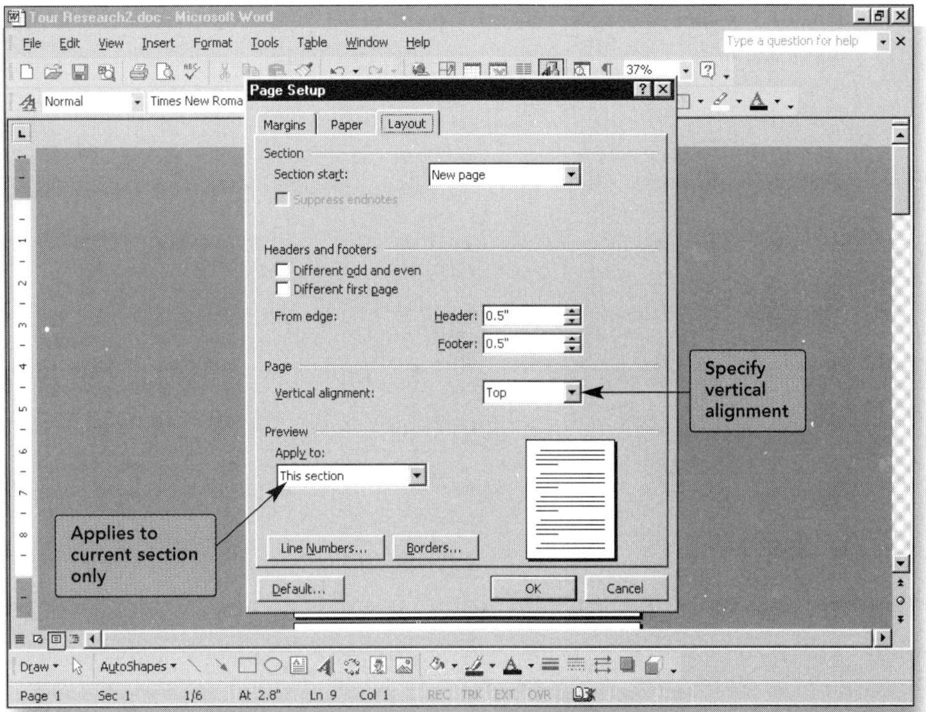

Figure 3.33

Additional Information

If you do not create a section break first, Word will automatically insert a section break for you if you change the formatting of selected text, such as inserting columns or centering selected text vertically on a page.

From the Vertical Alignment drop-down list box, you specify how the text is to be aligned on the page vertically. In addition, from the Apply To drop-down list box you need to specify what part of the document you want to be aligned to the new setting. Because you already divided the document into sections, this setting is already appropriately selected. You only need to specify the vertical alignment.

2 ● From the <u>V</u>ertical Alignment drop-down list, select Center.

● Click `OK`.

● Click 💾 to save the changes you have made to the document.

Your screen should be similar to Figure 3.34

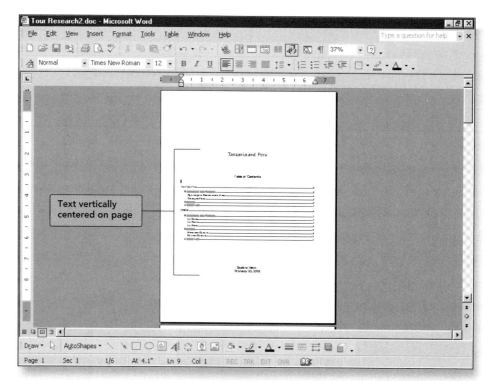

Text vertically centered on page

Figure 3.34

Now you can see that the text on the title page is centered vertically between the top and bottom margins. Word required a section break at this location because a different page format, in this case vertical alignment, was used on this page than the rest of the document.

Footnoting a Document

This document already includes parenthetical source references entered according to the MLA style for research papers. However, you still have several reference notes you want to include in the report as footnotes to help clarify some information.

concept 3

Footnote and Endnote

3 A **footnote** is a source reference or text offering additional explanation that is placed at the bottom of a page. An **endnote** is also a source reference or long comment that typically appears at the end of a document. You can have both footnotes and endnotes in the same document. Footnotes and endnotes consist of two parts, the note reference mark and the note text. The **note reference mark** is commonly a superscript number appearing in the document at the end of the material being referenced (for example, text). It can also be a character or combination of characters. The **note text** for a footnote appears at the bottom of the page on which the reference mark appears. The footnote text is separated from the document text by a horizontal line called the **note separator**. Endnote text appears as a listing at the end of the document.

Adding Footnotes

The first footnote reference you want to add is the height of Mt. Kilimanjaro. This note will follow the reference to the mountain at the end of the first paragraph in the Geography and Climate section for Tanzania. To identify where you want the footnote number to appear in the document, you position the insertion point at the document location first.

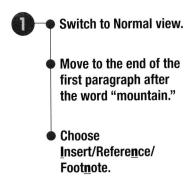

- Switch to Normal view.

- Move to the end of the first paragraph after the word "mountain."

- Choose Insert/Reference/Footnote.

Another Method

The keyboard shortcut to insert a footnote using the default settings is Alt + Ctrl + F.

Your screen should be similar to Figure 3.35

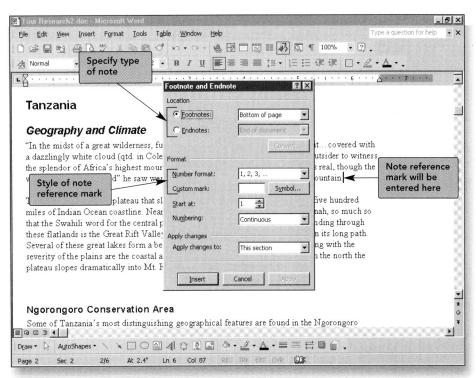

Figure 3.35

In the Footnote and Endnote dialog box, you specify whether you want to create footnotes or endnotes and the type of reference mark you want to appear in the document: a numbered mark or a custom mark. A custom mark can be any nonnumeric character, such as an asterisk, that you enter in the text box. You want to create numbered footnotes, so the default settings of Footnote and AutoNumber are acceptable.

②——● Click [Insert] .

Your screen should be similar to Figure 3.36

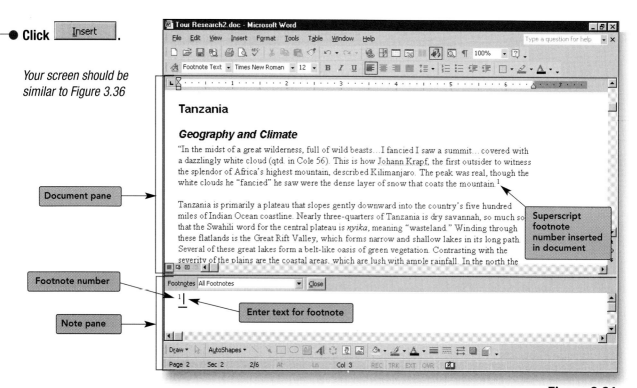

Document pane

Footnote number

Note pane

Figure 3.36

The document window is now horizontally divided into upper and lower panes. A **pane** is a portion of the document that you can view and scroll independently. The report is displayed in the document pane. The footnote number, 1, appears as a superscript in the document where the insertion point was positioned when the footnote was created. The **note pane** displays the footnote number and the insertion point. This is where you enter the text for the footnote. When you enter a footnote, you can use the same menus, commands, and features as you would in the document window. Any commands that are not available are dimmed.

3 ● **Type** Mt. Kilimanjaro is 19,340 feet high, making it the fourth tallest mountain in the world.

Your screen should be similar to Figure 3.37

Footnote text

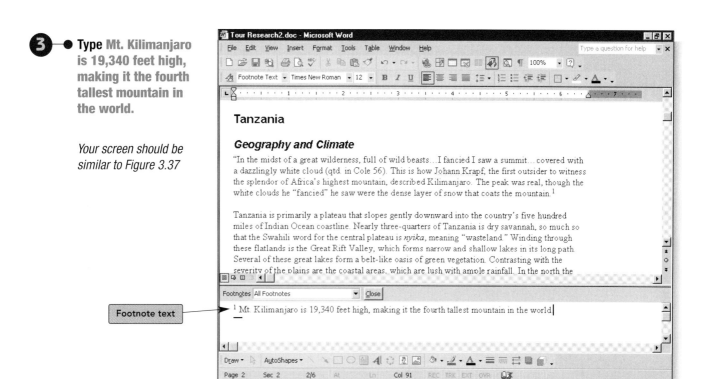

Figure 3.37

Using the Document Map

The second footnote you want to add is in the Geography and Climate section under Peru. To quickly move to that location in the document, you can use the Document Map feature. **Document Map** displays document headings, and is used to quickly navigate through the document and keep track of your location in it.

1 ● **Click** 🔲 **Document Map.**

Another Method
The menu equivalent is **View/Document** Map.

Your screen should be similar to Figure 3.38

Indicates all subordinate levels are displayed

Document Map pane displays headings in your document

Current location in document is highlighted

Hides/displays Document Map

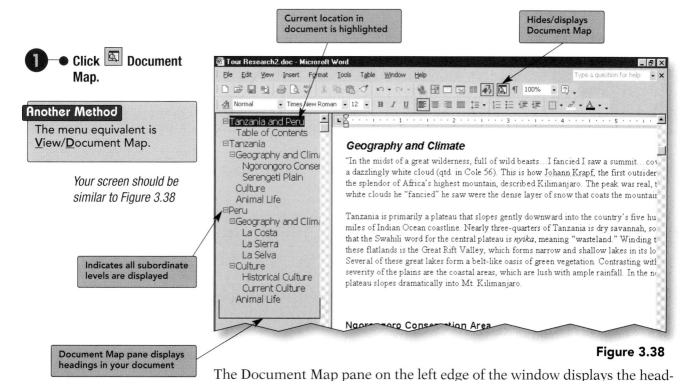

Figure 3.38

The Document Map pane on the left edge of the window displays the headings in your document. The document pane on the right displays the document in Normal view.

All text that is formatted with a heading style is displayed in the Document Map pane. Notice the ▬ symbol to the left of many of the headings in the Document Map; this indicates that all subordinate headings are displayed. A ▦ symbol would indicate that subordinate headings are not displayed. When your document does not contain any headings formatted with heading styles, the program automatically searches the document for paragraphs that look like headings (for example, short lines with a larger font size) and displays them in the Document Map. If it cannot find any such headings, the Document Map is blank. The highlighted heading shows your location in the document. Clicking on a heading in the Document Map quickly jumps to that location in the document.

2 ● **Change the zoom to Page Width.**

● **Click on La Sierra in the Document Map.**

Your screen should be similar to Figure 3.39

Selected heading

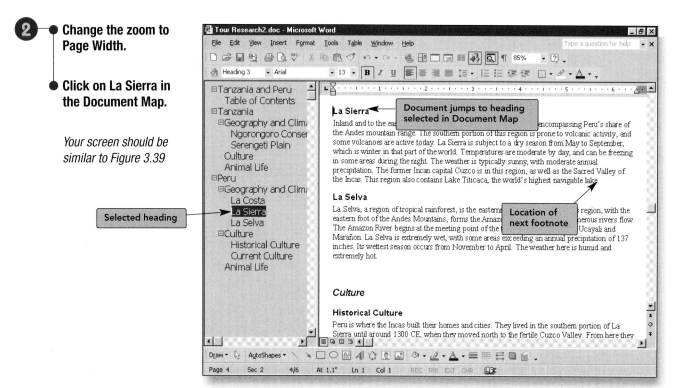

Figure 3.39

The selected heading is displayed at the top of the window and highlighted in the Document Map. You can now quickly locate the text you want to reference. You want to add a note about Lake Titicaca.

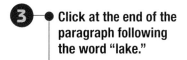

3 ● Click at the end of the paragraph following the word "lake."

● Choose **Insert/Reference/Footnote/** Insert.

Your screen should be similar to Figure 3.40

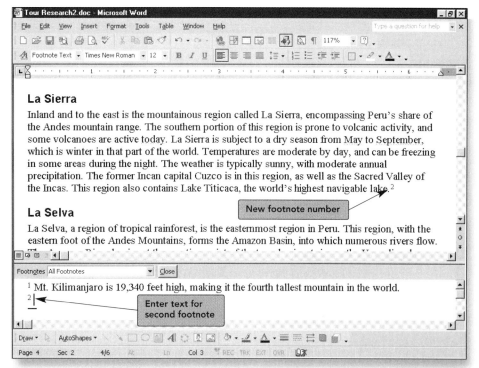

Figure 3.40

The footnote number 2 is automatically entered at the insertion point location. The note pane is active again, so you can enter the text for the second footnote. The Document Map pane is temporarily hidden while the note pane is displayed. When you close the note pane, the Document Map pane will be displayed again.

4 ● In the footnote pane, type **Lake Titicaca is 12,507 feet above sea level.**

Your screen should be similar to Figure 3.41

Additional Information

To delete a footnote or endnote, highlight the reference mark and press Delete. The reference mark and associated note text are removed, and the following footnotes are renumbered.

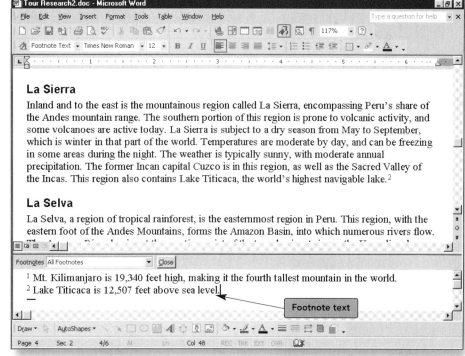

Figure 3.41

Now you realize that you forgot to enter a footnote earlier in the document, on page 2.

5 ● Click **Close** on the note pane.

● Click Ngorongoro Conservation Area in the Document Map.

● Move to the end of the first sentence of the first paragraph, following the word "Area."

● Insert a footnote at this location.

Your screen should be similar to Figure 3.42

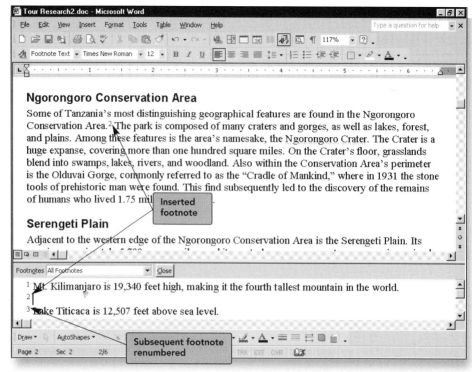

Figure 3.42

Notice that this footnote is now number 2 in the document, and a blank footnote line has been entered in the note pane for the footnote text. Word automatically adjusted the footnote numbers when the new footnote was inserted.

6 ● In the footnote pane, type **The Conservation Area is a national preserve spanning 3,196 square miles.**

Your screen should be similar to Figure 3.43

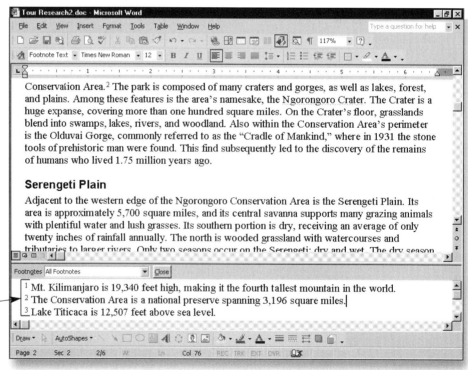

Figure 3.43

You are finished entering footnotes for now.

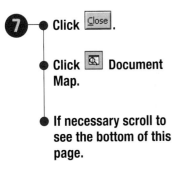

7 ● Click [Close].

● Click [🔍] Document Map.

● If necessary scroll to see the bottom of this page.

Your screen should be similar to Figure 3.44

Additional Information
You can hide and display the note pane any time by using the View/Footnotes command or by double-clicking on a note reference mark.

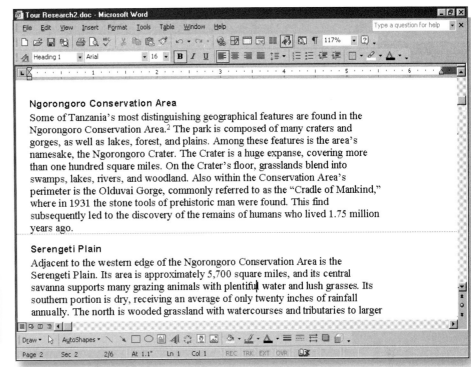

Figure 3.44

Viewing Footnotes

In Normal view, footnotes are not displayed at the bottom of the page. Instead, to see the footnote text, you point to the note reference mark and the footnote is displayed as a ScreenTip.

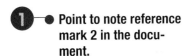

1 ● Point to note reference mark 2 in the document.

Your screen should be similar to Figure 3.45

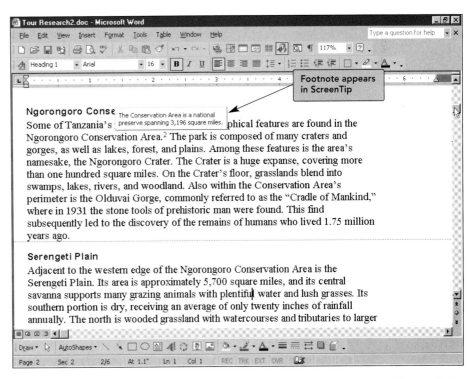

Figure 3.45

In Print Layout view, footnotes are displayed as they will appear when the document is printed.

2 • **Switch to Print Layout view and set the zoom to 75 percent.**

• **Scroll to the bottom of page 2 to see the footnotes.**

Additional Information
If you drag the scroll box, a ScreenTip will identify the page and topic that will be displayed when you stop dragging the scroll box.

Additional Information
If the zoom percentage is too small, the footnote numbers will not display correctly.

Your screen should be similar to Figure 3.46

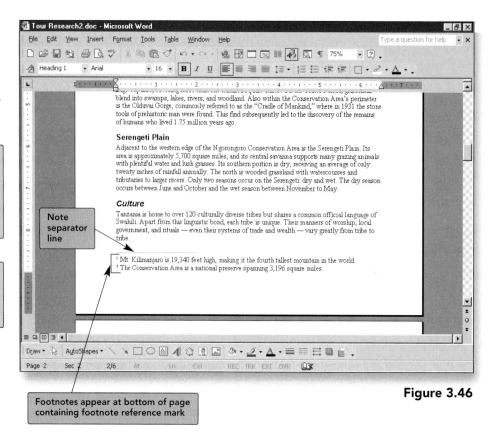

Note separator line

Footnotes appear at bottom of page containing footnote reference mark

Figure 3.46

The footnotes are displayed immediately above the bottom margin separated from the text by the note separator line. They appear at the bottom of the page containing the footnote reference mark.

Inserting a Footnote in Print Layout View

As you continue to check the document, you decide you want to explain the CE abbreviation following the date 1300 in the Historical Culture section. While in Print Layout view, you can insert, edit, and format footnotes just like any other text. After using the command to insert a footnote, the footnote number appears in the footnote area at the bottom of the page, ready for you to enter the footnote text.

Move the insertion point after "CE" in the second sentence below Historical Culture on page 4.

Insert a footnote at this location.

Type Common Era (CE) is the period dating from the birth of Christ.

Click 💾 Save to save the changes you have made to the document.

Your screen should be similar to Figure 3.47

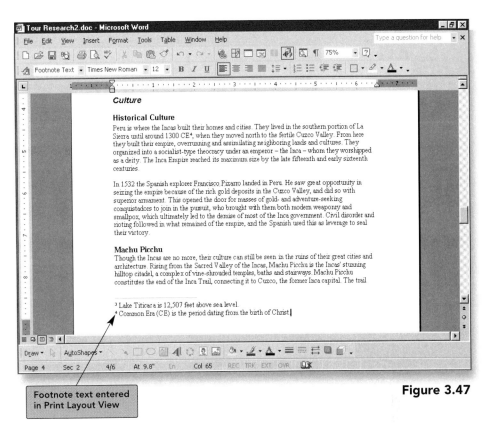

Footnote text entered in Print Layout View

Figure 3.47

Formatting Picture Layout

Next you want to add a picture in the report to complement the subject of the first topic. You want the text in the document where the picture will be inserted to wrap around the picture. To do this, you change the text-wrapping layout for the picture.

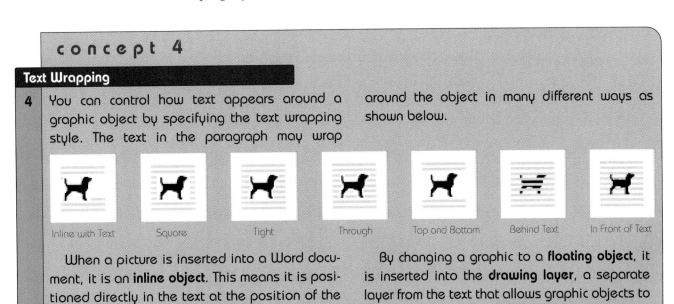

concept 4

Text Wrapping

4 You can control how text appears around a graphic object by specifying the text wrapping style. The text in the paragraph may wrap around the object in many different ways as shown below.

Inline with Text   Square   Tight   Through   Top and Bottom   Behind Text   In Front of Text

When a picture is inserted into a Word document, it is an **inline object**. This means it is positioned directly in the text at the position of the insertion point. It becomes part of the paragraph, and any paragraph alignment settings that apply to the paragraph also apply to the picture.

By changing a graphic to a **floating object**, it is inserted into the **drawing layer**, a separate layer from the text that allows graphic objects to be positioned precisely on the page. You can change an inline object to a floating picture by changing the wrapping style of the object.

You will insert the picture file wd03_Lions.jpg next to the second paragraph on page 2.

1 ● Use the Document Map to move to the Geography and Climate head under Tanzania.

● Move to the beginning of the second paragraph.

● Close the Document Map and change the zoom to Text Width.

● Insert the picture wd03_ Lions from your data files.

● Reduce the size of the picture to approximately 2 by 2 inches.

Additional Information
Dragging the corner handle maintains the original proportions of the picture.

● If necessary, display the Picture toolbar.

Your screen should be similar to Figure 3.48

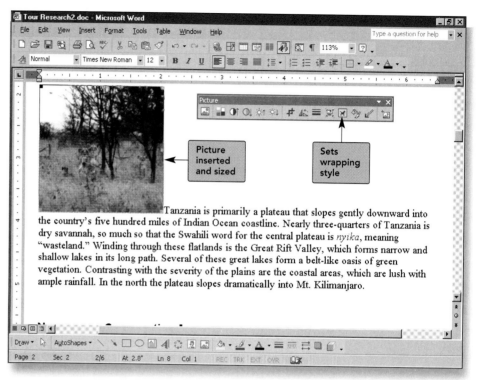

Figure 3.48

The picture has been inserted as an inline object and appears at the beginning of the paragraph like the first text characters of the paragraph. The text continues to the right of the picture.

Wrapping Text around Graphics

You want the text to wrap to the right side of the picture.

1 ● Click  Text Wrapping on the Pictures toolbar.

Another Method

The menu equivalent is Format/Picture/ Layout/Wrapping Style.

Your screen should be similar to Figure 3.49

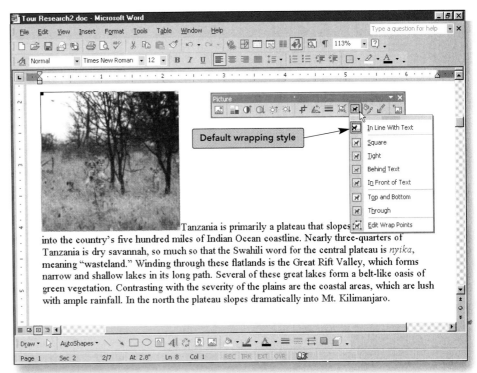

Default wrapping style

Figure 3.49

The default wrapping style, In Line with Text, is selected. You want to change the style to Square.

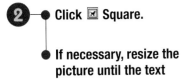

2 ● Click Square.

● If necessary, resize the picture until the text wraps around it as in Figure 3.50.

Your screen should be similar to Figure 3.50

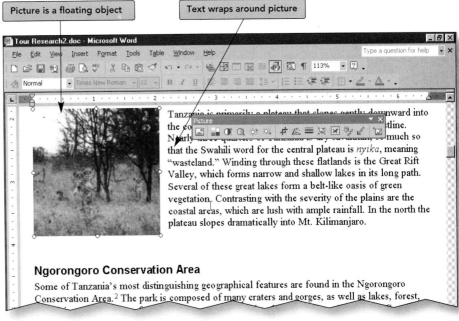

Picture is a floating object

Text wraps around picture

Figure 3.50

Additional Information

Sometimes it is easy to lose a floating object behind another. If this happens, you can press [Tab↹] to cycle forward or [⇧Shift] + [Tab↹] to cycle backward through the stacked objects.

The picture is changed to a floating object that can be placed anywhere in the document, including in front of or behind other objects including the text.

Because the picture is aligned with the left margin, the text wraps to the right side of the object. If you moved the picture, because the wrapping style is Square, the text would wrap around the object on all sides.

3 Move the picture to the center of the paragraph to see how the text wraps around it.

Your screen should be similar to Figure 3.51

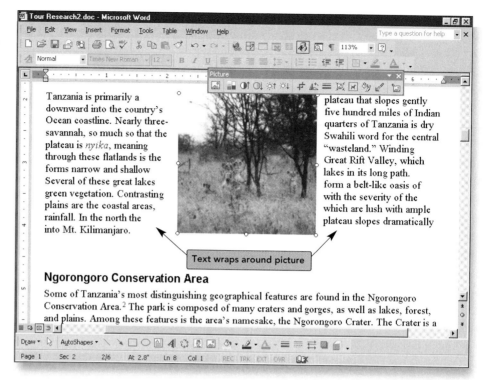

Figure 3.51

The text wraps on all sides of the object, depending on its location in the text.

4 Move the picture back to the left margin and aligned with the top of the paragraph. (See Figure 3.50).

● Insert the picture wd03_Parrots to the left of the first paragraph in the Animal Life section under Peru on page 5.

● Change the wrapping style to Square.

● Click 🖫 to save the document.

Your screen should be similar to Figure 3.52

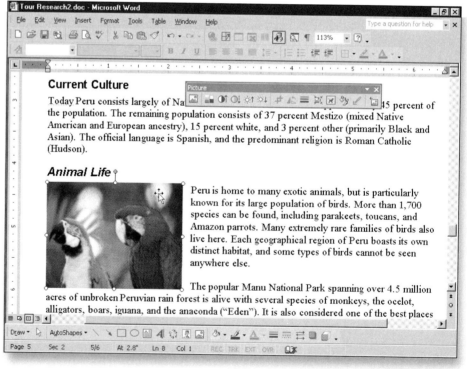

Figure 3.52

Referencing Figures

Referencing figures in a document helps the reader locate information quickly. Using captions and cross-references are two ways that you can link items together in a document. If the reader is viewing the document online, the captions and cross-references become hyperlinks to allow the reader to jump around in the document.

concept 5

Captions and Cross-References

5   A **caption** is a title or explanation for a table, picture, or graph. Word can automatically add captions to graphic objects as they are inserted, or you can add them manually. The caption label can be changed to reflect the type of object to which it refers, such as a table, chart, or figure. In addition, Word automatically numbers graphic objects and adjusts numbering when objects of the same type are added or deleted.

A **cross-reference** is a reference from one part of a document to related information in another part. Once you have captions, you can also include cross-references. For example, if you have a graph in one part of the document that you would like to refer to in another section, you can add a cross-reference that tells the reader what page the graph is on. A cross-reference can also be inserted as a hyperlink, allowing you to jump to another location in the same document or in another document.

Adding a Figure Caption

Next you want to add a caption below the picture of the lions.

1 ● **Move to the blank line below the lion picture.**

● **Choose Insert/Reference/Caption.**

Your screen should be similar to Figure 3.53

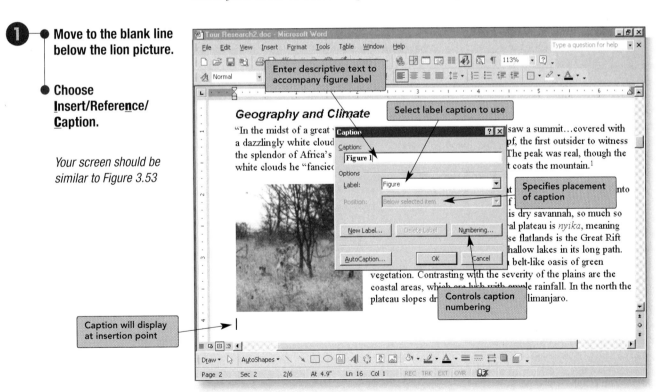

Figure 3.53

The Caption options are described in the table on the next page.

Option	Description
Label	Select from one of three default captions: Table, Figure, or Equation.
Position	Specify the location of the caption, either above or below a selected item. When an item is selected, the Position option is available.
New Label	Create your own captions.
Numbering	Specify the numbering format and starting number for your caption.
AutoCaption	Turns on the automatic insertion of a caption (label and number only) when you insert selected items into your document.

The most recently selected caption label and number appear in the Caption text box. You want the caption to be Figure 1, and you want to add additional descriptive text.

2 In the Caption text box, following "Figure 1," type **- Lions in the Serengeti**.

Click [OK].

Your screen should be similar to Figure 3.54

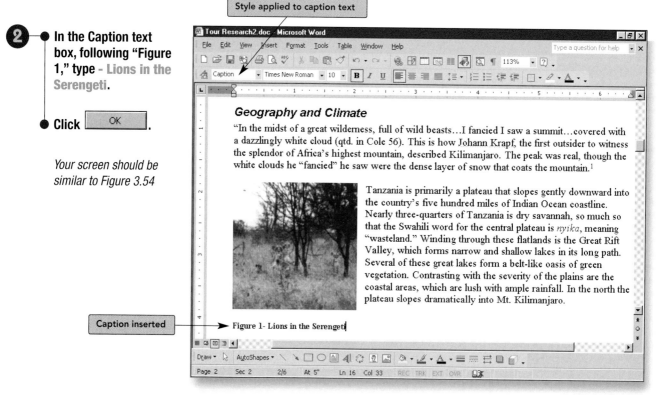

Figure 3.54

The caption label appears below the figure. It can be moved like any other text.

Adding a Cross-Reference

In the Animal section of the report, you discuss the animals found in the Serengeti. You want to include a cross-reference to the picture at this location.

1 ● Move to after the word "prey" in the third paragraph in the Animal Life section (page 3).

● Press Spacebar.

● Type (see .

● Press Spacebar.

● Choose Insert/Reference/ Cross-reference.

Your screen should be similar to Figure 3.55

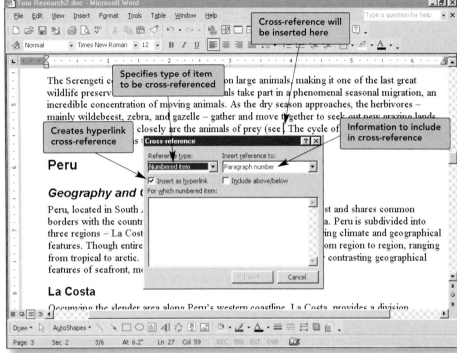

Figure 3.55

In the Cross-reference dialog box, you specify the type of item you are referencing and how you want the reference to appear. You want to reference the lions picture, and you want only the label "Figure 1" entered in the document.

2 ● From the Reference Type drop-down list box, select Figure.

● From the Insert Reference To drop-down list box, select Only label and number.

Your screen should be similar to Figure 3.56

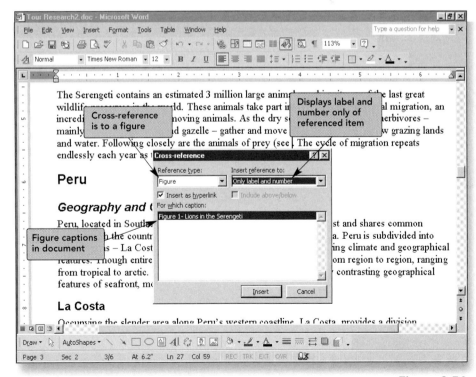

Figure 3.56

The For Which Caption list box lists all figure captions in the document. Because there is only one figure in this document, the correct figure caption is already selected. Notice that the Insert as Hyperlink option is selected by default. This option creates a hyperlink between the cross-reference and the caption. The default setting is appropriate.

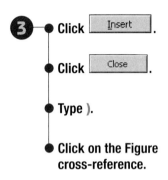

● Click [Insert].

● Click [Close].

● Type).

● Click on the Figure cross-reference.

Your screen should be similar to Figure 3.57

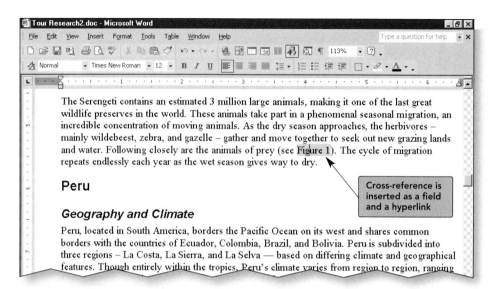

The Serengeti contains an estimated 3 million large animals, making it one of the last great wildlife preserves in the world. These animals take part in a phenomenal seasonal migration, an incredible concentration of moving animals. As the dry season approaches, the herbivores – mainly wildebeest, zebra, and gazelle – gather and move together to seek out new grazing lands and water. Following closely are the animals of prey (see Figure 1). The cycle of migration repeats endlessly each year as the wet season gives way to dry.

Peru

Geography and Climate

Peru, located in South America, borders the Pacific Ocean on its west and shares common borders with the countries of Ecuador, Colombia, Brazil, and Bolivia. Peru is subdivided into three regions – La Costa, La Sierra, and La Selva — based on differing climate and geographical features. Though entirely within the tropics, Peru's climate varies from region to region, ranging

> Cross-reference is inserted as a field and a hyperlink

Figure 3.57

A cross-reference is entered into the document as a field. Therefore, if you insert another picture or item that is cross-referenced, the captions and cross-references will renumber automatically. If you edit, delete, or move cross-referenced items, you should manually update the cross-references using Update Field. When you are working on a long document with several figures, tables, and graphs, this feature is very helpful.

Using a Cross-Reference Hyperlink

Next, you want to use the cross-reference hyperlink to jump to the source it references.

● Hold down Ctrl and click on the Figure 1 cross-reference.

Your screen should be similar to Figure 3.58

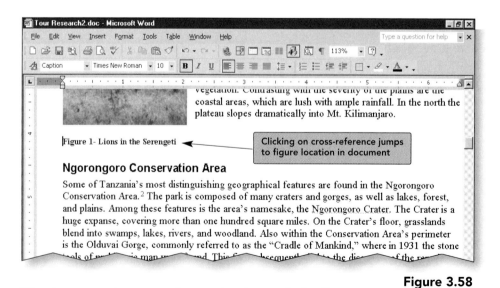

vegetation. Contrasting with the severity of the plains are the coastal areas, which are lush with ample rainfall. In the north the plateau slopes dramatically into Mt. Kilimanjaro.

Figure 1- Lions in the Serengeti

> Clicking on cross-reference jumps to figure location in document

Ngorongoro Conservation Area

Some of Tanzania's most distinguishing geographical features are found in the Ngorongoro Conservation Area.[2] The park is composed of many craters and gorges, as well as lakes, forest, and plains. Among these features is the area's namesake, the Ngorongoro Crater. The Crater is a huge expanse, covering more than one hundred square miles. On the Crater's floor, grasslands blend into swamps, lakes, rivers, and woodland. Also within the Conservation Area's perimeter is the Olduvai Gorge, commonly referred to as the "Cradle of Mankind," where in 1931 the stone tools of prehistoric man were found. This find subsequently led to the discovery of the re-

Figure 3.58

The document jumps to the caption beneath the figure.

Creating a Simple Table

Next you want to add a table comparing the rainfall and temperature data for the three regions of Peru.

concept 6

Table

6 A **table** is used to organize information into an easy-to-read format of horizontal rows and vertical columns. The insertion of a row and column creates a **cell** in which you can enter data or other information.

Tables are a very effective method for presenting information. The table layout organizes the information for readers and greatly reduces the number of words they have to read to interpret the data. Use tables whenever you can to make your documents easier to read.

The table you want to create will display columns for regions, rainfall, and temperature. The rows will display the data for each region. Your completed table will be similar to the one shown below.

Region	Annual Rainfall (Inches)	Average Temperature (Fahrenheit)
La Costa	2	68
La Sierra	35	54
La Selva	137	80

Inserting a Table

Word includes several different methods you can use to create tables. One method (Table/Convert/Text to Table) will quickly convert text that is arranged in columns into a table. Another uses the Draw Table feature to create any type of table, but is most useful for creating complex tables that contain cells of different heights or a varying number of columns per row. The third method, which you will use, initially creates a simple table consisting of the same number of rows and columns.

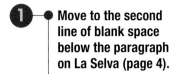

1 ● Move to the second line of blank space below the paragraph on La Selva (page 4).

● Click Insert Table (on the Standard toolbar).

Another Method

The menu equivalent is Table/Insert/Table

Your screen should be similar to Figure 3.59

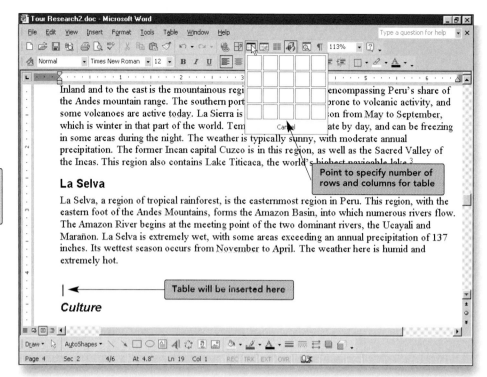

Inland and to the east is the mountainous regi... encompassing Peru's share of the Andes mountain range. The southern port... prone to volcanic activity, and some volcanoes are active today. La Sierra is ... on from May to September, which is winter in that part of the world. Tem... ate by day, and can be freezing in some areas during the night. The weather is typically sunny, with moderate annual precipitation. The former Incan capital Cuzco is in this region, as well as the Sacred Valley of the Incas. This region also contains Lake Titicaca, the world's highest navigable lake.[3]

Point to specify number of rows and columns for table

La Selva

La Selva, a region of tropical rainforest, is the easternmost region in Peru. This region, with the eastern foot of the Andes Mountains, forms the Amazon Basin, into which numerous rivers flow. The Amazon River begins at the meeting point of the two dominant rivers, the Ucayali and Marañon. La Selva is extremely wet, with some areas exceeding an annual precipitation of 137 inches. Its wettest season occurs from November to April. The weather here is humid and extremely hot.

Table will be inserted here

Culture

Figure 3.59

The Insert Table drop-down menu displays a grid in which you specify the number of rows and columns for the table. Moving the mouse pointer over the grid highlights the boxes in the grid and defines the table size. The dimensions are reflected in the bottom of the grid.

2 ● Point to the boxes in Insert Table drop-down grid to highlight a 3-by-3 section.

● Click on the lower right corner of the selection.

Your screen should be similar to Figure 3.60

Table of 3 rows and 3 columns is inserted

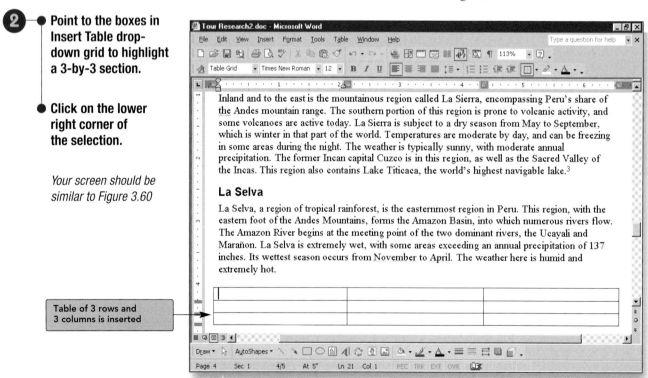

Inland and to the east is the mountainous region called La Sierra, encompassing Peru's share of the Andes mountain range. The southern portion of this region is prone to volcanic activity, and some volcanoes are active today. La Sierra is subject to a dry season from May to September, which is winter in that part of the world. Temperatures are moderate by day, and can be freezing in some areas during the night. The weather is typically sunny, with moderate annual precipitation. The former Incan capital Cuzco is in this region, as well as the Sacred Valley of the Incas. This region also contains Lake Titicaca, the world's highest navigable lake.[3]

La Selva

La Selva, a region of tropical rainforest, is the easternmost region in Peru. This region, with the eastern foot of the Andes Mountains, forms the Amazon Basin, into which numerous rivers flow. The Amazon River begins at the meeting point of the two dominant rivers, the Ucayali and Marañon. La Selva is extremely wet, with some areas exceeding an annual precipitation of 137 inches. Its wettest season occurs from November to April. The weather here is humid and extremely hot.

Figure 3.60

A table the full width of the page is drawn. It has equal sized columns and is surrounded by a black borderline.

Entering Data in a Table

Now you are ready to enter information in the table. Each cell contains a single line space where you can enter data. Cells in a table are identified by a letter and number, called a **table reference**. Columns are identified from left to right beginning with the letter A, and rows are numbered from top to bottom beginning with the number 1. The table reference of the top left-most cell is A1 because it is in the first column (A) and first row (1) of the table. The second cell in column 2 cell B2. The fourth cell in column 3 is C4.

	Jan	Feb	Mar	Total
East	7	7	5	19
West	6	4	7	17
South	8	7	9	24
Total	21	18	21	60

You can move from one cell to another by using the arrow keys or by clicking on the cell. In addition, you can use the keys shown in the table below to move around a table.

Additional Information

Pressing Tab ⇆ when in the last cell of a row moves to the first cell of the next row.

To Move To	Press
Next cell in row	Tab ⇆
Previous cell in row	⇧ Shift + Tab ⇆
First cell in row	Alt + Home
Last cell in row	Alt + End
First cell in column	Alt + Page Up
Last cell in column	Alt + Page Down
Previous row	↑
Next row	↓

The mouse pointer may also appear as a solid black arrow when pointing to the table. When it is a ↓, you can click to select the entire column. When it is ➚, you can click to select a cell. You will learn more about this feature shortly.

You will begin by entering the information for La Costa in cells A1 through C1. You can type in the cell as you would anywhere in a normal document.

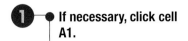

1 ● If necessary, click cell A1.

● Type La Costa.

● Press Tab ⇆.

● In the same manner, type 2 in cell B1 and 68 in cell C1.

● Continue entering the information shown below, using Tab ⇆ to move to the next cell.

Cell	Entry
A2	La Sierra
B2	35
C2	54
A3	La Selva
B3	137
C3	80

Your screen should be similar to Figure 3.61

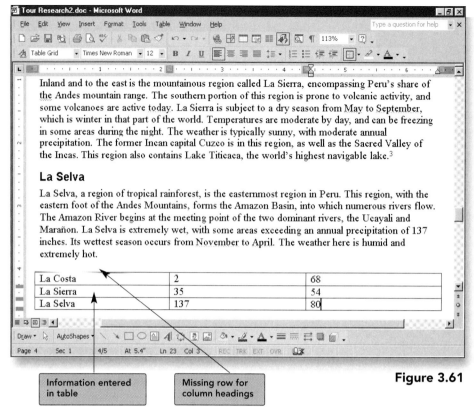

Inland and to the east is the mountainous region called La Sierra, encompassing Peru's share of the Andes mountain range. The southern portion of this region is prone to volcanic activity, and some volcanoes are active today. La Sierra is subject to a dry season from May to September, which is winter in that part of the world. Temperatures are moderate by day, and can be freezing in some areas during the night. The weather is typically sunny, with moderate annual precipitation. The former Incan capital Cuzco is in this region, as well as the Sacred Valley of the Incas. This region also contains Lake Titicaca, the world's highest navigable lake.[3]

La Selva

La Selva, a region of tropical rainforest, is the easternmost region in Peru. This region, with the eastern foot of the Andes Mountains, forms the Amazon Basin, into which numerous rivers flow. The Amazon River begins at the meeting point of the two dominant rivers, the Ucayali and Marañon. La Selva is extremely wet, with some areas exceeding an annual precipitation of 137 inches. Its wettest season occurs from November to April. The weather here is humid and extremely hot.

La Costa	2	68
La Sierra	35	54
La Selva	137	80

Information entered in table

Missing row for column headings

Figure 3.61

Inserting a Row

After looking at the table, you realize you forgot to include a row above the data to display the column headings.

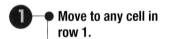

1 ● Move to any cell in row 1.

● Choose T**a**ble/**I**nsert/Rows **A**bove.

● Click in the new row to deselect the row.

Your screen should be similar to Figure 3.62

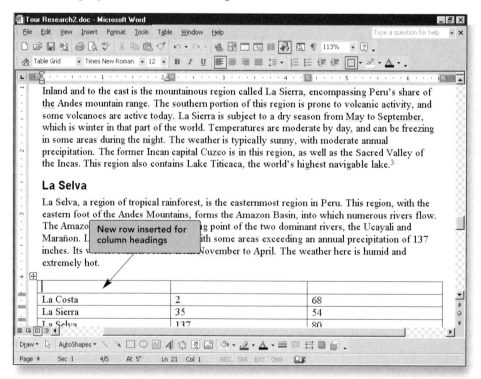

Inland and to the east is the mountainous region called La Sierra, encompassing Peru's share of the Andes mountain range. The southern portion of this region is prone to volcanic activity, and some volcanoes are active today. La Sierra is subject to a dry season from May to September, which is winter in that part of the world. Temperatures are moderate by day, and can be freezing in some areas during the night. The weather is typically sunny, with moderate annual precipitation. The former Incan capital Cuzco is in this region, as well as the Sacred Valley of the Incas. This region also contains Lake Titicaca, the world's highest navigable lake.[3]

La Selva

La Selva, a region of tropical rainforest, is the easternmost region in Peru. This region, with the eastern foot of the Andes Mountains, forms the Amazon Basin, into which numerous rivers flow. The Amazo[New row inserted for column headings]g point of the two dominant rivers, the Ucayali and Marañon. L[...]th some areas exceeding an annual precipitation of 137 inches. Its w[...]November to April. The weather here is humid and extremely hot.

La Costa	2	68
La Sierra	35	54
La Selva	137	80

Figure 3.62

Now you are ready to add the text for the headings.

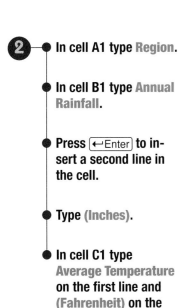

2 • In cell A1 type Region.

• In cell B1 type Annual Rainfall.

• Press ←Enter to insert a second line in the cell.

• Type (Inches).

• In cell C1 type Average Temperature on the first line and (Fahrenheit) on the second.

Your screen should be similar to Figure 3.63

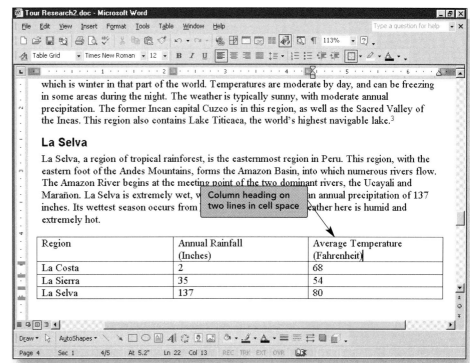

Figure 3.63

Sizing a Table

The table is much larger than it needs to be. To quickly reduce the overall table size, you can drag the resize handle □. This handle appears whenever the mouse pointer rests over the table. Once the table is smaller, you then want to center it between the margins.

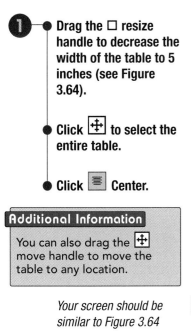

1 • Drag the □ resize handle to decrease the width of the table to 5 inches (see Figure 3.64).

• Click ⊞ to select the entire table.

• Click ▤ Center.

Additional Information

You can also drag the ⊞ move handle to move the table to any location.

Your screen should be similar to Figure 3.64

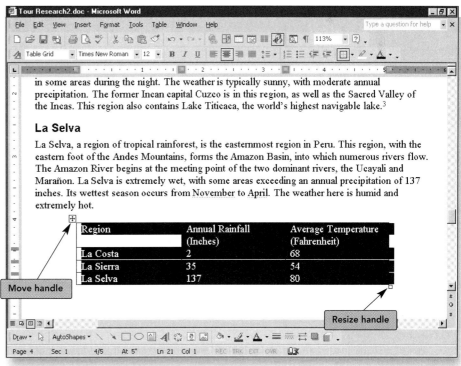

Figure 3.64

Formatting a Table

To enhance the appearance of the table, you can apply many different formats to the cells. This is similar to adding formatting to a document, except the formatting affects the selected cells only.

You want the entries in the cells A1 through C1, and B2 through C4, to be centered in their cell spaces. As you continue to modify the table, many cells can be selected and changed at the same time. You can select areas of a table using the Select command on the Table menu. However, it is often faster to use the procedures described in the table below.

Area to Select	Procedure
Cell 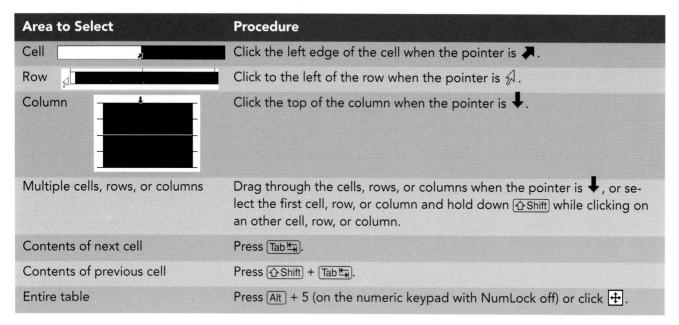	Click the left edge of the cell when the pointer is ➚.
Row	Click to the left of the row when the pointer is ➚.
Column	Click the top of the column when the pointer is ⬇.
Multiple cells, rows, or columns	Drag through the cells, rows, or columns when the pointer is ⬇, or select the first cell, row, or column and hold down ⬆Shift while clicking on an other cell, row, or column.
Contents of next cell	Press Tab⇥.
Contents of previous cell	Press ⬆Shift + Tab⇥.
Entire table	Press Alt + 5 (on the numeric keypad with NumLock off) or click ⊹.

1
- Select cells A1 through C1.
- Click ▤ Center.
- In the same manner, center cells B2 through C4.
- Click on any cell of the table.

Your screen should be similar to Figure 3.65

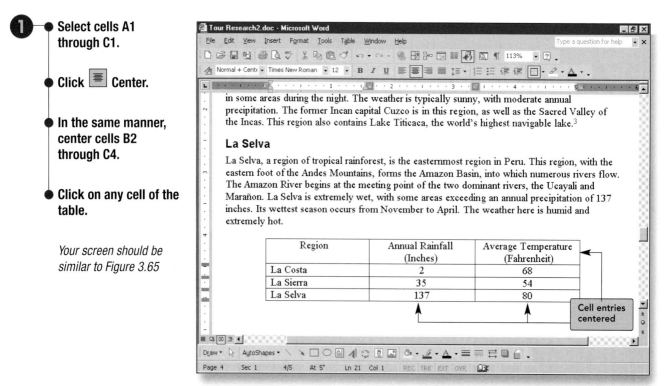

Figure 3.65

A quicker way to apply formats to a table is to use the table AutoFormat feature. This feature includes built-in combinations of formats that can be applied to a table. The AutoFormats consist of a combination of fonts, colors, patterns, borders, and alignment settings.

2 ● **Choose Table/Table AutoFormat.**

Your screen should be similar to Figure 3.66

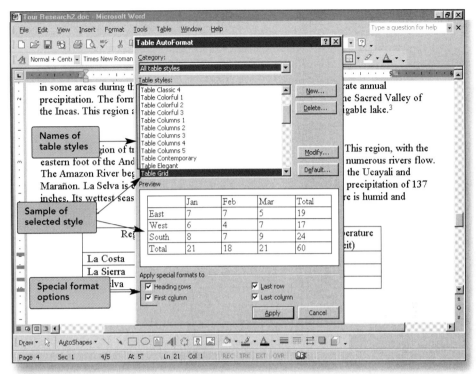

Figure 3.66

From the AutoFormat dialog box, you select the format design you want to apply to the table. The Preview area shows how the selected format will look.

3 ● **Select several names from the Table styles list and look at the samples in the Preview box.**

● **Select Table Colorful 2.**

● **Clear the First Column, Last Row, and Last Column special format options.**

● **Click** Apply **.**

● **Center the table again.**

● **Click outside the table to deselect it.**

● **Click** 🖫 **Save.**

Your screen should be similar to Figure 3.67

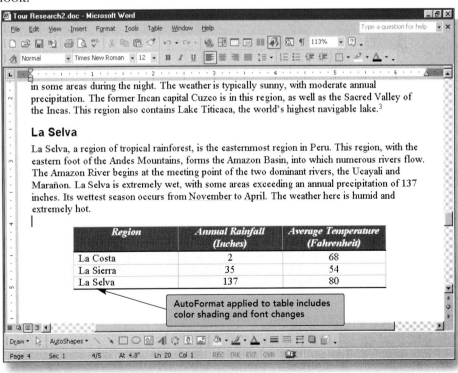

Figure 3.67

Additional Information

Use the Table Normal style to restore the default table style.

The table is reformatted to the new design. The table lines now appear gray, indicating they will not print and are only displayed to help you while entering data on screen. Color shading is applied to the top row along with a change in the text color and italics. Using AutoFormat was much faster than applying these features individually.

Sorting a List

Additional Information

MLA formatting for the Works Cited page also requires that the page is a separate numbered page with the title "Works Cited" centered 1 inch from the top margin. It should also be double-spaced, as is the entire report.

The last page of the report contains the list of works cited in the report. According to the MLA style, each work directly referenced in the paper must appear in alphabetical order by author's last name. The first line is even with the left margin, and subsequent lines of the same work are indented .5 inch. This page needs to be alphabetized and formatted. To quickly arrange the references in alphabetical order, you can sort the list.

concept 7

Sort

7 Word can quickly arrange or **sort** text, numbers or data in lists or tables in alphabetical, numeric, or date order based on the first character in each paragraph. The sort order can be ascending (A to Z, 0 to 9, or earliest to latest date) or descending (Z to A, 9 to 0, or latest to earliest date).

1 ● Move to the last page of the document.

● Select the list of references.

● Choose T**a**ble/**S**ort.

Your screen should be similar to Figure 3.68

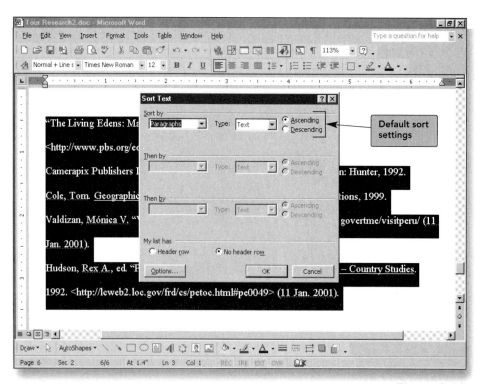

Figure 3.68

The table on the next page describes the rules that are used when sorting.

Sort By	Rules
Text	First, items beginning with punctuation marks or symbols (such as !, #, $, %, or &) are sorted.
	Second, items beginning with numbers are sorted. Dates are treated as three-digit numbers.
	Third, items beginning with letters are sorted.
Numbers	All characters except numbers are ignored. The numbers can be in any location in a paragraph.
Date	Valid date separators include hyphens, forward slashes (/), commas, and periods. Colons (:) are valid time separators. If unable to recognize a date or time, Word places the item at the beginning or end of the list (depending on whether you are sorting in ascending or descending order).
Field results	If an entire field (such as a last name) is the same for two items, Word next evaluates subsequent fields (such as a first name) according to the specified sort options.

When a tie occurs, Word uses the first non-identical character in each item to determine which item should come first.

The default Sort Text settings will sort by text and paragraphs in ascending order.

2 ● Click OK.

● Click 🄰 Styles and Formatting.

● Choose the Body Text Indent style.

● Close the task pane.

● Deselect the list of references.

Your screen should be similar to Figure 3.69

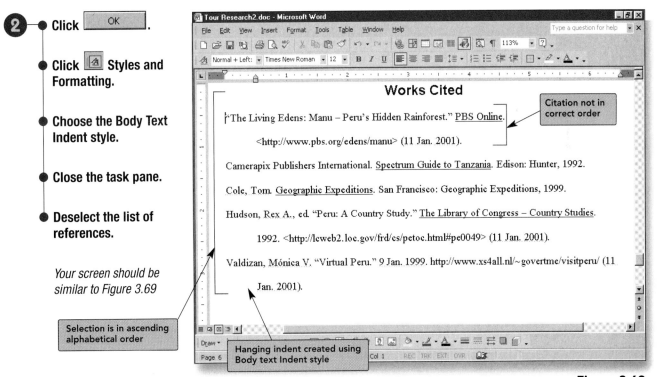

Selection is in ascending alphabetical order

Hanging indent created using Body text Indent style

Figure 3.69

The list is in ascending alphabetical order. Entries that are longer than one line appear with a hanging indent. Notice, however, that the citation for "The Living Edens . . ." is still at the top of this list. This is because Word sorts punctuation first. You will need to move this item to below the citation for Hudson.

3 ● Select the entire "The Living Edens . . ." citation and drag it to below the Hudson citation.

Your screen should be similar to Figure 3.70

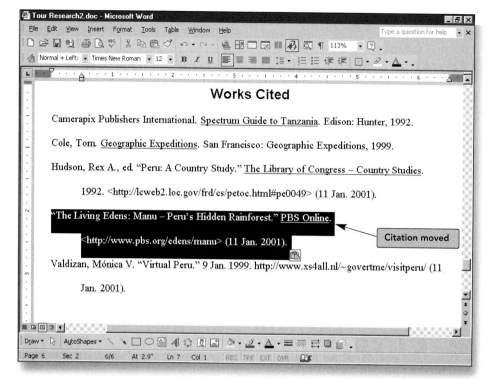

Figure 3.70

Creating Headers and Footers

Next you want to add information in a header and footer to the report.

concept 8

Header and Footer

8 Headers and footers provide information that typically appears at the top and bottom of each page in a document and helps the reader locate information in a document. A **header** is a line or several lines of text at the top of each page just above the top margin line. The header usually contains the title and the section of the document. A **footer** is a line or several lines of text at the bottom of every page just below the bottom margin line. The footer usually contains the page number and perhaps the date. Headers and footers can also contain graphics, such as a company logo.

The same header and footer can be used throughout a document, or a different header and footer can be used in different sections of a document. For example, a unique header or footer can be used in one section and a different one in another section. You can also have a unique header or footer on the first page, or omitted entirely from the first page, or use a different header and footer on odd and even pages.

Adding a Header

You want the report header to display your name and the page number.

1 ● Move to the Tanzania heading on page 2.

● Choose **V**iew/**H**eader and Footer.

Your screen should be similar to Figure 3.71

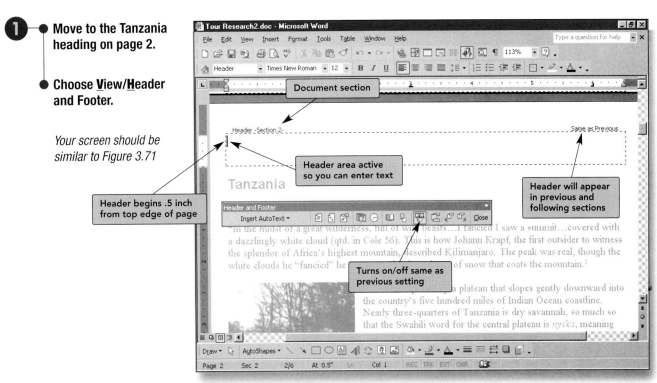

Figure 3.71

The document dims, the header area becomes active, and the Header and Footer toolbar is displayed. Notice that the information above the header area identifies the section location of the document where the insertion point is positioned, in this case, section 2. In addition, in the upper right corner the message "Same as Previous" is displayed. When this setting is on, the header in the sections before and after the section in which you are entering a header will have the same header. Because you do not want the title page in section 1 to have a header, you will turn off the Same as Previous option.

2 ● Click 🖳 **Same as Previous.**

Your screen should be similar to Figure 3.72

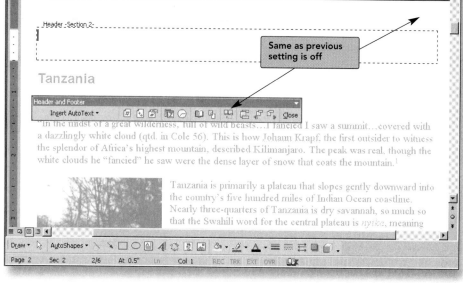

Same as previous setting is off

Figure 3.72

You type in the header as if it were a mini-document. The header and footer text can be formatted just like any other text. In addition, you can control the placement of the header and footer text by specifying where it should appear: left-aligned, centered, or right-aligned in the header or footer space. You will enter your name followed by the page number, right-aligned.

3 ● Type **your name.**

● Press [Spacebar].

● Click 🔢 **Insert Page Number.**

● Click 🔳 **Align Right.**

Another Method

You can also press [Tab⇥] once to center-align and twice to right-align the header text.

Your screen should be similar to Figure 3.73

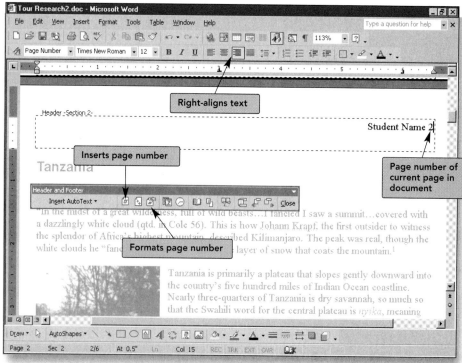

Right-aligns text

Inserts page number

Student Name 2

Page number of current page in document

Formats page number

Figure 3.73

The page number 2 is displayed, because that is the current page in the document. You do not want the title page included in the page numbering, but instead want to begin page numbering with the first page of section 2.

4 ● Click  **Format Page Number.**

Your screen should be similar to Figure 3.74

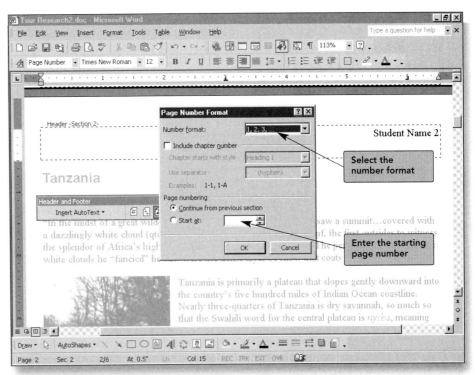

Figure 3.74

The Page Number Format dialog box is used to change the format of page numbers, to include chapter numbers, and to change the page numbering sequence. The default page numbering setting continues the numbering from the first section. To reset the page number sequence to begin section 2 with page 1,

5 ● **Choose Start At.**

● Click ___OK___ .

Your screen should be similar to Figure 3.75

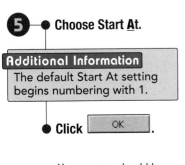

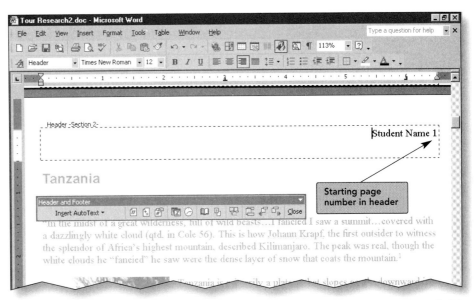

Figure 3.75

The header now displays "1" as the current page number.

Adding a Footer

You want to display the date in the footer. To quickly add this information, you will use an AutoText entry.

1
- Click 🔲 **Switch Between Header and Footer.**

- Click 🔲 **Same as Previous to turn off this option.**

- Click [Insert AutoText ▾].

- **Choose Created on.**

- **Right-align the entry.**

Your screen should be similar to Figure 3.76

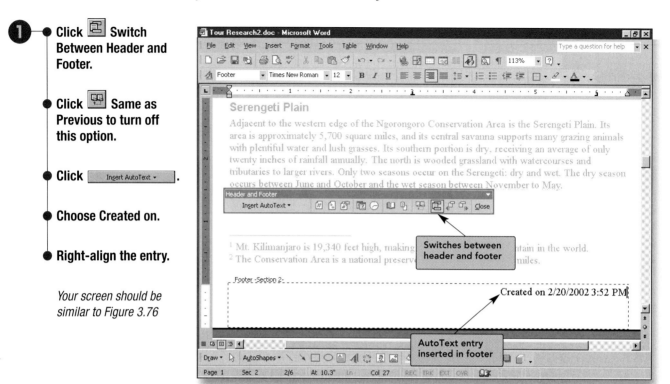

Figure 3.76

The AutoText entry is displayed followed by the date and time.

2 ● Close the Header and Footer toolbar.

● In section 2, scroll down to see the bottom of page 1 and the top of page 2.

Your screen should be similar to Figure 3.77

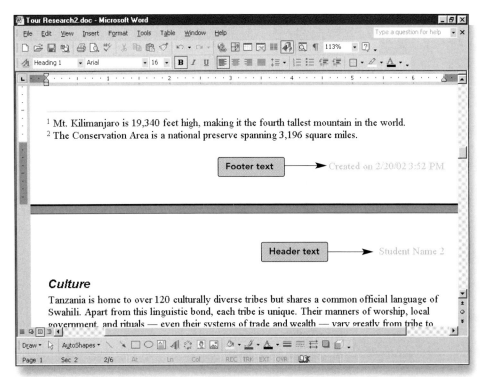

Figure 3.77

The document area is active again, and the header and footer text appears dimmed.

Checking the Document

Before you print the report, you want to check the spelling and grammar of the entire document, including the footnotes, header, and footer. You also want to check the formatting of the document for consistency. Many times when creating a long document, it is easy to format areas differently that should be formatted the same. For example, if your headings are mostly formatted as Heading 2 styles, but you accidentally format a heading with a Heading 3 style, Word can locate the inconsistent formatting and quickly make the appropriate correction for you. Using the formatting consistency checker can give your documents a more professional appearance.

Redisplaying Spelling and Grammar Errors

First you will turn on the display of spelling and grammar errors again and then spell and grammar check the document.

1 ● Move to the top of page 1 of section 2.

● Choose **Tools/Options/Spelling and Grammar.**

● Select Hide spelling errors in this document to clear the checkmark.

● Select H**i**de grammatical errors in this document to clear the checkmark.

● Click [OK] .

● Click [ABC] Spelling and Grammar.

● Choose I**g**nore All for all proper names, special terms and abbreviations. Respond appropriately to any other located errors.

● Click [OK] to end spelling and grammar checking.

Your screen should be similar to Figure 3.78

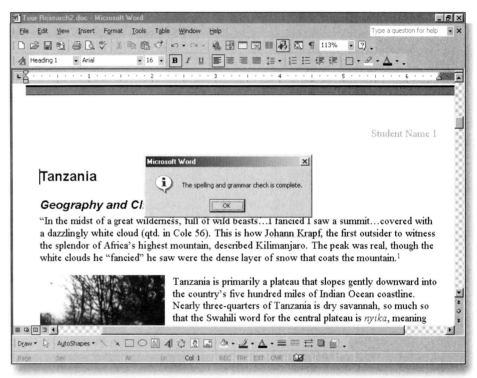

Figure 3.78

The spelling and grammar checker first checked the document text for errors, then footnotes, and finally headers anf footers.

Checking Formatting Inconsistencies

Next, you will turn on the feature to check for formatting inconsistencies. Word identifies inconsistencies with a blue wavy underline.

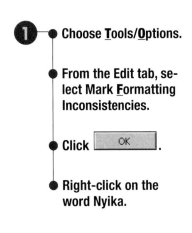

1 Choose **T**ools/**O**ptions.

● From the Edit tab, select Mark **F**ormatting Inconsistencies.

● Click [OK].

● Right-click on the word Nyika.

Your screen should be similar to Figure 3.79

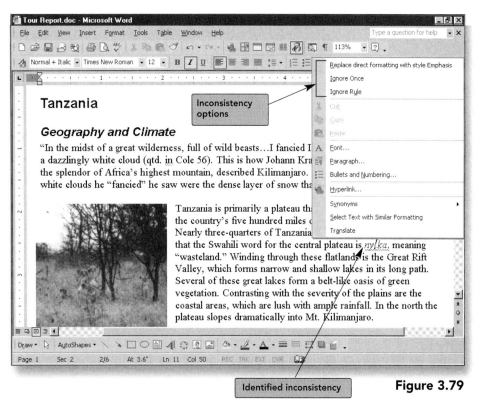

Figure 3.79

The first identified formatting inconsistency is for the italics applied to the word "nyika."

When checking for formatting inconsistencies, Word looks for occurrences of similar formatting that you have applied directly to text, of styles that contain additional direct formatting, and of direct formatting that matches styles that are applied elsewhere in the document. If two occurrences of formatting are markedly different, then they are not identified as inconsistent. However, in cases where the formatting is very similar, they are identified as inconsistent. In this case, the identified inconsistency is because the formatting was applied directly to the word using the italics feature, and the same result could be obtained by using the style Emphasis. Since changing this will not affect how the word looks, you will ignore the suggestion.

②━● **Choose Ignore Once.**

Your screen should be similar to Figure 3.80

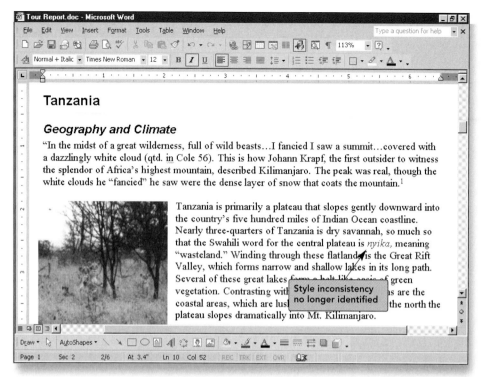

Figure 3.80

The wavy blue underline is cleared from the document.

③━● **Scroll to page 4 to see the next located occurrence in the Machu Picchu heading.**

● **Right-click on Machu Picchu.**

Your screen should be similar to Figure 3.81

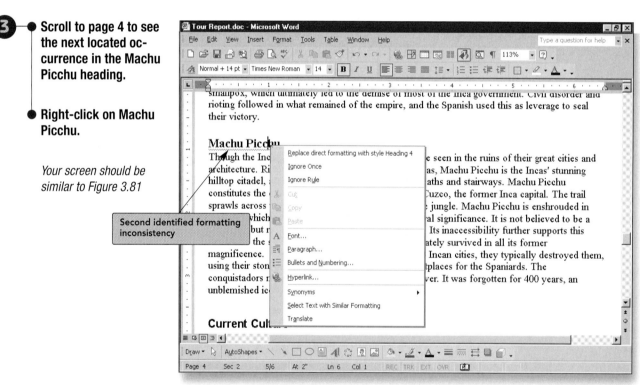

Figure 3.81

The suggested change is to replace the direct formatting of this text (14 points and bold) with the equivalent heading style. Because you want the topic to appear in the table of contents, you will replace the formatting with the Heading 4 style. (The last inconsistency is in the Works Cited heading. You want the heading to appear in the table of contents listing.)

4 ● Choose Replace direct formatting with style Heading 4.

● Move to the Works Cited page.

● Right-click on the Works Cited title.

Your screen should be similar to Figure 3.82

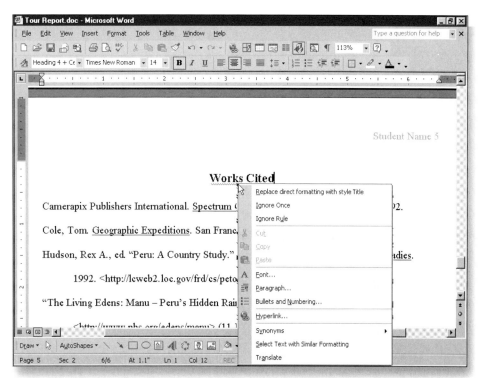

Figure 3.82

The suggested style change is to use the Title style. In this case, you want to change it to a Heading 1 style so it will appear in the table of contents. You will need to make this change directly.

5 ● Choose Heading 1 from the Styles and Formatting task pane list box.

● Click 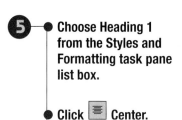 Center.

● Close the task pane.

● Choose tools/Options/ Edit/Mark formatting inconsistencies to turn off this feature.

Your screen should be similar to Figure 3.83

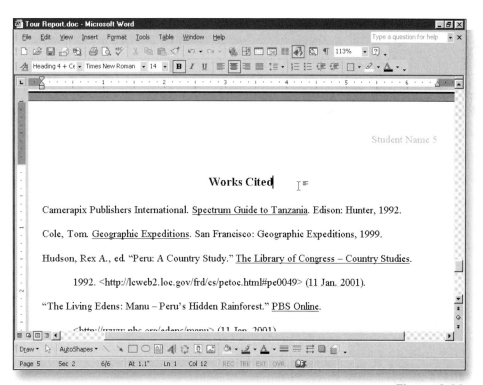

Figure 3.83

1 • Move to the top of the document.

• Right-click on the table of contents to display the shortcut menu.

• Choose **U**pdate Field.

Another Method

You can also press F9 to quickly update a field.

• Choose Update **e**ntire table.

• Click [OK].

• Scroll the window to see the entire table of contents.

• Click outside the table of contents to deselect it.

Your screen should be similar to Figure 3.84

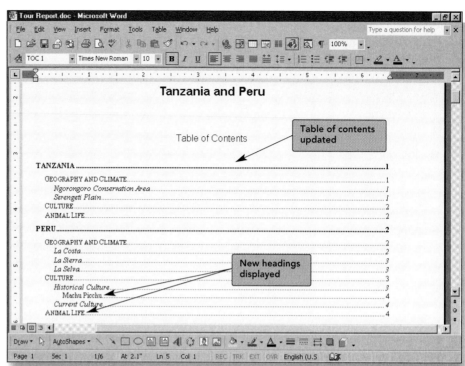

Figure 3.84

Updating a Table of Contents

You have made many modifications to the report since generating the table of contents, so you want to update the listing. Because the table of contents is a field, if you add or remove headings, rearrange topics, or make other changes that affect the table of contents listing, you can quickly update the table of contents. In this case, you have added pictures and a table that may have affected the paging of the document, and you changed two headings to heading styles. You will update the table of contents to ensure that the page references are accurate and that all headings are included.

The page numbers referenced by each table of contents hyperlink have been updated as needed and the two new topics are listed.

Printing Selected Pages

You are now ready to print the report.

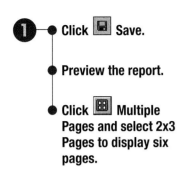

1 ● Click 🖫 Save.

● Preview the report.

● Click ▦ Multiple Pages and select 2x3 Pages to display six pages.

Another Method
The menu equivalent is View/Zoom/Many Pages.

Your screen should be similar to Figure 3.85

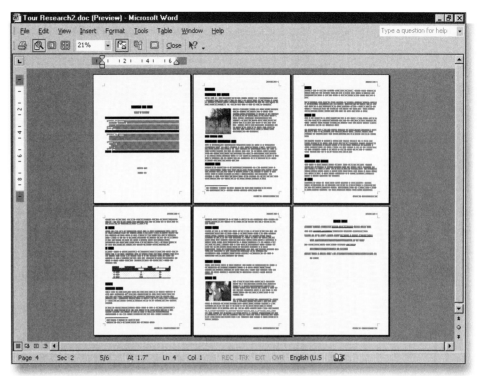

Figure 3.85

You would like to print only the first, second, fourth, and sixth pages of the document. To do this, you use the Print dialog box to select the pages you want to print. When printing pages in different sections, the page number and section number must be identified in the page range.

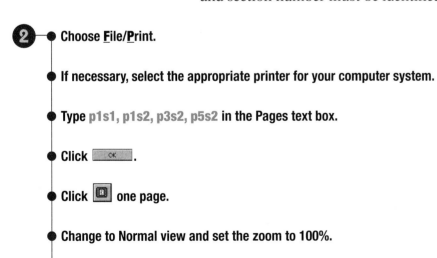

2 ● Choose File/Print.

● If necessary, select the appropriate printer for your computer system.

● Type p1s1, p1s2, p3s2, p5s2 in the Pages text box.

● Click OK .

● Click ▣ one page.

● Change to Normal view and set the zoom to 100%.

● Close the file and exit Word.

Your printed output should be similar to that shown in the case study at the beginning of the lab.

concept summary

LAB 3

Creating Reports and Tables

Style (WD3.6)

A **style** is a set of formats that is assigned a name.

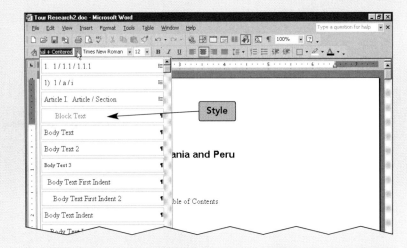

Section (WD3.25)

To format different parts of a document differently, you can divide a document into **sections**.

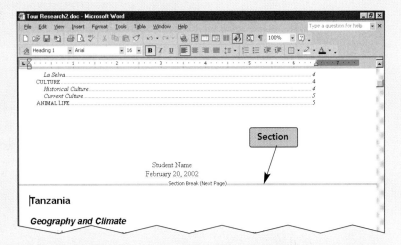

Footnote and Endnote (WD3.28)

A **footnote** is a source reference or text offering additional explanation that is placed at the bottom of a page. An **endnote** is also a source reference or long comment that typically appears at the end of a document.

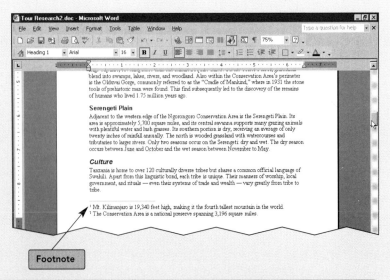

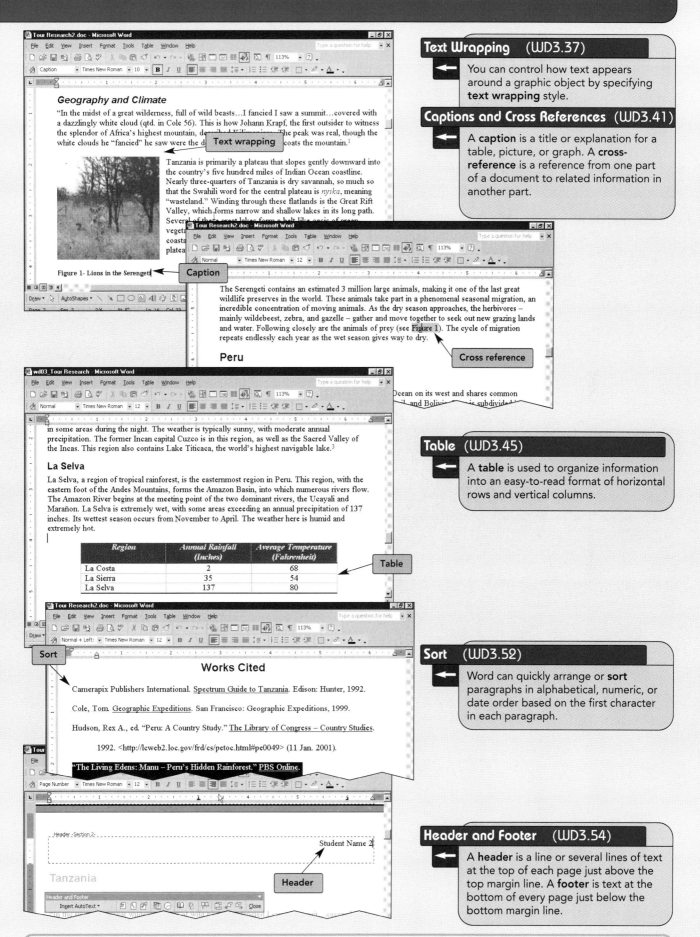

Text Wrapping (WD3.37)

You can control how text appears around a graphic object by specifying **text wrapping** style.

Captions and Cross References (WD3.41)

A **caption** is a title or explanation for a table, picture, or graph. A **cross-reference** is a reference from one part of a document to related information in another part.

Table (WD3.45)

A **table** is used to organize information into an easy-to-read format of horizontal rows and vertical columns.

Sort (WD3.52)

Word can quickly arrange or **sort** paragraphs in alphabetical, numeric, or date order based on the first character in each paragraph.

Header and Footer (WD3.54)

A **header** is a line or several lines of text at the top of each page just above the top margin line. A **footer** is text at the bottom of every page just below the bottom margin line.

lab review

LAB **3**

Creating Reports and Tables

key terms

caption   WD3.41

cell   WD3.45

character style   WD3.6

cross-reference   WD3.41

Document Map   WD3.31

drawing layer   WD3.37

endnote   WD3.28

floating object   WD3.37

footervWD3.54

footnote   WD3.28

header   WD3.54

heading style   WD3.6

inline object   WD3.37

note pane   WD3.30

note reference mark   WD3.28

note separator   WD3.28

note text   WD3.28

paragraph style   WD3.6

pane   WD3.30

section   WD3.25

section break   WD3.25

sort   WD3.52

style   WD3.6

table   WD3.45

table reference   WD3.47

mous skills

The Microsoft Office User Specialist (MOUS) certification program is designed to measure your proficiency in performing basic tasks using the Office XP applications. Getting certified demonstrates that you have the skills and provides a valuable industry credential for employment. After completing this lab, you have learned the following Microsoft Office User Specialist skills:

Skill	Description	Page
Inserting and Modifying Text	Apply character styles	WD3.6
Creating and Modifying Paragraphs	Apply bullet, outline, and numbering format to paragraphs	WD3.6
	Apply paragraph styles	WD3.6
Formatting Documents	Create and modify a header and footer	WD3.54
	Modify document layout and page setup options	WD3.25
	Create and modify tables	WD3.45
Managing Documents	Manage files and folders for documents	WD3.14

command summary

Command	Shortcut Keys	Button	Action
<u>F</u>ile/Page Set<u>u</u>p/Layout/<u>V</u>ertical Alignment			Aligns text vertically on a page
<u>V</u>iew/<u>D</u>ocument Map		🔲	Displays or hides Document Map pane
<u>V</u>iew/<u>H</u>eader and Footer			Displays header and footer areas
<u>V</u>iew/Foot<u>n</u>otes			Hides or displays note pane
<u>V</u>iew/<u>Z</u>oom/<u>M</u>any Pages		🔡	Displays two or more pages in document window
Insert/<u>B</u>reak/<u>P</u>age/Break	Ctrl + Enter		Inserts a hard page break
Insert/Page N<u>u</u>mbers			Specifies page number location
Insert/Refere<u>n</u>ce/Foot<u>n</u>ote	Alt + Ctrl + F		Inserts footnote reference at insertion point
Insert/Refere<u>n</u>ce/<u>C</u>aption			Inserts caption at insertion point
Insert/Refere<u>n</u>ce/Cross-<u>r</u>eference			Inserts cross-reference at insertion point
Insert/Refere<u>n</u>ce/In<u>d</u>ex and Tables/Table of <u>C</u>ontents			Inserts table of contents
F<u>o</u>rmat/<u>S</u>tyle		Normal ▾	Applies selected style to paragraph or characters
F<u>o</u>rmat/P<u>i</u>cture/Layout/Wrapping Style		🖼	Specifies how text will wrap around picture
F<u>o</u>rmat/<u>S</u>tyles and Formatting		🔳	Opens Styles and Formatting task pane
<u>T</u>ools/<u>O</u>ptions/View/ScreenTips			Turns off and on the display of ScreenTips
<u>T</u>ools/<u>O</u>ptions/Spelling & Grammar			Changes settings associated with the Spelling and Grammar checking feature
Ta<u>b</u>le/<u>I</u>nsert Table		🔲	Inserts table at insertion point
Ta<u>b</u>le/<u>I</u>nsert/Rows <u>A</u>bove			Inserts a new row in table above selected row
Ta<u>b</u>le/Con<u>v</u>ert/Te<u>x</u>t to Table			Converts selected text to table format
Ta<u>b</u>le/Table Auto<u>F</u>ormat			Applies selected format to table
Ta<u>b</u>le/<u>S</u>ort			Rearranges items in a selection into sorted order

Terminology

screen identification

1. In the following Word screen, letters identify important elements. Enter the correct screen element in the space provided.

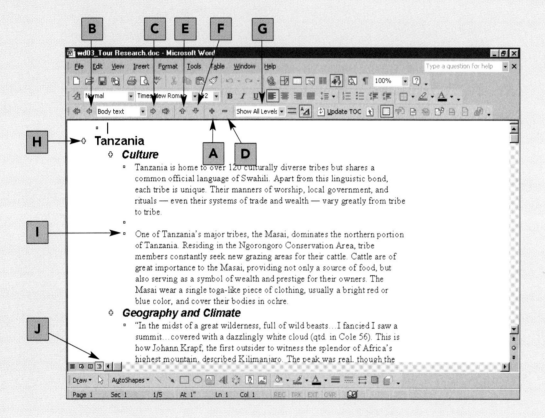

A. _____   F. _____

B. _____   G. _____

C. _____   H. _____

D. _____   I. _____

E. _____   J. _____

matching

Match the item on the left with the correct description on the right.

1. note pane	_____	**a.** text that appears at the bottom of each page below the bottom margin line
2. table of contents	_____	**b.** graphic placed at the insertion point
3. footer	_____	**c.** source reference displayed at the bottom of a page
4. caption	_____	**d.** lower section of workspace that displays footnote text
5. footnote	_____	**e.** instructs Word to end one set of format settings and begin another
6. section break	_____	**f.** a title or explanation for a table, picture, or graph
7. tight wrap	_____	**g.** a listing of the topics that appear in the document
8. Document Map	_____	**h.** text closely follows contours around a graphic
9. inline image	_____	**i.** reference from one part of the document to another part
10. cross-reference	_____	**j.** displays the headings in the document

multiple choice

Circle the correct response to the questions below.

1. Styles can be applied to _____.
   a. characters and paragraphs
   b. documents and paragraphs
   c. words and characters
   d. characters and documents

2. A _____ is inserted automatically when a new page is created in a document.
   a. hard page break
   b. section break
   c. soft page break
   d. page division

3. Source references or text offering additional explanation that are placed at the bottom of a page are _____.
   a. endnotes
   b. footnotes
   c. reference notes
   d. page notes

4. The graphic text-wrapping style(s) that can be used in Word are _____.
   a. inline
   b. square
   c. through
   d. all the above

5. A _____ is a title or explanation for a table, picture, or graph.
   a. statement
   b. cross-reference
   c. caption
   d. footnote

6. A cross-reference is a _____ to another location.
   a. caption
   b. hyperlink
   c. footnote
   d. endnote

7. Text sorted in _____ order appears alphabetically from A to Z.
   a. ordered
   b. descending
   c. ascending
   d. rescending

8. The _____ pane displays the headings in your document.
   a. Document Map
   b. Note
   c. Heading
   d. Outline

9. A _____ object is inserted in the drawing layer and can be positioned precisely on the page.
   a. fixed
   b. floating
   c. layered
   d. pasted

10. A(n)_____ displays information in horizontal rows and vertical columns.
    a. Document Map
    b. cell reference
    c. object
    d. table

true/false

Circle the correct answer to the following questions.

1. A style is a named group of formats.		True	False
2. Outline view is the best view to use while entering the body of a document.		True	False
3. The Document Preview pane displays the headings in your document.		True	False
4. A caption can be displayed below a graphic to identify the object.		True	False
5. A cross-reference can be placed within a document to refer back to a figure or other reference in the document.		True	False
6. A hyperlink allows you to jump to another location in a document, another document, or to the Web.		True	False
7. Outline view is used to apply different formats to different parts of a document.		True	False

8. A header is text that prints at the bottom of every page just above the
   bottom margin line.   True   False

9. Footnotes are source references or long comments that typically appear
   at the end of a document.   True   False

10. How text appears surrounding a graphic object depends on the
    text wrapping style.   True   False

Concepts

fill-in

1. A(n)_____ is a named set of formats that affects an entire paragraph.

2. A title or explanation for a table, picture or graph is a(n)_____.

3. Pictures are inserted by default as _____   _____.

4. When you change the wrapping style of a picture, the object changes to a(n)_____

   _____.

5. Use _____ in documents to reference from one part of your document to

   another.

6. The sort order can be either _____ or _____.

7. Headers are displayed _____ the top margin line and footers are displayed _____ the

   bottom margin line.

8. A table consists of horizontal _____, vertical _____, and _____.

9. A cross-reference _____ jumps to the referenced location in the document when clicked.

10. A(n)_____ is typically a source reference that appears at the end of a document.

discussion questions

1. Discuss the differences between footnotes and endnotes. When should notes be added to a
   document?

2. Use Help to learn more about how to position text and graphic objects on a page. Discuss how you
   can move and place graphic objects in a document. Discuss the different wrapping options.

3. Discuss how the Document Map can be used in a document. What must be present for the
   Document Map to display text?

4. Discuss the cross-reference and caption features. When would it be appropriate to use them in a document?

5. Describe the different methods you can use to create a table and explain when they should be used.

6. What is the significance of using a column and row format in tables? How are the rows and columns labeled?

Hands-On Exercises

rating system

★ Easy

★★ Moderate

★★★ Difficult

step-by-step

★ Creating an Outline

1. The University Recreation Center provides handouts on different topics related to exercising and health. You are just starting work on a new handout about how to prepare for a workout. To help organize your thoughts, you decide to create an outline of the main topics to be included. Your completed outline is shown here.

   a. Open a new blank document. Switch to Outline view. Turn on formatting marks.

   b. The topics you want to discuss are shown on the next page. Enter these topics at the outline level indicated, pressing ⎌Enter at the end of each.

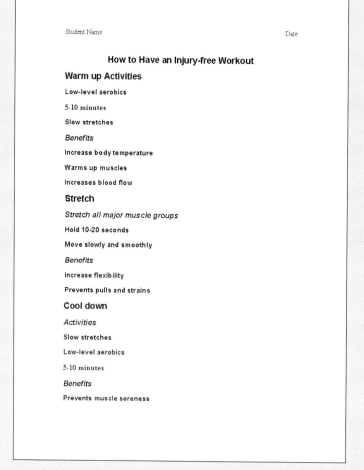

Stretch (Level 1)

Stretch all major muscle groups (Level 2)

Hold 10–20 seconds (Level 3)

Move slowly and smoothly (Level 3)

Do not bounce (Level 3)

Benefits (Level 2)

Increase flexibility (Level 2)

Prevent pulls and strains (Level 2)

Warm up (Level 1)

Activities (Level 2)

Low-level aerobics (Level 3)

5–10 minutes (Level 4)

Slow stretches (Level 3)

Benefits (Level 2)

Increases body temperature (Level 3)

Warms up muscles (Level 3)

Cool Down (Level 1)

Benefits (Level 2)

Prevents muscle soreness (Level 3)

Activities (Level 2)

Slow stretches (Level 3)

Low-level aerobics (Level 3)

5–10 minutes (Level 4)

   c. Move the "Warm up" topic and all subtopics above the "Stretch" topic.

   d. In the "Stretch" topic, change the subtopics "Increases flexibility" and "Prevent pulls and strains" to level 3.

   e. In the "Cool down" topic, move "Benefits" below "Activities."

   f. Insert a new level 3 line, **Increases blood flow**, as the last subtopic under warm-up benefits. Delete the "Do not bounce" topic.

   g. Turn off formatting marks. Switch to Normal view.

   h. Enter your name and the date centered in a header.

   i. Print the outline.

   j. Save the outline as Workout. Close the file.

★ Modifying an Outline

2. You are preparing a lecture for your class on the Internet and World Wide Web. You have started an outline of topics that you want to discuss, but it still needs some work. Your completed outline is shown here.

   a. Open the document wd03_Internet.

   b. Enter the title **The Internet and World Wide Web** above the list. Enter a blank line below the title. Apply the Title style to the title.

   c. Switch to Outline view.

   d. Change the levels of the following topics to the level indicated:
   CERN—Level 3
   Sends e-mail to and from a list of subscribers—Level 5
   Messages sent to your personal inbox—Level 5
   E-mail messages are not sent to your personal inbox—Level 5
   Messages are posted to news-group sites—Level 5
   Research—Level 3

   e. Demote the "Use the WWW" topic and all subtopics below it two levels.

   f. Delete the topic "E-mail messages are not sent to your personal inbox."

   g. Enter the new topic **Public discussions** as the first topic under "Newsgroups" (level 5).

   h. Move "Use the WWW" and all subtopics under it to below "Send E-mail."

   i. Enter your name and the current date right-aligned in a header.

   j. Switch to Print Layout view.

   k. Preview and print the outline.

   l. Save the outline as Internet2.

Student Name · February 20, 2002

Messages are posted to newsgroup sites

Chat groups

Direct "live" communications

Internet Relay Chat (IRC) is by far the most popular

Student Name · February 20, 2002

The Internet and World Wide Web

The Internet

Definition

History

Advanced Research Project Agency Network (ARPANET)

CERN

Uses

Send E-mail

Use the WWW

Definition

Applications

Communication

Shopping

Web Storefronts

Web Auctions

Research

Entertainment

Participate in Discussion Groups

Mailing Lists

Sends e-mail to and from a list of subscribers

Messages sent to your personal inbox

Newsgroups

Public discussions

★★ Creating a Table

3. You work for the town of Glendale and are putting together a list of the antique shops to give to visitors along with a map showing the location of each shop. You have entered the shop names, specialties, and map locations in a document. You now want to sort the list and display it as a table. Your completed table is shown here.

   a. Open the file wd03_Antique Shops.
   b. Enter the title **Glendale Antique Shops** above the list. Apply the Title style. Include a blank line below the title.
   c. Line up the columns of information by setting left tabs at the 1.5-inch and 3.5-inch positions on the ruler.
   d. Change the order of the list (excluding the heading line) so that it is sorted by the map location number in ascending order.
   e. Select the table text. Choose the Convert Text to Table command on the Table menu to convert the list to a table. Specify 3 columns as the table size, AutoFit to contents and to separate text at tabs.
   f. Apply a table AutoFormat of your choice to the table.
   g. Center the table.
   h. Color the title to match colors used in the table.
   i. Add a header to the document that displays your name left-aligned and the current date, right-aligned.
   j. Print the document.
   k. Save the document as Antique Shops2.

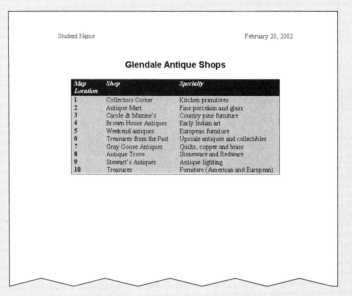

★★ Designing a Flyer

4. The Downtown Internet Cafe is planning a grand opening celebration. You have already started designing a flyer to advertise the event, but it still needs additional work. Your completed flyer is shown on the next page.

   a. Open the file wd03_Cafe Flyer.
   b. Change the left and right margins to 1 inch.
   c. Create the following table of data below the "Users pay . . ." paragraph.

Length of Time	Rate
Hour	$8.00
Half hour	$5.00

   d. Use Table/AutoFit/AutoFit to contents to size the table to the cell contents.
   e. Apply an AutoFormat of your choice to the table. Center the table.
   f. Add bullets to the four items under "The Downtown Internet Cafe combines." Add a different style bullet before the four items under "What to do at the Cafe."

g. Insert the picture wd03_coffee.wmf to the right of the first four bulleted items.

h. Insert the picture wd03_Computer User.wmf to the left of the second list of bulleted items.

i. Preview the document. Make any editing changes you feel are appropriate.

j. Enter your name and the date centered in the footer.

k. Save the document as Cafe Flyer2.

l. Print the document.

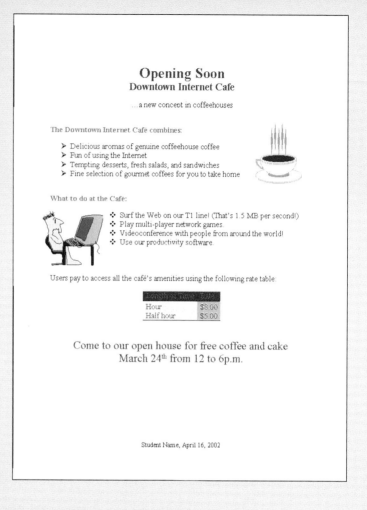

Formatting a Manuscript

★★ 5. You are a freelance writer and have written an article about the top ten scenic drives in the world.
★   You want to enhance the document before submitting it to several travel magazines. Your completed article is shown on the next page.

a. Open the file wd03_Scenic Drives.

b. Create a title page at the top of the document. Include the article title in Title style and your name and the current date centered below the title. Center the title page vertically.

c. Format the names of the top ten drives as Heading 1 styles. (*Hint:* use Format Painter.)

d. On a new page following the title page, add the heading **Table of Contents** formatted as Title style. Create a table of contents listing on this page. Use the Modern style and do not include the Title style headings in the listing.

e. Insert the picture wd03_Mountain to the left of the first paragraph in the Rocky Mountains section. Size the graphic appropriately and wrap the text to the right.

f. Add the following footnote to the end of the first sentence of the third paragraph: **This top 10 list was obtained from the Weissmann Travel Reports in the America Online Traveler's Corner**.

g. Number the pages, excluding the title page.

h. Preview the document and make any adjustments necessary.

i. Save the document as Scenic Drives2. Print the first 3 pages of the document.

Scenic Drives

Student Name
Date

Table of Contents

1

Top 10 Scenic Drives

The high road, it seems, is the road of choice: Routes through mountainous scenery dominated the nominations you sent in for Top 10 Scenic Drives. As one person wrote about the experience of hitting the top of one Rocky Mountain pass, "you'll think you've reached heaven."

Hyperbole competed with sentiment in many of the nominations we received; multiple exclamation points (AWESOME!!!!!) lined up as thick as billboards along an interstate, and in a few cases, memories of childhood drives revealed just how long it has been since the writer hit the road ("My strongest memories are from looking out the back window of my parents' station wagon").

For those whose memories of beautiful drives needs updating, let the following list of our top 10 picks for Scenic Drives, as nominated by online users and the correspondents and editors of Weissmann Travel Reports, serve as inspiration for your summer travel plans'. As usual, this month's ranking is not intended to be a popularity contest; while multiple nominations were taken into consideration when compiling the list, the final results also took into account the writers' ability to convey the beauty they traversed.

1. THE ROCKY MOUNTAINS

Three Rocky roads--Rocky Mountain National Park's Trail Ridge Road, Waterton-Glacier International Peace Park's Going to the Sun Road and the Icefields Parkway, located between Jasper and Banff National Parks in Alberta, Canada, were all nominated as the most scenic drive in the world. Each is lined with spectacular scenery, and for us to try to choose the "best" among them would be like saying that air is more important to human beings than water or food: They all have their strengths, and none could eliminate the others from contention. We're left with a three-way tie. Trail Ridge Road, the highest through-highway in the U.S., begins in Estes Park, Colorado, and winds along a route that takes in terrain ranging from ponderosa pine forests to tundra. Forested canyons, hanging valleys and glacial lakes punctuate the route. Going to the Sun Road, which runs for 50 miles/80 km from Lake McDonald to St. Mary, features stunning and inspiring vistas of alpine scenery (watch for the "Garden Wall," a landmark of the Continental Divide), while the Icefields Parkway is characterized by magnificent lakes, glacial ice fields, waterfalls

---

' This top 10 list was obtained from the Weissmann Travel Reports in the America Online Traveler's Corner.

2

Writing a Report

★ ★ **6.** You are a Physical Education major and have written a report on water exercises. The first page of
★   the document is where the table of contents will appear. Pages 2 through 4 contain the body of
your report. Several pages of your completed report are shown here. Use the features presented in
this lab to add the following to the report:

a. Open the file wd03_Water.

b. Create a new page at the beginning of
the document to be used as a title
page. Enter the report title, Acquatic
Fitness Routine, your name, and the date
centered on separate lines. Format the
report title using the title style.

c. Create a table of contents on the title
page below the date.

d. Center the title page vertically.

e. Insert the graphic wd03_Swimmer to the
left of the first paragraph of the report.
Wrap the text around the graphic.
Include a caption below the graphic.

f. Apply additional formats of your
choice to the report.

g. Include page numbers right-aligned in
a header. Do not number the
title page.

h. At the end of the document,
create a works cited page following the example in the lab.
Enter the following two reference sources:

McEnvoy, Joseph. *Fitness
Swimming: Lifetime Programs.*
Princeton: Princeton Book
Company Publishers, 1995.

President's Council on Physical
Fitness and Sports.
*AquaDynamics: Physical
Conditioning Through Water
Exercise.* Washington, DC:
Government Printing Office, 1981.

i. Save the document as Water2.
Print the report.

Aquatic Fitness Routine
Student Name
February 20, 2002

Table of Contents

Figure 1 In-pool Warm-up

In order to achieve and maintain the benefits of exercise, an aquatic exercise program must follow the main principles of a workout. It should begin with warm-up stretches on the pool deck, followed by an in-pool aerobic warm-up session. Then the actual conditioning activity begins, consisting of 20 to 30 minutes of vigorous "aerobic" activity. A cool-down period in the pool can end the session, although a toning period is recommended following the cool-down. The following section discusses the aquatic fitness routine in detail.

Warm-up Stretches

It is very important to include proper warm-up routines before each day's activity. Physiologically, the muscles need to be warmed slowly through increased circulation, and the heart rate needs to be raised gradually. Psychologically, each participant needs to begin to think about the workout and perhaps set some personal goals for the day. Warm-ups are also an important safety precaution. Cold, tight muscles are inefficient for a good workout and may tear with sudden movements.

A general idea to keep in mind while structuring a warm-up routine is to try to simulate the movements of the activity to be performed in the main body of the workout. The warm-up should simulate the workout movement but should be of a much lower intensity. Because of the nature of the exercises, they should be performed before entering the pool.

A good warm-up should move quickly but thoroughly from the top of the body to the bottom of the body. In lap swimming and aerobic workout, special attention should be given to these areas: shoulder complex, obliques, abdominal, groin, hamstrings, quadriceps, gastrocnemius.

Aerobic Warm-up Exercises

Once the participants have entered the pool, they need to slowly raise their heart rates and get their body temperatures acclimated to that of the pool. Some fun activities for a good aerobic warm-up are to walk, jog, skip, or hop back and forth the width of the pool. As further variation, participants can do front kicks or skips and hops across the pool width. Finally, long strides, called skiing, can be used across the pool width. There are several fun games, such as musical kick-board, water basketball, and tug of war, that may be appropriate for your group as an aerobic warm-up. These games should be played for approximately 5 minutes as a warm-up activity.

Conditioning Activities

Circuit Training: Circuit training is a conditioning activity using stations. Different activities are

Creating a FAQ

★ 1. The city Health Department receives a large number of calls concerning Alzheimer's disease. In response to the need for information on this topic, they are putting together a FAQ (Frequently Asked Questions) sheet with answers to the most frequently asked questions about the disease.
   - Open the file wd03_Alzheimer.
   - Use the Document Map to locate the headings in the document, and apply appropriate heading levels.
   - Number the list of ten warning signs.
   - Use the Format Painter to add bold and underlines to the first sentence of each of the ten warning signs.
   - Convert the scale for stages of Alzheimer's on the last page to a table (Use Table/Convert text to Table). Apply an AutoFormat of your choice to the table.
   - Display a page number at a position of your choice in the footer.
   - Include your name and the date in a header.
   - Save the document as Alzheimer2 and print the document.

Computers and Children

★ 2. You are an Elementary Education major and are writing a report about computers and children. You are in the final stages of finishing the report. Use the features presented in this lab to add the following to the report:
   - Open the file wd03_Computer.
   - Apply appropriate formats to the titles and headings.
   - Create a title page above the body of the report. Use appropriate styles, fonts, and sizes.
   - Locate and insert an appropriate clip art on the title page.
   - Center the title page vertically.
   - Add the footnote **Availability of products is limited to stock on hand** after "Look for:" in the section "Software for Kids."
   - Add page numbers to the report, excluding the title page.
   - Create a bulleted, sorted list of the five software titles at the end of the report.
   - Save the document as Computer2.
   - Print the document.

Preparing for a Job Search

★★ 3. You are graduating next June and want to begin your job search early. To prepare for how to get a job, locate three sources of information on this topic. Use your school's career services department, the library, newspaper, and magazine articles as sources. Begin by creating an outline of the topics you will include in the report. Using the outline, write a brief report about your findings. Include the following features in your report:
   - A title page that displays the report title, your name, the current date, and a table of contents.
   - The body of the paper should include at least two levels of headings and a minimum of three footnotes.
   - The report layout should include page numbers on the top right corner of every page (excluding the title page). The title page should be vertically aligned.
   - Include at least one picture with a caption and cross-reference.
   - Include a works cited page with an alphabetical list of your reference sources.
   - Save the report as Job Search and print the report.

Writing a Research Paper

★ ★ **4.** Create a brief research report (or use a paper you have written in the past) on a topic of interest to
★ you. The paper must include the following features:
- A title page that displays the report title, your name, the current date, and a table of contents.
- The body of the paper should include at least two levels of headings and a minimum of three footnotes.
- The report layout should include page numbers on the top right corner of every page (excluding the title page). The title page should be vertically aligned.
- Include at least one picture with a caption and cross-reference.
- Include a works cited page with an alphabetical list of your reference sources.
- Save the document as Research and print the report.

on the web

Computer viruses can strike at any time and can cause serious problems. Use the Web as a resource to learn more about them, then write a brief report defining computer viruses. Describe three viruses, what they do, and the effect they could have on a large company. The paper must include the following features:
- A title page that displays the report title, your name, the current date, and a table of contents.
- The body of the paper should include at least two levels of headings and a minimum of three footnotes.
- The report layout should include page numbers on the top right corner of every page (excluding the title page). The title page should be vertically aligned.
- Include at least one picture with a caption and cross-reference.
- Include a works cited page with an alphabetical list of your reference sources.
- Save the document as Computer Viruses and print the report.

Working Together: Word and Your Web Browser

Case Study

Adventure Travel Company

Adventure Travel Company has a World Wide Web (WWW) site. Through it they hope to be able to promote their products and broaden their audience of customers. In addition to the obvious marketing and sales potential, they want to provide an avenue for interaction between themselves and the customer to improve their customer service. They also want the Web site to provide articles of interest to customers. The articles, with topics such as travel background information and descriptions, would change on a monthly basis as an added incentive for readers to return to the site.

You think the flyer you developed to promote the new tours and presentations could be used on the Web site. Word 2002 includes Web-editing features that help you create a Web page quickly and easily. While using the Web-editing features, you will be working with Word and with a Web browser application. This capability of all Office XP applications to work together and with other applications makes it easy to share and exchange information between applications. Your completed Web pages are shown here.

Note: The intent of the Working Together tutorial is to show how two applications work together and to present a basic introduction to creating Web pages. More information about Web page creation is available in Lab 6 of the Introductory text.

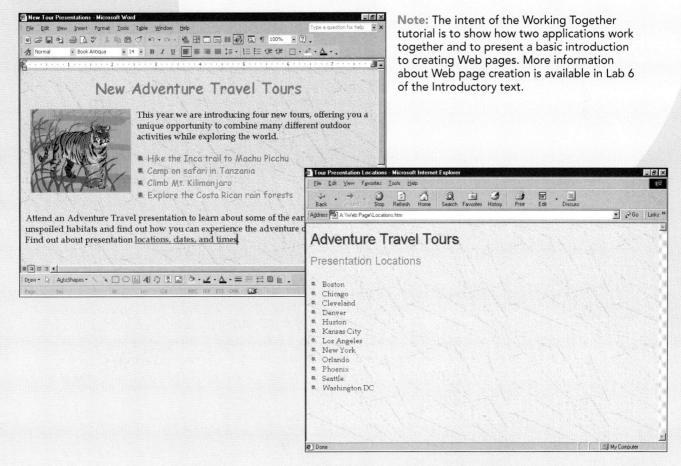

Saving a Word Document as a Web Page

You want to create a Web page on the company's Web site. A **Web page** is a document that can be used on the WWW. The Web page you create will provide information about the tour presentations. Word offers three ways to create or **author** Web pages. One way is to start with a blank Web page and enter text and graphics much as you would a normal document. Another is to use the Web Page Wizard, which provides step-by-step instructions to help you quickly create a Web page. Finally, you can quickly convert an existing Word document to a Web page.

Because the tour flyer has already been created as a Word document and contains much of the information you want to use on the Web page, you will convert it to a Web page document.

1 ● Start Word.

● Open the file wdwt_Tour Flyer **from the appropriate location.**

● **If necessary, close the New Document task pane.**

Your screen should be similar to Figure 1

Figure 1

Word converts a document to a Web page by adding HTML coding to the document. HTML **(Hypertext Markup Language)** is a programming language used to create Web pages. HTML commands control the display of information on a page, such as font colors and size, and how an item will be processed. HTML also allows users to click on hyperlinks and jump to other locations on the same page, other pages in the same site, or other sites and locations on the WWW. HTML commands are interpreted by the browser software you are using. A **browser** is a program that connects you to remote computers and displays the Web pages you request.

When a file is converted to a Web page, the HTML coding is added and it is saved to a new file with an .html file extension.

Choose File/Save as Web Page.

Your screen should be similar to Figure 2

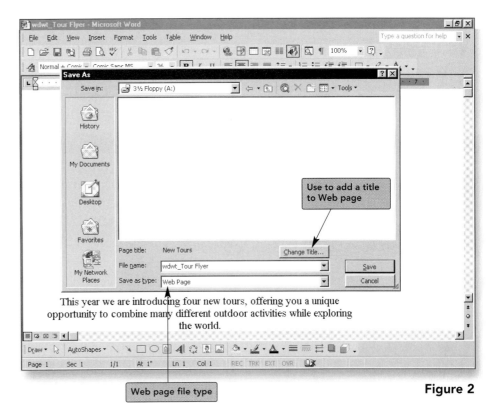

Use to add a title to Web page

Web page file type

Figure 2

The file type of Web Page is automatically specified. You want to save the Web page using the file name New Tour Presentations in a new folder. You also need to provide a title for the page. This is the text that will appear in the title bar of the Web browser when the page is displayed. You want the title to be the same as the file name.

● **If necessary, change the location to save to the appropriate save location.**

● **Create a new folder named Web Page.**

● **Change the file name to New Tour Presentations.**

● **Click Change Title...**

● **Change the title to New Tour Presentations.**

● **Click OK.**

● **Click Save.**

Your screen should be similar to Figure 3.

No margins

Text wraps to fit window

Web layout view

Figure 3

The flyer has been converted to an HTML document and is displayed in Web Layout view. Although the menu bar contains the same menus, Word customizes some menus, commands, and options to provide the Web page authoring features. This view displays the document as it will appear if viewed using a Web browser. This document looks very much like a normal Word document. In fact, the only visible difference is the margin settings. A Web page does not include margins. Instead, the text wraps to fit into the window space. However, the formatting and features that are supported by HTML, in this case the paragraph and character formatting such as the font style, type size, and color attributes, have been converted to HTML format.

Web Layout view does not display the HTML codes that control the formatting of the Web page. To view these codes, you will switch to HTML Source view.

4 ● Choose **V**iew/HTML Sourc**e**.

● If necessary, maximize the window.

Your screen should be similar to Figure 4

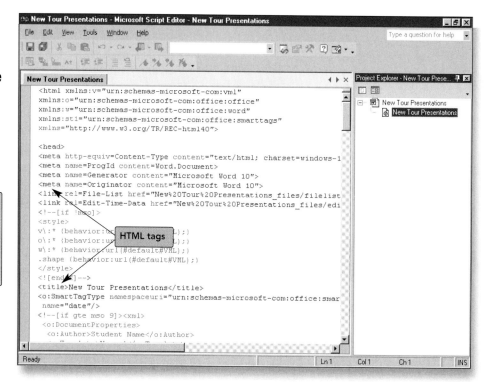

Figure 4

Every item on a Web page has properties associated with it that are encoded in HTML tags. **Tags** are embedded codes that supply information about the page's structure, appearance, and contents. They tell your browser where the title, headings, paragraphs, images, and other information are to appear on the page. Converting this document to HTML format using Word was a lot easier than learning to enter the codes yourself.

5 ● Click ☒ in the title bar to close the Microsoft Script Editor window.

The Web page is displayed in Web page view again.

Making Text Changes

Next you want to change the layout of the Web page so that more information is displayed in the window when the page is viewed in the browser. You will delete any unnecessary text first and change the paragraph alignment to left-aligned.

1 ● Select the entire Announcing heading line.

● Press Delete.

● Delete the last two paragraphs in the flyer and the AutoShape.

● Select all the text below the picture.

● Click ▤ Left.

● Add bullets preceding the list of four tours.

● Scroll to the top of the document.

Your screen should be similar to Figure 5

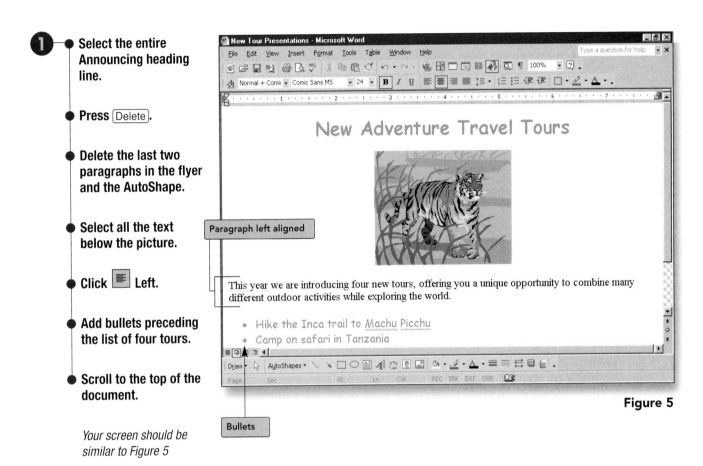

Paragraph left aligned

Bullets

Figure 5

Changing the Picture Layout

You still cannot view all the information in a single window. To make more space, you will move the picture to the left edge of the window and wrap the text to the right around it. Unlike a normal Word document, pictures and other graphic elements are not embedded into the Web page document. Instead they are inserted as inline objects. In an HTML file, an inline image is stored as a separate file that is accessed and loaded by the browser when the page is loaded. However, it can still be moved, sized, and formatted just like embedded picture objects.

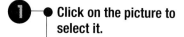

1
- Click on the picture to select it.
- If necessary, display the Picture toolbar.
- Drag the graphic to the T in This at the beginning of the first paragraph.
- Click 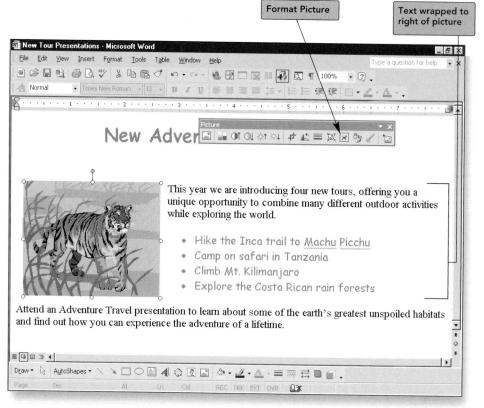 Format Picture.
- Open the Layout tab.
- Select Square.
- Change the horizontal alignment to Left.
- Click OK.

Your screen should be similar to Figure 6

Figure 6

Now almost all the information is visible. You will remove two of the blank lines from below the heading and reduce the size of the picture slightly.

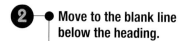

2
- Move to the blank line below the heading.
- Press Delete twice.
- Reduce the picture size slightly as in Figure 7.

Your screen should be similar to Figure 7

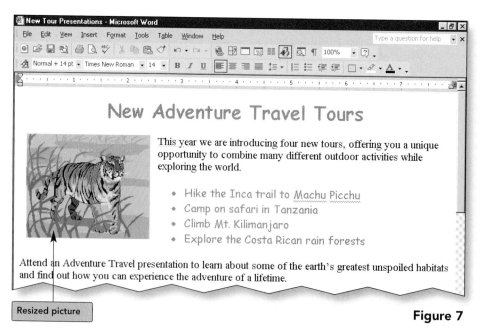

Figure 7

Applying a Theme

Because color and design are important elements of Web pages, you can add a background color and other special effects to a Web page. Many of these special effects are designed specifically for Web pages and cannot be used in printed pages. Like styles, Word includes many predesigned Web page effects, called **themes**, which you can quickly apply to a Web page.

Choose Format/Theme.

Your screen should be similar to Figure 8

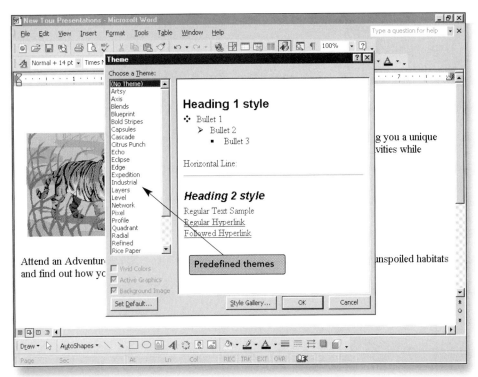

Figure 8

The Choose a Theme list displays the names of all the themes that are provided with Word. The preview area displays a sample of the selected theme showing the background design, bullet and horizontal line style, and character formats that will be applied to headings, normal text, and hyperlinks.

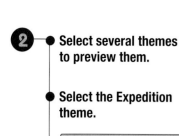

2 ● Select several themes to preview them.

● Select the Expedition theme.

HAVING TROUBLE?
If the Expedition theme is not available, try Axis or Nature.

● Click OK .

● Click [save icon] to save the changes you have made to the Web page.

Your screen should be similar to Figure 9

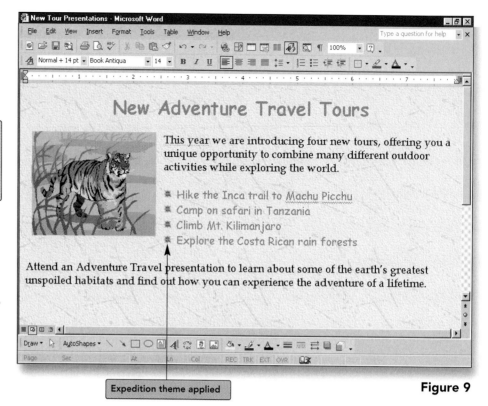

Expedition theme applied

Figure 9

The formatting settings associated with the selected theme are applied to the Web page.

Creating a Hyperlink

Next you want to create another Web page that will contain a list of presentation locations. You will then add a hyperlink to this information from the New Tour Presentations page. As you have learned, a hyperlink provides a quick way to jump to other documents, objects, or Web pages. Hyperlinks are the real power of the WWW. You can jump to sites on your own system and network as well as to sites on the Internet and WWW.

The list of tour locations has already been entered as a Word document and saved as a file named Locations.

1
● Open the file
wdwt_Locations.

● Save the document as a Web page to your Web Page folder with the file name Locations and a page title of Tour Presentation Locations.

● Apply the Expedition theme to this page.

● Save the page again.

Your screen should be similar to Figure 10

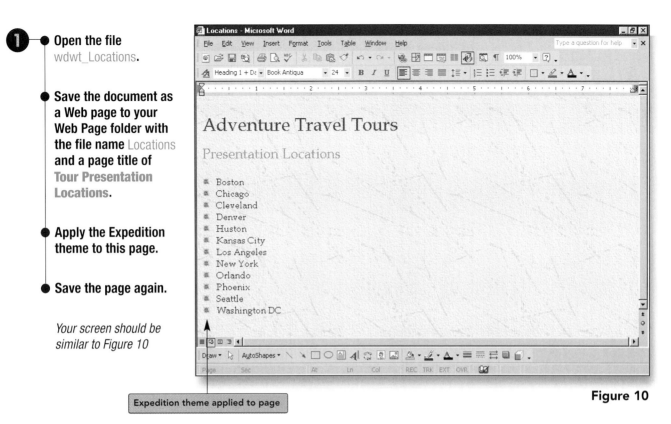

Expedition theme applied to page

Figure 10

Now you are ready to create the hyperlink from the New Tour Presentations page to the Locations page.

2
● Switch to the New Tour Presentations window.

● Add the following text, left aligned one line below the last paragraph: Find out about presentation locations, dates, and times.

● Select the text "locations, dates, and times."

● Click [icon] Insert Hyperlink (on the Standard toolbar).

Another Method
The menu equivalent is Insert/Hyperlink and the keyboard shortcut is Ctrl + K.

Your screen should be similar to Figure 11

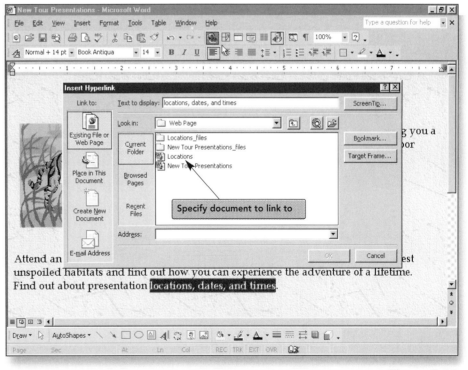

Specify document to link to

Figure 3.11

From the Insert Hyperlink dialog box, you need to specify the name of the document you want to the link connect to.

3 ● **If necessary, click** .

● **Click** [Current Folder].

● **Select** Locations.htm **from the file list.**

● **Click** [OK].

Your screen should be similar to Figure 12

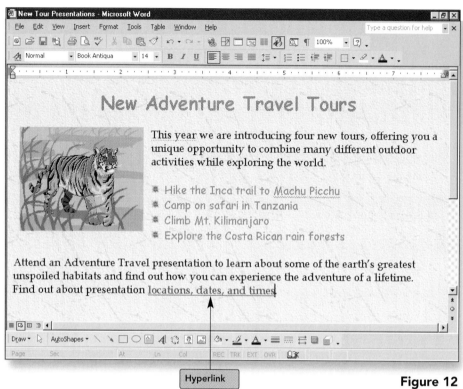

Hyperlink

Figure 12

The selected text appears as a hyperlink in the design colors specified by the theme.

4 ● **Hold down** [Ctrl] **and click the hyperlink.**

Your screen should be similar to Figure 13

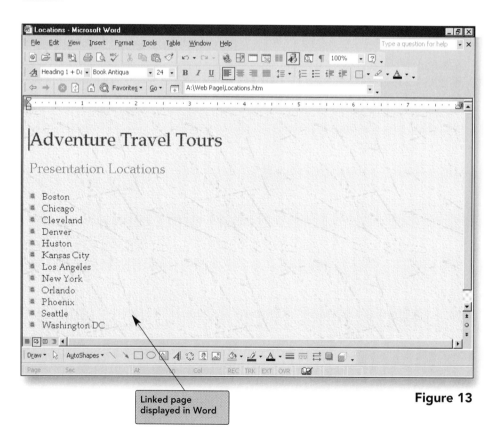

Linked page displayed in Word

Figure 13

Because the Locations document is already open in a window, clicking the hyperlink simply switches to the open window and displays the page. You plan to add hyperlinks from each location to information about dates and times for each location.

Previewing the Page

To see how your Web page will actually look when displayed by our browser, you can preview it in your default browser.

1 ● Click ⬅ **Back** to view the previous page.

● Choose **F**ile/We**b** Page Preview.

● If necessary, maximize the browser window.

● If Internet Explorer is your default browser and the Favorites bar is open, click ☒ in the Favorites bar to close it.

Your screen should be similar to Figure 14

Web page previewed in browser window

Figure 14

The browser on your system is loaded offline, and the Web page you are working on is displayed in the browser window. Sometimes the browser may display a page slightly differently than it appears in Web Page view. In this case, the bullets overlap the edge of the picture. If you do not like the change, you can return to Word and adjust the layout until it displays appropriately in the browser. In this case, however, you will leave it as it is.

2 ● Click on the hyperlink.

Your screen should be similar to Figure 15

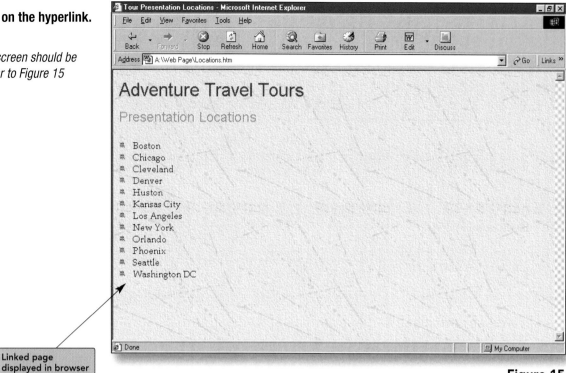

Linked page displayed in browser

Figure 15

The associated page is displayed in the browser. This page also looks fine and does not need any additional formatting.

3 ● Click 🗵 in the title bar to exit the browser program.

● Exit Word, saving the changes you made to both documents.

Making a Web Page Public

Now that you have created Web pages, in order for others to see them you need to make them available on the Internet. The steps that you take to make your pages public depend on how you want to share them. There are two main avenues: on your local network or intranet for limited access by people within an organization, or on the Internet for access by anyone using the WWW. To make pages available to other people on your network, save your Web pages and related files, such as pictures, to a network location. To make your Web pages available on the WWW, you need to either install Web server software on your computer or locate an Internet service provider that allocates space for Web pages.

lab review

Working Together: Word and Your Web Browser

key terms

author   WDWT1.2
browser   WDWT1.2

HTML (Hypertext Markup Language)   WDWT1.2
tag   WDWT1.4

theme   WDWT1.7
Web page   WDWT1.2

mous skills

The Microsoft Office User Specialist (MOUS) certification program is designed to measure your proficiency in performing basic tasks using the Office XP applications. Getting certified demonstrates that you have the skills and provides a valuable industry credential for employment. After completing this lab, you have learned the following Microsoft Office User Specialist skills:

Skill	Description	Page
Workgroup	Preview documents as Web pages	WDWT1.11
Collaboration	Save documents as Web pages	WDWT1.2

command summary

Command	Shortcut Keys	Button	Action
File/Save as Web Page			Saves file as a Web page document
File/Web Page Preview			Previews Web page in browser window
View/HTML Source			Displays HTML source code
Insert/Hyperlink	Ctrl + K	🔗	Inserts hyperlink
Format/Theme			Applies a predesigned theme to Web page

Hands-On Exercises

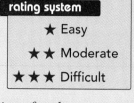

step-by-step

Adding a New Web Page

★ **1.** You want to continue working on the Web pages about the new tour presentations for the Adventure Travel Web site. Your next step is to create links from each location to information about each location's presentation date and times. Your completed Web page for the Los Angeles area is shown here.

a. Open the Web page file Locations you created in this lab.

b. Open the document wdwt_LosAngeles. Save the document as a Web page to your Web Page folder with the file name LosAngeles and a page title of **Los Angeles Presentation Information**.

c. Apply the same design theme to the new page. Change the title to a Heading 1 style. Add color to the table headings. Enhance the Web page with any features you feel are appropriate.

d. Two lines below the table add the text **Contact [your name] at (909) 555-1212 for more information**.

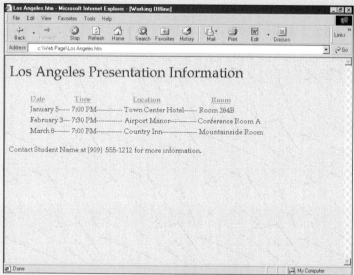

e. Create a link from the Los Angeles location to the Los Angeles page. Test the link.

f. Resave both Web pages and preview them in your browser. Print the Los Angeles Web page.

g. Exit the browser and Word.

Converting a Flyer to a Web Page

★★ **2.** To complete this problem, you must have created the document Executive Style in Hands-On Exercise 3 of Lab 1.

You have decided to modify the Executive Style flyer you created and convert the flyer into a Web page to add to your store's Web site. Your completed Web page is shown here.

a. Open the file Executive Style you created in Hands-On Exercise 3 in Lab 1.

b. Convert the flyer to a Web page and save it using the same file name in a new folder. Include an appropriate page title.

c. Delete the first title line.

d. Apply the Cascade theme to the page. (If this theme is not available, select another theme of your choice.)

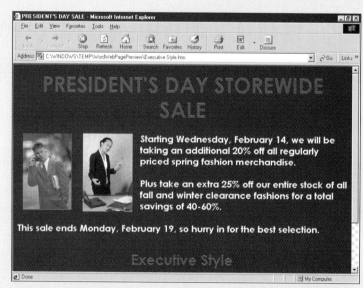

e. Break the paragraph into three paragraphs at each sentence, leaving a blank line between each. Change the three paragraphs to left-aligned.

f. Reduce the size of the pictures. Change the picture text wrapping style to square. Move the pictures to the left of the first two paragraphs. Size the pictures to fit next to the first two paragraphs.

g. Change the color of the title line to red.

h. Preview the page in your browser. Close your browser. Resave the Web page.

i. Use Print Preview to see how the page will appear when printed. The background and white text does not display. Change the text color to lime green and preview the page again. Print the Web page.

j. Exit Word without saving your changes to the page.

Advertising on the Web

★ ★ ★ **3.** To complete this problem, you must have completed Hands-On Exercise 4 in Lab 1. You would like to advertise your bed and breakfast inn on the Web. You plan to use the information in the advertisement flyer you created as the basis for the Web pages. Your completed Web pages are shown here.

a. Open the file B&B Ad. Convert the document to a Web page and save it as B&B in a new folder. Include an appropriate page title.

b. Cut the information from "Number of Rooms" to "Children" and paste it to a new Web page. Add the text Information and Rates above the list on the new page. Format it with a Heading 1 style. Center it above the list.

c. Save the new page to the folder with the file name Information. Title the page Information and Rates.

d. Apply the design theme Waves or a theme of your choice to both pages. Change the B&B name on the first page to a Heading 1 style. Add the text Information and Rates below the Host name to the first page and create a link from this text to the Information page. Test the link.

e. Change the layout of the first page to that shown here. Copy the graphic from the first page to the second and change the layout to that shown here.

f. Resave the Web pages and preview them in your browser.

g. Print the pages.

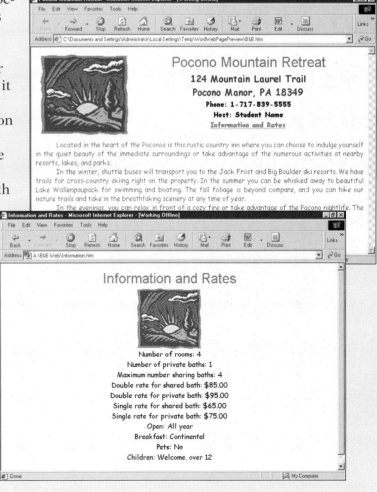

on your own

on your own

★ 1. **Learning about Web Design**

Use Word Help to learn more about Web pages and making Web pages public.

a. Search in Help for information on Web page design, Web layout, Web sites, and publishing Web pages.

b. Print the Help pages that might be appropriate for writing a report on using Word to create a Web site.

c. Write a one-page report in Word summarizing the information you found.

d. Include your name and the date in a header.

e. Save the report as Web Design. Print the report.

Creating a Newsletter

objectives

After completing this lab, you will know how to:

1.	Create and enhance a WordArt object.
2.	Modify character spacing.
3.	Create horizontal rules.
4.	Collect and paste multiple items.
5.	Modify styles.
6.	Create newsletter-style columns.
7.	Use hyphenation.
8.	Create sidebars.
9.	Add borders and shading to paragraphs.
10.	Create and link text boxes.
11.	Insert symbols and drop caps.

Use the WordArt feature to create an attractive headline.

Newsletter-style columns make newsletters easy to read as well as attractive.

Text boxes, graphics, color, and borders enhance the appearance of the newsletter.

Adventure Travel Tours

The Adventure Travel Tours manager is very pleased with the research you did on Tanzania and Peru. The company plans to feature tours to these areas in the next few months and wants to provide much of the information you gathered to clients. A good way to present this type of information is through a monthly newsletter. Newsletters allow businesses to present timely information. Unlike a flyer, whose purpose is to quickly attract attention and provide a small amount of information, a newsletter is designed to provide detailed information. Because newsletters are generally several pages long, you have enough space to paint a picture and tell a story.

After discussing the plans for the upcoming newsletters with the

Adventure Travel Tours manager, you have decided to make the African safari in Tanzania the focus of the next month's newsletter. In addition to using several topics from the material in the report on Tanzania, the newsletter will include various tips and facts about the country. You will also include some information about other upcoming tours and events.

In a newsletter, information must be easy to read and, more important, visually appealing. In this lab, you will use the WordArt and desktop publishing tools in Word 2002 to create the newsletter (shown left).

© Corbis

1
2
3
4
5
6
7
8
9
10
11

1	**WordArt** WordArt is used to enhance your documents by changing the shape of text and adding special effects such as 3-D and shadows.
2	**Special Drawing Effects** Special drawing effects, such as shadows and 3-D effects, can be easily added to text and graphics, including WordArt objects, to enhance the appearance of your document.
3	**Collecting and Pasting** Collecting and pasting is the capability of the program to store multiple copied items in the Office Clipboard and then paste one or more of them into another document.
4	**Newsletter-Style Columns** Newsletter-style columns display text so that it flows from the bottom of one column to the top of the next.
5	**Hyphenation** The hyphenation feature inserts hyphens in long words that fall at the end of a line, splitting the word between lines.
6	**Text Box** A text box is a graphic object that is a container for text or graphics.

Creating a Newsletter Headline

A newsletter commonly consists of two basic parts: the headline and the body (see the following figure). The headline, also called the nameplate or banner, is the top portion of the newsletter. It generally contains the name, issue or volume number, and publication date. It may also include a company logo, a line that announces the main subject or article included in the newsletter, and a brief table of contents. The body, which is the text of the newsletter, is commonly displayed in a two- or three-column format. Article headings often include subheadings that help organize the newsletter topics. The headline is often visually separated from the body by horizontal lines, called rules. Your sample newsletter will include many of these features.

The first thing you want to do is to create a headline for the newsletter. The headline will display the name of the newsletter, The Adventure Traveler, the date of publication, and the volume number.

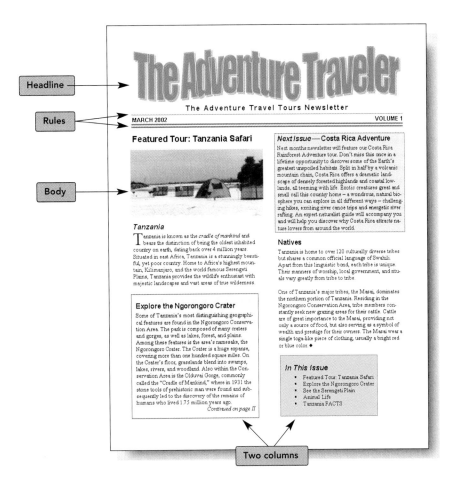

The text for the headline has already been entered for you.

1 • **Start Word.**

• **If necessary, maximize the Word application window.**

• **To see the headline text, open the file** wd04_Headline.

Your screen should be similar to Figure 4.1

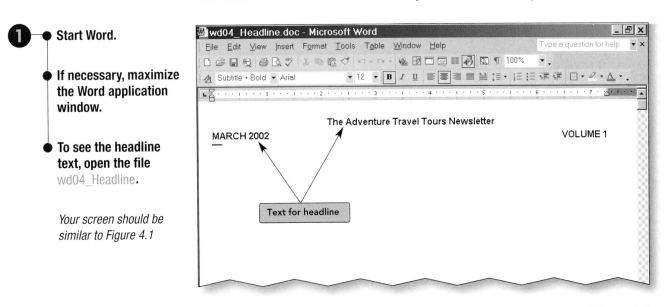

Figure 4.1

Using WordArt

You need to add the newsletter name at the top of the page headline. You will use the WordArt feature to make this name unique and more interesting.

WordArt

1 **WordArt** is used to enhance your documents by changing the shape of text and adding special effects such as 3-D and shadows. You can also rotate, flip, and skew WordArt text. The text that is added to the document using WordArt is a graphic object that can be edited, sized, or moved to any location in the document. In addition, it can be changed using the Drawing toolbar buttons.

You can use WordArt to add a special touch to your documents. However, you should limit its use to headlines in a newsletter or to a single element in a flyer. You want the WordArt to capture the reader's attention. Here are some examples of WordArt.

You will create a WordArt object consisting of the newsletter name for the headline. The Drawing toolbar is used to access the WordArt feature.

1 ● If necessary, display
the Drawing toolbar.

● Click 🔳 Insert
WordArt.

*Your screen should be
similar to Figure 4.2*

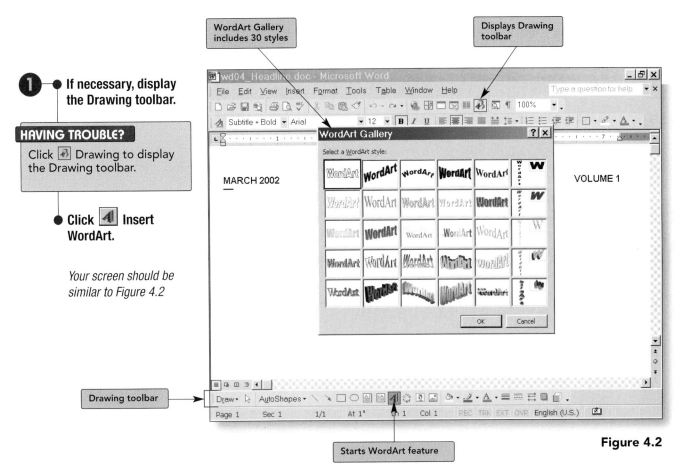

Drawing toolbar

Starts WordArt feature

Figure 4.2

In the WordArt Gallery dialog box, you first select one of the 30 styles or designs of WordArt you want to use for the headline. The styles consist of a combination of fonts, colors, and shapes and are just a starting point. As you will soon see, you can alter the appearance of the style by selecting a different color or shape, and by adding special effects.

2 ● Select [WordArt] (third
row, second column).

● Click OK.

*Your screen should be
similar to Figure 4.3*

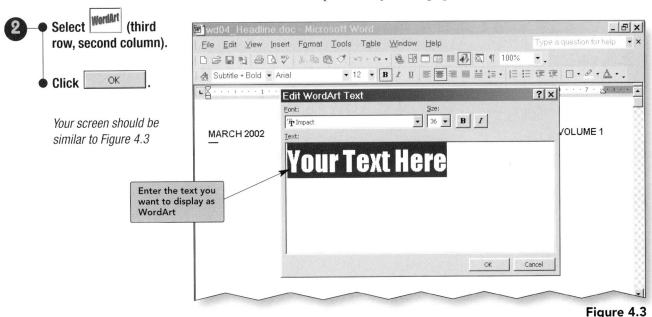

Enter the text you
want to display as
WordArt

Figure 4.3

Next, in the Edit WordArt Text dialog box, you need to replace the sample text with the text you want displayed using the selected WordArt design.

3 ● **Type** The Adventure Traveler.

● **Click** OK .

Your screen should be similar to Figure 4.4

Text you entered appears in selected WordArt style

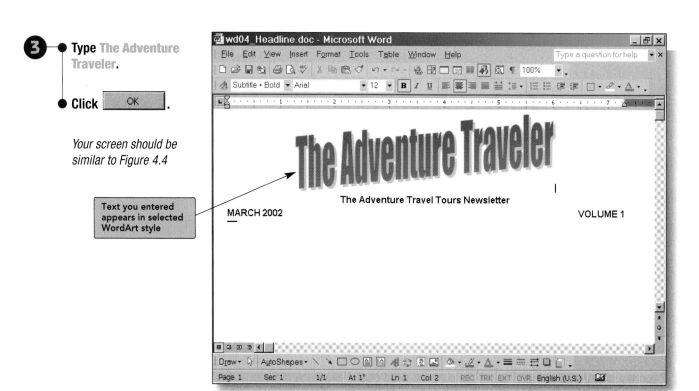

The Adventure Traveler

The Adventure Travel Tours Newsletter

MARCH 2002   VOLUME 1

Figure 4.4

Another Method

To review these features, refer to Concept 4: Text Wrapping, in Lab 3.

Now the words you entered are displayed in the selected WordArt style in the document. When a WordArt object is first inserted in the document, it has a default wrapping style of In Line with Text, assuming the formatting of the line into which it was inserted, in this case, centered.

Changing the WordArt Shape and Size

Now that you can see how the selected style looks in the document, you want to change the WordArt shape to make it more interesting. You can select from 40 different shapes provided in the WordArt palette and apply the shape to the selected object.

Whenever a WordArt object is selected, the WordArt toolbar is displayed. The WordArt toolbar buttons (identified below) are used to modify the WordArt.

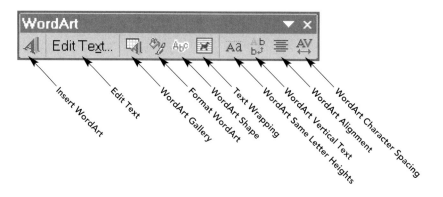

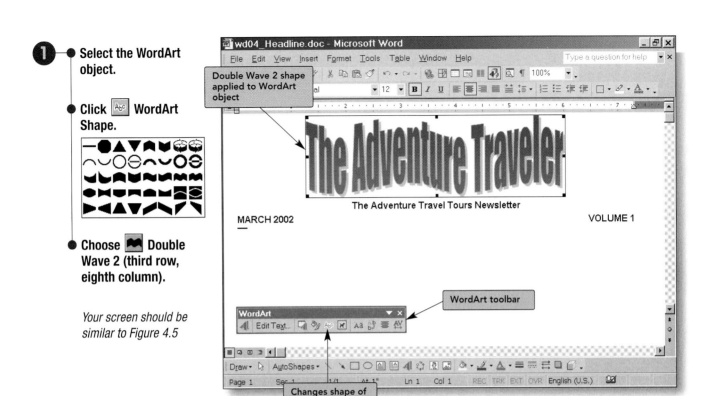

1 ● Select the WordArt object.

● Click [Abc] WordArt Shape.

● Choose [~] Double Wave 2 (third row, eighth column).

Your screen should be similar to Figure 4.5

> Double Wave 2 shape applied to WordArt object

> WordArt toolbar

> Changes shape of WordArt object

Figure 4.5

The selected shape is applied to the WordArt object. You also want the WordArt object to extend the full width of the text space between the margins. To do this you will increase its width.

2 ● Drag the middle sizing handle of the WordArt shape to increase the width as shown in Figure 4.6.

Another Method

You can also adjust the size to exact measurements using Format/WordArt/Size and entering values to specify an exact height and width.

Your screen should be similar to Figure 4.6

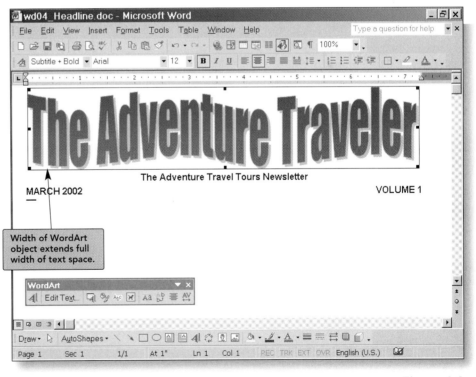

> Width of WordArt object extends full width of text space.

Figure 4.6

The WordArt is now the full text width of the page.

Changing the WordArt Fill and Line Color

Next you want to change the color of the WordArt characters to match the colors used in the company logo. You can easily do this using some of the special effects options that can be applied to graphic objects.

concept 2

Special Drawing Effects

2 Special drawing effects, such as shadows and 3-D effects, can easily be added to text and graphics, including WordArt objects, to enhance the appearance of your document. When you draw an object, a border automatically appears around it. You can change the thickness and color of the border. You also can fill a drawing object with a solid color, a gradient color, texture, or a picture. Adding shadows or 3-D effects gives depth to an object.

Use these effects in moderation. You want to capture the reader's interest with your graphics but not detract from your message.

---

1 ● Click  Format WordArt.

● Open the Colors and Lines tab.

Another Method

The menu equivalent is Format/WordArt/Colors and Lines.

Your screen should be similar to Figure 4.7

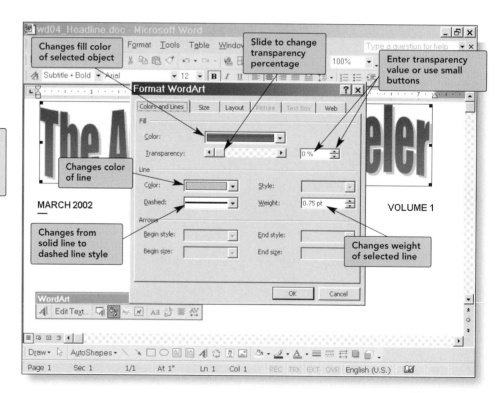

Figure 4.7

The default color and line settings for the selected WordArt design style are a purple gradient fill color set to 0 percent transparency with a light purple line color. When set, the transparency option makes the selected fill color less opaque, allowing the shadow color to bleed through. When set to zero, the color is solid or opaque. You want to use the corporate colors of green and blue in your newsletter. You will also set the transparency to 30 percent.

2
- Open the Fill **C**olor drop-down list and select  green (second row, fourth column) from the palette.

- Set the transparency to 30%.

- Open the Line C**o**lor palette and select Light Turquoise (fifth row, fifth column).

- Click [OK].

Your screen should be similar to Figure 4.8

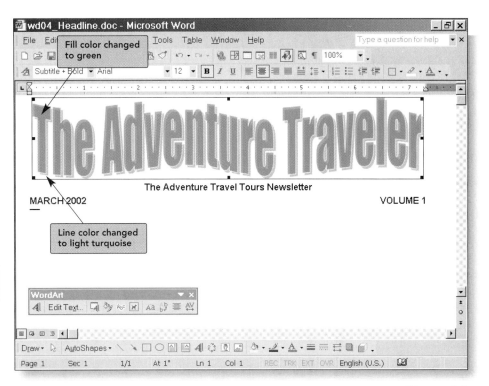

Figure 4.8

The selected fill and line colors are applied to the WordArt shape.

Modifying Character Spacing

Finally, you want to change the spacing of the characters in the WordArt object to be very close together. The character spacing for WordArt objects can be changed from the normal spacing (set at 100 percent) to closer together or wider apart. A larger percent value increases the spacing and a smaller percent value decreases the spacing. In addition, if the **kerning** setting is on, the spacing between particular pairs of letters it may be altered to improve the appearance of the text. You want to condense the spacing between characters as much as possible.

1 ● Click 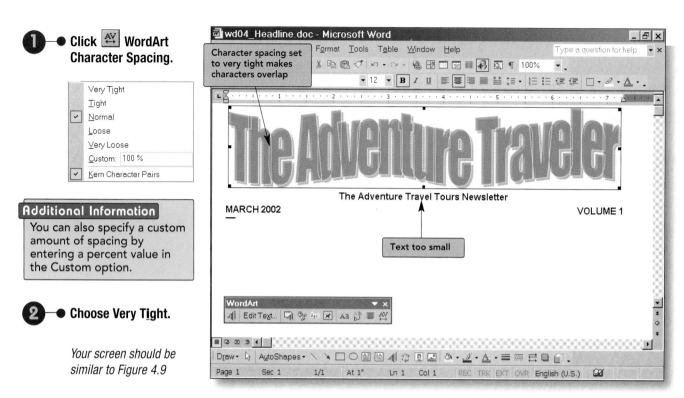 **WordArt Character Spacing.**

Very Tight
Tight
✓ Normal
Loose
Very Loose
Custom: 100 %
✓ Kern Character Pairs

Additional Information

You can also specify a custom amount of spacing by entering a percent value in the Custom option.

2 ● **Choose Very Tight.**

Your screen should be similar to Figure 4.9

Character spacing set to very tight makes characters overlap

Text too small

Figure 4.9

Now that the WordArt object is complete, the headline subtitle below it looks very small. You will make the font size larger and stretch the text to expand the character spacing.

3 ● **Select the subtitle line of text below the newsletter title.**

● **Choose Format/Font.**

● **Increase the point size to 14.**

● **Open the Character Spacing tab.**

Your screen should be similar to Figure 4.10

Stretches or compresses text horizontally as a percentage of its current size

Controls the amount of space between characters

Expands or condenses spacing between characters by the amount specified

Automatically adjusts kerning

Controls the amount by which text is raised or lowered

Selected text previewed

The Adventure Travel Tours Newsletter

Figure 4.10

The Character Spacing tab is used to expand or condense the space between characters by a specified amount. You can also kern characters above a specified point size. Expanding or condensing characters changes the space by an equal amount regardless of the font design. You can also specify the amount of space by which you want to expand or condense the spacing. The default setting is 1 point.

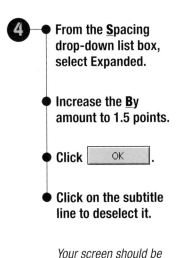

4
- From the **S**pacing drop-down list box, select Expanded.

- Increase the **B**y amount to 1.5 points.

- Click OK.

- Click on the subtitle line to deselect it.

Your screen should be similar to Figure 4.11

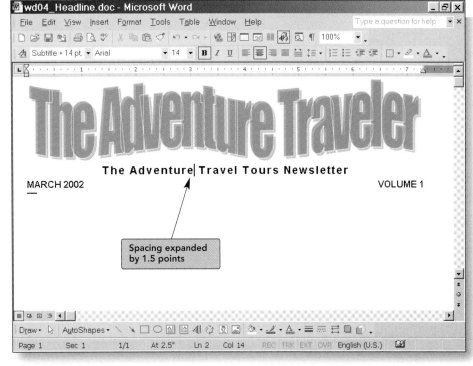

Figure 4.11

The spacing between characters has increased, making the headline subtitle more prominent.

Creating Horizontal Rules

Next you want the newsletter's issue identification information, which in this newsletter is the publication date and issue number, to be displayed between two horizontal lines or rules. Rules can be added to any side of a selected paragraph or object.

1 ● **Move to anywhere within the line of text containing the publication date and issue number.**

● **Choose Format/Borders and Shading.**

● **Open the Borders tab if necessary.**

Your screen should be similar to Figure 4.12

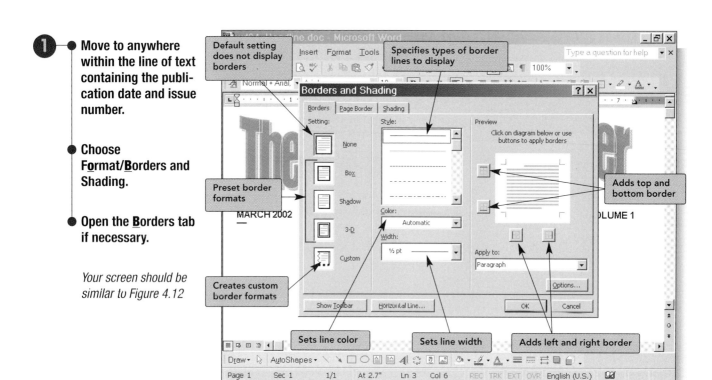

Figure 4.12

From the Borders and Shading dialog box, you can specify the style, color, weight, and location of the border. You can apply either a preset box border by selecting from the Settings options, or a custom border. You want to create a custom border that will display a 1.5-point single-line border in blue above the text, and a 3-point double-line border in blue below the text. As you specify the line settings, the Preview area will reflect your selections.

2 ● **Click [icon] Custom.**

Another Method

You can also specify border settings using the Tables and Borders toolbar.

● **From the Width drop-down list box, select 1½ pt.**

● **Open the Color palette and select Light Blue (third row, sixth column).**

● **Click [icon] Top Border.**

The dialog box on your screen should be similar to Figure 4.13

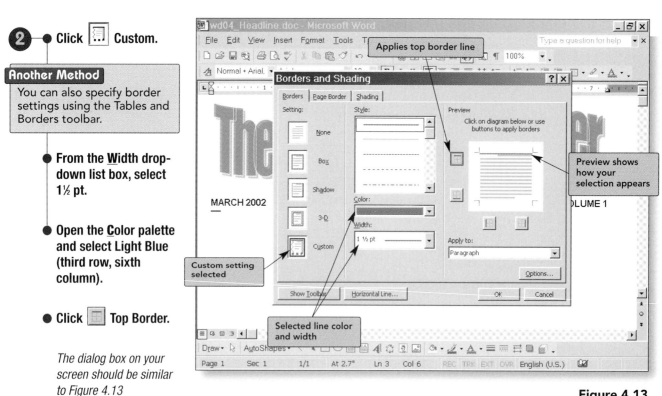

Figure 4.13

The Preview area of the dialog box shows how a top border line using the settings you specified will appear. Next you will add a double-line bottom border.

3 • From the **St**y**le** list box, select ————.

• From the **W**idth dropdown list, select 3 pt.

• From the **C**olor dropdown list, select Light Blue.

• Click  **Bottom Border**.

HAVING TROUBLE?
Use the None option to remove all border lines, or remove individual lines by selecting the border location again.

• Click ___OK___ .

• Save the headline as Newsletter Headline.

Your screen should be similar to Figure 4.14

Another Method
You can also create a single horizontal line by typing ⊡ three times and pressing (←Enter) and a double line by typing ⊟ three times and pressing (←Enter).

The Adventure Traveler

The Adventure Travel Tours Newsletter

MARCH 2002   VOLUME 1

Top and bottom border line create rule

Figure 4.14

The horizontal lines extend between the margins above and below the text in the color, style, and point size you specified. The newsletter headline is now complete and can be used with any newsletter.

Assembling the Newsletter from a Variety of Sources

Now you are ready to copy the headline into the document containing the text for the lead article of the newsletter. Following your manager's suggestions, you modified the report you wrote about Tanzania and Costa Rica by shortening the topic coverage and dividing the topics into several brief articles to be used in this and future newsletters. You saved the articles on different topics in separate files. In this month's newsletter, you will use the articles about the African Safari. You also have several other short topics to include in this month's newsletter saved in separate files. You will open files containing the main African safari articles and the other articles.

1 ● Open the file
wd04_Newsletter
Articles.

● If necessary, change
the view to Print
Layout and the zoom
to Page Width.

● Scroll through the text
to view the contents of
the document.

● Open the files wd04_Be
an Adventure Traveler,
wd04_Costa Rica
Adventure, **and**
wd04_Tanzania Facts.

Additional Information

Hold down Ctrl while
selecting multiple file names
to open multiple files at the
same time.

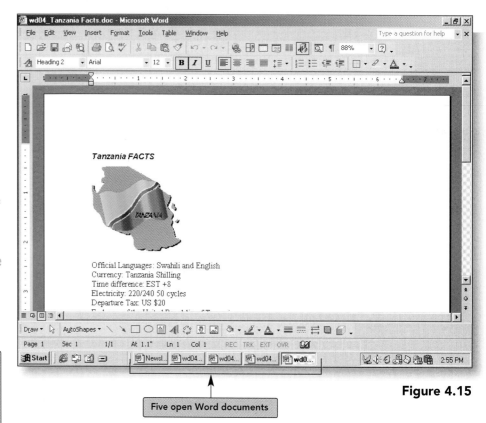

Figure 4.15

Five open Word documents

*Your screen should be
similar to Figure 4.15*

Using the Office Clipboard

You now have five open documents. You want to copy the newsletter banner into the document containing the African Safari article. In addition, you want to copy the information from the other three documents, Tanzania Facts, Costa Rica Adventure, and Be an Adventure Traveler, into this same file containing the lead article. You can copy and paste the selections one after the other, or you can use the Office Clipboard to collect multiple items and paste them into the document as needed.

concept 3

Collecting and Pasting

3 **Collecting and pasting** is the capability of the program to store multiple copied items in the Office Clipboard and then paste one or more of them into another document. For example, you could copy a chart from Excel, then switch to Word and copy a paragraph, then switch to PowerPoint and paste the two stored items into a slide in one easy step. This saves you from having to switch back and forth between documents and applications.

 The Office Clipboard and the System Clipboard are similar but separate features. The major difference is that the Office Clipboard can hold up to 24 items whereas the System Clipboard holds only a single item. The last item you copy to the Office Clipboard is always copied to the System Clipboard. When you use the Office Clipboard, you can select the items in any order to paste from any of the items stored.

 The Office Clipboard is available for all Office 2002 applications and non-Office programs if the Cut, Copy, and Paste commands are available. You can copy from any program that provides copy and cut capabilities, but you can only paste into Word, Excel, Access, PowerPoint, and Outlook.

Copying Multiple Objects to the Office Clipboard

First you will copy the headline to the Office Clipboard.

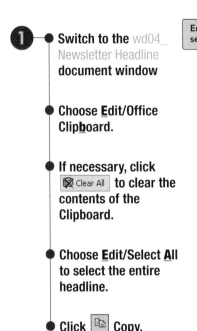

- **Switch to the** wd04_ Newsletter Headline **document window**

- **Choose** **E**dit/Office Clip**b**oard.

- **If necessary, click** 🗙 Clear All **to clear the contents of the Clipboard.**

- **Choose** **E**dit/Select **A**ll **to select the entire headline.**

- **Click** 📋 **Copy.**

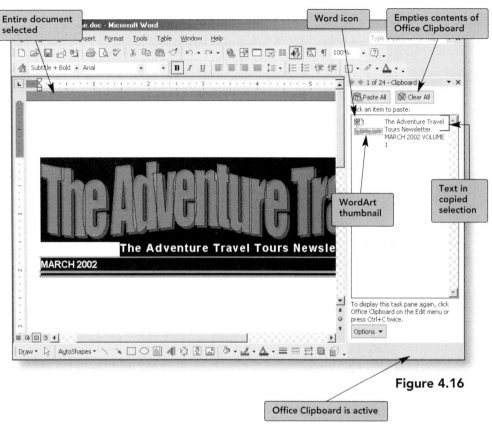

Figure 4.16

Another Method

You can also use [Ctrl] + A to select the entire document and [Ctrl] + C to copy the selection to the Clipboard.

Your screen should be similar to Figure 4.16

Additional Information

The Office Clipboard is automatically activated if you copy or cut two different items consecutively in the same program; copy one item, paste the item, and then copy another item in the same program; or copy one item twice in succession.

The 📋 Office Clipboard icon appears in the system taskbar to show that the Clipboard is active. It also briefly displays a ScreenTip indicating that 1 out of a possible 24 items was collected as the selection is copied.

📋 **1 of 24 - Clipboard**

The Clipboard task pane displays a Word icon representing the copied item, a thumbnail of the WordArt, and the first few words in the selection.

Next you will copy the contents of the Be an Adventure Traveler and Tanzania Facts documents into the Office Clipboard. If you open the Office Clipboard in the task pane in one program or document, it does not automatically appear when you switch to another program or document. However, it is still active and will continue to store copied items.

2 ● **Switch to the** wd04_ Be an Adventure Traveler **document.**

● **Select the entire file.**

● **Click** 📋 **Copy.**

● **Double-click** 📋 **Clipboard in the system taskbar.**

Your screen should be similar to Figure 4.17

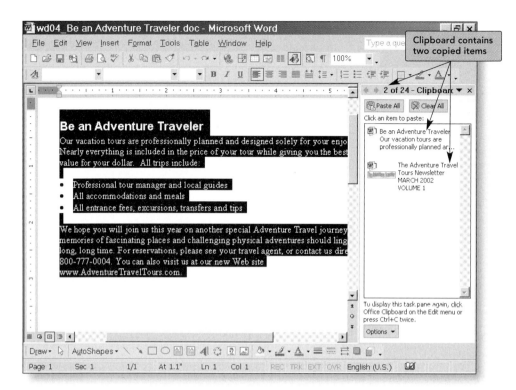

Figure 4.17

The second copied item was added to the Office Clipboard. The most recently added item is displayed at the top of the list.

3 ● **In a similar manner, copy the entire contents of the** wd04_ Tanzania Facts **and** wd04_Costa Rica Adventure **files to the Office Clipboard.**

● **Display the Office Clipboard task pane.**

Your screen should be similar to Figure 4.18

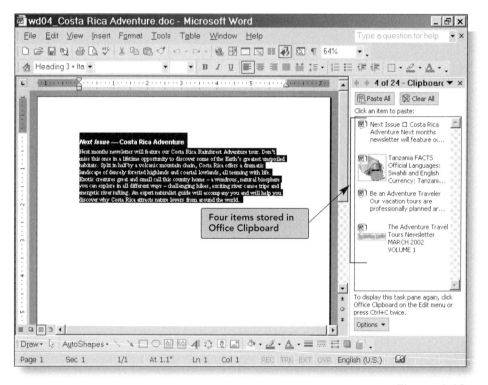

Figure 4.18

The Office Clipboard now contains four Word document icons.

Pasting Multiple Objects from the Office Clipboard

Now you are ready to paste the items into the main article document. You want to paste the headline first.

- **Switch to the** wd04_Newsletter Articles **document.**

- **If necessary, move to the beginning of the Featured Tour heading at the top of the document.**

- **Display the Office Clipboard task pane.**

- **Click on the newsletter headline item to paste it into the top of the document.**

Another Method

You could also select **P**aste from the item's shortcut menu.

Your screen should be similar to Figure 4.19

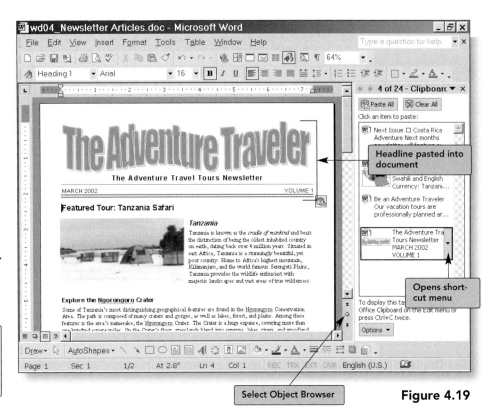

Figure 4.19

Another Method

You can also click 🔲 Select Object Browser and select the element to browse by from the menu.

Next you want to insert the information from the Be an Adventure Traveler file before the article about Animal Life. A quick way to move to specific elements in a document is to use **E**dit/**G**o To (or Ctrl + G), select the object type you want to go to (in this case Heading) and click Next or Previous to move to the next or previous occurrence.

2
- Choose **E**dit/**G**o To.
- Select Heading from the Go to what list box.
- Click [Next] 5 times to move to the Animal Life heading.

Additional Information

You can also type the name or number of the item in the Enter text box to move specifically to that item.

- Click [Close].
- Paste the Be an Adventure Traveler item from the Office Clipboard.

Your screen should be similar to Figure 4.20

Additional Information

The Office Clipboard Paste All option inserts the contents of all copied items in the order in which they were added to the Office Clipboard.

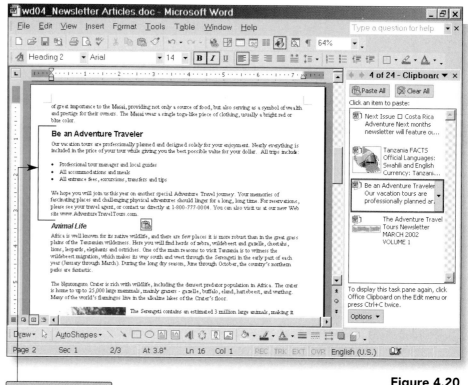

Second pasted item

Figure 4.20

The text for the newsletter already fills almost two pages and you still have more information to add to the document. To make the articles fit into the two-page newsletter format better, you decide to reduce the font to 11 points.

Modifying Styles

Because you plan to add more articles to this document, you will make the font change by modifying the Normal style for this document. Then, as new information is added, it will automatically be formatted using the settings associated with the modified style.

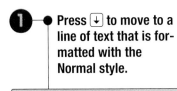

1 ● Press ⊥ to move to a line of text that is formatted with the Normal style.

HAVING TROUBLE?
Normal will appear in the Style toolbar button.

● Click 🅰 Styles and Formatting.

Another Method
The menu equivalent is Format/Styles and Formatting.

● Point to the Normal style name in the Styles and Formatting task pane.

Your screen should be similar to Figure 4.21

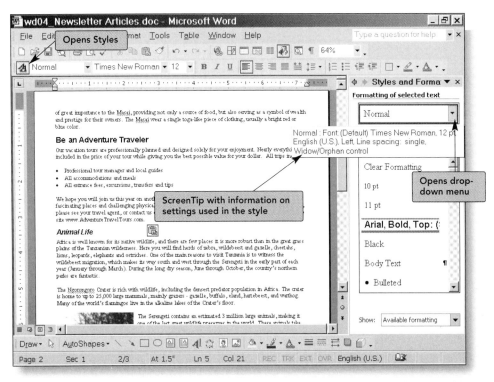

Figure 4.21

The Formatting of Selected Text box shows that the text of the current selection has the Normal style applied, and a ScreenTip displays information about the format settings used in the style.

2 ● Open the Formatting of Selected Text drop-down menu.

● Choose **M**odify.

Your screen should be similar to Figure 4.22

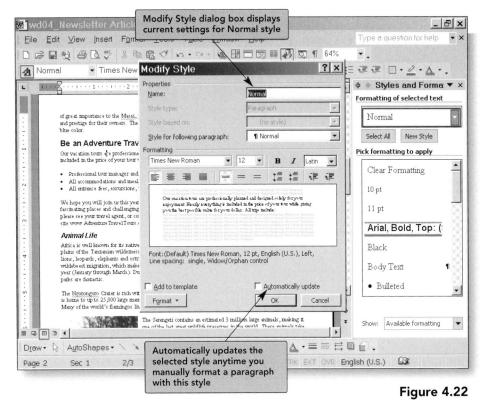

Figure 4.22

The current settings for the selected style are displayed in the Modify Style dialog box. After you modify the style, you can select Add to Template to add the modified style to the template used to create the document, which in this case is Normal. If you do not select this option, the Normal style is changed for the current document only. Selecting the Automatically Update option will automatically update the selected style anytime you manually format a paragraph with this style. It then applies the updated style to the entire document. You want to change the font size to 11 points for the current document only.

3 ● Select 11 from the size drop-down list box.

● Click [OK] .

Your screen should be similar to Figure 4.23

New Normal style applied

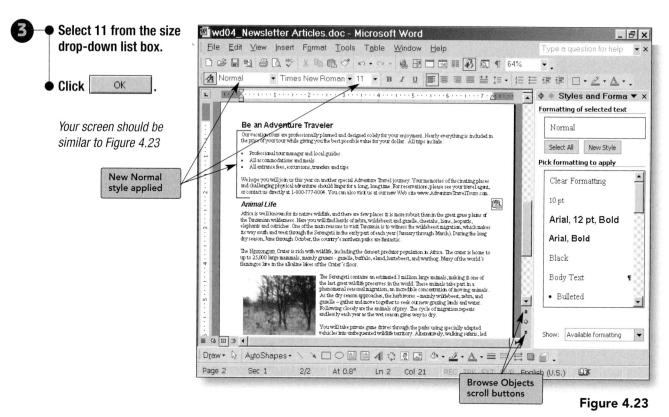

Browse Objects scroll buttons

Figure 4.23

The modified Normal style is applied to all paragraphs in the document that are formatted with the Normal style. Now you will insert the Costa Rica Adventure text above the Natives section in the document. Because you last specified Heading as the element to go to, you can quickly scroll the document by headings using the Browse Objects scroll buttons. These buttons scroll based on the last selected element type.

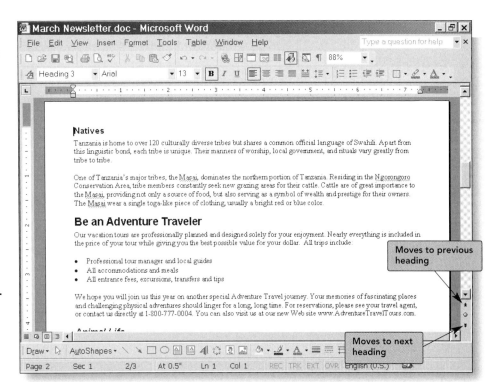

4 ● **Click ⬆ 3 times (in the scroll bar) to move to the Natives heading on page 1.**

● **Display the Office Clipboard task pane.**

● **Paste the Next Issue - Costa Rica Adventure item from the Office Clipboard.**

● **Close the Office Clipboard task pane.**

● **Save the revised document as** March Newsletter.

Your screen should be similar to Figure 4.24

Figure 4.24

The article content is pasted into the document and automatically converted to the new modified Normal style associated with this document.

Creating Newsletter-Style Columns

Now you are ready to format the newsletter articles so that they will be displayed in newsletter-style columns.

concept 4

Newsletter-Style Columns

4 **Newsletter-style columns** display text so that it flows from the bottom of one column to the top of the next. The Normal template has one column the full width of the margins, so the text appears to flow continuously from one page to the next. On occasion, the layout for your document may call for two or more columns on a page.

Newspapers, magazines, and newsletters are common applications for newsletter-style columns.

The optimum column width for reading comfort is 4.5 inches. In a newsletter, narrow columns help the reader read the articles more quickly, and you as the writer can fit information on a page in a visually pleasing arrangement. Note, however, that if you use more than four columns on an 8½-by-11-inch page, the columns will be too narrow and the page will look messy.

The Columns command on the Format menu is used to set the text format of a document to columns. With the Columns feature, you can change the text in the entire document to the new format. To affect only a portion of a document, you must divide the document into sections. Because you do not want the headline to appear in column format, you will create a section break below the headline.

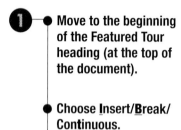

- Move to the beginning of the Featured Tour heading (at the top of the document).

- Choose **I**nsert/**B**reak/ Con**t**inuous.

- Click [OK].

HAVING TROUBLE?
Refer to Lab 3, Concept 2, to review section breaks.

Your screen should be similar to Figure 4.25

Section 2 of document

Figure 4.25

Although section break lines do not display in Print Layout view unless ¶ Show/Hide is selected, the status bar shows that the insertion point is positioned in section 2. The new section continues to the end of the document unless another section break is inserted.

Applying a Two-Column Layout

You want the newsletter to have two columns of text on the first page.

1 ● Choose F**o**rmat/
Columns.

● Select T**w**o from the
Presets area.

*Your screen should be
similar to Figure 4.26*

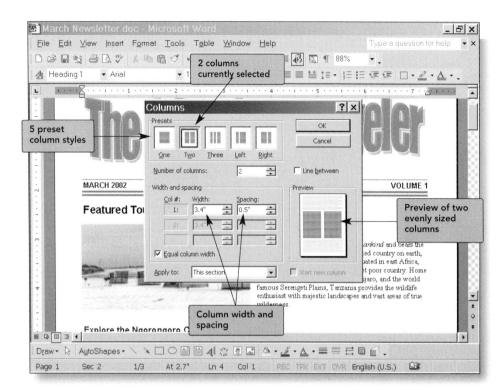

Figure 4.26

Using the Presets area, you can select up to three evenly spaced columns or
two unevenly spaced columns. If none of the preset styles is appropriate,
you can enter a number in the Number of Columns text box to create up to
14 columns.

The Number of Columns text box displays 2 as the selected number of
columns. Based on the number of columns you specify and your document's
left and right margin settings, Word automatically calculates the size of the
columns and the spacing between them. Using the default setting, the two
columns will be 3.4 inches wide, separated by 0.5 inch. The Preview box
shows how text will appear on the page using the specified column settings.

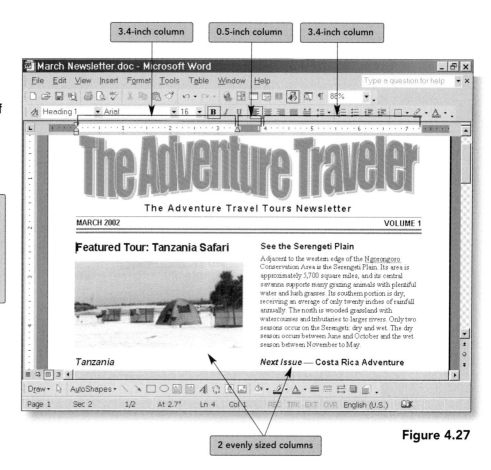

Figure 4.27

2 ● Click [OK].

● **Scroll to the bottom of the document to see the entire newsletter, then return to the top of the document.**

HAVING TROUBLE?
Do not be concerned if the text in your columns wraps differently than in Figure 4.27. This is a function of the selected printer on your system.

Your screen should be similar to Figure 4.27

The text is displayed as two evenly sized newsletter-style columns, with 0.5 inch of space between. The text at the bottom of the first column continues at the top of the second column. The column markers on the horizontal ruler show the size and spacing of each column.

Applying a Three-Column Layout

Additional Information
If you select the area of the text to be affected before setting the format to columns, Word automatically inserts a continuous section break at the beginning (and end, if necessary) of your selection.

Next you would like the second page of the newsletter to be in three-column format. You want a second page to begin with the advertisement "Be an Adventure Traveler." To force a new page and section, you will insert a New Page section break. Then you will format the section to three columns. Another way to specify columns is to use the 🔲 Columns button on the Standard toolbar. It allows you to specify up to six columns using the default column definitions.

1

- Move to the **Be an Adventure Traveler** heading.

- Choose **Insert/Break/Next Page/** OK .

- Click ▤ **Columns**.

- Click on the third column from the left.

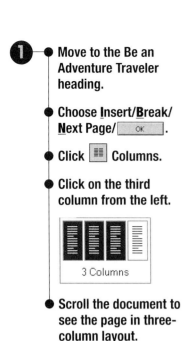

3 Columns

- Scroll the document to see the page in three-column layout.

Your screen should be similar to Figure 4.28

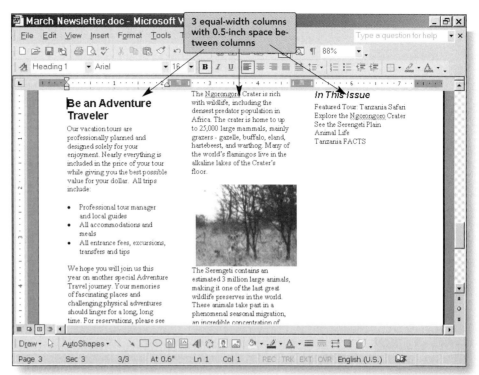

3 equal-width columns with 0.5-inch space between columns

Figure 4.28

Sizing Columns

The default width of 0.5 inch between the columns was appropriate for two columns, but seems too wide for three columns. You want to reduce the space between columns to 0.3 inch and maintain equal column widths.

1

- Choose **Format/Columns**.

- In the Width and Spacing section of the dialog box, reduce the **Spacing** to 0.3 for column 1.

- Select **Equal Column Width**.

- Click OK .

Another Method

You can also drag the column marker in the ruler to adjust the column size and spacing between columns.

Your screen should be similar to Figure 4.29.

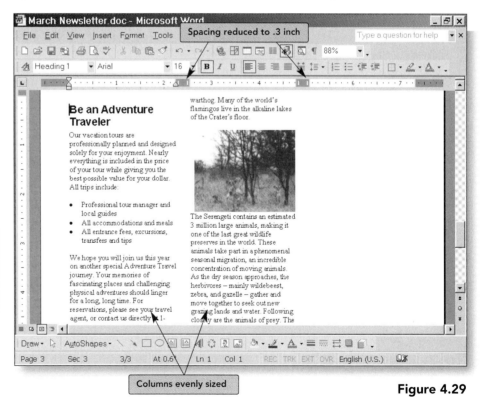

Spacing reduced to .3 inch

Columns evenly sized

Figure 4.29

The columns are equally sized with 0.3 inch between them. Because the columns are wider, there are only 2 full columns of text.

Using Hyphenation

Now that the layout is in columns, you notice that the lines have very uneven right margins. On lines of text where there are several short words, wrapping the text to the next line is not a problem. However, when long words are wrapped to the next line, a large gap is left on the previous line. To help solve this problem you will hyphenate the document.

concept 5

Hyphenation

5 The **hyphenation** feature inserts hyphens in long words that fall at the end of a line, splitting the word between lines. Because Word automatically moves long words that fall at the end of a line to the beginning of the next line, uneven right margins or large gaps of white space commonly occur in a document.

Using hyphenation reduces the amount of white space and makes line lengths more even, thereby improving the appearance of a document. The program inserts **optional hyphens**, which break the word only if it appears at the end of a line. Then, as you edit the document, the hyphenation is adjusted appropriately.

1 ● **Choose Tools/Language/ Hyphenation.**

Your screen should be similar to Figure 4.30

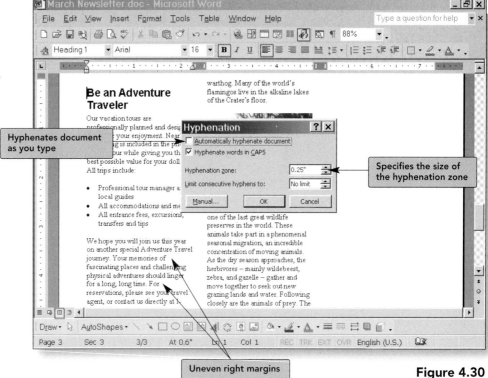

Figure 4.30

From the Hyphenation dialog box you can select the Automatically Hyphenate Document option, which lets Word set hyphenation for the entire document. You can also specify the size of the **hyphenation zone**, an unmarked space along the right margin that controls the amount of white space in addition to the margin that Word will allow at the end of a line. Making the hyphenation zone narrower (a smaller number) reduces the unevenness of lines by hyphenating more words, while making the zone wider (a larger number) hyphenates fewer words. Finally, you can specify whether words appearing in all capital letters should be hyphenated.

Additional Information

Use the [Manual...] button only if you want to be able to accept, reject, or change the proposed hyphenation of each word that Word is considering hyphenating.

2 ● Select **A**utomatically Hyphenate Document.

● If necessary, specify a hyphenation zone setting of 0.25 inch.

● Click [OK].

● Save the document again.

Your screen should be similar to Figure 4.31

HAVING TROUBLE?

Depending on your printer, different words may be hyphenated.

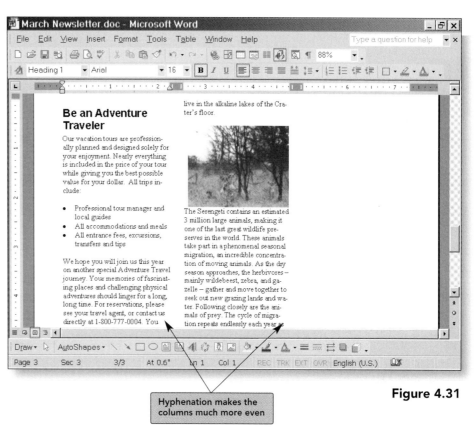

Hyphenation makes the columns much more even

Figure 4.31

Word has examined each line and determined where it is possible to hyphenate a word. Hyphenating the newsletter has made the column margins much less uneven. Word generally proposes accurate hyphenation. If you do not agree with how a word is hyphenated after it has been done, you can select the word and hyphenate it manually.

Creating Sidebars

You would like to set the Next Issue—Costa Rica Adventure article on the first page of the newsletter apart from the rest of the newsletter articles by adding a border and shading to the paragraph. An article you want to keep separate from other articles or information, and that highlights an article next to it, is called a **sidebar**. You can use a sidebar for such things as a list of contributors; addresses or contact information; a small self-contained story; a preview of the next issue; or a calendar or schedule.

Adding Borders and Shading to Paragraphs

First you will add the border around the article. To do this, you first select the text you want to include in the sidebar. When text is formatted into columns, you can use the mouse to move and select text just as in a document formatted with a single column. When you drag to select text in column layout, however, the selection moves from the bottom of one column to the top of the next.

1 ● **Move to the Next Issue —Costa Rica Adventure heading (on the first page).**

● **Select the text from the heading to the end of the paragraph.**

● **Open the** Border **drop-down menu (on the Formatting tool-bar).**

● **Choose** Outside Border.

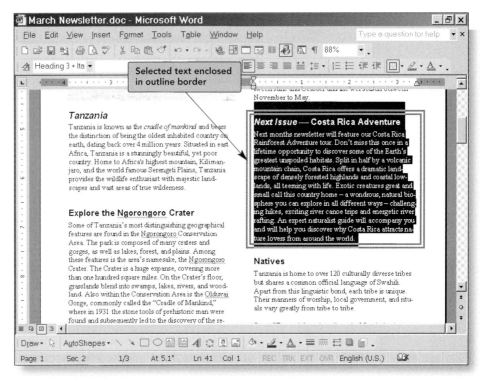

Figure 4.32

> **Another Method**
>
> The menu equivalent is Format/Borders and Shading/Borders/Box.

Your screen should be similar to Figure 4.32

The last-used border style, in this case a double 3 pt weight blue line, surrounds the selection. You want to change the border style to a single line. Then, to make the sidebar stand out even more, you will add a shading color to the box.

2 • Choose
F**o**rmat/**B**orders and
Shading/**B**orders.

• **Change the line style
to the single-line style
in blue and 1½ pt.
weight.**

• **Open the Sh**ading tab.

*Your screen should be
similar to Figure 4.33*

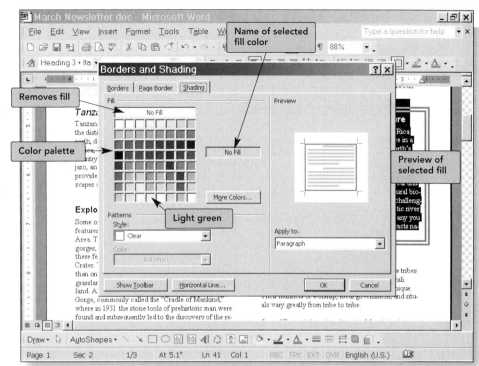

Figure 4.33

The Shading tab includes a color palette of fill colors. Selecting No Fill
removes a previously selected fill. The name of the selected color appears in
the text box to the right of the palette, and the preview area shows how the
selection will appear. The More Colors option opens another dialog box of
Standard and Custom colors from which you can select. The Apply To
option allows you to apply the color to the paragraph or selected text. The
default is to apply it to the paragraph containing the insertion point. If a
selection is made, the color is applied to the entire selection.

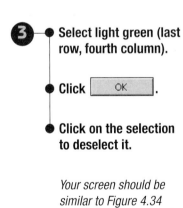

3 • **Select light green (last
row, fourth column).**

• **Click** OK **.**

• **Click on the selection
to deselect it.**

*Your screen should be
similar to Figure 4.34*

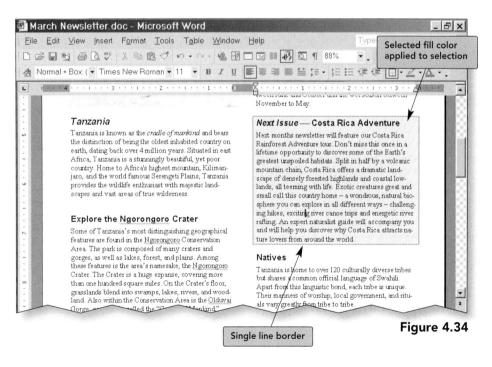

Figure 4.34

You also want to add the same border and shading to the Be an Adventure Traveler article on the third page. You can easily repeat the previous formatting by using the Repeat command.

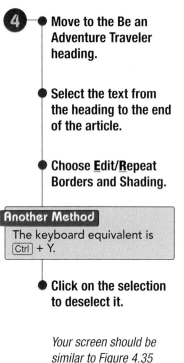

4 ● Move to the Be an Adventure Traveler heading.

● Select the text from the heading to the end of the article.

● Choose **E**dit/**R**epeat Borders and Shading.

Another Method

The keyboard equivalent is [Ctrl] + Y.

● Click on the selection to deselect it.

Your screen should be similar to Figure 4.35

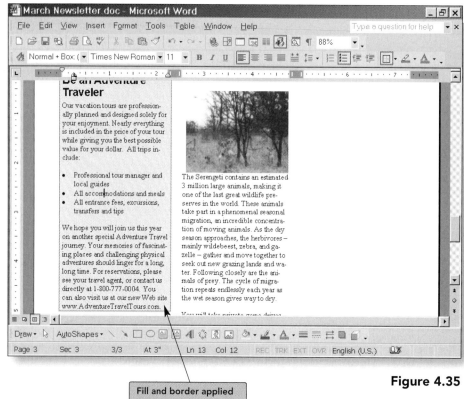

Fill and border applied

Figure 4.35

Creating Text Boxes

Next you want to add the information about the Tanzania Facts to the newsletter. Again, you would like to make this information stand out by displaying it as a sidebar. Another way to display information as a sidebar is to insert it in a text box.

concept 6

Text Box

6 A **text box** is a graphic object that is a container for text or graphics. Because text boxes are graphic objects, you can place them on the page as you would a picture or WordArt, and move and resize them. You can also add drawing features to text boxes to enhance their appearance.

When using newsletter-style columns, the text scrolls from the bottom of one column to the top of the next. If you want your newsletter to have specific objects in fixed places on the page, it is best to use text boxes and link those that need to flow from one page to the next. When you link text boxes together, the large articles will automatically flow into the correct text boxes on the other pages in the newsletter. Text that is contained in a single text box or linked text boxes is called a **story**.

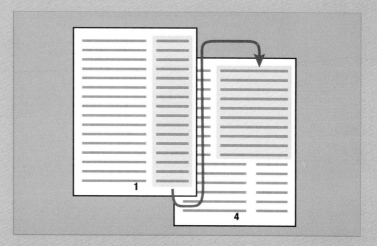

Generally, the first page of a newsletter should contain the beginnings of a main article and a secondary article, a sidebar with the newsletter contents, and perhaps a quote pulled from the article to capture the interest of someone just skimming the first page. The remainders of the articles are usually found on another page. All these elements can be entered into fixed text boxes in a template that you can use over and over so your newsletter looks the same every issue.

You will create a text box on the last page to contain the information about Tanzania and a map of the country.

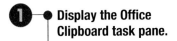

● Display the Office Clipboard task pane.

● Paste the Tanzania Facts item at the end of the second column on the last page.

● Click ![Clear All] to clear the contents of the Office Clipboard.

Additional Information
The System Clipboard is cleared also.

● Close the Office Clipboard task pane.

● Select the text beginning with the heading "Tanzania FACTS" and ending with "$45."

● Click 📄 Text Box.

Another Method
The menu equivalent is Insert/Text Box.

● Move the text box by dragging it to the top of the third column.

HAVING TROUBLE?
You may have to scroll the document to locate the text box.

Your screen should be similar to Figure 4.36

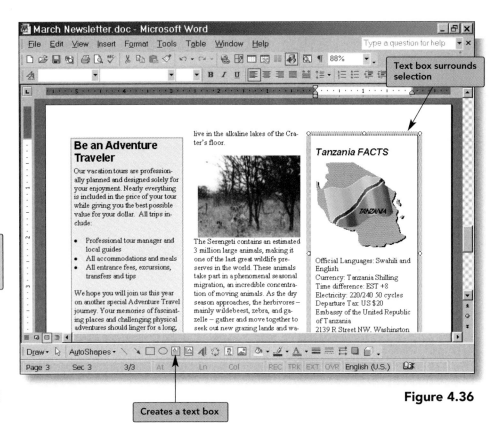

Creates a text box

Text box surrounds selection

Figure 4.36

The selected text is placed in a text box. The text is inserted using the new Normal font size of 11 points. In addition, the Text Box toolbar may be displayed. Its buttons (identified below) are used to link text boxes together so that text flows from one to the next. You will use this feature shortly.

Notice that when you moved the text box, all the objects inside the text box moved too. This is because the text box is a grouped object and is considered one graphic element. However, you can still format the text and size the graphic as separate items.

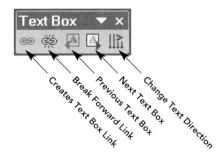

Formatting a Text Box

You will enhance the appearance of the text and text box next.

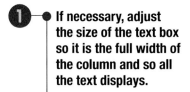

- **If necessary, adjust the size of the text box so it is the full width of the column and so all the text displays.**

- **Reduce the text size (excluding the heading) to 10 points and bold the text.**

- **Click 🖌️▼ Fill Color and select gold from the color palette.**

Additional Information

Because a text box is a drawing object, the Drawing toolbar buttons can be used to make these changes.

- **Click ✏️▼ Line Color and change the line color to blue.**

- **Center the entire contents of the text box.**

- **Deselect the text box.**

Your screen should be similar to Figure 4.37

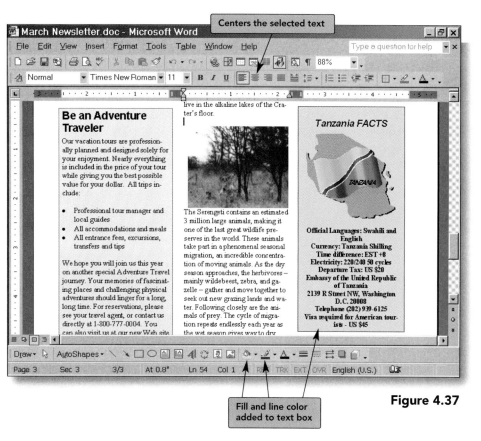

Figure 4.37

Next you want to include the listing of newsletter contents in a text box and move it to the first page of the newsletter.

2
- Select the heading "In This Issue" and the five lines of text that follow.

- Apply a text box to the selection.

- Fill the box with a color of your choice.

- Add a border with a color of your choice.

- Apply bullets to the five topics.

- Move the text box to the bottom of the column on page 2 as shown in Figure 4.38.

- Click outside the text box to deselect it.

Your screen should be similar to Figure 4.38

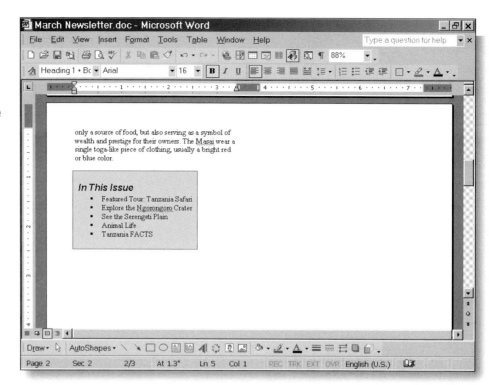

Figure 4.38

Now you would like to see the effects your changes have made to the layout and design of your newsletter.

3
- Change the zoom to Two Pages.

- Scroll down to see the third page.

- Scroll up to the first two pages again.

- Save the document again.

Your screen should be similar to Figure 4.39

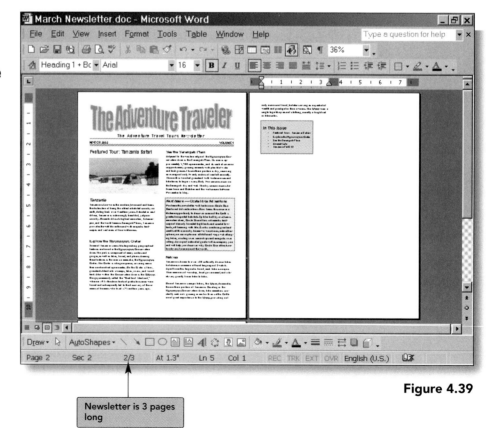

Newsletter is 3 pages long

Figure 4.39

The newsletter consists of three pages, with the second page only containing the end of the article on Natives and the text box. Once you have all the elements added to the newsletter, you will play with placement and size of the elements to make the entire newsletter fit on two pages.

Linking Text Boxes

As you look at the layout, you decide to make space on the first page by creating a linked text box for the two topics about the Ngorongoro Crater and the Serengetti Plain.

1 ● Change the zoom to Page Width.

● Move to the heading **Explore the Ngorongoro Crater** and select the text through the end of the **See the Serengetti Plain** article.

● Click 🖺 Text Box.

● Add a light yellow fill color and blue border to the text box.

● Reduce the size of the text box until only the first article is displayed in it.

● Change the zoom to Whole Page and position the text box as shown in Figure 4.40.

Your screen should be similar to Figure 4.40

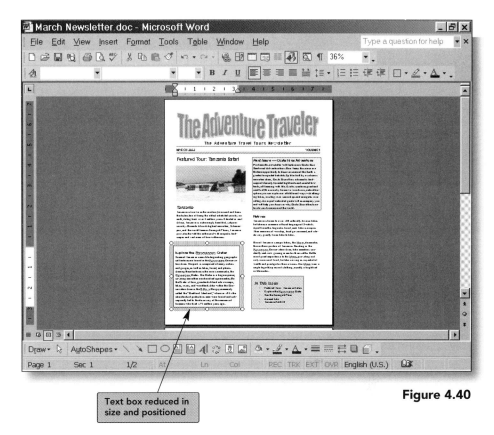

Text box reduced in size and positioned

Figure 4.40

Now you will create the second text box on page 2 where the remainder of the story will be displayed.

2 ● **Change the zoom to Page Width.**

● **Move to the bottom of column 2 of page 2.**

● **Click 🖼 Text Box.**

● **Press** ⌈Delete⌉ **to re-move the Drawing Canvas placeholder.**

Additional Information

When you create a text box without first selecting text, the Drawing Canvas appears and the mouse pointer changes to **+** so you can draw the text box.

● **Drag down and to the right to create a text box as shown in Figure 4.41.**

● **Add a light yellow fill color and blue border to the text box.**

Your screen should be similar to Figure 4.41

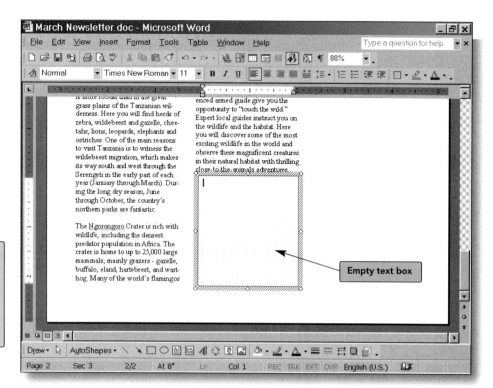

Figure 4.41

A text box created in this manner is inserted as a floating object. You want to change the wrapping style to Square. Then you will create a link be-tween the two text boxes so that the overflow information from the first text box will flow into the empty text box. The text boxes to which you link must be empty—they cannot contain text.

3 ● Choose F**o**rmat/Text Bo**x**/Layout/S**q**uare/ [OK].

Another Method

You can also right-click the text box border and select Format Text Bo**x** from the shortcut menu.

● Click on the Ngorongoro Crater text box on page 1 to select it.

● Click 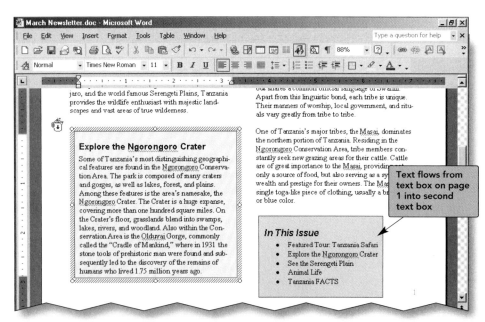 Create Text Box Link (in the Text Box toolbar).

Another Method

You can also select C**r**eate Text Box Link from the object's shortcut menu.

Your screen should be similar to Figure 4.42

Figure 4.42

The mouse pointer changes to an upright pitcher which indicates there is text that is not showing that can flow into another text box. You decide to go ahead and link the boxes.

4 ● Scroll the document and click on the blank text box on page 2.

Additional Information

The mouse pointer changes to a pouring pitcher to indicate that the text will be poured into the text box.

● Increase the size of the text box to fully display the text.

● Size the text box to the column width and position it at the bottom of the column.

Your screen should be similar to Figure 4.43

Additional Information

To move between text boxes in an article, select one of the text boxes and then click Next Text Box or Previous Text Box on the Text Box toolbar.

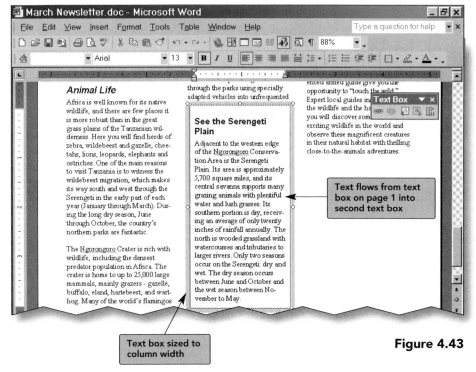

Figure 4.43

The overflow text from the first text box flows into the linked text box.

To indicate to the reader that the article is continued on another page, you will add a "Continued on" line to the bottom of the first text box and a "Continued from" line to the top of the second text box. You plan to use Roman numerals for the newsletter's page numbers and want the page reference to reflect this style.

4 ● **Move to the end of the first topic in the text box on page 1 and press** ←Enter.

HAVING TROUBLE?
If necessary, increase the length of the text box on page 1 to display the new line.

● **Type** Continued on page II.

● **Press** ←Enter **and type** Continued from page I.

● **Change the font style to italics and right-aligned for both lines.**

● **Change the zoom to Two Pages.**

● **Size and position the linked text boxes as shown in Figure 4.44.**

● **Save the newsletter again.**

Your screen should be similar to Figure 4.44

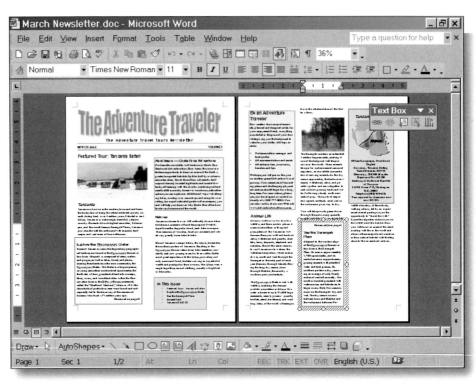

Figure 4.44

Finalizing the Newsletter

Now that the content and placement of articles in the newsletter is set, you want to add a few final touches to improve the appearance.

Inserting Symbols

One way to customize a newsletter is to place a small symbol at the end of each article to let the reader know that the article is finished and will not continue onto another page. You will add a symbol at the end of the article on page 1 and another at the end of the article on page 2.

1.
- Change the zoom to Page Width.

- Move to the end of the text in the second column on page 1.

- Choose **I**nsert/**S**ymbol.

- If necessary, open the **S**ymbols tab and select Symbol from the **F**ont drop-down list.

- Select the diamond symbol (see Figure 4.44).

- Click [Insert].

Your screen should be similar to Figure 4.45

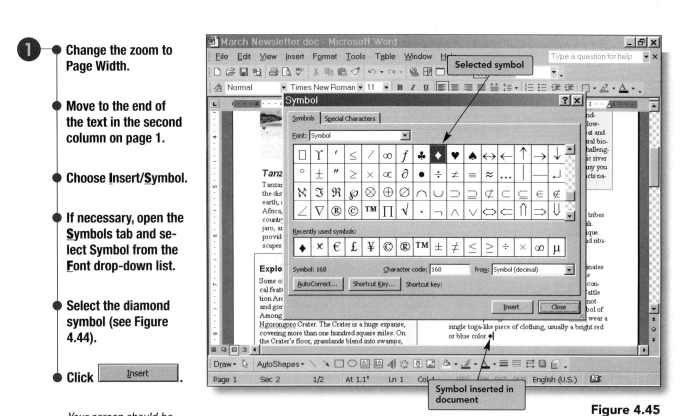

Figure 4.45

The dialog box remains open so you can insert additional symbols.

2.
- Move to the end of the text in column 3 on page 2 and insert the same symbol at this location.

- Click [Close] to close the dialog box.

Adding a Drop Cap

Finally, you would like to make the first letter of the first paragraph of the newsletter a drop cap. A **drop cap**, used most often with the first character in a paragraph, appears as a large uppercase character with the top part of the letter even with the line and the rest of the letter extending into the paragraph below it. The character is changed to a graphic object in a frame, and the text wraps to the side of the object.

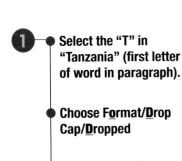

1 ● Select the "T" in
   "Tanzania" (first letter
   of word in paragraph).

● Choose F**o**rmat/**D**rop
   Cap/**D**ropped

● Decrease the lines to
   drop to 2.

● Click [OK] .

● Add the same style and
   size drop cap to the "A"
   of "Africa" at the beginning of the article under
   Animal Life.

Another Method

You can use **E**dit/**R**epeat or
F4 to quickly add the
second drop cap.

*Your screen should be
similar to Figure 4.46*

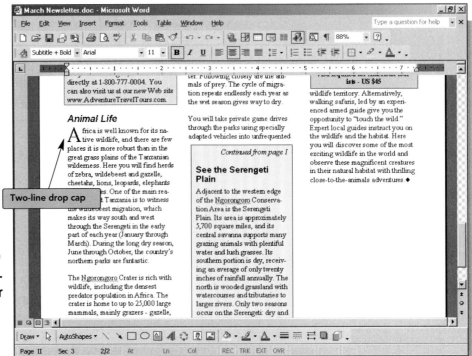

Figure 4.46

The drop-cap effect emphasizes the beginning of the paragraph and makes
the columns appear more like those in a magazine.

Adjusting the Layout

Now you need to check the newsletter layout and move text and graphic elements around on the page until the newsletter has an orderly yet interesting appearance.

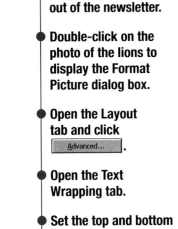

1 ● Switch to Two Pages
   zoom and check the layout of the newsletter.

● Double-click on the
   photo of the lions to
   display the Format
   Picture dialog box.

● Open the Layout
   tab and click
   [Advanced...] .

● Open the Text
   Wrapping tab.

● Set the top and bottom
   distance from the text
   to 0.1 inch.

● Click [OK] two
   times.

*Your screen should be
similar to Figure 4.47*

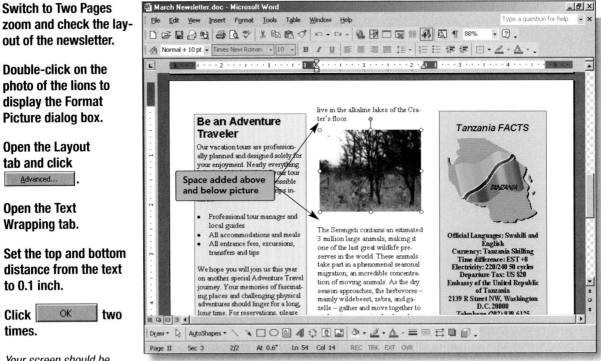

Figure 4.47

The added spacing around the pictures helps set it off from the running text. You will continue refining the layout.

2 ● Move the photo of lions to the top of column 2 on the second page.

● Insert a right-aligned page number in the footer using the uppercase Roman numeral format.

● Position and size the other graphic elements as needed so your newsletter is similar to that shown in Figure 4.46.

Your screen should be similar to Figure 4.48

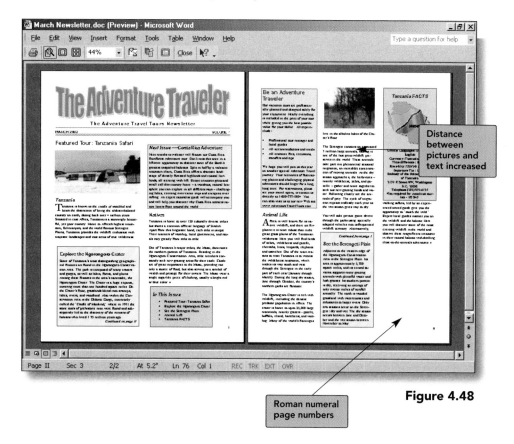

Distance between pictures and text increased

Roman numeral page numbers

Figure 4.48

Printing the Newsletter

As a final check before printing, it is a good idea to display the document in the Print Preview window to make sure that elements will print correctly.

1 ● Preview the document.

● If necessary, switch to Editing and make any changes to the layout as needed.

● Save the document again.

● Print the newsletter.

The printed copy of the newsletter should be similar to the document shown in the Case Study at the beginning of the Lab.

2 ● Exit Word, closing all open files.

Another Method
You can close all open documents without exiting the program by holding down ⇧Shift when opening the File menu and selecting Close All.

LAB 4

Creating a Newsletter

WordArt (WD4.6)

WordArt is used to enhance your documents by changing the shape of text and adding special effects such as 3-D and shadows.

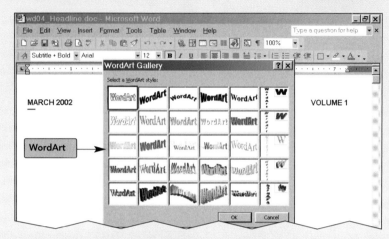

Special Drawing Effects (WD4.10)

Special drawing effects, such as shadows and 3-D effects, can be easily added to text and graphics, including WordArt objects, to enhance the appearance of your document.

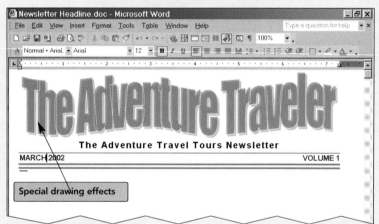

Collecting and Pasting (WD4.16)

Collecting and pasting is the capability of the program to store multiple copied items in the Office Clipboard and then paste one or more of them into another document.

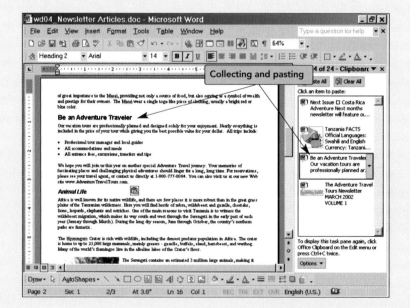

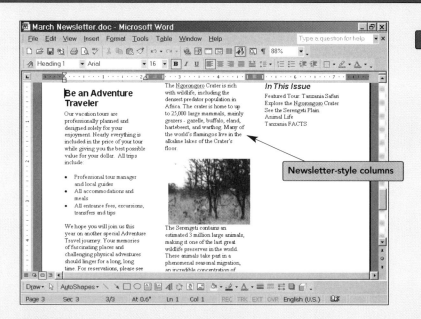

Newsletter-Style Columns (WD4.23)

Newsletter-style columns display text so that it flows from the bottom of one column to the top of the next.

Newsletter-style columns

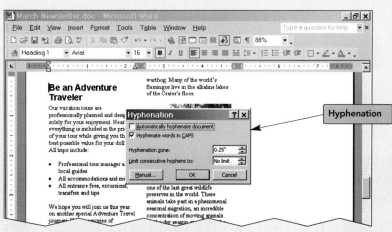

Hyphenation (WD4.28)

The hyphenation feature inserts hyphens in long words that fall at the end of a line, splitting the word between lines.

Hyphenation

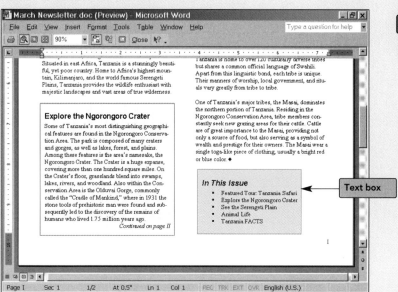

Text Box (WD4.33)

A text box is a graphic object that is a container for text or graphics.

Text box

key terms

collect and paste   WD4.16
drop cap   WD4.41
hyphenation   WD4.28
hyphenation zone   WD4.29
kerning   WD4.11
newsletter-style columns   WD4.23
optional hyphen   WD4.28

sidebar   WD4.29
story   WD4.33
text box   WD4.33
WordArt   WD4.6

mous skills

The Microsoft Office User Specialist (MOUS) certification program is designed to measure your proficiency in performing basic tasks using the Office XP applications. Getting certified demonstrates that you have the skills and provides a valuable industry credential for employment. After completing this lab, you have learned the following Microsoft Office User Specialist skills:

Skill	Description	Page
Inserting and Modifying Text	Insert, modify, and move text and symbols	WD4.17
Creating and Modifying Paragraphs	Modify paragraph formats	WD4.30
	Apply bullets, outline, and numbering format to paragraphs	WD4.36
Formatting Documents	Apply and modify column settings	WD4.23
	Modify document layout and Page Setup options	WD4.43
	Preview and print documents, envelopes, and labels	WD4.43
Managing Documents	Save documents using different names and file formats	WD4.15, WD4.23, WD4.29 WD4.36, WD4.40, WD4.43
Working with Graphics	Insert images and graphics	WD4.5, WD4.19

command summary

Command	Shortcut Keys	Button	Action
Edit/**R**epeat	Ctrl + Y		Repeats last action
Edit/Office Clip**b**oard			Activates Office Clipboard and displays the task pane
Edit/**G**oTo	Ctrl + G		Moves to specified location
Insert/**B**reak/Con**t**inuous			Inserts a section break and starts next section on same page as current section
Insert/**B**reak/**N**ext Page			Inserts a section break and starts next section on a new page
Insert/**S**ymbol			Inserts selected symbol
Insert/Te**x**t Box		▣	Inserts text box
F**o**rmat/**F**ont/Cha**r**acter Spacing			Changes spacing between characters
F**o**rmat/**B**orders and Shading			Adds borders and shadings to selection
		▣	Adds outside border
		▣	Adds top border
		▣	Adds bottom border
F**o**rmat/**C**olumns		▦	Specifies number, spacing, and size of columns
F**o**rmat/**D**rop Cap/**D**ropped			Changes character format as a dropped capital letter
F**o**rmat/**S**tyles and Formatting		▤	Displays Styles and Formatting taskbar from which you apply, create, or modify styles
F**o**rmat/W**o**rdArt/Size		▨	Sizes, rotates, and scales WordArt object
F**o**rmat/W**o**rdArt/Colors and Lines		▨	Applies fill and line color to WordArt object
F**o**rmat/Text B**o**x/Layout		▨	Changes wrapping style and alignment of text box
Tools/**L**anguage/**H**yphenation			Hyphenated document

Terminology

screen identification

In the following Word screen, letters identify important elements. Enter the correct term for each screen element in the space provided.

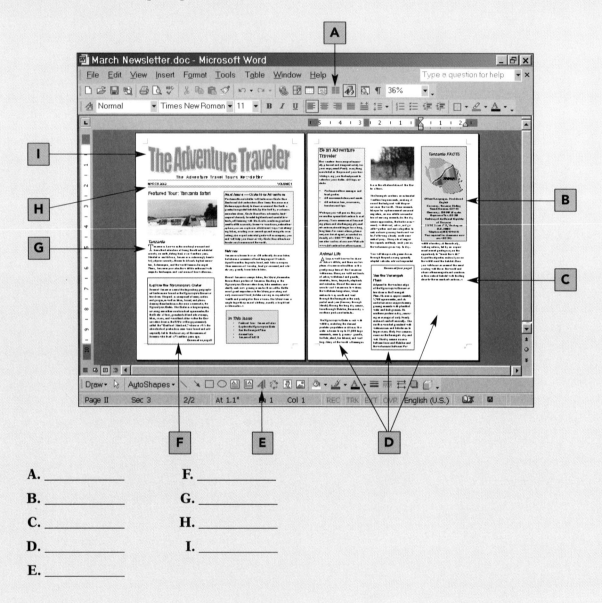

A. _____   F. _____

B. _____   G. _____

C. _____   H. _____

D. _____   I. _____

E. _____

matching

Match the item on the left with the correct description on the right.

1. ☺ _____   **a.** adjusts the spacing between particular pairs of letters

2. drop cap _____   **b.** creates a WordArt object

3. sidebar _____   **c.** creates a linked text box

4. ▣ _____   **d.** flows text from the bottom of one column to the top of the next

5. ◢ _____   **e.** an unmarked space along the right margin that controls the amount of white space in addition to the margin that Word will allow at the end of a line

6. kerning _____   **f.** sets apart an article from the article next to it

7. newsletter-style column _____   **g.** adds a top border line to selection.

8. ▦ _____   **h.** a large uppercase letter aligned with the top of a line and extending into the paragraph below it

9. ▤ _____   **i.** creates a text box

10. hyphenation zone _____   **j.** displays the Office Clipboard task pane

multiple choice

Circle the correct response to the questions below.

1. The feature that is used to enhance documents by changing the shape of text is called _____.

   a. WordArt
   b. WordWrap
   c. Art
   d. DrawShape

2. When an object that is _____ is moved, all objects inside the object move too.
   a. locked
   b. grouped
   c. fixed
   d. blocked

3. _____ adjusts the spacing between particular pairs of letters depending on the font design to improve the appearance of the text.
   a. Locking
   b. Floating
   c. Kerning
   d. Anchoring

4. Text that flows from the bottom of one column to the top of the next is said to be in _____ column format.
   a. newspaper
   b. newsletter-style
   c. adjusted
   d. fixed

5. Information you want to keep separate from other articles or information that highlights an article next to it is called a _____ article.
   a. sideline
   b. sidebar
   c. sidetrack
   d. sidestep

6. Word inserts _____ hyphens, which break the word only if it appears at the end of a line.
   a. fixed
   b. optional
   c. adjusted
   d. floating

7. You can also specify the size of the _____ zone, an unmarked space along the right margin that controls the amount of white space in addition to the margin that Word will allow at the end of a line.
   a. tab
   b. margin
   c. hyphenation
   d. border

8. _____ are graphic objects that are used to contain text or graphics.
   a. Text boxes
   b. List boxes
   c. Phrase boxes
   d. Display boxes

9. Text that is contained in a single text box or linked text boxes is called a(n) _____.
   a. article
   b. story
   c. item
   d. piece

10. A(n) _____, used most often with the first character in a paragraph, appears as a large uppercase character with the top part of the letter even with the line and the rest of the letter extending into the paragraph below it.
   a. decline character
   b. enlarged character
   c. drop cap
   d. character object

true/false

Check the correct answer to the following questions.

1. If you display the Office Clipboard in the task pane of one program or document, it automatically appears when you switch to another program or document.	True	False
2. Handles surround a WordArt object when it is selected.	True	False
3. You cannot change the thickness and color of a border.	True	False
4. WordArt can be changed using the Drawing toolbar buttons.	True	False
5. The Semitransparent option does not allow the shadow color to bleed through.	True	False
6. Kerning adjusts the spacing between particular pairs of letters depending on the font design.	True	False
7. Rules can be added to any side of a paragraph using the Lines toolbar.	True	False
8. When you link text boxes together, large articles will automatically flow into the correct text boxes on the other pages in a newsletter.	True	False
9. The last item you copy to the Office Clipboard is always copied to the Windows Clipboard.	True	False
10. The hyphenation feature inserts a hyphen in long words that fall at the end of a line to split the word between lines.	True	False

Concepts

fill-in

Complete the following statements by filling in the blanks with the correct terms.

1. The _____ feature is used to enhance your documents by changing the shape of text.

2. The _____ stores multiple copied items and the _____ holds one copied item.

3. A(n) _____ is a graphic object that is a container for text or graphics.

4. _____ reduces the amount of white space at the end of lines and makes line lengths more even to improve the appearance of a document.

5. _____ allow you to format a document to different column settings.

6. Text that flows from the bottom of one column to the top of the next is in _____ format.

7. A(n) _____ breaks a word only if it appears at the end of the line.

8. Text contained in linked text boxes is called a(n) _____.

9. _____ adjusts the spacing between pairs of letters based on the font design.

10. Shadows and 3-D effects are examples of _____.

1. How can WordArt enhance the look of a document? What types of documents are best suited for WordArt?

2. What types of special effects can be added to drawing objects? How do the special effects enhance the object?

3. How can newsletter-style columns enhance the look of a document? What types of documents are columns best suited for? How can the adjustment of widths, spacing, and hyphenation affect the layout?

4. How do linked text boxes differ from normal text boxes? When should you consider using a linked text box? When would it be appropriate to add a text box to a document?

step-by-step

Diet and Fitness Newsletter

★ **1.** The Lifestyle Fitness Club's newsletter for this month will focus on dietary concerns and fitness, along with this month's special sale item. The completed newsletter is shown here.

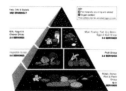

a. To create this newsletter, open the file wd04_Fitness Club Headline. Insert the [WordArt] WordArt object and center it below the main title. Enter the text UPDATE with top and bottom wrapping style.

b. Fill the WordArt object with orange and clear the Semitransparent check box. Change the line color to red. Apply the deflate shape and size appropriately.

c. Insert a shadow border of 3 points around the identification text.

d. Save the headline file as Fitness Headline2. Copy the entire file to the Clipboard. Close the file.

e. Open the file wd04_Fitness Club. Paste the headline text above the text in the Fitness Club file.

f. Move to the blank line below the bottom border line and insert a continuous section break.

g. Select the text below the bottom border and change to a two-column format. Then select the text beginning at the Fitness heading to the end of the document and format it to three columns. Change the spacing between the three columns to 0.3 for column 1 and choose equal column widths.

h. Apply automatic hyphenation to the entire document.

i. Create a text box that contains the text at the end of column 3 on page 2 beginning with the heading "Special of the Month" and ending with the word "description." Add a tan fill color and change the border color to black and increase the line weight to 3 pt.

j. Insert the clip art wd04_Exercise Bike beneath the "Special of the Month" heading. Size the graphic to fit the text box. Adjust the size of the text box to fully display the text.

k. Add the file wd04_Jogger clip art to the first paragraph below "Fitness" on page 2. Size the graphic to approximately 4 by 1.2 inches. Set the wrapping to Tight on both sides. Move the graphic to be displayed between the columns (see the figures for reference).

l. Add your name and the current date to the bottom of column 3 on page 2. Check the layout of your document and make adjustments as necessary. Save the document as Fitness Club Newsletter. Print the document.

Scenic Drives Newsletter

★ ★ **2.** The Adventure Travel agency devotes one issue of its newsletter annually to information about travel experiences from the car window. This year's car-window newsletter contains information on scenic drives around the United States and Canada. The completed newsletter is shown here.

The Adventure Travel Tours Newsletter

April 2002   VOLUME 2

This Adventure Travel Tours newsletter highlights several scenic drives in the US and Canada. For more information about the drives and accommodations call us at 1-800-555-0004 or visit our Web site at www.AdventureTravelTours.com.

Wisconsin's Kettle Moraine

The route follows the Kettle Moraine Scenic Drive developed and maintained by the Kettle Moraine State Forest staff. Along the way you're likely to learn more about glacial geology than you ever thought you'd know. You will travel many unmarked back roads, wandering all over in search of yet more glacial formations. It is likely to fill an enjoyable day of driving.

Lake Michigan

This drive tours the Lake Michigan shore from Sheboygan to Algoma, passing sand dunes, high bluffs, lighthouses, farms, and museums. The area's flavor and history are closely tied to the lake through fishing, sailing, and ship building. Special attractions: Kohler-Andrae State Park, Point Beach State Forest, the USS Cobia, lighthouses, museums, hiking, swimming, fishing, camping, wildlife watching.

Dahinda Illinois

Breathtaking fall scenery will usher you into this small community, a prime example of rural America at its finest; a small town with friendly folk always ready to visit. This is the only Scenic Drive stop along the Spoon River. The hilly timberland surrounding the river and nearby creeks, along with the vast area of river bottomland gives visitors a breathtaking view of Mother Nature's fiery fall colors.

Cohutta Loop

These 70 square miles of North Georgia wilderness are encompassed by the drive many refer to as the Cohutta Loop. For the outdoor enthusiast, this is heaven. The drive provides access to the largest wilderness area east of the Mississippi, abounds with walking trails and wildlife, and features occasional campgrounds as it follows the perimeter of the wilderness.

Columbia River

The Columbia River Gorge Loop is Oregon's most famous scenic drive. Drive along a two-lane country road that follows the contour of the land through open country and past towering basalt outcroppings. Along the route you'll find wineries that feature distinctive varieties, and picturesque surroundings. You will also pass dozens of waterfalls, and any number of hatcheries and dam fishways for viewing the fall salmon runs.

Washington State

Washington has the fastest growing wine region in the country; the effects of its geography, climate, and soil create a classic combination for growing premium grapes to produce wines achieving world class status. Wine lovers can sample the newest releases from twenty-two wineries in the Yakima Valley Appellation at their annual "Spring Barrel Tasting" in late April. As the fruit begins to ripen in mid-September, wineries throughout the state celebrate the harvest season with open houses and special events.

Hood Canal

Washington state visitors are drawn by the wonders of the ancient rain forests, the wildness of its ocean beaches, and the mysteries of the Hood Canal. Rich native cultures have inhabited the land for thousands of years, and a heritage deeply rooted in logging and fishing is evident at every turn. The National Park, with its majestic mountains, vast glaciers, and wilderness trails, lures hikers and climbers. Rushing rivers, pristine lakes, distinctive wildlife, old growth forests, and magnificent vistas offer unlimited opportunities for fishers, naturalists, and photographers.

Upcoming Adventure Tours

January ◆ **Ski the Canadian Wilderness**: Fulfills everyone's desire to explore and participate in the majestic outdoors of northern Alberta, the Yukon, and the Northwest Territories.

June ◆ **Vancouver Island**: No matter where you travel on Vancouver Island or the Gulf Islands, there is an abundance of interesting things to do and see.

September ◆ **Amazon River Excursion**: Imagine yourself exploring the upper reaches of the exotic Amazon, one of the world's greatest ecosystems, on a multilevel riverboat with private rooms. Spend your days relaxing in comfort on the upper deck and walking through the forest surrounded by sights and sounds most people have only imagined.

Student Name
Date

a. To create this newsletter, open the file wd04_Scenic Drives and the file Newsletter Headline you saved in this lab.

b. In the Newsletter Headline file, change the date to the current month and year. Increase the volume number by one. Copy the text from the Newsletter Headline file to the top of the Scenic Drives file. Adjust the WordArt so that it is displayed a half inch below the top edge of the page.

c. Insert the clip art image wd04_Road below the first paragraph. Size the clip art appropriately. (about 3" × 2") Change the wrapping style for the graphic to Top and Bottom. Center it horizontally.

d. Select all the text below the clip art and format it to two equal columns. Apply hyphenation to the selected text.

e. Use bold and italics for each of the scenic drive headings. Use bold for the headline "Upcoming Adventure Tours" and the names of the upcoming adventure tours. Replace the hyphens with diamond (◆) symbols to separate the month and tour names.

f. Insert a column break before the Dahinda, Illinois heading and another column break before Washington State scenic drive heading. Insert another column break before "Upcoming Adventure Tours." (Hint: To insert a column break select Break from the Insert menu and choose Column break.)

g. Insert the picture of wd04_Canada at the beginning of the "January ◆ Ski the Canadian Wilderness" paragraph. Size it to fit across half the column and wrap the text to the right.

h. Add the picture wd04_MtDoug at the beginning of "June ◆ Vancouver Island" and wd04_Huts at the beginning of "September ◆ Amazon River Excursion." Size and format these pictures as you did the Canada picture.

i. Add your name and the current date to the bottom of column 2 on page 2. Check the layout of your document and make adjustments to the text as necessary. Save the document as Scenic Drives Newsletter. Print the document.

Cafe Promotion Newsletter

★ ★ **3.** The Downtown Internet Cafe would like to use a newsletter to promote itself. The newsletter will highlight some of the things people can do at the cafe and describe four coffees the cafe plans to feature this month. The completed newsletter is shown here.

a. To create the newsletter, open the file wd04_Coffee. Create a WordArt headline at the top of the document with the words The Downtown Internet Cafe. Choose an appropriate shape and adjust the size to fit between the margins.

b. Center and bold A Newsletter for Coffee Lovers of the World below the WordArt. Format the line to 14 point and expand the character spacing to 1.5 points. Type and bold Spring 2002 Volume II on the next line. Add a right tab at the right margin and indent "Volume II" to this position.

c. Add a blank line above the date and volume line. Add appropriately colored borders above and below the date and volume text line.

d. Apply hyphenation to all the text in the file.

e. Insert a blank line below the issue identification text and insert a continuous section break.

f. Select the text beginning at the heading "Things to Do in the Cafe," and ending at "by technical area." Apply two-column format. Insert a page break before the heading "Coffee Reviews."

g. Apply the heading 3 style to the headings "Things to Do in the Cafe," "Services We Provide," and "Coffee Reviews." Add italics and underlines to the names of the four featured coffees in the Coffee Reviews article.

h. Add an appropriate color to each heading for the types of services provided.

i. Insert the clip art wd04_Conversation above "Things to Do at the Cafe" heading. Set the wrapping to top and bottom. Change the size of the graphic to 2.5 × 2.5 inches.

j. Adding the clip art caused the Consulting text to move to page 2, so you would like to display the text in a text box. Select the heading Services We Provide and all the text under that topic. Create a text box and size it to fully display the text. Remove the blank lines between each service and resize the box until it is displayed down the right side of page 1 under the heading.

k. You want to draw attention to the services discussed in the text box using a fill effect. Apply a two-color fill effect of your choice to the text box. (Hint: access these options in the Colors and Lines tab of the format dialog box. Choose Fill Effects from the color drop down list and select the two colors option.

l. Apply a three-column format to the text on page 2 with spacing of 0.3 inch and equal columns.

k. Insert the clip art wd04_Coffee Beans in front of the "Coffee Reviews." Increase the size of the Coffee Reviews text to 22 points.

l. Insert the clip art wd04_Coffee Cup at the bottom of column 3 on page 2.

m. Add your name and the current date to the bottom of column 3 on page 2. Check the layout of your document and make adjustments to the text as necessary. Save the document as Internet Cafe Newsletter. Print the document.

Survival Newsletter

★ ★ **4.** The National Parks Service places newsletters for hikers in park stores. This month's newsletter highlights hikes and survival skills. The completed newsletter is shown here.

The National Parks Service
A Publication for People That Explore Our Great Country.

FALL 2001   VOLUME 10

Central Oregon Cascades Hikes

Come discover a new path along the Deschutes River near Bend, hike to a hidden cave overlooking Mt. Jefferson, or prowl a gold-mining ghost town near Eugene! With 47 easy day hikes suitable for the whole family, and there's a variety of tougher trails too, and lots of backpacking options.

Short Hikes in California's Central Coast

The central coast of California is a hiker's dream, with miles of trails with stunning coastal views, easily accessible and beautiful any time of the year. Try short hikes in San Luis Obispo, Santa Barbara, and Ventura counties, plus the scenic Channel Islands.

Day Hikes of the California Northwest

Ninety four wonderful day hikes located from Marin to Crescent City, to Mount Shasta. Including Trinity Alps, Russian, Marble Mountain, and Yolla Bolla

Wilderness Areas. The local geology, flora and wildlife makes the trips most enjoyable.

Best Easy Day Hikes Olympics

Olympic National Park is home to a vast network of hiking trails. Easy-to-follow trails that take you to some of the area's most spectacular scenery without taking you to physical extremes.

Hiking California

Boasting a mild climate, incredible diversity and thousands of miles of hiking trails, California has something for every hiker. The hikes use routes varying from gentle inclines to rugged cross-country scrambles, including old favorites known to many and obscure routes known only to a few. Surveying the most awe-inspiring scenery in the state, trails will satisfy both beginning and veteran hikers.

Hiking the Cape Breton's Cabot Trail

Cape Breton's Cabot Trail includes 28 hiking trails from short hikes to longer day hikes. Discover whales, birds, animals, and flowers along the hiking trails.

Vermont and New Hampshire Hiking

Try some of the best hikes of Central Vermont, the Upper Valley of New Hampshire /Vermont. Including the Killington Peak Region the second highest peak in Vermont (4,242'). Trails include surrounding region, the Long Trail and Appalachian Trail. Also the Mt. Ascutney Trails, in and around the Mt. Ascuntey State Park. Hikes range from difficult to easy.

Utah's Favorite Hiking Trails

The Hikes range in length from a half-a-day stroll to Fisher Towers near Moab, to a four day walk around Brown Duck Mountain in the High Unitas area.

The National Parks Service

5 Basic Survival Skills

One of the most important elements to survival is between your ears.... your brain. Don't panic, use your wits and practice all elements of the 5 Basics before you may need to rely on them.

 FIRE can purify water, cook food, signal rescuers, provide warmth, light and comfort, help keep predators at a distance, and can be a most welcome friend and companion. Have a minimum of two ways to start a fire, one on your person at all times and the other in your gear.

 SHELTER is the means by which you protect your body from excess exposure from the sun, cold, wind, rain or snow. Anything that takes away or adds to your overall body temperature can be your enemy. Clothing is the first line of shelter protection, have the right clothes for the right environment. Always have a hat. Try and keep the layer closest to your body dry. Layers trap air and are warmer than one thick garment.

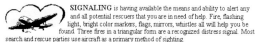 **SIGNALING** is having available the means and ability to alert any and all potential rescuers that you are in need of help. Fire, flashing light, bright color markers, flags, mirrors, whistles all will help you be found. Three fires in a triangular form are a recognized distress signal. Most search and rescue parties use aircraft as a primary method of sighting.

 FOOD/WATER are vital towards your survival. Ration your sweat not your water intake. Try to drink only in the cool of the evening. You can live up to three days without water. Do not eat plants you do not know. Never drink urine. Always assume that you will need extra food and water when you plan your trip. Pack energy bars and candy in your pockets at all time, just in case.

 FIRST AID is not just the basic medical needs, it is the primary way in which you act to survive. STOP means Sit, Think, Observe, and Plan. It is the most intelligent thing you can do when you realize you are lost or stranded. The most important element is to keep your brain functioning rationally; this is basic first aid for survival.

Student Name
Date

a. To create the newsletter, open the files wd04_Hikes, wd04_Park Headline, and wd04_Survival Skills. In the Park Headline file create a WordArt object with the text The National Parks Service. Color the WordArt green. Adjust the size of the WordArt appropriately.

b. Increase the font size of the remaining text to 14 points. Create a single green top border and a double green bottom border around the date and volume information.

c. Copy the text from the Hikes and Survival Skills documents to the Office Clipboard. Paste the Hikes text into the headline document one blank line below the bottom border.

d. Select all the text, excluding the headline, and format it to three columns with 0.3-inch spacing.

e. Bold the headlines for the different hikes.

f. Create a Next Page section break at the end of the paragraph on Utah's Favorite Hiking Trails. Add three blank lines to the top of page 2 and copy the WordArt object to the top of page 2.

g. Paste the Survival Skills text below the WordArt on page 2 and close the Office Clipboard. If necessary, change the format back to one column. Draw a double-line border under the WordArt on the second blank line. (You will need one blank line below the border to add more text.) Increase the size of the section heading and the five tips to 14 points and make them bold.

h. You would like to insert a clip art image in front of each tip. The pictures should be formatted tight to the text and appear on the left. Choose five appropriate clipart images from your ClipArt Gallery, or use the images wd04_Fire, wd04_Shelter, wd04_Signaling, wd04_Food&Water, wd04_First Aid. Add your name and the current date to the bottom of page 2. Check the layout of your document and make adjustments to the text as necessary. Save the document as National Parks Newsletter. Print the document.

Animal Angels Travel Newsletter

★ ★ **5.** Animal Angels, the volunteer group for the Animal Rescue Foundation, sends a monthly
★   newsletter to its members. This month's newsletter focuses on air travel issues. The completed
      newsletter is shown here.

Animal Angels

The Animal Rescue Foundation rescues unwanted pets from local animal shelters and finds fosters homes for them until a suitable adoptive family can be found. The Animal Angels volunteer group produces this newsletter to keep you informed on issues related to the animals we are dedicated to saving. This month's newsletter is dedicated to air travel with animals.

Is Your Pet Up for the Flight?

Before you make any travel arrangements check with your vet. Animals that are very young or old, pregnant, ill, or injured should generally not travel. Sometimes the best decision is not to fly with pets. Some animals do not function well in unfamiliar surroundings, and an unhappy pet can make a trip miserable for everyone.

Most vets agree that your pet should not be tranquilized during the flight. It creates an unnecessary risk of suffocation!

Choosing a Pet-friendly Airline...

When making your reservations, inquire about the airline's Animal Welfare and Transport Policies. All airlines must comply with the basic guidelines set forth by the Animal Welfare Act, but standards still vary between carriers. Also keep in mind the US Department of Agriculture prohibits animals from being kept in the hold or on the tarmac for more than 45 minutes when temperatures are above 85F or below 45F.

Your airline should certainly adhere to these standards, but a good airline may prohibit animals on flights to cities where temperatures exceed these limits.

Continued from page 1

You should be sure to reserve a spot for your pet; many airlines carry a limited number of animals per flight. Try to arrange a nonstop flight, this reduces the time your pet spends in the hold, and eliminates the possibility that your pet is placed on the wrong flight.

Verify the policy on layovers and delays. If you must have a lengthy layover, or encounter a delay, make sure you will have access to your pet; a good airline will allow you to check on your pet in these circumstances.

You may also want to inquire about hand-carrying and counter-to-counter shipping. Hand-carrying assures that your pet will not be subjected to conveyor belt accidents. Counter-to-counter shipping ensures that your pet will be loaded right before departure and immediately after arrival. There is usually a fee for counter-to-counter shipping, but it may be worth the price for peace of mind.

Thanks to all of our loyal supporters whose donations have made it possible for us to provide vaccinations and medications for rescued animals.

Keep in mind that the more information a carrier provides in response to your questions, the more likely your pet will be well cared for!

Buying a Pet Carrier

❖ The carrier should have hard sides, ventilation on at least two sides, and exterior rims to prevent blocked airflow.

❖ The carrier must be large enough for the pet to stand, turn around, and lie down comfortably. Your pet should easily be able to stand, turn around, and lie down inside the carrier.

❖ It should also be marked with a large, highly visible label reading "Live Animal," at least one inch tall, including arrows indicating the carrier's upright position. Never lock your pet's carrier before departure, in an emergency, airline personnel may need access to your pet.

❖ Finally, both the pet and the carrier should be well marked with the owner's name, address, and phone number, and the pet's updated health certificate.

Student Name
Date

a. To create the newsletter, open the file wd04_Air Travel. Create and center a WordArt headline at the top of the document with the words Animal Angels. Choose a design and colors of your choice and adjust the size appropriately.

b. Insert a border line of your choice below the WordArt object.

c. Apply a two-line drop cap to the "T" in "The" in the beginning of first paragraph. Add color to the drop cap to match the WordArt object.

d. Beginning at the heading "Is Your Pet Up for the Flight?", select the text and apply a two-column format.

e. Since the entire article on selecting an airline does not fit on page 1, you decide to create a linked text box. Select the material from the heading "Choosing a Pet Friendly Airline…" to "for!" Create a text box and size it to the width of the second column on page 1. Move the bulleted paragraph to page 2.

f. Move the note on tranquilization to the space above the text box in the second column of page 1.

g. Move the graphic of the dogs and suitcases to the bottom of column 1 on page 1. Resize the image appropriately.

h. Create a second text box on page 2 and size it to the width of the left column. Link the text boxes. Resize the text boxes as necessary and add the text continued from page 1 in italics and right-aligned at the top of the linked text box.

i. Change the border style on the text boxes to a line style of your choice. Then add color to each of the text boxes.

j. Adjust the layout as needed, and add your name and the date at the bottom of the second page.

k. Save the file as Air Travel Newsletter. Print the document.

Activity Newsletter

★ **1.** Prepare a two-page newsletter on an activity or club of interest to you. The newsletter should include the following features: WordArt, column format, linked text boxes, clip art and/or pictures. When you are finished, add your name and the current date to the last column on page 2. Check the layout of your document and make adjustments as necessary. Save the newsletter as Activity Newsletter and print the document.

Power Plant News

★ ★ **2.** As the Public Relations Officer for the local power company, you have been assigned a project to inform the public on issues related to the construction of a new power plant. As part of your campaign, you have been asked to create a newsletter to address community concerns. Your completed letter should have great visual appeal. Create a one-page newsletter with multiple graphic objects. Include your name and the date in the document. Save it as Power Plant Newsletter and print it.

Creating a Newsletter

★ ★ **3.** You are a physical education major and have written a report on water exercises. Open the file wd04_Water. Use this file to create a newsletter for students who use the pool at your school's recreation center. Use the features you have learned in Word, including WordArt, clip art, borders, colors, and text boxes, to create a newsletter that is both informative and visually appealing. When you are finished, add your name and the current date to the last column on page 2. Check the layout of your document and make adjustments as necessary. Save your file as Water Exercise Newsletter and print the document.

PTA Newsletter

★ ★
★ **4.** You are a member of the PTA at the local elementary school. The budget for the year has just been released and the parents are trying to accommodate requests from the teachers and staff for equipment and supplies. The parents decide that a fund raiser will be necessary. In order to fund the purchases, the school has decided to hold an old-fashioned ice cream social. You have volunteered to put together a newsletter to be distributed to the students advertising the event. Your completed newsletter should include WordArt, column format, and other graphic features. Add your name and the date to the top of the newsletter, save the newsletter as PTA Newsletter, and print the document.

Garden Newsletter

★ ★
★ **5.** The neighborhood that you live in has begun construction of a public garden in a previously vacant lot. You are the chairperson of the committee that raised the funds for the park. You and the other committee members have decided to distribute a newsletter updating the contributors and community on the park's progress. Your newsletter should have great visual appeal. Be sure to include WordArt and other graphic features, as well as photos of the garden. Add your name and the current date to the top of the newsletter. Save the document as Garden Newsletter and print it.

Creating a Personal Newsletter

Create a monthly newsletter with small articles on a topic of your choice. Use the Web or other resources to obtain information on your topic. Use the features you have learned in Word to create a newsletter that is both informative and visually appealing. Include features such as WordArt, clip art, borders, colors, and text boxes. When you are finished, add your name and the current date to the end of the document. Check the layout of your document and make adjustments as necessary. Save the document as My Newsletter and print it.

Creating Complex Tables and Merging Documents

LAB 5

objectives

After completing this lab, you will know how to:

1.	Use a template.
2.	Modify a field format.
3.	Insert graphics from the Web.
4.	Use the Draw Table feature to create and enhance a table.
5.	Merge cells.
6.	Change text orientation, table size, and page orientation.
7.	Insert a column.
8.	Perform calculations in a table.
9.	Add cell shading.
10.	Size rows and columns.
11.	Remove border lines.
12.	Create and modify a chart.
13.	Create an outline-style numbered list.
14.	Use the Mail Merge feature to create form letters.
15.	Print mailing labels and envelopes.

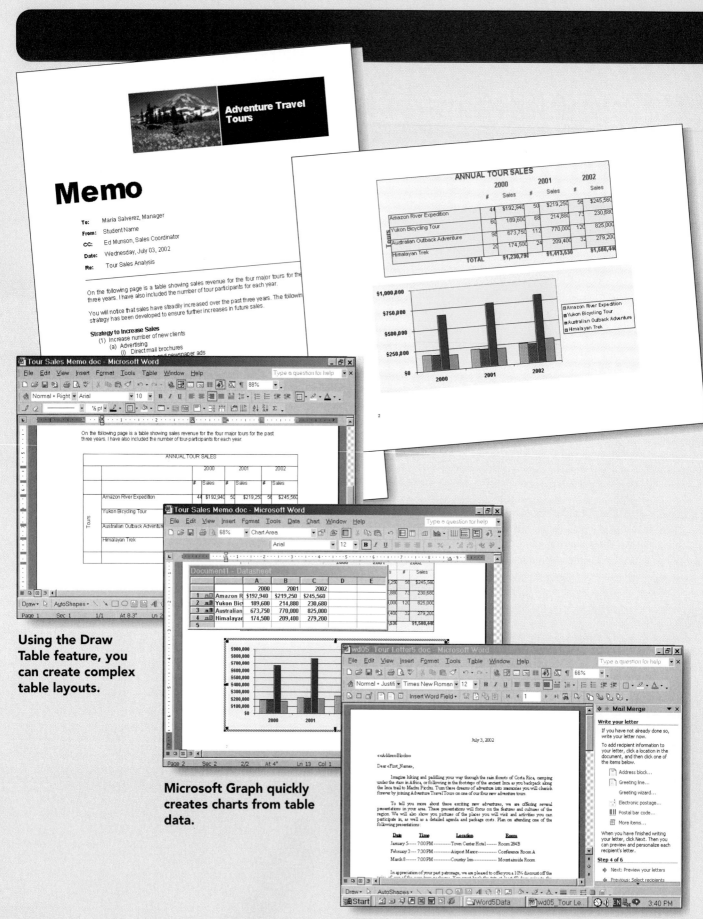

Using the Draw Table feature, you can create complex table layouts.

Microsoft Graph quickly creates charts from table data.

The Mail Merge feature helps you quickly generate a form letter.

Adventure Travel Tours

In addition to the four new tours, Adventure Travel Tours offers many established adventure tours. The four most popular tours are the Amazon River Expedition, the Yukon Bicycling Tour, the Australian Outback Adventure, and the Himalayan Trek. Your latest project for Adventure Travel Tours is to prepare a memo for the regional manager that contains a table showing the sales figures for these four major tours for the past three years. In addition, you want to include a strategy to increase sales for the four tours.

The manager has also asked you to personalize the letter you wrote about the new tours and presentations by including an inside address for each client and using his or her first name in the salutation. To do this, you will create a form letter. Form letters are common business documents used when the same information needs to be communicated to many different people. You will also create mailing labels for the letter and learn how to quickly address a single envelope.

© Corbis

concept overview

The following concepts will be introduced in this lab:

1	**Formulas and Functions**	Formulas and functions are used to perform calculations in tables.
2	**Charts**	A chart, also called a graph, is a visual representation of numeric data.
3	**Mail Merge**	The Mail Merge feature combines a list of data (typically a file of names and addresses) with a document (commonly a form letter) to create a new document.
4	**Data Source**	The data source file is a table of information that contains data fields in the columns and records in the rows.
5	**Field Name**	Field names are used to label the different data fields in the data source.

Using a Template

You would like to create the sales-figure memo using one of the pre-designed document templates included with Word. The templates are designed to help you create professional-looking business documents such as letters, faxes, memos, reports, brochures, press releases, manuals, newsletters, resumes, invoices, purchase orders, and weekly time sheets. Once you create a document from a template, you can change different elements to give it your own personal style.

1 ● **Start Word.**

Additional Information
Word displays the last two templates that were used in the New From Template list.

● **Click** 🔲 General Templates... **from the New Document task pane.**

● **Open the Memos tab.**

● **Select** 🔲 Contemporary Memo **.**

Your screen should be similar to Figure 5.1

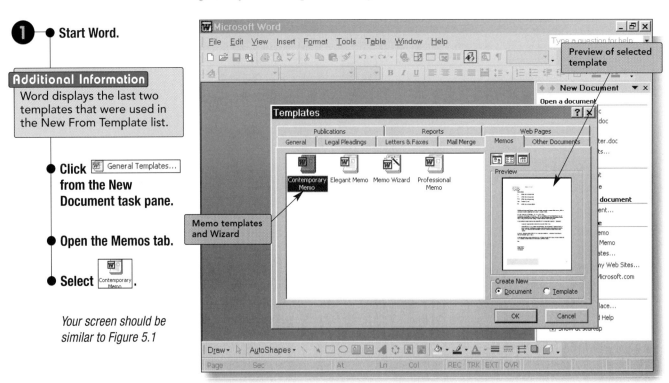

Figure 5.1

Additional Information
You will learn more about Wizards later in this lab.

Word has several memo templates and a Memo Wizard that guides you step by step through creating a memo. Document templates have a .dot file extension and are stored in the Templates folder. When opened, the file type changes to a Word document (.doc). This prevents accidentally overwriting the template file when the file is saved.

The Preview area displays how the selected memo template looks. You will use the Professional Memo template to create your memo.

② ● Double-click Professional Memo.

● Change the zoom to Page Width.

Your screen should be similar to Figure 5.2

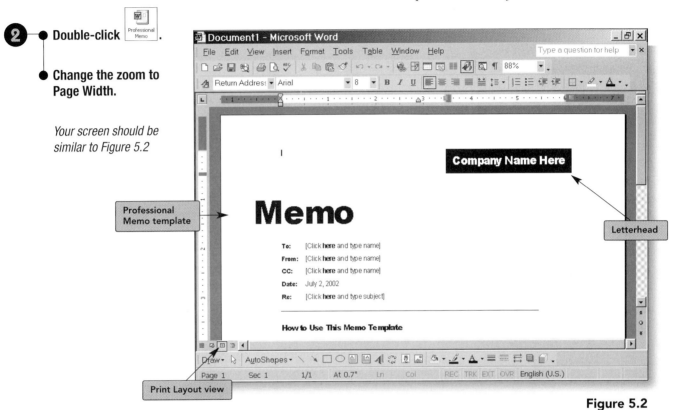

Figure 5.2

The memo template is opened as a Word document and is displayed in Print Layout view.

Replacing Template Placeholders

The template uses a single-row table to control the layout of the company letterhead. You will display the table gridlines and then replace the text in the table cell with the company name.

3 ● If necessary, choose **Table/Show Gridlines.**

● Select the text **Company Name Here.**

● Type **Adventure Travel Tours.**

Your screen should be similar to Figure 5.3

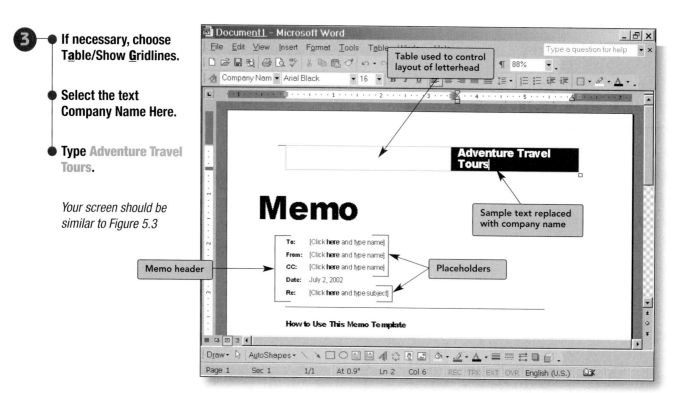

Figure 5.3

The next area in the memo template you need to modify is the memo header, which includes the name of the recipient, the sender's name, a carbon or courtesy (CC) recipient, the date, and a subject line. Notice that the date is the current system date. The text in brackets is a **placeholder** that tells you what information to enter. To enter text, click on the placeholder and type the information you want to include in your document. This feature is found in most templates.

4 ● Click the **To:** placeholder.

● Type **Maria Salverez, Manager.**

Your screen should be similar to Figure 5.4

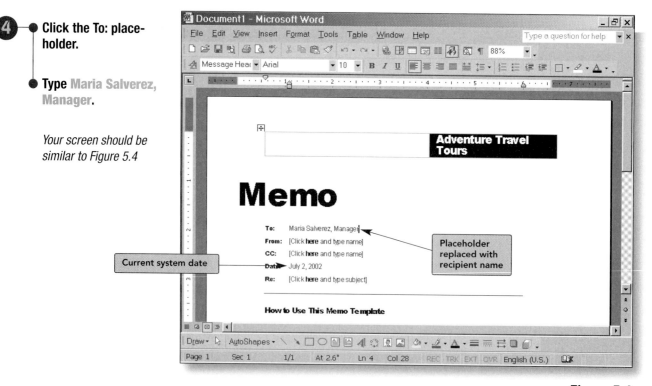

Figure 5.4

The placeholder is replaced with the name of the recipient. Notice that the Style list box displays "Message Header" as the default style; this sets the font to Arial and the size to 10 points.

5 ● **Replace the remaining four placeholders with the following:**

From: Your name

CC: Ed Munson, Sales Coordinator

Re: Tour Sales Analysis

Your screen should be similar to Figure 5.5

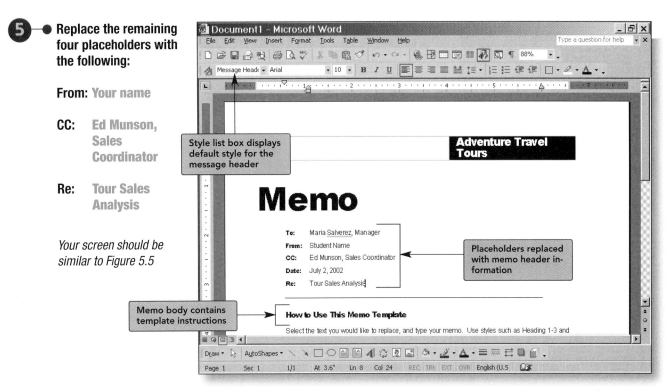

Style list box displays default style for the message header

Placeholders replaced with memo header information

Memo body contains template instructions

Figure 5.5

Next you want to enter the body of the memo. The memo template also includes instructions on how to use the template in the body of the memo. You will replace the template instructions with the information you want to include in the memo. However, because the template instructions are not placeholders, you first need to select the instructions to be deleted before typing the replacement text.

6 ● Click ¶ Show/Hide to turn on paragraph marks.

● Scroll the window to see the paragraph of template instructions in the body of the memo.

● Select the heading, the instructions paragraphs and the blank lines below the paragraph.

● Type the following text: On the following page is a table showing sales revenue for the four major tours for the past three years. I have also included the number of tour participants for each year.

● Press ←Enter twice.

Your screen should be similar to Figure 5.6

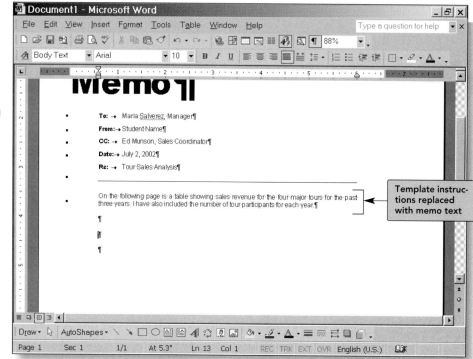

Figure 5.6

The template instructions are replaced with your own memo text.

Modifying Field Formats

The date in the memo template is a field that displays the current system date. You want to change the date format to include the day of the week. To do this, you need to edit the field format.

1 ● Right-click on the Date field.

● Choose **E**dit Field.

Your screen should be similar to Figure 5.7

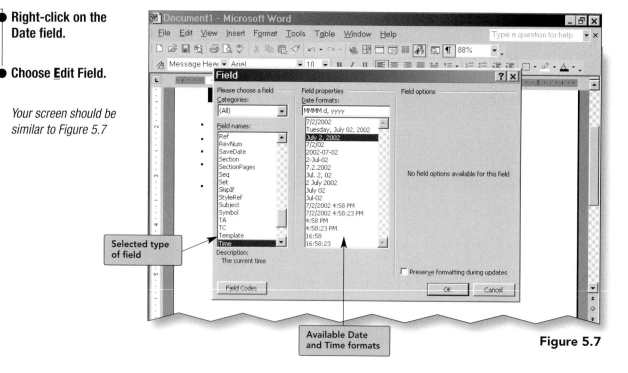

Figure 5.7

The Field dialog box displays a list of field names and formats for the selected field. Since the Date field is selected, the Time category is open and selected formats for date and time display in the Field Properties area.

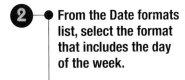

2 ● **From the Date formats list, select the format that includes the day of the week.**

● Click  OK .

Your screen should be similar to Figure 5.8

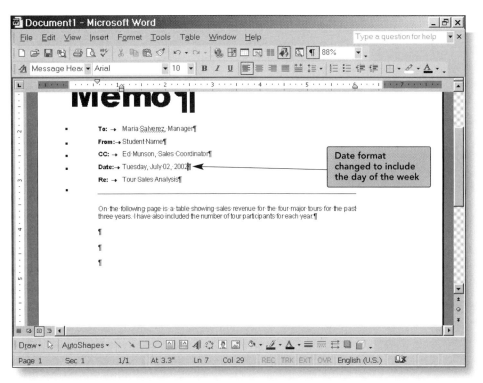

Date format changed to include the day of the week

Additional Information

If you type over the Date field with text, you will delete the field from the document and it will not update automatically.

Figure 5.8

Inserting Graphics from the Web

Next you want to add a graphic to the letterhead. If the Clip Organizer does not include a suitable graphic, you can go to the Microsoft Design Gallery Live Web site and download a picture. You will use this resource to locate a graphic.

Additional Information

If you are connected to the Internet, any search performed in the ClipArt task pane will automatically include the Microsoft Design Gallery Live Web site.

Note: This section requires an Internet connection. If you do not have this capability, insert the clip art graphic wd05_Mountain from your supplied data files and complete the instructions in Step 4 to size and position it.

1 ● Click in the table cell to the left of the company name.

● Click ■ Insert Clip Art (on the Drawing toolbar).

● Click 🌐 Clips Online.

● Enter the information as needed to connect to the Internet.

HAVING TROUBLE?
If an End User license agreement appears, click Accept to continue.

Your screen should be similar to Figure 5.9

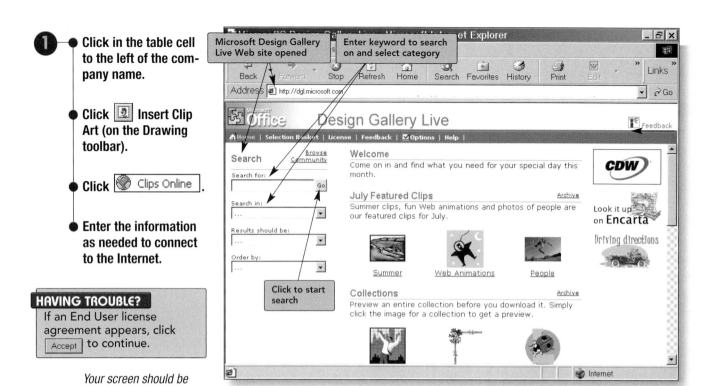

Figure 5.9

The browser on your system is started and the connection to the Microsoft Design Gallery Live Web site is made. The Design Gallery includes clip art, photos, sounds, and motion graphics that you can download and use in your documents. The easiest way to locate an item is to search on a keyword, just as you do in the Insert Clip Art task pane. You want to use a graphic of a mountain in the letterhead and will search using the keyword "mountain."

2 ● In the Search For text box, type mountain.

● From the Search In drop-down list, select Nature.

● Click Go.

Another Method
You can also press ←Enter to start the search.

Your screen should be similar to Figure 5.10

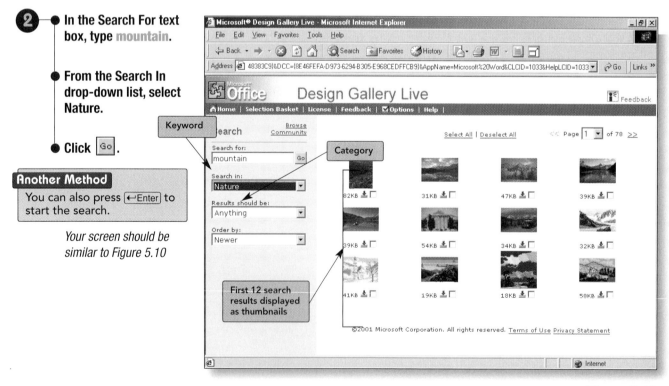

Figure 5.10

The Design Gallery displays the results of the search. Thumbnails of the first 12 items in the Nature category whose associated keyword matches the keyword you entered are displayed.

3 ● Click on a thumbnail to see an enlarged view.

● Select a picture of your choice, preview it, and click ⬇ to download it.

● If you are prompted, select the MPF (Office XP) format type, and click [Download Now!].

Your screen should be similar to Figure 5.11

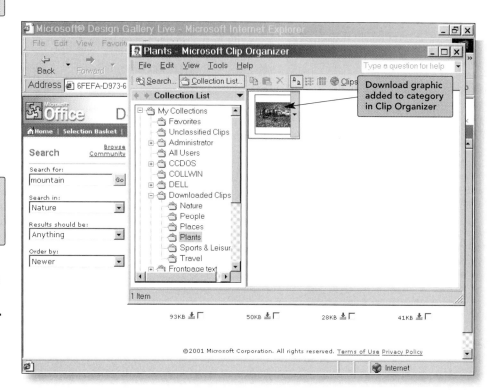

Figure 5.11

The picture is downloaded and added automatically to a category in the Clip Organizer on your system. The category it is added to is determined from the keywords associated with the picture. Next you want to insert the picture in the document.

4
- Display the Word document window.
- Display the Clip Organizer window.
- Drag the picture into the left cell of the letterhead table.

Additional Information

You can also drag a thumbnail displayed in the Insert Clip Art task pane into the document to insert it.

- Close the Insert Clip Art task pane.
- Select the picture and reduce its size to approximately 1.25 inches high by 2 inches wide.
- Size and position the letterhead table similar to as shown in Figure 5.12.

HAVING TROUBLE?

Refer to Lab 3, page WD3.49 to review sizing and moving tables.

Your screen should be similar to Figure 5.12

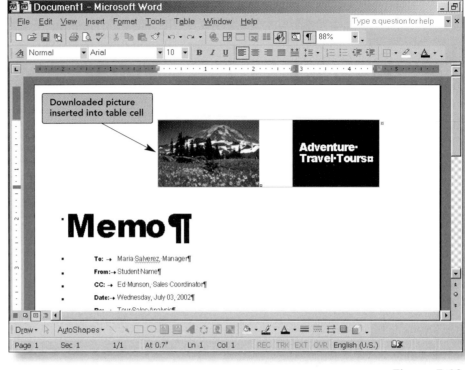

Figure 5.12

You will continue to refine the appearance of the letterhead later. For now, you want to save the changes you have made and continue to work on the memo content.

5
- Close the Clip Organizer window.
- Close the browser window and, if necessary, disconnect from the Internet.
- Save the document as Tour Sales Memo.

Creating a Complex Table

Next you want to create a table to display the tour sales data below the memo text. The table will display the data vertically (in columns) for the three years and horizontally (in rows) for the four tours and a total. Your completed table will be similar to the one shown below.

Additional Information

Refer to Lab 3, Concept 7, to review tables.

ANNUAL TOUR SALES

Tours		2000		2001		2002	
		#	Sales	#	Sales	#	Sales
	Amazon River Expedition	44	$192,940	50	$219,250	58	$245,560
	Yukon Bicycling Tour	60	189,600	68	214,880	73	230,680
	Australian Outback Adventure	98	673,750	112	770,000	120	825,000
	Himalayan Trek	20	174,500	24	209,400	32	279,200
	TOTAL		$1,230,790		$1,413,530		$1,580,440

You will use the Draw table feature to create this table. The Draw Table feature can be used to create any type of table, but is particularly useful for creating a complex table like this.

1 ● Move to the first blank line below the paragraph in the body of the memo.

Your screen should be similar to Figure 5.13

Current style

Location to create table

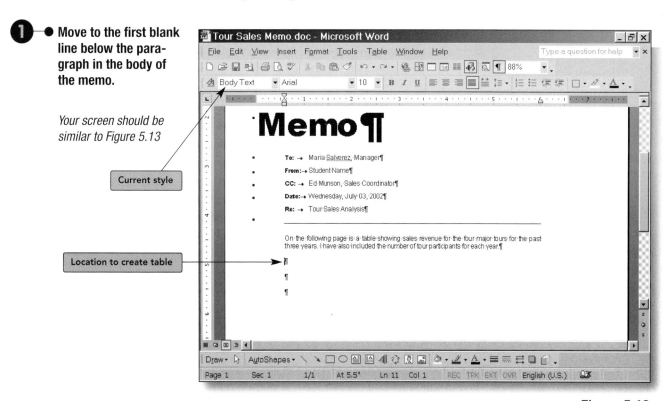

Figure 5.13

Notice that the Style list box shows "Body Text." The Body Text style includes formatting settings that will adversely affect the table that you are about to create at this location. You will change the style to Normal for the text after the memo body before creating the table. Then you will display the Drawing and Tables toolbar to help you create the table.

Table and Borders
toolbar

2 ● Select the three blank lines.

● From the Style drop-down menu, choose Clear Formatting.

● Click ¶ Show/Hide to hide the paragraph marks.

● Click 🗒 Tables and Borders (on the Standard toolbar).

● If necessary, move and dock the Tables and Borders toolbar below the Formatting toolbar.

Your screen should be similar to Figure 5.14

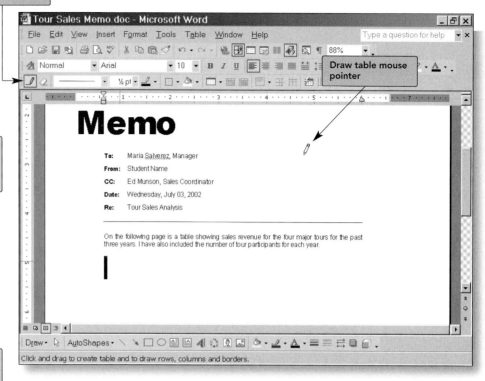

Figure 5.14

When the Tables and Borders toolbar is displayed, the Draw Table feature is automatically activated. Using Draw Table to create a table is like using a pen to draw a table. The mouse pointer changes to ✏ when positioned in the text area, and a dotted line appears to show the boundary or lines you are creating as you drag. First you define the outer table boundaries; then you draw the column and row lines.

The Tables and Borders toolbar buttons (identified below) are used to modify table settings.

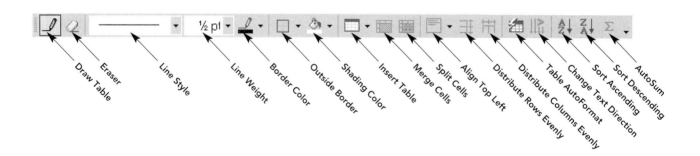

3 ● Click below the paragraph and drag downward and to the right to create an outer table boundary of approximately 3 inches high by 6 inches wide (refer to Figure 5.15).

● Drag the right indent marker on the ruler to the right margin of the table.

Your screen should be similar to Figure 5.15

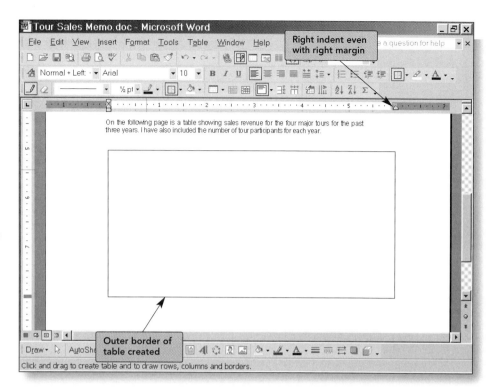

Figure 5.15

The outer border of the table is created. Next you need to add lines to create the columns and rows. When creating row or column lines, drag from the beginning boundary to the end to extend the line the distance you want. A dotted line appears in the ruler to show your position in the table as you draw. If you make an error, click 🔄 or 🖉 Eraser and drag over the line.

As you create the row and columns in the next step, refer to Figure 5.16 for placement. Do not be concerned if your table does not look exactly like Figure 5.16 when you are done as you will learn all about adjusting table rows and columns in following steps.

4 ● Add four vertical column lines at positions 0.5, 3, 4, and 5 on the ruler (see Figure 5.16).

● Draw seven horizontal lines to create the rows as shown in Figure 5.16. (Lines 4, 5, and 6 begin at the first column.)

● Click ✎ to turn off Draw Table.

Another Method
Typing in any cell will also turn off Draw Table.

Your screen should be similar to Figure 5.16

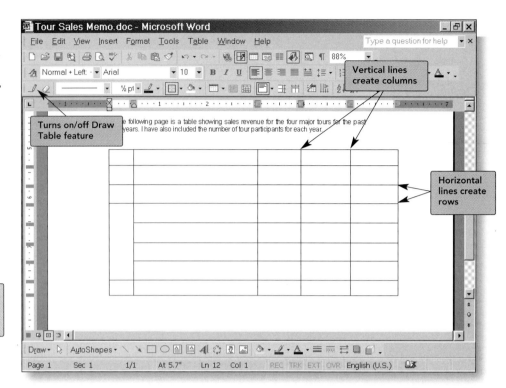

Figure 5.16

The table consists of eight rows and five columns. Now you are ready to enter information in the table.

5 ● Enter the labels and data in the cells as shown in Figure 5.17. Incliude $ symbols in row 4 Sales Values only.

Your screen should be similar to Figure 5.17

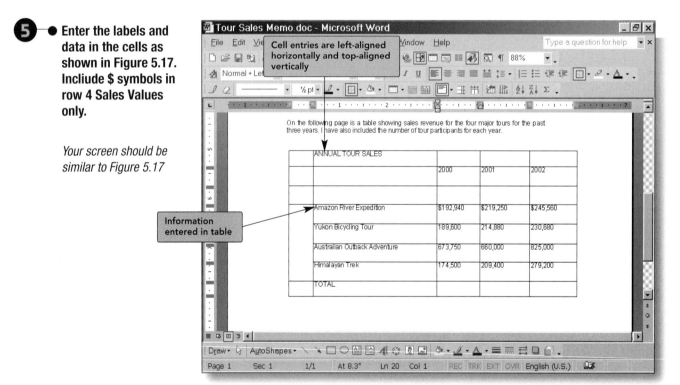

Figure 5.17

By default, entries in cells are left-aligned horizontally and top-aligned vertically in the cell space. You want to center the year headings and right-align the sales values.

6
- Select cells C2 through E2, containing the year headings.

- Click ≡ Center.

- Select the cells containing the sales values and right-align the values.

- Click in the table to deselect the cells.

Your screen should be similar to Figure 5.18

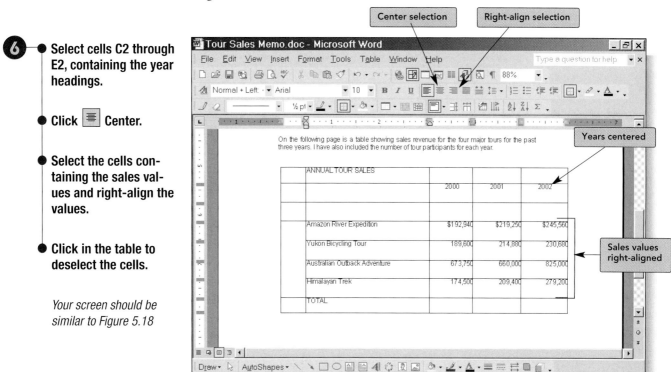

Figure 5.18

You will continue to add more formatting changes to improve the appearance of the table shortly.

Inserting a Column

You realize that you forgot to include columns for the number of people who took the tours in each year. To add this information, you need to insert three new columns to the left of the sales values. You can do this quickly using the Draw Table feature again.

1 ● Click 🖉 Draw Table.

● Using Figure 5.19 as a reference, drag to add three new columns at the 3.25, 4.25, and 5.25 positions extending from row 3 through row 7.

● Turn off the Draw Table feature.

Another Method

The Table/Insert/Columns to the left command will add a full height column to the left of the current column.

Your screen should be similar to Figure 5.19

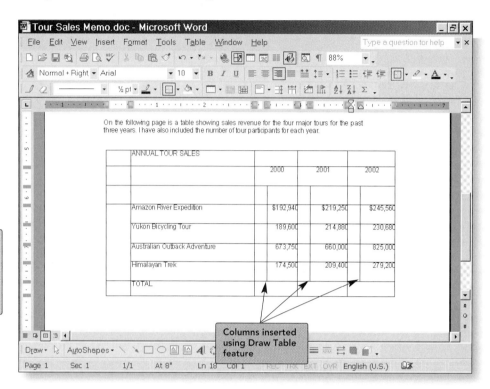

Figure 5.19

2 ● Choose Table/Table Properties/Table/ Options/Automatically resize to fit contents.

● Click [OK] twice.

● Type # in cells C3, E3, and G3.

● Type Sales in cells D3, F3, and H3.

● Enter the following values in the cells specified.

	Col C	Col E	Col G
Row 4	44	50	56
Row 5	60	68	73
Row 6	98	112	120
Row 7	20	24	32

If any of the sales values in your table wrap to a second line in a cell, this is because the cell width is too narrow to display the entry on a single line. In a Normal document template, the table properties are set to automatically resize to fit the cell contents. However, the Professional Memo template has this table property turned off. You will turn it on to fix this problem as well as to ensure that as you enter the data for the number of people in the tours, the columns will automatically resize to fit.

Your screen should be similar to Figure 5.20

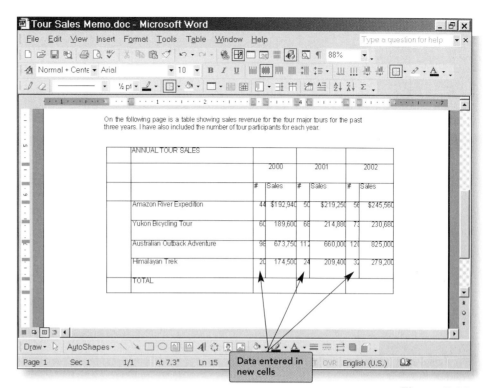

Figure 5.20

Performing Calculations in a Table

Now you want to calculate the sales revenue totals. Rather than adding the values for each column of data and entering them in the Total row, you can enter a formula to make this calculation for you.

concept 1

1 Formulas and functions are used to perform calculations in tables. A **formula** is an expression that contains any combination of numbers, fields resulting in numbers, table references, and operators. **Operators** specify the type of calculation to perform. The most common operators are + (add), − (subtract), * (multiply), and / (divide).

To use the operators, follow the common arithmetic laws: multiply and divide before adding and subtracting, and calculate whatever is in parentheses first. For example, the formula, 125 + D3 * D5 will multiply the value in cell D3 by the value in cell D5 and then add 125. If you want to add 125 to D3 and then multiply the result by D5, put 125 and D3 in parentheses: (125 + D3) * D5.

A **function** is a prewritten formula. One function you may use frequently is the SUM function. SUM calculates the total of a column of numbers. Other functions include:

Function	Description
AVERAGE	Calculates the average of a column of numbers
COUNT	Totals the number of cells in the column
MAX	Displays the maximum value in the column
MIN	Displays the minimum value in the column

To reference cells in formulas and functions, use a comma to separate references to individual cells and a colon to separate the first and last cells in a block. For example C1, C5 references the values in cells C1 and C5, whereas C1:C5 references the values in cells C1, C2, C3, C4, and C5.

The calculated result of a formula or function is displayed in the table cell containing the formula or function. The result of the calculation is a field.

Therefore, if the data in the referenced cells of the formula or function changes updating the field quickly recalculates the result.

The formulas and functions in Word let you create simple tables and spreadsheets for your documents. For larger, more complex spreadsheets, use Excel and then paste the spreadsheet into your document.

Calculating a Sum

You will enter a formula to sum the sales revenue values in the 2000 column of data.

1 ● Move to cell D8.

● Choose Table/Formula.

Your screen should be similar to Figure 5.21

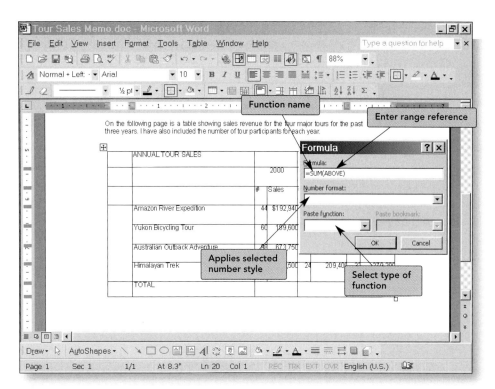

Figure 5.21

In the Formula dialog box, you enter the type of formula and the table cell references for the formula in the Formula text box. The function =SUM(ABOVE) is displayed by default because that is the only location of the cells containing values to sum. The range reference ABOVE will calculate a sum for all values directly above the current cell. Use the Paste Function list box to select the type of function you want, or type the function directly in the Function text box. From the Number Format drop-down list box, you can select a number style.

You want to sum the values in the range of cells D4 through D7 (D4:D7) and will replace ABOVE with the specific table cell references. You also want to format the numbers as currency.

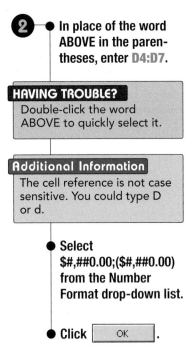

2 In place of the word ABOVE in the parentheses, enter **D4:D7**.

HAVING TROUBLE?
Double-click the word ABOVE to quickly select it.

Additional Information
The cell reference is not case sensitive. You could type D or d.

● Select **$#,##0.00;($#,##0.00)** from the Number Format drop-down list.

● Click [OK].

Your screen should be similar to Figure 5.22

Figure 5.22

Using the values in the specified cells of the table, the formula correctly calculates the result of $1,230,790.00. The value is displayed in the selected number format style. Because the SUM function is the most frequently used function, it has its own shortcut button. You will use the shortcut to calculate the sales total for 2001.

3 ● Move to cell F8.

● Click Σ AutoSum.

Your screen should be similar to Figure 5.23

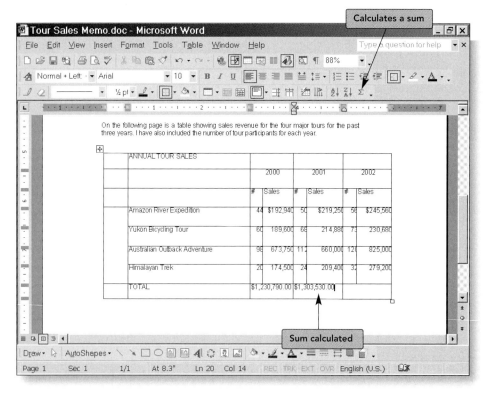

Figure 5.23

Using the Σ AutoSum button enters a SUM function that calculates the sum of all the numbers above the current cell. The calculated value of $1,303,530.00 is displayed in cell D8. It is also formatted as currency. This is because Word used the same format as the value in cell D4.

As you look at the total, you think it seems a little low and decide to check the values you entered for the year. You see that the Australian Outback Adventure value was entered incorrectly. It should be 770,000. Because the calculated result is a field, after changing the value in the cell, you can quickly update the calculation.

4 ● **Change the entry in cell F6 to** 770,000.

● **Move to cell F8 and press** F9 **to update the field.**

Another Method

You can also select <u>U</u>pdate Field from the field's shortcut menu.

Your screen should be similar to Figure 5.24

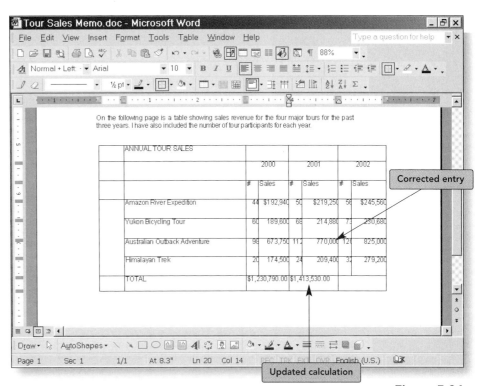

Figure 5.24

The correct calculated value of $1,413,530.00 is displayed in the cell. Next you need to enter the function to calculate the value for 2002. Additionally, you decide you do not want the two decimal places displayed for the three totals and will delete them.

5 ● Enter the function to calculate the total for 2002 in cell H8.

● Click in the field and delete the decimal and two decimal places from each of the three calculated results.

HAVING TROUBLE?
Click to the left of the decimal point and press Delete three times.

● Right-align the TOTAL label and total values.

● Save the document again.

Your screen should be similar to Figure 5.25

Additional Information
Because you did not change the format of the field, the decimal point and two decimal places will reappear if you update the field.

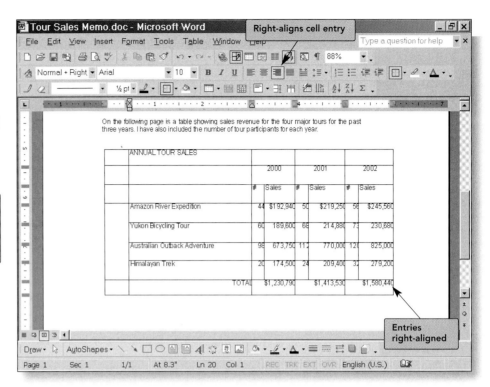

On the following page is a table showing sales revenue for the four major tours for the past three years. I have also included the number of tour participants for each year.

ANNUAL TOUR SALES		2000		2001		2002	
		#	Sales	#	Sales	#	Sales
Amazon River Expedition		44	$192,940	50	$219,250	58	$245,560
Yukon Bicycling Tour		60	189,600	68	214,880	73	230,680
Australian Outback Adventure		98	673,750	112	770,000	120	825,000
Himalayan Trek		20	174,500	24	209,400	32	279,200
	TOTAL		$1,230,790		$1,413,530		$1,580,440

Right-aligns cell entry

Entries right-aligned

Figure 5.25

Formatting the Table

The table is really taking shape. Now that the content of the table is complete, you want to improve its appearance by enhancing the title, adding color, increasing the text size, and modifying the border lines.

Merging Cells

After looking at the table, you decide to display the title centered over all columns of the table. To do this, you will combine the cells in the row to create a single cell and then center the label within the cell.

● Select row 1.

HAVING TROUBLE?
Click at the left edge of the row to select the entire row.

● Click 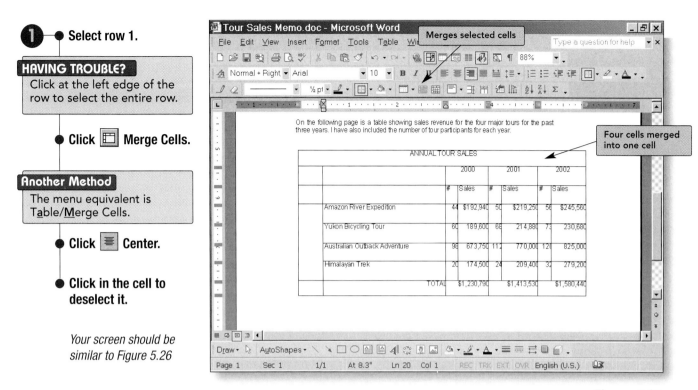 Merge Cells.

Another Method
The menu equivalent is Table/Merge Cells.

● Click ≡ Center.

● Click in the cell to deselect it.

Your screen should be similar to Figure 5.26

Figure 5.26

The four column dividers are eliminated, and the top row is one cell. The entry is centered in the cell space.

Changing Text Orientation

In cell A4 you want to display the heading "Tour." You also want the heading to appear centered and the orientation to be vertical within the cell space.

● Enter Tours in cell A4.

● Click Change Text Direction twice.

Another Method
The menu equivalent is Format/Text Direction/Orientation.

● Click Center.

Your screen should be similar to Figure 5.27

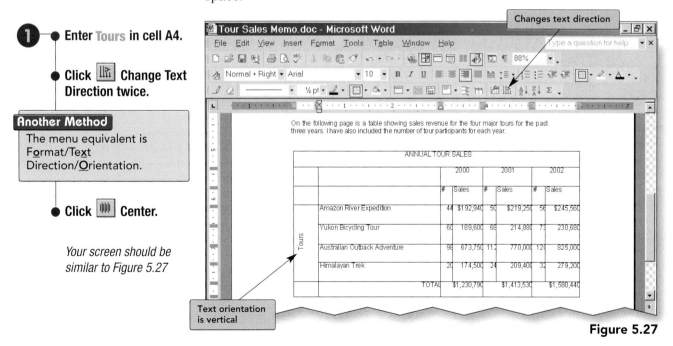

Figure 5.27

Adding Cell Shading

You will first add color shading to differentiate the areas of the table.

1 ● Select the entire table.

HAVING TROUBLE?

You can click ⊞, or drag, or use Table/Select/Table to select the entire table.

● Open the 🎨 ▾ Shading Color drop-down menu.

● Click [More Fill Colors...].

● If necessary, open the Standard tab.

Your screen should be similar to Figure 5.28

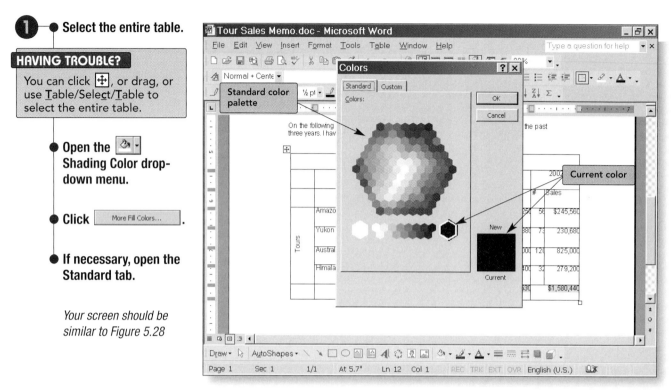

Figure 5.28

From the Colors dialog box, you can select from standard colors or create a custom color. The Standard tab palette includes many shade variations of the same colors that are included in the drop-down color palette list.

2 ● Select a color of your choice from the standard color palette.

● Click [OK].

● Select the tour names and sales values, and apply another color to the cells in this range.

Your screen should be similar to Figure 5.29

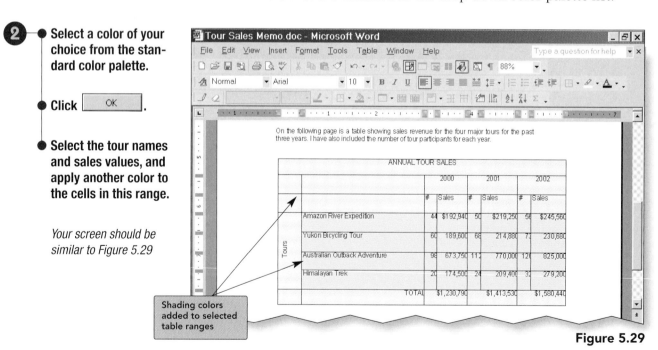

Figure 5.29

Next you want to enhance the text of the headings and the table data.

3

- Select the table title and increase the font size to 16 points, and add bold with a color of your choice.

- Select the year headings and increase the font size to 14 points, add bold and the same color as the title. Apply the same formats to the Tours label.

- Select the remaining text in the table and increase the font size to 12 points.

- Center and apply the same color to the # and Sales headings.

- Apply the same color and bold to the TOTAL label and values.

Your screen should be similar to Figure 5.30

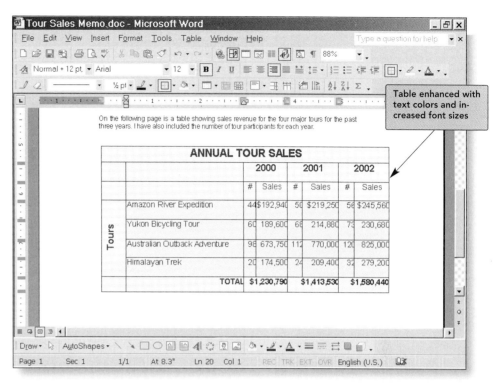

Table enhanced with text colors and increased font sizes

Figure 5.30

Changing Table Size and Page Orientation

Because the increased point size makes the table contents look crowded, you decide to make the entire table larger.

1

- Select the table.

- Drag the sizing handle to the right to increase the width of the table to the 7-inch position on the ruler.

Your screen should be similar to Figure 5.31

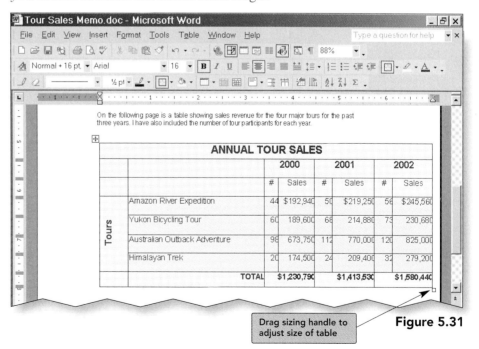

Drag sizing handle to adjust size of table

Figure 5.31

Now the table is too wide to fit easily within the width of the page. When text is wider than the width of the page, you can change the orientation of the page from **portrait**, in which text is printed across the width of the page, to **landscape**, in which text is printed across the length of the page.

Because the memo will look better in the current orientation of portrait, you decide to display the table on a separate page that will print in landscape orientation. To have different orientations within a document, you need to insert a section break first, and then apply the orientation to the section you want affected.

2 ● If necessary, insert a blank line above the table.

● Move to the blank line above the table.

● Insert a **N**ext Page section break.

● Choose **F**ile/Page Set**u**p/Landscape.

● Click OK .

● Change the zoom to Two Pages.

Your screen should be similar to Figure 5.32

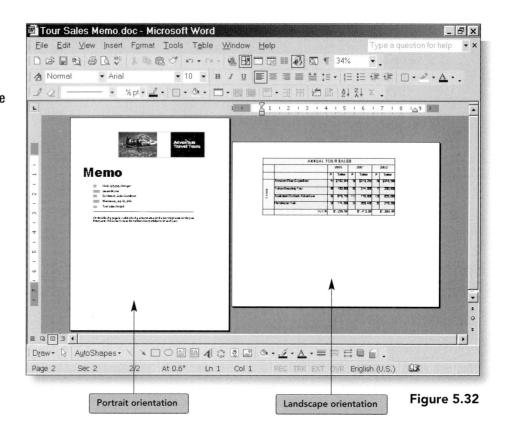

Portrait orientation   Landscape orientation   **Figure 5.32**

The entire table now easily fits across the width of the page.

Sizing Rows and Columns

You want to decrease the width of column A. To change the width of a column or row, point to the column divider line and drag it to the right or left to increase or decrease the column width, or up or down to increase or decrease the row height. A temporary dotted line appears to show your new setting.

1 ● Return the zoom to Page Width.

● Point to the right border of column A and drag to the left to decrease the column width to the minimum amount possible.

Additional Information

The mouse pointer appears as ↔ when you can drag to size a row or column.

Your screen should be similar to Figure 5.33

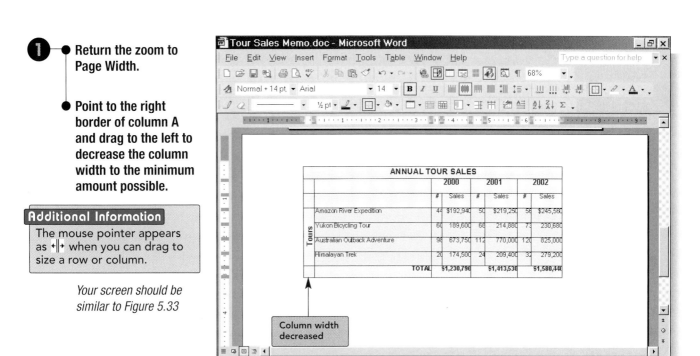

Figure 5.33

You also want to adjust the height of the rows to be equally sized.

2 ● Select the entire table.

● Click ⊞ Distribute Rows Evenly.

Another Method

The menu equivalent is Table/Autofit/Distribute Rows Evenly.

Your screen should be similar to Figure 5.34

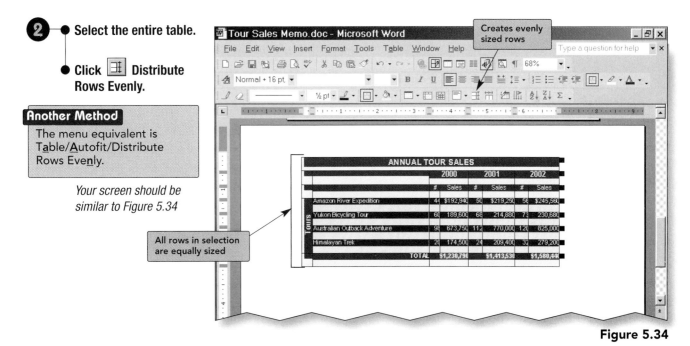

Figure 5.34

You also want the widths of the # columns to be the same and the widths of the Sales columns to be the same. However, because these columns are not adjacent, you cannot use the Distribute Columns Evenly feature. Instead, you need to specify the exact width for each column.

3 ● Select the 2000 #
column.

● Choose T**a**ble/Table
P**r**operties/Col**u**mn.

● Select Preferred
Width.

● Enter **.5** in the text
box.

*Your screen should be
similar to Figure 5.35*

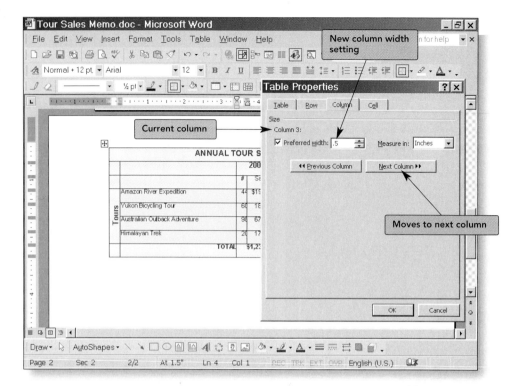

Figure 5.35

Notice the dialog box identifies the column as column number 3. You can
continue specifying settings for the other columns by moving to the column
and making the appropriate selections. When you are done, the new settings will be applied to the table.

4 ● Click [Next Column ▶▶]
twice to move to
column 5.

● Select Preferred Width
to accept the last en-
tered width setting.

● Move to column 7 and
set the width to 0.5
inch.

● In a similar manner,
set the column widths
for columns 8, 6, and 4
to 1 inch.

● Click [OK].

● Click on the table to
deselect the column.

*Your screen should be
similar to Figure 5.36*

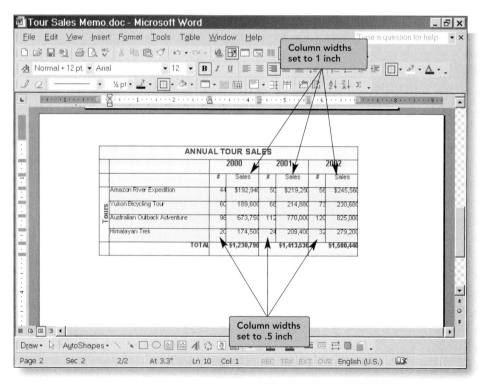

Figure 5.36

Removing Border Lines

When a table is created, single, black, 0.5-point solid-line borders are added by default around each cell. Once color and other formatting has been added to a table, you may no longer need all the border lines to define the spaces. You will remove the border line below row 1 first.

1 ● Move to row 1.

● Open the [ ] ▾ Border drop-down menu.

● Click [ ] bottom border to clear the border line.

Additional Information

The Border drop-down menu identifies the border lines that are used in a selected cell by highlighting them.

Your screen should be similar to Figure 5.37

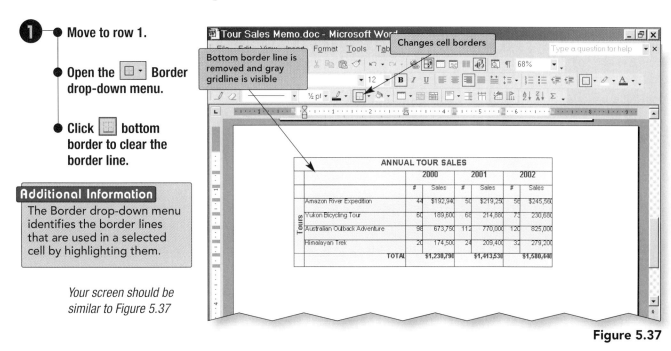

Figure 5.37

The border line is removed, but a gray gridline is still displayed. Gridlines are used to help you see the cell boundaries; however, they are not printed.

2 ● Remove the border lines from the cells as shown in Figure 5.38.

Your screen should be similar to Figure 5.38

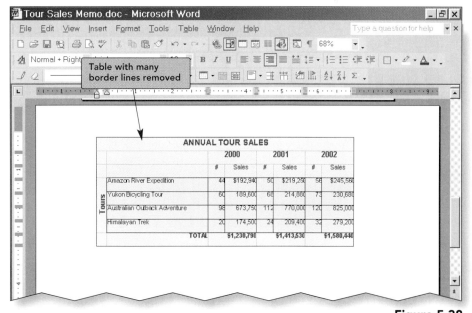

Figure 5.38

Finally, you want the table centered on the page.

Another Method

The menu equivalent is Table/Table Properties/Table/Center.

● When you are finished, close the Tables and Borders toolbar.

● Save the document again.

Your screen should be similar to Figure 5.39

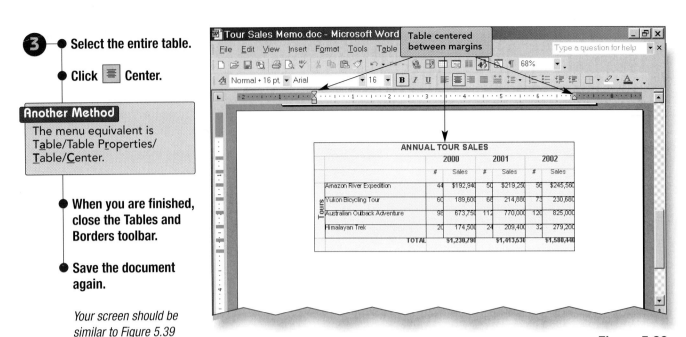

Figure 5.39

Creating a Chart

As you look at the data in the table, you decide to include a chart of the data below the table, to better show the trends in sales.

concept 2

Charts

2 A **chart**, also called a graph, is a visual representation of numeric data. Presenting data as a chart provides more impact than the data alone and makes it easier to see trends and comparisons. Word 2002 includes a separate program, Microsoft Graph, designed to help you create 14 types of charts with many different formats for each type.

Each type of chart represents the data differently and has a different purpose. It is important to select the type of chart that will provide the right emphasis to support the data. The basic chart types are described below.

Type of Chart	Description
Area	Shows the relative importance of a value over time by emphasizing the area under the curve created by each data series.
Bar	Displays categories vertically and values horizontally, placing more emphasis on comparisons and less on time. Stacked-bar charts show the relationship of individual items to a whole by stacking bars on top of one another.
Column	Similar to a bar chart, except categories are organized horizontally and values vertically.
Line	Shows changes in data over time, emphasizing time and rate of change rather than the amount of change.
Pie	Shows the relationship of each value in a data series to the series as a whole. Each slice of the pie represents a single value in a data series.

Most charts are made up of several basic parts, as described in the following table.

Part	Description
X axis	The bottom boundary of the chart, also called the category axis, is used to label the data being charted; the label may be, for example, a point in time or a category.
Y axis	The left boundary of the chart, also called the value axis, is a numbered scale whose numbers are determined by the data used in the chart. Each line or bar in a chart represents a data value. In pie charts there are no axes. Instead, the data that is charted is displayed as slices in a circle or pie.
Legend	A box containing a brief description identifying the patterns or colors assigned to the data series in a chart.
Titles	Descriptive text used to explain the contents of the chart.

Pasting Data from a Table

To specify the data in the table to use in the chart, you will copy the sales labels in row 3, the four tour names in column B, and the sales values for the three years in columns D, F, and H.

Select cells B3 through H7.

Click 📋 Copy.

Move to the blank line below the table.

Press ↵Enter.

Choose Insert/Object/ Microsoft Graph Chart.

Click [OK].

Your screen should be similar to Figure 5.40

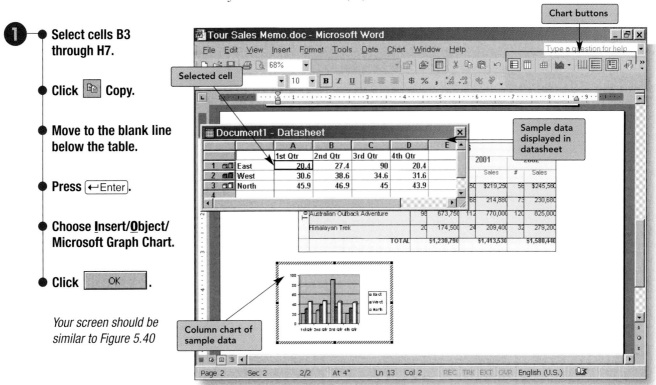

Figure 5.40

The Graph feature is activated and a table, called a **datasheet**, containing sample data is displayed in a separate window. A column chart using the sample data from the datasheet is inserted in the document. Notice that the datasheet displays the column letters A through E and row numbers 1 through 4 to label the cells in the table. The cell that is surrounded by the border is the selected cell and is the cell you can work in.

In addition to displaying sample data, the datasheet also contains place-holders for the row labels, which are used as the legend in the chart, and for the column labels, which are used as X-axis labels. The Standard toolbar also now includes buttons for working with charts.

Specifying the Chart Data

You need to replace the sample data in the datasheet with the data you copied from the table.

1
- Click in the cell in the top left corner of the Datasheet window.

- Click 🔲 Paste.

- Click on the selection to deselect it.

- Increase the size of the datasheet window to view all the data.

Your screen should be similar to Figure 5.41

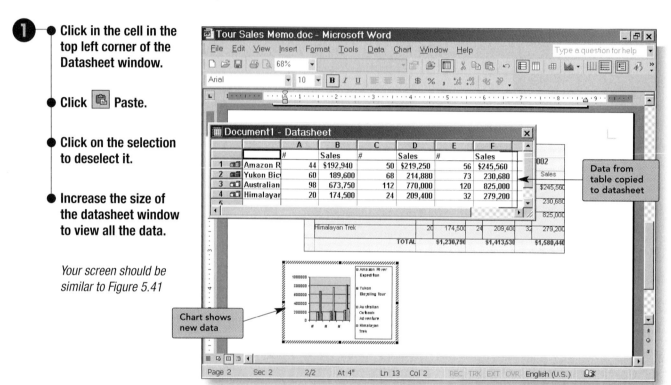

Figure 5.41

The data in the datasheet is updated to include the data from the table, and the chart reflects the change in data. Next you need to remove the three columns of data containing the number of participants and change the re-maining column headings to reflect the three years.

2 • Right-click column A and choose **Delete**.

• Delete the other two columns with # in the heading row.

• In the first row of column A, replace "Sales" with 2000.

• In the same manner change the "Sales" headings in columns B and C to 2001 and 2002.

Your screen should be similar to Figure 5.42

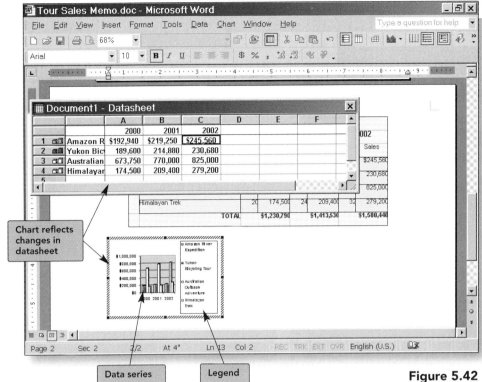

Data series   Legend

Figure 5.42

Each group of related data that is plotted in the chart is a **data series**. Each data series has a unique color or pattern assigned to it so that you can identify the different series. The **legend** identifies the color or pattern associated with each data series. As you can see, the values and text in the chart are directly linked to the datasheet, and any changes you make in the datasheet are automatically reflected in the chart.

Sizing the Chart

Now that the data is specified, you can close the datasheet. Then you will increase the size of the chart.

1 • Close the Datasheet window.

• Drag the right-corner and right-center sizing handles to increase the height and width of the chart.

• Click outside the chart to deselect it.

HAVING TROUBLE?
If the chart moves to page 3, reduce its size so that it stays on page 2.

Your screen should be similar to Figure 5.43

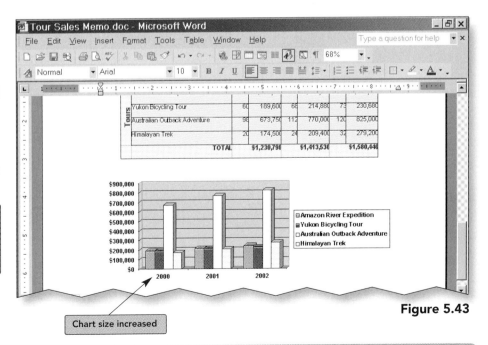

Chart size increased

Figure 5.43

Modifying the Chart

As you look at the chart, you decide you want to change it so the colors coordinate with the table in the memo. You also want to remove the 3-D effect on the chart, which is the default. To modify the chart, you need to activate the Graph application again. Then you can use the features on the Graph menu and toolbar to edit the chart.

1 ● **Double-click on the chart.**

● **If the datasheet is open, close it.**

Another Method

The menu equivalent is Edit/Chart Object.

Your screen should be similar to Figure 5.44

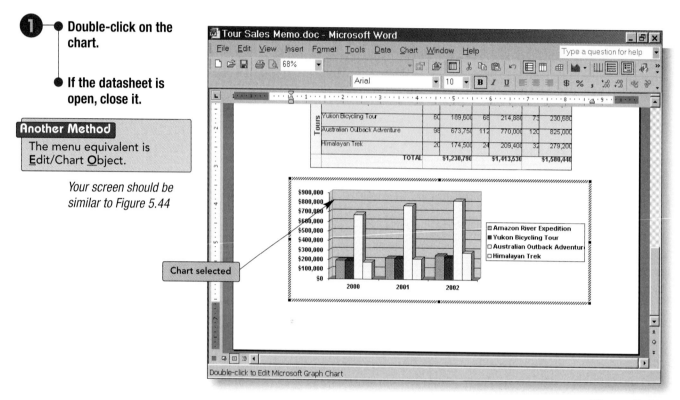

Figure 5.44

The chart object opens and the datasheet window is active. You want to change the color and appearance of the chart to match the colors in the table. First you will change the background color of the plot area.

2 • Right-click on the area behind the columns of data.

• Choose F**o**rmat Walls.

• From the Area color palette, select the same color that you used behind the data in the table.

• Click   OK   .

Your screen should be similar to Figure 5.45

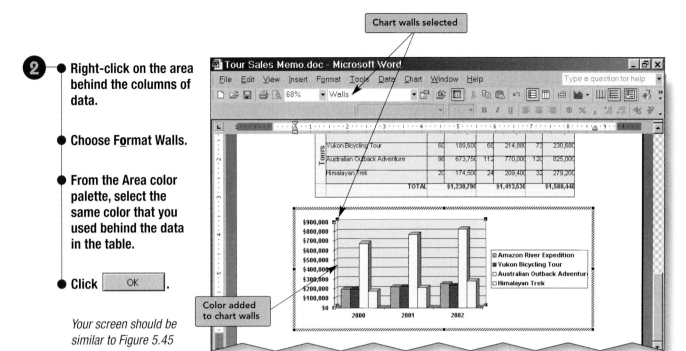

Figure 5.45

You also want to change the background color of the chart area.

3 • Right-click on the white background of the chart.

• Choose F**o**rmat Chart Area.

• From the Area color palette, select the same color you used in the table.

• Click   OK   .

Your screen should be similar to Figure 5.46

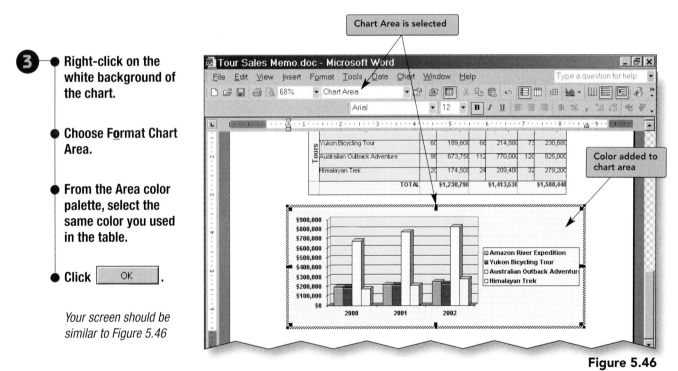

Figure 5.46

Next you will change the color of the columns.

4 ● Right-click on any one of the Australian Outback Adventure columns.

● Choose For̲mat Data Series.

● If necessary, open the Patterns tab.

Your screen should be similar to Figure 5.47

Default settings for selected data series

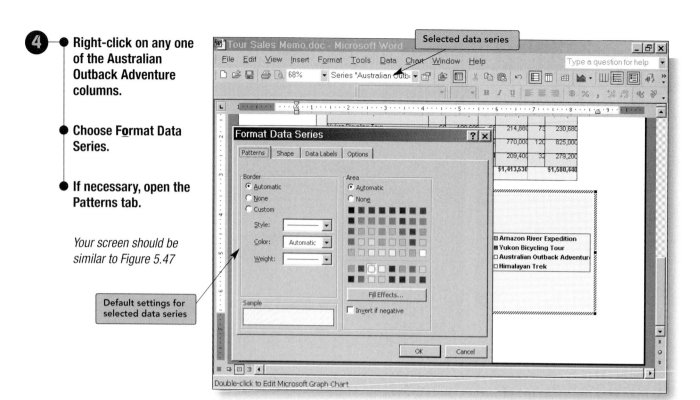

Figure 5.47

The Format Data Series dialog box is used to modify the appearance of the selected data series. The initial chart is created using the default chart colors. From the Patterns tab you can select different borders, fill colors, and patterns.

5 ● From the Area color palette, select a color that coordinates with the table.

● Click [OK].

● Repeat as needed for the other three data series.

Your screen should be similar to Figure 5.48

Data series color changed

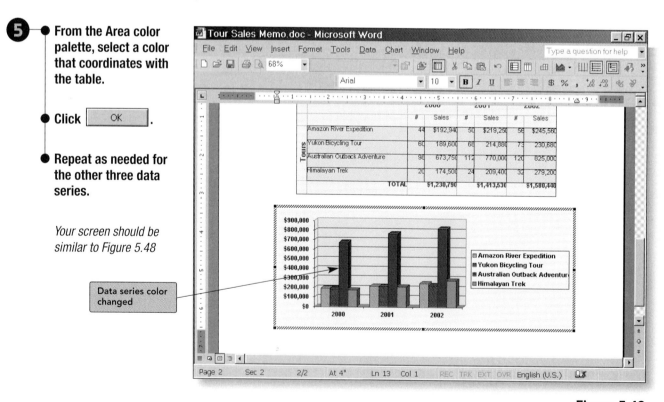

Figure 5.48

Next you want to change the type of column chart to display flat columns rather than 3-D columns.

6 • **Right-click on any one of the columns.**

• **Choose Chart Type.**

• **Select Clustered Column (row 1 column 1).**

• **Click** [OK].

Your screen should be similar to Figure 5.49

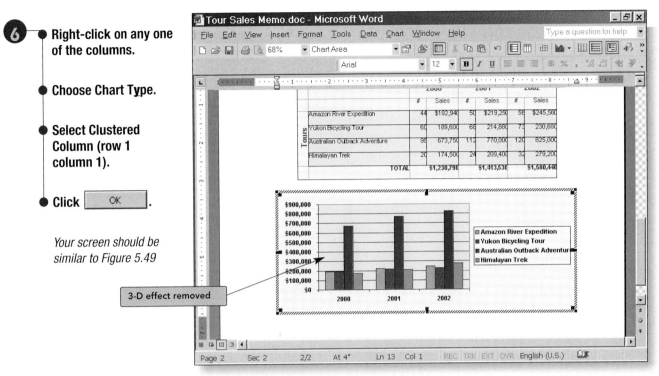

Figure 5.49

The 3-D effect has been removed from the columns. You also want to reduce the number of values that display on the Y axis. Currently because the values increment by 100,000, there are 9 values displayed. To reduce the number of values, you increase the incremental value.

7 • **Right-click anywhere on the Y axis.**

• **Choose Format Axis.**

• **If necessary, open the Scale tab.**

• **Type 250000 in the Major Unit text box.**

• **Click** [OK].

Your screen should be similar to Figure 5.50

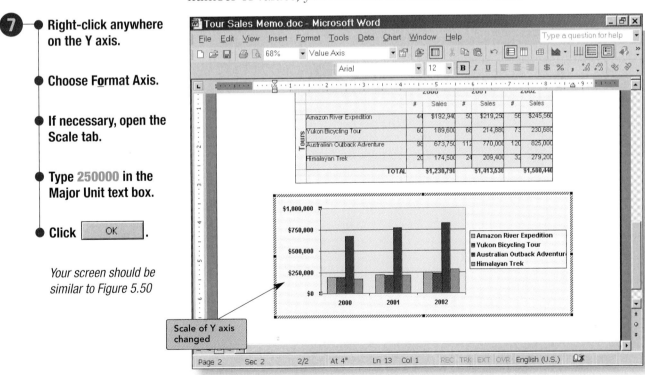

Figure 5.50

There are now only four values displayed along the Y-axis.

The last two changes you want to make are to reduce the font size of the text in the legend and to center the chart object.

8 • **Right-click on the legend.**

• **Choose F_ormat Legend.**

• **Open the Font tab and select 10 pt as the font size.**

• **Click** OK .

• **Click outside the chart to exit the Graph application.**

• **Select the chart object.**

• **Click** ≡ **Center.**

• **Deselect the chart object.**

• **Save the document again.**

Your screen should be similar to Figure 5.51

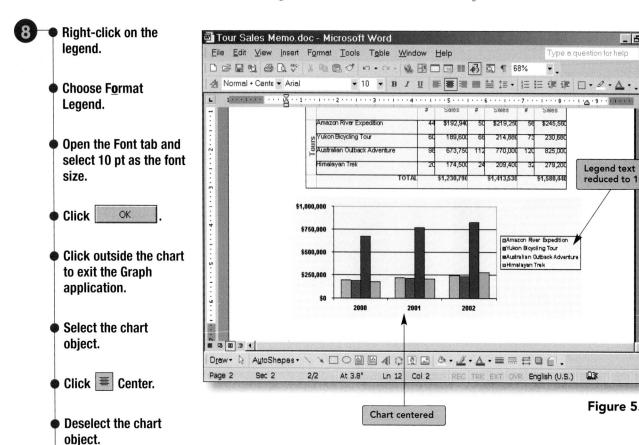

Figure 5.51

The changes you made to the chart greatly improve its appearance.

Creating an Outline-Style Numbered List

Now that you have created the table and chart, you want to include in the memo a strategy on how to increase sales for the four major tours. First you will add a lead-in paragraph, and then you will enter the proposed strategy to increase sales.

1 ● **Move to the end of the first paragraph in the memo.**

● **Set the zoom to Page Width.**

● **Press** ⏎Enter .

● **Change the style to Normal.**

● **Type:** You will notice that sales have steadily increased over the past three years. The following strategy has been developed to ensure further increases in future sales.

● **Press** ⏎Enter **twice.**

Your screen should be similar to Figure 5.52

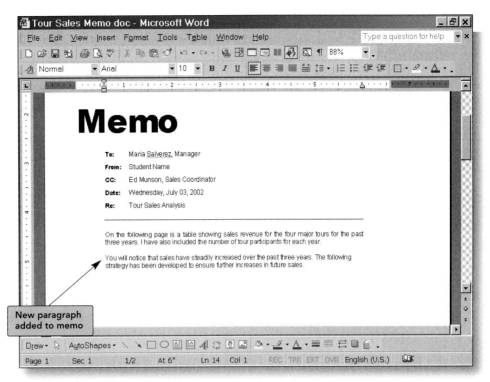

Figure 5.52

The strategy consists of several main points and corresponding subpoints. The best way to add this information to your memo is to use an outline-style numbered list.

2 ● **Type** Strategy to Increase Sales.

● **Press** ⏎Enter .

● **Choose Format/Bullets and Numbering.**

● **Open the Outline Numbered tab.**

Your screen should be similar to Figure 5.53

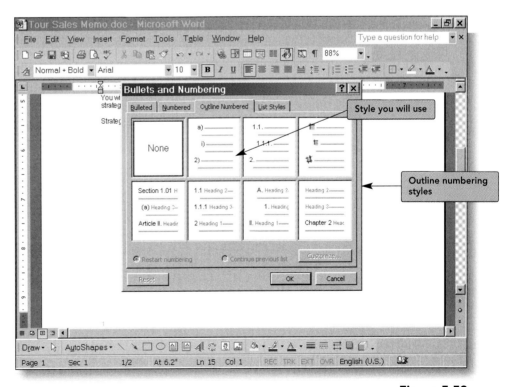

Figure 5.53

The Bullets and Numbering dialog box displays seven outline numbered-list styles. The first style to the right of None is the style you will use.

3 • **Select the first outline numbered-list style.**

• **Click** [OK].

• **Type Increase number of new clients.**

• **Press** [←Enter].

Your screen should be similar to Figure 5.54

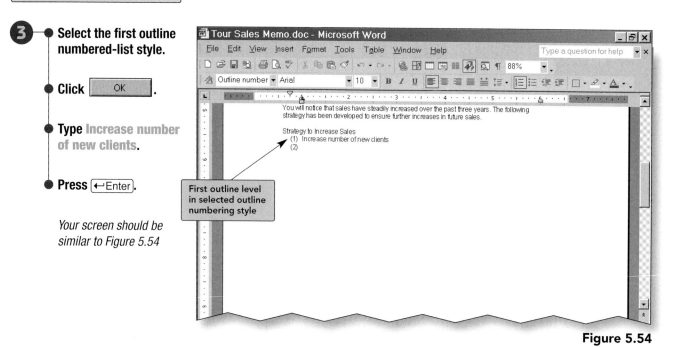

First outline level in selected outline numbering style

Figure 5.54

The outline number (1) in the selected style is inserted for the first line and the text following the outline number is automatically indented to the 0.25-inch position. The next line is automatically numbered (2) for the second entry at the same outline level. Next, however, you want to add the list of strategies for the first topic under the first topic heading. They will be entered at lower outline levels.

4 • **Press** [Tab].

• **Type Advertising.**

• **Press** [←Enter].

• **Press** [Tab].

• **Type Direct mail brochures.**

• **Press** [←Enter].

• **Type Magazine and newspaper ads.**

• **Press** [←Enter].

• **Type Web ads and specials.**

• **Press** [←Enter].

Your screen should be similar to Figure 5.55

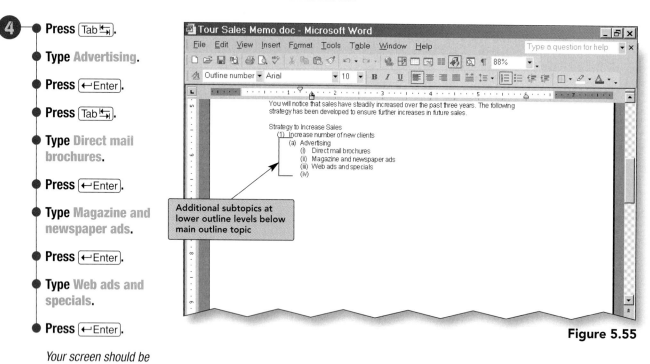

Additional subtopics at lower outline levels below main outline topic

Figure 5.55

Each time you press Tab ⇆ to indent a line, the next line indents to the 0.25-inch position and the outline numbering level is demoted to the next lower numbering level. That completes the first category. To add the second and third categories, you need to promote the outline numbering level by decreasing the indent.

5 • Press ⇧Shift + Tab ⇆.

• **Enter the following three items:**

(b) Participate in "travel fairs"

(c) Offer presentations to specialty groups (biking, hiking, etc.)

(d) Expand Adventure Travel Web site

• **Press ←Enter.**

• **Press ⇧Shift + Tab ⇆.**

Your screen should be similar to Figure 5.56

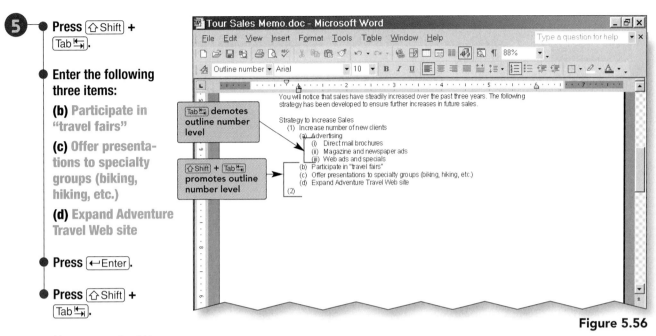

Figure 5.56

The outline level is at the first numbering level and you are ready to enter the second main strategy to increase sales by increasing repeat business.

6 • **Complete the memo by entering the following topics at the levels shown:**

(2) Increase repeat business

(a) Follow-up surveys

(b) Thank-you letters

(c) Newsletter

• **Press ←Enter.**

• **Click ☰ to turn off Outline Numbering.**

• **Bold the heading above the outline numbered list.**

Your screen should be similar to Figure 5.57

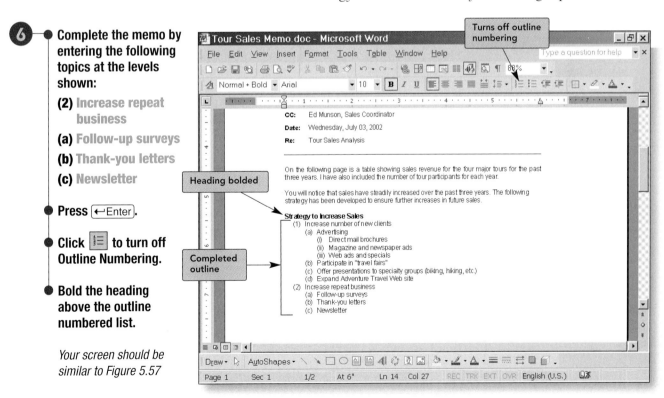

Figure 5.57

The memo is now complete. The final change you want to make is to fix the letterhead so there is no white space between the picture and the company name.

7 ● Move the right indent marker in the ruler for the left table cell to the right column margin.

● Drag the left border of the right cell to the left to increase the size of the cell.

Your screen should be similar to Figure 5.58

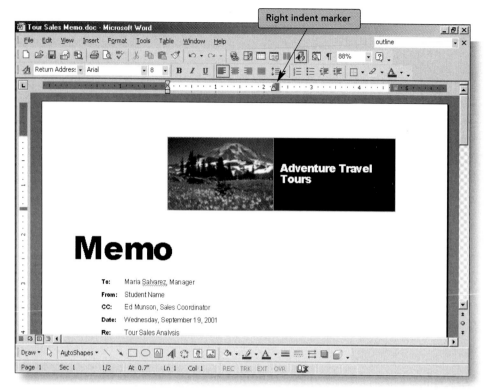

Figure 5.58

8 ● Preview and then prin the memo.

● Save and close the file.

The letterhead looks much better. Your completed memo should look like the memo shown here.

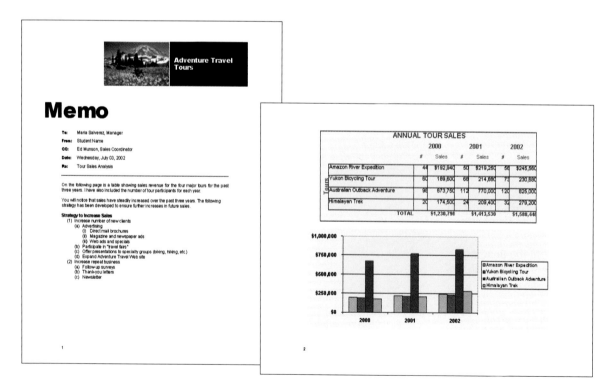

Note: If you are running short on time, this is an appropriate place to end this session.

Using Mail Merge

Recall that your second project is to personalize the letter you wrote about the new tours and presentations by including each client's name and address information in the inside address and his or her first name in the salutation. To do this you will use the Mail Merge feature to create a personalized form letter and mailing labels to be sent to all clients.

---

concept 3

Mail Merge

3 The **Mail Merge** feature combines a list of data (typically a file of names and addresses) with a document (commonly a form letter) to create a new document. The names and addresses are entered (merged) into the form letter in the blank spaces provided. The result is a personalized form letter.

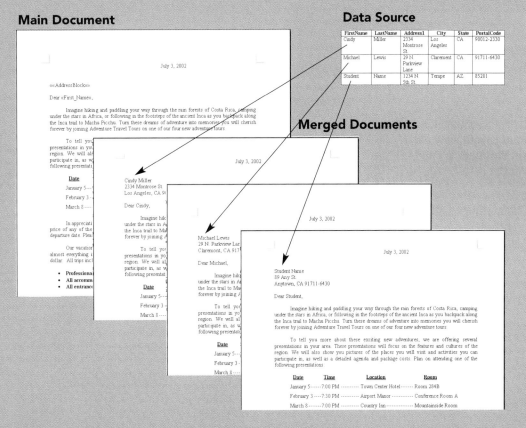

Mail Merge usually requires the use of two files: a main document and a data source. The **main document** contains the basic form letter. It directs the merge process through the use of merge fields. A **merge field** is a field code that controls what information is used from the data source and where it is entered in the main document. The **data source** contains the information needed to complete the letter in the main document. It is also called an **address file** because it commonly contains name and address data.

In addition to the templates, Word 2002 includes many wizards to help you create documents. A **wizard** asks you questions and then uses your answers to automatically lay out and format a document such as a newsletter or resume. You will use the Mail Merge Wizard to take you step by step through the process of creating a form letter. The four steps are:

1. Open or create a main document.

2. Open or create a data source with individual recipient information.

3. Add or customize merge fields in the main document.

4. Merge data from the data source into the main document to create a new, merged document.

Another Method

You can also use the icons on the Mail Merge toolbar instead of the Mail Merge Wizard to create a merge document. Choose <u>T</u>ools/L<u>e</u>tters and Mailings/Show Mail Merge <u>T</u>oolbar.

You will open the tour letter as the main document and create the data source of clients' names and addresses. Then you will add the merge fields to the main document. When you perform the merge, Word takes the data field information from the data source and combines or merges it into the main document.

Creating the Main Document

You are going to use an existing letter as the main document. This letter is similar to the tour letter you saved as Tour Letter2 in Lab 2.

1
● **Open the file**
wd05_Tour Letter5.

● **If necessary, switch to Print Layout view and set the zoom to Page Width.**

● **Choose <u>T</u>ools/L<u>e</u>tters and Mailings/<u>M</u>ail Merge Wizard.**

Your screen should be similar to Figure 5.59

Additional Information

Notice that the date in the letter on your screen is automatically updated to the current system date. This is because a Date field was entered in the document.

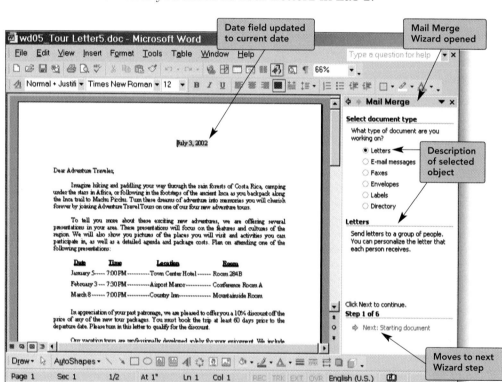

Figure 5.59

The Mail Merge task pane contains the wizard that will guide you through creating the form letter. The first selection you need to make is to specify the type of document you want to create. An explanation of the selected document type is displayed below the list of options.

2 • **If necessary, select Letters.**

• **Click**
⇨ Next: Starting document .

Your screen should be similar to Figure 5.60

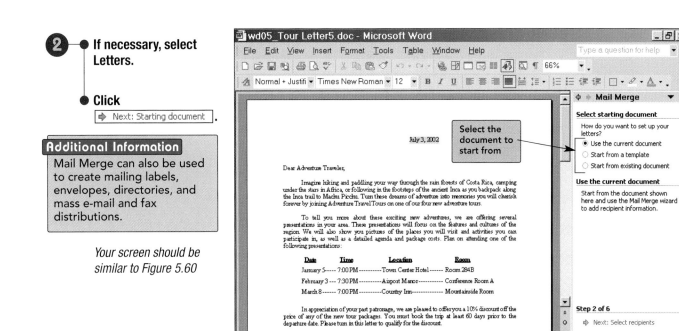

Figure 5.60

In the next step of the wizard, you need to identify the starting document. Since you already opened the file containing the letter you want to use, you will select the "use the current document" option.

3 • **If necessary, select Use the current document.**

• **Click**
⇨ Next: Select recipients .

Your screen should be similar to Figure 5.61

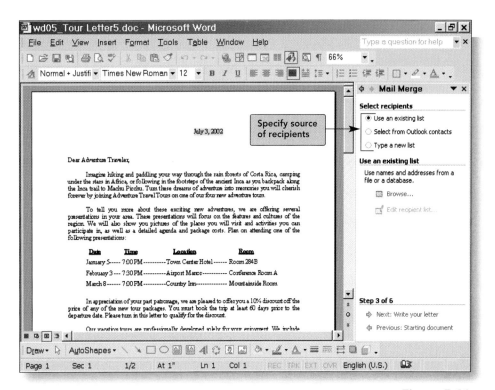

Figure 5.61

Creating the Data Source

Next you select the recipients to use as the data source for the mail merged document. You can use an existing list, select from your Outlook contacts, or type a new list.

---

concept 4

Data Source

4 The data source is a table of information that contains data fields in the columns and records in the rows. A **data field** is a category of information. For example, a client's first name is a data field, the last name is a data field, the street address is another data field, the city a fourth data field, and so on. All the data fields that are needed to complete the information for one person (or other entity) are called a **record**. Each record is displayed in a row of the table. Commonly, a database table created using a database application is used for the data source. However, the recipient list can also be created using Word.

You are going to type a new recipient list.

1 • Select **Type a new list**.

• Click [▦] **Create...** .

Your screen should be similar to Figure 5.62

Common field names

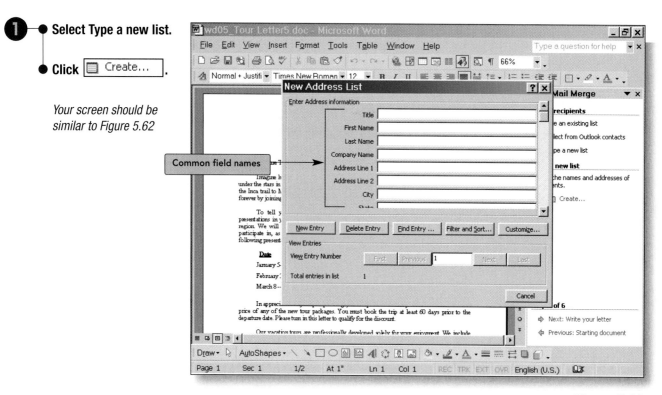

Figure 5.62

The New Address List dialog box is used to specify the field names for the data that will be entered in the recipient list.

Commonly used form-letter field names are displayed in the New Address List list box. You can remove from the list any field names that you do not need in your letter, or you can add field names to the list or rename the field names. In this case, you will remove several field names from the list.

2 ● **Click** Customize... .

The dialog box on your screen should be similar to Figure 5.63

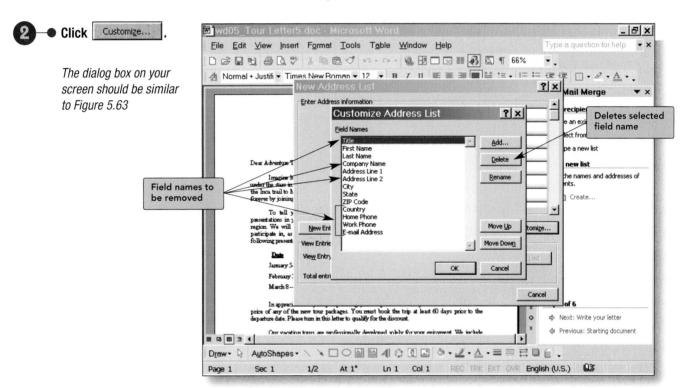

Figure 5.63

Additional Information

The Move Up and Move Down buttons let you rearrange the order of the fields.

Because you only need basic address information, you will remove any extra field names. Since the title field name is already selected, you will delete it first.

3 ● Click [Delete] to remove the Title field from the list.

● Click [Yes] to confirm the deletion.

● Select and remove the following field names: **Company Name, Address Line 2, Country, Home Phone, Work Phone and E-mail Address.**

● Click [OK].

Your screen should be similar to Figure 5.64

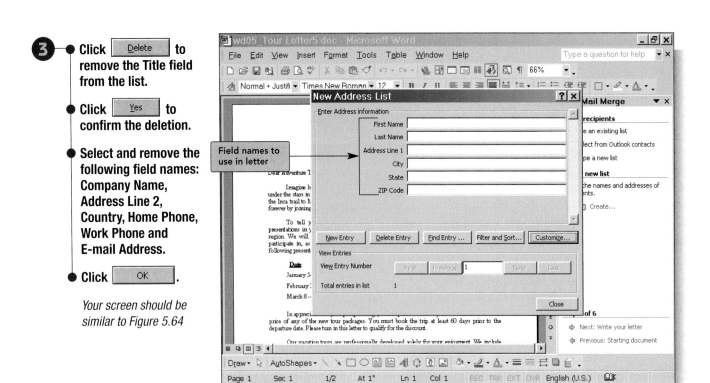

Figure 5.64

The New Address List dialog box now displays only the six field names to use in the letter, and text boxes for entering the data for each record. The data must be entered exactly as you want it to appear in the letter. If you do not have the information you need to complete a field, you can leave it blank. You will enter the data for the first field of the first record, the client's first name.

4 ● Click in the First Name field.

● Type **Cindy**.

● Press [Tab] or [↵Enter].

● Enter the following information for the remaining fields of this record:

Last Name:	Miller
Address Line 1:	2334 Montrose St.
City:	Los Angeles
State:	CA
ZIP Code:	90012-2330

● If you see any errors in the field data, move back to the entry and edit it.

Your screen should be similar to Figure 5.65

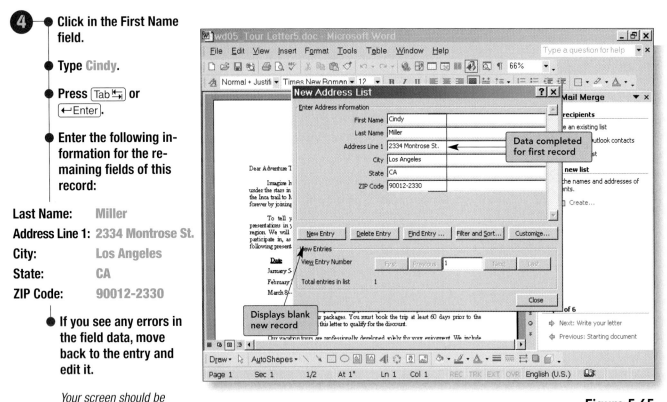

Figure 5.65

Next you will add this record to the data source file and display a new blank data form.

5 • Click [New Entry].

• Enter the field data for the second record using the information:

First Name: Michael
Last Name: Lewis
Address Line 1: 29 N. Parkview Lane
City: Claremont
State: CA
ZIP Code: 91711-6430

Your screen should be similar to Figure 5.66

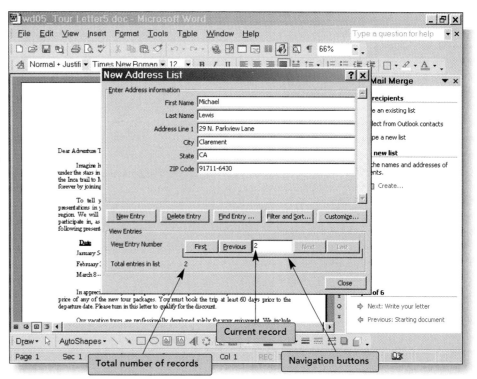

Figure 5.66

Notice that the View Entries area shows the number of records entered into the recipient list. The four record navigation buttons allow you to move among existing records in the list.

6 • Click [New Entry].

• Enter your name and address as the third record in the data source.

• Use the record navigation buttons to move to each of the records and verify the data you entered. If necessary, correct any errors.

• Click [Close].

• Save the address list as Client List to your data file location.

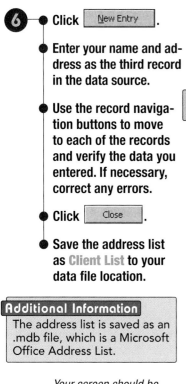

Additional Information

The address list is saved as an .mdb file, which is a Microsoft Office Address List.

Your screen should be similar to Figure 5.67

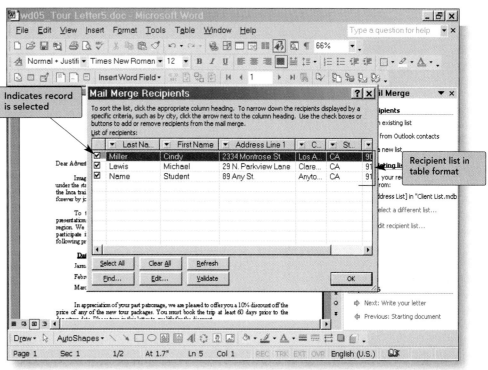

Figure 5.67

The Mail Merge Recipients dialog box is displayed along with the Mail Merge toolbar, shown below.

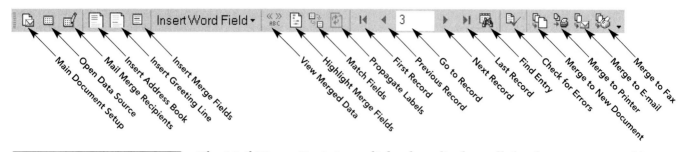

The number of records you enter in the data source file is limited only by your disk space. At any time, you can add more records using the Data Form as you just did.

The Mail Merge Recipients dialog box displays all the data you entered in a table format. The field names are displayed as the top row of the table, and each record is displayed as a row. You can sort the list or edit the data before you perform the merge. All the records are checked, indicating they are selected and will appear in the Mail Merge.

7 ● **Click** OK .

Your screen should be similar to Figure 5.68

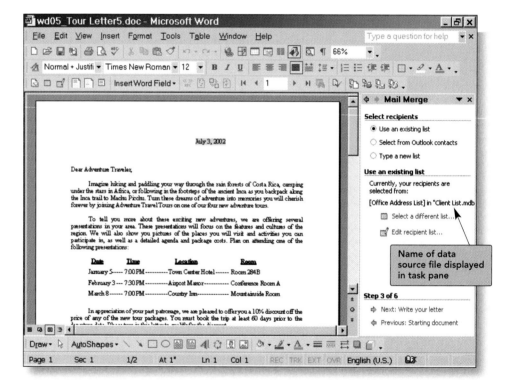

Figure 5.68

Now the list that you created appears as the current list in the task pane. You will use this recipient list and advance to the next step.

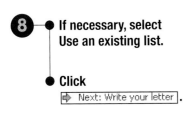

8 ● **If necessary, select Use an existing list.**

● **Click**
⇨ Next: Write your letter .

Your screen should be similar to Figure 5.69

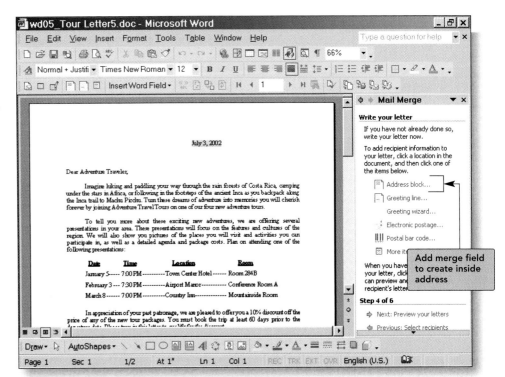

Figure 5.69

Entering Merge Fields in the Main Document

The next step is to create your letter, if you have not done so already, and to include the recipient information in it. How will Word know where to enter the client's name and other source data in the main document? Word uses merge fields to do this. Merge fields direct the program to accept information from the data source at the specified location in the main document. To prepare the letter to accept the fields of information from the data source, you need to add merge fields to the letter.

The letter needs to be modified to allow entry of the name and address information for each client from the data source. The inside address will hold the following three lines of information, which are the components of the address block:

> First Name Last Name
> Address Line 1
> City, State Zip Code

The first line of the inside address, which will hold the client's full name, will be entered as line 5 of the tour letter. A merge field needs to be entered in the main document for each field of data you want copied from the data source. The location of the merge field indicates where to enter the field data. First you need to position the insertion point on the line where the client's name and address will appear.

1 • Move to the blank line above the salutation.

• Click [Address block...]

Your screen should be similar to Figure 5.70

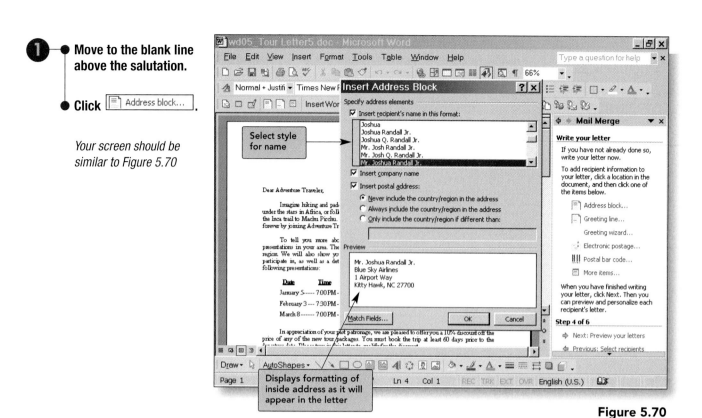

Select style for name

Displays formatting of inside address as it will appear in the letter

Figure 5.70

The Insert Address Block dialog box has many options for customizing the appearance of the fields. The Preview area displays how the Address Block will appear in the letter.

2 • Choose the example "Joshua Randall Jr." as the format for the recipient's name.

• Click Insert company name to deselect it.

• Click [OK].

Another Method

You can also click [ ] Insert Address Block on the Mail Merge toolbar or [ ] Insert Merge Fields and insert the merge fields one at a time.

Your screen should be similar to Figure 5.71

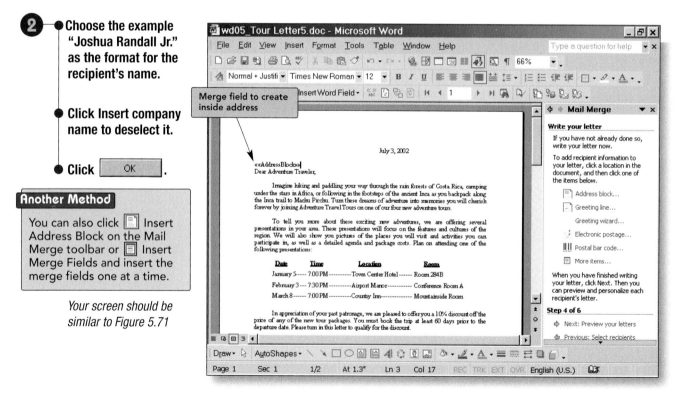

Merge field to create inside address

Figure 5.71

The merge field <<Address Block>> is displayed at the insertion point in the main document. It is a field code that instructs Word to insert the information from the data fields (from the data source) at this location in the main document when the merge is performed.

3
- Enter a blank line between the Address Block merge field and the salutation.

- Select "Adventure Traveler" in the salutation.

- Click ▣ Insert Merge Fields (on the Mail Merge toolbar).

- Select the First Name merge field.

- Click Insert .

- Click Close .

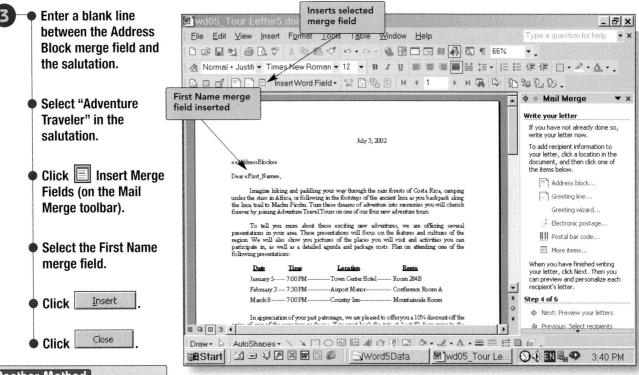

Figure 5.72

Another Method

You can also select the entire salutation and click Greeting line... in the Mail Merge task pane to access several options for formatting the salutation.

Additional Information

The same merge field can be used more than once in the main document.

Your screen should be similar to Figure 5.72

Previewing the Merged Letter

The next step is to see how the form letter will appear with the merged data.

1 ● **Click**

   ⇨ Next: Preview your letters ▸.

Another Method

You can also click 〈ABC〉 View Merged Data on the Mail Merge toolbar.

Your screen should be similar to Figure 5.73

Data from record 1 inserted in place of merge fields

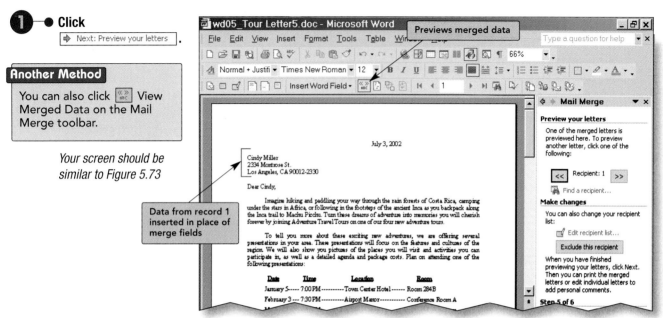

Figure 5.73

The data from the first record of the address list is displayed in place of the merge fields.

2 ● **Click** >> **to see the address information for the next recipient in the letter.**

● **Change the zoom to Two Pages.**

Your screen should be similar to Figure 5.74

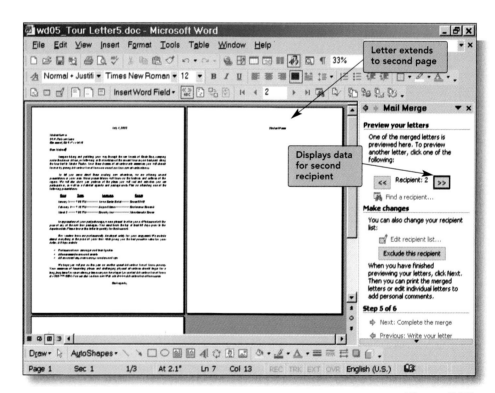

Figure 5.74

With the addition of the address information, the form letter no longer fits on one page. You can easily fix this using the shrink to fit feature to make the letter fit on one page.

3 • Click 🔍 Print Preview.

• Click 🗐 Shrink to Fit.

Your screen should be similar to Figure 5.75

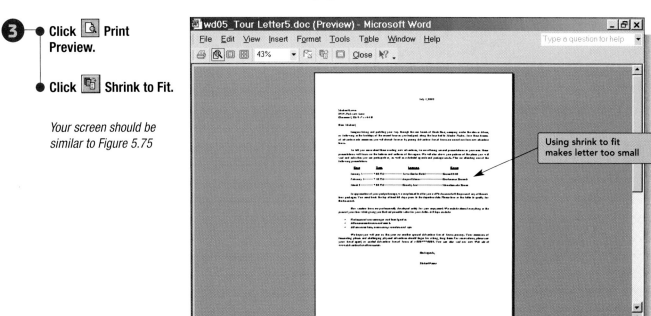

> Using shrink to fit makes letter too small

Figure 5.75

The reduced letter now appears too small. You decide to undo the Shrink to Fit change and manually adjust the font size to make it more appropriate.

4 • Choose **E**dit/**U**ndo Shrink to Fit.

• Close the Print Preview window.

• Select the letter only.

• Reduce the font size to 11 points.

• Deselect the selected text.

• Save the letter as Tour Main Document.

Your screen should be similar to Figure 5.76

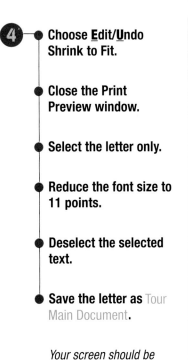
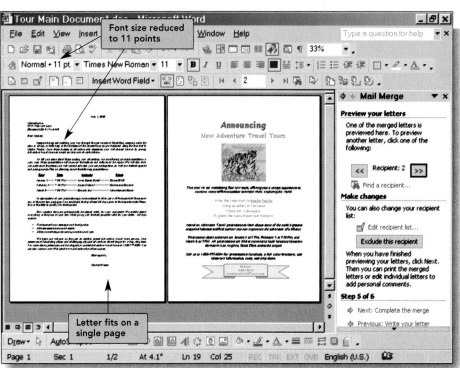

> Font size reduced to 11 points

> Letter fits on a single page

Figure 5.76

Performing the Merge

Now that you have created the main document and data source document, you are ready to combine them to create the new personalized tour letter. During this process a third file is created. The original main document and data source file are not altered or affected in any way. The third file is the result of merging the main document with the data source file.

1 ● **Click**

⇨ Next: Complete the merge .

Another Method

You can also click 🔲 Merge to New Document on the Mail Merge toolbar.

Your screen should be similar to Figure 5.77

Merged document

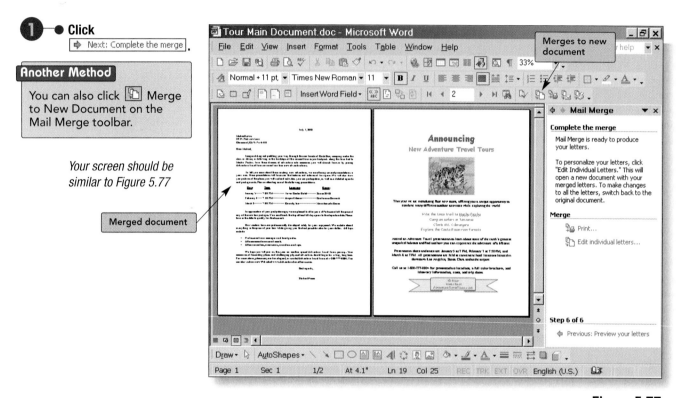

Figure 5.77

From the Mail Merge task pane box, you can personalize the letters before you print them. You can also direct the merge to output the form letters to e-mail or a fax if your system is set up to include these features. Finally, if you do not want every record in your data source to receive a copy of the form letter, you can specify a range of records to merge or criteria for records to meet.

Printing the Merged Letter

You can also specify the records you want to send a letter to. In this case, you only want to print the letter that contains your name and address, which is record 3.

1 • Click  .

• Click in the From field and type 3.

• Click in the To field and type 3.

• Click ⬚ OK ⬚ .

• Make the necessary selections from the Print dialog box for your system.

• Click ⬚ OK ⬚ .

Your printed output should be similar to that shown here.

2 • Close the Mail Merge task pane.

• Close the Mail Merge toolbar.

• Return the zoom to Page Width.

• Save the merged document as Tour Merge Document to your data file location.

• Close all document windows, saving the files as necessary.

July 3, 2002

Student Name
89 Any St.
Anytown, CA 91711-6430

Dear Student,

Imagine hiking and paddling your way through the rain forests of Costa Rica, camping under the stars in Africa, or following in the footsteps of the ancient Inca as you backpack along the Inca trail to Machu Picchu. Turn these dreams of adventure into memories you will cherish forever by joining Adventure Travel Tours on one of our four new adventure tours.

To tell you more about these exciting new adventures, we are offering several presentations in your area. These presentations will focus on the features and cultures of the region. We will also show you pictures of the places you will visit and activities you can participate in, as well as a detailed agenda and package costs. Plan on attending one of the following presentations:

Date	Time	Location	Room
January 5	7:00 PM	Town Center Hotel	Room 284B
February 3	7:30 PM	Airport Manor	Conference Room A
March 8	7:00 PM	Country Inn	Mountainside Room

In appreciation of your past patronage, we are pleased to offer you a 10% discount off the price of any of the new tour packages. You must book the trip at least 60 days prior to the departure date. Please turn in this letter to qualify for the discount.

Our vacation tours are professionally developed solely for your enjoyment. We include almost everything in the price of your tour while giving you the best possible value for your dollar. All trips include:

• **Professional tour manager and local guides**
• **All accommodations and meals**
• **All entrance fees, excursions, transfers and tips**

We hope you will join us this year on another special Adventure Travel Tours journey. Your memories of fascinating places and challenging physical adventures should linger for a long, long time. For reservations, please see your travel agent, or contact Adventure Travel Tours at 1-800-777-0004. You can also visit our new Web site at www.AdventureTravelTours.com.

Best regards,

Now each time you need to send tour letters, all you need to do is edit the client data source file and issue the Merge command. Because the Date field was used, the date line will change automatically.

Printing Mailing Labels

Now that the form letter is ready to be sent to clients, you want to create mailing labels for the envelopes. To create mailing labels for your form letter, you will use the Mailing Label Wizard.

1 ● Choose **F**ile/**N**ew.

● Click 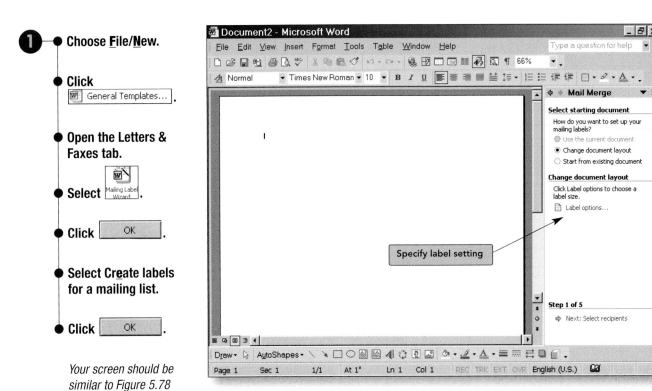 General Templates... .

● Open the Letters & Faxes tab.

● Select [Mailing Label Wizard].

● Click [OK].

● Select C**r**eate labels for a mailing list.

● Click [OK].

Your screen should be similar to Figure 5.78

Figure 5.78

The Mail Merge task pane displays with a blank document. The Wizard first needs to know how you want to set up the mailing labels. The default will use the new blank document as the starting document. You can also choose to use another existing document. The next step is to select a ready-to-use mail merge template.

2 ● Click [Label options...].

Your screen should be similar to Figure 5.79

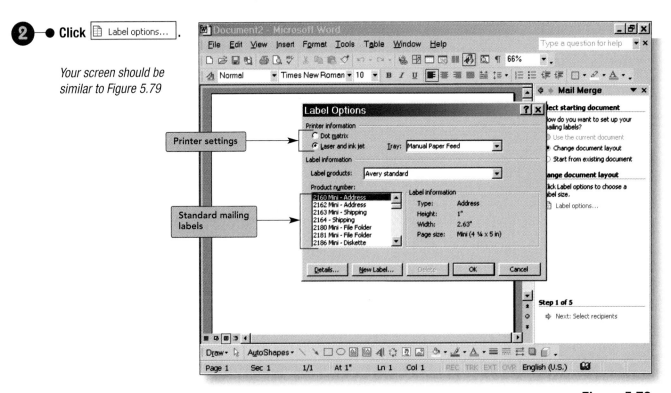

Figure 5.79

The Label Options dialog box displays the type of printer and the manufacturer of mailing labels. Avery Standard is the default. The Product Number list shows all the types of labels for the selected manufacturer.

3 ● **Select 5260-Address.**

● **Click** `OK`.

Your screen should be similar to Figure 5.80

> Blank label layout for selected type of label

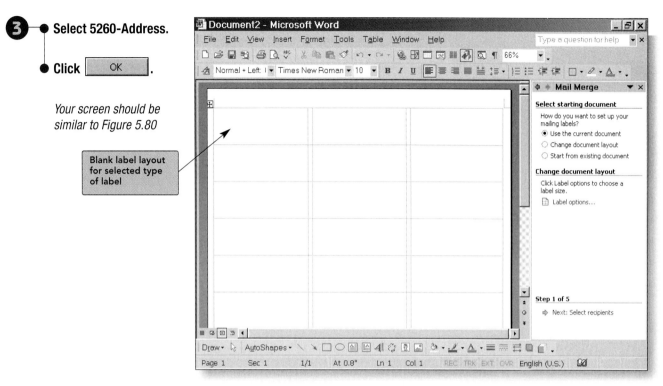

Figure 5.80

The main document is now set up to create mailing labels. You will use the Client List, which is the same data source you used for the merged letter.

4 ● **Click** `Next: Select recipients`.

● **Click** `Browse...`.

● **Select** Client List **from your data files.**

● **Click** `Open`.

● **From the Mail Merge Recipients dialog box, click** `OK`.

● **Click** `Next: Arrange your labels`.

Your screen should be similar to Figure 5.81

> Recipient list identified

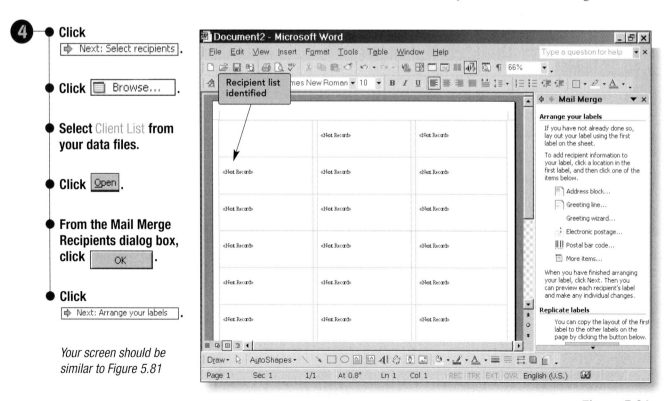

Figure 5.81

Next you set up the first label on the sheet and replicate that setup to the rest of the labels.

5 • Click [Address block...].

• **Select a format for the recipient's name.**

• **Deselect Insert company name.**

• Click [OK].

• Click [Update all labels].

HAVING TROUBLE?
Scroll the task pane to see this button.

Your screen should be similar to Figure 5.82

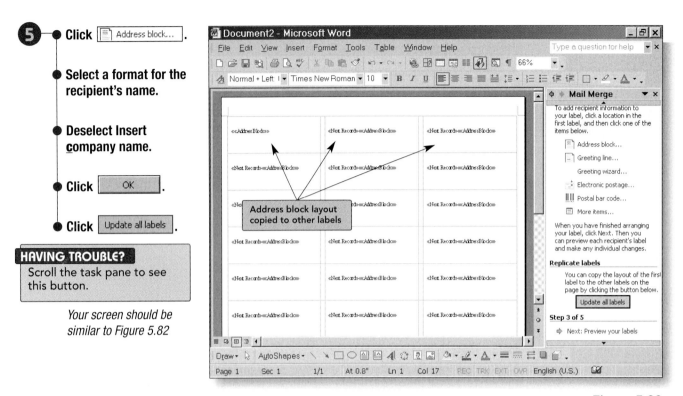

Figure 5.82

Next you will preview the labels before you perform the merge.

6 • Click [Next: Preview your labels].

HAVING TROUBLE?
You may need to scroll the task pane to see this option.

Your screen should be similar to Figure 5.83

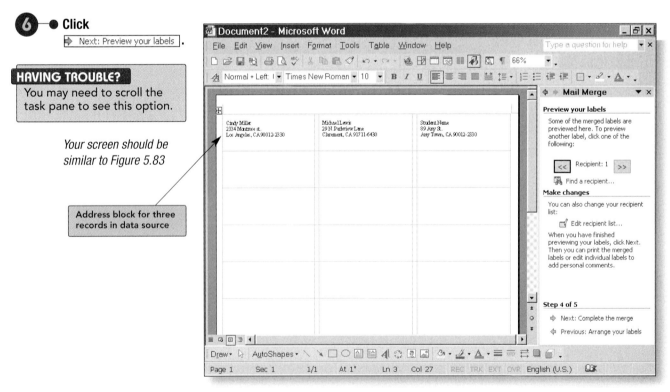

Figure 5.83

Check that the addresses fit on the label. The labels look good, so you can complete the merge and, if you wanted, print the labels. Instead, you will save the merged label file. Now when you send tour letters, you can create mailing labels using the same data source as the letter.

7 ● Click ⟶ Next: Complete the merge .

● **Save the document as** Tour Mailing Labels.

● **Close the Mail Merge task pane and close the document.**

Preparing and Printing Envelopes

Sometimes you may want to quickly address a single envelope. To see how this feature works, you will address an envelope for one of the letters in the Tour Merge Document file.

1 ● **Open the file** Tour Merge Document **file.**

● **If necessary, change the zoom to Page Width.**

● **Copy the inside address of the letter.**

● **Choose Tools/Letters and Mailings/Envelopes and Labels.**

● **If necessary, open the Envelopes tab and select the entire entry in the Delivery Address text box.**

● **Press** Ctrl **+ V to paste the address in the Delivery Address text box.**

Your screen should be similar to Figure 5.84

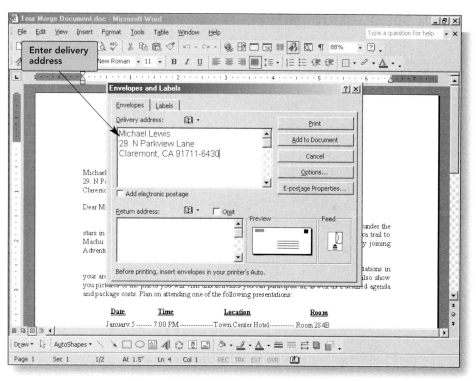

Figure 5.84

To complete the information for the envelope, you need to add the return address. Then you will check the options for printing and formatting the envelope.

2 ● Enter your name and your school's address in the Return Address text box.

● Click [Options...].

● If necessary, open the **E**nvelope Options tab.

Your screen should be similar to Figure 5.85

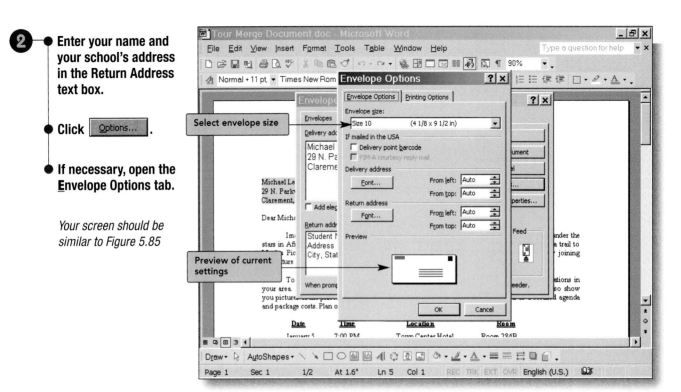

Figure 5.85

Using the Envelope Option dialog box, you can change the envelope size and the font and placement of the delivery and return addresses. The Preview area shows how the envelope will appear when printed using the current settings.

3 ● Open the Envelope Size drop-down list.

Your screen should be similar to Figure 5.86

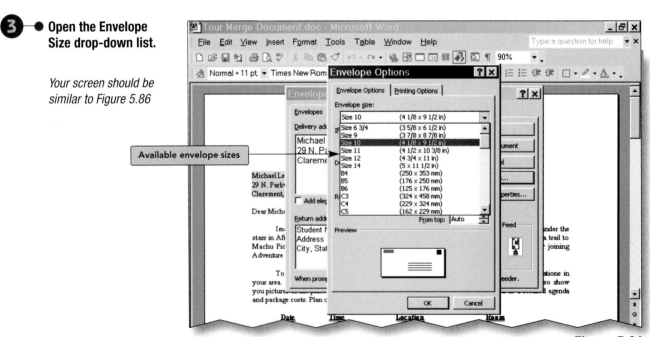

Figure 5.86

The default envelope size of 10 is for standard 8½-by-11-inch letter paper. This is the appropriate size for the letter. Next you will check the print options.

4 ● Open the **P**rinting Options tab.

Your screen should be similar to Figure 5.87

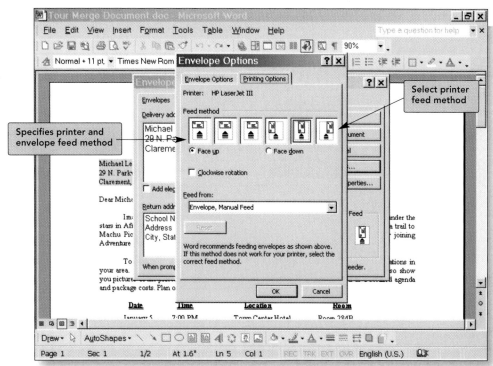

Figure 5.87

The options in this tab are used to specify how the envelope is fed into the printer. Word automatically selects the best option for the selected printer. You do not need to change any of the envelope options. Next you will print the envelope. Before printing, you would need to insert the correct size envelope in the printer. However, you will simply print it on a sheet of paper.

5 ● Close the dialog box.

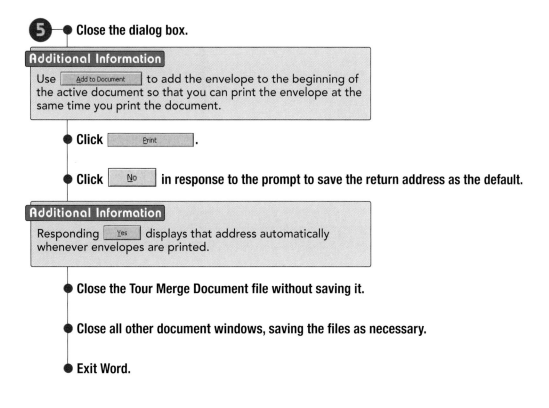

Additional Information

Use | Add to Document | to add the envelope to the beginning of the active document so that you can print the envelope at the same time you print the document.

● Click | Print |.

● Click | No | in response to the prompt to save the return address as the default.

Additional Information

Responding | Yes | displays that address automatically whenever envelopes are printed.

● Close the Tour Merge Document file without saving it.

● Close all other document windows, saving the files as necessary.

● Exit Word.

LAB 5

Creating Complex Tables and Merging Documents

Formulas and Functions (WD5.20)

Formulas and functions are used to perform calculations in tables.

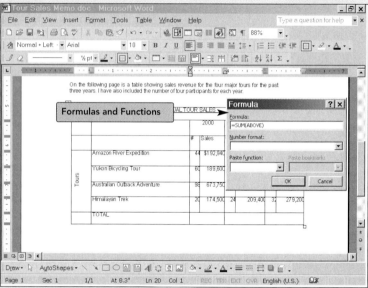

Charts (WD5.32)

A chart, also called a graph, is a visual representation of numeric data.

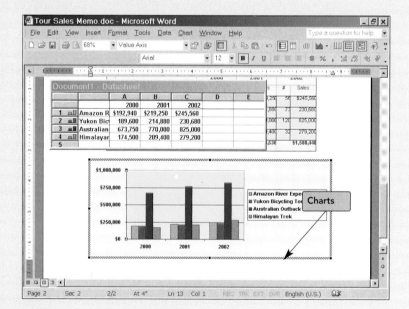

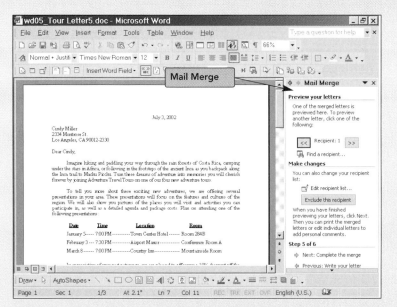

Mail Merge (WD5.45)

The Mail Merge feature combines a list of data (typically a file of names and addresses) with a document (commonly a form letter) to create a new document.

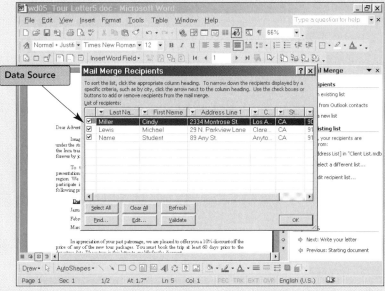

Data Source (WD5.48)

The data source file is a table of information that contains data fields in the columns and records in the rows.

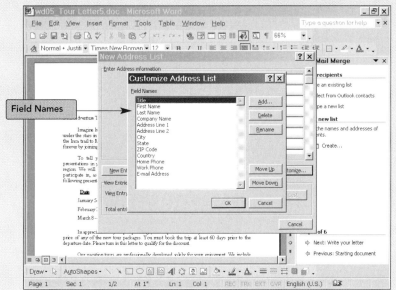

Field Name (WD5.49)

Field names are used to label the different data fields in the data source.

LAB **5**

Creating Complex Tables and Merging Document

key terms

address file WD5.45	legend WD5.35
chart WD5.32	Mail Merge WD5.45
data field WD5.48	main document WD5.45
data series WD5.35	merge field WD5.45
data source WD5.45	operator WD5.20
datasheet WD5.33	placeholder WD5.6
field name WD5.49	portrait WD5.28
formula WD5.20	record WD5.48
function WD5.20	wizard WD5.46
landscape WD5.28	

mous skills

The Microsoft Office User Specialist (MOUS) certification program is designed to measure your proficiency in performing basic tasks using the Office XP applications. Getting certified demonstrates that you have the skills and provides a valuable industry credential for employment. After completing this lab, you have learned the following Microsoft Office User Specialist skills:

Skill	Description	Page
Inserting and Modifying Text	Enter and format Date and Time	WD5.8
Creating and Modifying Paragraphs	Apply bullet, outline, and numbering format to paragraphs	WD5.40
Formatting Documents	Modify document layout and Page Setup options	WD5.28
	Create and modify tables	WD5.13
	Preview and print documents, envelopes, and labels	WD5.59, WD5.63
Managing Documents	Create documents using templates	WD5.4
Working with Graphics	Insert images and graphics	WD5.9
	Create and modify diagrams and charts	WD5.32

Command	Button	Action
File/**N**ew/GeneralTemplates/ Letters & Faxes/Mailing Label Wizard		Starts Mailing Label Wizard to create mailing labels
Edit/Chart **O**bject/**E**dit		Opens Chart object for editing
View/**D**atasheet		Displays Datasheet table for Open Chart object
Insert/**O**bject/Microsoft Graph Chart		Creates a chart in the document
F**o**rmat/Bullets and **N**umbering/ O**u**tline Numbered		Applies the selected outline number style to the text
F**o**rmat/Te**x**t Direction/**O**rientation		Changes direction of text in a table
Tools/Le**t**ters and Mailings/ **M**ail Merge Wizard		Starts Mail Merge Wizard
Tools/Le**t**ters and Mailings/ Show Mail Merge **T**oolbar		Displays Mail Merge toolbar
Tools/Le**t**ters and Mailings/ **E**nvelopes and Labels/**E**nvelopes		Creates and prints delivery and return address on envelopes
Table/Draw Ta**b**le		Creates a table using Draw Table feature
Table/**I**nsert Columns		Inserts new columns in a table
Table/**M**erge Cells		Merges cells in a table
Table/Sele**c**t/**T**able		Selects entire table
Table/**A**utofit/Distribute Rows Eve**n**ly		Evenly sizes selected rows
Table/F**o**rmula		Inserts a formula into a table
Table/Show **G**ridlines		Displays gridlines in a table
Table/Table P**r**operties/**T**able/**C**enter		Centers the selected table
Table/Table P**r**operties/**T**able/**O**ptiona/ Automatically resi**z**e to fit contents		Automatically resizes columns in the table to fit text or graphic
Table/Table P**r**operties/Col**u**mn		Adjusts width of selected columns

Terminology

In the following Word screen, letters identify important elements. Enter the correct term for each screen element in the space provided.

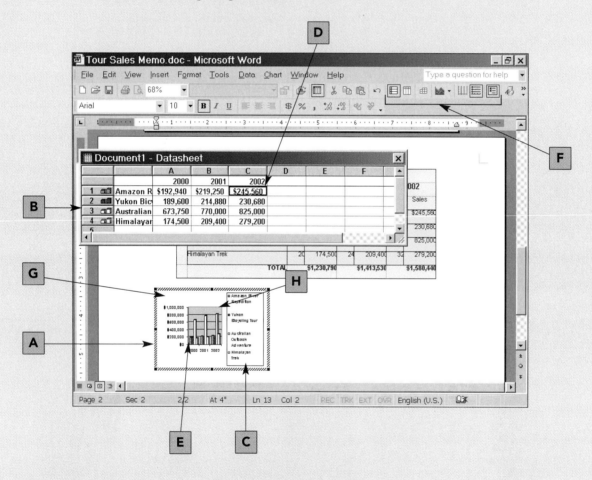

A. _____   E. _____

B. _____   F. _____

C. _____   G. _____

D. _____   H. _____

Match the item on the left with the correct description on the right.

1. placeholder _____ **a.** all the data fields that are needed to complete the information for one person

2. portrait _____ **b.** orientation of the page, in which text is printed across the width of the page

3. address file _____ **c.** each group of related data that is plotted in the chart

4. record _____ **d.** contains the information needed to complete the letter in the main document

5. legend _____ **e.** a table containing sample data

6. data series _____ **f.** asks you questions and then uses your answers to automatically lay out and format a document

7. landscape _____ **g.** orientation in which text is printed across the length of the page

8. data source _____ **h.** text that marks the space and provides instructions for text to be entered in that location

9. datasheet _____ **i.** the file that supplies the data in a mail merge

10. wizard _____ **j.** identifies the color or pattern associated with each data series

multiple choice

Circle the correct response to the questions below.

1. A(n) _____ contains any combination of numbers, fields resulting in numbers, table references, and operators.
   a. expression
   b. calculation
   c. formula
   d. function

2. _____ orientation prints the text across the length of the page.
   a. Margin
   b. Picture
   c. Portrait
   d. Landscape

3. The _____ feature combines a list of data with a document to create a new document.
   a. Mail Format
   b. Mail Join
   c. Mail Manage
   d. Mail Merge

4. The _____ document contains the text that will become the basis of a form letter.
   a. letter
   b. data source
   c. address file
   d. main

5. The _____ contains the information needed to address and complete a form letter.
   a. letter
   b. data source
   c. address file
   d. main

6. All the data fields that are needed to complete the information for one person are called a _____.
   a. field
   b. record
   c. file
   d. row

7. _____ names are used to label each data field in the data source.
   a. Row
   b. Record
   c. Field
   d. File

8. A(n) _____asks questions and then uses your answers to automatically lay out and format a document.
   a. template
   b. placeholder
   c. wizard
   d. merge

9. A formula uses _____to specify the type of calculation to perform.
   a. cell references
   b. table references
   c. operators
   d. fields

10. A(n) _____ is used in the main document for each item from the data source that is inserted.
    a. placeholder
    b. record
    c. row
    d. data field

Check the correct answer to the following questions.

1. Text in a placeholder tells the user what information to enter.   True   False
2. A function is an expression that contains numbers only.   True   False
3. Text that is printed with landscape orientation is printed across the width of the page.   True   False
4. The Mail Merge feature combines a file of names and addresses with a document form letter to create a new document.   True   False
5. The data source document contains the basic form letter.   True   False
6. A merge field is a field code that controls what information is used from the main document and where it is entered in the data source.   True   False
7. The data source contains the information needed to complete the letter in the main document.   True   False
8. All the data fields that are needed to complete the information for one person are called a record.   True   False
9. Field names are used to label each data field in the data source.   True   False
10. A wizard asks you questions and then uses your answers to automatically lay out and format a document, such as a newsletter or resume.   True   False

lab exercises

Concepts

fill-in

Complete the following statements by filling in the blanks with the correct terms.

1. The left boundary of the chart is known as the _____.

2. The Graph feature activates a table called the _____.

3. Commonly used form-letter _____ are displayed in the New Address List list box.

4. The data source is a table of information that contains data _____ and _____ in the rows.

5. _____ requires the use of two files: a main document and a data source.

6. The data source can also be called the _____.

7. A(n) _____ is a visual representation of a chart.

8. SUM is a prewrittten _____.

9. A(n) _____ can only contain letter, numbers, or the underline character.

10. You can also use the icons on the Mail Merge toolbar instead of the Mail Merge _____ to create a merged document.

discussion questions

1. There are several methods you can use to create a table. Describe each and explain when they would be used.

2. What is the significance of using a column-and-row format in tables? How are the rows and columns labeled?

3. Describe the use of formulas and functions in tables. What advantage do they offer over entering fixed values?

4. Describe how the Mail Merge feature works. What are some advantages of using Mail Merge?

5. What steps are used to create a data source file? How is the data used in a main document?

Hands-On Exercises

rating system

★ Easy

★★ Moderate

★★★ Difficult

step-by-step

Yoga Memo

★ **1.** The Adventure Travel Tours manager has fielded several requests from clients seeking Yoga retreats. She has asked you to gather information on yoga packages the agency could offer. You did some research and found several resorts that offer such packages. You would like to send a memo to the manager with an update on your progress. The completed memo is shown here.

    a. Open a new file with the Professional Memo template.

    b. Replace "Company Name Here" with **Adventure Travel Tours**. Insert the wd05_Mountain picture in the left table cell. Size the picture and table appropriately.

    c. Enter the following in the placeholders:

        To: **Manager, Adventure Travel**
        From: **[Your Name]**
        CC: **Tour Director**
        Re: **Yoga Retreats**

    d. Remove the template instructions from the memo body and enter the following:

> **I researched several yoga retreats that meet our client requests. Now I am working on a document that will provide our agents with the information about the retreats. I plan to format the document as below. If you have any questions or would like me to provide additional information to the agents please let me know.**
>
> **Kripalu Center for Yoga and Health**
>
> **This Center emphasizes the gentle and slow Kripalu style of yoga on its 300 acres of meadows and hills. A variety of yoga programs are offered for beginners through advanced practitioners.**

    e. Draw a table with the appropriate number of columns and rows to hold the following data. Place the table below the descriptive paragraph.

Valid Dates	Price/Person	Minimum Stay	Yoga
June 3–Sep 7	$239/night	2 Nights	Kripalu
Dec 3–Jan 23	$305/night	5 Nights	Svaroopa Yoga
April 1–May 1	$363/night	4 Nights	Raja Yoga
Aug 6–Aug 12	$415/night	6 Nights	Partner Yoga

Memo

To: Manager, Adventure Travel
From: Student Name
CC: Tour Director
Date: September 27, 2001
Re: Yoga Retreats

I researched several yoga retreats that meet our client requests. Now I am working on a document that will provide our agents with the information about the retreats. I plan to format the document as below. If you have any questions or would like me to provide additional information to the agents please let me know.

Kripalu Center for Yoga and Health

This Center emphasizes the gentle and slow Kripalu style of yoga on its 300 acres of meadows and hills. A variety of yoga programs are offered for beginners through advanced practitioners.

VALID DATES	PRICE/PERSON	MINIMUM STAY	YOGA
June 3 – Sept 7	$239/night	2 Nights	Kripalu
Dec 3 – Jan 23	$305/night	5 Nights	Svaroopa
April 1 – May 1	$363/night	4 Nights	Raja
Aug 6 – Aug 12	$415/night	6 Nights	Partner

1

f. Select each column and drag the right indent marker to the right edge of each column. Center cells B1 through D5.

g. Increase the font size of all the text in the memo to 12 points. Apply the Elegant AutoFormat to the table. Size the table rows and columns as necessary. Center the table in the memo.

g. Add color as you like to the memo. Save the document as Yoga Memo. Print the document.

Membership Memo

★ 2. The Lifestyle Fitness Club is preparing a memo containing a summary of membership data for the four stores. The most effective way to present the data is to use a table and chart. The completed memo with the table and chart are shown here.

a. Open a new file with the Professional Memo template.

b. Replace "Company Name Here" with Lifestyle Fitness Club. Adjust the size of the cell to display the text on one line.

c. Enter the following in the placeholders:
To: Brian Birch, Owner
From: [Your Name]
CC: Kathy Roth, Assistant Manager
Re: Membership Totals

d. Replace the template instructions from the memo body with the following:
The data you requested comparing the total memberships for the years 1999 through 2001 for the four clubs is shown below.

e. Select all the blank lines below the sentence and clear the format (use Clear Formatting on the Style list).

f. Draw table approximately 2 by 6 inches. Add four columns and 6 rows to accommodate the information shown in the table below.

g. Enter the data into the table shown here.

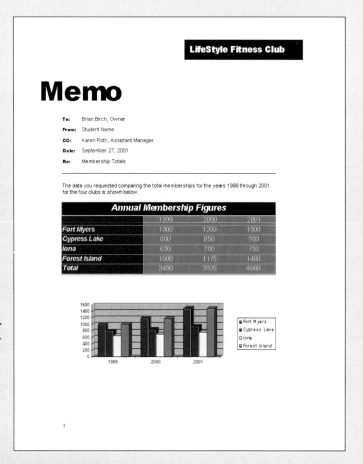

	Col. A	Col. B	Col. C	Col. D
Row 1		1999	2000	2001
Row 2	Fort Myers	1000	1200	1500
Row 3	Cypress Lake	800	850	950
Row 4	Iona	650	700	750
Row 5	Forest Island	1000	1175	1480
Row 6	Total			

h. In cell B6 enter a formula that sums the column, excluding the year in row 1. Enter the same type of formula in columns C and D.

i. Insert a new row at the top of the table. Merge the cells to make one cell. Center the table title Annual Membership Figures in the new cell. Increase the size of the title text to 16 points.

j. Increase the font size of the remaining table data to 12 points. Center-align the numbers and the year headings.

k. Select cells B2 through D7 and distribute the columns evenly. Select rows 2 through 7 and distribute the rows evenly. Format the table using colors and other effects of your choice. Center the table in the memo.

l. Add a chart below the table showing the growth for the four locations for the three years. Chart the data by columns. Adjust the size of the chart to match that of the table. Apply colors and patterns to match the table.

m. Format the memo as you like.

n. Save the document as Membership Memo. Print the document.

Video Club Membership Letter

★ ★ **3.** The Video Tower sends membership cards to all its new members. Since new people open new memberships every day, the owners would like you to create a form letter that can be used when the permanent membership cards are sent. One of your completed merge letters is shown here.

a. Open the file wd05_Video Tower Letter.

b. Using the Mail Merge Wizard, create a form letter from the current document. Create a data source file that contains the fields needed to enter the data shown below. Name the file Video Data Source. Enter the following records and one more that contains your name.

First name:	Stephanie	Rhett
Last name:	Manahan	Owens
Address1:	2931 Campus Dr.	3957 W. University Ave.
City:	St. John	Pleasant
State:	WI	FL
Zip Code:	53205-6911	33301-7985

c. In the Video Tower Letter document, create an inside address by inserting data source merge fields above the salutation. In the salutation replace "Member" with the First Name merge field.

d. Merge the data source and main document files. Save the merged letters as Video Merge Document. Print the letter that contains your name.

September 19, 2001

Student Name
555 Campus Lane
University Town, CA 55555

Dear Student:

Thank you for joining Video Tower and becoming one of our most valued members. Here's your new Video Tower card! Using your new card is as easy as 1-2-3

1. Please sign your new card in ink with your usual signature.

2. If you have an old card or a temporary card, destroy it immediately.

3. Always carry your new Video Tower card with you.

Your new card identifies you as a member and guarantees you a pleasant experience at any of The Video Tower locations throughout the country.

You can begin using your new Video Tower card with your very next visit. In appreciation for becoming a Video Tower member, you will receive 10% off the first purchase you make in our multimedia shop. Please turn in this letter at the time the discount is given.

Additionally, each month you will receive The Video Tower Update, a newsletter about new products, movie trends, and upcoming events. The newsletter will also include announcements of special sale days for our members only. If you have questions about an event, call 1-800-555-9838 or come in and speak to the Customer Service representative.

We are the leading video store in the country with a tradition of personal, friendly service. As you use your new Video Tower membership card, you will discover the many conveniences that only our members enjoy.

We are delighted with the opportunity to serve you and we look forward to seeing you soon.

Sincerely,

The Video Tower Manager

Volunteer Recruitment Memo

★ ★ **4.** Animal Angels plans to send a letter to all the veterinarians in the area to enlist their help in the placement and care of homeless animals. Your completed form letter is shown here.

a. Open the file wd05_Vet Letter to see the letter text. Create a WordArt object that contains the words Animal Angels. Center and place the WordArt at the top of the document. Enter three blank lines below the WordArt.

b. Right-align the current date as a field. Enter four blank lines after the date.

c. Use the active document to create a form letter. Create a data source named Vet Data Source that contains the following fields:

> Title
> First Name
> Last Name
> Address1
> City
> State
> Zip Code

d. Enter the following records:

> Dr. Joel Allen
> 316 River St.
> Claremont, NH 03702
>
> Dr. Matthew Smith
> 452 Valley View Dr.
> Newport, NH 03706
>
> Dr. Deana Walter
> 409 Laurel Rd.
> Claremont, NH 03707

Animal Angels

April 4, 2001

Dr. Joel Allen
316 River St.
Claremont, NH 03702

Dear Dr. Allen:

Animal Angels strives to make a difference in the quality of life of homeless pets. This is achieved on a daily basis through the immediate care of these animals, but there is so much that still needs to be done.

Animal Angels has identified five specific things you can do to help us meet the needs of this homeless population:

1. Increase exposure to local humane organizations resulting in higher placement rates.
2. Provide a low cost spay/neuter program to the general public.
3. Subsidize extraordinary medical expenses for animals referred by local humane groups.
4. Participate in the regional lost and found service.
5. Help educate the public on owner responsibility through presentations, displays, and literature.

Take this opportunity to make a difference!

For more information or copies of the Animal Angel Newsletter to distribute to your clients please call us at 1-800-555-8888.

Sincerely,

Student Name

e. In the main document, insert fields representing the names and addresses above the first paragraph. Insert a salutation line that contains "Dear" and the title and last name from the data source file.

f. Insert an appropriate closing to the letter and type your name as the sender.

g. Merge the main document and the data source. Save the merge letters as Vet Merge Document. Print the letters.

Bonus Club Memo

★★ **5.** The Downtown Internet Cafe manager asked you to create a letter to send to members of the
★ bonus awards program. The body of the letter has already been created. One of the merge letters
you will create is shown below.
  a. Open the file wd05_Cafe Bonus.
  b. Draw a table with the appropriate number of columns and rows to hold the following data.
  Place the table below the second paragraph. Enter the information shown below into the table.

Bonus Awards					
	Hours				
	20	50	75	100	150+
Award	Free coffee refill	Free bagel	One free hour online time	Two free hours online time	One free hour online time for each additional 25 hours
	Or free bagel	Or free half hour online time	Or free coffee and bagel	Or free coffee and bagel on next four visits	Or free coffee and bagel per visit for each additional 10 hours

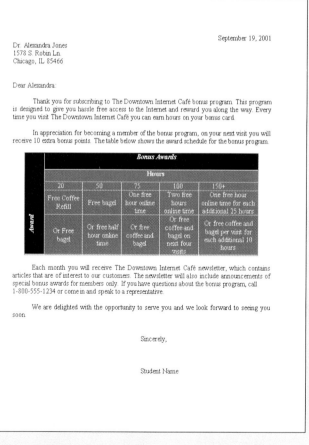

  c. Apply format features you learned in this lab, including text alignment and colors to the table. Size the table rows and columns as necessary, and center the table.
  d. Use the wizard to create a form letter. Create a data source named Cafe Data Source that contains the following fields:

  Title
  First Name
  Last Name
  Address1
  City
  State
  Zip Code

  e. Create three records in the Cafe Data Source file.
  f. In the main document, insert fields representing the names and addresses above the first paragraph. Replace the word "Member" in the salutation line with the member's first name from the data source file. Insert your name in the closing.
  g. Merge the main document and the data source. Save the merged letters as Cafe Merge Document. Print the letters.

lab exercises

on your own

Leisure Activity Newsletter

★ 1. According to the Yankelovich study printed in the *Yankelovich Monitor Minute*, Americans are seeking more creative outlets through their home and family. You feel this information would be of interest to the people to whom you send a monthly newsletter. Use the information provided below to create an attractive table. Use the features you learned in the lab to enhance the appearance of the table. When you are finished, enter your name and the current date below the table. Save the document as Leisure Activities and print the document.

Activity	Boomers	Xers
Do-it-yourself projects	54%	50%
Home improvements	52	38
Gardening	39	18
Cooking from scratch	32	23
Raising children	53	29
Cooking for fun	39	33
They wish for more:		
Get-togethers with friends	52	43
Family get-togethers	49	37
Watching movies/videos	22	17

New Car Research

★★ 2. Your friend is excited about his new car and has gotten you interested in buying a new car. You have narrowed down your options to those shown below. Use the data to create a table that contains the make, model, fuel efficiency, and selling price. Add text to the document with a short description of the features that attract you to your favorite vehicle on the list. Enter your name and the current date at the end of the document. Save the document as New Car Info and print the document.

Make	Model	MPG (City/Hwy)	Retail
Toyota	Echo	34/41	$12,685
Honda	Insight	61/68	$19,716
Volkswagen	Jetta	42/49	$18,520
Nissan	Altima	21/28	$19,160

Hand Washing Data

★ ★ **3.** You work at the American Society for Microbiology and have received a request for data on hand washing. Create a memo using the Professional Memo Template. Add the paragraph below to the body of the memo. Address the memo to your instructor and include your name and the date in the memo placeholders. Then use the data below to create a table, with headings for city, sex, and percentage of hand washers. Include it in the memo you will send in response to the request. Add color and formatting of your choice to the table. Save your completed memo as Hand Washing and print it.

Recent studies done by the American Society for Microbiology conclude that only 60% of Americans using public restrooms wash their hands. These findings are inconsistent with polling that suggested 98% of Americans wash their hands after using the restroom. Field observations demonstrate that the percentage of hand washers varies by city and sex. I have included the data from our studies in the table below.

City	% Women	% Men
Chicago	83	60
San Francisco	80	75
Atlanta	64	60
New Orleans	64	55
New York	49	35

Movie Data Research

★ ★ **4.** For your marketing class, you have been asked to create a report on historical movie promotions. To inform the rest of your team about the results of your research, use a Memo Template with appropriate fields and include a table, using the data below, that displays the current movies, the number of weeks they have been in theaters, and the gross revenue of each. Be sure to include a chart of your findings. When you are finished, format the table and chart in an attractive manner. Save the document as Movie Data and then print the document.

Movie	Weeks in Theater	Gross Revenue	Year
The Exorcist	24	$204 Billion	1973
Star Wars	21	$461 Billion	1977
Gone with the Wind	30	$200 Billion	1939

Frequent Flyer Letter

★ ★ 5. Your job with a new low-cost airline company is to manage the company's frequent flyer program.
★ Use the features you learned in this lab to create a form letter to be sent to new customers of your
airline's frequent flyer program. Put the program information provided below into a table, and
then enhance the table. Enter your name as the signature name on the letter. Create at least three
addresses in the data source file. When you are finished, save the document as Frequent Flyer Letter.
Print the document.

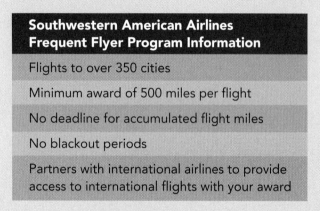

Southwestern American Airlines Frequent Flyer Program Information
Flights to over 350 cities
Minimum award of 500 miles per flight
No deadline for accumulated flight miles
No blackout periods
Partners with international airlines to provide access to international flights with your award

on the web

Researching Job Opportunities on the Web

Use the Web to locate three advertisements for jobs of interest to you in your field. Using the
Letter Wizard, create a cover letter appropriate for each position. Include features you learned in
this and other tutorials to make a professional-looking document. Use Resume Wizard to create a
current resume for yourself. Include all the information that might help you secure one of the
positions you are interested in. When you are finished, save the document as Cover Letter and Resume.
Print the documents.

Creating a Web Site

objectives

After completing this lab, you will know how to:

1.	Plan and design a Web site.
2.	Use the Web Page Wizard.
3.	Preview a Web site.
4.	Create and size frames.
5.	Add backgrounds.
6.	Group objects.
7.	Use tables to control layout.
8.	Insert lines, animated graphics, and diagrams.
9.	Insert absolute and relative hyperlinks.
10.	Create a Web form.
11.	Use supporting folders.

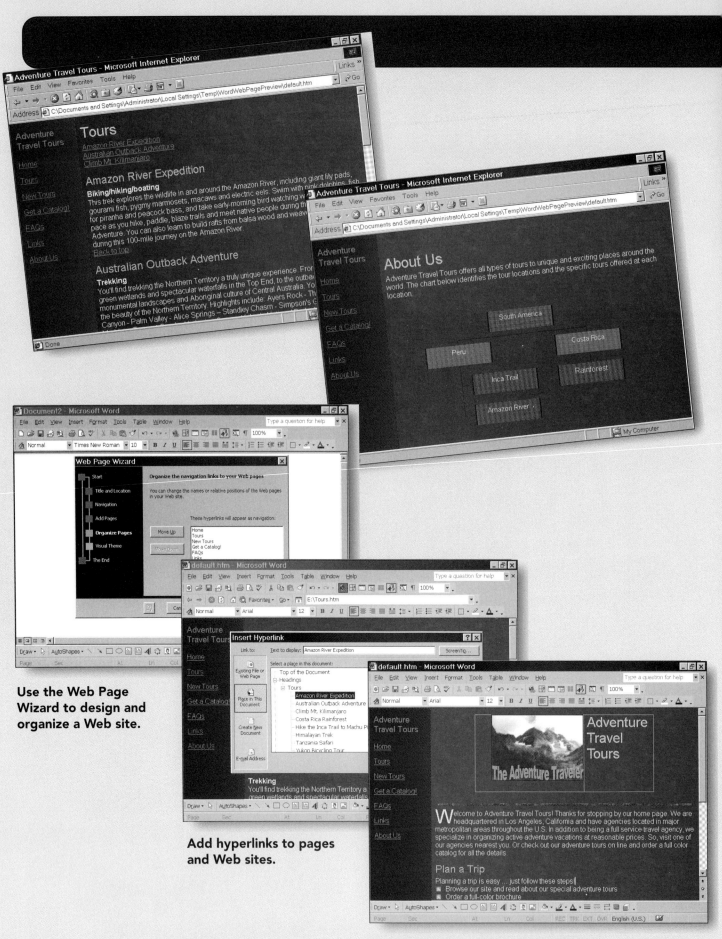

Use the Web Page Wizard to design and organize a Web site.

Add hyperlinks to pages and Web sites.

Enhance pages with graphics, animations and themes.

Adventure Travel Tours

The manager of Adventure Travel Tours has noticed that the company Web site has become disorganized as new items have been added to the site. In addition, the site has an inconsistent look—different colors and styles have been used as pages have been added. You have been asked to evaluate the site for content, organization, and style and to develop a new overall design and layout for the site as well as a new structure for the site content.

You are very excited about working on this project as you recently attended a seminar on Web page design and layout. You learned about how to organize a site to make it both efficient and attractive. Additionally, the seminar demonstrated how these features could be created using Word. You will use Word to create the new Web site shown below.

© Corbis

Planning and Designing Web Sites

The Adventure Travel Tours Web site consists of several Web pages. These pages contain a list of tours, tour descriptions, a catalog request form, a newsletter, and links to other Web sites. Like all Web sites, the Adventure Travel Tours site opens with a home page that links to the additional pages.

concept 1

Home Page

1 The top-level or opening page of a Web site is called the **home page**. It is displayed by default when a user visits your Web site. A large site may have many home pages. The home page usually contains an introduction to the site along with hyperlinks that allow users to jump to another location on the same page, to another page in the same site, or to another page on a different site altogether.

Because the home page is the first page people see when visiting a site, it is very important that it is well designed. After looking at the existing home page and the organization of the Adventure Travel Tours site, you have decided to redesign the entire site.

When creating or authoring a Web page, you want to make the page both attractive and informative. You also want it to be easy to use, and you want it to work right. It is therefore important to plan the design of the Web site and the pages it will include. Web page design includes planning the text content of the page and the addition of elements such as graphic objects, images, art, and color, which can make the page both attractive and easy to use.

Graphic objects, images, art, and color are perhaps the most important features of Web pages. They entice the user to continue to explore the Web site. Other elements, such as animation, scrolling banners, blinking text, audio, and video can be added to a Web page to make it even more dynamic.

With all these elements, it is easy to add too many to a page and end up with a cluttered and distracting mess. Keep the following design tips in mind when authoring your own Web pages:

- The text content of your page is the single most important element. Text should be readable against the background. Check for proper spelling and grammar.

- Background colors and patterns add pizzazz to a page, but be careful that they do not make the page hard to read. Also keep in mind that more complex patterns take longer to download, and that many users have 256-color monitors, on which higher resolution colors will be lost.

- To speed up downloading, keep graphics simple and avoid busy animations and blinking text. A good suggestion is to keep the file size of images less than 100K. Smaller is even better.

- Page dimensions should be the same as the browser window size. Many users today have large monitors with the screen resolution set to 600 by 800 pixels. Some, however, still have 15-inch screens with the screen resolution set to 640 by 480 pixels. A page designed with 600 by 800 pixels will be too large for their screens. To solve this problem, many professional sites include a JavaScript program that determines the user's screen dimensions and dynamically resizes the page width. Older versions of browser programs may not support JavaScript; therefore, designing a Web page for 640 by 480 resolution is still the safest approach.

- In general, keep pages to no longer than two to three screens' worth of information. If a page is too long, the reader has to remember too much information that has scrolled off the screen.

- At the bottom of each page, include navigation links back to the home page and other major site pages so users will not get lost. Also include text links (alternative text) for users who have turned off graphics loading in their browsers to improve downloading speed.

- Get permission before using text, sounds, and images that are copyrighted. Copyright laws and infringement fines apply to pages posted on the Internet.

After a discussion with the marketing manager about the content and features that Adventure Travel Tours wants to include in the Web site, you drew a sample home page layout that you feel may be both interesting and easy to use (shown here). Your plans are to include separate pages for company information, tour descriptions and itinerary, frequently asked questions (FAQs), ordering catalogs and booking tours, a photo album, and links to other travel-related sites.

You have created a Word document containing the text for the home page. You have also prepared several other documents to use in the Web site, including the Web page you already created about the four new tours. Now you are ready to start creating the web site.

Using the Web Page Wizard

Word offers three ways to create Web pages. You can start with a blank Web page. You can convert an existing Word document to hypertext markup language (HTML), which you did in Working Together following Lab 3. Finally, you can use the Web Page Wizard to help you quickly create a Web site. The Web Wizard is a guided approach that helps you determine the content and organization of your Web site through a series of questions. Then it creates a Web site based on the answers you provide.

Starting the Web Page Wizard

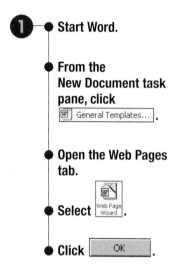

1
- **Start Word.**

- **From the New Document task pane, click** 🗔 General Templates... **.**

- **Open the Web Pages tab.**

- **Select** 🗔 Web Page Wizard **.**

- **Click** OK **.**

Your screen should be similar to Figure 6.1

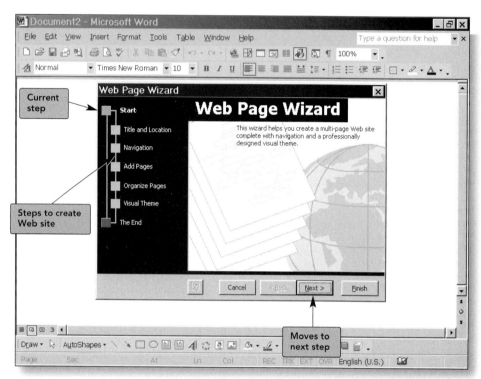

Figure 6.1

The opening dialog box of the Web Page Wizard briefly describes how the feature works. As the wizard guides you through creating the Web site, the left side of the window shows you which step you are on in the outline. The green box identifies the current step. Clicking Next > moves to the next step.

2 ● Click [Next >] .

Another Method

You can also click on an outline box to move to that step.

Your screen should be similar to Figure 6.2

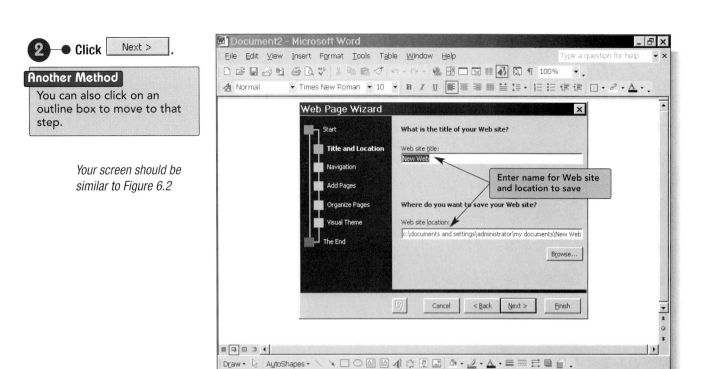

Figure 6.2

The second wizard dialog box asks you for the name of your Web site and the location where you want to save it.

3 ● **In the Web Site Title text box, type Adventure Travel Tours.**

● **If necessary, change the location to store the Web site to your data file location.**

HAVING TROUBLE?

You can type in the path directly or click [Browse...] to quickly select the location.

● Click [Next >] .

Your screen should be similar to Figure 6.3

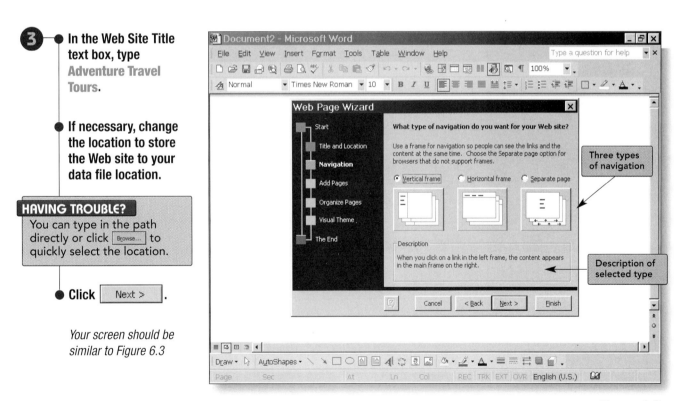

Figure 6.3

Setting Site Navigation

The third wizard dialog box asks you for the type of navigation you want to use. Most Web sites use frames to make navigation easier.

---

concept 2

Frame

2 A Web page can be divided into sections, called **frames**, that display separate Web pages. Because each one can display different information, frames not only make the Web site more organized but allow users to access the information more easily. The frames for a Web site are held in a special **frames page** container. The frames page serves as the file name for the collection of frames; it is invisible to the users viewing the Web site.

You can use frames to create a header for your Web site that appears on each page in the site. You can also create a table of contents in the left frame that displays hyperlinks to the main pages of a Web site. It stays on the screen while the right frame, often called the main frame, displays the contents of the page the hyperlink points to.

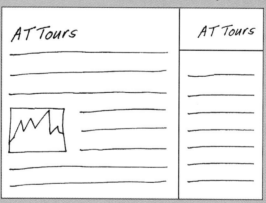

Table of contents frame on left, main frame on right

Header frame on top, table of contents frame on left, main frame on right

Main frame on left with two small frames on right

Although frames can make navigation in your Web site easier, having too many can make it difficult to read the screen. Use as few frames as possible. Many people have browsers that cannot display frames, so you may want to consider creating a nonframe version to accommodate those users.

Your choices are to create a frame to the left or at the top of the home page. A vertical frame on the left side can display links to topics that, when selected, appear in the main frame on the right. A horizontal frame at the top of the screen can contain links to topics that, when selected, appear below the frame. You can also set up your Web site without frames so that the navigation is limited to browsers' Back and Forward buttons.

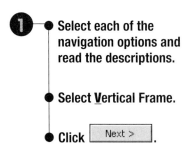
Additional Information

Refer to the discussion of hyperlinks in the Working Together section following Lab 3.

1 ● Select each of the navigation options and read the descriptions.

● Select **V**ertical Frame.

● Click Next > .

Your screen should be similar to Figure 6.4

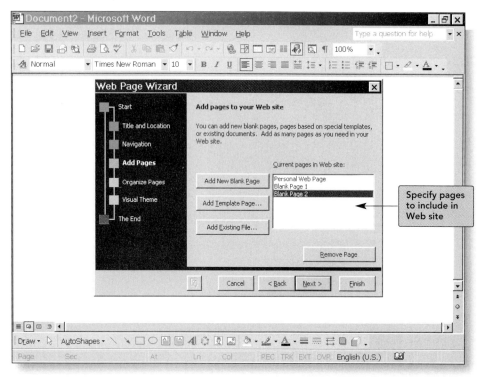

Figure 6.4

Creating Pages

The fourth wizard dialog box asks you to specify the pages to include in your Web site. By default, the wizard offers a Personal Web Page template and two blank pages. You want to remove the Personal Web Page template and include a home page using the text in the document ATT Home Page, which has already been created. You also want to include pages for the following: new tours, a list of all tours and descriptions, frequently asked questions (FAQs), ordering catalogs and booking tours, and links to other travel-related sites.

The three option buttons, described below, are used to specify the type of page to insert and the source of any contents you want included in the pages.

Option	Effect
Add New Blank Page	Creates a blank page
Add Template Page	Creates a page with suggested contents
Add Existing File	Creates a page containing the contents of the selected file

First you will remove the Personal Web Page and add a page using the text in the ATT Home Page document.

1 ● Select **Personal Web Page.**

● Click [Remove Page] .

● Click [Add Existing File...] .

● **If necessary, change the location to the location of your data files.**

● Select the file wd06_ATT Home Page.

● Click [Open ▾] .

Your screen should be similar to Figure 6.5

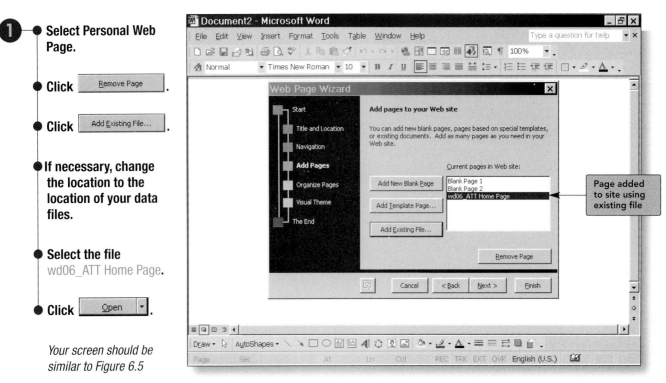

Figure 6.5

The list box displays the name of the file on which this page will be based. Next you want to add a page for the frequently asked questions. Word includes a template for a FAQs page.

2 ● Click  .

Your screen should be similar to Figure 6.6

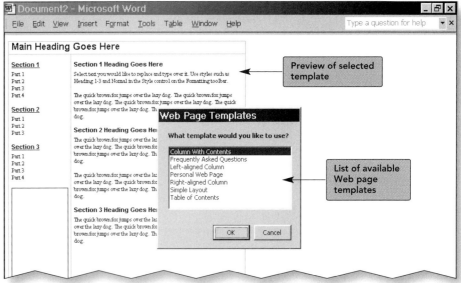

Figure 6.6

The Web Page Templates box lists the seven different templates you can use to create a Web page. The selected template is displayed behind the dialog box in the window. You want to use the Frequently Asked Questions template to create the FAQs page.

3 • Click on each template to view it.

• Select Frequently Asked Questions.

• Click [OK].

Your screen should be similar to Figure 6.7

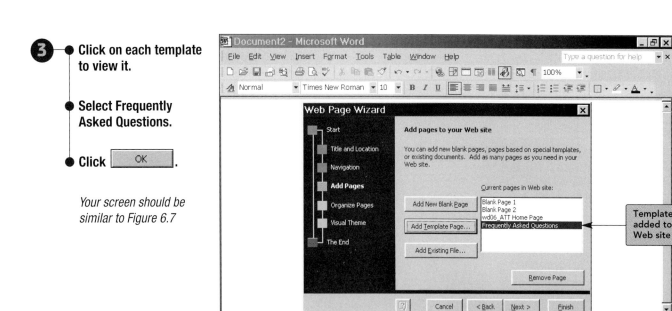

Template added to Web site

Figure 6.7

The page is added to the list and you are returned to the Web Page Wizard. Next you want to add two more pages from existing file content. The first is a list of all tours and a brief description, and the second is a Web page file about the new tours, similar to the one you created in the first Working Together lab. You will also add another blank page that you will add information to.

4 • Click [Add Existing File...].

• If necessary, change the location to your data disk.

• Select wd06_Tour List.

• Click [Open ▾].

• In the same manner, add the wd06_New Tours.htm file to the list.

• Click [Add New Blank Page] to add another new blank page.

Your screen should be similar to Figure 6.8

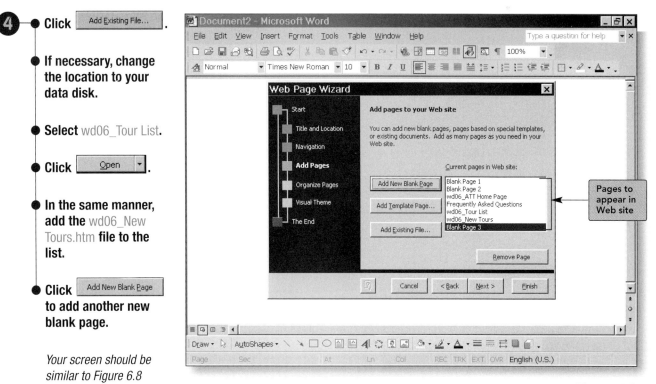

Pages to appear in Web site

Figure 6.8

Organizing and Naming Pages

You are halfway finished with your Web site structure. The next step is to organize the Web pages.

 Click [Next >].

Your screen should be similar to Figure 6.9

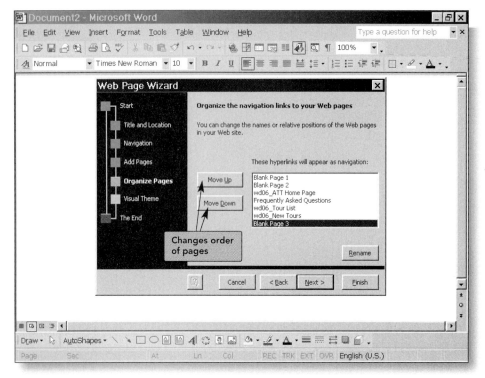

Figure 6.9

You need to specify the order in which the pages will appear as links in the table of contents frame. The ATT Home Page document contains the information you want displayed on the home page, so you need to move it to the top of the list. You want the Tours page second, the New Tours page third, a blank page fourth, the FAQs page fifth, and two more blank pages to be sixth and seventh.

- **Select** wd06_ATT Home Page.

- **Click** [Move Up] twice.

- **In a similar manner, move the other pages to the following order:**

  wd06_Tour List

  wd06_New Tours

  Blank page 1

  Frequently Asked Questions

  Blank page 2

  Blank page 3

  Your screen should be similar to Figure 6.10

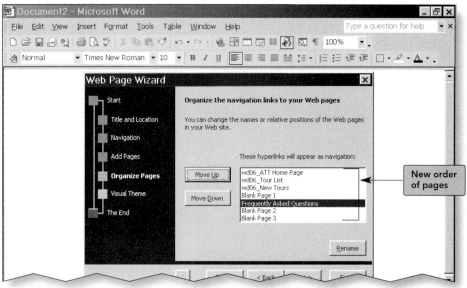

Figure 6.10

Now that the pages are in the right sequence, you want to give them more descriptive names. Each name will be used as the link in the contents frame. First you will rename the wd06_ATT Home Page to Home.

3 ● **Select** wd06_ATT Home Page.

● **Click** Rename .

Rename Hyperlink

What is the name for this page?

| wd06_ATT Home Page |

OK   Cancel

● **Type** Home **in the Rename Hyperlink dialog box text box.**

● **Click** OK .

● **Using this same procedure, rename the remaining pages using the names shown below.**

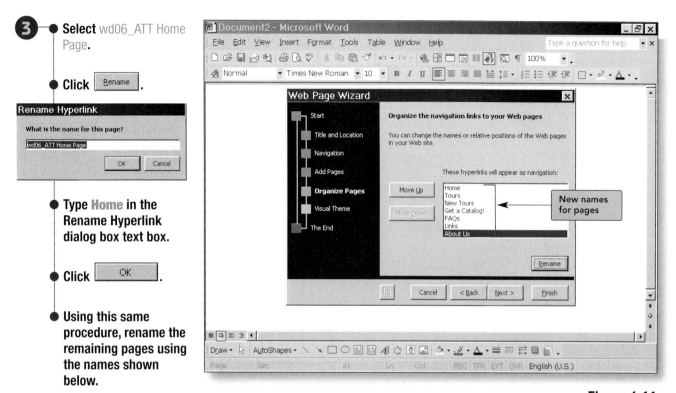

Figure 6.11

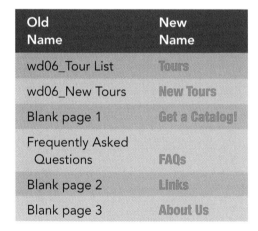

Old Name	New Name
wd06_Tour List	Tours
wd06_New Tours	New Tours
Blank page 1	Get a Catalog!
Frequently Asked Questions	FAQs
Blank page 2	Links
Blank page 3	About Us

Your screen should be similar to Figure 6.11

Selecting a Theme

Your Web site structure is almost finished. The last step in the process is to select a theme for the site. The theme you select here will be applied to all the pages in your site at once. You can also apply themes to individual pages, as you did in the first Working Together section.

1 Click [Next >].

Click [Browse Themes...].

Select several themes and view a sample of them in the dialog box.

Select Artsy.

Your screen should be similar to Figure 6.12

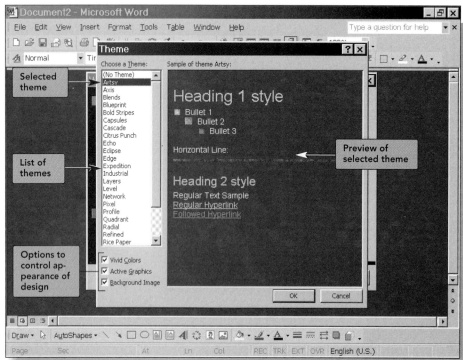

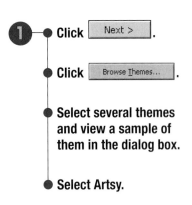

Figure 6.12

The three options under the Theme list box are used to control the appearance of the page. Choose Vivid Colors when you want to brighten the theme. Choose Active Graphics if you plan to include any animation. Background Image is selected by default. You want to brighten the theme colors and you plan to include animation. The name of the selected theme appears in the wizard text box. Now you are finished setting up the structure for the Web site and the last step is to create it.

2 If necessary, select Vivid **C**olors.

If necessary, select Active **G**raphics.

Click [OK].

Click [Next >].

Click [Finish].

After a few moments, your screen should be similar to Figure 6.13

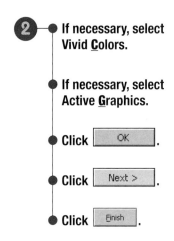

Figure 6.13

All the pages in the Web site are created and the home page is displayed. The Frames toolbar opens automatically. It can be used to add or delete frames to existing pages. The Web site name appears at the top of the contents frame, followed by the page names in the order you specified while using the wizard. Each page name is a link to the associated page. The design elements from the Artsy theme are applied to the page and affect the frame background, heading and body text styles, hyperlink colors, and bullets and horizontal lines.

Previewing the Web Site

Next you want to preview the site in a browser.

1 ● Choose **File/Web** Page Preview.

● **Maximize the browser window.**

Your screen should be similar to Figure 6.14

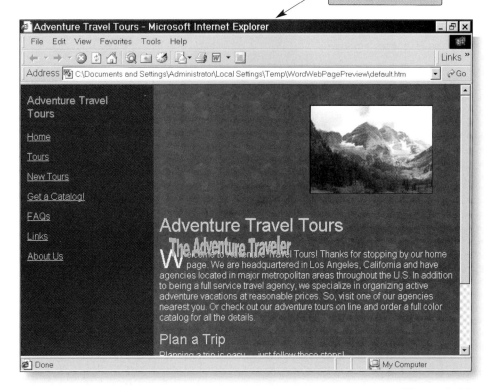

Browser loaded offline and current Web page is displayed

Figure 6.14

Additional Information

Offline viewing does not connect you to the Internet.

The browser on your system is loaded offline, and the Web page you are working on is displayed in the browser window. As you can see, the page appears different in the browser window than it did in the Word document window. It is important as you create your Web pages to preview them and make adjustments to the page so that they display correctly in the browser.

As you look at the home page, you decide you want to reduce the width of the contents frame and change its background color. You also want to combine the WordArt text with the picture and display the company name to the right of the picture. To view the other pages in the Web site, you click the links in the contents frame.

2 ● Click the **Tours** link in the contents frame.

Your screen should be similar to Figure 6.15

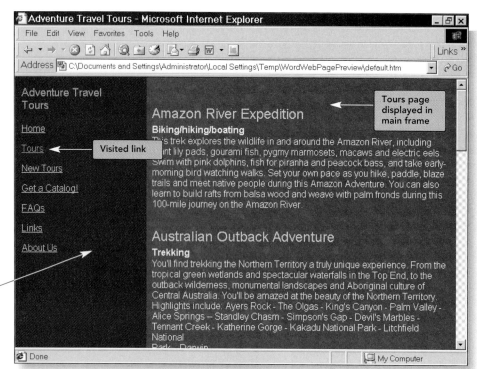

Figure 6.15

The Tours page is displayed in the main frame, while the table of contents remains fixed on the screen. This makes it easy to navigate to other pages within the site. Notice that the Tours link has changed to a different color, indicating it is a visited link. This page displays the contents of the wd06_Tour List file. Again you have several changes you want to make to this page.

3 ● Click the **New Tours** link.

● Click the **Get a Catalog!** link.

● Click the **FAQs** link.

Your screen should be similar to Figure 6.16

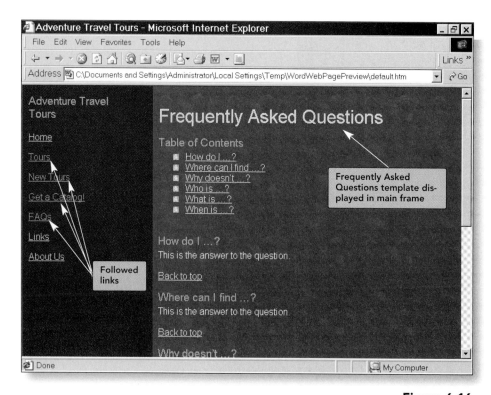

Figure 6.16

This page contains the Frequently Asked Questions template. Like other templates, it provides a suggested layout and ideas for content that you replace with your own information.

4 ● Click on the other links to view the associated pages.

● Click on the Word default.htm button in the taskbar to switch to the Word document window.

HAVING TROUBLE?
Point to the taskbar button to see the window name in a ScreenTip.

As you open the Web pages in Word, each page opens in a separate window. The window names are Default.htm:#, with the number representing the order in which they were opened. If only one window is open, it does not have a number.

Formatting a Web Page

You want the background of the table of contents frame to blend in better with the theme colors used in the main frame. Even though you applied a theme to the Web site, you can change the background of a page or frame. A **background** is a color or design that is displayed behind the text on the page. You can change the background to another color or select a background image, pattern, or texture, called a **wallpaper**.

Adding a Background

You will change the background of the contents frame to another color. Because you do not plan to add or remove frames, you can close the toolbar.

1 ● Close the Frames toolbar.

● Click in the contents frame to make it active.

● Choose Format/ Background/Fill Effects.

● Open the Gradient tab and select **T**wo colors.

● Select Dark Blue as Color 1 and Gray–50% as Color 2.

● Select **V**ertical as the shading style.

● Select the bottom left Variants style.

Your screen should be similar to Figure 6.17

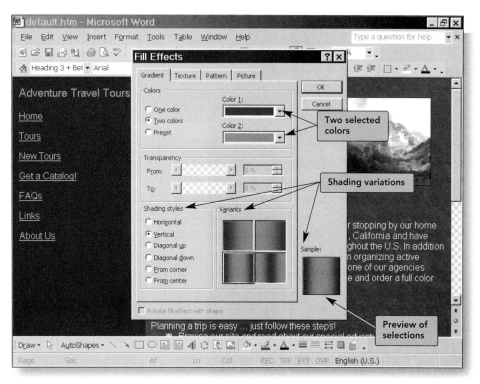

Figure 6.17

The Sample provides a preview of your selections.

② Click [OK].

Your screen should be similar to Figure 6.18

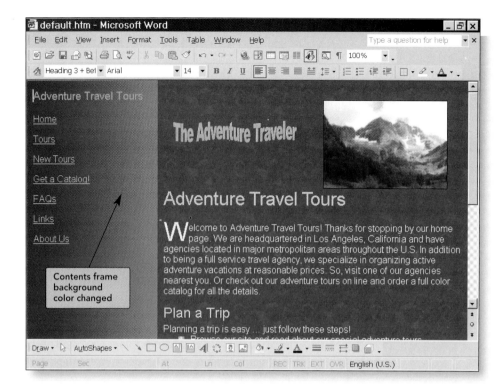

Figure 6.18

The selected background gradient is applied to the contents frame only.

Sizing a Frame

Next you need to adjust the width of the contents frame. Generally, you want the main frame to be as large as possible to display the maximum amount of page content. Reducing the size of the contents frame will make the main frame larger.

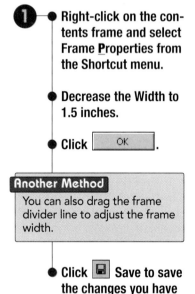

① ● Right-click on the contents frame and select Frame **P**roperties from the Shortcut menu.

● Decrease the Width to 1.5 inches.

● Click [OK].

Another Method
You can also drag the frame divider line to adjust the frame width.

● Click 🖫 Save to save the changes you have made to the contents frame page.

Your screen should be similar to Figure 6.19

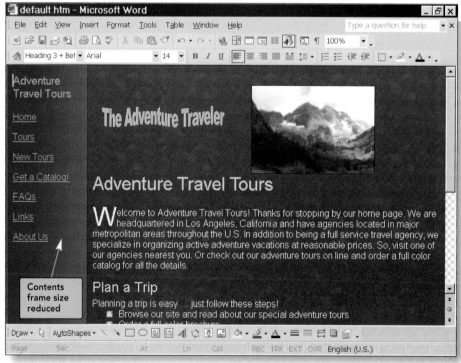

Figure 6.19

Grouping Objects

You decide that the home page would look better if the WordArt text were combined with the mountain picture. To do this, you will combine a WordArt object with a picture object by grouping them.

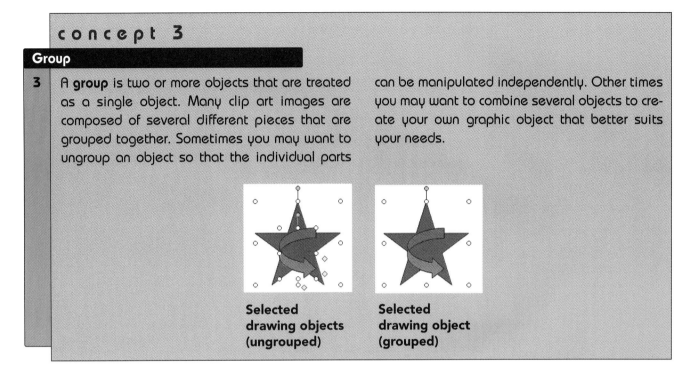

concept 3

Group

3 A **group** is two or more objects that are treated as a single object. Many clip art images are composed of several different pieces that are grouped together. Sometimes you may want to ungroup an object so that the individual parts can be manipulated independently. Other times you may want to combine several objects to create your own graphic object that better suits your needs.

Selected drawing objects (ungrouped)

Selected drawing object (grouped)

1 ● Select and move the WordArt object over the picture object.

Your screen should be similar to Figure 6.20

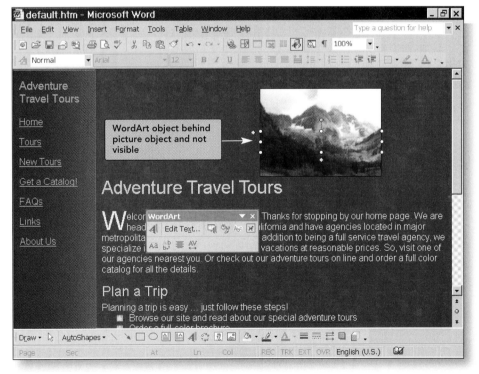

Figure 6.20

Notice that the WordArt object is not visible. This is because the objects were inserted as floating objects in the drawing layer so that they can be positioned precisely on the page, including in front of and behind other objects. As floating objects are added to a document, they stack in layers and may overlap. You can move floating objects up or down within a stack using the Order button on the drawing toolbar. Sometimes it is easy to lose a floating object behind another. If this happens you can press [Tab ↹] to cycle forward or [⇧ Shift] + [Tab ↹] to cycle backward through the stacked objects until the one you want is selected. You need to move the WordArt object to the front of the stack.

2 ● Click [Draw ▾].

● Choose O**r**der/Bring to Front.

Another Method
You can also right-click on the object and select the order from the shortcut menu.

Your screen should be similar to Figure 6.21

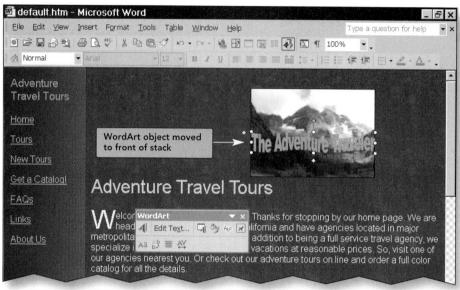

Figure 6.21

The WordArt object is now at the top of the stack and is visible over the picture. You want the WordArt displayed centered at the bottom of the picture. You also want to group the two objects to create a single object.

3 ● Hold down [⇧ Shift] and click on the picture.

● Click [Draw ▾].

● Choose **A**lign or Distribute/Align **B**ottom.

● Click [Draw ▾].

● Choose **A**lign or Distribute/Align **C**enter.

● Right-click on the selection and select **G**rouping from the shortcut menu.

● Choose **G**roup

Another Method
You can also select Group from the [Draw ▾] drop-down menu.

Your screen should be similar to Figure 6.22

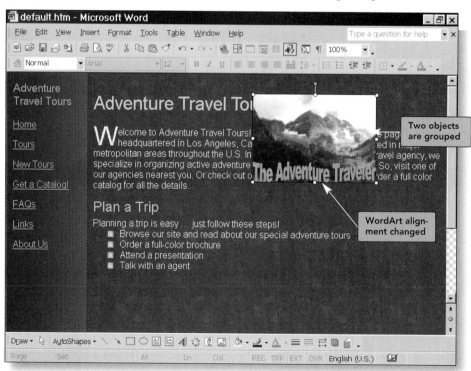

Figure 6.22

The text is now centered at the bottom of the picture. Also, because you have grouped the two objects, when you move and size the object it will act as a single object.

Next you need to change the wrapping style of the object.

4 ● **Change the text wrapping style to Top and Bottom.**

● **Click outside the object to deselect it.**

Your screen should be similar to Figure 6.23

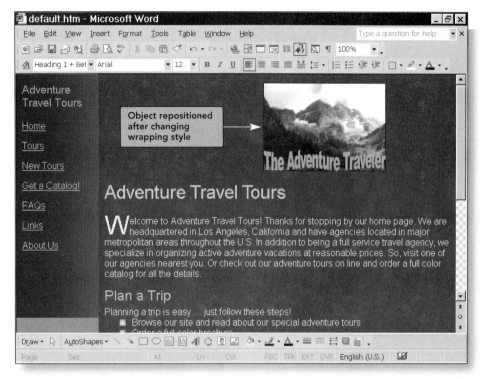

Figure 6.23

Using Tables to Control Page Layout

The next change you want to make is to display the company name to the right of the picture in the home page. Unlike a regular document, in which you could use columns to display text side by side, a Web page requires a table to control the page layout. The table allows you to place items in different locations on the Web page. You will create a one-row, two-column table to hold the two items. Then you will move the text and picture into the appropriate cells of the table.

1 ● **Click on the blank line above the Adventure Travel Tours title.**

● **Click 🔲 Insert Table and create a table that is 1 row by 2 columns.**

● **Select the picture, and cut and paste it into the left cell of the table.**

● **Select the company name, and cut and paste (or drag) this selection into the right cell of the table.**

Your screen should be similar to Figure 6.24

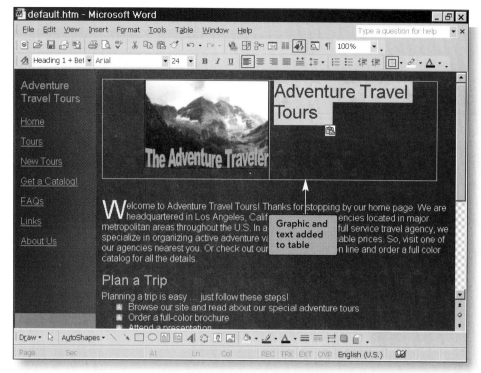

Figure 6.24

The picture and company name need to be in the center of the page. Since you are using the table as a layout tool, you need to center the table. You also want to turn off the display of the border lines.

2 ● **Size the table as in Figure 6.25.**

● **Select the table and center it.**

● **Remove all the table border lines.**

Your screen should be similar to Figure 6.25

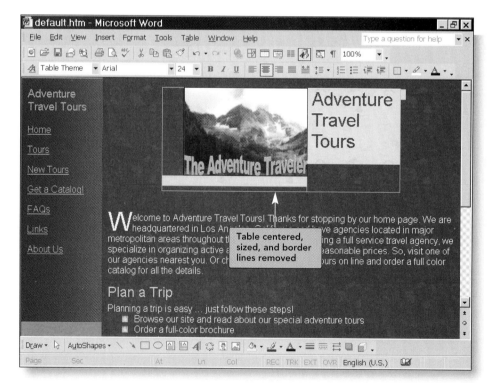

Figure 6.25

The table displays the picture and company name side by side, centered in the main frame. The table gridlines are still displayed.

Adding and Modifying Graphics

Graphics on a Web page add interest and present information in a more visually appealing manner. The major kinds of graphics found on Web pages include icons, lines or bars, bullets, photographs, and animated GIFs. You should be aware that some graphics, such as photographs, will take time to load in a browser window.

At the moment, Web browsers can display only two types of graphic files: GIF and JPG. These are compressed file formats that load fairly quickly in a browser window. If the graphics you create or add to your Web page are in a different format, Word converts them to GIF files when you save the Web page.

Inserting a Horizontal Line

You want to include a graphic horizontal line below the table on the home page to further separate the heading from the page content and to make the page more interesting. A line design is included with the theme, but because the Word document file you used for this page did not contain a horizontal line, the line in the theme was not used. You need to first add a horizontal line and then reapply the theme to change it to the graphic line associated with the theme.

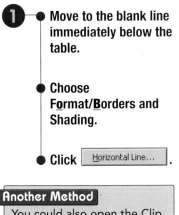

● **Move to the blank line immediately below the table.**

● **Choose Format/Borders and Shading.**

● **Click** [Horizontal Line...] .

Another Method

You could also open the Clip Organizer and add a line from the Web Dividers category.

Your screen should be similar to Figure 6.26

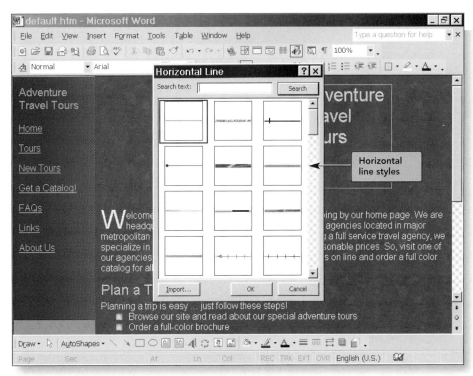

Figure 6.26

2 ● Select and insert any line style from the Horizontal Line dialog box.

Your screen should be similar to Figure 6.27

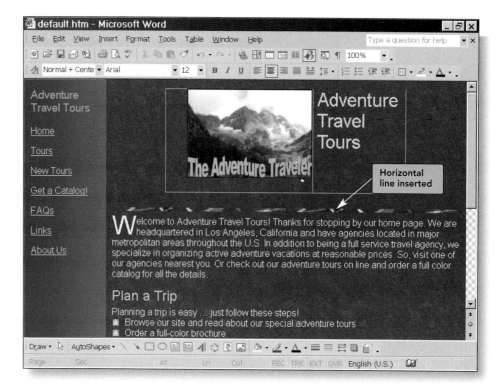

Figure 6.27

The selected line style is displayed the full width of the main frame. However, it is not the style that is associated with the theme. You will reapply the theme to update the line style to the one used in the theme. You will then need to remove the table border lines again.

3 ● Choose Format/Theme.

● If necessary, select the Artsy theme.

● Click [OK].

● Remove the table border lines again.

● Click 🖫 Save to save your changes to the page.

Your screen should be similar to Figure 6.28

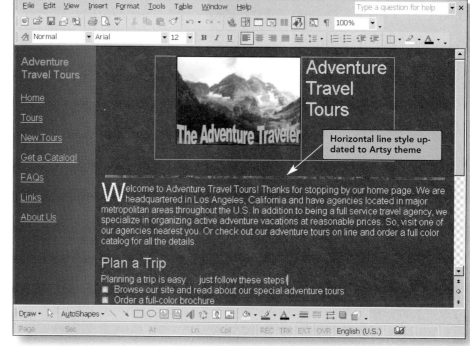

Figure 6.28

A new horizontal line designed for use with the selected theme replaces the horizontal line you inserted.

Inserting Animated Graphics

Next you will work on the Links page. Because you still do not have all the content ready for this page, it is common practice to indicate that a page is under construction by inserting either text or a clever graphic. You will first replace the sample text on this page with a page title.

1
● Click in the contents frame.

● Press (Ctrl) and click **Links**.

● Replace the sample text with **Links** and apply the Heading 1 style to the word.

Additional Information
The styles associated with the theme are displayed in the Style drop-down list.

● Insert two blank lines below the heading.

Your screen should be similar to Figure 6.29

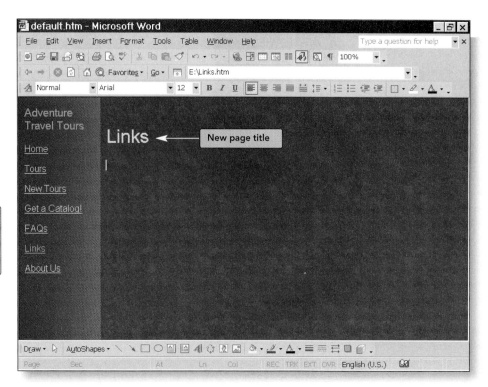

Figure 6.29

Next you will add two animated graphics to show that it is under construction.

2
- Insert the picture file wd06_Construction.

- If necessary, expand the object to fully display the graphic.

- Center the graphic on the page.

- Press ⏎Enter.

- In the same manner, add the picture file wd06_Elephant Walking and center it on the page.

- Save the page.

Your screen should be similar to Figure 6.30

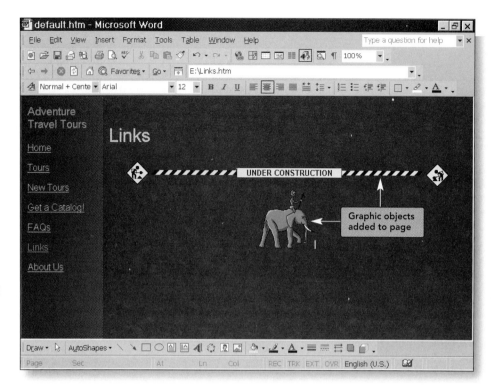

Figure 6.30

Because you are editing the Web page in Word, you cannot see the animation. To see the animation, you need to view the page in the browser. Since the browser is still open, you can simply switch to the browser window.

3
- Switch to the browser window.

- Click **Links** to display the page.

Your screen should be similar to Figure 6.31

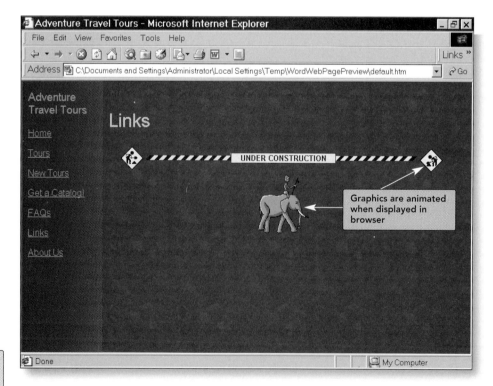

Figure 6.31

HAVING TROUBLE?
If the updated page is not displayed, click 🔲 in Internet Explorer or 🔲 in Netscape Communicator.

You should see the animation in the two graphics now.

Inserting a Diagram

The next page you will work on is the About Us page. On this page you want to include an overview to the tours and locations. You could type a list of locations and tours, but to make it more visually appealing you decide to create a diagram to display the information.

concept 4

Diagram

4 A **diagram** is a graphic object that can be used to illustrate concepts and to enhance your documents. Diagrams are based on text rather than numeric information. There are six predesigned diagrams you can use. The type of diagram you choose depends on the purpose of the diagram and the type of concept you want to illustrate. The table below describes the diagram types and uses.

Type	Use
Cycle	Shows a process that has a continuous cycle
Target	Shows steps toward a goal
Radial	Shows relationships of elements to a core element
Venn	Shows areas of overlap between and among elements
Pyramid	Shows foundation-based relationships
Organization	Shows hierarchical-based relationships

Additionally, you can create flowcharts (or flow diagrams) using a combination of AutoShapes on the Drawing toolbar, including flowchart shapes and connectors. Flowcharts show a process that has a beginning and an end.

You will enter an introductory paragraph on the About Us page and then create a diagram to display the tour information.

1 ● Switch to the Word document window.

● Open the About Us page.

● Replace the sample text with About Us and apply a Heading 1 style.

● Insert a blank line below the heading.

● Type: Adventure Travel Tours offers all types of tours to unique and exciting places around the world. The chart below identifies the tour locations and the specific tours offered at each location.

● Press [←Enter].

● On the Drawing toolbar click [icon].

Another Method
The menu equivalent is Insert/Diagram.

Your screen should be similar to Figure 6.32

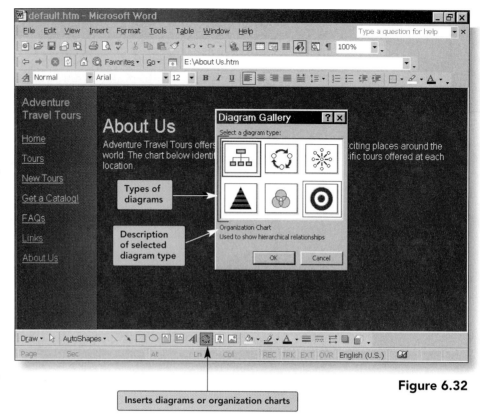

Figure 6.32

The Diagram Gallery dialog box asks you to select a type of diagram. The best type of diagram to represent the tour information is an organization chart. Typically, organization charts are used to illustrate a working unit within a company; however, they can be used to illustrate any type of concept that consists of a hierarchal organization.

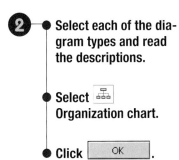

2
- Select each of the diagram types and read the descriptions.

- Select 🔲 Organization chart.

- Click ‍ OK ‍ .

Your screen should be similar to Figure 6.33

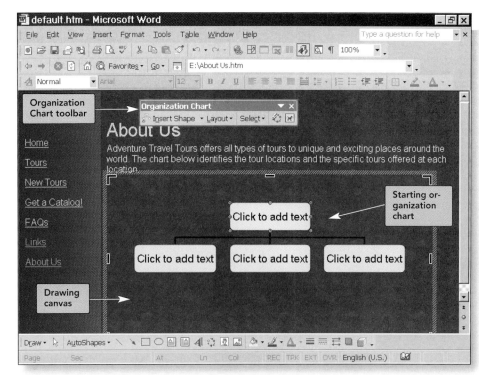

Figure 6.33

A starting organization chart consisting of boxes arranged in a hierarchy is displayed. A drawing canvas surrounds the entire chart and keeps all pieces of the chart together as a unit. The shapes you can use in an organization chart and what they represent are described below.

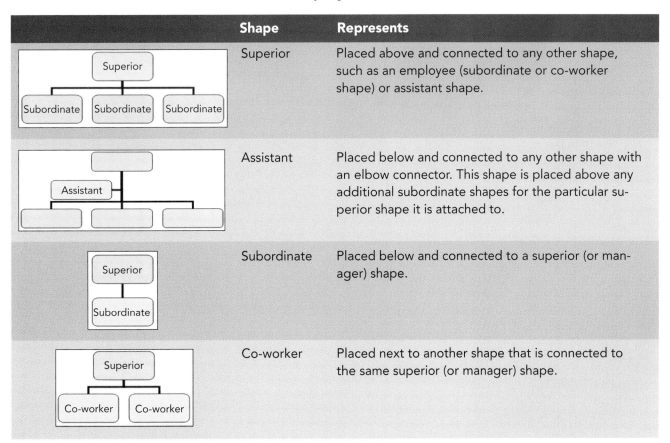

	Shape	Represents
	Superior	Placed above and connected to any other shape, such as an employee (subordinate or co-worker shape) or assistant shape.
	Assistant	Placed below and connected to any other shape with an elbow connector. This shape is placed above any additional subordinate shapes for the particular superior shape it is attached to.
	Subordinate	Placed below and connected to a superior (or manager) shape.
	Co-worker	Placed next to another shape that is connected to the same superior (or manager) shape.

Additionally, the Organization Chart toolbar is automatically opened. It contains buttons to add shapes, modify the layout, and enhance the chart.

You will create separate organization charts to illustrate the tour locations for each of the continents. The first chart you will create will show the South American tours. The completed diagram is shown below.

You will enter text for the first two levels. Since you only need two boxes at the second level, you will also delete a box.

3 • Type **South America** in the top box.

• Click ☰ .

• Click in the second level box on the left.

• Type **Peru**.

• In the middle box, type **Costa Rica**.

• Click on the edge of the third box and press Delete .

Your screen should be similar to Figure 6.34

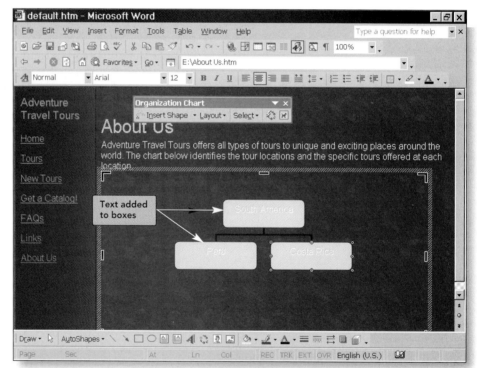

Figure 6.34

Next you need to add two subordinate shapes below the Peru shape to contain the names of the two tours. As you add shapes, the diagram will automatically resize to fit the drawing area. If you do not want the diagram to resize, you can expand the drawing canvas before adding more shapes. You can expand the drawing area by dragging the drawing canvas handles, or by using the options in the [Layout ▾] drop-down menu described below.

Option	Effect
Scale the Organization Chart	Increases the size of both the chart and the drawing canvas.
Fit Organization Chart to Contents	Reduces the size of the drawing canvas to fit the size of the chart.
Expand Organization Chart	Increases the size of the drawing canvas to add space around the chart.

You will let the chart resize to the current drawing canvas size, as there is still plenty of space.

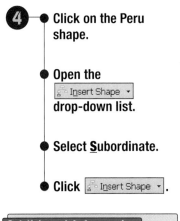

4 ● **Click on the Peru shape.**

● **Open the** [Insert Shape ▾] **drop-down list.**

● **Select Subordinate.**

● **Click** [Insert Shape ▾].

Additional Information

The default selection for Insert Shape is Subordinate.

Your screen should be similar to Figure 6.35

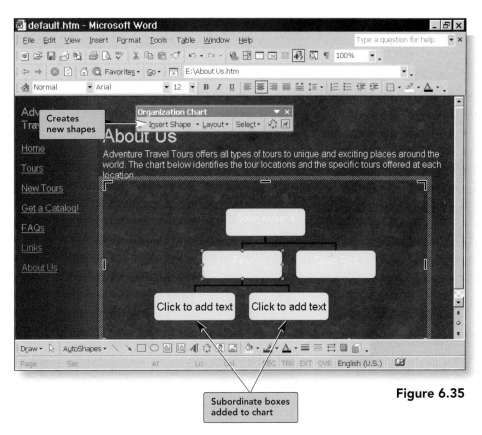

Subordinate boxes added to chart

Figure 6.35

The two new shapes are added in a horizontal line subordinate to the selected shape. You decide to change the layout of this grouping so the subordinate shapes line up in a column below the superior shape. The four types of layouts are described in the following table.

Layout	Description
Standard	Subordinate shapes line up horizontally below the superior shape.
Both Hanging	Subordinate shapes hang in columns both to the left and right of the superior shape.
Left Hanging	Subordinate shapes hang in columns to the left of the superior shape.
Right Hanging	Subordinate shapes hang in columns to the right of the superior shape.

5 ● Open the Layout ▾ drop-down list.

● Select **R**ight Hanging.

Your screen should be similar to Figure 6.36

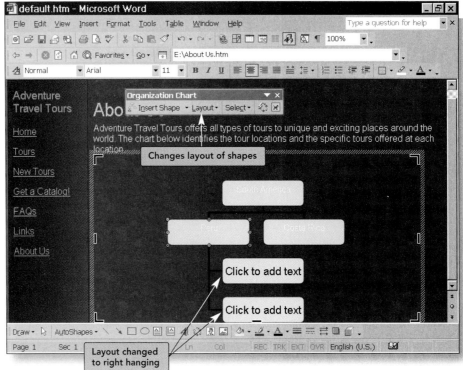

Figure 6.36

Now you will add the tour names to the two new subordinate shapes. Then you will add a subordinate shape below the Costa Rica shape for the Rainforest tour.

6
- In the first subordinate shape below Peru, type Inca Trail.

- Enter Amazon River in the second subordinate shape.

- Add a subordinate shape below Costa Rica and include the text Rainforest.

Your screen should be similar to Figure 6.37

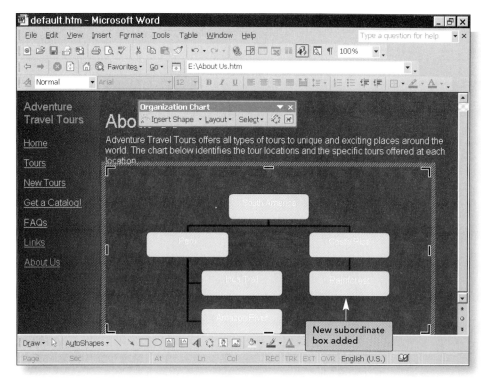

Figure 6.37

Finally, you want to change the style of the chart. There are 15 different Autoformat styles consisting of different shape designs and colors from which you can select.

7
- Click 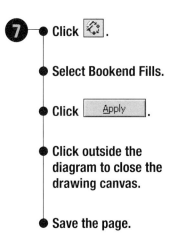.

- Select Bookend Fills.

- Click Apply.

- Click outside the diagram to close the drawing canvas.

- Save the page.

Your screen should be similar to Figure 6.38

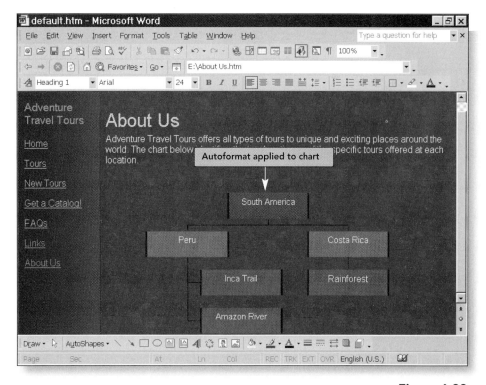

Figure 6.38

Inserting Hyperlinks

The next page you want to work on is Tours. The Tours page contains a brief description of several tours. You want to create a table of contents for the tour descriptions at the top of the page. Then you want to make each table of contents item a hyperlink so the reader can quickly go to a specific tour description in the page. The type of link you will create is a relative link.

concept 5

Absolute and Relative Links

5 When you create a hyperlink in a document, you can make the path to the **destination** (the element you go to from a hyperlink) an absolute link or a relative link. An **absolute link**, also called a **fixed link**, identifies the file location of the destination by its full address, such as c:\Word Data File\Sales.doc. Fixed links usually are used only if you are sure the location of the object will not change. A relative link identifies the destination location in relation to the location of the HTML file. A **relative link** is based on a path you specify in which the first part of the path is shared by both the file that contains the hyperlink and the destination file.

Hyperlinks to other Web sites should typically use a fixed file location that includes the full path to the location or URL of the page. All URLs have at least two basic parts. The first part presents the protocol used to connect to the resource. The **protocol** is the set of rules that control how software and hardware on a network communicate. The hypertext transfer protocol (http), shown in the example below, is by far the most common. The protocol is always followed by a colon (:). The second part of the URL presents the name of the server, the computer where the resource is located (for example, www.adventuretraveltours.com). This is always preceded by two forward slashes (//), and each part of the path is separated by a single forward slash (/).

$$\underbrace{\text{http://}}_{\text{protocol}}\underbrace{\text{www.adventuretraveltours.com}}_{\text{server}}$$

You will enter a heading at the top of the page and then create the links for the first three tour descriptions.

1 ● Open the Tours page.

● Type Tours at the top of the page and apply the Heading 1 style to the word.

● Press ←Enter.

● Type the following three topic headings on separate lines:

Amazon River Expedition

Australian Outback Adventure

Climb Mt. Kilimanjaro

● Select the text "Amazon River Expedition."

● Click 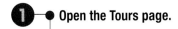 Insert Hyperlink (on the Standard toolbar).

Your screen should be similar to Figure 6.39

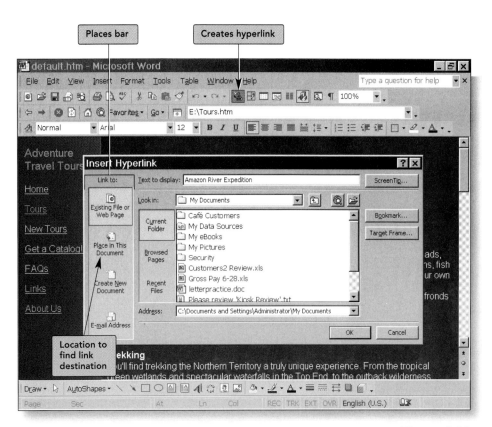

Figure 6.39

From the Insert Hyperlink dialog box, you first need to specify the type of link from the Places bar. The four options are described below.

Option	Effect
Existing File or Web Page	Creates a link in an existing Web page or file.
Place in This Document	Creates a link to a place in the active file.
Create New Document	Creates a link to a file that you have not created yet.
E-mail Address	Creates a link that allows users to create an e-mail message with the correct address in the To line.

Linking within the Document

You need to create a link to a location in the active document. Then you need to select the location in the document to which the link will jump. The list box will display a tree diagram showing an outline of the information in the current page. From the outline you select the heading you want to link to. If you wanted the linked information to display in a different frame, you would need to select the name of the frame in which you want the document to appear. By selecting the name from the list, you are creating a relative link.

1 ● Select Place in This Document.

● Select the "Amazon River Expedition" topic heading from the list box.

HAVING TROUBLE?
If the list of tour names is not displayed, click ⊞ next to Tours to expand the list.

Your screen should be similar to Figure 6.40

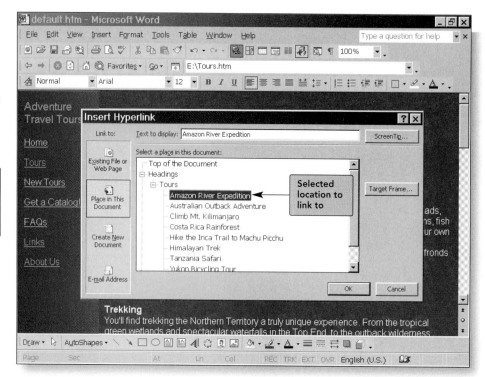

Figure 6.40

You can also assign a tip to be displayed when you point to the hyperlink using the ScreenTip option. If you do not enter text for the ScreenTip, Word uses the path to the file as the ScreenTip.

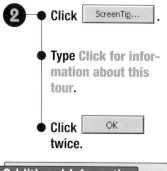

2 ● Click ScreenTip... .

● Type Click for information about this tour.

● Click OK twice.

Additional Information
This type of link is also called a **target link** because it targets a heading or other object on a page.

Your screen should be similar to Figure 6.41

Figure 6.41

The text appears in the hyperlink colors associated with the theme. Next you will create hyperlinks for the other two topics, and then you will test them.

3 ● In the same manner, create links and ScreenTips for the other two topics.

● Follow each of the links, ending with the Climb Mt. Kilimanjaro link.

Your screen should be similar to Figure 6.42

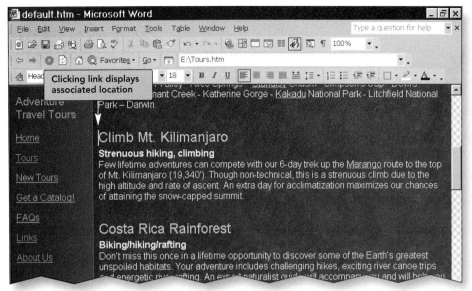

Figure 6.42

As you used each of the links, the section of the page associated with the link displays near the top of the frame. These links are relative links because they indicate a location to jump to relative to the location of the link. For example, if you move the text associated with the link to another location on the page, the link will still take you to the original location in the page, regardless of the information displayed at that location.

After each topic was displayed, you had to scroll back to the top of the page to access the listing again. To make navigation easier, include links back to the top of the page. This allows the reader to jump to the top instead of using the scroll bar.

4 ● Move to the blank line below the Mt. Kilimanjaro description.

● Type Back to top.

● Select the text "Back to top" and create a link to the Tours heading.

Your screen should be similar to Figure 6.43

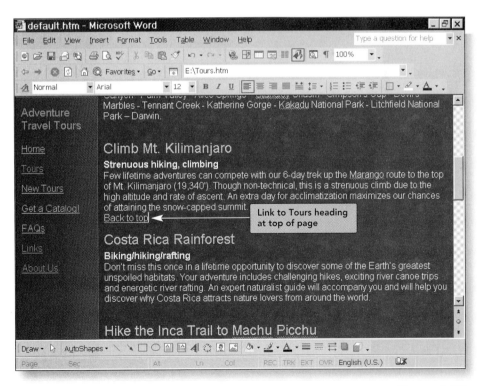

Figure 6.43

You want to include the same link below each of the descriptions. To do this quickly, you can copy the link.

5
- **Copy the Back to top link (do not include the blank line at the end of the text).**

- **Use the Back to top link to return to the top of the page.**

- **Paste the Back to top link at the end of the Amazon River and Australian Outback tour descriptions.**

- **Test the links.**

- **Save the page.**

Your screen should be similar to Figure 6.44

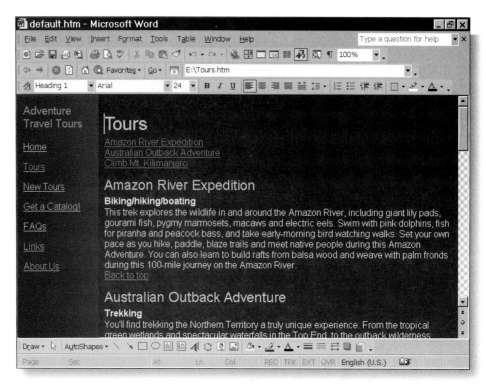

Figure 6.44

Linking to a Web Site

On the Links page, you want the first link to be to a Web site that provides weather reports for locations around the world. As these links are beyond your control, it is your responsibility to check these links periodically to ensure that they are still viable links.

First you will add a horizontal line below the page title and another heading then you will create the link to the Web site.

1
- Display the Links page again.
- On the blank line under Links, click ▦ ▾ Borders to open the Borders drop-down menu.
- Click ▤ to insert the Artsy style horizontal line.
- Press ↵Enter, type Travel Resources, and apply a Heading 2 style to the text.
- Press ↵Enter.
- Type World Weather Report: Clickable map giving you local weather anywhere in the world.
- Press ↵Enter.

Your screen should be similar to Figure 6.45

Web page window name

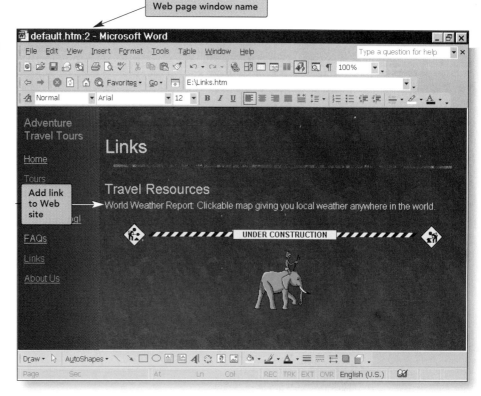

Figure 6.45

Next you will create the link to the World Weather Report page on the World Wide Web.

2 ● Select the text "World Weather Report."

● Click  Insert Hyperlink.

● Select **E**xisting File or Web Page.

● In the Address text box, enter http://www.intellicast. com/LocalWeather/ World/.

● Click [OK].

Another Method

You could also click [Web Page...] to browse the Web to locate the site and enter the address if you are connected to the World Wide Web.

● Save the page.

● Switch to the browser window.

● Click [Refresh].

● Point to the link.

Your screen should be similar to Figure 6.46

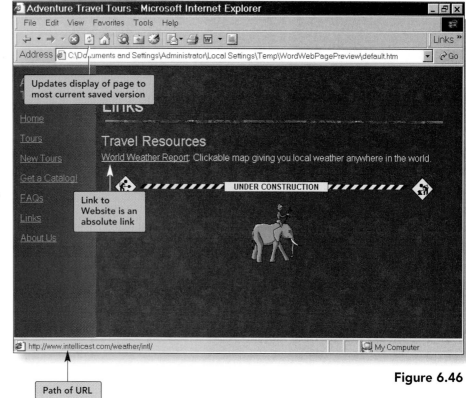

Figure 6.46

The status bar displays the full path of the URL. This link is an absolute link to a Web page document. Clicking on a hyperlink to a page directs the browser to get the page from the server and display it. You will try out this link at the end of the lab.

You also want to see how the ScreenTips you entered for the hyperlinks on the Tours pages work.

3 ● Click Tours.

● Point to any of the topic hyperlinks.

Your screen should be similar to Figure 6.47

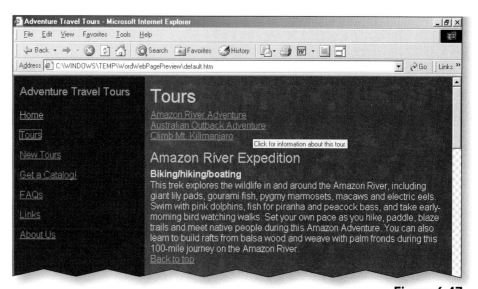

Figure 6.47

Linking to an E-mail Address

You also want to include a hyperlink on the home page, so readers can send an e-mail to Adventure Travel Tours to request specific information.

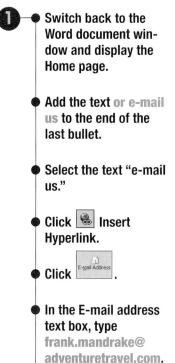

- Switch back to the Word document window and display the Home page.

- Add the text **or e-mail us** to the end of the last bullet.

- Select the text "e-mail us."

- Click  Insert Hyperlink.

- Click [E-mail Address].

- In the E-mail address text box, type **frank.mandrake@ adventuretravel.com**.

Another Method

If this e-mail address appears in the Recently used list you can select it rather than type in the address.

- Click [OK].

- Save the page.

Your screen should be similar to Figure 6.48

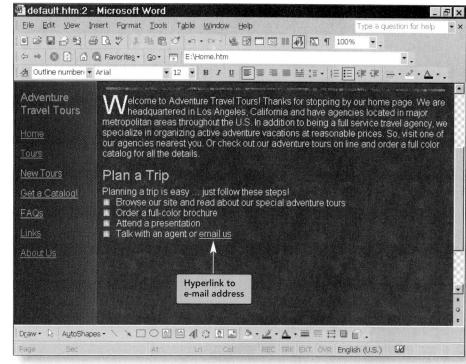

Figure 6.48

When the user clicks on the hyperlink, a new e-mail message window will open. The e-mail address you entered will appear in the To line. The user can then submit a question to the company.

Creating a Web Form

Finally, on the Get a Catalog! page, you want to add a form that allows users to order a catalog.

concept 6

Form

6 **Forms** are used in Web pages to get information or feedback from users or to provide information. Using forms makes your Web site interactive. The user completes the information requested in the form and then clicks a Submit button on the form, which sends the information in the form back to the Web server. The information is processed and a response is sent back to the user and displayed in another page in the browser window. For example, a company that sells golf clubs may provide a form in which users can enter the type of golf club they want to purchase. Then they submit the form, which sends their request to the Web server. The database is searched and the results of the search are returned to the user and displayed in a Web page. Other forms are used to collect information, as in the case of a customer survey. The information submitted from the form is stored on the site's Web server for later use. This type of form is often called a mailto form, because the results are submitted via an e-mail address.

Forms require additional support files and Web server support. When creating forms for use in a Web site, you should work with your network or Web site administrator.

After considering the information you need, you have designed the form shown below.

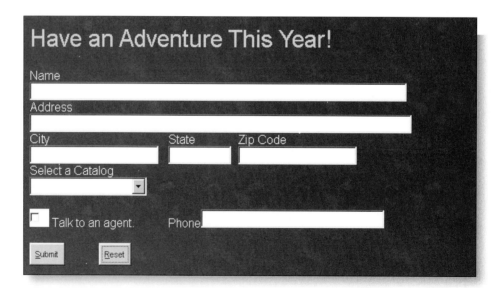

A form is created just like any other Web page document, with the addition of the form controls. **Controls** are graphic objects that are designed to automate the process of completing information in the form. There are 11 standard form controls that are used to enter different types of information. Just as in a paper form, there are fill-in boxes, check-off boxes, and selections from lists. You will use the following form controls:

Form Control	Use
Check box	Allows selection of more than one item.
Drop-down box	Displays available choices in a list.
Text box	Allows users to enter one line of text.
Reset	Clears entries in the form.
Submit	Submits the data in the form to the specified location.

You will enter a heading for the form and add text labels and controls to specify the information to be entered in the form.

1 ● **Display the Get a Catalog! page.**

● **Replace the sample text with Have an Adventure This Year! and apply a Heading 1 Style.**

● **Press ⏎Enter twice.**

● **Type Name and press ⏎Enter.**

● **Display the Web Tools toolbar.**

● **If necessary, close the Web toolbar.**

Your screen should be similar to Figure 6.49

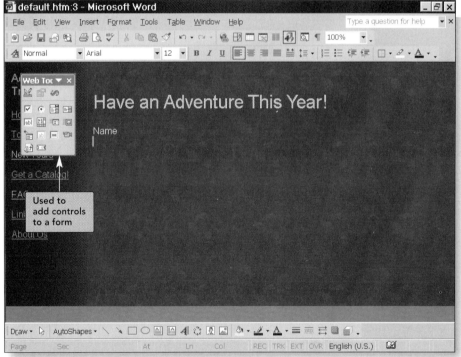

Used to add controls to a form

Figure 6.49

You use the Web Tools toolbar to add various form controls to a Web page.

Adding a Textbox Control

The first control you want to add to the form is a text box in which the user will enter his or her name.

1 ● Click [abl] Textbox.

● Size the text box object as shown in Figure 6.50.

Your screen should be similar to Figure 6.50

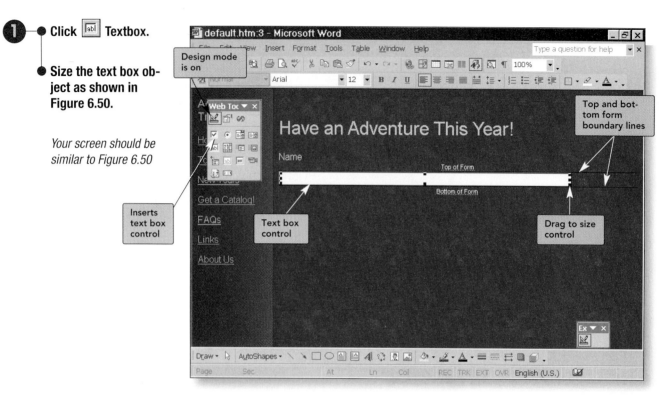

Figure 6.50

A blank Textbox control has been added to the form. Using a Web Tools button automatically turns on Design mode in which you can insert controls into the page. The [🗹] button turns Design mode on and off.

Notice that a Top of Form and Bottom of Form boundary line is displayed above and below the control. The boundaries define the area containing the form controls and appear only in Design mode. As you continue to add more controls, they will appear within the boundaries. A Web page can have more than one form, each contained within its own form boundaries.

2 ● Press ⏎Enter.

● Type Address and press ⏎Enter.

● Add and size another Textbox control as shown in Figure 6.51.

● Add the City, State, and Zip Code labels and Textbox controls as shown in Figure 6.51.

HAVING TROUBLE?
Use Tab⇆ to separate the labels and controls.

Your screen should be similar to Figure 6.51

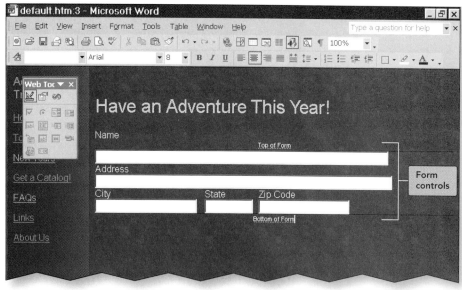

Figure 6.51

Adding a Drop-Down Box Control

Next you want to include a Drop-Down box control from which a catalog selection can be made. When inserting a Drop-Down box control, you also need to enter the list of items to be displayed when the Drop-Down box is opened. You will enter the names of the three catalogs in the list.

1 ● On a blank line below the City control, type Select a Catalog.

● Press ⏎Enter.

● Click 🖽 Drop-Down Box.

● Click 🖾 Properties.

Your screen should be similar to Figure 6.52

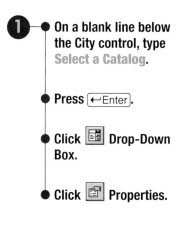

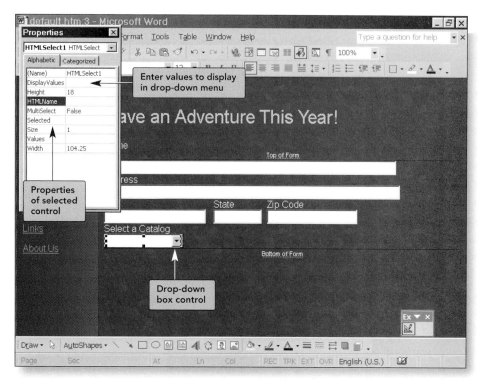

Figure 6.52

Additional Information
Control properties are also used to manage how data is communicated to the Web server.

In the Properties dialog box, you need to type the values you want to display when the Drop-Down box is opened. The values are separated with a semicolon without any blank spaces between titles.

2

- Click in the Display Values text box.

- Type **African Adventures;South American Adventures;Far East Adventures**.

- Click **X** to close the Properties dialog box.

- Press **←Enter** twice.

Your screen should be similar to Figure 6.53

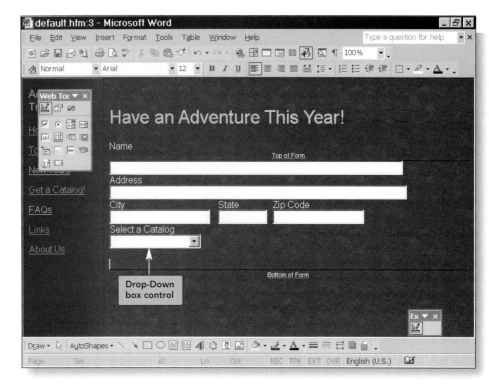

Drop-Down box control

Figure 6.53

Adding a Checkbox Control

Last, you want to add a Checkbox control that allows the user to request that an agent call him or her with more information.

1

- Click ☑ Checkbox.

- Click to the right of the control and enter a space.

- Type **Talk to an agent**.

- Press **Tab** twice.

- Add the label **Phone** and another Textbox control for a phone number, as shown in Figure 6.54.

Your screen should be similar to Figure 6.54

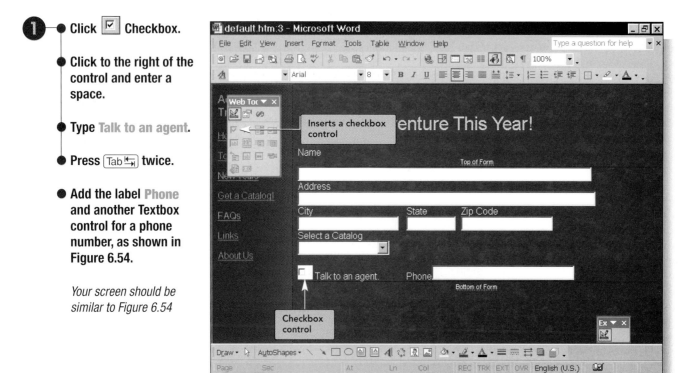

Inserts a checkbox control

Checkbox control

Figure 6.54

Adding Buttons

Now that all the necessary information is entered, you need to add two buttons: one to submit the form and another to clear it. A form should always include a Submit control, otherwise there is no way to send the information to the Web server. As part of the Submit button, you need to provide the e-mail address to which the form will be sent when submitted.

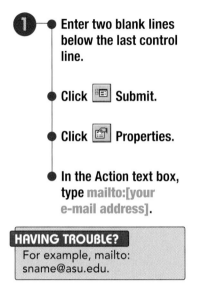

1 • Enter two blank lines below the last control line.

• Click 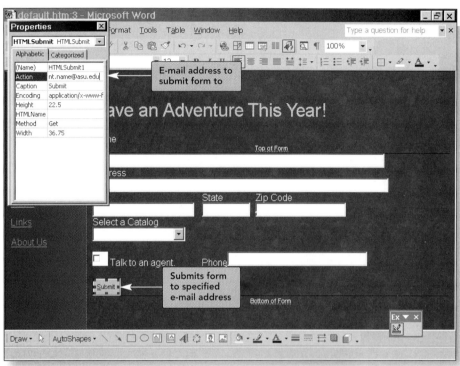 Submit.

• Click Properties.

• In the Action text box, type mailto:[your e-mail address].

> **HAVING TROUBLE?**
> For example, mailto: sname@asu.edu.

Your screen should be similar to Figure 6.55

Figure 6.55

Next you will add a button to clear the form.

2 • Click  to close the Properties dialog box.

• Move to the space after the Submit button.

• Press Tab ⇥.

• Click Reset.

• Click Exit Design Mode

• Close the Web Tools toolbar.

Your screen should be similar to Figure 6.56

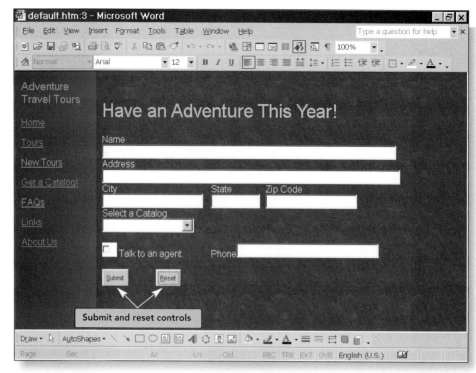

Figure 6.56

Previewing the Web Form

Now you want to preview the form.

1 • Save the page.

• Switch to the browser window.

• Display the Get a Catalog! page.

Your screen should be similar to Figure 6.57

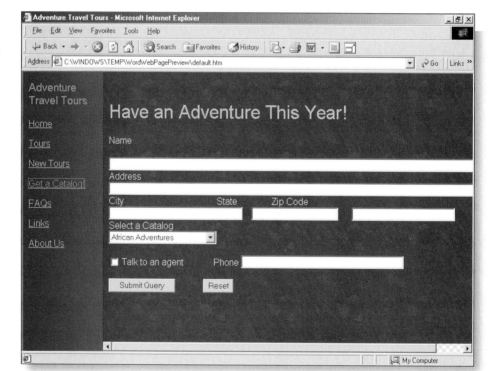

Figure 6.57

When you view the page in the browser, it may not appear exactly as it does in the Word document. For example, in Figure 6.57, the State and Zip Code labels do not display correctly over the boxes. Always view your Web pages in a browser and make any modifications before you make the pages public.

2 ● Return to the Word document and adjust the form as needed.

HAVING TROUBLE?
To edit a form, redisplay the Web tools toolbar and click 🖉 to turn on Design Mode.

● Move the Name label into the Form control boundary above the Textbox control.

● Enter a blank line between the Address and City control lines as in Figure 6.58.

● Save the form and redisplay it in the browser.

HAVING TROUBLE?
Don't forget to refresh the display of the browser window.

Your screen should look similar to Figure 6.58

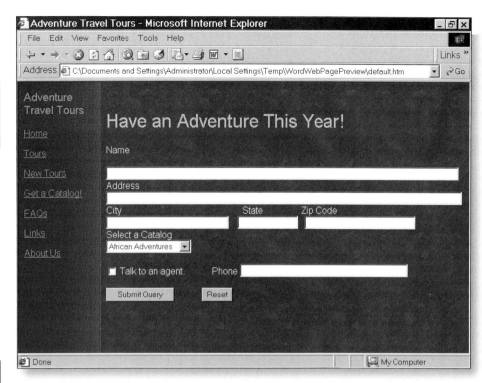

Figure 6.58

Next, you will use the form to request a catalog.

3 ● Move to each item in the form and enter the information requested for yourself. Select the **Far East Adventures** catalog.

HAVING TROUBLE?
Press (Tab ⇆) or click on a text box to move from one item to the next in the form.

● Print the completed form using the Print command on your browser (**F**ile/**P**rint).

● If you have Internet access, click the link to the World Weather Report on the Links page.

● Close the browser.

● Exit Word, saving all Web page documents when prompted.

Before making your Web site available for others to see, you should make sure that all of the links work correctly. In addition, because all browsers do not display the HTML tags in the same way, it is a good idea to preview your Web site using different browsers. Many of the differences in how browsers display a page are visual, not structural.

Using Supporting Folders

Each page in your Web site has a supporting folder that contains all the elements on the page, such as images and hyperlinks. You can view the folders that were created in the Exploring window.

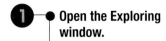 **Open the Exploring window.**

HAVING TROUBLE?
Select Explore from the My Computer icon shortcut menu.

● **Change the location to the location of your data files.**

Your screen should be similar to Figure 6.59

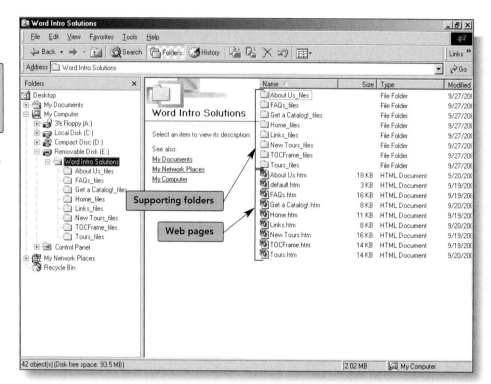

Figure 6.59

Also notice the document Default.htm included in the file list. This file is the frames page that controls the display of the frames for the Web site on the screen. If you want to view the Web site in Word again, open this file so that the pages will display correctly. Additionally, when creating Web sites, it is best to create them in their own folder so that the pages and supporting folders are organized in one location and so that files with the same names are not overwritten.

By default the name of the supporting folder is the name of the Web page plus an underscore (_) and the word "files." For example, the Links supporting folder name is Links_files. All supporting files, such as those for bullets, graphics, and background, are contained in the supporting folder. Any graphics that were added to the page that were not already JPG or GIF files are converted to that format.

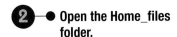

2 ● **Open the Home_files folder.**

Your screen should be similar to Figure 6.60

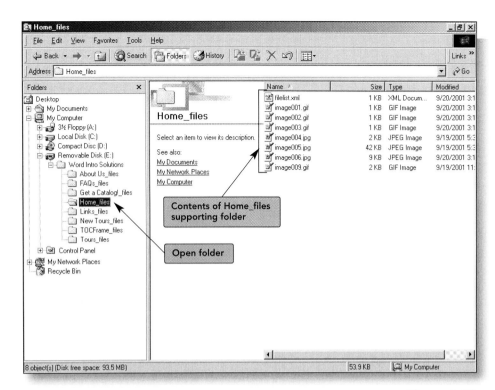

Figure 6.60

The Home_files folder contains nine graphic elements. Each graphic has been renamed "image000." The number is assigned in the order the element was added to the page.

3 ● **Close the Exploring window.**

When you move your files to place on a server, you need to include the HTML file and the associated supporting folder that contains all the elements on the page. If you do not, the page will not display correctly. If this folder is not available when the associated HTML page is loaded in the browser, the graphic elements will not be displayed.

LAB 6
Creating a Web Site

Home Page (WD6.4)

The top-level or opening page of a Web site is called the **home page**.

Home page

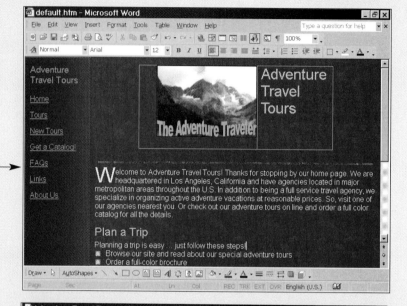

Frame (WD6.8)

A Web page can be divided into sections, called **frames**, that display separate Web pages.

Frame

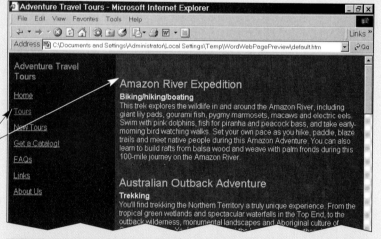

Group (WD6.19)

A group is two or more objects that are treated as a single object.

Group

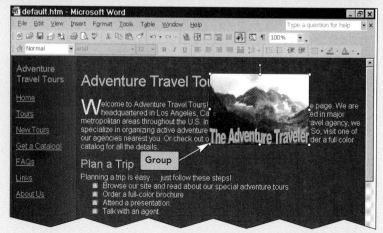

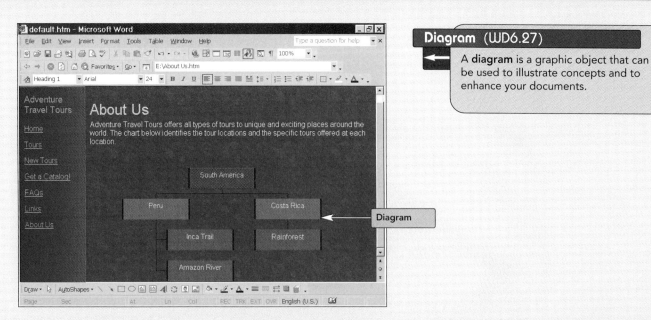

Diagram (WD6.27)

A **diagram** is a graphic object that can be used to illustrate concepts and to enhance your documents.

Diagram

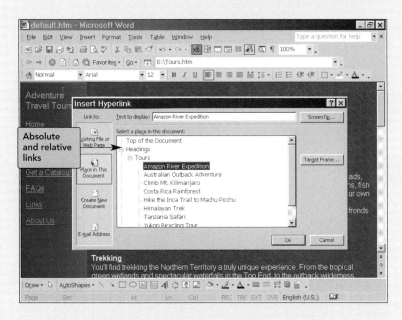

Absolute and Relative Links (WD6.34)

When you create a hyperlink in a document, you can make the path to the destination an **absolute link** or a **relative link**.

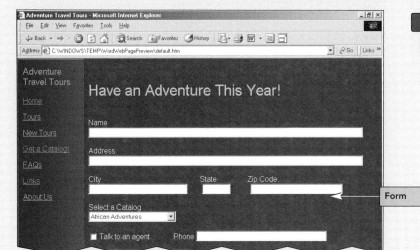

Form (WD6.41)

Forms are used in Web pages to get information or feedback from users or to provide information. Using forms makes your Web site interactive.

Form

key terms

absolute link WD6.34	fixed link WD6.34	home page WD6.4
background WD6.17	form WD6.41	protocol WD6.34
controls WD6.43	frame WD6.8	relative link WD6.34
destination WD6.34	frames page WD6.8	target link WD6.36
diagram WD6.27	group WD6.19	wallpaper WD6.17

mous skills

The Microsoft Office User Specialist (MOUS) certification program is designed to measure your proficiency in performing basic tasks using the Office XP applications. Getting certified demonstrates that you have the skills and provides a valuable industry credential for employment. After completing this lab, you have learned the following Microsoft Office User Specialist skills:

Skill	Description	Page
Creating and Modifying Paragraphs	Apply paragraph styles	WD6.35
Formatting Documents	Create and modify tables	WD6.21
Working with Graphics	Create and modify diagrams and charts	WD6.27
Workgroup Collaboration	Convert documents into Web pages	WD6.9

command summary

Command	Shortcut Key	Button	Action
Word			
File/**N**ew/General Templates /Web Pages/Web Page Wizard			Creates a new Web site
File/We**b** Page Preview			Displays saved Web page in a browser window
Insert/Dia**g**ram		⟳	Inserts a diagram
F**o**rmat/**B**orders and Shading /**H**orizontal Line			Adds graphic horizontal line to Web page
F**o**rmat/Background/**F**ill Effects			Applies background color to selection
F**o**rmat/T**h**eme			Applies a predesigned theme to Web page
Draw Drop-Down Menu			
Draw ▾ **O**rder/Bring to Fron**t**			Brings object to front of stack
Draw ▾ **G**roup			Creates a group from selected objects
Draw ▾ **U**ngroup			Ungroups a grouped object
Draw ▾ Regr**o**up			Regroups an ungrouped object
Organization Chart Toolbar			
I**n**sert Shape/**S**ubordinate			Inserts a shape below the selected superior shape
Layout/**R**ight Hanging			Hangs subordinate shapes to right of superior shape
Layout/**E**xpand Organization Chart			Expands drawing canvas around organization chart
Web Tools Toolbar			
Checkbox		☑	Allows selection of more than one item
Drop-Down box		⊞	Displays available choices in a list
Textbox		abl	A box where you can enter one line of text
Text Area		⊞	A box where you can enter more than one line of text
Reset		⊞	Clears entries in form
Submit		⊞	Submits data in form to specified location

lab exercises

Terminology

screen identification

1. In the following Word screen, letters identify important elements. Enter the correct term for each screen element in the space provided.

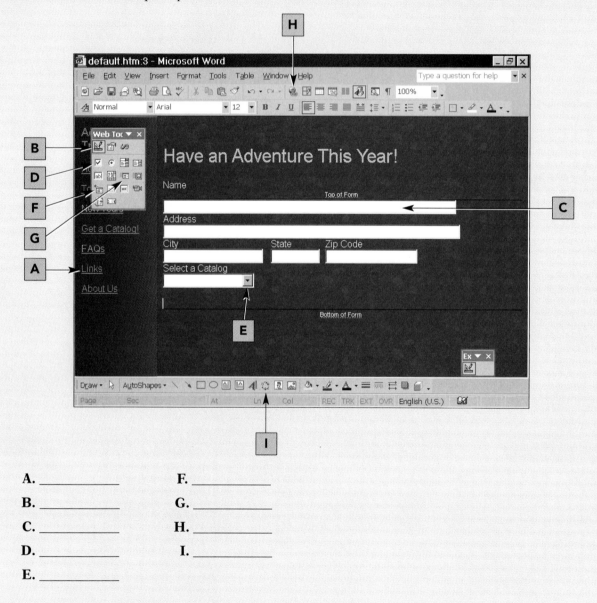

A. _____ F. _____

B. _____ G. _____

C. _____ H. _____

D. _____ I. _____

E. _____

matching

Match the item on the left with the correct description on the right.

1. home page   _____ a. two or more objects that are joined together as a single object

2.   _____ b. creates an organization chart

3. hyperlink   _____ c. allows users to jump to other locations

4.   _____ d. below a superior shape

5. absolute link   _____ e. identifies the location of a hyperlink by its full address

6.   _____ f. creates a diagram

7. page   _____ g. basic document of the World Wide Web

8. form   _____ h. inserts a horizontal line

9. subordinate   _____ i. an interactive element used to gather information from users

10. group   _____ j. top-level page

multiple choice

Circle the correct response to the questions below.

1. _____ are based on text rather than numeric information.
   a. charts
   b. diagrams
   c. pages
   d. forms

2. A(n) _____ is two or more objects that are treated as a single object.
   a. combination
   b. group
   c. block
   d. collection

3. A Web page divided into sections that display separate Web pages is said to contain _____.
   a. panes
   b. sections
   c. frames
   d. forms

4. A(n) _____ is a color or design that is displayed behind the text on the page.
   a. window
   b. background
   c. backdrop
   d. environment

5. Images, patterns, or texture placed behind text on a Web page is called _____.
   a. wallpaper
   b. background
   c. backdrop
   d. imaging

6. A(n) _____ link identifies the file location of the destination page by its full address.
   a. relative
   b. absolute
   c. followed
   d. destination

7. The _____ diagram shows steps toward a goal.
   a. pyramid
   b. organization
   c. cycle
   d. target

8. The _____ shape is below and connected to any other shape with an elbow connector.
   a. subordinate
   b. superior
   c. co-worker
   d. assistant

9. _____ are commonly used in Web pages to get information or feedback from users.
   a. Links
   b. Text boxes
   c. Frames
   d. Forms

10. The top-level or opening page of a site is called the _____ page.
    a. introduction
    b. index
    c. home
    d. site

true/false

Circle the correct answer to the following questions.

1. A diagram can not be used to illustrate concepts.   True   False
2. Form controls are used to automate the input of information.   True   False

3. Controls can only be added when Design mode is on.	True	False
4. A Web page can be divided into forms that display separate Web pages.	True	False
5. An organization chart shows hierarchical-based relationships.	True	False
6. Wallpaper is a color or design that is displayed behind the text on the page.	True	False
7. A relative link identifies the file location of the destination by its full address.	True	False
8. Hyperlinks to other Web sites should typically use a fixed file location.	True	False
9. Backward slashes (\\) are used to separate the protocol from the rest of the address.	True	False
10. Web pages use frames to get information or feedback from users.	True	False

Concepts

fill in

Complete the following statements by filling in the blanks with the correct answers.

1. The top-level or opening page of a Web site is called the _____.

2. A(n) _____ is two or more objects that are treated as a single object.

3. _____ are used to make it easier to navigate in a Web site.

4. A graphic object that can be used to illustrate concepts is a(n) _____.

5. An organization chart is used to illustrate _____ relationships.

6. A(n) _____ is a color or design that is displayed behind the text on the page.

7. A(n) _____ is a graphic object that automates a procedure.

8. Hyperlinks to other Web sites should typically use a fixed file location that includes the full path to the location or address of the page, called the _____.

9. When you create a Web page, all the elements on the page are stored in a(n) _____.

10. _____ are used in Web pages to get information or feedback from users or to provide information.

discussion questions

1. Discuss three attributes of a well-designed Web page.

2. Discuss frames and their advantages and disadvantages.

3. Discuss absolute and relative hyperlinks and when to use them.

4. Discuss supporting folders and why they are created.

5. Discuss diagrams and provide examples of when you use the different types.

Hands-On Exercises

step-by-step

The Sports Company Web Site

★★ 1. The Sports Company is a discount sporting goods store. You are working on a summer internship
★ with the company and have been asked to help design and build a Web site for the company. This
site will contain fitness-related information and links to products the company sells over the
Internet. Much of the information for the site has already been saved in Word document files.
When you are finished, the completed home page and Newsletter page should look similar to the
ones shown here.

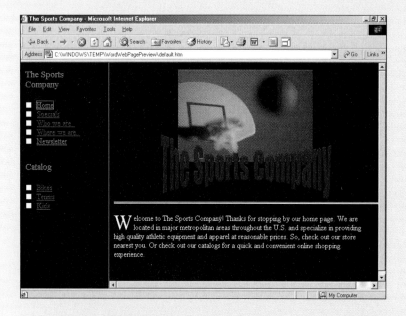

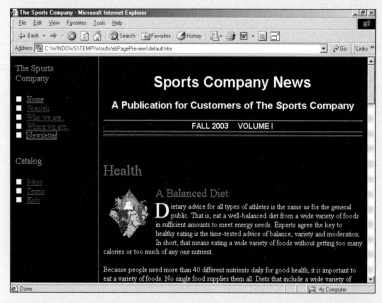

a. Open the file wd06_Home Page Text in Word. Reduce the size of the photo to approximately 2 by 3 inches. Center the WordArt above it. Center the whole graphic object on the page. Change the text wrapping style to Top and Bottom.

b. Center the WordArt object below the title as shown in the example. If necessary change the order so the photo is behind the WordArt. Group the objects.

c. Center the graphic object on the page. Change the text wrapping style to Top to Bottom. Reduce the size of the object to approximately 2 by 3 inches.

d. Save the document as Home Page Text2. Close the file.

e. You will use the Web Page Wizard to create the rest of the Web site. Start the wizard and enter the title **The Sports Company**. Specify a new folder as the location to save the Web site.

f. Select Vertical Frame for type of navigation.

g. Remove the Personal Web Page. Add the Home Page Text2 and wd06_SCNewsletter files. Add four new blank pages.

h. Move the Home Page Text2 file to the top of the list and rename the page **Home**. Rename the 6 blank pages with these titles: **Specials**, **Who we are . . .**, **Where we are . . .**, **Bikes**, **Tennis**, and **Kids**. Rename the SCNewsletter to **Newsletter** and move the newsletter page above Bikes.

i. Choose the Refined theme with vivid colors and active graphics, but without the Background Image. Finish the wizard. Preview the Web site. Switch back to Word.

j. Change the color of the WordArt to match the theme. Insert a horizontal line below the graphic and above the text in the main frame. If necessary, reapply the theme to update the horizontal line to the theme line. Add a drop cap to the W in the main frame using the Wrap 2 Lines setting.

k. Insert a blank line above "Bikes" in the table of contents frame and insert the word **Catalog**. Format the word as a Level 3 heading.

l. Delete the blank lines between the first five links. Insert a bullet in front of each link. In the same manner, insert bullets before the last three links. Adjust the spacing and bullets as necessary. Adjust the size of the contents frame as needed.

m. Open the Newsletter page and delete the graphic at the top of the page. Change the color of the lines above and below Fall 2003 to match the theme. Make any other necessary adjustments to the layout and spacing.

n. Create a link to the American Dietetic Association at www.eatright.org. Insert the link on the line following the sentence below the Food Pyramid. Add your name as a link to your e-mail address at the end of the newsletter

o. Preview the Web site and make any necessary adjustments to the pages. Print the Home page and the Newsletter page. Close all documents.

Animal Angels Web Site

★★ **2.** Animal Angels, the volunteer group for the Animal Rescue Foundation, would like a Web page to help attract volunteers and inform people about abandoned and adoptable pets. The home page has already been started and saved as an HTML document. You will enhance the page and add links to other pages. The completed home page and form are shown here.

a. Open the file wd06_Pets Home Page in Word. Create links from the text in the left column to the headings in the center column. Insert a Return to Top link after each section in the middle column.

b. In the "Pets Available for Adoption" section, insert one image of each kind of animal after the names (you can use wd06_Puppies, wd06_Cat, wd06_Parrots, and wd06_Lizard or one image of your choice). Size the images appropriately. Change the font size and left align the categories. Create a link from each of the pictures to four new pages that have the same location. (Hint: Use the Create New Document option on the Insert Hyperlink dialog box.) Name the new pages the same as the animal. Choose the Edit New Document Later option so that the new pages do not open.

c. Apply the Blends theme to the Web page.

d. Preview the page in your Web browser. Adjust any layout problems as needed.

e. Insert some blank lines above both the right and left columns to move them down below the Animal Angels title in the center column. Make the Pets of the Day and Upcoming Events Heading 3 style.

f. Insert an image of your choice above the links in the right column to add visual interest. Replace the Animal Angels title with a WordArt design of your choice.

g. Create a link called Become a member at the end of the list in the left column to a new page. Name the file Member and open the file for editing. Apply the Fixed theme with vivid colors to the new page.

h. On the Member page, you will create a form in which users can enter information so that Animal Angels can put them on its mailing list. Enter and center the title Become an Animal Angel. Apply the Heading 1 style.

i. Open the Web Tools toolbar. Enter the following text in the document.

For more information on becoming an Animal Angel please fill in the following fields. We will mail you a membership package. If you have a question please provide your e-mail address and a note in the comment box and we will be happy to e-mail a reply to you.
Full Name:
Street Address:
City:
State:
Zip Code:
E-mail Address:
Comments:

j. Insert text boxes next to the labels. Use the Text Area control for the Comments. Size and position the text boxes appropriately based on the type of input. Insert Reset and Submit buttons at the bottom of the form.

k. Close the Web Tools toolbar. Add the text Questions? Contact followed by your name as a link to your e-mail address at the end of the form.

l. Save the changes you have made to the pages and print the home and form pages.

Updating The Downtown Internet Cafe Site

★★ **3.** Evan, the owner of the Downtown Internet Cafe, has not updated its Web site in quite some time. He feels the old site is dated and would like you to completely redesign the site. He would like to have a list of services the cafe offers, as well as an online coffee store. Evan has provided you with all the new content and some recent photos taken at the cafe. Your completed Web pages should be similar to those shown here.

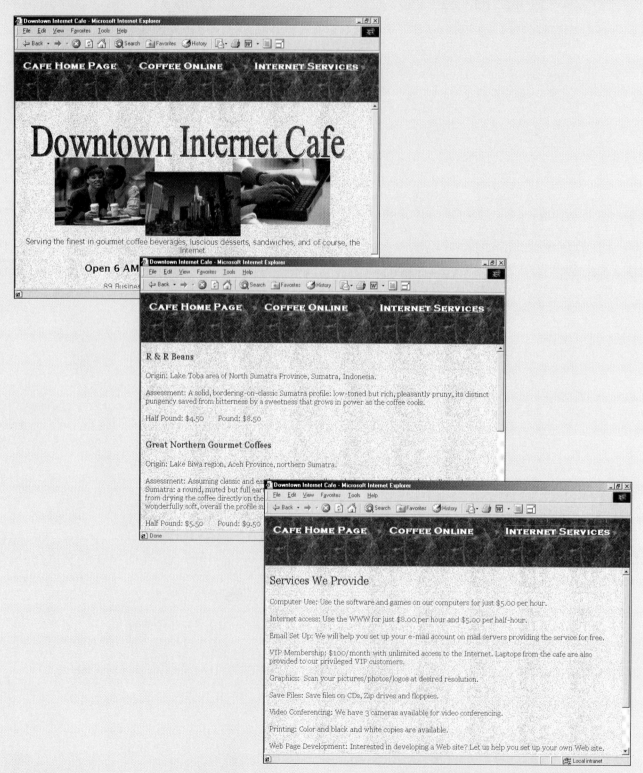

a. Begin the Web site using the Web Page Wizard. Title the Web page Downtown Internet Cafe. Choose horizontal navigation. Rename the default web pages: Cafe Home Page, Coffee Online, and Internet Services. Add the Layers visual theme with vivid colors and background image and finish the wizard.

b. Examine the new layout and add the Layers theme to the horizontal frame across the top of the site. Decrease the size of the frame to approximately 1 inch.

c. Delete the "Main Heading Goes Here" text. Insert a WordArt object (the example uses the style in the first column, fourth row) with the text Downtown Internet Cafe. Change the font to Times New Roman. Size and center the object as shown in the example figure. Change the shadow color to gray. (Hint: The shadow color options are available on the Drawing toolbar under the Shadow Settings menu). You now decide to change the fill color from Paper bag to Brown Marble. Change the wrapping style to Behind Text.

d. Delete all the default text below the photos. You now decide that some recent photos from the cafe would be appropriate for the site. Insert the files wd06_Computer, wd06_City, and wd06_Patrons. Change the layout to Behind Text. Arrange them as shown in the example and group the photos. Use Web page preview to examine the changes you have made so far. Save the file as a Web page called Downtown Internet Cafe Site.

e. With the new photos in place you feel the horizontal frame could use some formatting changes. Delete the Cafe name from the frame. Remove the table borders and use the brown marble texture to fill in the background.

f. Change the font color of the hyperlinks to white, the font to Copperplate Gothic Bold and use a 16 pt font size. Preview your changes in your browser.main window of the Coffee Online page. Close the wd06_Online Coffee file.

g. You like the changes you have made to the layout and now decide to change the content. Enter and center the following text below the photos:

Serving the finest in gourmet coffee beverages, luscious desserts, sandwiches and, of course, the Internet.

Open 6 AM to 11 PM every day of the week!

89 Business Parkway, Suite 102, Chicago, IL, 86512
(555) 555-CAFE

h. Preview your changes in your browser. Return to the document and adjust the text until it displayed appropriately in the Web preview. You are happy with the page so far and decide to create the Coffee Online and Internet Services pages.

i. Click on the Coffee Online page to begin editing it. Delete the default text. Insert the file wd06_Coffee Online. Remove the sentence above the R&R Beans heading. Preview your changes in your browser. Make any necessary layout adjustments.

j. Click on the Internet Services page to begin editing it. Delete the default text. Insert the file wd06_Services. Make the first sentence a Heading 2 style. Return to the Home page.

k. You like the layout of the Home page, but would like to emphasize the text at the bottom of the page. Apply the Lucida Sans font to the text. Bold the sentence that gives the cafe hours. Increase the font size of this line to 16 pt.

l. Add your name as an e-mail address link as the contact at the bottom of the home page. Save the file and print the pages.

Creating a Personal Web Site

★★ 4. Now that you have practiced your Web page design skills you have decided to create a Personal
★ Web Site. You will create a home page that highlights your interests and include a mini-biography.
Be sure to include pictures and graphics and utilize the many formatting techniques available to
you. You will also create a page about one of your insterests or hobbies. Although your completed
home page will be personalized, it should be similar to that shown here.

a. Plan the design of your home
page. You may want to visit other
personal home pages on the Web
to get an idea of what you like
and do not like for your page.
You may also consider using the
Personal Web Page template provided with Word to help you get
started.

b. Develop a Word document that
contains the text of your home
page.

c. If necessary, save the Word docu-
ment as an HTML document, or if you use the template, copy and paste the information from
your document into the appropriate locations.

d. Apply a theme of your choice. Modify the background colors or theme to suit your design.

e. Add clip art, pictures, and animation to your home page. If you have access to a scanner, you
can scan pictures to insert. You can also use the Web to locate graphics and animations. Use
tables as necessary to align your text and pictures or clip art.

f. Add a link from your home page to another page. Include a brief description of the content.
This page should be formatted similarly to your home page.

g. If possible, load your home page to a server so others can enjoy your work.

h. Save the file as My Home Page and print both pages.

Computer Virus Web Site

★★
★

5. You are a graduate student and have received an assistantship to work with a university professor. The professor has assigned students a research project on computer viruses. You have been asked to create a Web page for inclusion on the class Web site that describes computer viruses and includes links to Web sites that discuss viruses. The pages you will create should be similar to the pages shown here.

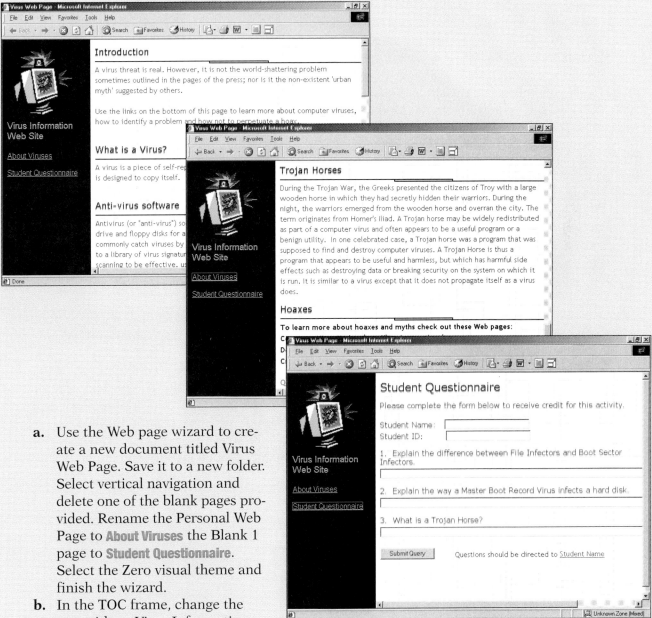

a. Use the Web page wizard to create a new document titled Virus Web Page. Save it to a new folder. Select vertical navigation and delete one of the blank pages provided. Rename the Personal Web Page to **About Viruses** the Blank 1 page to **Student Questionnaire**. Select the Zero visual theme and finish the wizard.

b. In the TOC frame, change the page title to Virus Information Web Site. Change the theme of the main frame from the Zero theme to the Modular theme.

c. You have already prepared the text for the main page and would like to insert it now. Select all the text in the main frame and insert the file wd06_Virus Text Page. Delete the blank line above the Introduction heading. Insert a horizontal line below the Introduction heading. If necessary, reapply the Modular theme to format the horizontal line appropriately.

d. Copy and paste the horizontal line below each of the headings in the main frame. Insert four blank lines above the title in the TOC frame. Insert the graphic file wd06_Virus. Change the wrapping style to Top and Bottom. Size and center the graphic over the title.

e. View the Web page in Web Page Preview and make any necessary layout adjustments so that the page displays correctly in your browser.

f. In the Hoaxes section of the main frame add the following text:

To learn more about hoaxes and myths check out these Web pages.
Computer Virus Myths—http://kumite.com/myths/
Don't Spread That Hoax!—http://www.nonprofit.net/hoax/hoax.html
Create Your Own Hoaxes—http://www.cao.com/hoax/

g. Next you will create the student questionnaire. Click on the Student Questionnaire hyperlink. Change the main frame to the Modular visual theme. Delete the default text. Enter and center the title Virus Questionnaire. Apply the Heading 1 style.

h. Below the title, create the form by entering the following text. Add controls as appropriate (see the example at the beginning of the exercise).

Please complete the form below to receive credit for this activity.
Student Name
Student ID
1. Explain the difference between File Infectors and Boot Sector Infectors.
2. Explain the way a Master Boot Record Virus infects a hard disk.
3. What is a Trojan Horse?

i. Insert a submit button that links to your e-mail address. Apply the Heading 4 style to the form directions and text box labels. Check your changes in Web Page Preview. make any required layout adjustments.

j. Your page is almost finished. All you need to do is finish adding the text to the Virus Home Page. Insert the file wd06_Trojan Horses below the Trojan Horse heading. The file also contains information on antivirus software—move this paragraph under the appropriate heading. The new paragraphs have different formatting. Select both paragraphs and choose Clear Formatting from the Styles and Formatting Drop Down Menu.

k. Check your changes in Web Page Preview and make any needed layout adjustments. Print the two pages.

Revising Your Personal Web Site

★ **1.** To complete this problem, you must have completed Step-by-Step Exercise 4 in this lab and created your personal Web site. After designing your home page, you would like to know how others feel about what you added to your page. A good way of asking for input is to use a feedback form. With this form you can ask visitors to respond to questions. Create a feedback form in the same visual style as your home page. Enhance the page using lines, borders, and pictures as appropriate. Link the feedback form to your home page. Print the form page.

Creating a Fan Site

★ **2.** Because the Web is open to anyone who has a computer and Internet access, there are many unofficial Web sites for popular television shows. People create Web pages to let others know what they like or dislike about a show. Design and create a Web site with the title My TV Site for the show of your choice. Include clip art, pictures, and animation to enhance the site. Link your site to other official and unofficial Web sites for the same or similar shows. Create frames that are appropriate for your design. Create additional pages that are links from your home page that give your views of the characters on the show. Print the pages.

Enhancing Adventure Travel Tours' Web Page

★★ **3.** To complete this problem, you must have created the Adventure Travel Tours Web site in this lab. Open the Adventure Travel Web site. Create links to the other topics on the Tours page and add additional Back to Top links. Use a table to make the list of tour links display in two columns at the top of the page. Add a link to a new page that provides a detailed itinerary for one of the tours. (Use the Web to get itinerary information.) Add additional links and descriptions on the Links page that would be of interest to travelers. Add information to the FAQs page using information provided in the wd06_Tour FAQs document. Add an organizational chart and text to the About Us page that includes length of time in business, number of locations, philosophy, and objectives. Edit the hyperlink on the New Tours page to display the Presentations Locations.htm page you created in the first Working Together tutorial, if available. Apply the Nature theme to this page. Adjust the layout on all the pages as necessary. Print the Itinerary and Tour FAQs pages.

Creating a School Club Website

★★ **4.** The members of a club at your school have asked you to create a Web site that will inform fellow
★ students and club members about their activities. Choose a club or an organization you are familiar with and create a Web site titled Club Website that includes information on the club history, its recent activities (include photos), faculty sponsor, calendar of events, and a mascot of your choice. Be sure to include an organizational chart for the club officers and links to your school's home page. The club has also asked that the site be colorful and include photos. When you have completed the site, print the home page.

Expanding the Animal Angels Web Site

★★ **5.** To complete this exercise you must have completed Step-by-Step Exercise 4 in Lab 4 and Step-by-
★ Step Exercise 2 in Lab 6. You have been asked by the Animal Angels to include the monthly newsletter as a feature on the Web site. You decide that the newsletter should be reformatted for the Web. Reformat the content for the Web site and include new graphics. Apply a theme of your choice to the page and make any necessary adjustments to the layout. Finally, print the new page.

on the web

Evaluating Web Design

Do some research on the Web on the topics of your choice. Once you have some ideas of good and bad page design, create a Web page titled Web Evaluation that gives information on Web page design. Consider using frames to hold the lists of links to pages you felt were of good design as well as pages that in your opinion had bad page design. Add clip art, pictures, and animation to your page as needed. Use an appropriate background color or wallpaper. When you are finished, print the page(s) you created.

Working Together 2: Linking and Document Collaboration

Case Study

Adventure Travel Company

The manager for Adventure Travel Tours has asked you to provide a monthly status report for the bookings for the four new tours. You maintain this information in an Excel worksheet and want to include the worksheet of the tour status in a memo each month. You will learn how to share information between applications while you create the memo.

You are also working on developing a brochure for the Mt. Everest tour. Writing documents, such as travel brochures and newsletters, is often not a solo effort. One person is typically responsible for assembling the document, but several people may be involved in writing and/or reviewing the text. You will learn about the collaboration features in Word 2002 that make it easy to work on a group project.

Linking an Excel worksheet to a Word document allows the Word document to be quickly updated when data in the worksheet changes.

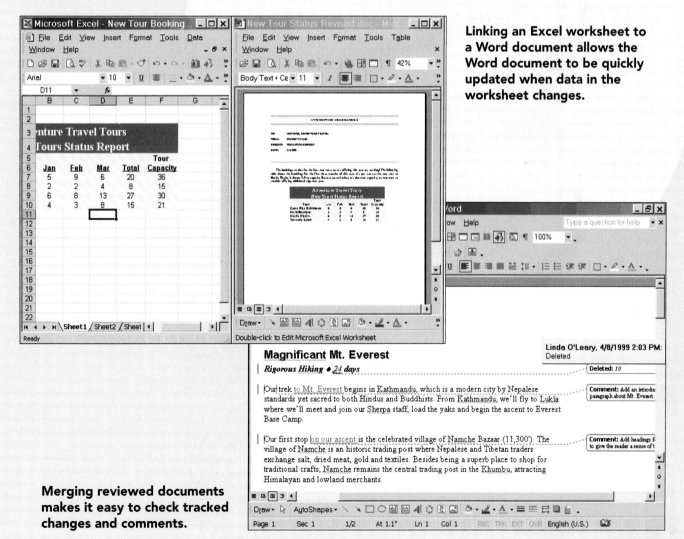

Merging reviewed documents makes it easy to check tracked changes and comments.

WDWT2.1

• Sharing Information between Applications

All Microsoft Office applications have a common user interface such as similar commands and menu structures. In addition to these obvious features, the applications have been designed to work together, making it easy to share and exchange information between applications.

The memo to the manager about the new tour status has already been created using Word. However, you still need to add the Excel worksheet data to the memo.

1 ● **Start Word and open the file** wdwt2_New Tour Status.

● **In the memo header, replace "Student Name" with your name.**

● **Change the zoom to Page Width.**

● **Save the file as** New Tour Status Revised.

Your screen should be similar to Figure 1

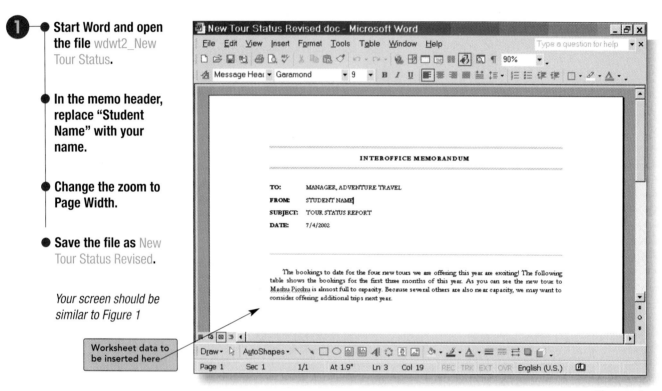

Figure 1

Linking an Excel Worksheet

You will insert the worksheet data below the paragraph. To insert the information from the Excel workbook file into the Word memo you need to open the workbook file and copy the worksheet range.

1 ● **Start Excel and open the workbook file** wdwt2_New Tour Bookings.xls**.**

● **Save the file as** New Tour Bookings Linked**.**

● **Tile the two open windows vertically.**

● **Select the worksheet range A3 through F10.**

● **Click** 🖹 **Copy to copy the selected range to the System Clipboard.**

● **Switch to the Word document window and move to the blank space below the paragraph.**

Your screen should be similar to Figure 2

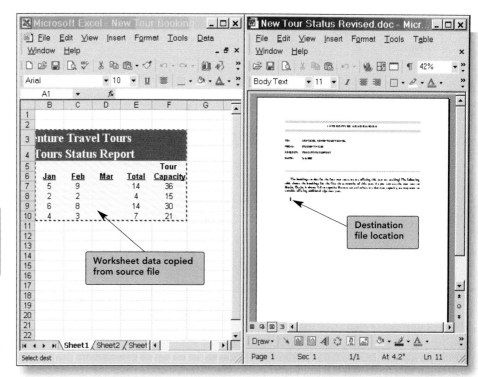

Figure 2

You will insert the worksheet into the memo as a linked object. A **linked object** is information created in one application that is inserted into a document created by another application while maintaining a link between the files. When an object is linked, the data is stored in the **source file** (the document it was created in). A graphic representation or picture of the data is displayed in the destination file (the document in which the object is inserted). A connection between the information in the **destination file** to the source file is established by the creation of a link. The link contains references to the location of the source file and the selection within the document that is linked to the destination file.

When changes are made in the source file that affect the linked object, the changes are automatically reflected in the destination file when it is opened. This is called a **live link**. When you create linked objects, the date and time on your machine should be accurate. This is because the program refers to the date of the source file to determine whether updates are needed when you open the destination file.

You will make the worksheet a linked object, so it will be automatically updated when you update the data in the worksheet.

2 ● Choose **E**dit/Paste
Special.

● Select Paste L**i**nk.

*Your screen should be
similar to Figure 3*

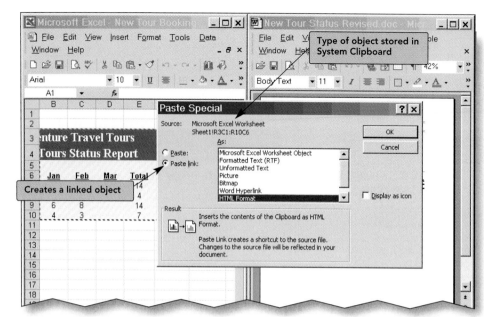

Figure 3

The Paste Special dialog box displays in the Source area the type of object contained in the Clipboard and its location. From the As list box, you select the type of format in which you want the object inserted into the destination file. The Result area describes the effect of your selections. In this case, you want to insert the object as an Excel Worksheet object, and a link will be created to the worksheet in the source file. Selecting the Display as Icon option changes the display of the object from a picture to an icon. Then to open or edit the object, you would double-click the icon. You need to change the type of format only.

3 ● Select Microsoft Excel
Worksheet Object.

● Click ⬚OK⬚.

● Select the worksheet
object and center it
below the paragraph.

*Your screen should be
similar to Figure 4.*

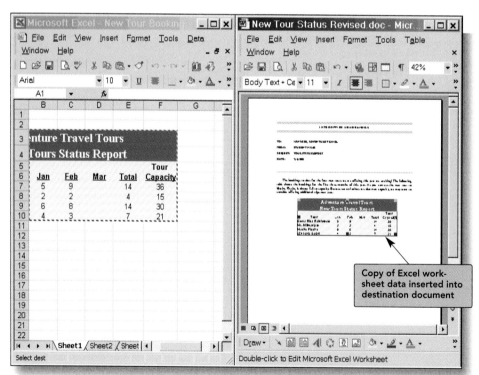

Figure 4

Updating a Linked Object

While preparing the memo, you received the tour booking for March and will enter this information into the worksheet. To make these changes, you need to switch back to Excel. Double-clicking on a linked object quickly switches to the open source file. If the source file is not open, it opens the file for you. If the application is not open, it both opens the application and the source file.

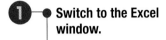

Another Method

The menu equivalent is Edit/Linked Object.

1 ● Switch to the Excel window.

● Enter the values for March in the cells specified.

D7 6
D8 4
D9 13
D10 8

● Press ⏎Enter.

Your screen should be similar to Figure 5

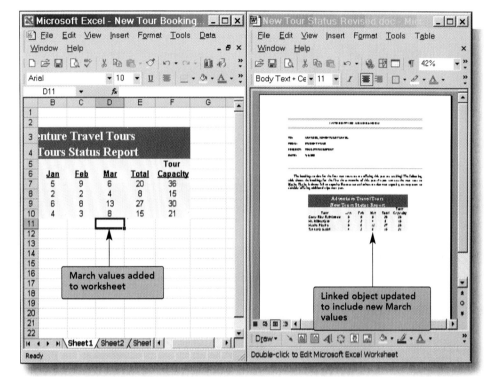

Figure 5

The worksheet in the memo reflects the changes in data. This is because any changes you make to the worksheet in Excel will be automatically reflected in the linked worksheet in the Word document.

2 ● Undo the tiled windows.

● Exit Excel, saving the worksheet file.

● Print the memo.

● Close and save the Word document.

Linking documents is a very handy feature, particularly in documents whose information is updated frequently. If you include a linked object in a document that you are giving to another person, make sure the user has access to the source file and application. Otherwise the links will not operate correctly.

Using Collaboration Features

Your second project is to review a document that a co-worker wrote for the new brochure being developed on the Africa Safari tour. You want to enter your suggested changes in the document and return it to the author. Word 2002 offers several features that make collaboration on documents easy and efficient.

Tracking Changes to a Document

To show the author what changes you are suggesting, you will use the Track Changes feature. When this feature is turned on, each insertion, deletion, or formatting change that is made to a document is identified or tracked.

Reviewing toolbar

1 ● **Open the** wdwt2_Camping Safari file.

● **If necessary, switch to Print Layout view at 100% zoom.**

● **Save the file as** Camping Safari Edited.

● **Choose Tools/Track Changes.**

Another Method

The keyboard shortcut is Ctrl + ⇧Shift + E.

Your screen should be similar to Figure 6

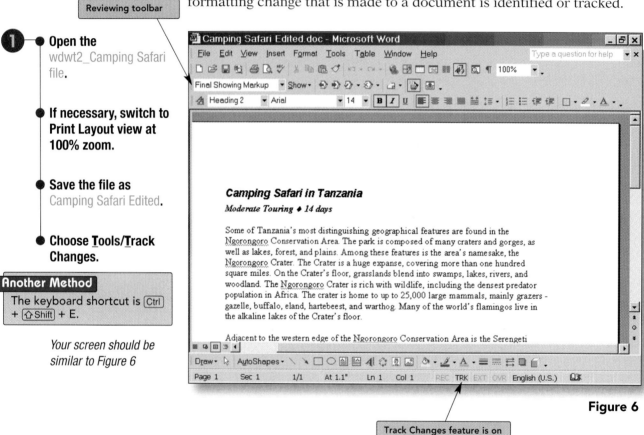

Track Changes feature is on

Figure 6

When Track Changes is enabled, "TRK" appears in the status bar and the Reviewing toolbar shown below is displayed. Now, any changes you make to the document will be marked to show the **tracked changes.**

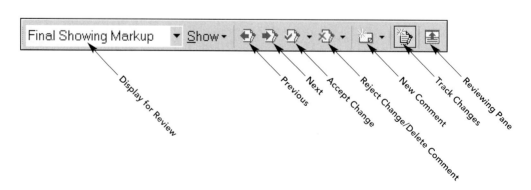

2 ● **Move to the end of the third sentence, after the word "Crater" and before the period.**

● **Select the following text until you reach the end of the word "covering."**

● **Press** Delete.

● **Type** , which covers.

Your screen should be similar to Figure 7

HAVING TROUBLE?
If revision marks are not displayed, choose View/Markup to turn on this feature.

Additional Information
The balloons appear only in Print Layout and Web Layout views.

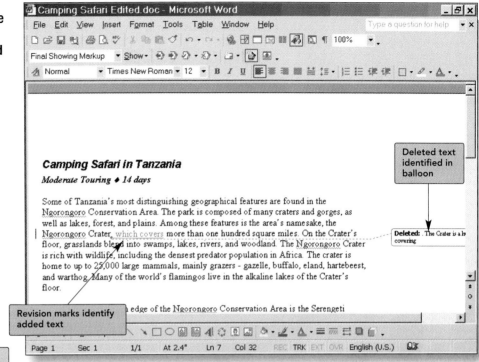

Figure 7

Different **markup** elements are used to identify the changes. The inserted text is identified with a red underline called a **revision mark** that indicates an insertion was made. The text you deleted is displayed in a **balloon** in the right margin. Dotted lines connect the balloons to the text that was changed.

The next change you want to make is to change the word "Crater" to all lowercase characters when it appears by itself.

3 ● **Highlight the "C" in the word "Crater" in the next sentence.**

● **Type a lowercase** c.

● **Make the same change to the word "Crater" in the last sentence of this paragraph.**

● **Point to any revision mark.**

Your screen should be similar to Figure 8

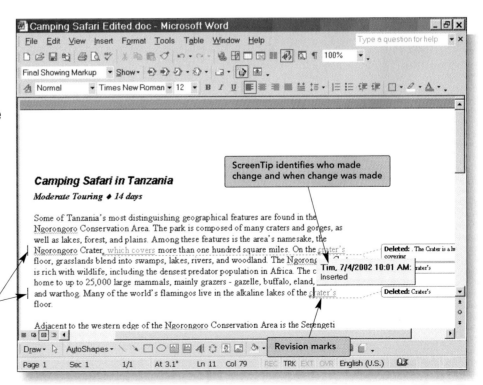

Figure 8

The change is identified with a revision mark and the deletion appears in the balloon. Pointing to a revision mark displays a ScreenTip with information about who made the change and when the change was made. The lines of the document that have been changed are identified with a vertical rule along the outside margin. The different markup elements help preserve the layout of the document while changes are being tracked.

Adding Comments

You want to add a comment before you send the document to the author. A **comment** is a note that can be added to a document without changing the document text. You will add a comment suggesting that there should be more information about the activities and camping experiences that will be encountered on the safari.

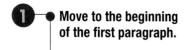

1 ● **Move to the beginning of the first paragraph.**

● **Click** 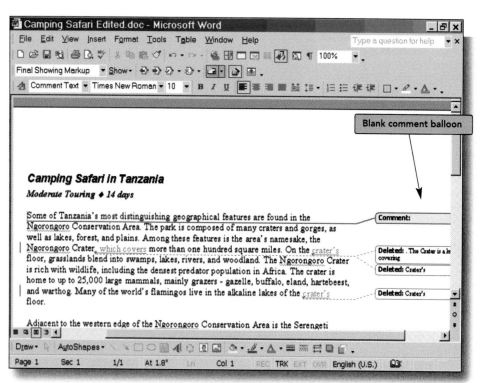 **New Comment on the Reviewing toolbar.**

Another Method

The menu equivalent is Insert/Comment.

Your screen should be similar to Figure 9

Figure 9

Another Method

You can also click 🔳 to display the Reviewing pane where you can type a comment. To close the Reviewing pane, click 🔳 again.

A blank **comment balloon** is displayed in the margin and a line connects it to the location where you inserted the comment. Next you need to add the text of the comment.

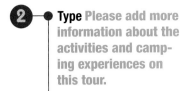

2 • **Type** Please add more information about the activities and camping experiences on this tour.

• **Click** [icon] **to turn off Track Changes.**

Your screen should be similar to Figure 10

Another Method
You can also record comments using [icon] New Comment/Voice Comment. You must have sound capabilities and a microphone to record and listen to recorded comments.

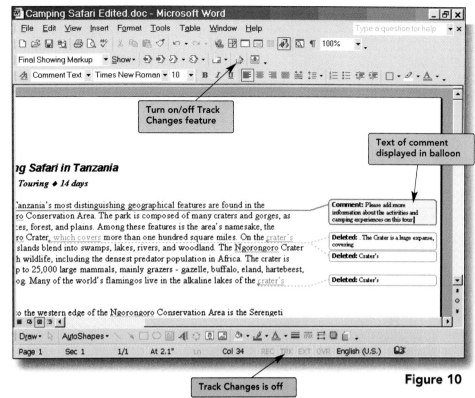

Turn on/off Track Changes feature

Text of comment displayed in balloon

Comment: Please add more information about the activities and camping experiences on this tour.

Deleted: . The Crater is a huge expanse, covering

Deleted: Crater's

Deleted: Crater's

Track Changes is off

Figure 10

Now, any further changes you make will not be tracked.

Adding Text Animation

You only reviewed the first few paragraphs and want to indicate where you stopped in the document. A clever way of marking the document is with animated text.

1 • **Move to the blank line after the first paragraph.**

• **Type** I stopped reviewing here.

• **Select the text and apply a font color of your choice.**

• **Choose Format/Font/Text Effects.**

Your screen should be similar to Figure 11

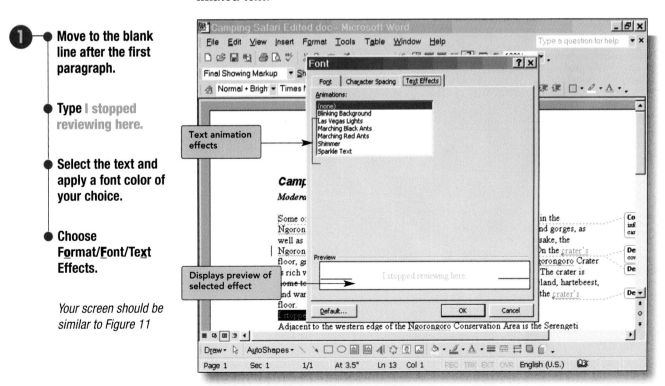

Text animation effects

Displays preview of selected effect

Font

Font | Character Spacing | Text Effects

Animations:
(none)
Blinking Background
Las Vegas Lights
Marching Black Ants
Marching Red Ants
Shimmer
Sparkle Text

Preview

I stopped reviewing here.

Default... | OK | Cancel

Figure 11

The available effects are listed in the Animations list box, and a sample of the animation effect associated with the selected text appears in the Preview area. Since no effect has been applied yet, the text is not animated.

2 ● **Select each effect to preview how it will appear.**

● **Select Las Vegas Lights.**

● **Click** OK **.**

● **Deselect the text.**

● **Save the document.**

Your screen should be similar to Figure 12

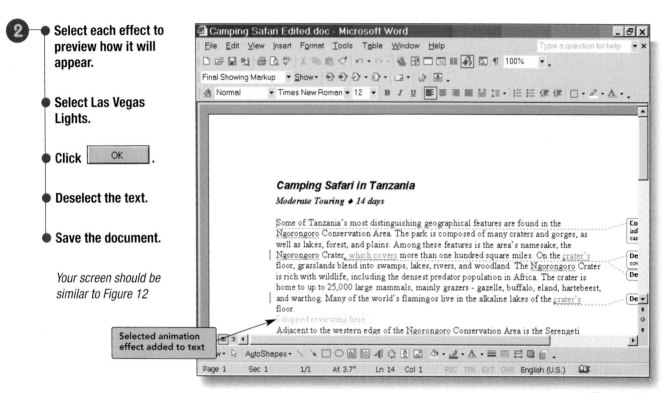

Selected animation effect added to text

Figure 12

The text will blink when viewing the document, but the animation effect will not print.

Sending a Document via E-mail

Next you will return the edited document to the author. The most efficient way is via e-mail with the document as an attachment. An **attachment** is a file that is sent with the e-mail message but is not part of the e-mail text. You open the attachment with the application in which it was created.

Note: Skip this section if you do not have Microsoft Outlook installed on your system.

1 ● Choose **F**ile/Send
To/M**a**il Recipient (as
Attachment).

● Maximize the e-mail
window.

*Your screen should be
similar to Figure 13*

File name of
attachment

Message area

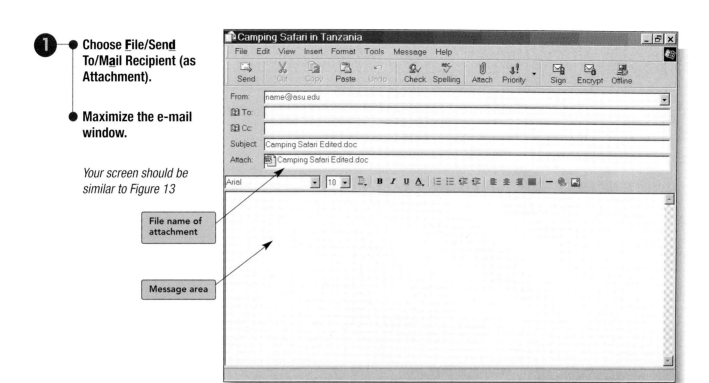

Figure 13

An e-mail window is displayed in which you can address your e-mail message. Notice that the Subject and the Attach fields show the filename of the attached document. The extension indicates the application in which the file will open, which is helpful to know.

Sends message

2 ● In the To field, type
your e-mail address.

● In the message area,
type: Please consider
these comments to
your attached docu-
ment.

*Your screen should be
similar to Figure 14*

Recipient's e-mail
address

Body of e-mail
message

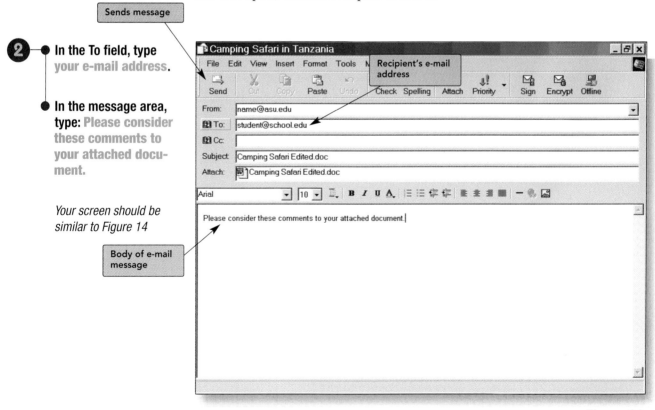

Figure 14

Now you are ready to send the message. If you have access the Internet, you could click to send the e-mail message. Instead, you will save it to be sent at a later time.

3
- **Choose File/Save As and save the message as** Safari e-mail.
- **Click ☒ to close the e-mail window.**
- **Close the Reviewing toolbar.**
- **Close the Word document.**

Reviewing Documents

While checking your e-mail for new messages, you see that two co-workers have returned a document you snet to them to review with their comments and tracked changes. You have downloaded the attachments and saved them as files on your system. Now you want to review the suggested changes.

Comparing and Merging Documents

When you receive multiple reviewer comments for the same document, the easiest way to review them is to merge the documents together. You will open the first reviewed document.

1
- **Open** wdwt2_Everest Changes 2.

- **If necessary, switch to Print Layout view.**

- **Scroll the document to see the changes.**

Your screen should be similar to Figure 15

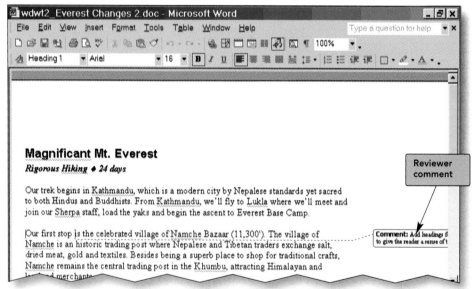

Figure 15

This reviewer only inserted one comment. To make sure that the reviewer did not change the document without using the Track Changes option, you will compare this document to the original using the Legal Blackline option. When you use Legal Blackline, Word compares the documents and creates a third document showing what changed between the two. The documents being compared are not changed.

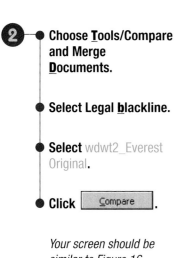

② • Choose **T**ools/Compare and Merge **D**ocuments.

• Select Legal **b**lackline.

• **Select** wdwt2_Everest Original.

• **Click** 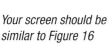 Compare .

Your screen should be similar to Figure 16

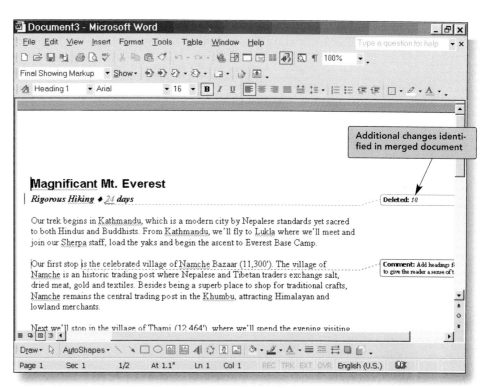

Additional changes identified in merged document

Magnificant Mt. Everest

Rigorous Hiking ◆ 24 days

Deleted: 10

Our trek begins in Kathmandu, which is a modern city by Nepalese standards yet sacred to both Hindus and Buddhists. From Kathmandu, we'll fly to Lukla where we'll meet and join our Sherpa staff, load the yaks and begin the ascent to Everest Base Camp.

Our first stop is the celebrated village of Namche Bazaar (11,300'). The village of Namche is an historic trading post where Nepalese and Tibetan traders exchange salt, dried meat, gold and textiles. Besides being a superb place to shop for traditional crafts, Namche remains the central trading post in the Khumbu, attracting Himalayan and lowland merchants.

Comment: Add headings to give the reader a sense of t

Next we'll stop in the village of Thami (12,464') where we'll spend the evening visiting

Figure 16

A new document is created showing the differences in the reviewed document from the original document. The next step is to merge this new document with the other reviewer's document so you can review all the changes together.

③ • Save the document as Everest Changes 3.

• Choose **T**ools/Compare and Merge **D**ocuments.

• Select Legal blackline to deselect it.

• **Select** wdwt2_Everest Changes 1.

• **Click** Merge ▼ .

• If necessary, switch to Print Layout view.

Your screen should be similar to Figure 17

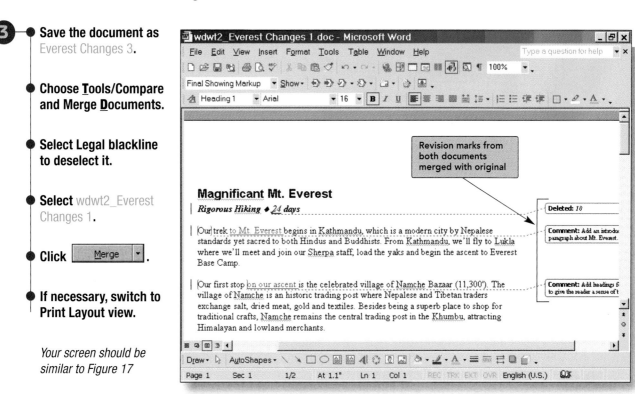

Revision marks from both documents merged with original

Magnificant Mt. Everest

Rigorous Hiking ◆ 24 days

Deleted: 10

Our trek to Mt. Everest begins in Kathmandu, which is a modern city by Nepalese standards yet sacred to both Hindus and Buddhists. From Kathmandu, we'll fly to Lukla where we'll meet and join our Sherpa staff, load the yaks and begin the ascent to Everest Base Camp.

Comment: Add an introductory paragraph about Mt. Everest.

Our first stop on our ascent is the celebrated village of Namche Bazaar (11,300'). The village of Namche is an historic trading post where Nepalese and Tibetan traders exchange salt, dried meat, gold and textiles. Besides being a superb place to shop for traditional crafts, Namche remains the central trading post in the Khumbu, attracting Himalayan and lowland merchants.

Comment: Add headings to give the reader a sense of t

Figure 17

The revision marks and comments from both documents are now combined with the wdwt2_Everest Changes 1 document. Word automatically assigns unique colors to the comments and tracked changes made by the first eight reviewers who revise a document. You would like to see who the reviewers are.

4 ● **Point to the first balloon.**

Another Method

You can also select Reviewers from the Show▾ drop-down menu on the Reviewing toolbar.

Your screen should be similar to Figure 18

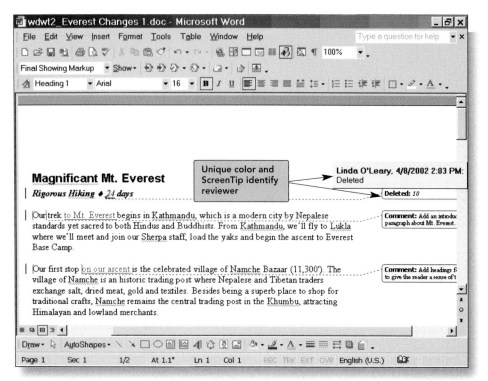

Figure 18

A ScreenTip displays the reviewer's name and the date of the change.

Accepting or Rejecting Changes to a Document

Before you begin to review the individual changes, you want to view the document in several different ways. The different views are described below.

Option	Effect
Final Showing Markup	Displays the final document with the insertions underlined and the deletions indicated in the revision balloons.
Final	Displays how the document would appear if you accepted all the changes.
Original Showing Markup	Displays the original document with the deletions underlined and the insertions indicated in the revision balloons.
Original	Displays the original unchanged document so you can see how the document would look if you rejected all the changes.

You want to see how the document would look if you accepted all changes.

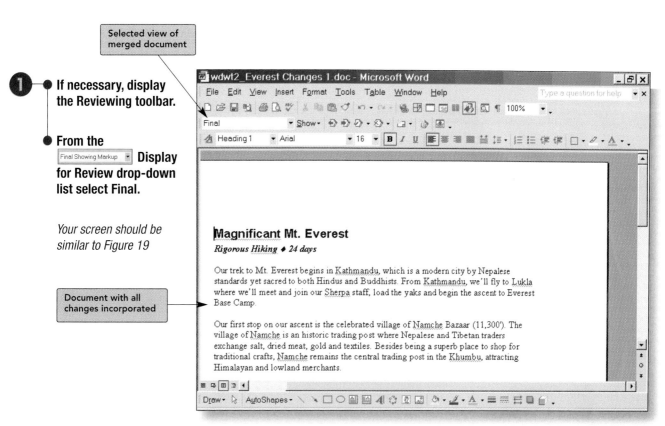

Selected view of merged document

① ● If necessary, display the Reviewing toolbar.

● From the [Final Showing Markup ▼] **Display for Review drop-down list select Final.**

Your screen should be similar to Figure 19

Document with all changes incorporated

Figure 19

The document appears as it would look if you accepted all changes and ignored all the comments. Next you want to see the original document before the changes were made.

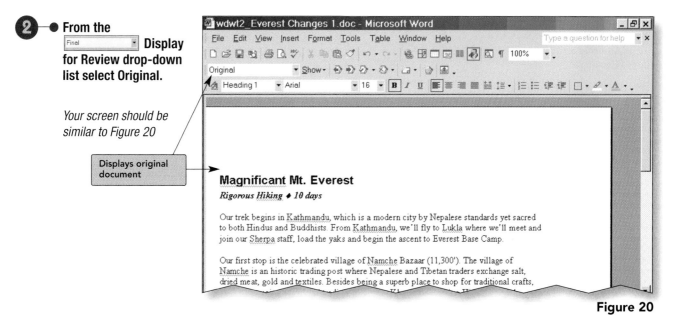

② ● From the [Final ▼] **Display for Review drop-down list select Original.**

Your screen should be similar to Figure 20

Displays original document

Figure 20

The original document appears without the suggested changes. You can quickly switch between the document views to check the changes. You want to display the final document with markups and review each change individually.

- **From the** [Original ▼] **Display for Review drop-down list select Final Showing Markup.**

- **Click** 🔳 **Reviewing Pane.**

- **Click** 🔁 **Next.**

Additional Information

Clicking 🔁 moves to the previous change or comment.

Your screen should be similar to Figure 21

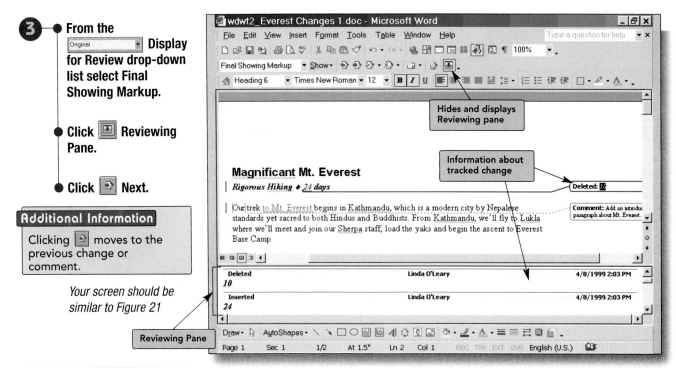

Figure 21

Additional Information

Often Word cannot display the complete text of a change or comment in a balloon, and it is necessary to view the comments in the Reviewing Pane.

The Reviewing Pane is displayed at the bottom of the document window and the information about the first change is displayed. The first tracked change to delete the number 10 is highlighted. Since this tour is 24 days in length, you want to accept the change.

4

- **Click** 🔁 **Accept Change.**

Your screen should be similar to Figure 22

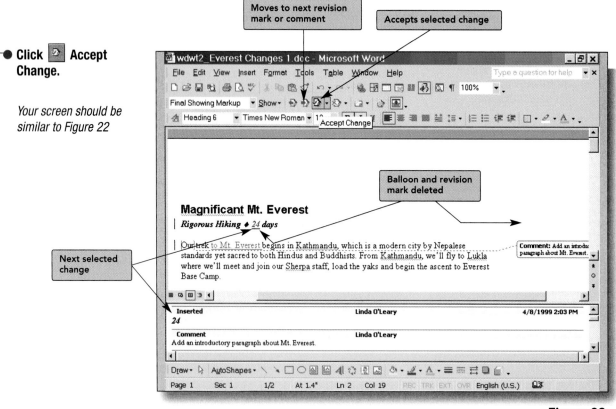

Figure 22

The number 10 is deleted along with the revision mark and the balloon. The next suggested change, to insert the number 24, is highlighted. Again, this is correct and you want to accept the change.

5 • **Click ⟳ Accept Change.**

Your screen should be similar to Figure 23

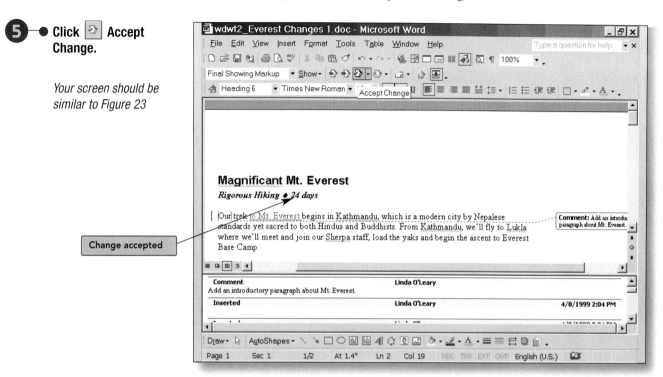

Figure 23

The number 24 is added to the document and the revision mark is removed. The next change is a comment. You will address the comments after you review the changes. For now you will bypass the comment, go to the next change, and accept the insertion of the words "to Mt. Everest."

6 • **Click ➡ Next 3 times.**

• **Click ⟳ Accept Change.**

Your screen should be similar to Figure 24

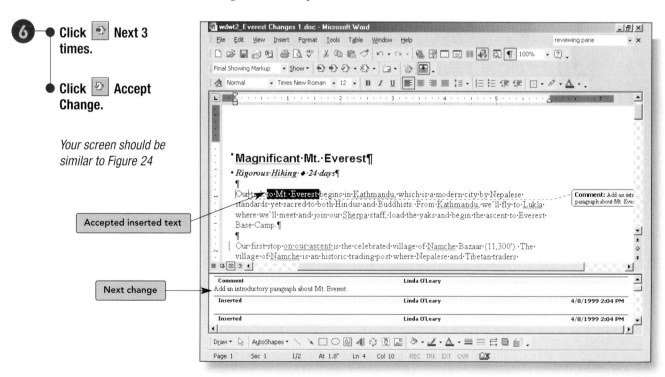

Figure 24

The next change is to insert "on our ascent". You feel this change is unnecessary and you will reject it.

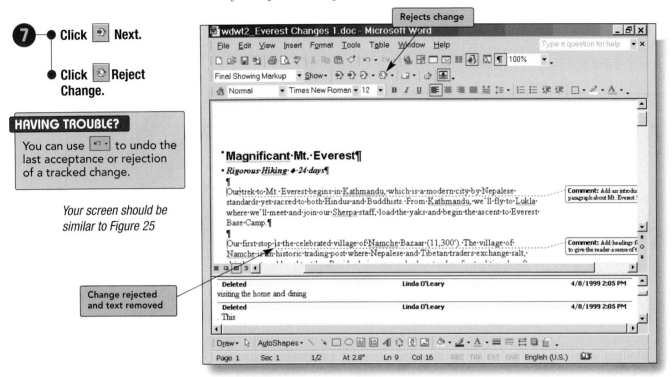

Figure 25

7 ● Click 🔁 **Next.**

● Click 🔁 **Reject Change.**

HAVING TROUBLE?

You can use ↩ ▾ to undo the last acceptance or rejection of a tracked change.

Your screen should be similar to Figure 25

The rest of the changes in the document are acceptable. You will accept all the remaining changes and then look at the comments.

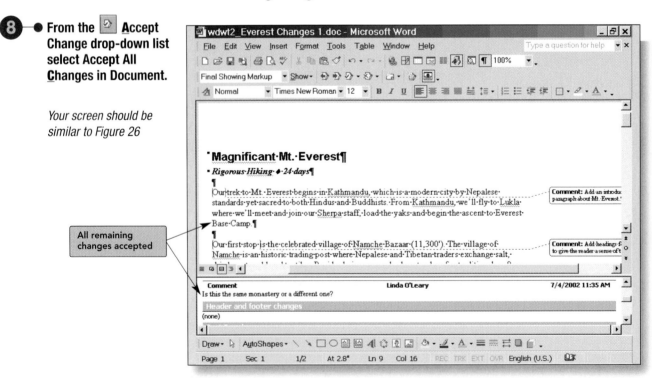

Figure 26

8 ● From the 🔁 **Accept Change drop-down list select Accept All Changes in Document.**

Your screen should be similar to Figure 26

Now, the only review item left is the comments.

Reviewing Comments

In the first comment, the reviewer wants you to add an introductory paragraph about Mt. Everest. This sounds like a good suggestion. In fact, you already have a paragraph you had written and saved in a separate file that you can add to the document that will take care of this.

1

● **Move to the beginning of the first paragraph.**

● **Insert the file** wdwt2_Everest Paragraph.

● **Right-click on the comment balloon.**

● **Choose Delete Comment from the shortcut menu.**

Your screen should be similar to Figure 27

Paragraph inserted

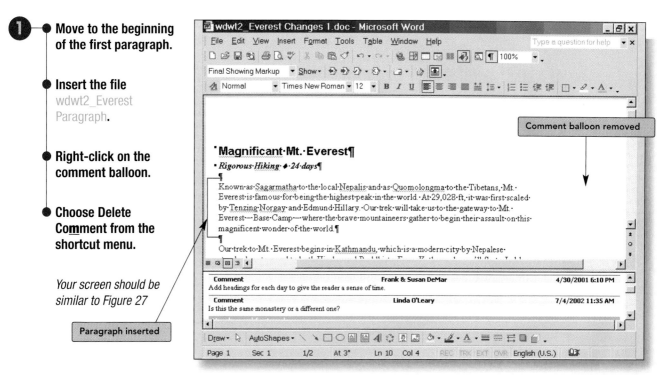

Figure 27

You feel the remaining comments require some discussion with the reviewers and will leave them in the document for now.

2

● **Click** 📄 **to close the Reviewing Pane.**

● **Close the Reviewing toolbar.**

● **Add your name and the current date in a header.**

● **Save the document as** Everest Brochure Revised.

● **Print the document.**

● **Exit Word, saving all documents as needed.**

Collaborating Online

In addition to collaboration through the exchange of documents and accepting and rejecting tracked changes, there are two other ways that you can collaborate with many reviewers at once. The first way is to hold an online meeting using the Microsoft NetMeeting feature. Each person you invite to the online meeting must also be running NetMeeting to receive your invitation.

In an online meeting, you are in control of the collaboration. Each person in the meeting can add comments to the document in real time, if you give them access. When you turn on collaboration, each person in the online meeting can take turns editing the document. The person whose turn it is to edit the document is the only one whose mouse will operate, and their initials will appear next to the mouse pointer.

The second way to collaborate is by using the Web Discussions feature, which needs to be set up by a system administrator. It enables you and other people to insert comments into the same document at the same time. This makes your job as document author much easier. You can see all the comments made by the reviewers, and they can too. Thus, if there is a discrepancy with the comment, the reviewers can discuss it among themselves.

Working Together 2: Linking and Document Collaboration

key terms

attachment   WDWT2.10
balloon   WDWT2.7
comment   WDWT2.8
comment balloon   WDWT2.8
destination file   WDWT2.3

linked object   WDWT2.3
live link   WDWT2.3
markup   WDWT2.7
revision marks   WDWT2.7
source file   WDWT2.3

mous skills

The Microsoft Office User Specialist (MOUS) certification program is designed to measure your proficiency in performing basic tasks using the Office XP applications. Getting certified demonstrates that you have the skills and provides a valuable industry credential for employment. After completing this lab, you have learned the following Microsoft Office User Specialist skills:

Skill	Description	Page
Workgroup Collaboration	Compare and merge documents	WDWT2.12
	Insert, view, and edit comments	WDWT2.8, WDWT2.16, WDWT2.19

command summary

Command	Shortcut Keys	Button	Action
Word			
File/Sen**d** To/**M**ail Recipient (as Attachment)			Sends the document as an e-mail attachment
File/Sen**d** To/**M**ail Re**c**ipient (for Review)			Sends the document as part of body of e-mail message
Edit/Paste **S**pecial/Paste L**i**nk			Pastes contents of Clipboard as a linked object
Edit/Linked **O**bject			Edits selected linked object
View/M**a**rkup			Displays/hides markup elements
Insert/Co**m**ment			Adds a note to the document
F**o**rmat/**F**ont/**T**ext Effects			Adds animation to selected text
Tools/**T**rack Changes	Ctrl + ⇧Shift + E		Marks changes to document
Tools/Compare and Merge **D**ocuments			Combines documents and identifies differences
Reviewing Toolbar			
		Final Showing Markup ▾	Displays merged document in different views
			Accepts highlighted change
			Rejects highlighted change or deletes selected comment
			Inserts a new comment
			Displays or hides Reviewing pane
E-mail Window			
File/Save **A**s			Saves e-mail message to name and location specified
File/**S**end		Send	Sends e-mail message to recipient

lab exercises

Hands-On Exercises

step-by-step

Payroll Department Memo

★ **1.** Karen works for a large hotel chain in the payroll department. She has recently created a new time sheet to be used to track hours worked and wants to send a memo informing department managers of the new procedure. She also wants to include a copy of the time sheet from Excel in the memo. The completed memo is shown below.

    a. Start Word and open the document wdwt2_Time Sheet Memo.

    b. In the memo header, replace the From placeholder with your name.

    c. Start Excel and open the workbook file wdwt2_Time Sheet.xls. Link the range containing the time sheet to below the first paragraph in the Word memo. Center the time sheet in the memo.

    d. You still need to complete the sample by entering the hours worked on Saturday. In the excel Worksheet, enter 4 as the Saturday hours worked.

    f. Save the Excel workbook as Time Sheet. Exit Excel.

    g. Save the Word document as Time Sheet Linked. Preview and print the document.

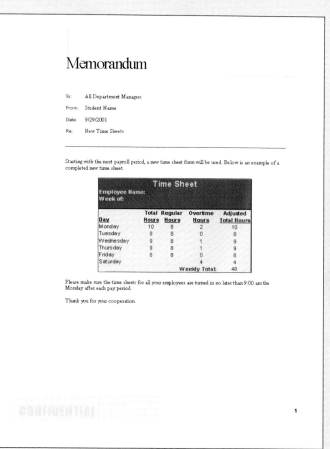

New Customer Memo

★ ★ **2.** You work for The Sports Company, a sporting goods retail store, as an Associate Manager. The credit card department has sent you a draft of a letter to be sent to new credit card customers and has asked for your input. You will use the Track Changes feature to indicate your revisions. The letter with the revision marks will look like that shown below.

a. Start Word and open the document wdwt2_Credit Card Letter.

b. Turn on Track Changes while editing the document.

c. Make the following changes to the document:

■ Add **Sports Company** following the word "new" (second sentence of first paragraph).

■ Begin a new paragraph with the sentence "It will identify you…" (last sentence, second paragraph).

■ Change the text "It will identify" to **Your new credit card identifies**.

■ Insert the contents of the file wdwt2_Credit Card Paragraph below the third paragraph.

■ Highlight the second paragraph and add the comment: **Change to itemized list**.

■ Replace the placeholder in the closing with your name.

d. Turn off Track Changes.

e. Save the revised letter as Credit Card Letter Revised and print the letter.

Updating Adventure Travel Tours' Web site

★ ★ **3.** You have been working on the content of the FAQ page for the Adventure Travel Tours Web site and have sent it out for review to several co-workers for input. You recently received one of the reviews back and want to update the document with the suggested changes. The revised FAQ document is shown here.

    a. Open the file wdwt2_Draft FAQs.

    b. Turn on the tracking feature to accept/reject changes and respond to each suggested change as you think appropriate.

    c. In response to the comment about the minimum numbers of participants, add the following: Our minimum is usually 6, but varies by trip. Delete the comment.

    d. In response to the comment to change the note to an answer, add an appropriate question heading and revise the note accordingly. Format the question heading like the others. Delete the comment.

    e. Turn off the Track Changes feature.

    f. Add your name and the current date to the header.

    g. Save the file as FAQs Revised.

Student Name
Date

Answers to Frequently Asked Questions

How long have you been in business?
For over 15 years, Adventure Travel Tours has been offering adventures to the most intriguing destinations in the world.

What kind of trips are offered?
We have adventures that range from easy get-aways to challenging treks. We explore the world on foot, by kayak or raft, bicycle, 4-wheel drive, cruise ship or a combination of these vehicles! If you are a novice, we can teach you to kayak, or to safely summit a mountain.

How do I know what each trip is like?
This Web site provides full details of each trip. If you still have questions, call us at 1-800-555-3344, or email us at AdventureTraveler@AdventureTravelTours.com. We would be happy to discuss our adventure trips with you!

What is your maximum group size?
We keep our groups small - usually less than 16 participants. Our minimum is usually 6, but it varies by the trip.

What if I am traveling alone?
About half of our trip participants are individuals traveling alone. We also have people traveling with a friend, a spouse, or their entire family! We get single men as well as single women traveling with ATTours. It is a safe, convenient way to experience a new part of the world.

How are accommodations handled if I am a single traveler?
Prices are based on double occupancy. If you are traveling alone, and wish to share accommodations, we will assign a roommate if one is available. If you request single accommodations, or if a roommate cannot be found, you are requested to pay the single supplement. Single rooms are limited, and are based on availability.

Can I be comfortable doing adventure travel?
Adventure travel and physical comfort can go hand-in-hand. Join us for a hike through the Black Forest and you will sleep in charming inns and dine in many fine restaurants. If you prefer mountaineering, these amenities will, of course, be unavailable. But our camping trip arrangements are and comfortable. For example, our African safari trips provide spacious sleeping tents, a dining tent and a shower tent. Hot water is available, and a full camp staff takes care of all the chores!

Who are your guides?
Our skilled guides are skilled in their field (mountain climbing, sea kayaking, cycle touring, etc.). Besides running and leading our own trips, we hire local experts to lead our trips. These men and women know their homeland intimately, and are enthusiastic and accommodating. They "show you the ropes" and encourage you every step of the way!

What's the food like?
On hotel and inn-based trips we dine in local restaurants and have the pleasure of experiencing a variety of local cuisine. We eat equally well on our camping trips, which feature an abundance of fresh and delicious food. On high altitude climbing trips a combination of fresh food and freeze-dried is used. All water used for cooking and drinking is purified by filter or it is boiled.

Command Summary

Command	Shortcut	Button	Action
File/New	Ctrl + N	☐	Opens new document
File/New/General Templates /Web Pages/Web Page Wizard			Creates a new Web site
File/New/GeneralTemplates/ Letters & Faxes/Mailing Label Wizard			Starts Mailing Label Wizard to create mailing labels
File/Open	Ctrl + O	☞	Opens existing document file
File/Close	Ctrl + F4	☒	Closes document file
File/Save	Ctrl + S	💾	Saves document using same file name
File/Save As			Saves document using a new file name, type and/or location
File/Save as Web Page			Saves file as a Web page document
File/Web Page Preview			Previews Web page in browser window
File/Page Setup			Changes layout of page including margins, paper size, and paper source
File/Page Setup/Layout/Vertical Alignment			Aligns text vertically on a page
File/Print Preview		▣	Displays document as it will appear when printed
File/Print	Ctrl + P	🖨	Prints document using selected print settings
File/Send To/Mail Recipient (as Attachment)		✉	Sends the document as an e-mail attachment
File/Send To/Mail Recipient (for Review)			Sends the document as part of body of e-mail message
File/Exit	Alt + F4	☒	Exits Word program
Edit/Undo	Ctrl + Z	↶ ▾	Restores last editing change
Edit/Redo	Ctrl + Y	↷ ▾	Restores last Undo or repeats last command or action
Edit/Repeat	Ctrl + Y		Repeats last action
Edit/Cut	Ctrl + X	✂	Cuts selected text and copies it to Clipboard
Edit/Copy	Ctrl + C	🖺	Copies selected text to Clipboard
Edit/Office Clipboard			Activates Office Clipboard and displays the task pane

Command	Shortcut	Button	Action
Edit/**P**aste	Ctrl + V	📋	Pastes text from Clipboard
Edit/Paste **S**pecial/Paste Li**n**k			Pastes contents of Clipboard as a linked object
Edit/Select All	Ctrl + A		Selects all text in document
Edit/**F**ind	Ctrl + F		Locates specified text
Edit/R**e**place	Ctrl + H		Locates and replaces specified text
Edit/Linked **O**bject			Edits selected linked object
Edit/**G**oTo	Ctrl + G		Moves to specified location
Edit/Chart **O**bject/**E**dit			Opens Chart object for editing
View/**N**ormal		▤	Displays document in Normal view
View/**W**eb Layout		▦	Shows document as it will appear when viewed in a Web browser
View/**P**rint Layout		▣	Shows how text and objects will appear on the printed page
View/**O**utline		▤	Shows structure of document
View/Tas**k** Pane			Displays or hides task pane
View/**T**oolbars			Displays or hides selected toolbar
View/**R**uler			Displays or hides horizontal ruler
View/**S**how Paragraph Marks			Displays or hides paragraph marks
View/**D**ocument Map		▦	Displays or hides Document Map pane.
View/**H**eader and Footer			Displays header and footer areas
View/**F**ootnotes			Hides or displays note pane
View/Ma**r**kup			Displays/hides markup elements
View/**D**atasheet			Displays Datasheet table for Open Chart object
View/**Z**oom		100% ▾	Changes onscreen character size
View/**Z**oom/**P**age width			Fits display of document within right and left margins
View/**Z**oom/**W**hole Page			Displays entire page onscreen
View/**Z**oom/**M**any Pages			Displays two or more pages in document window
View/HTML Sour**c**e			Displays HTML source code
Insert/**B**reak/**P**age break	Ctrl + ↵Enter		Inserts hard page break
Insert/**B**reak/Con**t**inuous			Inserts a section break and starts next section on same page as current section
Insert/**B**reak/**N**ext Page			Inserts a section break and starts next section on a new page
Insert/Page N**u**mbers			Specifies page number location
Insert/Date and **T**ime			Inserts current date or time, maintained by computer system, in selected format
Insert/**A**utoText			Enters predefined text
Insert/**A**utoText/AutoTe**x**t/ **S**how AutoComplete suggestions			Turns on AutoText feature

Command	Shortcut	Button	Action
Insert/Symbol			Inserts selected symbol
Insert/Comment		🗂	Adds a note to the document
Insert/Reference/Footnote	Alt + Ctrl + F		Inserts footnote reference at insertion point
Insert/Reference/Caption			Inserts caption at insertion point
Insert/Reference/Cross-reference			Inserts cross-reference at insertion point
Insert/Reference/Index and Tables/ Table of Contents			Inserts table of contents
Insert/Picture/Clip Art			Inserts selected clip art at insertion point
Insert/Picture/From File			Inserts selected picture into document
Insert/Picture/AutoShapes		AutoShapes ▾	Inserts selected AutoShape
Insert/Diagram		🔁	Inserts a diagram
Insert/Text Box		📄	Inserts text box
Insert/Object/Microsoft Graph Chart			Creates a chart in the document
Insert/Hyperlink	Ctrl + K	🔗	Inserts hyperlink in Web page
Format/Font/Font/Font		Times New Roman	Changes typeface
Format/Font/Font/Size		12	Changes type size
Format/Font/Font/Color		A	Changes type color
Format/Font/Font/Font Style/Italic	Ctrl + I	I	Makes selected text italic
Format/Font/Font/Font Style/Bold	Ctrl + B	B	Makes selected text bold
Format/Font/Font/ Underline style/Single	Ctrl + U	U	Underlines selected text
Format/Font/Text Effects			Adds animation to selected text
Format/Font/Character Spacing			Changes spacing between characters
Format/Paragraph/Indents and Spacing/Special/First Line			Indents first line of paragraph from left margin
Format/Paragraph/Indents and Spacing/Alignment/Left	Ctrl + L	▤	Aligns text to left margin
Format/Paragraph/Indents and Spacing/Alignment/Centered	Ctrl + E	▤	Centers text between left and right margins
Format/Paragraph/Indents and Spacing/Alignment/Right	Ctrl + R	▤	Aligns text to right margin
Format/Paragraph/Indents and Spacing/Alignment/Justified	Ctrl + J	▤	Aligns text equally between left and right margins
Format/Paragraph/Indents and Spacing/Alignment/Line Spacing			Changes amount of space between lines
Format/Theme			Applies a predesigned theme to Web page
Format/Style		Normal ▾	Applies selected style to paragraph or characters
Format/Picture/Layout/Wrapping style			Specifies how text will wrap around picture
Format/Bullets and Numbering		⬛⬛	Creates a bulleted or numbered list

Command	Shortcut	Button	Action
Format/Borders and Shading			Adds borders and shadings to selection
		▣	Adds outside border
		▤	Adds top border
		▥	Adds bottom border
Format/Borders and Shading /Horizontal Line			Adds graphic horizontal line to Web page
Format/Background/Fill Effects			Applies background color to selection
Format/Theme			Applies a predesigned theme to Web page
Format/Columns		▦	Specifies number, spacing, and size of columns
Format/Tabs			Specifies types and positions of tab stops
Format/Drop Cap/Dropped			Changes character format as a dropped capital letter
Format/Styles and Formatting		▨	Opens Styles and Formatting task pane
Format/Reveal Formatting			Opens Reveal Formatting task pane
Format/WordArt/Size		▨	Sizes, rotates, and scales WordArt object
Format/WordArt/Colors and Lines		▨	Applies fill and line color to WordArt object
Format/Text Box/Layout		▨	Changes wrapping style and alignment of text box
Format/Text Direction/Orientation		▥	Changes direction of text in a table
Tools/Spelling and Grammar	F7	▨	Starts Spelling and Grammar tool
Tools/Language/Thesaurus	Shift + F7		Starts Thesaurus tool
Tools/Track Changes	Ctrl + ⇧Shift + E		Marks changes to document
Tools/Compare and Merge Documents			Combines documents and identifies differences
Tools/Language/Hyphenation			Specifies hyphenation settings
Tools/Letters and Mailings/ Mail Merge Wizard			Starts Mail Merge Wizard
Tools/Letters and Mailings/ Show Mail Merge Toolbar			Displays Mail Merge toolbar
Tools/Letters and Mailings/ Envelopes and Labels/Envelopes			Creates and prints delivery and return address on envelopes
Tools/AutoCorrect Options/ Show AutoCorrect Options buttons			Displays or hides AutoCorrect options
Tools/Customize/Options/Show Standard and Formatting toolbars on two rows			Displays Standard and Formatting toolbars on two rows
Tools/Options/Edit/Overtype mode	Ins	OVR	Switches between Insert and Overtype modes

Command	Shortcut	Button	Action
Tools/**O**ptions/View/**A**ll		¶	Displays or hides formatting marks
Tools/**O**ptions/View/Scr**e**enTips			Turns off and on the display of screen tips
Tools/**O**ptions/View/**A**ll	Ctrl + Shift	¶	Displays or hides special characters
Tools/**O**ptions/Edit/**O**vertype mode		OVR	Switches between insert and overtype modes
Tools/**O**ptions/Spelling & Grammar			Changes settings associated with the Spelling and Grammar checking feature
T**a**ble/Draw Ta**b**le			Creates a table using Draw Table feature
T**a**ble/**I**nsert Table			Inserts table at insertion point
T**a**ble/**I**nsert Columns			Inserts new columns in a table
T**a**ble/**I**nsert/Row **A**bove			Inserts a new row in table above the selected row
T**a**ble/Sele**c**t/**T**able			Selects entire table
T**a**ble/**M**erge Cells			Merges cells in a table
T**a**ble/Table Auto**F**ormat			Applies selected format to table
T**a**ble/Con**v**ert/Te**x**t to Table			Converts selected text to table format
T**a**ble/**S**ort			Rearranges items in a selection into sorted order
T**a**ble/F**o**rmula			Inserts a formula into a table
T**a**ble/Show **G**ridlines			Displays gridlines in a table
T**a**ble/Table P**r**operties/**T**able/**C**enter			Centers the selected table
T**a**ble/Table P**r**operties/**T**able/**O**ptiona/ Automatically resi**z**e to fit contents			Automatically resizes columns in the table to fit text or graphic
T**a**ble/Table P**r**operties/Col**u**mn			Adjusts width of selected columns
T**a**ble/**A**utofit/Distribute Rows Eve**n**ly			Evenly sizes selected rows
Help/Microsoft Word **H**elp		?	Opens Help window
Dr**a**w ▾ **O**rder/Bring to Fron**t**			Brings object to front of stack
Dr**a**w ▾ **G**roup			Creates a group from selected objects
Dr**a**w ▾ **U**ngroup			Ungroups a grouped object
Dr**a**w ▾ Regr**o**up			Regroups an ungrouped object
Insert Shape/**S**ubordinate			Inserts a shape below the selected superior shape
Layout/**R**ight Hanging			Hangs subordinate shapes to right of superior shape
Layout/**E**xpand Organization Chart			Expands drawing canvas around organization chart
Checkbox		☑	Allows selection of more than one item
Drop-Down box			Displays available choices in a list
Textbox		abl	A box where you can enter one line of text

Command	Shortcut	Button	Action
Text Area			A box where you can enter more than one line of text
Reset			Clears entries in form
Submit			Submits data in form to specified location

Glossary of Key Terms

absolute link A link that identifies the file location of the destination file by its full address. Also called a fixed link.

active document The document containing the insertion point and that will be affected by any changes you make.

active window The window you can work in identified by a highlighted title bar, the insertion point, and scroll bars.

address file The data source file used in a merge; it typically contains name and address data to be combined with the main document.

alignment The positioning of paragraphs between the margins: left, right, centered, or justified.

antonym A word with the opposite meaning.

attachment A file that is sent along with an e-mail message, but is not part of the e-mail text.

author The process of designing and creating a Web page.

authoring The process of creating a Web page.

AutoComplete A feature that recognizes commonly used words or phrases and can automatically complete them for you if chosen.

AutoCorrect A feature that makes basic assumptions about the text you are typing and automatically corrects the entry.

AutoFormat The feature that makes certain formatting changes automatically to your document.

automatic grammar check The feature that advises you of incorrect grammar as you create and edit a document, and proposes possible corrections.

automatic spelling check The feature that advises you of misspelled words as you create and edit a document, and proposes possible corrections.

AutoShape A ready-made shape that is supplied with Word.

AutoText A feature that provides commonly used words or phrases that you can select and quickly insert into a document.

background A color or design applied behind the text on a Web page.

balloon A box that displays markup elements such as comments and tracked changes in the margin of the document.

browser A program that connects to remote computers and displays Web pages.

bulleted list Displays items that logically fall out from a paragraph into a list, with items preceded by bullets.

caption A title or explanation for a table, picture, or graph.

case sensitive The capability to distinguish between uppercase and lowercase characters.

cell The intersection of a column and row where data is entered in a table.

character formatting Formatting features, such as bold and color, that affect the selected characters only.

Character style A combination of any character formats that affect selected text.

chart A visual representation of numeric data. Also called a graph.

clip art A collection of graphics that is usually bundled with a software application.

collect and paste The capability of the program to store multiple copied items in the Office Clipboard and then paste one or more of the items.

comment A note that can be added to a document without changing the document text.

comment balloon A balloon that displays the text of a comment.

controls Graphic objects designed to automate the process of completing a form.

cross-reference A reference in one part of a document to related information in another part.

cursor The blinking vertical bar that shows you where the next character you type will appear. Also called the insertion point.

custom dictionary A dictionary of terms you have entered that are not in the main dictionary of the Spelling Checker.

data field Each category of information in the data source.

data series Each group of related data that is plotted in the chart. Each data series has a unique color or pattern assigned to it so that you can identify the different series.

datasheet The data validation restrictions you place on a field.

data source The file that supplies the data in a mail merge.

default The initial Word document settings that can be changed to customize documents.

destination The location to which text is moved or copied.

destination file A document in which a linked object is inserted.

diagram A graphic object that can be used to illustrate concepts and to enhance documents.

Document Map Displays the headings in the document.

document window The area of the application window that displays the contents of the open document.

drag and drop A mouse procedure that moves or copies a selection to a new location.

drawing layer The layer above or below the text layer where floating objects are inserted.

drawing object A simple object consisting of shapes such as lines and boxes.

drop cap A large, uppercase character with the top part of the letter even with the line and the rest of the letter extending into the paragraph below it.

edit The process of changing and correcting existing text in a document.

embedded object An object, such as a picture graphic, that becomes part of the Word document and that can be opened and edited using the program in which it was created.

endnote A reference note displayed at the end of the document.

end-of-file marker The horizontal line that marks the end of a file.

field A placeholder code that instructs Word to insert information in a document.

field code The code containing the instructions about the type of information to insert in a field.

field name A name used to label each data field in the data source.

field results The results displayed in a field according to the instructions in the field code.

fixed link A link that identifies the file location of the destination by its full address. Also called an absolute link.

floating object A graphic object that is inserted into the drawing layer and which can be positioned anywhere on the page.

font A set of characters with a specific design. Also called a typeface.

font size The height and width of a character, commonly measured in points.

footer The line or several lines of text at the bottom of every page just below the bottom margin line.

footnote A reference note displayed at the bottom of the page on which the reference occurs.

form Collection of fields on a Web page that are used to get information or feedback from users.

format To enhance the appearance of the document to make it more readable or attractive.

Format Painter The feature that applies formats associated with the current selection to new selections.

formatting marks Symbols that are automatically inserted into a document as you enter and edit text and that control the appearance of the document.

Formatting toolbar The toolbar that contains buttons representing the most frequently used text-editing and text-layout features.

formula Table entry that does arithmetic calculations.

frame A division of a window that can be scrolled separately.

frames page The container for frames in a Web site. The frames page serves as the file name for the collection of frames. It is invisible to the user when viewing the Web site.

function A prewritten formula that performs a calculation automatically in a table.

global template The normal document template whose settings are available to all documents.

graphic   A non-text element in a document.

group   Two or more objects that are treated as a single object.

hard page break   A manually inserted page break that instructs Word to begin a new page regardless of the amount of text on the previous page.

header   The line or several lines of text at the top of each page just above the top margin line.

heading style   A style that is designed to identify different levels of headings in a document.

home page   The top-level or opening page to a site.

HTML (Hypertext Markup Language)   A programming language used to create Web pages.

hyperlink   A connection to locations in the current document, other documents, or Web pages. Clicking a hyperlink jumps to the specified location.

hyphenation   Inserts a hyphen (-) in long words that fall at the end of a line to split the word between lines.

hyphenation zone   An unmarked space along the right margin that controls the amount of white space in addition to the margin that is allowed at the end of a line.

inline object   An object that is inserted directly in the text at the position of the insertion point, becoming part of the paragraph.

Insert mode   Method of text entry in which new characters are inserted into existing text, which moves to the right to make space for the new characters; the text on the line is reformatted as necessary.

insertion point   The blinking vertical bar that shows you where the next character you type will appear on the line. Also called the cursor.

kerning   Adjusting the spacing between particular pairs of letters, depending on the font design.

landscape   Orientation in which text is printed across the length of page

leader characters   Solid, dotted, or dashed lines that fill the blank space between tab stops.

legend   A box containing a brief description that identifies the patterns or colors assigned to the data series in a chart.

line spacing   The vertical space between lines of text.

linked object   Information created in a source file from one application and inserted into a destination file of another application while maintaining a link between files.

live link   A linked object that automatically reflects in the destination document any changes made in the source document when the destination document is opened.

Mail Merge   A feature that combines a text document with a data document or file containing names and addresses to produce a merged document or form letter.

main dictionary   The dictionary of terms that comes with Word 2002.

main document   The document that contains the basic form letter with merge fields in a merge operation.

markup   Elements used to identify changes made to a document when Track Changes is on.

menu   Method used to tell a program what you want it to do.

menu bar   A bar that displays the menu names that can be selected.

merge field   A field code that controls what information is used from the data source and where it is entered in the main document.

newsletter-style columns   The arrangement of text in a document so that it flows from the bottom of one column to the top of the next column.

Normal template   The document template that is opened when you start Word.

note pane   Lower portion of the window that displays footnotes.

note reference mark   A superscript number or character appearing in the document at the end of the material being referenced.

note separator   The horizontal line separating footnote text from main document text.

note text   The text in a footnote.

numbered list   Displays items that convey a sequence of events in a particular order, with items preceded by numbers or letters.

object   An item that can be sized, moved, and manipulated.

operator   Specifies the type of calculation to perform. The most common operators are + (add), – (subtract), * (multiply), and / (divide).

optional hyphen   A hyphen that is inserted automatically when a word is broken between two lines because the full word did not fit.

outlined numbered list   Displays items in multiple outline levels that show a hierarchical structure of the items in the list.

Overtype mode   Method of text entry in which new text types over the existing characters.

page break   Marks the point at which one page ends and another begins.

page margin   The blank space around the edge of the page.

pane   A split portion of the document window that can be scrolled independently.

paragraph formatting   Formatting features, such as alignment, indentation, and line spacing, that affect an entire paragraph.

paragraph style   A combination of any character formats and paragraph formats that affect all text in a paragraph.

picture   An illustration such as a scanned photograph.

placeholder   Text in a template that marks the space and provides instructions for the text that should be entered at that location.

point   Measure used for height of type; one point equals 1/72 inch.

portrait   Orientation of the page, in which text is printed across the width of the page.

protocol   The rules that control how hardware and software on a network communicate.

record   All the fields of data that are needed to complete the main document for one entity in a merge operation.

relative link   Identifies the destination location in relation to the location of the HTML file.

revision marks   Red underlines that identify where an insertion was made while Track Changes is on.

ruler   The ruler located below the Formatting toolbar that shows the line length in inches.

sans serif font   A font, such as Arial or Helvetica, that does not have a flair at the base of each letter.

scroll bar   A window element located on the right or bottom window border that lets you display text that is not currently visible in the window. It contains scroll arrows and a scroll box.

section   A division into which a document can be divided that can be formatted separately from the rest of the document.

section break   Marks the point at which one section ends and another begins.

section cursor   A colored highlight bar that appears over the selected command in a menu.

select   To highlight text.

selection rectangle   The rectangular outline around an object that indicates it is selected.

serif font   A font, such as Times New Roman, that has a flair at the base of each letter.

shortcut menu   A menu of the most common menu options that is displayed by right-clicking on the selected item.

sidebar   An article set off from other articles or information that highlights an article next to it.

sizing handles   Black squares around a selected object that can be used to size the object.

SmartTag   A feature that recognizes data such as names, addresses, telephone numbers, dates, times, and places as a particular type. The recognized item can then be quickly added to a Microsoft Outlook feature.

soft page break   A page break automatically inserted by Word to start a new page when the previous page has been filled with text or graphics.

soft space   A space automatically entered by Word to align the text properly on a single line.

sort   To arrange alphabetically or numerically in ascending or descending order.

source   The location from which text is moved or copied.

source file   The document that stores the data for the linked object.

source program   The program in which an object was created.

Standard toolbar   The toolbar that contains buttons for the most frequently used commands.

status bar   A bar displayed at the bottom of the document window that advises you of the status of different program conditions and features as you use the program.

story   Text that is contained in a single text box or linked text boxes.

style   A set of formats that is assigned a name.

synonym   A word with a similar meaning.

tab stop   A marked location on the horizontal ruler that indicates how far to indent text when the [Tab ⇆] key is pressed.

table   Displays information in horizontal rows and vertical columns.

table reference   The letter and number (for example, A1) that identify a cell in a table.

tag   An HTML code embedded in a Web page document that supplies information about the page's structure.

target link   Link that targets a heading or object on a page.

task pane   A pane that provides quick access to features as you are using them.

template   A document file that includes predefined settings that can be used as a pattern to create many common types of documents.

text box   Container for text or graphics.

theme   Predesigned Web page effects that can be applied to a Web page to enhance its appearance.

Thesaurus   Word feature that provides synonyms and antonyms for words.

thumbnail   A miniature representation of a picture.

toolbar   A bar of buttons commonly displayed below the menu bar. The buttons are shortcuts for many of the most common menu commands.

tracked changes   Insertions, deletions, and formatting changes that are made to a document while Track Changes is on.

TrueType   A font that is automatically installed when you install Windows.

typeface   A set of characters with a specific design. Also called a font.

Uniform Resource Locator (URL)   a fixed file location that includes the full path to the location or address of the Web page.

wallpaper   A background consisting of an image, pattern or texture.

Web page   A document that uses HTML to display in a browser.

wizard   A guided approach to creating special types of documents, such as Web sites, consisting of a series of dialog boxes in which you specify settings. The wizard creates a document based on your selections.

word wrap   A feature that automatically determines where to end a line and wrap text to the next line based on the margin settings.

WordArt   A supplementary application included with the Word program that is used to enhance a document by changing the shape of text, adding 3-D effects, and changing the alignment of text on a line.

Data File List

Supplied/Used File	Created/Saved As
Lab 1	
	Flyer
wd01_Flyer2	Flyer3
wd01_Elephants (graphic)	
Step-by-Step	
1.	Dress Code
2.	Top Stresses
wd01_Stress (graphic)	
3.	Executive Style
wd01_Executive1 (graphic)	
wd01_Executive2 (graphic)	
4.	B&B Ad
wd01_Sunshine (graphic)	
5. wd01_Making Sushi	Making Sushi2
wd01_sushi (graphic)	
On Your Own	
1.	Career Report
2.	Reunion
3.	Lab Rules
4.	PomPom
5.	Cruise Flyer
On the Web	
1.	Writing Tips
Lab 2	
wd02_Tour Letter	Tour Letter2
wd02_ Flyer4	
Step-by-Step	
1. wd02_Cleaning Checklist	Cleaning Checklist2
2.	Career Fair
3. Making Sushi2 (from Lab 1, PE 5)	Making Sushi3
wd02_Rice	
4. wd02_Thank You Letter	Thank You Letter2
5. wd02_Coffee Flyer	Coffee Flyer2

Supplied/Used File	Created/Saved As
On Your Own	
1.	Internship Letter
2.	Insurance Comparison
3.	To Do List
4.	New Staff Memo
5.	For Sale Flyer
On the Web	
1.	Election Results
Lab 3	
wd03_Tour Research	Tour Research2
	Research Outline
wd03_Lions (graphic)	
wd03_Parrots (graphic)	
Step-by-Step	
1.	Workout
2. wd03_Internet	Internet2
3. wd03_Antique Shops	Antique Shops2
4. wd03_Cafe Flyer	Cafe Flyer2
wd03_coffee (graphic)	
wd03_Computer User (graphic)	
5. wd03_Scenic Drives	Scenic Drives2
wd03_Mountain (graphic)	
6. wd03_Water	Water2
wd03_Swimmer (graphic)	
On Your Own	
1. wd03_Alzheimer	Alzheimer2
2. wd03_Computer	Computer2
3.	Job Search
4.	Research
On the Web	
1.	Computer Virus
Working Together	
wdwt_Tour Flyer	New Tour Presentations
wdwt_Locations	Locations
Step-by-Step	
1. Locations (from WT Lab)	LosAngeles
wdwt1_LosAngeles	
2. Executive Style (from Lab 1, PE 3)	Executive Style
3. B&B Ad (from Lab 1, PE 4)	B&B
On Your Own	
1.	Web Design

Supplied/Used File	Created/Saved As
Lab 4	
wd04_Headline	Newsletter Headline
wd04_Tanzania Facts	
wd04_Be An Adventure Traveler	March Newsletter
wd04_Costa Rica Adventure	
wd04_Newsletter Articles	
Step-by-Step	
1. wd04_Fitness Club Headline	Fitness Headline2
wd04_Fitness Club	Fitness Club Newsletter
wd04_Exercise Bike	
wd04_Jogger	
2. wd04_Scenic Drives	Scenic Drives Newsletter
Newsletter Headline (from Lab 4)	
wd04_Road	
wd04_Canada	
wd04_MtDoug	
wd04_Huts	
3. wd04_Coffee	Internet Cafe Newsletter
wd04_Conversation	
wd04_Coffee Beans	
wd04_Coffee Cup	
4. wd04_Hikes	National Parks Newsletter
wd04_Park Headline	
wd04_Survival Skills	
wd04_Fire	
wd04_Shelter	
wd04_Signaling	
wd04_Food & Water	
wd04_First Aid	
5. wd04_Air Travel	Air Travel Newsletter
On Your Own	
1.	Activity Newsletter
2.	Power Plant Newsletter
3. wd04_Water	Water Newsletter
4.	PTA Newsletter
5.	Garden Newsletter
On The Web	
	My Newsletter
Lab 5	
wd05_Mountain	Tour Sales Memo
wd05_Tour Letter5	Client List

Supplied/Used File	Created/Saved As
	Tour Main Document
	Tour Merge Document
	Tour Mailing Labels
Step-by-Step	
1. wd05_Mountain	Yoga Memo
2.	Membership Memo
3. wd05_Video Tower Letter	Video Data Source
	Video Merge Document
4. wd05_Vet Letter	Vet Data Source
	Vet Merge Document
5. wd05_Cafe Bonus	Cafe Data Source
	Cafe Merge Document
On Your Own	
1.	Leisure Activities
2.	New Car Info
3.	Hand Washing
4.	Movie Data
5.	Frequent Flyer Letter
	Default
On The Web	
1.	Cover Letter and Resume
Lab 6	
wd06_ATT Home Page	Adventure Travel Tours Web Site
wd06_Tour List	
wd06_New Tours	
wd06_Construction	
wd06_Elephant Walking	
wd06_New Tours	
Step-by-Step	
1. wd06_Home Page Text	Home Page Text2
wd06_SCNewsletter	Sports Company Web Site
2. wd06_Pets Home Page	Animal Angels Web Site
wd06_Parrots	
wd06_Cat	
wd06_Puppies	
wd06_Lizard	
3. wd06_Patron	Downtown Internet Cafe Web Site
wd06_Laptop	
wd06_City	
wd06_Services	
wd06_Coffee Online	Cafe Home Page2

Supplied/Used File	Created/Saved As
4.	My Home Page
5. wd06_Virus Text Page	Virus Web Site
wd06_Virus	
wd06_Trojan Horses	
On Your Own	
1. My Home Page (from exercise 4)	(expansion of personal web site)
2.	My TV Site
3. Adventure Travel Web site (from Lab 6)	(expansion of Adventure Travel Tours Web Site)
wd06_Tour FAQs	
4.	Club Web Site
5.	(expansion of Animal Angels Web Site)
On The Web	
	Web Design
Working Together 2	
wdwt2_Camping Safari	Camping Safari Edited
wdwt2_New Tour Bookings.xls	New Tour Bookings Linked
wdwt2_New Tour Status	New Tour Status Revised
wdwt2_Everest Original	Everest Changes3
wdwt2_Everest Changes1	Everest Brochure Revised
wdwt2_Everest Changes2	Safari e-mail
wdwt2_Everest Paragraph	
Step-by-Step	
1. wdwt2_Time Sheet Memo	Time Sheet Linked
wdwt2_Time Sheet.xls	Time Sheet
2. wdwt2_Credit Card Letter	Credit Card Letter Revised
wdwt2_Credit Card Paragraph	
3. wdwt2_Draft FAQs	FAQs Revised

Reference 2

MOUS Skills

Word Core Certification

Standardized Coding Number	Activity	Lab Exercises			
		Lab	Page	Step-By-Step	On Your Own
W2002-1	**Inserting and Modifying Text**				
W2002-1-1	Insert, modify, and move text and symbols	1	1.2,1.39	1,2,3,4,5	1,2,3,5
		2	2.12,2.14,2.20	1,3,4,5	2,5
		4	4.17	1,2,3,4,5	1,2,3,4,5
		6		1,2,3,4,5	1,2,3,4,5
W2002-1-2	Apply and modify text formats	1	1.46	1,2,3,4	1,2
		2	2.44	1,2,5	
W2002-1-3	Correct spelling and grammar usage	1	1.18,1.23	1,2,3,4,5	
		2	2.5,2.10	1,4	
W2002-1-4	Apply font and text effects	1	1.50	1,2,3,4,5	2
		2	2.41, 2.42	2,3,5	
W2002-1-5	Enter and format Date and Time	2	2.24	2,3,4	1
		5	5.8	1,2,3,4,5	1,2,3,4,5
W2002-1-6	Apply character styles	3	3.6	1,2,3,4,5	1,2,3,4
W2002-2	**Creating and Modifying Paragraphs**				
W2002-2-1	Modify paragraph formats	1	1.53	1,3,4,5	1,2,4
		2	2.28,2.31	1,2	
		4	4.30	1,2,3,4,5	1,2,3,4,5
W2002-2-2	Set and modify tabs	2	2.35	2,5	2,5
		4	4.30	2	
		5	5.40	1,2,3,4,5,	1,2,3,4,5
W2002-2-3	Apply bullet, outline, and numbering format to paragraphs	2	2.46	3,4	1,2,4,5
		3	3.6	1	1,2
		4	4.36	2	
		5	5.40	1,2,3,4,5,	1,2,3,4,5
W2002-2-4	Apply paragraph styles	3	3.6,3.18	1,3,4,5	1,3,4
		6	6.35		
W2002-3	**Formatting Documents**				
W2002-3-1	Create and modify a header and footer	3	3.54	2,3,4,5	1,2,3,4
W2002-3-2	Apply and modify column settings	4	4.23	1,2,3,4,5	1,2,3,4,5
W2002-3-3	Modify document layout and Page Setup options	2	2.18,2.28	1,2,3	
		3	3.27	5,6	4,3
		4	4.43	1,2,3,4,5	1,2,3,4,5
		5	5.28	1,2,3,4,5	1,2,3,4,5

Standardized Coding Number	Activity	Lab	Page	Lab Exercises	
				Step-By-Step	On Your Own
W2002-3-4	Create and modify tables	3	3.45,3.51 3.48,3.50	5,6	1,2,3,4
		5	5.13	1,2,3,4,5	1,2,3,4,5
		6	6.21	3	
W2002-3-5	Preview and print documents, envelopes, and labels	1	1.61,1.62	1,2,3,4,5	
		2	2.55,2.57	1,2,3,4	
		3	3.65		1,2,3,4
		4	4.43	1,2,3,4,5	1,2,3,4,5
		5	5.59,5.63	1,2,3,4,5	1,2,3,4,5
W2002-4	**Managing Documents**				
W2002-4-1	Manage files and folders for documents	3	3.14		
W2002-4-2	Create documents using templates	1	1.7		
		5	5.4	1,2,3,4,5	1,2,3,4,5
		6		1,2,3,4,5	1,2,3,4,5
W2002-4-3	Save documents using different names and file formats	1	1.28,1.44		
		WT	2	2,3	
		4	4.15,4.23 4.29,4.36 4.40,4.43	1,2,3,4,5	1,2,3,4,5
		5		1,2,3,4,5	1,2,3,4,5
		6		1,2,3,4,5	1,2,3,4,5
W2002-5	**Working with Graphics**				
W2002-5-1	Insert images and graphics	1	1.55	2,3,4,5	2,3,4,5
		4	4.5,4.19	1,2,3,4,5	1,2,3,4,5
		5	5.9	1,2,3,4,5	1,2,3,4,5
W2002-5-2	Create and modify diagrams and charts	5	5.32	1	3
		6	6.27		
W2002-6	**Workgroup Collaboration**				
W2002-6-1	Compare and merge documents	WT2	2.12	1,2,3	
W2002-6-2	Insert, view, and edit comments	WT2	2.8,2.16, 2.19	1,2,3	
W2002-6-3	Convert documents into Web pages	WT		2,11	2,3
		6	6.9	1,2,3,4,5	1,2,3,4,5